American Presidential Elections

Michael Nelson

John M. McCardell, Jr.

THE ELECTION OF THE EVANGELICAL

JIMMY CARTER, GERALD FORD, AND THE PRESIDENTIAL CONTEST OF 1976

DANIEL K. WILLIAMS

76

UNIVERSITY PRESS OF KANSAS

Published by the University Press of Kansas (Lawrence, Kansas 66045), which was organized by the Kansas Board of Regents and is operated and funded by Emporia State University, Fort Hays State University, Kansas State University, Pittsburg State University, the University of Kansas, and Wichita State University.

Library of Congress Cataloging-in-Publication Data

Names: Williams, Daniel K., author.
Title: The election of the evangelical : Jimmy Carter, Gerald Ford, and the presidential contest of 1976 / Daniel K. Williams.
Description: Lawrence, Kansas : University Press of Kansas, [2020] | Series: American presidential elections | Includes bibliographical references and index.
Identifiers: LCCN 2019025983
ISBN 9780700629121 (cloth)
ISBN 9780700629138 (epub)
Subjects: LCSH: Presidents—United States—Election—1976. | Party affiliation—United States—History—20th century. | Republican Party (U.S. : 1854–)—History—20th century. | Democratic Party (U.S.)—History—20th century. | United States—Politics and government—1974–1977. | Christianity and politics—United States—History—20th century. | Carter, Jimmy, 1924– | Ford, Gerald R., 1913–2006.
Classification: LCC E868 .W55 2020 | DDC 324.973/0924—dc23

LC record available at https://lccn.loc.gov/2019025983.

British Library Cataloguing-in-Publication Data is available.
Printed in the United States of America

10 9 8 7 6 5 4 3 2 1

The paper used in this publication is recycled and contains 30 percent postconsumer waste. It is acid free and meets the minimum requirements of the American National Standard for Permanence of Paper for Printed Library Materials Z39.48–1992.

CONTENTS

EDITORS' FOREWORD

When Donald J. Trump won the 2016 presidential election by positioning himself as an anti-Washington outsider, he was imitating a forty-year-old strategy that Jimmy Carter, a one-term Georgia governor who had never held national office, pioneered in 1976. Carter was a Democrat, but his campaign strategy proved so successful that for the next forty years both Republicans and Democrats borrowed a page from his playbook and won the White House by presenting themselves as outsiders who promised to shake up the Washington establishment.

In the quarter century after World War II ended in 1945, presidential elections were dominated by senators and vice presidents (most of whom—like Harry S. Truman, Lyndon B. Johnson, and Richard M. Nixon—had been senators before becoming vice president). The reason is that Cold War–era voters trusted the federal government and valued the experience acquired by senators and vice presidents in dealing with national security issues.

In the aftermath of the Vietnam War and the Watergate scandal of the late 1960s and early 1970s, voters' trust in Washington soured. Eventually, this distrust extended to political leaders of any kind. In 1992 voters showed a willingness to consider a presidential candidate whose experience featured business and celebrity, not government and politics. Running as an independent, Ross Perot led the polls during much of the spring and finished with nearly 20 percent of the national popular vote—the largest share for a candidate running as neither a Republican nor a Democrat since former president Theodore Roosevelt won 28 percent in 1912. In 2016 voters actually elected Donald J. Trump, a celebrity businessman who swept the primaries to secure the GOP nomination and earned a clear majority in the Electoral College.

As an alternative to both Washington politicians and outsider nonpoliticians, Carter represented an intermediate figure. In 1976 he trumpeted his experience as a one-term former governor of Georgia, confident that voters were willing to look beyond the usual talent pool of senators and vice presidents but not yet ready to devalue experience in government at any level. As Daniel K. Williams reports, Carter repeatedly told voters, "I'm not a member of Congress. So I'm not responsible for letting that horrible mess develop."

As an unfamiliar kind of candidate in 1976—Georgia had never produced a president and was embedded in the Deep South, a region whose last president had been Zachary Taylor of Louisiana in 1848—Carter was a long shot. He came from behind to win the Democratic nomination, partly because his message as an outsider resonated with the anti-Washington mood of the electorate and partly because, ideologically, his many opponents were either to his left, like Representative Mo Udall of Arizona and Senator Fred Harris of Oklahoma, or to his right, like Governor George C. Wallace of Alabama and Senator Henry "Scoop" Jackson of Washington State.

Charging straight up the middle with appeals that extended in both ideological directions of his party, Carter then went on to narrowly defeat the incumbent president, Gerald R. Ford, in November. Ford was a longtime Washington politician whose bid for the Republican nomination in 1976 was almost derailed by another former governor, Ronald Reagan of California. Ford was also the nation's first chief executive who had never been elected president or vice president. He was appointed to the vice presidency under the recently enacted Twenty-Fifth Amendment when Spiro T. Agnew resigned in response to one scandal, and he ascended to the presidency when President Nixon resigned in response to another.

Scholars and other political observers differ about how successful Carter's policies as president were. But few dispute that he was an unpopular leader during much of his term. In 1980 Carter was defeated by Reagan in the largest electoral vote landslide in history against an incumbent president: 489 to 49. Reagan was the second governor in a row to be elected. He was later followed by Governor Bill Clinton of Arkansas in 1992 and 1996 and Governor George W. Bush of Texas in 2000 and 2004. The trend toward outsider status continued with the election of Barack Obama, a US senator but also the first president in history who was not a white male, in 2008 and 2012. The trend was then taken to its furthest (so far) extreme with Trump's election in 2016.

Williams's account of the 1976 election is both suspensefully written and scrupulously researched. It offers a sure guide to the historical hinge on which voters' swing from valuing Washington experience to disdaining such experience took place. And it accurately locates 1976 as one of the most important presidential elections in history.

Michael Nelson
John M. McCardell, Jr.

PREFACE

A CONTEST OF VALUES AND PARTY IDENTITY

For those who lived through it, the 1976 presidential contest was like no other. What many supposed in late 1974 would be a relatively predictable competition between two heavyweights—the incumbent president and the nation's best-known Democrat, Senator Ted Kennedy—instead became a nail-biting contest among multiple candidates. On the Republican side, President Gerald Ford was nearly unseated by primary challenger Ronald Reagan. Indeed, the outcome of the contest between Reagan and Ford was not decided until the Republican National Convention in August. On the Democratic side, the winner of the primaries turned out to be dark-horse candidate Jimmy Carter, a one-term Georgia governor who became the first presidential nominee from the Deep South in more than a century. Carter did not win the nomination without a fight. He waged primary battles against nearly a dozen other Democrats, not all of whom were easy to finish off. In fact, on June 8, the final day of the primaries, there were still three other Democrats who were winning delegates. Carter's victory in the general election in November was also unusually close—the narrowest electoral vote margin in the previous half century. But when it was all over, Carter became the first president elected from the Deep South since 1848, the first governor without Washington experience to win the White House since 1912, and the first president ever elected on a claim of being "born again."[1]

Given the excitement of the campaign and Carter's improbable rise to power, the journalists who covered the election believed they had just witnessed the political story of a lifetime, and they were eager to publish comprehensive campaign narratives that explained "how Jimmy won." Within months of Carter's Election Day victory, several journalistic accounts of the campaign appeared, including, most notably, Jules Witcover's 650-page tome *Marathon*. These were quickly followed by several books specifically on the Carter campaign, which, in the late 1970s, seemed to be the most interesting aspect of the election.[2] Several of these books offered rollicking narratives featuring a classic David and Goliath story of Carter versus the political establishment, along with accounts of his victory over an improbable cast of colorful also-rans.

Carter's Democratic primary opponents included not only the usual senators and governors but also a one-eyed Mormon former professional basketball player, an Oklahoma senator who portrayed himself as a man of the people by conducting his campaign while camping in trailer parks, and a housewife from Long Island who had never run for office before but became the first female presidential candidate to qualify for Secret Service protection. There was also Sargent Shriver, a Kennedy brother-in-law and Peace Corps founder, competing with Alabama governor George Wallace, the symbol of a racially charged demagoguery. And, of course, if journalists were looking for colorful figures, there was Carter himself, a peanut farmer–turned–politician who offered his own challenge to political convention. When Carter convened his press conference to announce that he had won enough delegates to claim the party's nomination, he showed up to the formal event in blue jeans and a casual shirt—his usual attire on the farm, he said.[3]

The journalists who published the first campaign narratives uncovered some fascinating stories, but they missed the election's most far-reaching significance: its effect on the nation's parties and the values those parties represented. Most of the journalistic accounts of the 1976 election were written only months after Carter's improbable victory, and at the time, pundits did not sense the rightward shift in the nation's politics; therefore, they did not frame their narratives of the election to explain such a shift. Democrats, after all, had not only won the White House but had also held on to comfortable majorities in both houses of Congress. The idea that Reagan would emerge from his primary defeat to take control of the Republican Party and usher in a conservative revolution did not occur to any of the pundits. Nor did they realize that Carter would be the last Democrat to win nearly the entire South or that he would be the last candidate of any political party to put together a winning coalition that included black Christians, white southern evangelicals, and northern Catholics and Jews. There was no reason to think that the 1976 election was an ideologically significant moment—and certainly not a sign of a conservative shift in the nation's politics. And there was no reason to think that the election of the most overtly evangelical presidential candidate in decades was necessarily a harbinger of America's political future—despite *Newsweek*'s decision to call 1976 the "year of the evangelical."[4]

But in the early twenty-first century, after decades of liberal Democratic defeats and conservative Republican victories in presidential and congressional elections, historians began to reexamine the 1970s for clues to both the conservative movement's rise to power and white evangelicals' increasing influence on national politics. Beginning with Bruce J. Schulman's *The Seventies: The Great Shift in American Culture, Society, and Politics* (2001) and continuing with Thomas Borstelmann's *The 1970s: A New Global History from Civil Rights to Economic Inequality* (2012), Rick Perlstein's *Nixonland: The Rise of a President and the Fracturing of America* (2008), and *The Invisible Bridge: The Fall of Nixon and the Rise of Reagan* (2014), historians have portrayed the 1970s as a decade of rapid retreat from the unrealized promise of Robert F. Kennedy's 1968 presidential campaign and the rise of a new social conservatism that threatened to undermine the early gains of second-wave feminism. In Laura Kalman's words, there was a "right star rising." Perhaps the title of the leading anthology of historical scholarship on the politics of the 1970s says it all, summarizing the new historical consensus on the direction of the nation's politics: *Rightward Bound: Making America Conservative in the 1970s*.[5]

At the same time, historians have been quick to portray the rightward shift in the 1970s as a troubled and fiercely contested movement—a product of polarization and backlash, rather than a new national consensus. It was, as the title of Daniel T. Rodgers's intellectual history suggests, both an age of individualism and an "age of fracture." American women were "divided" over "family values" and even their own rights, Marjorie J. Spruill explains. Americans concerned about the family were living in "fear of national decline" and were looking for someone to blame for the nation's ills, as Natasha Zaretsky demonstrates. The emerging "culture wars" were "a war for the soul of America" as Americans fought over whether to accept or reject the social changes of the 1960s, Andrew Hartman argues. The troubled economy and the shift "from factories to finance" exacerbated this national divide. If the 1970s were the "last days of the working class" and a time when Americans living paycheck to paycheck were worried about "stayin' alive" (as the title of Jefferson Cowie's monograph suggests), perhaps it was no surprise that they brought their anger into the political realm.[6]

But despite all the historical studies on the cultural polarization and conservative political trends of the 1970s, most historians of postwar American politics have not yet figured out how to incorporate the 1976 presidential election into this narrative. Relying on contemporary journalistic accounts that minimize the ideological issues at stake in the contest, they have settled for long-standing portrayals of the election as a relatively meaningless contest between two lackluster bumblers: a Republican incumbent who squandered his outside chance of victory with a clumsy statement that there was "no Soviet domination of Eastern Europe," and a Southern Baptist peanut farmer who threw away his lead and nearly lost the election by granting an interview to *Playboy* magazine that replaced his squeaky-clean reputation with the image of a man awkwardly struggling to explain the "adultery in [his] heart."[7] The polarizing cultural issues behind these news flashes—the national debate over sexual morals that made Carter's *Playboy* interview so polarizing and the divisions over détente that framed the context for Ford's gaffe—are often forgotten amidst the chuckles over the candidates' missteps. And if these issues of significance are glossed over in most accounts of the 1976 election, the larger debates about the future of the parties are usually omitted entirely. Hardly anyone covering the election of 1976 has considered what the primary contests between Carter and his Democratic rivals signaled for the future of their party or what the last-minute decision of several liberal Republicans not to challenge Ford for the GOP nomination (as they had initially planned) meant for the fate of the Republicans. From the perspective of the early twenty-first century, the 1976 election looks like an odd anomaly: a bygone moment when the evangelical candidate with strong support from his fellow Southern Baptists was a Democrat, and the Republican candidate was a social moderate whose wife loudly proclaimed her support for *Roe v. Wade* and who was able to win culturally liberal states like Oregon, California, and New Jersey while losing Ohio, Texas, and nearly the entire South.

But the 1976 election was a pivotal turning point. It was both the last of the New Deal–era elections, which always split along regional and socioeconomic class lines, and a harbinger of a new culturally polarized politics that differentiated the parties according to values-based ideologies. This book traces that watershed moment by doing what no other study of the 1976 election has done: it explains how and why the primary campaigns and the events leading up to the general election reshaped both the Democratic and Republican Parties in ways that reflected the nation's cultural divisions. Americans in the 1970s were engaged in a polarizing national debate over shifting cultural mores; deep divisions over race, gender, religion, and sexuality were played out in heated policy disagreements over busing, abortion, and the Equal Rights Amendment. Even debates over foreign policy and the tax code reflected deeper conflicts over personal and national values. Many Americans sensed that something had gone badly wrong with the country during the previous five or ten years. In the wake of the Watergate scandal, the loss in Vietnam, the energy crisis, and the worst economy since the Great Depression, many Americans longed for a moral leader who could restore the country's unity and national purpose and, perhaps above all, its moral compass. The 1976 election took place in the midst of bicentennial observances, but for many Americans, the anniversary of the country's founding was a time not for proud celebration but for sober contemplation, because the nation seemed to have lost its way.

Carter, to a greater extent than most of the other Democratic hopefuls, recognized that many voters cared more about values than specific policy prescriptions, and he thought he could transcend the nation's growing cultural divide and unify Americans of different political ideologies by making the election a referendum on his own personal character rather than a set of potentially contentious policy proposals. That approach worked for a while. African Americans, whose already precarious economic situation was rapidly becoming worse, thought they saw in Carter the qualities of compassion and empathy that were required to fulfill the unrealized promise of the civil rights movement. White evangelicals believed he would be a Christian chief executive who would bring spiritual values to the White House. And large numbers of Americans in both the North and the South, among both whites and blacks, were looking for a president who would be the opposite of Richard Nixon, and they thought Carter might fit the bill. In 1972 a majority of American voters had trusted Nixon's promise of "law and order," and he had betrayed that trust. When Carter promised "I will never lie to you," some voters were skeptical, but for many others, the Democrat's moral credentials—his church involvement, his marriage and family life, his southern identity, and his status as a Washington outsider—were enough to persuade them to elect a dark-horse candidate who had virtually no chance of victory when he first entered the race.[8]

But Carter was not the only one who tapped into the national yearning for moral values. Reagan did the same when he denounced Ford's alleged refusal to stand up to the Soviet Union. Ford likewise did so when he made his own reputation for honesty and decency a central component of his campaign. And the Democratic and Republican Platform Committees engaged in a similar endeavor when they reshaped their parties' positions on abortion, racial justice, and the morality of the nation's foreign policy. This is where Carter faced an unpleasant surprise: the platform committee debates revealed a polarization over values that could not be resolved merely by a candidate's personal character. Even before his election, Carter found himself somewhat at odds with his party, which, on both economic and social issues, was being pulled in a very different direction from the one he had originally intended.

In the months leading up to the 1976 election, it was not apparent to observers that the Republican Party would become the party of the cultural right and the Democratic Party the party of the cultural left. The Democrat who was raising more money than any of his rivals in early 1975 was Alabama segregationist George Wallace, while on the Republican side, the incumbent vice president was the strongly pro-choice, socially liberal Nelson Rockefeller.[9] But over the course of the 1976 campaign, a partisan reorientation occurred, even if no one sensed it at the time. In winning his party's nomination and then the presidency, Carter wrested power away from Wallace-following conservative Democrats in the South, and he also convinced party centrists to accept a platform that pulled the party to the left on social issues such as abortion. On the Republican side, Ford found that to defeat Reagan, he had to reluctantly agree to a platform that pulled the party to the right. Because of the events of 1976, the presidential contests of the 1980s offered voters a clear ideological choice between candidates—for instance, between conservative Republican Ronald Reagan and liberal Democrat Walter Mondale, not between a conservative Democrat like Lloyd Bentsen (let alone George Wallace) and a moderate Republican like Howard Baker.

The contrast between the parties' platforms was even more distinct. This is not what observers expected. The conventional wisdom was that the Democratic Party had learned from its mistake with George McGovern in 1972 and would avoid veering too far to the left, while the Republican Party, by denying the nomination to Reagan, was pursuing a sensible course that would allow Ford and other candidates to practice the politics of moderation. But this is not what happened. Both parties were pulled to extremes during the election year, even though both nominees were centrists. Conservatives in the Republican Party wrote a platform that endorsed an antiabortion constitutional amendment, rescinded the party's previous call for restrictions on handguns, and pushed the party to the right on racial issues and foreign policy in ways that almost directly repudiated the Ford administration's record. At the same time, Democrats adopted a platform that endorsed *Roe v. Wade,* and they forced Carter to accept liberal economic promises that were at odds with his fiscally conservative inclinations. Both Ford and Carter tried to reach for the political center, but the national conventions and party platforms created a different narrative for 1976: a story of cultural, ideological, and, ultimately, partisan polarization that would prevent any future Democratic candidate from sweeping the South, as Carter did. By Election Day 1976, the two candidates were already out of step with their parties. Ford and Carter were in some ways the last moderates to win their parties' nomination; never again would the Republican Party nominate someone as socially moderate as the pragmatic midwestern Episcopalian Gerald Ford, and never again would the Democratic Party nominate someone as fiscally and socially conservative as the Southern Baptist Jimmy Carter.[10] Instead, the two parties would continue to nominate candidates who matched the distinctly different values they first adopted in 1976.

To understand why this partisan transformation occurred despite the candidates' positions, I have gone beyond the election-year headlines and examined the political behavior of voter groups and partisan ideologues. I have examined the particular coalitions that supported each candidate and analyzed how these coalitions reshaped their party. For that reason, much of this book focuses on the primary campaigns and the partisan debates that led up to the general election, because it was in the primary contests and the party conventions that both the Republican and the Democratic Parties were reshaped in 1976. By the time the general election took place, both candidates had been forced to conform to the new ideological orientations of their respective parties in ways they had not anticipated a few months earlier. And both candidates ultimately proved to be ineffective in stopping or transcending the forces of partisan polarization. Indeed, partisan polarization proved to be Carter's undoing in 1980, as he found himself squeezed from both the right and the left and challenged both inside and outside of his own party.

By examining the 1976 election in the larger context of the nation's cultural and ideological polarization, we can understand the contest not merely as a series of brilliant strategic moves and tragic missteps by the major candidates but also as a reflection of much larger conversations about the nation's future direction and place in the world. The election was partly about a national debate over economic policy, but it was about other anxieties as well—anxieties that would reshape the nation's parties and shift the United States to the right. If we want to understand the election of Ronald Reagan in the 1980s and George W. Bush and Donald Trump in the twenty-first century, we might start by examining the cultural polarization that surfaced in the 1976 election. And if we want to understand why Democratic presidential candidates would never again carry the South and would not win another national popular vote majority until 2008, we might find clues by analyzing why blue-collar and rural voters supported Carter in 1976—and why he was unable to meet their expectations once he was in office. By looking at this larger context, we can see that there was a much more momentous story occurring in 1976 than merely "how Jimmy won." In fact, this election solidified a partisan debate about nothing less than the nation's values and identity—a debate that would continue for decades. By the time the 1976 election was over, it almost did not matter whether the evangelical Democrat won or lost, because regardless of the outcome, the contest over the nation's values that was at the heart of this election would only grow more polarizing, and the bitter ideological debates that resulted would ensure that neither party would ever be the same again.

ACKNOWLEDGMENTS

This book would not have been possible without the support of numerous individuals and institutions.

First, I am grateful to Mike Nelson, coeditor of the University Press of Kansas's American Presidential Elections series, for inviting me to write this volume. Without his support, this book would never have been written, and without his careful editor's eye, I might not have discovered several potentially embarrassing mistakes that appeared in the first draft of the manuscript. I am grateful for Mike's superb knowledge of American political history and his careful attention to detail. He proved to be an ideal editor for this volume.

I am also grateful for two grants that enabled the timely completion of research for this book: a Gerald R. Ford Foundation Research Grant, which financed a trip to the Gerald R. Ford Library in Ann Arbor, Michigan, and an Award for Excellence in Research from the University of West Georgia's College of Arts and Humanities, which included a travel grant that partly covered a trip to the Ronald Reagan Presidential Library and the Hoover Institution. In addition, I am grateful for an Artists-in-Residency Writing Fellowship at Serenbe, Georgia, which provided a one-week stay at a secluded cabin, where I was able to write without interruption and get a substantial start on the first draft. I am grateful for the encouraging support I received from my colleagues, department chair, and college dean at the University of West Georgia, all of whom applauded the project and, in some cases (especially Pauline Gagnon) helped me secure funding for it.

I am also grateful to Mary Ziegler, Chapman Rackaway, and an anonymous peer reviewer for giving up some of their time to read my work carefully and offer helpful comments.

Because I started this project long after completing my PhD, my dissertation adviser Jim Patterson was not directly involved, but I could still sense his influence on my thinking. To whatever extent I have succeeded in maintaining an evenhanded tone, supporting my assertions with solid data, and writing an engrossing narrative, I owe a debt of thanks to Jim for his teaching and mentoring and his consistent example of what it means to be a conscientious and dedicated historian.

Finally, I am thankful for the support of my family throughout the research and writing process. My wife and intellectual confidant, Nadya, encouraged me to take on this project, and she gave me supportive and helpful feedback on early drafts of the chapters. Her constant reassurance and love were a continual blessing. I am also thankful for our baby daughter and our two sons, without whom this book might have been completed slightly earlier but with much less satisfaction or lasting joy. Our family will have wonderful memories of the summer travels we took in conjunction with some of the archival research for this project. If, as I argue in this volume, our political choices often reflect our values as much as our economic or material interests, it seems appropriate that this book could not have been written without a loving spouse and children who, in different ways, call me back to reflect on the values I consider most important.

1 TWO-PARTY CHAOS

The resignation of President Richard Nixon on August 9, 1974, decimated the Republican Party and ensured that the 1976 election would be different from any presidential contest Americans had seen before. As Nixon gave his final trademark two-finger victory salute and bid good-bye to a bewildered and angry nation, he left the presidency in the hands of a man who had never won a national—or even a statewide—election. Gerald Ford had served as a Michigan congressman for decades before becoming Nixon's vice president, and he was well liked among his constituents and congressional colleagues, but he had not been on the ticket during Nixon's reelection campaign in 1972. He joined the Nixon administration in 1973, after the resignation of disgraced vice president Spiro Agnew. He had never waged a national campaign, nor had he ever had to appeal to voters outside of his strongly conservative district in Grand Rapids. The 1976 election would be, in large measure, a referendum on Ford's performance, but he had only a few months to prepare before campaigning began. He would enter the race without the support of many of his fellow Republicans. Indeed, before Nixon's plane even reached California, some Republicans were already mulling the possibility of challenging Ford for the nomination.

Nixon's resignation created a power vacuum that offered politicians from both parties an opportunity to address the new cultural debates and economic crises that threatened to divide the nation. The 1976 election was, after all, the first presidential contest since the energy crisis of 1973 and the crippling stagflation that followed. It was the first election since *Roe v. Wade* legalized abortion across the nation. It was the first election in which newly mobilized gay rights activists were ready to fight for partisan recognition of their cause. It was the first presidential election in which the Equal Rights Amendment (ERA) was a contentious campaign issue, thanks to the polarizing conflict between feminist advocates of the amendment and conservative Catholic activist Phyllis Schlafly's anti-ERA campaign. It was the first election since the withdrawal of US troops from Vietnam and the subsequent collapse of the South Vietnamese government in Saigon. In short, the presidential contest would take place amid the worst economic conditions since the Great Depression, with Americans facing rising food prices, constant uncertainty about the oil supply, and the highest unemployment rate in decades. In addition, there was the cultural division over the painful legacy of Vietnam to contend with—a divide that would play out in debates over détente, the Panama Canal, and the status of eastern Europe. As if all this were not enough, the presidential campaign rallies would repeatedly be interrupted by antiabortion protesters, and the convention halls of both parties would be filled with women's rights activists who wanted to ensure that the nominees held the line on the ERA.[1]

In the midst of these cultural debates, both parties had to figure out their own ideological identities and reposition themselves to appeal to voters who were plagued by economic uncertainty and divided by the cultural debates rending the nation. With the economy in shambles and confidence in the government at an all-time low, no one was inclined to pay deference to Ford's incumbency; to both Republicans and Democrats, he seemed to be a vulnerable target. And so, within days of Nixon's resignation, the 1976 campaign unofficially began, with politicians of all stripes exploring the possibility of challenging Ford for the White House. Whether they fully realized it or not, their campaigns were not only about who should be the nation's chief executive but also about what the ideological identities of the two parties should be.

THE REPUBLICANS

For Republicans, it was a question of whether the GOP should be a center-right party that supported business interests, a balanced budget, and civil rights or whether it should move farther to the right, abandon its moderation on social issues, and exchange its policy of détente with the Soviet Union for a more hawkish hard-line anticommunism. It was a question of whether the party should merely try to hold the line on deficit spending or take an axe to the social welfare programs that were becoming increasingly unpopular with many conservative whites. And it was a question of whether the party would remain at least a moderate supporter of women's rights or embrace a different set of values.

Ford called himself a "conservative," but his conservatism was not the same as the right-wing ideology of California governor Ronald Reagan and his conservative activist supporters. When Ford described himself as a conservative, he meant that he wanted to balance the federal budget, promote private industry, and preserve international peace while modestly increasing defense spending. But to a growing group of Republicans who identified with the conservative movement, this was not enough. The readers of conservative magazines such as *National Review* or, farther to the right, *Human Events* wanted a stronger stance against international communism and a more concerted effort to roll back the programs of President Lyndon Johnson's Great Society. Many of them were angry that the Republican Party had acquiesced to the Democrats' social welfare programs and had nominated moderate centrists in every presidential contest since 1940, with the single exception of Barry Goldwater in 1964.

Reagan, who had replaced Goldwater as the standard-bearer for the conservative wing of the party, had briefly attempted to wrest the nomination away from Nixon in 1968, and it was well known that, after abandoning that effort, he had set his eyes on a more serious run for the White House in 1976. Having devoted his time, in the words of the *Los Angeles Times,* to "filling GOP speaking engagements and scouting his chances for the Republican presidential nomination in 1976," Reagan was in no mood to cede the nomination to the untested newcomer Ford. "What happens between now and 1976 (regarding the presidential race) will be dependent on his conduct in that office," he told a *Los Angeles Times* reporter less than four days after Ford was sworn in as president.[2] The message was clear: Reagan was putting Ford on notice. He would be watching for any deviation from conservative orthodoxy in the White House and would consider the party nomination fair game if Ford disappointed conservatives. That disappointment came only a few weeks later when Ford selected New York governor Nelson Rockefeller, the leading figure of the liberal wing of the party, as his vice president.

Many conservatives felt beleaguered because they were still insurgents, not power brokers, in the party. Though their numbers were growing, their place in the GOP was still uncertain. Their strength came from voters in the Sun Belt—especially Southern California and Arizona. This region, which had become Republican only after World War II, was far removed from the historical centers of Republican influence in the Midwest and Northeast. Their standard-bearer in 1964, Barry Goldwater, had suffered a landslide defeat in his contest against President Lyndon Johnson. To centrist and liberal Republicans, that failure served as confirmation that the conservative wing of the party was not the face of the GOP's future. To conservatives, though, it was just the beginning of their strategy for party takeover. Nixon had skillfully held the conservatives at bay through a combination of strategic White House appointments of a few young conservatives and rhetorical support for cultural conservatism. Once Nixon was gone, some of the conservatives were restless, and they looked to Reagan as their most likely champion.[3]

But to take over the party, conservatives would have to address the internal divisions in their movement. On college campuses, some of the young Republicans who identified with the conservative movement were libertarians who supported abortion rights and opposed the draft. They were attracted to Goldwater's and Reagan's complaints about the growth of the federal government and their championship of individual freedom. But the conservative movement also owed much of its early growth to middle-class whites who worked in the defense industry and were strong anticommunists and supporters of military buildup. Others—especially middle-class white Christian mothers—joined the conservative movement because they were concerned about the erosion of traditional Christian values. They wanted to restore prayer in public schools or even legislate against abortion—a stance that both Goldwater and many of the college-aged Republicans opposed. While they were out of power, it was easy for conservatives to downplay their differences, but any viable conservative candidate of the 1970s would have to take stands on these controversial issues, and that could threaten the unity of an already fissiparous movement.[4]

Conservatives were not the only Republicans who were unhappy about the direction of their party and who dreamed of getting Ford off the ticket in 1976. Two of the party's more liberal members—Senator Charles "Chuck" Percy of Illinois and Senator Charles "Mac" Mathias of Maryland—explored presidential runs, with Mathias going so far as to put his name on the Republican primary ballot in Massachusetts. And rumors were circulating that the nation's best-known liberal Republican, perennial candidate Nelson Rockefeller, might make a final bid for the White House, despite being Ford's vice president. Not to be outdone, a rapidly rising star in the moderate wing of the party—Senator Howard Baker of Tennessee—also began flirting with the idea of a primary challenge. Baker told one potential rival for the nomination in early 1975, when Ford had been in office less than six months, "I expect we'll be seeing a lot of each other in New Hampshire next year."[5]

As the economy stagnated and Ford struggled with a Democratic Congress that opposed his fiscal policies, his troubles escalated. When he pardoned Nixon a month into his tenure, whatever honeymoon he had enjoyed with the public ended instantly, as people began to link him with the corruption of the Nixon administration. His public approval ratings dropped by more than twenty points and never fully recovered.[6] Ford's vulnerability seemed to offer conservatives the opportunity they had been waiting for: they could try to wrest control of the Republican Party—assuming that the liberals and centrists in the party did not seize the initiative themselves.

The Republican Party's identity was hotly contested partly because Watergate had destroyed whatever institutions were holding it together. The party suffered landslide defeats in the midterm elections of 1974. Republicans in the Ninety-Fourth Congress held only 38 seats in the Senate and only 144 of the 435 seats in the House of Representatives. By 1976, only 22 percent of voters identified as Republicans, compared with 46 percent who identified as Democrats. Not since Herbert Hoover's presidency during the Great Depression had the GOP suffered such major reversals. New Right activist Richard Viguerie predicted that "in ten years, there won't be a dozen people in this country calling themselves Republicans."[7] Could a Republican candidate in 1976—whether Ford or one of his challengers—defy the odds and rehabilitate the party? And if so, what would a post-Nixon GOP stand for?

Nixon had been on the ballot in every presidential election except for one between 1952 and 1972. For twenty years, he had defined Republican Party politics, moving from the right wing to the center, rescuing the party from the liberalism of Rockefeller and the conservatism of Goldwater. Even in the wake of personal defeats, he had managed to position himself as the face of the party's future. But with Nixon's ignominious departure, a significant portion of the party had gone with him. The 1976 election would be a test of whether the party could reinvent itself and whether that reinvention would reshape the party's ideological foundation.

THE DEMOCRATS

Democrats should have been jubilant about their prospects in 1976, but their party was so deeply fractured that it made the Republicans' feuds seem like a garden tea-party conversation in comparison. The party had not managed to elect a president since Lyndon Johnson, and the legacy of the Vietnam War that had tarnished his administration still divided the party. In 1968 protests over the war rocked the Democratic National Convention, and Johnson's protégé, Vice President Hubert Humphrey, was nominated amid the pandemonium. Dissenting antiwar delegates were outraged that their party's nominee was a representative of the Johnson administration who had not won a single primary. In 1972 the antiwar forces bested Humphrey and traditional party leaders, but their standard-bearer, George McGovern, went on to suffer the biggest landslide defeat in any presidential election up to that time: he lost forty-nine states and carried only Massachusetts and the District of Columbia. Three weeks after Nixon's resignation, *New York Times* political reporter R. W. Apple Jr. concluded that the prospects of a Democrat defeating Ford to retake the White House in 1976 were "fairly gloomy."[8]

The problem was not that Ford was a formidable candidate or that the Democrats were unpopular but rather that the Democratic Party was so riven that its conservative and liberal factions were at war with each other. For more than three decades after Franklin Roosevelt's landslide victory in 1932, Democrats had been firmly in the center of American politics, and they had repeatedly won elections with a coalition of working-class voters who believed in labor unions, a government social safety net, and defense against international communism. Two-thirds of Catholics and an overwhelming number of northern urban residents joined African Americans and a somewhat unreliable coalition of southern whites to give Democrats control of the White House for twenty-eight of the thirty-six years between 1932 and 1968. But debates among various groups of Democrats over civil rights, the Vietnam War, feminism, and sexuality factionalized the party and threatened to deprive the Democrats of future victory. When the party stood for economic growth, for the security of white male–headed households, and against communism, it had been easy to win elections. But now that the social movements of the 1960s threatened to upset this delicate balance by introducing new concerns into the political equation, Democrats squared off against each other along racial, generational, and ideological lines, fighting with members of their own party over which set of values they should embrace.[9]

On one side were the McGovern Democrats—social liberals whose political consciousness had been forged in the antiwar movement and who took liberal positions on women's rights, abortion, busing, and foreign policy. They supported universal health insurance, progressive income taxation, and an expansion of civil rights policy. These voters tended to be younger and better educated than other Democrats, and they cared more about civil rights than about labor unions. On the opposite side was George Wallace, the Alabama governor who had been the public face of southern opposition to desegregation in the 1960s. Wallace had run for president three times before, and he was preparing another campaign in 1976. By the summer of 1975, he had raised more money than all his rivals combined—a sign of his continuing appeal among social conservatives in his party. Wallace could muster the support of only about 25 percent of Democrats; however, the number of Democrats opposed to McGovern-style social liberalism and willing to back a moderately conservative candidate was far larger and probably amounted to a majority in the party. As Lloyd Bentsen, another conservative southern Democrat (but not so far to the right as Wallace), pointed out, 57 percent of Democratic voters classified themselves in public opinion surveys as "moderates or conservatives." Indeed, in the summer of 1972, when McGovern was running on a liberal platform of opposition to the Vietnam War, 50 percent of Democrats favored an *increase* in defense spending, 47 percent opposed legalizing abortion, and 73 percent objected to the use of busing to achieve school integration. Sixty-nine percent said that they opposed amnesty for draft evaders.[10]

Perhaps it was not surprising that the Republicans' charge that McGovern was the candidate of "acid, amnesty, and abortion" doomed his campaign. This was the case not just among Republican voters but among more than a third of Democratic voters as well. These anti-McGovern Democrats included northern Catholics, Southern Baptists, and large numbers of midwesterners who were disturbed by their party's liberal drift. Their willingness to cross party lines and vote for Nixon gave the Democratic Party the most humiliating defeat it had ever experienced in a presidential race.[11]

The Democrats' problem, it seemed, was that they had ignored warnings that whites wanted the party to become more socially conservative. In 1970, two years before the Nixon-McGovern race, political analysts Richard Scammon and Ben Wattenberg argued in their book *The Real Majority* that the center of the electorate—that is, the "real majority" that was key to winning elections—was to the right of the Democratic Party on social issues and to the left of the Republican Party on economics. Nixon heeded that advice, but McGovern took the opposite course. He and his supporters pushed the party much farther to the left on social issues, angering many labor union members, northern Catholics, and southern Democrats who had long been attracted to the Democratic Party's economic promises. He won only 31 percent of the white vote nationwide, only 29 percent of the white southern vote, and only 22 percent of the white Protestant vote. And he performed more poorly among Catholics than any previous Democratic presidential candidate.[12]

If judged by voting returns, the Democratic Party's most loyal supporters were now African Americans, but many of them also felt ignored and beleaguered. Although 25 percent of the nation's Democrats were black—and although 82 percent of black voters cast their ballots for McGovern in 1972—several of the nation's leading civil rights leaders believed that the Democratic Party showed little interest in their concerns, and they pleaded with Democratic politicians to reverse this apathy. Fourteen percent of blacks were unemployed, and their economic situation was deteriorating. Court decisions and a grassroots political movement against busing to achieve desegregated schools had deprived blacks of some of the political gains of the 1960s. "We have traveled a long way since a President stood in the well of Congress and proclaimed 'We Shall Overcome,' and it's all been in the wrong direction," complained Vernon Jordan, president of the National Urban League.[13]

Black voters cared most strongly about two issues: jobs and civil rights. The vast majority took strongly liberal positions on both, and for that reason, most pundits considered them "liberal." But their interests were an uneasy fit for many of the white Democrats who also laid claim to the liberal label. The younger generation of white rights-conscious liberals invariably claimed to support civil rights for blacks, but they often made environmentalism, foreign policy, and women's rights higher priorities, and they sometimes put less emphasis on creating jobs than on reforming government. The "bread-and-butter" New Deal liberals of the northern cities might have seemed a better fit for African American interests, but their strong opposition to busing and their close alliances with white-dominated labor unions that had long discriminated against blacks alienated some black voters. Surveys of black Democrats in the mid-1970s revealed that their preferred presidential candidate was either Hubert Humphrey or Ted Kennedy, both of whom offered a return to the liberalism of the previous decade, when civil rights, poverty relief, and jobs creation had been priorities of the national Democratic Party.[14] Neither Humphrey nor Kennedy was a declared candidate in 1976, and with their absence from the field, it seemed unlikely that any presidential contender could excite blacks.

Black voter turnout—which was always slightly lower than white turnout—was declining, and many blacks were pessimistic about the prospects of making substantive political gains in 1976.[15] Unlike in 1972, when Representative Shirley Chisholm (D-NY) had won a few delegates as the first black woman to run for the Democratic Party's presidential nomination, there were no black presidential contenders in 1976. And, as some blacks noted, even the moderately liberal Democrats seemed a lot more concerned about placating the Wallace voters than advancing black interests. Most blacks were not willing to vote for President Ford or any other Republican—especially because they blamed their dire economic situation on the Ford administration's policy of fiscal austerity—but unless the Democratic Party paid more attention to their concerns, they were prepared to stay home on Election Day or give the Democratic nominee only tepid support.[16]

If blacks had relatively little influence on presidential politics, their power in Congress may have been even more limited. African Americans held only 17 of the 435 seats in the House of Representatives and only a single Senate seat. The majority of the blacks in Congress came from northern cities that were experiencing a rapid white flight. Only three represented districts in former Confederate states.[17] With the exception of Atlanta and a few other cities, conservative whites still controlled the Democratic Party in most of the South, and they exerted a powerful dampening effect on the party's rights-conscious liberalism.

After 1974 the Democrats still controlled Congress by overwhelming margins, but they did so only because congressional races were regional; candidates could take positions that matched the particular inclinations of their districts. Indeed, when it came to political ideology, the regional differences in the country were even more pronounced than the partisan divisions. In the Senate, southern Democrats voted with the conservatives 79 percent of the time—making them, on average, even more conservative than the Republicans, who voted with conservatives only 69 percent of the time. In contrast, northern Democrats had a mere 19 percent conservative voting record. In New York, a liberal Democrat like Bella Abzug could win election to the House of Representatives on a platform of unapologetic feminism and outspoken support for gay rights, while in Alabama, Democrat Walter Flowers, chairman of Wallace's 1972 presidential campaign, could win a seat in Congress on exactly the opposite platform. But in a national election, could one candidate unite all these factions? Many Democrats thought not. "The fact is, we just don't have two or three people who can appeal across the divisions in our party," Democratic National Committee (DNC) executive director Robert Keefe declared in September 1974.[18]

THE CHALLENGES AND OPPORTUNITIES FOR BOTH PARTIES

Both parties entered the 1976 election season with serious weaknesses, and both faced a seemingly insurmountable challenge in uniting their various factions. Even worse, many Americans had become disillusioned with politics and the two-party system altogether. By the fall of 1975, only 28 percent of Americans approved of "the way the United States Congress is handling its job," while 54 percent expressed disapproval. Democrats were almost as likely as Republicans to excoriate Congress, even though both the House and the Senate were under solid Democratic control. Regardless of their party affiliation, American voters—especially those of the younger generation—demonstrated an increased willingness to split their tickets at the voting booth, and a growing number refused to identify with any party at all. According to National Election Studies (NES) surveys, 37 percent of American voters in 1976 classified themselves as Independents—up from 28 percent only ten years earlier. Many eligible voters simply boycotted politics, refusing to show up at the polls. The voter turnout rate in the 1972 presidential election was only 56 percent—down from 63 percent in 1968 and 64 percent in 1960. In the 1974 midterm election, only 39 percent of voters participated, compared with 47 percent four years earlier. In the aftermath of Watergate, the Nixon and Johnson administrations' prevarications about the Vietnam War, and the cavalcade of congressional sex scandals uncovered by a new post-Watergate breed of investigative journalists, Americans' disillusionment with the political system was hardly surprising. In 1974 only 36 percent of Americans said they trusted government—down from 76 percent a decade earlier.[19]

Voters' cynicism about the major parties was coupled with a general pessimism about the future. Forty-four percent of Americans expected that in 1976, the nation's bicentennial year, American power would "decline," while only 42 percent expected it to increase; at the same time, 63 percent expected "Russian power" to increase, and 65 percent predicted the same for "Red China." Most Americans expected the nation's economic situation to worsen. Seventy percent of respondents to a Gallup poll conducted in December 1975 believed that 1976 would be a year of "economic difficulty," with 57 percent specifically predicting "rising unemployment."[20]

And yet, in the midst of such despair and disillusionment among the general public, a record number of presidential aspirants decided to run in 1976 and attempt to appeal to a cynical electorate. In February 1975, a full year before the first primary, *New York Times* columnist Tom Wicker calculated that there were a dozen Democrats who might make "some serious effort at the nomination." Wicker considered this number unusually high, but in fact, his count was a little low, omitting several candidates who eventually entered the race.[21]

There were at least three reasons why so many candidates decided to throw their hats in the ring. The first was a change in campaign finance rules. The 1976 election was the first in the nation's history in which there were strict limits on fund-raising and expenditures. Under the Federal Election Campaign Act of 1974, passed in the wake of Watergate, no one could donate more than $1,000 to a presidential candidate, and no candidate could spend more than $10 million in the primaries and another $12 million in the general election. A candidate could apply for matching funds from the US government after raising $5,000 in small donations (that is, no more than $250) from voters in at least twenty states. These new rules favored dark-horse candidates and those with popular appeal, and they limited the power of candidates with ties to big donors and corporate wealth. Any candidate who had the time to go out on the hustings and start raising cash could qualify for federal matching funds and run a presidential campaign on the cheap, without worrying about being overshadowed by party regulars with large fund-raising operations. In the 1972 race, Nixon had spent $57 million and McGovern $39 million.[22] This time, each candidate's expenditures were capped at a much lower figure. These spending limits made a presidential race conceivable for little-known candidates who would not have had much of a chance if forced to compete against well-financed political heavyweights.

A second reason for the large number of candidates was a change in the DNC's rules governing party primaries. Until the 1970s, party primaries meant little; only a few states held them, and they were sometimes treated as little more than "beauty contests," since convention delegates were often not bound to vote in accordance with their state's primary results. The real nomination work occurred at the conventions, not in the primary contests. Thus, candidates who wanted to make a serious run for the nomination usually entered only a few primaries to demonstrate their popular appeal; they focused most of their efforts on winning the support of party bosses. John F. Kennedy secured his party's nomination in 1960 after winning only three primaries; Adlai Stevenson did so in 1956 after winning only one; and Hubert Humphrey did so in 1968 after winning none. But the rise of binding, winner-take-all primaries in the early 1970s changed the political equation, allowing an outsider like George McGovern to clinch his party's nomination in 1972 based almost entirely on his success in the primaries. The DNC then changed its rules and declared winner-take-all primaries illegal. Instead, any candidate who received at least 15 percent of the votes in a state primary could win a share of that state's delegates. At least thirty states were expected to hold primaries in 1976, and the others planned to hold caucuses that were open to grassroots party members.[23] Thus, the convention delegates for both Republicans and Democrats would be chosen by the voters. Although the Republicans continued to hold a number of winner-take-all primaries, the Democrats' refusal to do so meant that even candidates who had only marginal appeal might win a few delegates and be able to stay in the race until the convention. Many people believed that getting 15 percent of the vote in a small state would not be difficult. New Hampshire, for instance, had only 115,000 registered Democratic voters, and only a fraction of them were expected to show up for the party primary.[24] Any candidate with a few months' time on his hands and the determination to knock on a lot of doors in some of the larger New Hampshire towns might convince a few thousand people to vote for him and thus start winning delegates.

But the third and final reason so many candidates entered the race in 1976 was the exciting opportunity it offered for almost any candidate to remake the nation's politics. With McGovern's crushing defeat and Nixon's startling resignation throwing each of the parties into disarray, the political slate had been wiped clean, and all the old assumptions were up for renegotiation. Any candidate could conceivably win his party's nomination and remake the party in his image. At the beginning of the 1976 campaign, it was not entirely clear which party would oppose abortion and which would support *Roe v. Wade,* or which party would support détente and which would oppose it. Both parties had serious presidential contenders on both sides of these issues. The 1976 presidential election was a contest to decide the ideological identity of the two parties and the future of American politics. With the prospects so immense and the stakes so high, there was no shortage of candidates who wanted to try their hand at the game.

2 THE DEMOCRATIC FIELD IN 1974

Nearly all Democrats, regardless of ideology, had one major goal as they contemplated the upcoming 1976 election: avoid a repetition of the McGovern debacle. George McGovern's nomination in 1972 had split the party by alienating the traditionalists, who deserted the Democrats in droves on Election Day. McGovern not only lost the "Solid South"—which had never before voted so monolithically Republican in a presidential race—but also faced defeat in almost every other state in the nation, including his own. The party could not afford another McGovern-like candidate.[1] But there was no party consensus on exactly how to avoid this. As the various factions of the Democratic Party debated the causes of the McGovern loss, they contested not only the future of the party but also the meaning of the word "liberal."

Was a liberal someone who favored protecting labor unions and promoting large government spending programs, such as the New Deal and the Great Society, while opposing the feminist and antiwar movements? Or were liberals those people who opposed the Vietnam War and supported civil rights for African Americans, even if labor unions meant little to them? This was the struggle the Democratic Party faced in the mid-1970s—a struggle that pitted younger, white, college-educated, suburban McGovern voters against older, religiously conservative, lifelong Democrats who resented what the younger voters had done to their party. The struggle between these two factions of very different "liberals" played out in televised shouting matches on the floors of the Democratic National Conventions in 1968 and 1972 and, less dramatically, in voting booths in state primary elections. No one doubted that the rifts were real and deep, and no one knew how to mend them.

For the many Democrats who were older, working class, or religiously conservative, McGovern represented a turn away from the ideals of Franklin D. Roosevelt and Harry Truman, which they wanted to resurrect. The party won elections when it defended labor unions, the military, and the social values of white working-class families, they thought. McGovern lost because he had exchanged traditional New Deal, bread-and-butter liberalism for the rights-conscious liberalism of feminists, antiwar activists, and blacks. He faced repudiation from union leaders who had never before endorsed a Republican, and he performed more poorly among Catholics than any Democratic presidential candidate up to that time. In the vernacular of the day, he lost the "middle American" vote by a landslide—or, what a later generation would call the "social conservative" vote. White voters who attended traditionally oriented churches (whether Catholic or Protestant), favored traditional gender roles, disliked the antiwar "hippies," supported the military, blamed blacks for riots in the inner cities, and worried about the rising crime rate and the sexual revolution were highly unlikely to vote for McGovern, even if—as was often the case—they were lifelong Democrats. For the millions of social conservatives in the Democratic Party, the answer to the McGovern debacle was clear: the party could not nominate another rights-conscious liberal. Some of these social conservatives found a champion in Alabama governor George Wallace, who in 1974 was already preparing for his next presidential race and riding high in the polls.

GEORGE WALLACE

Wallace had run for president three times before, and he had more name recognition than almost any other aspirant for the Democratic presidential nomination. An assassination attempt during his 1972 presidential campaign had left him paraplegic and confined to a wheelchair, but that did not deter his goal of winning the White House. Although he was in constant pain—the *New York Times* reported in November 1974 that he was in "tragically weak physical shape," with massive hearing loss and rapidly deteriorating eyesight in addition to the numerous maladies resulting from the bullet wound—he discovered that he was an even more effective campaigner by mail than he had been on the stump.[2] In 1968 and 1972 his presidential campaign stops had been raucous rallies often attended by tens of thousands of cheering supporters. Now, many of those same people, sitting in their living rooms and reading Wallace's direct-mail appeals, rallied around him once again.

Wallace used his mailing list of two million supporters from the 1972 campaign to continue to solicit small contributions. By 1975, that effort was being managed by Richard Viguerie, a young, populist, conservative Catholic from Texas who was considered the national master of direct-mail fund-raising. As a result, Wallace raised $3 million in 1975. After paying $2 million for fund-raising costs, he was left with a net return of $1 million—far more than any other candidate had raised at that stage in the race. Ninety-two percent of the money came from donations of less than $100, with most contributions amounting to no more than $25. Wallace received two thousand pieces of mail a day and was already getting about $1,500 a day in small donations by November 1974—a rate that would increase as his campaign progressed.[3] In the third quarter of 1975, for instance, Wallace led all other candidates in fund-raising by garnering $842,319 from 15,636 individuals—more than twice as much as Ronald Reagan's $395,793 and nearly twice as much as Wallace's nearest Democratic rival, Henry M. "Scoop" Jackson. It was even more than the $685,939 raised by President Ford, who relied on the deep pockets of well-heeled Republican contributors.[4]

Wallace portrayed himself in his fund-raising letters as the candidate of the common person. Embracing the slogan "Trust the People," he depicted his effort as a fight against the "liberal politicians" in his party who had nominated McGovern. His campaign was a last-ditch effort to reclaim the party for those who believed in the principles it had championed before "left-wing socialistic policies" produced "forced busing," "government bureaucracy," "new giveaway social programs," "higher prices and taxes," and "rampant crime." Though he no longer endorsed racial segregation, he still positioned himself as the candidate of an aggrieved white working class that was paying the price for liberal social initiatives through rising crime rates and higher taxes. This was a message with national appeal, he believed; the alienation felt by Alabama Baptists was paralleled by the anxieties of culturally conservative Catholics in other regions. In Boston, he talked about busing; in South Florida, he talked about abortion and Cuban

Figure 2.1. Alabama governor George Wallace campaigning for the 1976 Democratic presidential nomination. (Courtesy of Alabama Department of Archives and History)

communism. Against the advice of his campaign manager, he decided to make a serious bid to win the Massachusetts primary, hoping to beat the liberal Democrats on their home turf in the only state McGovern had carried in 1972.[5]

In doing so, Wallace took positions that closely presaged the rhetoric adopted by Jerry Falwell's Moral Majority and other Religious Right organizations in the next election. Although Wallace, like many southern Protestants of the early 1970s, had once supported abortion rights, he now espoused a pro-life position, becoming the only major Democratic contender in 1976 to support a constitutional amendment to ban abortion. He championed school prayer and excoriated the Supreme Court for ruling to restrict it. He denounced the proliferation of pornography. He lashed out at bloated welfare rolls, charging that "15–25 per cent" of the people on welfare were "completely ineligible." He called for a return of the death penalty (which the Supreme Court had recently restricted) and advocated a tough law-and-order approach to combating crime. He also denounced foreign aid programs and détente and promised a strong, hawkish stance against communism. "We ought to have bombed them out of existence up in North Viet Nam," he declared in 1975. "People say that would be barbaric, but if we had done it when some of them first said it, it wouldn't have cost one-tenth or one-fifteenth the lives that have been lost—and we would have won." Although the emphases of his campaign varied from state to state, the theme of populist opposition to elite bureaucratic attacks on commonsense moral norms always predominated. As one advertisement that ran in South Carolina in January 1976 proclaimed, voters should support Wallace if they shared his concerns about "forced busing, constant taxation of the average citizen, welfare loafing, foreign aid giveaways, decaying moral standards, unemployment, crime in the streets, soft courts, uncaring judges and many other issues."[6]

Wallace's defense of the military and his cultural traditionalism caused many, both in the 1970s and today, to view him as a conservative.[7] Several liberal analysts of the mid-1970s classified him with Reagan; both the *New Leader* and the *Nation* predicted that Reagan and Wallace would join forces for a third-party ticket in the fall. But despite the significant overlap between Reagan's and Wallace's proposals, their ideology had different foundations. Wallace was not merely Reagan with a southern accent; he was, first and foremost, a populist. His was a campaign of the "people" versus the Washington "elite," and he grounded his proposals in the claim that he was standing up for the poor against uncaring, misguided bureaucrats. Most of the "limousine liberals," he wrote, "had never known privation in their lives. . . . I believe those of us who have known poverty can better understand the poor than the self-flagellating liberals who were born with silver spoons in their mouths." Like Reagan, he railed against high tax rates on the middle class—denouncing the "bureaucrats" who were wasting the "working man's money"—but unlike Reagan, he took a special interest in attacking corporate power along with government bureaucracy. For much of the 1970s, one of his chief projects as Alabama governor was to fight utility rate increases. He never abandoned his faith in the New Deal, and he held out hope that he could save the Democratic Party from the wrong turn it had made in the 1960s. But he frequently advocated the idea that both the national culture and the government in Washington had departed markedly from the values of the founding fathers and that the nation therefore needed to be "saved" by a mass movement of common people who would "stand up for America."[8]

His supporters may have been even more favorably disposed toward large federal programs than he was. Though some Wallace supporters were movement conservatives who liked Reagan and could move comfortably between the right wings of the Republican and Democratic Parties, most were culturally conservative Democrats who hated "welfare" but still believed in large government programs to help those who were deserving. One survey of voters in the 1976 primaries showed that 61 percent of Wallace supporters favored an *increase* in "government spending for health, education, [or the] poor." Fifty-three percent said they wanted to "strengthen Social Security," even if it required "higher taxes." Sixty-seven percent supported "federal job guarantees." Their number-one concern was not the "size of the federal government" (only 5 percent of Wallace voters cited this concern, compared with 11 percent of Reagan supporters) but the "state of the economy"; 50 percent listed this as their primary reason for supporting Wallace. Seventy-five percent of Wallace supporters said they were "dissatisfied" with the state of the economy, and more of them expected the economy to get worse than to get better. In fact, Wallace voters were less likely than supporters of any other candidate to say they were "satisfied" with the nation's economic condition.[9]

Wallace may have believed that he could win the Democratic presidential nomination, but no one else in the party outside of his campaign thought this was possible. Even though some polls in 1975 showed him at the head of the Democratic pack, and even though he led all candidates in fund-raising, he was by far the most polarizing Democrat in the race. Nearly one-third of Democrats said they would "always oppose" Wallace in any hypothetical matchup, and another 17 percent expressed a generally unfavorable view of him. As one pollster for Jimmy Carter's campaign concluded in 1975 after examining the survey data, "Wallace has a fairly solid 20–25% base of support among Democrats but not much potential to increase that support . . . Wallace's strongest support comes from old people, less well-educated voters, and southerners." Indeed, even in his home region, "he just barely gets a majority of Democratic votes in the South"—probably because he had extremely limited support among African Americans and because moderately liberal white Democrats and younger, college-educated voters in the South likewise hated him.[10] His only hope for the nomination was a permanently divided field that would allow him to win a consistent plurality of the vote and continue to collect delegates in the party's proportional representation system. But even then, he could not prevail without a majority of the delegates, and that seemed highly unlikely, given the strong opposition to his candidacy from all other wings of the party.

Even if Wallace could not win the nomination, the Democratic Party could not afford to ignore his constituency. Many pundits expected him to gain enough delegates to influence the platform and shift the party to the right. He could also act as a spoiler in the race—a prospect that many Democrats feared. If Wallace voters boycotted the party, the Democrats would lose the presidential race, just as they had in 1968, when Wallace's third-party candidacy likely drew off a sufficient number of Democratic votes to throw the election to Richard Nixon. If Democrats wanted to win the White House, they had to keep this from happening, which meant they had to appeal to Wallace's socially conservative (but economically liberal) voters and prevent Wallace from getting very far in the race.

HENRY "SCOOP" JACKSON

One candidate who believed he could appeal to Wallace voters was Senator Henry M. Jackson of Washington State, known to his friends and supporters as "Scoop." Jackson was the oldest Democratic candidate in the race (he would turn sixty-four in 1976) and had the longest political career by far. He had been in Congress since 1941 and had run for president once before, in 1972. Many of the party's institutions were behind him, and he seemed well positioned to win a large share of the primary votes. Throughout 1975 he surpassed all his rivals except for Wallace in fund-raising. He was popular with labor unions, Jews, and many northeastern Catholics. George Meany, president of the AFL-CIO and the most politically prominent labor leader of the 1970s, supported him, as did civil rights leader Bayard Rustin. Jackson also enjoyed the endorsement of numerous colleagues in Congress. His campaign, according to the *New York Times,* was well greased with money from large Democratic donors and was "the most highly organized" among the Democratic presidential aspirants. He had earned a reputation as an intelligent, hardworking senator who was an expert in many fields, especially defense and energy policy, which seemed especially relevant in the wake of the nation's massive energy crisis. "Probably no other man or woman in Congress has so powerful—though not uncontroversial—a voice on so many leading issues," the

Figure 2.2. Senator Henry M. "Scoop" Jackson with young campaign volunteers. (University of Washington Libraries, Special Collections, UW 27865z)

Washington Post declared in July 1974. "Certainly he is one of two or three Democrats at the top of everyone's list of possibles."[11]

Jackson thought he had a viable strategy for winning the nomination by relying on the traditional bases of Democratic support. Labor union endorsements, which McGovern had pointedly failed to secure, were still seen as essential for any viable Democratic presidential campaign. By locking up the support of labor in the northeastern corridor, Jackson hoped to win a lot of the early delegate-rich primaries in big industrial states like Pennsylvania. Then, with the support of Jewish and Catholic voters in New York and Massachusetts, where he enjoyed strong leads, he expected to emerge as a favorite for the nomination.[12]

In some ways, Jackson was a thoroughly orthodox Democrat in the mold of Lyndon Johnson and the Great Society. The *New York Times* characterized him as "very much in the vein of the nineteen-fifties liberal pushing for more, more, more as the cure to all problems." He had a "long record of support for labor, civil rights legislation and massive government programs, including those to assist the troubled cities"—a record that seemed ideally suited to win the support of liberal voters and traditional Democrats. His theme for the 1976 campaign would be the economy, he promised. He would relentlessly press for government jobs programs and greater economic intervention to secure full employment.[13]

Some aspects of Jackson's political platform reminded people of Senator Hubert Humphrey, another northern liberal senator who had supported large government programs for years. However, Jackson had two fatal flaws that made him the inveterate enemy of the younger generation of rights-conscious liberals who had supported McGovern. He was an outspoken opponent of court-ordered busing and an ardent Cold Warrior who supported an increase in defense spending. Wallace's campaign staff viewed Jackson as their biggest competitor for the culturally conservative Democrats they needed to win, but the stances that attracted some Wallacites to Jackson made him anathema to many liberal McGovernites.[14]

The busing issue had hurt Jackson with liberals during his run for the party nomination in 1972, and for this reason, he had resolved not to stress this issue in 1976. In fact, the question of busing was more symbolic than substantive, because no elected politician—not even the president—could stop a court order from being enforced. President Gerald Ford, for instance, repeatedly criticized court-mandated busing, yet it continued unabated during his term in office. Even so, the issue had emotional appeal because it pitted civil rights against parental rights and possibly children's well-being—giving rise to strong emotions on both sides. The conflict began in 1971 when the Supreme Court ruled in *Swann v. Charlotte-Mecklenburg Board of Education* that communities could achieve court-mandated desegregation of schools by busing white children to predominantly black schools across town and, in turn, busing black children from inner-city neighborhoods to white schools in the suburbs. The result would be the immediate desegregation of schools—a goal that had never been fully realized, even seventeen years after *Brown v. Board of Education*. But many white parents did not see it that way. To them, the *Charlotte-Mecklenburg* decision destroyed neighborhood schools and disrupted family life by forcing children to leave their communities for what the parents viewed as an inferior educational experience in a different part of the city. The result was outrage. Throughout the North, angry parents formed antibusing organizations, such as Louise Day Hick's Restore Our Alienated Rights (ROAR) in Boston. In Pontiac, Michigan, antibusing protesters dynamited ten empty school buses. Very few parents approved of such violence, but millions were hoping for a politically peaceful end to busing. Seventy-four percent of Americans opposed the use of busing to achieve school desegregation, according to a Roper opinion poll taken in late 1975. Even among blacks, busing received mixed reviews; only 45 percent of African Americans approved of it. The strongest opponents of busing included large Democratic constituencies, such as white, working-class Catholics in northern cities. In fact, only 14 percent of all Democrats approved of busing, according to the Roper survey.[15]

Given its widespread unpopularity, one might have thought that opposition to busing would be a safe position for a politician to take. And it was—for conservatives. On the Republican side, busing received strong criticism from both Reagan and Ford throughout the 1976 campaign, and on the Democratic side, Wallace made opposition to busing one of his major issues. But because busing was a court-mandated civil rights measure, any liberal who attacked it risked having his progressive bona fides called into question and might even be characterized as a racist. Jackson protested that he had an "impeccable" voting record on civil rights legislation, having supported all the major civil rights initiatives of the previous two decades. But in the view of many progressives, he squandered this achievement by pandering to white suburban racism and vehemently opposing the major school desegregation measure of the 1970s. African Americans took a similar view. An *Ebony* magazine poll of more than 1,500 black elected officials taken in the summer of 1974 showed that Jackson was the preferred presidential nominee for only 3 percent of them.[16]

Perhaps Jackson could have gotten away with a nuanced, cautious critique of busing. Perhaps he could have said that he supported its intent but wanted to see its implementation revised, as liberal candidates such as Sargent Shriver did. But by making busing his target issue in 1972 and denouncing it vociferously to win the votes of disgruntled white parents that civil rights liberals suspected of racism, Jackson probably destroyed whatever chance he had of getting support from the McGovern wing of the party. His voting record on civil rights might have been "good enough," but according to the liberal magazine the *Nation,* Jackson had "become in recent years something of a Kleagle for the Chamber of Commerce kind of racism that hides under ledger sheets. He has become a leading spokesman for opponents of the sort of racism that is thought to hurt real estate values."[17] He would continue to win a lot of votes from white working-class and suburban parents who shared his views—and he would even win primaries in 1976 based largely on his opposition to busing—but popularity among these constituencies could not compensate for the strong opposition he now faced from rights-conscious liberals who believed he did not represent the values of the Democratic Party. And by the time of the 1976 campaign, liberal Democrats thought they had an even more potent reason to hate Jackson: his stance on defense. On that issue they went after him with a vengeance, determined to do whatever was necessary to block him from winning the nomination.

The rights-conscious McGovern wing of the Democratic Party of the 1970s was forged in opposition to the Vietnam War. Some of the liberal Democrats who were born in the 1940s cut their political teeth in college antiwar organizations of the New Left, such as Students for a Democratic Society. Many then entered party politics in 1968 by supporting Eugene McCarthy or Robert F. Kennedy—both of whom made opposition to the Vietnam War their signature issue. Liberal Democrats lost their fight to nominate an antiwar candidate in 1968, but they got their revenge in 1972 when McGovern, who promised an immediate end to the Vietnam War and amnesty for draft evaders, won the nomination.

Jackson supported the Vietnam War for its entire duration. Worse, even when the war was over, he called for increases in defense spending to continue the fight against communism around the globe. Although he was willing to support détente with the Soviet Union in the abstract, he was critical of Nixon's and Ford's negotiations with the Soviet Union because he believed they had given up too much. Any material assistance the United States gave to the Soviet Union must be accompanied by Soviet disarmament, he believed. Because the Nixon and Ford administrations had not insisted on this, the United States was "subsidiz[ing] the Soviet industrial-military complex." Jackson coupled his opposition to Soviet power with unconditional support for Israel. This made him the favorite of many Jewish voters and helped him raise money from some wealthy supporters of Jewish causes, but most liberals only scoffed. Support for Israel may have been the only defense cause liberals favored, but outside of Jewish circles, a commitment to protect Israel was not a sufficiently high priority to compensate for the cardinal sin of being a foreign policy hawk.[18]

Liberal Democrats could not stand the thought of having a presidential nominee whose stances on defense and foreign policy were to the right of the Republican president's. They made stopping Jackson one of their highest priorities. "When Goldwater lost in 1964, he retained a veto over the 1968 candidate," one liberal Democrat told the *New York Times* in November 1974. He explained that McGovern Democrats had earned the right to exercise a similar "veto" power. "We're going to have that veto in 1976, and we're going to use it against Jackson."[19]

The irony was that in opposing Jackson as a "conservative," McGovern Democrats embraced candidates who were far less liberal on economic questions. On economic matters, Jackson fit the mold of Lyndon Johnson: there was no problem that more government spending could not solve. But that was the trouble, the progressives believed; Jackson was too much like Johnson in all his stances—including his disastrous belief in a military buildup—and he represented everything they had spent the last eight years fighting against. Jackson's blend of policy positions—a faith in government spending as a way to counter recession and aid the less fortunate, combined with a firm adherence to the ideals of the Cold War—might have made him an ideal Democratic candidate in the early 1960s. But in the mid-1970s his time had passed, at least as far as the party's new liberals were concerned. The liberals of the 1970s gave much less weight to economic liberalism than Jackson did, and they placed a much higher priority on the moral issues of peace and human rights. Their priorities no longer reflected the thinking of the New Deal era—the predominant ideology when Jackson was a young man. They embraced the ideology of the late 1960s, when civil rights and antiwar protests seemed far more urgent than the formation of large government programs.

Jackson was born in 1912, and he would have cast his first presidential ballot for Franklin Roosevelt in the midst of the Great Depression. He entered Congress on the eve of World War II and then spent his career in the House and Senate supporting the Cold War military buildup of the 1950s and 1960s. He witnessed the poverty of the Depression firsthand, and he lived through the patriotic fervor of the Second World War, the Truman Doctrine, the Marshall Plan, and the Korean War. For the most part, the liberal Democrats were born in the 1930s, 1940s, and 1950s. They were too young to remember the Depression or much of World War II; they came of age at a time of widespread middle-class prosperity but increasing concern about civil rights and the morality of the Vietnam War. For them, a liberal political agenda was not primarily about providing a social safety net for the less fortunate and a strong defense for the nation—as it had been for the Truman administration and for Senator Jackson. Rather, it was about protecting fundamental human rights and committing the United States to a moral foreign policy by reducing the military-industrial complex. Perhaps without fully realizing it, the new generation of post–Vietnam War liberals had changed the definition of what it meant to be a liberal, and Jackson—a thoroughly orthodox liberal by the standards of the previous decade—was now a "conservative" in their view.

For this reason, the nation's major liberal magazines, including the *Nation*, the *Progressive*, and the *New Republic*, singled out Jackson for nearly unparalleled excoriation. They thought they could largely ignore Wallace, secure in the belief that he could never win the Democratic nomination. But because Jackson's candidacy showed greater promise, and because they were afraid he might become their party's standard-bearer, they denounced him in the strongest terms, portraying him as an advocate of the Far Right. In a March 1976 Gallup poll, 35 percent of Democrats said they would cross party lines and vote for Ford in a contest between Jackson and the incumbent president. Even McGovern had not been so unpopular among members of his own party. "If Sen. Jackson is nominated by the Democrats, they will risk a split in their ranks comparable to the split in 1968," declared the *New Republic*.[20]

Yet Jackson, who defined liberalism along economic rather than cultural lines, insisted that despite touches of social conservatism or hawkish views, his voting record and ideological leanings were by no means right wing. "I have sometimes been portrayed as a conservative candidate, which I regard as a phony and misleading label," he declared. He intended to reach out to African Americans and appeal to them with his "unblemished civil rights voting record," he said.[21] Yet regardless of his protestations, it was clear that Jackson would never bridge the divide between the McGovern voters and the social conservatives in the party. His only chance of winning the nomination would be to sideline the new generation of liberals who had taken over the party in 1972. And they were determined to use all their resources to make sure that did not happen.

EDWARD "TED" KENNEDY

Was there a candidate who could bridge the divisions between labor union leaders, socially conservative northern urban Catholics, Wallace-leaning southern Protestants, young McGovern liberals, and the 25 percent of Democrats who were African American? The consensus among Democratic strategists in the fall of 1974 was that only one candidate could do that: Senator Edward M. "Ted" Kennedy. "He alone," the *New York Times* declared in September 1974, "seems capable of bridging the divide between the new and old left." For that reason, he was "everybody's front-runner." In the "view of most Democrats," the *Times* concluded, his broad-based support within the party would probably "guarantee him the nomination if he should seek it." Every public opinion poll showed him well ahead of any potential rival for the Democratic nomination; a Gallup poll taken in April 1974, for instance, showed Kennedy receiving 44 percent support, compared with only 17 percent for his nearest rival, George Wallace, and only 8 percent for Jackson.[22] In fact, Kennedy was so popular that several of the other potential presidential aspirants, including Jackson and Senator Walter Mondale (D-MN), openly conceded that he probably could not be stopped if he decided to seek the nomination.[23]

Kennedy had impeccable liberal credentials; indeed, he was the country's most politically prominent liberal, the leading voice in the Senate for universal health care and a passionate advocate of civil rights. But he also drew support from all other wings of the party, including many social conservatives. National polls showed that if Kennedy did not run, Humphrey would pick up nearly one-third of the Kennedy vote, but Wallace would receive the second largest portion, with most of the remainder split nearly evenly among Jackson, McGovern, and Edmund Muskie.[24] For northern Catholics, the attraction of a Kennedy candidacy was that he was one of their own—a scion of an Irish Catholic family from New England who understood the concerns of the white working class. He would continue the unfinished presidency of his older brother, whom they had strongly supported. For African Americans, he was a civil rights advocate and social justice leader who came from the same family as their favorite president. And for millions of "middle Americans" who lamented the country's loss in Vietnam and the cultural divisions that tarnished their nation, Kennedy likewise reminded them of his brother Jack, and they hoped he could restore the country to its former greatness, before it had been torn apart by the cultural conflict of the late 1960s and the economic stagnation of the 1970s.

Ted was forty-two years old in 1974—only a few months younger than Jack had been in 1960 and exactly the same age as Bobby when he

Figure 2.3. Senator Ted Kennedy. (Library of Congress, Prints & Photographs Division, U.S. News & World Report Magazine Collection, LC-DIG-ppmsca-50448)

entered the presidential race in 1968. He had the same forceful square jaw as Jack and the same youthful appeal as Bobby. His stylish mane of dark hair had not yet turned gray, and his athletic frame had not yet become portly. Ted was never quite the orator that his older brothers were (at his worst, his sentences were rambling and barely coherent), but when he was in top form, he could use his booming baritone and his Boston brogue to call for social justice in a way that seemed to resurrect the inspiring speeches of Jack and Bobby. In his best moments, he conjured up the mythical Kennedy image that so many Americans desperately wanted to believe was real.

Perhaps the ideologically divided groups that longed for Kennedy to run were naïve to think that he could satisfy their radically different interests. The wistful nostalgia for JFK's Camelot and Bobby's unfinished campaign was so strong in the mid-1970s that Democrats of all ideological stripes wanted to trust in Ted to save the country. In the aftermath of the polarizing and seemingly pointless Vietnam War, the Watergate scandal, and the economic and energy crises that had left the nation with its highest unemployment rate since the Great Depression, it was easy for many Americans to believe that if either JFK or

Bobby had lived, the problems of the 1970s would not have developed. When a November 1975 Gallup poll asked respondents to name the three greatest presidents of all time, John F. Kennedy topped the list, beating out Abraham Lincoln, Franklin Roosevelt, and George Washington. He was especially admired by African Americans and lower-income or lower-educated Americans; he was the choice of 86 percent of nonwhites who responded to the survey, along with 59 percent of those with only a high school education.[25]

Despite his own personal scandals, Ted Kennedy's family name earned him a certain mantle of respect, but much to the surprise and consternation of his backers, he decided not to capitalize on it. Even though nearly everyone agreed that the Democratic nomination was his for the asking, he took himself out of the running with an official announcement of his noncandidacy on September 23, 1974. His declaration that he would not be a candidate in 1976 was "firm, final and unconditional," he declared.[26] His disavowal of any interest in the race was headline news; the *New York Times* made it the focus of five separate articles and editorials the next day, in addition to printing a full transcript of his statement.

Kennedy's stated reason for not entering the race was that he "could not make a full commitment to the campaign for the Presidency." "I simply cannot do that to my wife and children and other members of my family," he said. This excuse sounded vague and unconvincing to the people who had expected him to be a shoo-in for the nomination, and they wondered what Kennedy's real motivations were. Perhaps he feared an assassination attempt, some speculated, and who could blame him? His mother had given that as her reason for not wanting Ted to run. He was the last surviving son in a family that had lost two sons to assassination already. But many hoped that Kennedy was simply biding his time, waiting for the opportune moment—perhaps even the convention itself—to enter the race and unite a fractured party around his candidacy. Pollsters continued to include Kennedy's name in their presidential candidate opinion polls throughout 1975, and there was widespread speculation (or wishful thinking) among many Democrats that Kennedy might enter the race at the last minute. All the polls showed him well ahead of all potential Democratic rivals, often by double digits. Polls also showed that he was the only Democrat who could handily win the general election over a Republican rival.[27]

But, as Kennedy explained decades later, there was more on his mind than the fear of assassination, although he conceded that he worried about the impact such a death would have on his family. He was more concerned about his son, Teddy Jr., who suffered from a rare form of bone cancer that required a leg amputation and numerous months of intensive, specialized medical treatment. How could he abandon his son to go out on the campaign trail? He was also experiencing marital tension at home. It was rumored (probably correctly) that he had engaged in a series of affairs, and his wife was battling depression and a drinking problem. "Joan and I remained together largely for the children," he later wrote, "and I worried about her role in the campaign."[28] In fact, the Kennedys would divorce in 1982.

There was also the shadow of Chappaquiddick to reckon with, and it was uncertain what impact that would have on the race. Even Democrats who supported Kennedy wondered how much his candidacy would be hurt by public memories of his actions during that infamous night in 1969 when, after leaving a summer party on Cape Cod with twenty-seven-year-old Mary Jo Kopechne, he drove his car off an unlit bridge into the water and then swam ashore, leaving his passenger to drown and failing to notify the police. At the time, some thought this would end Kennedy's political career. Indeed, Kennedy, who received a suspended jail sentence for his actions, raised the possibility himself in a public statement immediately after the incident. Yet it did not deter Massachusetts voters from reelecting him to the Senate with 61 percent of the vote the following year. Although a solid majority of Kennedy's constituents in Massachusetts did not believe his actions disqualified him from office, there was no doubt that the media, in the post-Watergate era, would cover the issue extensively during the presidential campaign, and Kennedy was reluctant to drag his family through that. His wife already blamed Chappaquiddick for both the miscarriage she suffered a month after the incident and at least some of her alcohol abuse, and the stress of the additional press scrutiny would be too much for her, he thought. Although public opinion polls indicated that, for a large number of Democrats, Chappaquiddick was not a disqualifier, there was no way to know if that sentiment would change after Americans were subjected to months of media discussion of the issue. "If there is a Watergate backlash, Kennedy may be its victim," the *Washington Post* declared in September 1974, hours before Kennedy took himself out of the running. He was the "one politician who seems to suffer most from the public's heightened concern over political morality."[29]

Faced with all these concerns, Kennedy decided that he and his family could not withstand a presidential campaign, no matter how desperately party leaders begged him to run. But there was another reason: Ted knew that the clamor for his candidacy was really just a longing for the myth of Jack and Bobby. It was the Kennedy mystique that motivated voters to consistently select Ted as their top candidate—not any real understanding of him or his policy positions. And Ted could never live up to those expectations. "Jack's and Bobby's great legacies inspired me, but cold reason told me that I could not run as their surrogate, nor could I govern as their templates," he wrote in his memoir years later. "The eras that shaped them," he astutely concluded, "had passed." The nation could not return to Camelot.[30]

Kennedy's assessment was probably correct. Though it is impossible to know for certain, it seems unlikely that his widespread popularity could have withstood a rigorous campaign in the divisive mid-1970s. As Kennedy's positions on controversial matters such as abortion, busing, foreign policy, and other issues became more widely known, his broad coalition probably would have started to fragment. In Boston, he was already losing some of the working-class Catholic support he had traditionally relied on because of his support for busing. Two weeks before he issued his official disavowal of interest in the presidential race, 10,000 antibusing protesters disrupted his appearance in Boston and prevented him from delivering his prepared remarks to the crowd.[31] There was every reason to suspect that many of the working-class, socially conservative Catholics in neighboring states who longed for him to enter the presidential race would have become similarly disillusioned when they found out he disagreed with them on many key issues. And as his family life and personal behavior became daily headline news, it is likely that his popularity would have dropped. This does not mean that Kennedy could not have won his party's nomination; it is quite likely that he would have. And it does not mean that he could not have beaten the relatively unpopular Gerald Ford. But the contest would have been much more grueling than most observers assumed at the time, and Kennedy did not want the stress.

MORRIS "MO" UDALL

Kennedy's refusal to run left the Democrats without an obvious liberal alternative. Some had assumed that Minnesota senator Walter Mondale, whose voting record was even more liberal than Kennedy's and who was popular with labor unions, would be a leading contender for the nomination. However, after briefly exploring a presidential run, Mondale issued a statement in the fall of 1974 declaring that he would not be a candidate. In a realistic assessment of how stressful a two-year presidential campaign would likely be in an era of investigative journalism and a newly created national primary system, Mondale decided he was "not willing to go through fire" to become president. He still had three school-age children living at home, and he valued his family vacations. Besides, with his poll numbers stuck in the single digits in the fall of 1974, his prospects for winning the nomination were not as promising as some of his early backers had hoped. His liberal position on busing doomed his candidacy in the South, pundits thought, and his lack of personal charisma made it hard to attract the support of young McGovernites, despite his liberal record.[32]

Without an obvious liberal front-runner, pollsters in 1975 usually drew on names from the past when querying respondents about their liberal Democratic preferences. They asked the public's opinion about George McGovern, Edmund Muskie, and Hubert Humphrey, assuming that one or more of these men would emerge as a leading candidate in 1976. McGovern and Muskie made no overtures to enter the race. Humphrey seriously entertained the idea but decided to forgo the early primaries, thinking that he could be drafted at the convention if none of the other candidates won a majority of the delegates. With Kennedy, McGovern, Muskie, Mondale, and Humphrey off the ballot, liberals who wanted an alternative to Jackson and Wallace had to turn to lesser-known candidates who were not yet household names.

The first of these lesser-known liberals to officially enter the presidential race was Arizona congressman Morris K. "Mo" Udall. Self-deprecating and candid—he frequently joked about the prospects of a candidate named Mo Udall being elected to the nation's highest office—Udall promised to be a liberal of a different sort. Unlike the old liberals of the East Coast and the Midwest, he was not closely tied to labor unions (he had voted for a right-to-work law in 1965); nor did he have any connection to northeastern Catholics or to blacks in large northern cities or the southern states, even though he was a strong believer in civil rights. He was a suburban liberal from Goldwater country, and he had been elected by appealing to a new generation of libertarian-leaning liberals in the Southwest. He had been an early opponent of the Vietnam War, breaking with President Johnson on the

Figure 2.4. Representative Morris K. "Mo" Udall. (Library of Congress, Prints & Photographs Division, U.S. News & World Report Magazine Collection, LC-DIG-ppmsca-53229)

issue in 1967. As chair of the House Environmental Subcommittee, he was a leading advocate in Congress for environmental preservation, which, along with "integrity" in government in the wake of Watergate, was his central campaign issue. He strongly favored national health insurance. He was also a pioneer in crafting campaign finance reform legislation. He took a more liberal stance on abortion than almost any other candidate in the race, saying that he favored unrestricted abortion rights. And, unlike most of the other pro-choice Democrats who claimed to be personally opposed to abortion, Udall had no private scruples about the practice.[33]

In essence, Udall was the type of liberal the young McGovernites might love—someone who cared more about the rights-based issues of human equality, clean government, environmentalism, and peace than about the bread-and-butter issues of the New Deal liberals. His "natural constituency" was the "environmental community," a member of his campaign staff determined, which meant that his campaign message would be highly critical of the "exponential growth" that was producing "exurban sprawl" and "sapping the planet." Unlike Jackson and the Great Society liberals, Udall did not believe there would be endless funds for large government programs. "Since the end of World War II, we have constructed our economic life on a religion of waste," he wrote. "We must now rebuild that economy on the imperative of scarcity." The solutions would likely be technocratic and environmentally sensitive, he thought; the government would need to invest in efforts to find new energy sources and prosecute the large oil companies under antitrust laws. The nation would also have to reduce its defense budget and its military commitments.[34]

At fifty-two, Udall was a full decade older than Ted Kennedy, but they had both entered Congress in the same term, during the presidency of JFK, and Udall's political views had been shaped by the 1960s generation. In age, he might have been one of the older candidates in the race—less than three years younger than Wallace—and like most men of his generation, he had served in World War II, but his ideology appealed to a younger group of liberal voters whose politics had been shaped not by FDR and the New Deal but by JFK, Bobby Kennedy, Martin Luther King Jr., and George McGovern. They were impressed by his unblemished record for straight talk and personal honesty and by his passionate advocacy of all the causes they cared about. Udall did not hesitate to wrap himself in the McGovern mantle, despite the risks this entailed. "In 1972, a decent and forthright liberal was nominated for the Presidency but failed to make it to the White House," stated one of his early campaign letters targeting liberals in New York and Massachusetts. "Now is the time . . . to insure that in 1976 we go all the way."[35]

But, as Udall admitted, he had no fund-raising apparatus, and he was not well known outside his own state. Most Democrats who were familiar with the name Udall were likely thinking of Mo's older brother Stewart, who had served as secretary of the interior in the Kennedy administration (and was now Mo's campaign manager). In addition, Udall was a member of the House of Representatives, not a senator or a governor, and no member of the House had been elected president since James Garfield's victory in 1880. "Mr. Udall's candidacy is clearly a long shot," the *New York Times* observed in May 1974, when he announced his entry in the race. Udall, true to his candid nature, agreed. He had launched his campaign only at the urging of twenty-seven of his House colleagues, and unlike most candidates, he did not promise to win. "I have considerable doubt about whether this will fly or not," he conceded to a reporter when he launched his campaign.[36]

Udall had another problem that did not get as much press coverage: his complicated relationship with his religion. He came from a long line of Mormons and had been raised in the Church of Jesus Christ of Latter-day Saints. However, as a young man serving in World War II, he broke with the church because of its opposition to equality for blacks, and he had not been a practicing member of the faith for decades. Thirty years later, this same commitment to "human equality" led him to become a strong proponent of the Equal Rights Amendment, another cause the LDS Church leadership opposed. After distancing himself from the LDS Church, Udall also abandoned its strictures on personal behavior. For years, he made it a practice to enjoy a daily drink, and he laced his speech with profanity—behaviors frowned on by the Mormons. In another breach of church rules, he got divorced in the late 1960s and then married the twice-divorced Ella "Tiger" Royston, an "irreverent" advocate of liberal causes who wore pantsuits on the campaign trail when all the other candidates' wives played it safe and wore conservative dresses. Udall never joined another church, so his break with the Mormons left him without a religious tradition.

When asked about his faith, he admitted feeling no "personal need for organized religion."[37] To young, white McGovern progressives, that did not matter, and for some, his willingness to defy his church's racist tenets probably enhanced his credibility. McGovern, after all, had abandoned the conservative Methodism of his youth and embraced secularism as an adult, and most liberal Democrats did not seem to mind. But McGovern had also lost the votes of religious traditionalists by overwhelming margins. Udall would likewise discover that his inability to speak in a religious vernacular would hurt him among more Democrats than he might have expected.

Udall thus entered the Democratic presidential race without much money and with little name recognition or a natural base of support among any Democratic constituency other than McGovern liberals. Nor did he conform to stereotypes of presidential appearance or behavior. Kennedy had been graced with the good looks of the Kennedy clan, and Jackson, with his tailored suits and neatly groomed silver hair, looked like the Hollywood version of an older, respectable senator. But Udall's lanky, six-foot-five-inch frame, southwestern drawl, skewed ties, floppy hair, long, sun-worn, craggy face, and glass eye (a relic of a childhood injury) reminded one *New York Times* reporter of a "rodeo hand." With characteristic good humor, Udall pointed out that his glass eye and awkward height had prevented him from getting any dates in high school, and he had been fighting against the odds ever since. "I'm a one-eyed Mormon Democrat from conservative Arizona," he said, "and you can't have a higher handicap than that."[38]

Udall received little press coverage at first, and he barely registered in the public opinion polls for more than a year. But while journalists ignored him, he doggedly built a base of support in New Hampshire and Massachusetts by knocking on one door at a time, convincing liberal voters that he was the candidate to represent their interests. For many younger, white, college-educated liberals who had supported McGovern, Udall was the right sort of candidate—witty, self-deprecating, unswervingly honest, and correct on all the issues. But few expected that his brand of liberalism could unite the fractious Democratic Party. Udall would have no chance in the South, most pundits assumed, and even in the North, his brand of liberalism was not popular outside of college towns and a few affluent suburban areas where college-educated workers in the technology sector appreciated his environmentalism and technocratic approach.[39] This was not a promising path to victory.

THE OTHER CANDIDATES

By early 1975, numerous other Democratic politicians were exploring a presidential bid. Fred Harris, a forty-four-year-old one-term senator from Oklahoma who had run unsuccessfully in 1972, entered the ring again and attempted to stake out a position to Udall's left, casting himself as the most liberal of the candidates. In the style of a prairie populist, the former Oklahoma senator focused on attacking corporate wealth and promising to return power and money to the people through a more progressive income tax and substantially higher corporate tax rates. "The whole question for 1976 is who is going to run this country and who will the economy serve—us or the rich people and big corporations," he declared in December 1974 when he announced his candidacy.[40]

News reports initially treated Harris as a strong second-tier candidate who had a better-than-even chance of besting Udall in the contest to wrap up the votes of the McGovernite wing of the party. But despite the fanfare that greeted his announcement, Harris's campaign quickly foundered because of a lack of funds and an inability to expand his base of support beyond a small cadre of left-leaning young people. His decision to run his populist campaign from his Winnebago camper and to spend each night in a public campground may have attracted attention as a publicity stunt, but it also made it hard to consider him a serious presidential contender. Although Harris "appealed to the restless young voter," journalist Jules Witcover wrote, "he always seemed more like the head of some rag-tag, blue-jeaned cult of the disaffected than a political statesman able to lead all segments of society."[41]

Harris was correct in his assessment that, in the aftermath of Watergate, Democratic voters wanted a candidate who eschewed the trappings of Washington power and was willing to roll up his shirtsleeves and carry his own luggage. His extreme aversion to convention, though, was probably a step too far, as was his embrace of a strongly anticorporate agenda at a time when many voters, even among the McGovernite liberals, were becoming more comfortable with a technocratic, capitalist economy.[42] Although Harris managed to stay in the race through the first round of primaries, his poll numbers remained in the low single digits.

While Harris was trying, unsuccessfully, to outflank Udall on the left, other presidential aspirants were attempting to pick up votes among the much larger constituency of centrist Democrats. Pennsylvania governor Milton Shapp, the first Jewish presidential candidate, entered the race expecting to appeal to traditional New Deal economic liberals with his strong record of support for labor unions and a platform centered on economic issues. Two southerners—Senator Lloyd Bentsen of Texas and former North Carolina governor Terry Sanford—hoped to appeal to white moderates in the South who wanted a less polarizing nominee than George Wallace. But Shapp was a lackluster campaigner with little of the charisma that voters wanted from a presidential candidate in the television age. Bentsen likewise had trouble gaining traction outside his own state. Although he hoped his fiscal conservatism would appeal to pro-business centrist Democrats across the nation, he found that his personal wealth and close alliance with Texas oil interests were serious liabilities at a time when high gas prices, economic stagnation, and unpleasant memories of President Lyndon Johnson made many Democrats reluctant to elect another rich Texan as president. Sanford, who had earned a progressive reputation on civil rights while serving as governor of North Carolina in the early 1960s, did well in early fund-raising and could count on support in his own state, but his low poll numbers elsewhere made it difficult to envision a path to victory. His candidacy likely would have foundered if he had pressed on, but after being hospitalized with chest pains, he decided to withdraw from the race before the first primary votes were cast, becoming the first declared Democratic presidential candidate to drop out.[43]

At the end of 1974 the Democratic race was still wide open, and pundits were talking about numerous others who might enter the race, including Governor Reubin Askew of Florida, Senator Birch Bayh of Indiana, and even Julian Bond, a civil rights activist and Georgia state legislator who was still a few weeks shy of his thirty-fifth birthday.[44] Whether any of these candidates could transcend the regional and ideological divisions in the Democratic Party to win the nomination was still very much in doubt. Ultimately, several of them, including Askew and Bond, decided to stay out of the race. But a number of other unexpected candidates jumped in, reasoning that without a clear front-runner, the nomination could go to anyone.

Most likely, experts predicted, the lesser-known candidates would never amount to more than regional favorites, but they would split the vote, meaning that no one would win a majority of delegates in the primaries. The nomination would therefore be decided at a brokered convention, where the delegates would likely select an established politician with national stature, such as Hubert Humphrey or Ted Kennedy. Despite all the hoopla, the primary races might settle nothing.[45] But this did not deter numerous dark-horse candidates from entering the primary contests, hoping they could accomplish the improbable and transcend party divisions to capture the nomination. One of the many who thought he could do this was one-term Georgia governor Jimmy Carter, whose personal ambition and self-confidence made up for his lack of national name recognition. By the fall of 1974, he had already put together a campaign operation that he believed could defeat all the other politicians in the race.

3 JIMMY CARTER ENTERS THE RACE

In November 1972, immediately after George McGovern lost the presidential election by a landslide, Hamilton Jordan, a twenty-eight-year-old aide to Georgia governor Jimmy Carter, sent his boss a fifty-three-page strategy memo detailing how Carter could win the next presidential race by becoming the Democratic standard-bearer in 1976. It was an audacious move. The 1972 election was barely over, and Carter was less than two years into the governorship. He had never served in national office, had no experience with the Democratic Party outside of Georgia, and came from a state that had never produced a president. He was a southerner, and southern Democrats had generally not been taken seriously as presidential candidates. The last time the country elected a president from the Deep South was 1848, when General Zachary Taylor of Louisiana won on a Whig ticket. But Jordan knew that Carter was ambitious and had been mulling a White House run. Jordan, too, could dream big, and he believed in his boss. Like Carter, he had grown up in South Georgia and wanted to prove that the region could be a contender in national politics. And like Carter, he was a shrewd strategist. His positive assessment of Carter's prospects contravened conventional wisdom—yet it highlighted a truth that most other candidates and political strategists had overlooked.

"Perhaps the strongest feeling in this country today is the general distrust and disillusionment of government and politicians at all levels," Jordan told Carter. "The desire and thirst for strong moral leadership in this nation was not satisfied by the election of Richard Nixon. It is my contention that this desire will grow in four more years of the Nixon Administration." For that reason, Carter, a political unknown, had a greater chance of winning the presidency than the Democrats' expected front-runner, Ted Kennedy. Although Kennedy had "tremendous political assets" and was the "only visible candidate at present who has the ability to bridge the gap between the McGovern constituency and traditional Democratic Party members," the "unanswered questions of Chappaquiddick" were at odds with the "national desire for trust and morality in government" and would severely handicap a Kennedy campaign. "Senator Kennedy can win the nomination much easier than he can win the presidency," Jordan noted.[1] Democrats might be able to forgive Kennedy's irresponsible behavior, but those outside the party could not.

Following Jordan's political strategy, Carter decided to base his presidential campaign not on issue positions or even on his political record but on his moral character. He would run as the antithesis of both Richard Nixon and Ted Kennedy. At a time when Henry Jackson was running on his governmental résumé, Mo Udall was campaigning on a set of progressive issues, and George Wallace was reaching out to voters with a cultural appeal, Carter's campaign was premised on the claim that his character and biography made him best suited to deliver the "moral leadership" that Nixon had not and Kennedy could not.

Carter gave voters at least two reasons to trust his moral character. First, and most important: he was not a Washington politician. With the exception of the popular general Dwight Eisenhower, nearly all presidential candidates of the past half century had come from the Senate, the presidential cabinet, or the vice presidency, or they had served as governors of populous states such as New York. Carter was different, and he made that difference his chief selling point. His campaign advertising portrayed him as a peanut farmer, proudly showing him in rolled-up sleeves and blue jeans as he sat atop a tractor. He never tired of recounting stories that highlighted his lack of national name recognition, knowing that journalists could not resist passing them on. News stories about Carter, for instance, frequently noted that when he appeared on *What's My Line?* in 1973, none of the panelists recognized him. And when he told his mother he was running for president, her first response was, "President of what?"[2] Such stories, which continued to evolve during the campaign, were a perfect fit for the strategy Carter and Jordan created in 1972, and they succeeded in cloaking Carter's intense political ambition with an aura of "aw shucks" innocence and down-home southern charm.

Carter cited his regional roots and religious devotion as the second major testament to his character. If American voters were longing for a moral candidate in the aftermath of Watergate, who better than a Southern Baptist Sunday school teacher from small-town Georgia? Carter seemed to epitomize the values of Andy Griffith's Mayberry while projecting an image of youthful vigor and business-minded efficiency that led voters to consider him a voice for a new generation. It was a politically potent combination, and both Jordan and Carter knew it. If voters were drawn to Ted Kennedy because his youth, good looks, and family name reminded them of JFK, Carter—who was almost as young and arguably as handsome—could likewise resurrect the image of JFK by flashing his trademark toothy smile and brushing back a wisp of his fashionably moppish hair.[3] And unlike Kennedy, Carter had a squeaky-clean reputation.

THE MAKING OF JIMMY CARTER

By all accounts, Carter was a straight arrow.[4] He faithfully attended church each Sunday and served as a deacon and a Sunday school teacher. He enjoyed an extraordinarily close working relationship with his wife, Rosalynn, whom he treated as a political partner and confidant. He drank very little and was never seen under the influence, and despite serving in the navy during the 1940s, when cigarettes were ubiquitous, he did not smoke. He had what was, in some ways, an ideal résumé for a politician—an excellent academic record, a naval career on nuclear submarines, and a stint managing his father's peanut farm. He could thus credibly claim (as he did in his campaign advertising) to be a businessman, a southern farmer, a nuclear engineer, a naval officer, and a community leader. He was the ultimate Washington outsider who also had the experience needed to appeal to voters and make informed decisions as chief executive.

According to his close associates, Carter had extraordinary confidence in his own abilities. Some observers—and, to a certain extent, Carter himself—attributed this to the serenity he gained from his Christian faith and his assurance that he was doing the Lord's will.[5] His decision in 1972 to explore a run for the presidency was only the most audacious example of an ambitious streak he had exhibited throughout his

Figure 3.1. Jimmy Carter speaking at a campaign event. (Library of Congress, Prints & Photographs Division, U.S. News & World Report Magazine Collection, LC-DIG-ppmsca-09744)

life. While growing up on the family farm in Plains (population about five hundred), he worked hard to advance himself, with the goal of leaving Plains and seeking better opportunities elsewhere—including, as he told some of his friends at the time, becoming governor of Georgia. When he enrolled at the US Naval Academy, it seemed that his dreams of travel and achievement would come true. He graduated sixtieth in a class of more than eight hundred, so he definitely had above-average abilities, but his ambitions were even greater; eventually, he hoped to become the US chief of naval operations. Although his academic skills were strong, they were not quite strong enough to accomplish all the goals he imagined for himself. He was deeply disappointed (later using the word "depressed" to characterize his state of mind) when he was rejected for a Rhodes scholarship. Nevertheless, despite occasional setbacks, Carter generally got what he wanted. For seven years, he and Rosalynn relished the opportunity to travel to various places in the United States as he fulfilled his duties as a naval officer. While living in the North, they came to reject the South's code of racial segregation. Rosalynn became especially enamored with their new life and never wanted to go back to Plains. But in 1953, when Jimmy's father died, he resigned from the navy and returned to Plains to manage the family peanut farm. As the oldest son, he was fulfilling his filial duty. But as some of his later biographers noted, the move also ideally positioned him for a shot at one of his longtime objectives: the governorship of Georgia. For the rest of his political career, he cast himself as a small businessman and a man of the soil who could be trusted.[6]

Carter entered local politics almost as soon as he returned to Georgia. Within three years, he was serving on the county school board and the Sumter County Chamber of Commerce; he was vice president of the Plains Lions Club, a Sunday school teacher at Plains Baptist Church, and scoutmaster of his son's troop. His refusal to support the Southern Baptist Convention's antialcohol stance hampered his desire to serve as church deacon, but by 1962, his upstanding moral life and clear commitment to the Christian faith were sufficient to overcome the objections of congregants, and he was elected to this church office. The same year, he won election to the state senate as the more progressive candidate in the race.

Carter was more liberal on civil rights than most white Georgians at the time, but he cautiously avoided an open confrontation with the segregationist practices of his region. Instead, he preferred to ameliorate racial injustices gradually, while also promoting clean government and fiscal prudence, reflecting his inclinations as a successful small businessman who now had nearly half a million dollars in assets. As a school board member in the aftermath of *Brown v. Board of Education,* he did not directly oppose school segregation—a course that was "unthinkable and pointless" in his community and would have "spelled financial ruin" for him, according to longtime associate and biographer Peter Bourne; instead, he pursued the more moderate course of increasing funding for black schools.[7] At the Plains Baptist Church, he cast an unpopular vote in 1966 in favor of opening membership to blacks, when nearly every other member voted against the proposal. Carter took this as an indication that the whites in his community were not ready to accept his racially progressive views. As a state senator, he avoided controversies over race and focused on the less contentious cause of economic development, as long as it accorded with his fiscally conservative instincts. He quickly developed a reputation as one of the hardest working state legislators. Having naïvely vowed on the campaign trail to read every bill before it came up for a vote, he had to take a speed-reading course to gain the requisite skills to peruse the thousand or so bills considered in each legislative session and fulfill his promise. But he had no intention of staying in the state legislature for long. He seriously considered a campaign for Congress but chose instead to run for governor in 1966.

His loss in the Democratic gubernatorial primary to the notorious racist Lester Maddox sent him into another depression. With the help of his faith-healing sister Ruth Carter Stapleton, he was "born again" and transformed from a mere "church Christian" into someone who genuinely wanted to follow Jesus. Full of newfound evangelistic zeal, Carter traveled to Pennsylvania to participate in a door-knocking campaign to share his Christian faith. He also embarked on a frenzy of theological and philosophical reading, finding particular inspiration in the political theology of Reinhold Niebuhr, which convinced him that the divinely ordained purpose of politics was to "establish justice in a sinful world." He had been a moderate progressive on race, but now he became more deeply committed to the cause of both civil rights and poverty relief. His sights were still set on the Georgia governorship; indeed, his determination was bolstered by his conviction that the Lord had called him to a political career. "I believe God wants me to be the best politician I can possibly be," he later wrote.[8]

Despite his born-again experience and conviction that he was doing the Lord's work in politics, Carter's second run for the governorship was tainted by racially tinged doublespeak that critics later cited as proof that he was not as honest as he claimed. In a state that was sharply divided along racial lines, Carter's campaign strategy in 1970 was to cast his opponent, the moderate former governor Carl Sanders, as a wealthy, out-of-touch elitist and a racial liberal, even though Carter himself was privately far more committed to civil rights than his campaign advertising suggested. In a controversial move that would cloud Carter's reputation for years, his campaign used photographs of Sanders celebrating with black athletes to target white conservative voters. Carter later denied any knowledge of these ads, but they were produced by members of his staff in conjunction with the advertising agency hired by his campaign.[9]

After portraying himself as slightly to the right of his opponent, Carter reversed course as soon as he was elected and began to establish a progressive record on race that nicely positioned him as a potential Democratic presidential nominee. Declaring in his inaugural address that "the time for racial discrimination is over," he appointed an unprecedented number of African Americans to governmental positions in Georgia and hung a portrait of Martin Luther King Jr. in the Georgia statehouse, inviting his newfound supporters Martin Luther King Sr. ("Daddy" King) and Coretta Scott King to join him at the ceremony.[10] His black allies included a few other members of the Atlanta civil rights establishment—most notably, Andrew Young, a Georgia congressman, former executive director of the Southern Christian Leadership Conference, and a close associate of "Daddy" King's famous son.

Carter's greatest passion proved to be governmental efficiency. He was proud of implementing zero-based budgeting, a procedure that required each state agency to offer a line-by-line defense of its budget requests, rather than simply asking for a certain percentage increase based on previous expenditures. This emphasis on cutting the fat in government might have marked Carter as a fiscal conservative, but his aversion to deficits was not accompanied by a hostility to government spending in general. He believed that eagle-eyed attention to detail in budgeting would allow him to use taxpayers' money more efficiently to fund necessary programs. Environmental conservation especially interested him, perhaps because of his career in agriculture and his experience with nuclear energy.

Whatever else he was, Carter was clearly not a traditional New Deal liberal or an old-fashioned southern Democrat. A decade earlier or a decade later, he might have been marked as a conservative because of his commitment to fiscal austerity. But in the 1970s he could plausibly market himself as a progressive because of his commitment to environmental preservation and racial justice. He was a southern white who broke the mold of the southern white politicians who preceded him. By allying himself with African American civil rights leaders, he demonstrated the racially egalitarian promise of what the "New South" could become.

He was a pious, Bible-reading Baptist—more devout than his parents and most other Carter family members—but culturally, he was well to the left of center. He took an egalitarian position on women's rights at a time when many culturally conservative Southern Baptists opposed the Equal Rights Amendment and women's ordination. His favorite theologian, Niebuhr, was neither a Baptist nor a conservative, and he supplemented his theological readings with Dylan Thomas's poetry, William Faulkner's novels, and Bob Dylan's folk-rock lyrics, which aroused his social consciousness.[11] Reporters were regularly impressed by his wide range of reading material and his "eclectic curiosity." "Mr. Carter may be one of the smartest men to run for President in a long time," the *New York Times* would declare in early 1976. "He is well read and well educated, an Annapolis graduate out of Georgia Tech who is comfortable discussing nuclear fission or existentialism."[12]

Because Carter was a quick study with a higher acumen than most other politicians, he began to seriously contemplate a presidential bid after observing the parade of lackluster Democratic contenders in 1972. "Jimmy knew a lot more about a lot of things than did these men who were running for president," Rosalynn Carter recalled.[13] His initial reason for running was not one particular cause or issue position; rather, it was the conviction that he was better equipped to run the country than any of his potential opponents. As he asked in the title of his 1975 autobiography, paraphrasing a question Admiral Hyman Rickover had posed to him nearly three decades earlier, "Why not the best?"[14]

Some of Carter's advisers doubted that he would be able to convince northern Democrats to vote for him, especially if his issue positions were more conservative than those of party activists. Peter Bourne, an English-born, McGovern-supporting liberal who was a Carter confidant and one of the earliest supporters of his presidential bid, warned him in August 1974 that "to get the delegate support that you will need for the nomination you must move significantly to the left." But Hamilton Jordan did not agree. In the wake of McGovern's massive loss, he believed the party would not want to nominate another liberal. Kennedy's "very liberal image and record" would hurt him, he predicted, at a time when "the political pendulum is swinging back toward the middle."[15] In such a political climate, Carter's centrism would be an asset.

In reality, Carter was remarkably uninterested in ideology. More than anything, he was a technocrat, believing that scientific know-how and technological efficiency could solve social problems. In the 1970s he was in the vanguard of public opinion in thinking that government waste was a central part of the nation's problems. He could thus channel the fiscally conservative, antigovernment critiques of Ronald Reagan while also positioning himself as an environmentally friendly progressive in the mold of Mo Udall. In the mid-1970s this was exactly what many progressive Democrats wanted.

The press did not realize it yet, but in the post-Watergate era, many of the young suburban white professionals who were the future of the Democratic Party were just as skeptical about big government as Carter was. A survey of Democratic Party telethon donors showed that although these people were overwhelmingly liberal on some issues, such as civil rights and national health insurance (70 percent had supported McGovern in 1972, 87 percent favored government-funded health care, and 70 percent approved of protests as a means of dissent), 76 percent of them thought the federal government "wastes a lot of money." The Carter campaign quickly seized on these survey results as justification for a populist strategy of attacking government spending, even while proposing new government programs. "The surprising fact is that Telethon givers—who are mostly partisan Democrats—are extremely alienated from the government," Rick Hutcheson noted in a memo to Hamilton Jordan. Carter, he thought, could appeal to these sentiments more effectively than the other candidates because, unlike most of his rivals—including progressives Mo Udall and Fred Harris—he had never been a part of the federal government and could thus claim to be the consummate outsider. "I'm not a member of Congress," Carter told audiences in a not-so-subtle dig against most of his Democratic rivals. "So I'm not responsible for letting that horrible mess develop."[16]

Carter could adopt an anti-Washington stance because he was both a new-style southern Democrat and a governor. While the leading

Figure 3.2. Jimmy Carter greeting supporters in his hometown of Plains, Georgia. (Library of Congress, Prints & Photographs Division, U.S. News & World Report Magazine Collection, LC-DIG-ppmsca-09752)

Democrats in Congress—especially northern liberals such as Ted Kennedy, Hubert Humphrey, and Tip O'Neill—were strong advocates of national health insurance, government job-creation programs, and other large spending measures that expanded the federal bureaucracy, many Democratic governors resented Washington's growing power and the pressure it put on their states. In 1975 the Democratic Governors Conference produced a position paper that complained about the "unresponsiveness, high costs and inefficiency of the Federal Government." "The Federal Government has become so large, unwieldy, and unavailable that it can no longer adequately respond to the basic needs of our citizens or adjust to new conditions and problems," the Democratic governors stated. Unlike Ronald Reagan and other right-wing Republicans, neither the other Democratic governors nor Carter viewed the federal bureaucracy as an enemy that needed to be destroyed, but they did want to radically trim and reshape it to make it far more efficient. This was especially true in the Sun Belt, a region that included the pro–free market Southwest and the culturally conservative South, both of which had experienced rapid economic growth for the past three decades. Southern Democrats, in particular, were a conservative breed; the southern Democrats in the House of Representatives voted with conservative Republicans 63 percent of the time in 1975. This was not merely because of racial issues, as some suspected. Even as Carter's own generation of New South politicians distanced themselves from the entrenched segregationist politics of their predecessors and built biracial coalitions, their support for higher defense spending (a leading driver of economic growth in the postwar South) and lower taxes brought them into coalitions with conservative Republicans.[17] Like Carter, the younger Democratic politicians in the South had been too young to vote during the New Deal and had come of age in an era of strong regional economic growth that gave them more faith in private industry than public programs.

CARTER'S ANTI-WASHINGTON CAMPAIGN STAFF

If there was one thing that united Carter's campaign staff, it was their iconoclastic disdain for Washington politics and their fierce personal loyalty to Carter and their belief that he was the man who could shake up the Washington establishment. Most of them were significantly younger than Carter, and most were fellow Georgians who had been part of his campaign team since at least 1970, if not 1966. Having spent their entire lives in Georgia, they shared Carter's deep southern drawl, but they also echoed his desire to transcend the racial prejudice and resistance to change that, in their view, had hindered the progress of their region. Carter, who was not yet fifty in 1972, was not considered old, but the leaders of his campaign staff were almost a full generation younger and, for the most part, more liberal than he was, especially on cultural issues. Too young to remember World War II or the beginning of the Cold War, they had formed their political consciences in the fires of the civil rights movement and the antiwar protests of the late 1960s, and they had gravitated toward Carter because they believed he represented their vision of a new type of political leadership for southern whites who wanted to repudiate the racial conservatism represented by Lester Maddox and Herman Talmadge.

Hamilton Jordan, the head of campaign operations, was still in his twenties when he became the architect of Carter's presidential campaign strategy. Born in 1944, he grew up in deeply segregated Albany, Georgia—a focal point for civil rights protests during his senior year of high school. He became a political science major at the University of Georgia, where he supported Carter's 1966 gubernatorial bid. Jordan believed that Carter could unify the rural and urban South and bring racial reconciliation to a state that was still haunted by segregation. A postcollege stint in Vietnam, where he was exposed to Agent Orange, deepened his skepticism of conventional politicians and heightened his desire to promote the career of a fresh, anti-Washington political maverick. Jordan believed so strongly in Carter that when the Plains native ran for governor again in 1970, Jordan managed the campaign. Two years later, he encouraged Carter to run for president.[18]

Carter's press secretary, Jody Powell, was only a year older than Jordan and a fellow South Georgia native. Like Jordan, he had studied political science and was an early supporter of Carter's political ambitions, supporting his first gubernatorial bid in 1966 and then playing a leading role in his second campaign in 1970. Powell then joined Carter's gubernatorial administration as his press secretary.[19]

Jordan and Powell were the nucleus of the early campaign. They proofread Carter's speeches, coordinated campaign strategy, and formulated long-term goals. As the official head of campaign operations, Jordan had a hand in nearly all strategizing memos, but in recognition of his importance, Powell was usually brought into the conversations as well, especially when they concerned matters of policy. Carter's campaign team included several other young southern liberals with a similar perspective. Lawyer Stuart E. "Stu" Eizenstat, who had lived in Atlanta since he was eight months old, had served as issues director for Carter's 1970 gubernatorial campaign and performed the same role for his presidential bid. Rick Hutcheson, whom Jordan recruited for the team, was the youngest of the group. Although he was only twenty-four years old in 1975 and still attending graduate school, he was brought in to plan campaign strategy and delegate outreach.[20]

All these people appreciated Carter's independent style, and most viewed themselves as challengers to the Washington establishment. Jordan, a political maverick with a reputation for casual dress and violations of proper decorum, was especially attracted to this sentiment. He wanted Carter to run as an anti-Washington centrist who would be able to upend the establishment in both parties. Powell, a Southern Baptist who shared Carter's churchgoing habit but not his piety, was a chain-smoking, hard-drinking, profane southern populist who appreciated Carter's championship of the neglected interests of the poor rural whites of the South. Bourne and Eizenstat (who described himself as a "JFK progressive") were the most liberal of the group, and they urged Carter to move to the left on issues of foreign policy and economics. Bourne was slightly older than some of Carter's other close aides (he was born in 1939) and was already an established physician; he was a cultural liberal who shared neither Carter's evangelical faith nor his moral prudery. In the words of the *Washington Post,* he was "a doctor who had earned his liberal stripes as a civil-rights activist, who worked in San Francisco's Haight-Ashbury free clinic, helped found Vietnam Veterans against the War after a stint doing research on combat stress in Vietnam and favored decriminalization of marijuana and heroin maintenance to ease the pain of terminal cancer patients." Like Jordan, he was an early supporter of Carter and one of the first to encourage him to run for president.[21]

Carter's innermost circle of campaign advisers consisted entirely of whites, but he also relied heavily on a few prominent black civil rights activists—especially Andrew Young. Eventually, at the height of the primary campaign, blacks would account for 13 percent of Carter's paid campaign staff, but Young in particular was relied on to shore up support among African Americans and white progressives whenever Carter's civil rights credentials were called into question.[22]

Though most of the people in Carter's inner circle were left of center, there were two or three possible exceptions: Bert Lance, Charles Kirbo, and, at least on economics, Robert Lipshutz. Lance, the chief executive of a $280-million-a-year Georgia bank, had been a fund-raiser for Carter since 1970. Like both Bourne and Jordan, he claimed he had been the first to urge Carter to run for president. But unlike some of Carter's other close associates, he was a budget hawk who insisted throughout the campaign that Carter was really a fiscal conservative, regardless of what his liberal advisers said. Kirbo, the fifty-eight-year-old éminence grise of the group and the one Carter described as his "closest friend," was a fiscally conservative South Georgia native, a partner in an Atlanta law firm, and chairman of the Georgia Democratic Party. He had been a strong supporter of Henry Jackson in 1972 and, like Jackson, had supported the American cause in Vietnam to the end. Some in Carter's circle worried that Kirbo would push their candidate to the right, but Lipshutz, a middle-aged Atlanta lawyer and the campaign's treasurer, noted that the fiscally conservative views he shared with Lance, Kirbo, and, he assumed, Carter himself were perfectly compatible with social liberalism, especially on civil rights. Indeed, this was probably true. Carter's campaign leaned to the right on economic matters and to the left on cultural and social issues. But, more than anything, the Carter campaign in its early months was characterized by a lack of ideological cohesion or emphasis on the candidate's policy proposals. Kirbo urged Carter to avoid making policy issues his main focus and to orient his campaign around the theme of restoring trust in government.[23]

This was what Carter wanted to do anyway, and it worked to his advantage because it allowed him to pull together a diverse coalition of people who were unsure of his precise policy positions but who appreciated the image of technocratic know-how and youthful optimism he projected. This coalition included not only his inner circle but also a large group of fellow Georgians who believed in his intelligence and personal honesty and wanted to do everything they could to send him to the White House. In the early days of the campaign, the vast majority of both staff and money came from Georgia, and many who committed themselves to Carter were motivated more by faith in his leadership abilities and personal character than by a specific platform.[24] In the aftermath of Watergate and in the midst of a prolonged economic downturn, they were convinced that the system in Washington was badly broken, and they had faith that their governor could fix it.

To gain national credentials within the party for his presidential bid, Carter volunteered for a term as the Democratic National Committee's campaign chair and also secured a place for himself on the newly formed Trilateral Commission, a foreign policy discussion group chaired by Columbia University professor Zbigniew Brzezinski. The DNC post set Carter up with useful contacts in the national party apparatus and put him in touch with people who were masters of the party's new delegate selection rules, a critical piece of knowledge for anyone competing in the newly established primary system. The Trilateral Commission gave him foreign policy experience and credentials, which would be important prerequisites for a credible presidential bid, and it also led to a long-term reliance on Brzezinski's advice on foreign affairs.[25] Despite this experience, though, Carter still viewed himself as an outsider to the Washington establishment, which he considered an asset.

CARTER'S ENTRY INTO THE RACE

When Carter officially declared his candidacy in December 1974, he introduced his campaign with a speech calling for efficiency in government and an end to bureaucratic waste. "The mechanism of our government should be understandable, efficient and economical," he declared. "We must give top priority to a drastic and thorough revision of the federal bureaucracy. . . . Tight businesslike management and planning techniques must be instituted and maintained." He touted his implementation of zero-based budgeting in Georgia as proof of his commitment to trim all unnecessary fat from the bloated government bureaucracy, and he pledged his support for "utilizing the full authority and personal involvement of the President himself" to do something similar at the national level. Yet, unlike Reagan and conservative Republicans, Carter did not question the value of social service programs or the principles behind the Great Society of the previous decade. Instead, he claimed that an aggressive deficit hawk could make these programs much more efficient. The government could manage the nation's energy resources more efficiently, and it could rein in the costs of health care. He expected that congressional Democrats would pass a program of national health insurance (which was Senator Ted Kennedy's top priority and a central goal of the Democratic Party), and he supported the idea. Yet his main priority was not creating such a program but ensuring that any national health care program that was created would include cost controls.[26]

The hallmark of Carter's speech, though, was not his call for government efficiency but his promise to restore trust in the nation's government. Coming only a few months after Nixon's resignation and Ford's pardon, Carter's emphasis was a brilliant move—and one that no other Democratic candidate had the foresight to echo to the same degree. "With the shame of Watergate still with us and our 200th birthday just ahead, it is time for us to reaffirm our ethical and spiritual and political beliefs," he declared. "There must be no lowering of these standards, no acceptance of mediocrity in any aspect of our private or public lives. . . . The confidence of people in our own government must be restored. . . . There is a simple and effective way for public officials to regain public trust—be trustworthy!"[27]

Carter thus made his campaign, to a nearly unprecedented degree, a referendum on his character. If his main stated reason for running was to restore trust in the government, his own trustworthiness would be a central issue in his campaign. He therefore opened his speech with a paragraph designed to prove to American voters that he was an honest, competent man. This was new ground for a presidential speech, and Carter's inner circle was unsure how to best pull it off.

Carter wanted to appeal to his Christian faith as proof of his character, but some of his closest advisers disagreed. When Carter wrote the first draft of the speech announcing his candidacy, he included the introductory line, "I am a Christian, and will try at all times to exemplify the finest aspects of my faith." Carter's campaign aides objected to the phrase, which they thought was inappropriate in a secular nation and a religiously pluralistic society. "I strongly feel that [this line] should be deleted," Eizenstat, who was Jewish, wrote in a memo to Carter and others in the inner circle. "If you want to get this across in order to underscore your ethical message, I think that you can state that you are a deeply religious man and feel that this would be an important factor that will guide you in your campaign and as President. However, as currently stated, I think that this would be offensive to many people and comes across a little too much as 'Old South.'"[28]

Carter took the advice to heart and wrote a new introduction that was thoroughly pluralistic and buried the reference to his Christianity in a long list of other attributes. "We Americans are a great and diverse people," he wrote in the third draft of his speech's introductory paragraph. "We have a right to develop different interests and responsibilities. For instance, I am a farmer, an engineer, a planner, a scientist, a governor and a Christian. Each of you is an individual and different from all the others. Yet we Americans have shared one thing in common: a belief in the greatness of our country."[29] But even this seemingly innocuous, incidental reference to Carter's faith was too much for his closest advisers, who were afraid that any declaration of Carter's Christianity—even in the context of a clear affirmation of the nation's religious pluralism—would doom his bid for the Democratic nomination. Jody Powell crossed out "Christian" on his draft copy and substituted the phrase "church member"—a change that highlighted Carter's civic commitment to a local institution rather than his personal faith. "Vote was 2–1," he wrote in the margin. "Those people who control all the newspapers and financial institutions won."[30]

If, as seems likely, Jordan cast the one vote in favor of the word "Christian"—with Powell and Eizenstat voting against—his political instincts were once again superior to those of his two colleagues. Although Jordan was an irreverent rebel with a self-professed penchant for the occasional indulgence in "sin" after hours, he understood the political appeal of Carter's religion.[31] Candidates' personal faith commitments would receive far more press coverage in 1976—"the year of the evangelical," according to *Newsweek*—than ever before, and Carter would prove more adept than other candidates in using his personal faith to enhance his political appeal. But back in the fall of 1974, it was difficult for some of his advisers to foresee this. To them, Carter's insistence on the term "Christian" threatened to undermine his national appeal, especially among younger progressives, and it would make it difficult to convince northern Democrats that he was more than a southern regional candidate.

Carter astutely ignored these admonitions and insisted on using the term "Christian" in the introductory paragraph of his announcement speech. The reference was brief and subtle, and it was couched in a ringing endorsement of the nation's religious and ideological pluralism, but it was there nonetheless. The speech also included one biblical quotation, used in passing to illustrate a point about "national purpose." Carter had originally wanted to explicitly link his Christian faith to his commitment to integrity, but the final version of his speech made this point subtly. For evangelical Christians, Carter's opening reference to his Christian faith and his casual invocation of a quotation from the Bible were enough to signal that he was one of their own and that his integrity and strong interest in government ethics were expressions of his Christian values. And for voters outside of Carter's religious circle, the religious references were brief and innocuous enough that they did not suggest religious sectarianism or an inappropriate injection of religion into politics. Secular voters could read Carter's lengthy discussion of the need to hold government to a high ethical standard as an expression of progressive values and the right message for a nation that was less than a year removed from Watergate.

Progressive voters—who tended to be more northern and more secular than Carter's base—could find much to like in Carter's speech. His foreign policy views were almost identical to those expressed in the *Nation*. "The time for American intervention in all the problems of the world is over," he stated. There would be no more Vietnam Wars. The United States "cannot retreat into isolationism," he said, and it must be committed to preserving the "integrity of Israel," but its foreign policy should focus on building partnerships, not intervening militarily. Carter also called for a reduction in energy consumption and a commitment to environmental protection. On issues of social welfare policy, one might have expected that Carter's strong inclinations toward deficit reduction would prevent him from being a Great Society–style liberal, but he claimed that a more efficiently run government could affordably deliver all the services favored by Democratic Party liberals, including their new favorite cause: national health care. Washington bureaucrats had wasted the people's money, but Carter would reform the system and channel the people's resources toward the things they really wanted. "Is a practical and comprehensive national health program beyond the capacity of our American government?" he asked. "I think not. . . . Is a comprehensive education program beyond the capacity of the American people? I think not."[32]

Left-of-center liberals were heartened and intrigued. A *New York Times* article the next day noted that Carter had a reputation as a "progressive force in racial matters" and as an "effective reformer of Georgia's cumbersome bureaucracy." Perhaps he was "just another Democratic dark horse," but he might be a "Southern-style Kennedy." Newspaper editorials across the nation concurred. "He seems to be of the young, modest, progressive mold of politicians who since 1970 have been enjoying growing success in the United States," the *Albuquerque Journal* declared. And in Iowa, the liberal-leaning John McCormally, editor of the *Burlington Hawk Eye,* declared in December 1974 that Carter was his favorite candidate. He was a "progressive politician" who displayed "the right touch of liberalism without being suicidally radical."[33]

Even some conservatives liked him. Syndicated columnist Roscoe Drummond, who generally expressed moderate Republican views, suggested that Carter would be a "distinctive, effective and appealing contender for the Democratic nomination." "He is sophisticated but not afraid to talk about recovering traditional values and morals," Drummond wrote. And his experience as a "nuclear scientist" had taught him to take a realistic approach to the reduction of nuclear weapons, insisting on "on-site inspection" of other countries' nuclear arsenals before agreeing to reduce the US supply. Other conservatives lauded Carter's commitment to reducing the federal budget deficit. In Minnesota, the *Red Wing Republican Eagle* commended Carter's "anti-inflation, anti-recession posture," saying that his "tight money policy" demonstrated his "willingness to tackle the largest special interest bloc within his own party."[34]

The new campaign finance law offered Carter a way to position himself as fiscally responsible, progressively reform-minded, and ethically pure, while also playing to his strengths as a Washington outsider without the monied connections of more established candidates such as Henry Jackson. Under the old system, which imposed no limits on the amount of money candidates could raise or spend, Carter almost certainly would have been at a disadvantage, given his limited financial connections outside the South, and he would have had trouble competing against nationally known senators. But the new rules leveled the playing field by limiting both the total amount a candidate could raise and the amount individuals could contribute. By capping individual contributions at $1,000, the new rules encouraged candidates to raise money from middle-income voters rather than from well-heeled party donors. This worked to Carter's advantage, but so did the spending limits. Under the old system, a candidate with a large campaign war chest could purchase massive amounts of television advertising, drowning out the messages of poorly financed candidates. But under the new system, no candidate could afford many TV ads, so during the primaries, at least, campaigning would consist largely of small-scale events, a few radio spots, and a relentless effort to get noticed by the local media. The new campaign finance laws were a godsend for Carter's candidacy.[35]

But the $1,000 limit on individual donations also made it more important than ever to have numerous fund-raising contacts. Fund-raising thus became a central focus of Carter's campaign in 1975. For much of the year, the majority of Carter's campaign contributions came from Georgia, which meant that the campaign had to be relentless in seeking donations from local people. "Supporters in Georgia . . . need to be systematically and regularly soaked for money," Rick Hutcheson noted in a memo to Carter's inner circle in July 1975. At the same time, the campaign made every effort to raise money for Carter in other states—especially California and New York. Carter regularly visited California for fund-raising purposes in 1975, but the campaign also relied on direct-mail appeals to solicit small donations from northern Democrats. The out-of-state fund-raising efforts were critical to the campaign's financial well-being, but they also helped Carter test the political waters by identifying what sort of voters might want him in the White House. In the spring of 1975 a marketing firm employed by the campaign found that it was easier for Carter to raise money from liberal donors—that is, people who had donated to George McGovern's campaign or who subscribed to a progressive magazine—than from those who were "middle of the road." Carter was frequently described in the press as a "moderate," but by early 1975, his out-of-state money was already beginning to come disproportionately from Democratic voters who were left of center. By August, more than half his funds were coming from out of state, which meant that Carter was now a nationally competitive candidate who could appeal to northern liberals.[36]

As the campaign recognized, Carter did not have to be the most liberal Democratic candidate to win the support of the party's progressive wing; he merely had to convince liberals that he was the most liberal person who could win the nomination and the election. Everyone knew that Udall and Harris were more liberal than Carter, but it was also common wisdom that neither of those candidates could win a single southern state—and perhaps not many northern ones either. Most northern votes would come from blue-collar workers, who were almost as socially conservative as their southern counterparts. The Carter campaign's message to party progressives who questioned the Georgia governor's commitment to progressive causes was that those causes would have a better chance of advancing with a Democratic centrist who could win the presidency than with a left-leaning McGovernite who could not. When the *Village Voice,* for instance, expressed skepticism about Carter's progressive commitments in January 1976, Andrew Young, whose liberal credentials (especially on civil rights) were impeccable, explained why he felt comfortable backing Carter. "You are probably right in questioning Jimmy's doctrinaire liberalism," he told the editors of the *Village Voice,* "but progressive politics in 1976 must be based on a 'tough mind and a tender heart,' and efficient pragmatism built on a foundation of sounder values and a sensitive loving spirit."[37]

CARTER'S ISSUE POSITIONS

To many national observers unfamiliar with New South Democrats, Carter's candidacy seemed to defy traditional ideological categories. For this reason, his position statements received unusually close scrutiny from both supporters and critics, and their creation sparked a lot of internal debate among his close associates. Several members of his campaign staff wanted Carter to adopt a more overtly progressive stance, believing that this would gain him credibility in the North without costing him very many votes in the South. "He will never frighten away the majority of moderates in the party regardless of what positions he is likely to take that are attractive to the left," a campaign strategy memo from May 1975 declared. "His southern background gives him great flexibility."[38]

Accordingly, Stu Eizenstat, Carter's issues position coordinator, began to craft policy statements that echoed liberal Democratic Party orthodoxy. But he ran into a problem: Carter's own positions, especially on economic issues, were not as progressive as some of his campaign staffers wanted, and he refused to be pushed to the left. Although Carter enjoyed meeting with the policy experts participating on the issues committees Eizenstat formed, he often marginalized Eizenstat and his staff in the end and plotted an independent course that deviated substantially from mainstream views in the Democratic Party.[39]

Carter's approach to inflation and unemployment was a case in point. In the fall of 1974 both inflation and unemployment were increasing—an unprecedented phenomenon that economists dubbed "stagflation." Having never faced this situation before, policymakers disagreed on which problem to tackle first. Keynesian economic models suggested that it might be difficult to lower unemployment without risking an increase in inflation, and conversely, any reduction in inflation would likely come at the cost of higher unemployment. In keeping with their New Deal heritage, liberals argued that unemployment was by far the greater of the two evils and should be given priority. Eizenstat's memo echoed this Democratic Party orthodoxy: unemployment, not inflation, should be the government's main concern, and deficit spending was not a problem as long as the additional spending generated economic growth. At the time, the Democrats' leading proposal to lower the unemployment rate was the Humphrey-Hawkins full employment bill, which committed the government to creating jobs directly through public works programs. Eizenstat's memo endorsed the concept.[40]

But Carter was reluctant to endorse the Humphrey-Hawkins bill because it cut against his inclination to be a deficit hawk. He promised to make a balanced budget a central priority, and he was committed to fighting inflation. The Humphrey-Hawkins bill in its original incarnation would have "created too much new bureaucracy," he said, but he suggested that he might favor a revised version of the bill—though he was vague on the details. By endorsing the concept of a government commitment to create full employment—a central promise of Humphrey-Hawkins—and by declaring that "every person has a right to a decent job," he sounded like a Great Society liberal in the mold of

Figure 3.3. Jimmy Carter working aboard his campaign plane. (Library of Congress, Prints & Photographs Division, U.S. News & World Report Magazine Collection, LC-DIG-ppmsca-09757)

Hubert Humphrey, but by criticizing the specific terms of the bill and arguing that it was imperative to balance the budget, Carter retained his image as a fiscal conservative. While the Humphrey-Hawkins bill called for increased public works programs to create jobs that were not available in the private sector, Carter believed that public works projects were acceptable only in an "extreme case" and favored increased federal spending on research and development instead, so that the private sector could remain the "primary supplier of jobs." He wanted to reduce federal interference in the business sector, not increase it. "My philosophic commitment is to a freer economy," he declared.[41]

Likewise, on taxes he projected a centrist image, calling for a "sweeping change in the tax structure" that would lower taxes for "middle and low income families" while also closing corporate tax loopholes that had encouraged corporations to relocate manufacturing plants overseas. In other words, Carter promised to pursue the priorities that were important to most working-class and middle-class families: lower taxes, a balanced federal budget, lower inflation, and full employment, with a "decent job" for every American. And all this, he believed, could be accomplished while ending the "horrible bureaucratic mess" in Washington.[42] Unlike Humphrey and other veterans of the party's Great Society years, Carter believed that he could enact more New Deal–Great Society priorities without creating New Deal–style government growth; indeed, he would *reduce* the overall size of government even while creating massive new government programs, such as national health insurance. It was this belief that allowed him to get the votes of both Democratic Party progressives and fiscal conservatives while also aiming for a broad swath of the middle class. Progressives and traditional Democratic liberals could take heart in Carter's spending promises and his endorsement of their two major, financially costly priorities—national health insurance and government spending to create full employment. Fiscal conservatives could take comfort in Carter's pledge to do this on the cheap and balance the budget within four years, even while lowering taxes for most American families. And centrist middle-class voters could believe that a vote for Carter would give them the best of all possible worlds—better jobs, reduced taxes, and an end to bloated government waste. All this was based on the assumption that a president could find enough money for all these new programs and tax cuts simply by growing the economy and trimming "waste" from the federal budget and that mere efficiency would be the key to expanding the federal government's activities while simultaneously reducing its size.

On foreign policy and the environment, Carter sounded like a progressive, and it was these two issues—along with his record on civil rights—that enabled him to make a bid for left-of-center votes and dollars. Carter had been slow to oppose the Vietnam War, and he had given the official nominating speech for Henry Jackson, one of the party's most outspoken hawks, at the 1972 Democratic National Convention, but by 1975, he had moved sharply to the left on this issue, and his foreign policy proposals now sounded very similar to Ted Kennedy's. Like Kennedy, he called for a human rights–based foreign policy, a strengthening of détente, denuclearization, an end to use of the CIA to effect regime change, and greater caution in the use of military force.[43]

To a greater degree than other Democrats, Carter invoked moral imperatives to describe his foreign policy vision. He rejected the moral claims invoked to justify the United States' Cold War fight against international communism—indeed, in the eight-page transcript of a foreign policy speech he gave in May 1975, the word "communism" never appears—but, like the raison d'être for his entire presidential candidacy, his vision for America's new role in the world was deeply moralistic and grounded in principles of trustworthiness and personal character. "Our influence and respect should go beyond our military might . . . and be based on the fact that we are right, and fair, and decent, and honest, and truthful," he declared.[44] Like the presidential candidate himself, the nation would never tell a lie to other countries.

Many progressives shared Carter's belief that the CIA's activities and the Vietnam War—and, by extension, Secretary of State Henry Kissinger's willingness to turn a blind eye to human rights abuses—were immoral. On foreign policy, they considered Carter a kindred spirit; his views on foreign affairs "decidedly place him in the liberal wing of the Democratic Party," the *New York Times* declared.[45]

On several other issues, Carter's position was a blank slate. In June 1975, six months after Carter declared his candidacy, Rick Hutcheson noted that the campaign still lacked Carter's position statements on several major controversial issues, including gun control, abortion, and capital punishment. Although Carter disputed the accusation, some of his opponents in the Democratic primaries—especially Mo Udall—charged that he was deliberately evasive on the issues in the hope of picking up votes from all sides. Carter repeatedly insisted that he was specific and forthright in stating his positions on issues and that any vagueness on policy matters would soon be cleared up when he released more detailed position statements, but his critics were correct in noting that his campaign was unusually slow in putting out such statements and even when it did so, the statements were often ambiguous. Carter was far more specific in his criticisms of Ford's handling of the economy than he was in his own promises of economic relief. When pledging tax relief for "working people," for instance, he did not specify the amount of the tax cuts or the income brackets that would be eligible for them; nor did he say whether he would offset these tax cuts with higher taxes on the wealthy. He called for public spending to create full employment but did not say how much he would spend or how he could implement this plan while still fulfilling his promise to balance the budget.[46]

By the end of 1975, Carter had staked out a position on most of the major cultural issues, and in general, he took a moderately progressive line. He endorsed *Roe v. Wade,* which marked him as pro-choice on abortion. He favored the decriminalization of marijuana. He promised a "blanket pardon" for Vietnam draft evaders that sounded so much like amnesty that even he had to admit "there was not much difference." He "strongly supported" the Equal Rights Amendment and endorsed federally funded day care. He advocated gun control, although he described his position as one that avoided "extreme" or "misguided" regulations; his stance coupled a requirement for handgun registration and a ban on "Saturday night specials" with a promise to leave hunting rifles alone. He gave qualified support to the use of busing to achieve school integration but insisted that student participation must be voluntary. On the death penalty, he was more centrist than liberal, supporting it in limited circumstances. But, as he pointed out, because of court decisions, there had been no executions in the United States since 1967, so capital punishment was largely a moot issue in presidential politics.[47]

Despite a few minor deviations from the progressive line, Carter's positions on cultural issues were far enough to the left for the *Nation* to describe him as a "liberal on racial and social justice issues, a conservative in government management." The *Boston Globe* called him a "kind of Kennedy Southerner" who was "a liberal on civil rights, on the environment and social justice and a conservative on taxation and budget matters"—in other words, "a liberal but not so liberal as to turn away conservatives." More precisely, Carter could be described as a deficit hawk who nevertheless accepted the Democratic Party's promises (albeit without enthusiasm) to create new federal programs and as a moderate liberal on social issues who still maintained a strait-laced, Southern Baptist image that endeared him to some cultural conservatives. Progressives in 1975 noted these apparent contradictions, but many found him acceptable anyway because they believed that his inclinations were compatible with theirs, even if his southern political context had thus far prevented him from fully acting on his progressive views.[48]

While Carter's image of fiscal restraint and social liberalism may have endeared him to some Democratic progressives, polls indicated that this stance was precisely the opposite of what most voters wanted. An analysis by the Democratic National Committee's Political Research Division concluded in January 1975 that "traditionally Democratic 'liberal' *economic* positions have the support of a broad majority," while on contentious "social issues" such as "marijuana legalization," "a majority sometimes favors the 'conservative' position."[49] The winning strategy for a Democrat in 1976 was therefore to embrace economic liberalism and at least moderate social conservatism—which McGovern had not done in 1972 and Carter was not yet doing in early 1975. To become a viable general election candidate, Carter would likely have to reposition himself. But his first challenge was to win the nomination, and it was still unclear whether his image as a socially liberal fiscal conservative would help him or hurt him in that endeavor.

CARTER'S CAMPAIGN STRATEGY

Carter's plan for winning the nomination focused heavily on two early-primary states: New Hampshire and Florida. If he could defeat most of his northern rivals in New Hampshire and deliver a decisive blow to George Wallace in Florida, he would win instant recognition as a front-runner.

The strategy may have been sensible, but for most of 1975, it appeared that Carter's chances of achieving his goal were low. In May, five months after his official entry into the presidential race, internal polling by the Carter campaign showed that nationally, only 3 percent of voters supported him. Carter enjoyed stronger support in the South than in other areas of the country, but his support paled in comparison to Wallace's; according to the poll, Wallace received 35 percent of the southern vote and Carter only 7 percent. And Carter's favorability rating in the South was only 26 percent. The best news that Carter could take from this survey was that 33 percent of southern voters—and more than 50 percent of voters in much of the North—said they had never heard of him. This meant there might be numerous undecided voters who could be convinced to support him once they heard his message. But four months later, after repeated trips to the early-primary or early-caucus states of Iowa, New Hampshire, and Florida, Carter's prospects had not improved. An NBC News poll of Democratic voters in New Hampshire in September 1975 showed Carter tied for eighth place, with only 3 percent of the vote. The *New York Times* grouped Carter with Fred Harris in October 1975, saying that both were "long shots" for the nomination.[50]

But the Carter campaign was not fazed. Although Carter's poll numbers were low in New Hampshire, his campaign team knew that doing well in the state would not be as difficult as it appeared. There were only 115,000 Democrats in New Hampshire, and most of them were concentrated in Manchester and a few other industrial towns near the Massachusetts border. It would thus be relatively easy for Carter's campaign team, which had limited financial resources but plenty of time and an abundance of volunteers, to personally talk to nearly every one of these Democrats. Carter was also helped by two other factors: the favorite candidate of New Hampshire Democrats—Ted Kennedy—was not running, and Henry Jackson, who had more support among New Hampshire Democrats than most of the other declared candidates, had decided not to campaign there so that he could focus his efforts on Massachusetts and New York. New Hampshire offered only seventeen delegates, a paltry sum in a contest in which more than one thousand were needed to win, whereas the larger Democratic strongholds of Massachusetts and New York, where Jackson was also popular, promised to be much richer prizes. But what Jackson failed to realize was that the New Hampshire contest was not about winning delegates but about winning media coverage. Carter knew that if he could score an upset in New Hampshire, his face would suddenly be on the cover of the nation's newsweeklies and he would receive an unprecedented amount of free television coverage. His campaign's financial troubles would be over, and he would instantly be recognized as a nationally competitive candidate, even if his delegate prize amounted to barely 1 percent of the total needed for the nomination. Furthermore, if Carter did well in New Hampshire, he would prove that he was not merely a southern regional candidate. For months, Jordan scheduled as much of Carter's time in New Hampshire as possible, complaining whenever the candidate took side trips to Massachusetts or other neighboring states.[51]

Although Jordan initially minimized Iowa's importance relative to New Hampshire, Carter also invested a lot of time in the Hawkeye State, where he capitalized on his image as a farmer and Washington outsider. Some of Carter's campaign staff worried about this, believing that any time Carter spent in Iowa—which they thought he might win anyway, without a lot of campaigning—would take away valuable time in New Hampshire.[52] Iowa was a low-delegate state, but what most campaign managers in the 1976 election failed to consider was that the timing of a caucus or primary mattered far more than the delegate count. Because Iowa was scheduled to hold the first precinct caucuses in the nation, its results would get far more publicity than those in other states. "Money can't buy the kind of press we'll get if JC finishes first in the precinct caucuses," Tim Kraft, the campaign's national field director, told Jordan in August 1975. A victory in Iowa could give Carter the momentum to "not only win in New Hampshire, but win big," added David Frye, the midwestern field desk coordinator. In the end, Carter followed Kraft and Frye's advice, and he slowly began to build a base of support in Iowa through repeated personal visits. In October he stunned the national press, which still routinely referred to him as a "dark-horse candidate," by taking first place in an Iowa straw poll, which meant that despite his low national poll numbers, he was now the man to beat in Iowa.[53] The same was not yet true in New Hampshire, where no poll showed Carter finishing first. But in the fall of 1975 New Hampshire was not Carter's only concern; he was investing as many resources as possible in Florida, which had become his campaign's top priority because of the tantalizing opportunity to defeat Wallace in a direct match.

CARTER AS THE SOUTHERN ANTI-WALLACE

George Wallace had positioned himself as the quintessential outsider ever since his first presidential run in 1964, and he had the national name recognition that Carter lacked. None of the national Democratic Party leaders or presidential aspirants liked Wallace, but no one knew how to finish him off either. Convinced that the South would only support a conservative southerner, most of the other candidates—especially Udall—largely bypassed the region.[54]

But because the Carter campaign was based in the South and staffed almost entirely by southerners, it had a different view of Wallace. An internal Carter campaign document from May 1975 asserted that, in reality, "most Southern opinion leaders consider themselves moderates" and were "ashamed of the image Wallace projects of the South." Wallace's favorability ratings among white southerners might momentarily be high, but his support was based primarily on his regional identity and anti-Washington image rather than his racial views. As Atlanta financial consultant Ezra Mintz, an early adviser to the Carter campaign, told campaign advertising manager Jerry Rafshoon in December 1974, "I believe a great deal of the Wallace vote comes from people who do not see themselves as racists but people who are sick of the 'elite liberals' that try to 'tear down our country.'" If Carter could channel those sentiments in a "respectable" way and give southerners a chance to elect an antiracist southerner to the presidency, few white southerners would be able to resist this chance to "redeem" their region. Carter could count on the votes of nearly all the region's moderate and liberal whites, along with the black vote; he could likewise appeal to a few cultural conservatives who might favor Wallace by convincing them that the Alabaman could never win the nomination but Carter could. If Carter could knock Wallace out of the race long before the convention, he could capture the lion's share of the southern vote and emerge as a formidable figure on the national political scene, earning both the respect and the gratitude of northern liberals, who would view his antiracist stance as sufficient proof that he was at least moderately progressive.[55]

Initially, besting Wallace at his own game had not been the focal point of Carter's campaign strategy. In the earliest stage of the Carter campaign, in November 1972, Hamilton Jordan had not expected Wallace to be a candidate; he had assumed that the severe injuries Wallace had sustained in the attempt on his life six months earlier would prevent him from running for president again. But by early 1975, Wallace was outpacing all other candidates in fund-raising, and it became apparent that he would not only run but also be a formidable candidate. This was a blessing in disguise for the Carter campaign, because it deterred most other candidates from campaigning in the South, thus giving Carter the chance to challenge Wallace directly. Initially, the Carter campaign had thought that Senator Lloyd Bentsen of Texas and former North Carolina governor Terry Sanford would be vying with Carter for the white southern vote, and some journalists speculated that Florida governor Reubin Askew would enter the race as well. But Askew decided not to run, Bentsen's campaign quickly folded, and Sanford's never got off the ground, leaving the South to Carter and Wallace as the northern and western candidates made only limited efforts in a small number of southern states. This presented Carter with an "enormous opportunity," suggested an internal campaign strategy memo from the spring of 1975. "To show strength against Wallace in his own region is to appear a giantkiller."[56]

Carter adopted a delicate approach to the Wallace vote: On the one hand, he had to campaign in the South with an appeal to the socially conservative blue-collar voters who were attracted to Wallace and convince them that he shared their values. On the other hand, he had to repudiate Wallace in the North and use his defeat of the Alabama governor to convince northern liberals that he was the antithesis of the southern populist whom they considered their inveterate enemy. The key to doing that, campaign strategists believed, was for Carter to distance himself from Wallace's racism, even while embracing his patriotism, his southern pride, and his socially conservative anti-Washington rhetoric. Carter also insisted that Wallace could never win the presidency, whereas he could. Playing off the Wallace slogan "Send them a message," he asked southern whites, "Why send a message when you can send a president?"[57]

CARTER'S ANTI-WASHINGTON MESSAGE

The Carter campaign could simultaneously appeal to Wallace voters and anti-Wallace progressives because of its conviction that, in the end, these two divergent wings of the Democratic Party could unite around the message that Washington was broken and needed to be fixed. Despite Carter's high regard for Reinhold Niebuhr, the neo-orthodox theologian who wrote at length about original sin and human evil, his campaign was based on an optimistic view of the innate goodness of "the people." Washington bureaucracy was the problem, but "the people" had the answers, if only they could be freed from the red tape and corruption in Washington. Carter recognized that many voters were angry, but he believed he could channel that anger not toward bitterness—as Wallace seemed to do—but toward positive solutions that would restore the nation's original goodness before Watergate and the Vietnam War.

Ted Sorensen, President John F. Kennedy's former speechwriter, crafted a speech for Carter a few weeks before the New Hampshire primary that encapsulated this anti-Washington theme and packaged it in the glowing rhetoric of American patriotism reminiscent of Kennedy's stirring oratory. "I sincerely believe that our country can enjoy a government that relies on fewer bureaucracies, less secrecy, a smaller White House staff, less centralization in Washington and, above all, more unvarnished truth and non-partisan integrity than we have seen in the last ten years," Sorensen wrote for Carter. The speech continued:

> In short, when I look at what ails this country, I have to say that government right now is part of the problem. But I believe it should be part of the solution. Perhaps I am an optimist. Some will say I am a dreamer. But I believe in the American dream, 200 years after independence, because it has come true in my own life. I believe in the vitality of this nation, its people, its business enterprises and farms, its young folks and workers, because for over a year I have been traveling through this land and listening to the people and drawing renewed inspiration from them.[58]

Fifteen years earlier, Kennedy had called for Americans to sacrifice their own interests for the Cold War liberal state. Now, if Sorenson and Carter were successful, there would be a new torchbearer for the Democratic Party with a somewhat different message—a message that was far more skeptical about the federal government but that retained Kennedy's essential faith in the American people. Carter's showing in New Hampshire would test whether Democratic voters were ready for this anti-Washington message.

4 THE REPUBLICANS

When Gerald Ford took the oath of office on August 9, 1974, the race for the 1976 Republican presidential nomination was already well under way, and Ford had done nothing to prepare for it. He was not yet sure that he would run for a full term in 1976, and some of his potential rivals in the Republican Party assumed (or at least hoped) he would not. The first of Ford's potential Republican challengers, Senator Charles Percy, had already announced his presidential campaign six months before Ford took office, and another one—Governor Ronald Reagan of California—was waiting in the wings, ready to enter the race at any moment.

Ford was vulnerable to a challenge not only because he was an unelected president and the economy was floundering but also because his own party was badly divided. There were at least three major factions in the GOP: liberals, centrists, and conservatives. Both the left and right wings of the party considered Ford, a centrist (or moderate conservative), to be a potential enemy.

The conflict among the party's factions had been brewing for decades. In the 1940s and 1950s the party's liberal wing, which accepted most of the Democrats' New Deal social programs, exercised a controlling influence over party conventions, but by the late 1950s, a small but rapidly growing coterie attempted to challenge both liberals and moderates within the party. The Republican Party had always had members who were well to the right of New York governor Thomas Dewey and the other northeastern liberals who dominated party conventions in the 1940s, but it was only in the late 1950s and early 1960s that these self-styled "conservatives" created the organizations (Young Americans for Freedom), magazines (*National Review* and *Human Events*), and political networks that made them a distinct movement within the party. The new conservatives were far from ideologically homogeneous. Their unofficial leader within the GOP was Arizona senator Barry Goldwater, a popular speaker who energized both conservative southern Democrats and western and northern Republicans with a message of free-market libertarianism and strong anticommunism. When Goldwater wrested the presidential nomination from party liberals in 1964, conservatives were ecstatic, but their dream ended with a landslide loss: Goldwater carried only six states—five in the Deep South plus his home state of Arizona. Liberals and centrists in the party blamed Goldwater's "extremism"; his history of bellicose rhetoric toward the Soviet Union, combined with his opposition to the Civil Rights Act of 1964, made him anathema to almost everyone except right-wing ideologues and southern racists, they thought. The fact that Goldwater won 87 percent of the vote in Mississippi while losing by wide margins nearly everywhere else showed how reactionary the Goldwater platform was, party liberals believed. But conservatives took a different view. They blamed Goldwater's loss on the unwillingness of his liberal Republican rivals, such as New York governor Nelson Rockefeller, to support him, and they vowed revenge.[1]

For a brief moment, Richard Nixon managed to hold the party's liberals and conservatives together. Having long been a staunch anticommunist, but having also served as vice president in the centrist Eisenhower administration, Nixon had credibility with both the liberal and the conservative factions. Neither side fully trusted him, but neither side directly opposed him either. In 1968 the conservatives attempted to nominate a new standard-bearer—California governor Ronald Reagan, who had launched his political career with a Goldwater campaign speech in 1964 and then entered state politics as a Goldwater-style conservative—but they quickly switched to Nixon's side when they realized their efforts lacked party support. Liberals, too, decided to support Nixon after their own favored candidate, Rockefeller, failed in his presidential quest. On the campaign trail, Nixon sometimes sounded like a cultural conservative as he called for "law and order," and as president, he placated the party's right wing by escalating the bombing in Vietnam and showing little tolerance for antiwar protesters. But he also elevated party liberals Elliot Richardson, William Ruckelshaus, and, above all, Henry Kissinger (a longtime Rockefeller supporter) to positions of influence in the administration. He surprised many Republicans with his liberal initiatives, which included the Environmental Protection Agency (EPA), the Occupational Safety and Health Administration (OSHA), the National Endowment for the Arts, and the first major federal affirmative action program. He negotiated the first arms limitation agreement with the Soviet Union since the beginning of the Cold War, and he became the first American president to visit China.[2]

Some of the party's conservatives were anxious about Nixon's foreign policy shifts—objecting especially to détente with the Soviet Union. One conservative (Representative John Ashbrook of Ohio) even mounted a primary challenge against Nixon in 1972, which the president easily beat back. But despite their misgivings, conservatives gave Nixon strong support in the general election because his campaign had successfully tarred Democrat George McGovern as a cultural liberal who was out of step with "middle America."[3] As a candidate who favored an immediate end to the Vietnam War and who enjoyed the support of feminists and left-leaning young people, McGovern was the candidate of "amnesty, acid, and abortion," Republicans charged. The tactic worked. Nixon won the electoral votes of forty-nine states, leaving McGovern with only Massachusetts and the District of Columbia; the hapless Democratic candidate could not even win a majority in his home state of South Dakota.

But this temporary Republican unity vanished as soon as the election was over. As Nixon became embroiled in the Watergate scandal, the economy started to founder. The energy crisis of 1973 caused oil prices to quadruple and ushered in a round of high inflation and high unemployment that would plague the nation for the rest of the decade. Conservatives and liberals within the Republican Party could not agree on how to solve these economic problems. They also disagreed on almost everything else, from the appropriate policy toward the Soviet Union to women's rights and civil rights. Conservative Republican Phyllis Schlafly mobilized women across the South and Midwest to fight the Equal Rights Amendment (ERA), while other Republican women, including Betty Ford, supported the ERA and gave feminism at least a moderate endorsement. And on abortion, the party included both supporters and opponents of *Roe v. Wade,* the 1973 decision issued by Nixon-appointed Supreme Court justice Harry Blackmun that quickly attracted the ire of social conservatives both inside and outside the GOP. Some conservative Republicans saw an opportunity to reach out to conservative Democrats and form a new coalition in opposition to the liberals in their party. The Republican liberals, for their part, were determined to save their party from a conservative faction that they believed would destroy it with anachronistic and dangerous ideas. And the centrists were desperate to find someone to carry on Nixon's project of uniting the two disparate factions under one party banner. In early 1973 the leading contender for this role was Spiro Agnew, Nixon's tough-talking, controversial vice president.

SPIRO AGNEW'S EARLY LEAD

Speculation about Agnew's plans for 1976 began even before the ballots had been counted in 1972. Two days before Election Day 1972, the *Washington Post* published an article about Agnew's prospects for the presidency and noted that although he was still being coy about his plans for 1976, he was clearly interested in the White House and, according to one of his aides, was working on establishing an image as a "centrist" and a "national rather than a partisan figure"—a "strategy," the *Post* observed, that "is likely to form the basis of Agnew's battleplan to win the presidency in 1976." Five months later, in April 1973, a Gallup poll showed Agnew at the top of the pack of potential Republican contenders for the 1976 presidential nomination, receiving the support of 35 percent of Republicans, compared to 20 percent for Ronald Reagan and 15 percent for John Connally.[4]

To a greater degree than most Republicans, Agnew had the potential to appeal to all wings of the party and forge the broad-based coalition that had secured Nixon's landslide reelection victory. Throughout the 1960s, as governor of Maryland, Agnew had been a liberal Republican and a Rockefeller acolyte. In fact, he had chaired the National Draft Rockefeller Committee in early 1968, hoping to give his party a more liberal candidate than Nixon, a sign of his political leanings at the time. But he also had a reputation as a hard-nosed law-and-order candidate, which appealed to conservatives. In Maryland, he gave a no-nonsense response to angry blacks who instigated race riots in Cambridge and Baltimore, saying that it would be state policy to "immediately arrest any person inciting to riot."[5] When Nixon selected Agnew as his running mate in 1968, the Maryland governor adopted the role of attack dog, lashing out at reporters with colorful invectives and occasionally using a racial slur. Combining the culturally conservative appeal of George Wallace with a willingness to steer a Nixonian centrist course on foreign policy and the economy, Agnew, the son of a Greek immigrant, seemed to be the best candidate to carry on Nixon's strategy of forging a majority through an appeal to white southerners and northern Catholic ethnics.

But Agnew also had obvious liabilities. His rhetoric was harsh and mean-spirited rather than presidential, and while some voters admired his toughness, few considered him likable. Both his aides and the *Washington Post* assumed that he would need to reinvent himself as a more moderate, conciliatory statesman to be considered presidential material. His staff hoped that a diplomatic trip to the Soviet Union would burnish his image, and they were helping him tone down the inflammatory rhetoric that had made him a political lightning rod. Despite these efforts, Agnew was already so controversial that he had almost been denied a spot on the 1972 ticket. Nixon had hoped to replace him with former Texas governor and treasury secretary John Connally. In the end, perhaps fearing that dumping Agnew would be seen as an affront to the cultural conservatives who still liked him, Nixon decided to keep him on the ticket, thus paving the way for Agnew to proceed with plans to capture his party's nomination in 1976—a project that Nixon scorned in private conversations with his aides. Although Agnew was the Republican front-runner in the spring of 1973, he was widely disliked outside of the party. A Gallup poll taken in April 1973 showed him losing by 22 points in a hypothetical matchup with Senator Ted Kennedy.[6]

But it was Agnew's ethical lapses rather than his controversial political statements that ended his presidential aspirations. Within weeks of Nixon's second inauguration, a federal grand jury in Baltimore began investigating charges that Agnew had received hundreds of thousands of dollars in bribes during his term as governor of Maryland. In October 1973 Agnew pleaded "no contest" to charges of bribery and tax evasion and resigned as vice president.[7] His political career was over.

Republicans then cast about for a possible consensus nominee for 1976. Nixon had hoped that Connally would be his successor. The Texan was popular in the South and was generally viewed as a conservative who could appeal to the Sun Belt version of the party's right wing. But Connally was a recent convert to the party (he officially became a Republican in early 1973, although he had campaigned for Nixon the previous year), and many Republicans distrusted him. Democrats in Congress hated Connally for abandoning their party and vowed that they would not let Nixon select him to replace Agnew.[8]

Instead, Nixon selected Gerald Ford, the hardworking House Republican minority leader who had an impeccable ethical reputation and had earned the respect of congressional colleagues from both parties. But Ford was largely unknown on the national scene, and even his own party members did not consider him a shoo-in for the presidential nomination in 1976. By late 1975, it would be apparent that Ford's major challenge for the nomination would come from the right wing of his party, but in 1974 it seemed that the greater danger might be a challenge from party liberals, who had felt constrained under Nixon and did not want to see the GOP move further to the right under Ford. Liberal Republican politicians began gearing up for a primary challenge even before Nixon's resignation in August 1974, and they continued their presidential preparations after Ford became president.

THE LIBERAL REPUBLICANS

Many expected the leading liberal contender for the party's nomination in 1976 to be Nelson Rockefeller, given his three previous presidential bids in the 1960s and his stature as one of the party's best-known figures. The wealthy New York governor had long been the leader of the liberal wing of the GOP, advocating a progressive probusiness approach that combined government support of corporate interests with liberal stances on civil rights, abortion, women's rights, and national health care. For Rockefeller, an art connoisseur and Ivy League–educated son of America's wealthiest family, the government played a vital role in ensuring that everyone had an opportunity to enjoy the blessings of life. As he said, "If you don't have good education and good health, then I feel society has let you down."[9]

Rockefeller wanted to be president in 1960, but he failed to take sufficient action to challenge Nixon. He then made a more serious attempt to stop conservative Barry Goldwater from getting the nomination in 1964. But by then, Rockefeller's 1962 divorce and prompt remarriage to a much younger woman (the former wife of a family friend and rumored to have had an affair with Rockefeller while still married) scandalized many Republican voters and contributed to his defeat in the primaries. Rockefeller also failed to win the party's nomination in 1968. Still, he seemed inclined to try again in 1976. Recognizing that a viable bid for the Republican nomination would require him to win over at least a few Sun Belt conservatives, he began taking trips to the South to convince party officials that he was not their enemy. He took a hard-line stance on crime, sending a thousand state troopers to quell a revolt at the Attica state prison in 1971, a move that earned him praise from law-and-order conservatives and condemnation from liberals. In 1973 he signed some of the toughest drug laws in the country. The Ripon Society, the leading organization for liberal Republicans, issued a gentle rebuke to its erstwhile hero. Southern Republicans, by contrast, decided to take a second look at the man they had once dismissed as a Yankee liberal. Clarke Reed, the Mississippi state Republican Party chairman who was supporting Ronald Reagan, acknowledged that Rockefeller was someone "we can live with," and he predicted that if Rockefeller won the nomination, he would be able to carry the South in the general election.[10]

This was a start, but it was still a far cry from a promise of southern support for a Rockefeller bid in the primaries. "Rocky's image as a liberal Republican will be hard to erase," declared the right-wing magazine *Human Events* in January 1974. Demographic trends did not favor his candidacy. In 1960, when Rockefeller had first toyed with the idea of running for president, New York was still the nation's most populous state, and the center of Republican Party influence was in the Northeast. But now California had surpassed New York in size, the South had started to join the GOP, and the party's center of influence was moving toward the Sun Belt, with rising stars such as Reagan and Connally emerging as potential party leaders, along with the aging Arizona conservative Goldwater. Perhaps the time for a liberal New York governor to be the Republicans' presidential nominee had passed. And perhaps, in an era of skepticism about government and corporate wealth, a philandering, aging political insider whose very name invoked an image of wealth, privilege, and power would have a difficult time appealing to voters. Many conservative Republicans still considered Rockefeller their enemy because of his liberal record and opposition to Goldwater in 1964, and many progressive Democrats were just as angry over his state's drug laws and his response to the Attica prison uprising. According to Gallup polls taken in 1973 and early 1974, he garnered only between 11 and 18 percent of the Republican vote, with nearly all of that support coming from the Northeast. Among Republicans in the South and West, Rockefeller's poll numbers were stuck at 5 percent, compared to nearly 50 percent for Reagan.[11] Yet despite his liabilities, Rockefeller was a personable, glad-handing campaigner whose charm could win over skeptics, and as the governor of New York (second only to California in population and political power), he had long been one of the most influential Republicans in the nation. He could not be counted out in 1976. But neither could he be counted in.

True to form, Rockefeller adopted a coy approach and refused to discuss his presidential plans. In February 1974 one of the most liberal members of the party, Senator Charles Percy of Illinois, grew tired of Rockefeller's dithering and announced his own candidacy to give liberal Republicans a chance to stop the party's drift to the right. By March, his presidential exploratory committee had raised $135,000, including some large contributions from television ratings company president A. C. Nielson and a few other corporate magnates. Percy even collected a small amount of Rockefeller family money when his daughter, the wife of John D. Rockefeller IV (Nelson's nephew and a liberal Democrat), sent his campaign a check for $3,500.[12]

Though scorned by conservative members of the GOP as Democrats in disguise, liberal Republicans may have been the most consistent defenders of the party's original principles. Like many of the Republicans of Abraham Lincoln's generation, they believed in a party that used the powers of government to promote civil rights and manufacturing interests. The liberal Republicans included a number of business executives and heirs to corporate fortunes, and they viewed themselves as thoroughly pro-business. Their movement's national political leaders included plenty of people (besides Rockefeller) with strong ties to the corporate world: Michigan governor George Romney, the former president of American Motors Corporation; Pennsylvania representative (and future senator) John Heinz, whose father was heir to the Heinz ketchup fortune; and Connecticut senator Lowell Weicker, son of a national pharmaceuticals company executive. Percy himself was the former president of Bell & Howell Corporation. While their party's libertarian right wing believed that free enterprise would prosper if the government did nothing to intervene in the economy, liberal Republicans—in accordance with the GOP's historic support for high tariffs in the late nineteenth and early twentieth centuries—believed in a more productive partnership between business and government. Like the Republicans of Lincoln's generation, they favored expanded government aid to education. They did not want to dismantle the large government programs of the New Deal and the Great Society; instead, they wanted to manage those programs responsibly. They were often more liberal than Democrats on issues of reproductive rights; some of them, like Rockefeller, had long been family-planning advocates and leaders in the early call for the legalization of abortion. Especially among the younger generation of Republican liberals, such as Senator Mark Hatfield of Oregon and Representative Pete McCloskey of California, opposition to the Vietnam War had come to define their movement. And they were strong supporters of civil rights legislation. Some of them, such as Senator Charles "Mac" Mathias of Maryland, had played a leading role in creating the landmark civil rights legislation of the 1960s, including the Civil Rights Act of 1964, and their votes had been crucial to its passage.[13] Others, like McCloskey, were cosponsors of the environmental legislation of the early 1970s. They also viewed themselves as advocates of clean government; they supported campaign finance reform legislation and were among the first in their party to break with President Nixon over the Watergate scandal.

Their relationship with Nixon was strained. McCloskey openly broke with Nixon over Vietnam, and Hatfield publicly criticized the president. But other liberal Republicans took jobs in the administration; Romney served as Nixon's secretary of the Department of Housing and Urban Development, and even Rockefeller seemed to be angling for a post. Liberal Republicans appreciated Nixon's achievement of détente with the Soviet Union and his initiative to open relations with China, and they appreciated many of his administration's more liberal domestic programs, including affirmative action policies, environmental legislation, and landmark laws such as Title IX to secure gender equality. But they were disturbed by Nixon's divisive campaign rhetoric, some of which was written by populist conservative speechwriter Patrick Buchanan. Nixon sometimes governed to the left of center, but on the campaign trail he hewed to the right, especially on social issues. He seemed to delight in dividing Americans and appealing to cultural conservatives, even while claiming to be a centrist above the fray of partisan division. This was precisely what a Republican candidate should not do, liberal Republicans thought.[14]

Like the Whigs of the early nineteenth century, liberal Republicans abhorred ignoble appeals to divisions based on social class, race, and religion. Even Edward Brooke, the only African American Republican senator, insisted that he was not a "national leader for the

Negro people." Most shunned sectarian religious appeals, preferring to champion the separation of church and state while invoking generic themes such as "the brotherhood of man and fatherhood of God"—a phrase Rockefeller used so often that journalists simply referred to it by its acronym: BOMFOG. Wary of creating any division in their party, many liberal Republicans objected to even the term "liberal," claiming they were pragmatic centrists who favored the principles the GOP had always championed. As political scientist Nicol Rae notes, liberal Republicans' reluctance to define themselves as a faction or to draft a statement of principles—in contrast to the conservatives in the party—probably hurt their movement.[15] But in the view of liberal Republicans, they were not a movement; they were simply champions of the historic principles of the Republican Party—updated, of course, for the needs of the 1970s—and they viewed the right-wingers in the party as dangerous interlopers. In their view, the conservatives in the party were the usurpers. Ronald Reagan had been a Democrat until the 1960s, and Strom Thurmond had not switched his party registration until 1964. Jesse Helms waited until the beginning of the 1970s to become a Republican. But nearly all the liberal Republicans had been lifelong members of the GOP, and several came from families whose Republican lineage extended back to the nineteenth century.

This largely explained why the liberal Republicans did not become Democrats, even when the center of gravity in their party began shifting to the right. Although a few younger liberal Republicans, such as New York mayor John Lindsay, switched to the Democratic Party in the early 1970s, most of the liberals in the GOP—especially the older ones—were not ready to bolt because the culture and institutions of the Republican Party were embedded deeply in their DNA. Their ethnic, cultural, and social class background differed from that of the Democrats. Disproportionately northeastern, overwhelmingly Protestant, and heavily patrician, they did not fit into a Democratic Party that was still associated with urban ethnics, southern segregationists, and the politics of class division. Of the seventeen Republican senators who earned an Americans for Democratic Action (ADA) rating of 30 percent or higher in 1972, the only non-Protestant was New York's Jewish senator Jacob Javits; more than half were Episcopalians, Methodists, Unitarians, or Congregationalists—the mainline denominations that for more than a century had controlled many of the nation's elite colleges and universities and whose members had long enjoyed a close relationship with the liberal wing of the GOP. Fifteen of the seventeen liberal Republican senators had attended elite colleges and universities as undergraduates or law students, with ten holding degrees from Harvard, Yale, Columbia, Georgetown, Boston University, or New York University. Although some liberal Republicans came from the West Coast or from the industrial cities of the Midwest, most had lived their entire lives in the Northeast. Eleven of the seventeen liberal Republican senators represented states in New England or the northeastern coastal corridor that stretched from Delaware to Maine, and none represented Sun Belt states. They came from states where Protestant blue bloods were Republicans and Catholic ethnics were Democrats. Of the six Democratic senators representing New England states in 1972, four were Catholic and one was Jewish. Most upper-crust liberal Protestants were not likely to join this group.[16]

Liberal Republicans also had philosophical differences with the Democrats that dissuaded them from switching parties. They strongly resented the Democrats' class-based appeals and their willingness to divide the electorate into competing ethnic alliances. As advocates of "clean" government, they abhorred the Democratic political machines that had long controlled the politics of the North's largest cities. They objected to the Democrats' attacks on "big business" and corporate wealth. And they believed that the Republican Party could offer more fiscally prudent management than the Democrats, even while providing social services more effectively. Above all, they were technocratic managers who believed they could offer a fiscally responsible, efficient oversight of the New Deal social welfare state without engaging in the corruption, class warfare, irresponsible spending, and bloated bureaucratic waste that, in their view, typified Democratic administrations. As Jacob Javits told the Ripon Society in 1975, the Republican Party, at its best, stood for a mandate of "equal opportunity, the productivity of the American free enterprise system and the need for being hard headed about money."[17] This was something the Democrats did not offer, and it was worth defending. Rather than switch parties, they attempted to seize control of their own party—a party that their opponents, the self-styled conservatives, had already begun to claim as their own.

By the 1970s, liberal northern Republicans were a minority in a party whose demographic base was rapidly shifting to the Sun Belt. The seventeen liberal Republican senators in 1972 were outnumbered by the twenty-eight who were conservative (defined as those whose

ADA rating was below 30 percent). Many of these conservatives came from different regions of the country and had different cultural backgrounds than the liberal Republicans. Seven were from the West, five were from the states of the old Confederacy, and ten were from the Midwest or Great Plains. Only four were from the northeastern corridor. They also differed from the liberals in their educational and social class backgrounds. Whereas most of the liberal Republicans had obtained their degrees at elite private universities or northeastern liberal arts colleges, more than half (sixteen of twenty-eight) of the conservative Republicans had been educated at public universities, and only seven (25 percent) had attended one of the Ivies. The conservatives were far more suspicious of governmental institutions than the liberals were, and they were far less likely to support increased United Nations funding or expanded environmental legislation.[18]

Although the liberal Republicans faced a threat from the party's growing right wing, Javits and his fellow liberals believed that the GOP's institutional heritage was on their side and that they would be able to defend it. "I don't believe that most Republicans are ready to sell out their reliance on the principles of Lincoln, Teddy Roosevelt, Tom Dewey, Wendell Willkie, and Dwight Eisenhower," Javits said. But if a "neanderthal wing" of the party was allowed to take over, Republicans would face "defeat," because only a party that appealed to young people, women, and minorities—which the conservativism of Reagan and Goldwater did not—could survive into the future.[19] But demographic trends were on Reagan's side, not Javits's. While Percy was collecting a small pile of donations from wealthy corporate leaders for his 1976 presidential campaign, Reagan, the new de facto leader of the conservative wing of the party, was drawing much larger crowds, raising far more money, and gaining a lot more popular appeal. It was enough to make Javits fear for the future of the GOP.

REAGAN'S CONSERVATIVE CHALLENGE

Throughout Nixon's presidency, Reagan acted as the cheerful prod from the right, leading a national populist movement to reclaim the Republican Party for the conservatives. As a movie actor in the 1940s, he had been a New Deal Democrat, but his opposition to communism and his dislike of the postwar era's high taxes pushed him to the right. In 1960 he supported Nixon in his race against Kennedy. In 1962 he officially changed his party registration to Republican, and in 1964 he made his national debut as a conservative spokesperson with his pro-Goldwater speech "A Time for Choosing." The forcefully delivered speech led some to view Reagan as the new face of the conservative movement, a role Goldwater had held for five years. With the support of the newly mobilized white suburban conservatives in Orange County and other parts of Southern California, Reagan won a surprise victory in the governor's race in 1966, catapulting him to a position of national political influence. Although Reagan's actions were not consistently conservative, he was a popular governor; his occasional tax increases or expansions of state government services did nothing to diminish his standing among conservatives because his rhetoric remained staunchly opposed to Washington deficit spending. After making a brief, hesitant attempt to win the Republican nomination in 1968, he was widely viewed as a serious contender for the 1976 race. Reagan quickly became the nation's most sought-after conservative speaker as he traveled the country headlining Young Americans for Freedom (YAF) conferences, National Association of Manufacturers gatherings, and other conservative forums.[20]

Reagan's message was simple and consistent: Washington was broken, and federal spending (especially out-of-control social welfare spending) was the cause of the nation's economic problems. Those problems would be fixed only when someone had the courage to end the high taxation, federal regulations, and deficit spending that prevented the common worker from enjoying the fruits of his labor. Reagan had preached this antigovernment gospel even during the prosperous years of the mid-1960s, but in the midst of the high inflation rates and rising unemployment of the 1970s, it seemed more credible than ever. "There's one cause of inflation and one alone," he repeated in speech after speech, "government continuing to spend more money than it takes in."[21]

In Reagan's view, both Republicans and Democrats had lost sight of what had made the country great. "The essence of the American Revolution was a system that produced a limited government and the ultimate in individual freedom consistent with an orderly society," he told a YAF convention in July 1974. And the key to perpetuating this vision of the founders was free enterprise, untrammeled by government regulation. "Our system of free enterprise sparkplugged by the hope of economic reward has lifted more burdens from the backs of more people than any other system the world has ever known," he declared. But "government programs multiplying like spores of a fungus have brought an inflation that robs our people of their dream of a good life." With his folksy speaking style peppered with jokes and anecdotes—along with a ream of statistics and ideological pronouncements culled from conservative publications such as *Human Events,* which he read religiously—Reagan could sound like both an optimist and an alarmist at the same time. He was profoundly optimistic when he expressed his faith in free enterprise and individual initiative, but when it came to the growth of government, he was almost apocalyptic, as reflected by the military metaphors he used to describe the conservative movement's campaign. "The ongoing struggle is for survival of the free market system," he said. "So far, we have been fighting a kind of a defensive, rear guard action. Step by step we have retreated much farther than we know." But it was not too late. Conservatives could still rise up and save the country from destruction by government bureaucracy.[22] If government regulations were simply repealed, entrepreneurs would be free to drill more oil and extract more resources domestically, and the United States would no longer face an energy crisis. In the area of defense, the same principles applied: the Vietnam War could have been won, but government bungling in the Kennedy and Johnson administrations had prevented the military from going "all out for victory."[23]

This was a populist message that pitted the people against the evils of an out-of-control government bureaucracy, and it suited the public mood at a time when Watergate, economic stagnation, and defeat in Vietnam had eroded Americans' confidence in the federal government. But Reagan did not simply echo popular sentiment; he also attempted to redirect it. As Republican pollster Dick Wirthlin told Reagan in July 1974, Americans' new suspicion of bureaucratic power made them skeptical of not only the president and Congress but also private-sector corporations—which did not bode well for Reagan and his message of free enterprise. In 1973 only 33 percent of Americans expressed a "moderate" or "high" approval of business (compared with 52 percent in 1967). Ralph Nader had become a folk hero, Wirthlin explained, and polls indicated that "people favor regulation of business by government." Reagan sought to recast this populist narrative. No longer would "Sir Ralph," as he derisively called Nader, be the heroic giant-slayer; the real heroes were the practitioners of free enterprise, who would save the economy from the true villain—government bureaucracy—if they could only break free of the regulatory shackles that prevented them from realizing their full potential.[24]

Reagan was an unusually charismatic speaker, and he used his folksy charm to both win votes and raise money on the speaking circuit. He was a popular headliner at fund-raisers. In 1974 he brought in $1.5 million for the GOP by giving speeches across the country to audiences totaling more than 100,000 people. As soon as Reagan's term as governor ended in January 1975, he devoted even more time to what he called the "mashed-potato circuit" of speaking engagements, and this time, he was free to plow the profits into his own political ambitions. He financed the salaries of a small campaign staff by charging $5,000 per speech. All this was part of a larger plan. In early November 1974, shortly before Reagan left the governor's office in Sacramento, his staff drew up a document titled "Ronald Reagan: A Program for the Future." Reagan's immediate objectives, according to the document, included the following: "strengthen and consolidate leadership as *the* national political spokesman," "actively pursue new avenues of media visibility," "continue 'newsmaker' image," and "enhance foreign affairs credibility." His operations would be managed by a small secretarial and managerial staff as well as a "steering committee" that would maintain a "political advisory group" and provide "continuous evaluation of the national situation re 1976."[25] The document did not directly mention a campaign for the presidency, but it hardly needed to. The intent was clearly to make sure that Reagan was well positioned for a campaign, should he decide to take the plunge.

Reagan continued to insist throughout 1974 and much of early 1975 that he had not made up his mind about a run for president in 1976, yet he followed most of the prescriptions laid out in his campaign advisers' strategy document, and his speeches and writings helped him build a loyal cadre of followers who were eager to see him campaign for the White House. He was especially popular in the Sun Belt. In the fall of 1973 and spring of 1974, even before his gubernatorial term ended, he traveled through the South multiple times, speaking to Republican activists and winning their heartfelt loyalty. "I don't think I've applauded so much since a Goldwater rally," one Mississippi committeeman said in November 1973 after listening to Reagan expound on welfare, the size of government, and the need for patriotic values. "At this point Reagan is head over heels in front." And in 1975, when Reagan began to broaden his speaking opportunities and reach out to conservative Democrats as well as Republicans, his popularity only increased. "You have an enormous following of Americans who are conservative and who see in you our hope to give our country new guidance and new ideals," a forty-six-year-old naval reserve officer from South Carolina wrote to Reagan in July 1975. "I hope and pray to God that you will accept the mantle of leadership and the challenge that faces you in your ascendancy to the Presidency." Others expressed similar adulation. Reagan's speech in Raleigh, North Carolina, was "one of the most memorable nights of my life," a young sales executive declared in an effusive letter to Reagan. "I have never heard a more forceful, enlightening, nor truthful talk. . . . You have my support."[26]

The reasons these letter writers gave for flocking to Reagan's still-undeclared campaign echoed the themes of his speeches. They were worried about the "welfare giveaway programs" that would "bankrupt this country" and the "weakening of our Defense posture in relation to that of the Soviet Union." "I'm SICK of big expensive government," wrote an older Californian who identified himself as a "Conservative" who was "no longer a Republican." He continued:

> I've been reading where the money goes and it is ridiculous. I'm SICK of healthy people cheating on welfare because the jobs they can get are demeaning to them. I'm SICK of old folks and others who have worked hard all their lives being taxed out of their homes while those on welfare fare well, and pay no taxes. It is said that by the year 2000, half of us will be supporting the other half. . . . Mr. Reagan can stop all this.[27]

Reagan's early supporters were overwhelmingly white and disproportionately male. (Indeed, when Reagan entered the New Hampshire primary a few months later, one polling firm reported that he was running 8 percentage points ahead among men but 2 points behind among women, which was "one of the strongest gender divides seen in any campaign.")[28] Later polls showed that once he officially entered the race, his support came disproportionately from the less educated, but the people who wrote to him in early 1975 were solidly middle class. They were small-business owners, retired military officers, and white-collar workers; most of them identified as Republicans, but they were disillusioned with the leaders in both parties and viewed Reagan as the last chance to save the nation. A small number were senior citizens, but most were middle-aged or younger. Too young to have voted for Franklin Roosevelt but old enough to remember the Cold War–inspired national unity of the 1950s, they were alarmed by both the cultural direction of the country and the shocking increase in social welfare spending.

Indeed, in the early 1970s the nation's welfare spending was increasing at a pace that far outstripped the inflation rate (which most conservatives also considered disturbingly high). According to official federal government figures, the growth in federal, state, and local welfare expenditures in 1975 was the "largest single-year increase" in American history—larger than at the peak of the New Deal or the Great Society. Fifty-eight percent of all state, local, and federal spending was now devoted to "social welfare." Most of this money went toward health insurance and Social Security, not food stamps or Aid to Families with Dependent Children, but this distinction was largely lost on Reagan supporters, who blamed the lower value of their dollars and their higher tax bills on "welfare bums."[29]

In general, Reagan's supporters were more conservative than libertarian—that is, more worried about deficit spending and social welfare programs than about government regulations, although the growth of any sector of government other than defense disturbed them. They were not "Christian conservatives," in the sense that they belonged to an explicitly religious political movement, but they were often traditionalist in their values. As one fifty-two-year-old lifelong Michigan Republican told Reagan, he had grown up as an Episcopalian and a Thomas Dewey supporter, and though he was "not a religious fanatic," he lamented that "'WE' have lost our country schools and along with that, the reading of the scripture in all classrooms." This writer was so perturbed about the loss of traditional values and American economic dominance that he confessed to voting for George Wallace once, which, he admitted, "could have been a foolish move on my part." He would be much more comfortable with Reagan, he believed.[30]

The frequency with which some of Reagan's correspondents mentioned Wallace as a viable option suggests an overlap between the two voter constituencies. Certainly, some on the left believed there was. Both Reagan and Wallace appealed to people who were angry with the Washington establishment, and both men frequently made welfare recipients and government bureaucrats the target of their rhetoric. Both ran populist campaigns, but there was a distinction between the two candidates' messages. Wallace believed that a reassertion of white southern values could save the nation, while Reagan placed a much greater emphasis on free enterprise. Reagan's supporters tended to be younger, more Republican, and less southern than Wallace's core constituency. Despite these differences, some of Reagan's supporters considered Wallace the best second choice and would much rather cast a ballot for him than for any mainstream Republican. Some expressed a few reservations about Wallace's history of overt racism, but most did not.[31]

Reagan's supporters doubted that any other politician from their party could effectively champion conservative principles. "The party no longer has any clear meaning," one Reagan enthusiast declared in a letter of support. "It has people in it like Rockefeller (nitwit), Ford (incompetent as President, and trying to please the liberals by outspending the spenders), etc." Indeed, William Rusher, publisher of the *National Review*—the magazine founded by William F. Buckley Jr. two decades earlier as the mouthpiece of the conservative movement—encouraged Reagan in 1975 to leave the GOP and launch a third-party campaign for the presidency. Rusher believed that conservatives stood a better chance with "Wallace people" outside of the GOP than with the Republican Party of Nixon, Rockefeller, and Ford. But Reagan dismissed such concerns. He favored, he said, "a new second party"—a Republican Party that would "return to its original and basic philosophy" of "fiscal responsibility, limited government, and a common sense approach to national security, as well as to safety in our own neighborhoods."[32]

Reagan spoke so often of party reform, and he had such a large following urging him to run for the White House, that it seems hard to imagine he ever seriously considered *not* campaigning in 1976. A few months before Nixon's resignation, he held a meeting with his staffers and a few Republican operatives and polled them on whether he should try for the presidency. The unanimous consensus was that he should. But then, when Nixon resigned, Reagan hesitated. According to all of Reagan's associates, he was genuinely ambivalent about whether he should challenge Ford for the nomination. Several of Reagan's advisers encouraged him to enter the race, believing that if the economy continued to falter, Ford would likely decide not to run if it appeared he could not win. In that case, they believed, Reagan would probably face a head-to-head match against Rockefeller or a group of liberal or moderate Republicans, and he stood a good chance of winning the nomination as champion of the party's conservatives. As Reagan toured the South in the fall of 1974, he was greeted by thousands of cheering spectators chanting "Reagan for president" and crowding the platform after his speeches to encourage him to enter the race. By October 1974, he had, according to news reports, already identified his chief campaign strategist—young Republican lawyer John Sears, who had worked in the Nixon White House and was eager to try his hand at presidential campaign management by steering Reagan to victory—and, in the words of the *New York Times,* he was "actively pursuing the possibility" of a presidential run.[33] The Ford White House hoped to dissuade Reagan from making a challenge that would be costly for the president and divisive for the party. But Reagan had too much support to back away.

GERALD FORD AND THE CONSERVATIVES

Ford considered himself a conservative, and he believed that he shared most of Reagan's views. In 1973, during his last year in Congress, he had earned an ADA rating of zero, which should have solidified his conservative credentials. Within a week of becoming president, he announced that cutting spending to bring inflation under control—the key theme of Reagan's speeches—would be a top priority in his administration. He repeatedly vetoed spending bills that the Democratic Congress sent him, racking up sixty-six vetoes during his brief time in office—more than any of his three immediate predecessors.[34]

But Reagan did not give Ford any credit for this; instead, he capitalized on conservatives' growing unease with Ford's policies in other areas. During his first month in office, Ford made conservatives anxious by offering conditional amnesty to Vietnam War draft dodgers and by expressing a willingness to endorse some form of national health insurance—policies that Reagan staunchly opposed.[35]

Ford faced even greater criticism from the right because of his selection for vice president. As soon as Ford took office, numerous Republicans in Congress, as well as many members of the general public, wrote to Ford with recommendations for vice president. Not surprisingly, these suggestions reflected the ideological leanings of the correspondents. Reagan and Goldwater were the top choices of conservatives, while Rockefeller was a favorite among liberals in the party. But former Texas congressman George Bush, who was then serving as chair of the Republican National Committee and had a reputation as a pragmatic centrist conservative, received the most support from Republican members of Congress, governors, and White House staff. Ford gave Bush serious thought and may have considered him one of the two or three finalists for the position; Bush was one of the few candidates for whom Ford requested an FBI background check. Yet in the end, Ford, a career legislator, did not pick Bush, perhaps partly because White House aides thought he lacked the necessary executive experience for the job. Instead, Ford selected someone with unsurpassed executive experience—the man who had been governor of New York for fourteen years. Rockefeller could help Ford win support from constituencies where the president might be expected to fare poorly—including urban areas, the Northeast, and among liberals and minorities—but more than that, he brought a wealth of governmental knowledge that could benefit Ford, who was conscious of his own lack of experience in the workings of the executive branch. Ford envisioned Rockefeller as a full partner in the administration, and he offered him an unprecedented opportunity to take a leading role in managing domestic policy.[36]

Ford did not anticipate the immediate political fallout from giving such a prize to the leader of the party's liberal wing. He may have won a few friends among liberals in both parties, who cheered the selection. Ted Kennedy sent Ford a note of congratulations immediately following the announcement, saying that he looked forward to Rockefeller's "rapid confirmation." But conservatives interpreted Ford's selection of Rockefeller to be his second in command as a stab in the back—a sign that the new president was an enemy of their movement. "I could hardly have been more upset if Ford had selected Teddy Kennedy," exclaimed Richard Viguerie, the New Right activist who was orchestrating George Wallace's direct-mail fund-raising operation. The American Conservative Union called the nomination a "mistake" and a "disaster." Pro-life activists from both parties were also upset; within two weeks of the selection, the White House was deluged with mail from angry right-to-lifers denouncing Ford's choice of an advocate of abortion rights to be his vice president. This is exactly what Senator Jesse Helms, one of the most outspoken conservatives in the Senate, had predicted. "The President is bound to realize he'll alienate a lot of conservative Republicans if he does nominate Rockefeller," he had warned a few days before Ford made the announcement.[37]

Although movement conservatives were angry about the Rockefeller selection from the beginning, most conservatives in the party leadership were willing to give Ford's choice the benefit of the doubt, despite their private reservations. The chair of the Republican Party in

Virginia expressed personal "disappointment in the choice," but Rockefeller tried to be conciliatory, meeting with the southern GOP party chairs and assuring them that he was not their enemy. Clarke Reed of Mississippi said that while most in the South would have preferred Reagan or Goldwater, Rockefeller was actually inclined to pay more attention to the South than many people assumed. And Goldwater himself, whose presidential campaign a decade earlier had been an attempt to deny Rockefeller his party's presidential nomination, initially said he would support Ford's vice-presidential choice.[38]

But then, during Rockefeller's confirmation hearings in the Senate, it was discovered that he had given public officials nearly $2 million in "gifts" that many considered bribes, and he had recently taken advantage of loopholes to avoid paying income tax. Damaged by these revelations, Rockefeller became a target for both liberals and conservatives and never fully recovered. Goldwater withdrew his support, as did several other conservatives. Some of the more liberal members of Congress, in a show of righteous indignation against unbridled wealth and corruption, treated Rockefeller harshly during his questioning. After three months of hearings, Congress finally voted to confirm the former New York governor as vice president, but Rockefeller soon attracted the ire of several White House officials, most notably chief of staff Donald Rumsfeld, who tried to use his position to limit Rockefeller's influence on the president. Rockefeller never enjoyed the close working relationship or expanded authority Ford had promised.[39] And his position continued to stoke the fires of a conservative revolt against the president.

While the congressional hearings over Rockefeller's nomination were still in progress, Ford did the one thing that inflicted the greatest damage on his public approval ratings over the course of his presidency and instantly ended his honeymoon with the American people: he pardoned Richard Nixon. Before the pardon, Ford seemed to many Americans like a breath of fresh air. In an effort to distance himself from the regal aloofness and pretentiousness of the Nixon administration, he instructed the Marine Corps band not to play "Hail to the Chief" when he entered the room at state functions; instead, the band should play the University of Michigan fight song. The press noted with admiration that the new president toasted his own English muffins in the morning and that he was not embarrassed to be photographed in his pajamas. Journalists generally lauded Ford's political actions during his first few weeks in office as well. During that time,

Figure 4.1. President Gerald Ford with Vice President Nelson Rockefeller and Secretary of State Henry Kissinger. (Courtesy of Gerald R. Ford Presidential Library)

Ford reached out to groups that Nixon had alienated, deliberately inviting some of the people on Nixon's infamous "enemies list" to meet him at the White House. He made a point of emphasizing that he would be the president of all Americans, not merely the conservatives he had represented during his time in Congress. And although some conservatives became suspicious of Ford after only a few days in the White House, most Americans welcomed his willingness to reach across the aisle. A Gallup poll taken during the second week of Ford's presidency showed him ahead of Ted Kennedy by more than 20 points in a hypothetical election matchup, with a public approval rating of 71 percent. But Ford's public approval rating instantly dropped to 50 percent when he pardoned Nixon, and it continued to drop during the next few months. He averaged only a 46 percent approval rating for the rest of his time in office.[40]

The Nixon pardon damaged Ford because, in the minds of many Americans, it linked him to the corruption of the previous administration. Shortly before the pardon, a Gallup poll had surveyed Americans' attitude toward a presidential pardon if Nixon were "brought to trial and found guilty," and it found that a majority of Americans opposed the idea. But Ford's action went beyond this: he pardoned

Nixon *without* a trial. Only 36 percent of Americans agreed with the president that Nixon "should not be tried for possible criminal charges." Ford thus put himself on the wrong side of public opinion, and he did so in a clumsy way by failing to prepare even his staff—let alone the public or congressional leaders—for the pardon and its ramifications. For the rest of his life, Ford insisted that his motivation had been to heal the nation, and he believed that subjecting Nixon to a public trial would have only compounded the damage of Watergate. But a majority of Americans disagreed with Ford's reasoning. Worse, many suspected—almost certainly erroneously, but not entirely without justification—that the pardon was part of a secret deal negotiated to secure Ford's appointment as vice president. From this point on, the press was more hostile toward Ford, and the public regarded him with a lot more cynicism. The sharp-edged, staunchly conservative *Manchester Union Leader* began calling him "Jerry the Jerk." *Harper's,* in a more believable image, pictured him as Bozo the Clown. And *Saturday Night Live* comedian Chevy Chase began to parody the president as a bumbler, accidently stapling his ear or jamming pencils into his hand. Because Ford, who suffered from a damaged knee, experienced a few well-publicized tumbles in real life—crashing into the snow while skiing, for instance, or stumbling while exiting Air Force One and falling on the tarmac—the image stuck, and Ford's stumbling became a metaphor for the political problems of his presidency.[41]

Ford's determination to fight inflation with austerity measures quickly brought him into conflict with the Democratic Congress. When Ford took office, the inflation rate was 14 percent and the unemployment rate was 5.2 percent and quickly rising. The growth rate of the gross domestic product (GDP), which had averaged about 6 percent per year in the mid-1960s and 5 percent per year briefly in the early 1970s, was now negative for the first time in more than a decade. By the standards of the latter half of the decade, the economic situation was not particularly bleak, but in the early 1970s Americans were still used to the high growth rates and low inflation and unemployment rates of the 1950s and 1960s, and they feared for the economic future. "Mr. Ford assumes the office of the Presidency against the most treacherous economic and financial backdrop in the post–World War II years," investment manager and economist Henry Kaufman declared in August 1974.[42]

Ford decided that inflation was a higher priority than unemployment, and at first, most Americans agreed. In September 1974, the month after Ford took office, 81 percent of Americans said that the "most important problem facing this country today" was the "high cost of living." But voters seemed to have little confidence that Ford or his party would be able to bring inflation under control; only 18 percent thought the Republicans were better equipped than the Democrats to address the issue. Undeterred by this public skepticism, Ford embarked on an anti-inflation campaign that he dubbed "Whip Inflation Now," which he hoped would be known by its optimistic-sounding acronym. The president began sporting a "WIN" button on his lapel and encouraged others to do the same. Fighting inflation, he believed, meant tackling the large government deficits that drove up interest rates, thus producing inflation. In an effort to cut deficit spending, he vetoed congressional spending bills and urged Congress to pass a tax increase. His goal was to balance the budget within one year, he said.[43]

Inflation did drop, from 14 percent in August 1974 to 11.8 percent in January 1975 to 6.7 percent in January 1976. It would fall to 5.2 percent by the time Ford left office in January 1977. But voters gave the president little credit for the improvement. In 1976, even though the inflation rate had been cut in half during Ford's short time in office, public opinion polls indicated that Americans believed, by a 10-point margin, that Democratic candidate Jimmy Carter was better equipped than Ford to fight inflation. They were almost evenly divided over whether Ford or Reagan would be more successful in bringing inflation under control. Furthermore, they were becoming more concerned about unemployment. By January 1975, Americans were almost evenly split over whether inflation or unemployment was the most urgent issue for the government to address.[44]

The Democrats agreed with workers that unemployment was the greater issue, and they minimized the dangers of inflation, focusing instead on stimulating the economy and providing more jobs. Inflation, they thought, was a greater concern to the wealthy, while unemployment had a much greater impact on the working class. They faulted Ford for pursuing measures that would slow the economy to bring inflation under control, accusing him of throwing people out of work simply to balance the budget.

They also disputed the Republicans' theory about the causes of inflation. Those causes were complex, they believed, and although deficit spending could be a contributing factor at a time of full employment, when "pump priming" might overstimulate the economy, this was unlikely to be the case during a recession; instead, the government's deficit spending would fuel consumer demand, which would then be channeled into additional jobs and higher wages. In a time of economic downturn, therefore, the government needed to focus on stimulus spending to create jobs and generate economic growth. And if inflation was a problem, the president could pressure large businesses to decrease their prices. "The only effective way to fight inflation is to stand up to the rich and powerful interests in this country . . . to stand up against outrageous price increases and against anti-competitive practices that fuel inflation," Senator Walter Mondale told the AFL-CIO. Ford, he charged, was afraid to do that because he was unwilling to challenge the business interests that were his political allies.[45]

With no worries about the federal deficit—but with a belief that the full powers of government were required to address the issue of unemployment—Democrats in Congress passed bills to implement government jobs programs, stimulus spending, and tax cuts to put more money in consumers' pockets. After the sweeping Democratic victories in the 1974 midterm elections, the Democrats had more seats in Congress than at any point since the 1930s, and they were determined to use their supermajorities to pursue their party's economic vision. Ford vetoed as much Democratic legislation as he could. Democrats charged that he was vetoing the very measures that would provide relief to the working poor and stimulate economic growth. Because the Republican White House and the Democratic Congress differed in their views on the causes of the nation's economic problems, and because they had opposing views on how to remedy the situation, they were constantly at loggerheads over budgetary matters. Even when Ford decided, somewhat reluctantly, to give up his idea of a tax increase—which had no chance of passing—and endorse a tax cut, Democrats disagreed with him. Ford favored tax relief that helped primarily business investment rather than consumers, because he thought that giving a tax cut to industry was the best way to create jobs. Congressional Democrats, by contrast, subscribed to a classic Keynesian economic view (that is, modeled on the theories of British economist John Maynard Keynes of the

1930s), which held that the key to fighting recession was to give money to consumers rather than suppliers. Democrats therefore favored large tax cuts for workers—a move that Ford believed would increase the deficit, fail to stimulate the economy, and exacerbate inflation.

Thus, Democrats entered the campaign season determined to fight Ford on the economy. This, in fact, was the focus of Henry Jackson's campaign. Adopting the Democrats' traditional Keynesian assumptions about how the economy worked, he blasted Ford for allowing the unemployment rate to rise and for vetoing measures that would have helped workers. Like Mondale, he promised that the Democrats would return the country to the prosperity of the Kennedy-Johnson years of the 1960s if they were given a chance to enact the liberal Democratic policy of Keynesian-style stimulus spending.

While congressional Democrats disputed Ford's basic economic premises, Reagan focused his criticism on the president's actions. Unlike the Democrats, he did not challenge Ford's assumptions about how the economy worked; in fact, he thoroughly agreed with Ford's thinking that deficit spending was the primary or even the sole cause of inflation. But he portrayed Ford as a weak leader who lacked the backbone to apply his axe to the bloated federal budget. "Balancing the budget is like protecting your virtue; you've got to learn to say no," he said. Such charges stuck because, although inflation rates moderated, both the unemployment rate and the federal deficit continued to increase—often by rates that people considered alarming at the time. In 1974, when Ford took office, the federal budget deficit was $22 billion a year (only 0.4 percent of GDP), but it rose to $176 billion (3.3 percent of GDP) in 1975 and to $228 billion (4.1 percent of GDP) in 1976.[46]

Ford had promised a balanced budget, and he made it his highest priority to reach that goal, but despite his efforts, the size of the deficit, if measured as a percentage of GDP, was the worst the country had seen since the 1940s.[47] He blamed Congress for the outcome. Congressional Democrats, in turn, blamed him for blocking their efforts to improve the economy and eventually eliminate the need for such high deficit spending. And Reagan Republicans blamed Ford for both the poor economy and the high deficit spending, believing that if their candidate had been in the White House, none of this would have happened.

Ford was puzzled by this reaction because he considered himself a fiscal conservative whose views on most issues did not differ radically from Reagan's. Accordingly, when Ford announced his campaign for reelection in July 1975, campaign manager Bo Callaway insisted that the president would run as a representative of the center–right wing of his party, where he could appeal to conservatives, and there was no need to attack Reagan on the issues. "Every effort should be made to keep the campaign from becoming an ideological debate," Callaway directed the campaign staff. "It should be emphasized that the President is strongly supported by both moderates and conservatives and that as a candidate his quality transcends ideological considerations."[48]

Despite Callaway's assurances, conservative Republicans in Congress suspected that Ford was not one of them. His conservative congressional voting record no longer mattered; what concerned them was that, in their view, he had moved to the left to appease party liberals. They did not intend to follow Ford because they believed that a drift to the left, at a time when they perceived the electorate to be moving to the right, would be political suicide as well as a betrayal of their core principles. "For 25 years Congressman Ford was more conservative than the American public. Now the American public is getting more conservative and President Ford is getting more liberal," Republican representative Bud Shuster, from a conservative district in rural southwestern Pennsylvania, complained to Ford campaign staffer Leo Thorsness.[49]

Both the liberals and the conservatives in the GOP complained that if Ford moved away from their positions, the Republican Party would lose votes. In a sense, both were right. In much of the Northeast, it was clear that if the party adopted the socially conservative positions and libertarian economic views that were popular in other parts of the country, the Republican Party would be finished as a viable force in the region. But in the Sun Belt and the Mountain West, it was clear that moderate or liberal Republicanism would be no match for the Goldwater-Reagan version and that Ford and the Republicans needed to move to the right if they wanted to mobilize voters. "Middle America is to the right of the Republican Party," Idaho representative Steve Symms told a Ford campaign aide in December 1975, in a complaint that was typical of conservative Republicans outside the Northeast. "Jerry needs to run to the right where basic constituents are. That is the thinking of people who will be at the convention."[50]

Conservative Republicans from the Sun Belt, the Mountain West, and rural areas complained not only about Ford's lack of success in balancing the budget and fixing the economy but also about his liberal foreign policy and cultural views. Ford signaled his desire to continue Nixon's policy of détente with the Soviet Union by retaining Secretary of State Henry Kissinger and giving him broad authority to take the lead in setting foreign policy, just as he had during the Nixon years. In the summer of 1975 Ford achieved another breakthrough in amity with the Soviet Union when he negotiated the Helsinki Accords, which affirmed US respect for existing territorial boundaries in eastern Europe. Most Americans supported détente. In April 1975, 56 percent said they approved of Kissinger's performance as secretary of state. This decreased slightly, to 48 percent, the following year, but even then, after months of Reagan's rhetorical attacks on the secretary of state, more Americans approved than disapproved of his job performance. Among Democrats, independents, and Republicans who supported Ford, Kissinger's approval ratings were positive. But among Reagan Republicans, the numbers were reversed: 46 percent disapproved of his job performance, while only 40 percent approved.[51]

Reagan's hawkish foreign policy views and criticisms of détente were not shared by most Americans or even most Republicans. A July 1976 Gallup poll showed that among Republicans, only 23 percent believed that Reagan would do a better job than Ford of "dealing with the Soviet Union," while 52 percent thought that Ford would do a better job. Yet in conservative congressional districts, Republicans on the right had a different picture of public opinion. "Kissinger is an Albatross around the neck of Ford," Alaska congressman Don Young told Thorsness in November 1975. The Ford campaign's polling in Colorado revealed much the same sentiment in the Mountain West. "Secretary Kissinger is not favorably perceived at this time in Colorado by reason of his longevity as well as his association with the Nixon Administration," the campaign's internal guide to Colorado strategy noted in April 1976. Even as Ford headed into the general election, shoring up his support among Republicans in conservative districts who disagreed with his foreign policy was still a concern. "We are doing below our normal vote with people in the Midwest and West who cite foreign policy as an important issue," a Ford campaign pollster warned White House Domestic Council director Mike Duval on October 1, 1976. "Those same people do not like Kissinger." While admitting that those people were "on the ideological extremes," he believed their lack of support could hurt the president in the general election. "The public wants us to be number one and wants to see evidence that détente benefits us," he said.[52]

On cultural issues Ford also alienated conservatives in the Sun Belt, despite his socially conservative leanings. Although he was a member of the Episcopal Church, a denomination often associated with more liberal cultural stances, for decades he had represented a socially conservative Michigan congressional district that included numerous Dutch Reformed Calvinists from the Grand Rapids area, so he thought he understood the priorities of social conservatives. During his last year in Congress, he had cosponsored an antiabortion constitutional amendment proposal to rescind *Roe v. Wade* and return abortion policy to the states. He had also been a supporter of a constitutional amendment to allow prayer in public school classrooms. But as president, he seemed to embrace the leftward cultural drift of the northern wing of the Republican Party. Both he and First Lady Betty Ford strongly supported the Equal Rights Amendment, which was then coming under fire from a conservative anti-ERA campaign led by Illinois Republican Phyllis Schlafly. He appointed pro-choice, pro-ERA Iowa Republican Mary Louise Smith as the first female chair of the Republican National Committee. Combined with his selection of a longtime abortion rights advocate as his vice president, the move seemed to signal that Ford was distancing himself from his former opposition to *Roe v. Wade*.[53]

Then, in August 1975, Betty Ford called *Roe* "the best thing in the world . . . a great, great decision" in an interview on CBS's *60 Minutes*. That comment made the White House the target of regular picketing by pro-life activists, most of whom were Catholic and from the North—especially those large industrial states whose electoral votes Ford would need in a general election. The First Lady's remark, coming at the beginning of Ford's reelection campaign, was not well timed to reinforce her husband's campaign strategy. Pro-life activists, led by March for Life organizer Nellie Gray, coordinated monthly protests outside the White House, with picketers carrying signs that read, "Betty, we don't want the right to kill." For months afterward, the First Lady continued to be confronted by pro-life protesters whenever she campaigned for her husband. As Gray said, pro-lifers intended to make abortion the "number one political issue in next November's elections."[54]

But two other comments by Betty Ford in the same interview did even greater damage to her husband's cause among cultural conservatives. She said she would not object or be "surprised" if her eighteen-year-old daughter was having "an affair," and she said she was "sure" her young-adult children had all "probably tried marijuana." She even admitted that she "probably" would have tried marijuana herself if it had been widely available when she was young, because youthful experimentation with marijuana was comparable to having "your first beer or your first cigarette." For socially conservative voters who had tarred George McGovern as the candidate of "amnesty, acid, and abortion," the First Lady's comments put the Ford administration on the wrong side of the nation's cultural divide. Callaway reported that at meetings with state Republican leaders and potential donors in early September 1975, "Mrs. Ford's comments frequently came up and a great deal of the comment was very negative and, in some cases, even bitter." Six months later, the furor had not ended. "Republican women are still mad about Betty Ford's attitude toward sex and drugs," conservative Republican representative Carlos Moorhead of California told the Ford campaign in March 1976. The First Lady's comments were especially damaging to Ford's cause among conservative southern Protestants, who had supported Nixon in the last election but now considered Ford their enemy. Bob Jones Jr., president of the fundamentalist college in Greenville, South Carolina, that bore his father's name, denounced Ford as "not fit to run the nation." Some of his school's top administrators enlisted in Reagan's campaign—the first time they had taken such an active role in a presidential election.[55]

Yet, like nearly every controversial stance in the Ford campaign, what one group of Republicans saw as a negative proved to be popular with another. Betty Ford's remarks may have exacerbated the cultural drift toward Reagan, but they earned her plaudits from other voters who liked the idea of an outspoken, socially progressive, independent woman in the White House. Although Callaway encountered widespread anger at the First Lady in areas outside the Northeast, he discovered that she was extremely popular among Republicans in New Hampshire. "We believe it is top priority that Mrs. Ford return to New Hampshire," Callaway told his fellow campaign managers Dick Cheney and Rogers Morton in February 1976, shortly before the state's primary. "Her first visit was extremely well received, and she is highly thought of by the people in the State. . . . Our people very much want her and consider her one of the most valuable assets for building momentum in the campaign."[56]

REAGAN FORGES A CONSERVATIVE COALITION

Technically, Ford's official declaration of his candidacy came before Reagan's, and Reagan was not officially in the race when Ford organized his campaign team in July 1975. But in reality, even though he was not yet a declared candidate, Reagan's campaign was already well under way. As soon as his second term as California governor ended in January 1975, Reagan embarked on the speaking circuit in earnest, and sometime in the spring (no one recalls exactly when) he made up his mind to run. In July, at about the same time Ford launched his campaign, a cadre of Reagan's associates formed the organization Citizens for Reagan, which worked under the leadership of Nevada senator Paul Laxalt to raise money for the Reagan campaign. To avoid the campaign finance laws, they operated as an independent interest group working for an officially undeclared candidate and did all their work outside of Reagan's direct oversight. But whenever a potential contributor inquired about Reagan's intentions, they assured the supporter that "there is no doubt in our minds" that Reagan would announce his candidacy later that year. By the end of September, the group had raised more than $300,000 in small donations, with nearly 30 percent of it coming from California conservatives. By the end of October, the funds had increased to more than $500,000.[57]

The staff list of Citizens for Reagan read like a roster of Reagan's former staffers from his time as governor in Sacramento. His former press secretary, fifty-one-year-old Lyn Nofziger, a small-government conservative whom journalist Jules Witcover described as a "galloping McKinleyite," was one of the leading members of the organization, as was thirty-eight-year-old Michael Deaver, who had served as the second most powerful person on Reagan's gubernatorial staff. Deaver brought in his friend Pete Hannaford, a forty-three-year-old California conservative who had made an unsuccessful run for Congress. Thirty-nine-year-old Stanford economics professor Martin Anderson also joined the campaign team to offer policy advice in support of free enterprise, as did thirty-eight-year-old California government administrator James Lake. But the lead role in the campaign went to someone who was neither a Californian nor a conservative: thirty-five-year-old Washington, DC, lawyer John Sears. In fact, Sears had no prior association with Reagan. He had served in the Nixon White House and was known as a liberal Republican, so he might have been expected to support Ford or even some other liberal Republican challenger to the left of the administration. But Sears cared more about campaign strategy than ideology, and above all he wanted to take the leading role in running a campaign. He knew the Ford White House would never give him this opportunity, so he decided his only opportunity for campaign management would probably come from the popular California governor. Whatever ideological compromises he had to make were worth it, he thought, because he was convinced that Reagan was a candidate who could win. Sears's lack of ideological fervor made him a bit of a black sheep among the true believers in the Reagan campaign, but the other members of Citizens for Reagan revered him as a brilliant thinker, and they knew they needed his help. Even though he showed up drunk to his first interview (he was a heavy drinker at the time), they still put him in charge of the campaign.[58]

Sears believed that Reagan could not afford to compete everywhere, so the campaign decided to forfeit several large states in the Northeast and Midwest and devote its limited resources to the South and West. Despite receiving pleas from conservatives in New York and New Jersey to let them organize there, the campaign decided not to run delegate slates in states where Ford's grip on Republican Party organizations was too strong. Instead, the Reagan campaign would focus nearly all its efforts on a few key early primaries and then rely on a strong showing in the rest of the South and West to knock Ford out of the race. Although the campaign had no way of knowing it at the time, the path that Sears outlined for victory—with a strong emphasis on New Hampshire and Florida, along with the South—bore a distinct resemblance to the one Hamilton Jordan orchestrated for Carter. According to the plan, Reagan would defeat Ford in New Hampshire in a close race; then he would win a primary victory in Florida, where he had plenty of support from conservatives and could pick up a lot of votes from Cuban Americans in Miami with his strong anticommunist rhetoric and criticism of Ford's policy of détente with the Soviet Union. In the fall of 1975 Reagan campaign strategists encouraged Republican officials in Florida to adopt a winner-take-all rule for the spring 1976 primary because they hoped to deliver a powerful blow to the Ford campaign in the state. Reagan would then go on to sweep the South (which supplied 606 of the 1,130 delegates needed to win), starting with a critical victory in North Carolina, where the Reagan campaign concentrated a lot of its organizational strength. Reagan would win the western states and finish the primary season with a victory in California on June 8. Because the Reagan campaign was challenging an incumbent Republican president with an antiestablishment message that appealed to a lot of conservative Democrats who wanted to see a change in Washington,

Reagan was expected to do better in states that allowed crossover voting by Democrats. This plan conceded so many delegates in the Northeast and Midwest that it left no room for error, but if Reagan really won all the states Sears hoped he could carry, he would be assured of the nomination.[59]

William Rusher encouraged Reagan to attack Ford's policies directly, a strategy that seemed well suited to an ideologically driven campaign. Reagan, after all, had been carping about Ford's policies almost since the moment he was sworn into office, and Reagan had regularly used his weekly syndicated newspaper columns and radio broadcasts, along with his speeches, to chastise Ford for not being conservative enough. Even when Ford's policies seemed to follow Reagan's recommendations, as they did in January 1975 when the president authorized a tax cut, Reagan complained that the measures were insufficient. The tax cuts were not accompanied by spending cuts, he said, so they would result in inflation. But once Reagan's campaign began in earnest, he avoided attacking the president directly because, his campaign claimed, he did not want to divide the Republican Party. Instead, staffers planned for Reagan to run an upbeat, hopeful campaign that focused on his image as a Washington outsider who had made California a success by cutting the welfare rolls, balancing the state budget, and returning money to the people through tax cuts. "Governor Reagan's very lack of prior dealings with the Congress and the rest of the 'Washington Establishment' is what will make him an outstanding President," Sears wrote in September 1975 to a Republican in Tennessee who was trying to decide between Ford and Reagan. "Governor Reagan will come to Washington without having any pre-conceived ideas or prior loyalties to members of the Congress or the bureaucracy. He will be free to act, as he was in California, in what he believes are the best interest of the people and the country."[60]

Reagan's early campaign advertising stressed the same themes. Reagan, who was "not a member of the Washington Establishment," was campaigning on three main principles, one of Laxalt's fund-raising letters declared. He was running because "government in Washington has grown much too large," because "American military strength must be second to none," and because "rising crime and the attack on the American family must be stopped."[61] With these themes, his candidacy wove together the concerns of libertarians, defense hawks, and social conservatives. He could pick up the votes of everyone from Goldwater-style conservative Republicans to Wallace-supporting Democrats, with a few Jackson-style critics of détente added for good measure.

Regardless of whether they came from the libertarian or socially conservative wing of the conservative coalition, Citizens for Reagan volunteers viewed themselves as party insurgents taking on the establishment, and their fund-raising letters read like a call to arms for an ideological movement whose goal was nothing less than saving the nation from destruction. "We are opposed by the powerful forces that have brought us the Welfare way of life, the largest Federal budget proposal ever proposed or enacted, total amnesty for draft dodgers and deserters, a weak foreign policy, our first defeat in war," a July 1975 fund-raising letter from Oklahoma Citizens for Reagan declared. "What might we see next? Giving away the Panama Canal? Clothing Stamps with abuses as wild as in the Food Stamp Program? Gun registration, possibly confiscation? Ever increasing Federal deficits? . . . WHERE WILL IT END???" "It will end," the letter promised, "when America has that for which she has long cried . . . LEADERSHIP"—something that only Ronald Reagan could provide.[62]

REAGAN'S CONSERVATIVE ISSUE POSITIONS

For the libertarian wing of the conservative movement, Reagan offered unrelenting attacks on government bureaucracy and the welfare system, which were his principal targets in numerous campaign speeches. The attacks on welfare appealed to older Wallace supporters, but if phrased in the language of individual liberty and freedom from government bureaucracy, they also resonated with many college students and young conservative activists.

Reagan was sixty-four years old (two years older than Ford) in 1975, and by the time of the New Hampshire primary he would be sixty-five, yet he found it easier to appeal to young Republicans than to older ones. Libertarian-leaning college students and recent college graduates had been the backbone of the conservative movement since William F. Buckley Jr. first started organizing college conservatives in the 1950s and early 1960s. Reagan had long enjoyed a close relationship with Young Americans for Freedom, a conservative campus organization founded by Buckley in 1960. He also received support from leaders of other campus Republican organizations such as the Young Republicans; Youth for Reagan national director Roger Stone had recruited members of this group with the promise that Reagan's campaign would be the "most exciting and challenging Presidential campaign of the century." While Ford could appeal to older conservatives with a message of stability and fiscal prudence, Reagan's promise to radically trim the size of government and usher in an era of sweeping change appealed to young voters on the right who were cynical about government in the post-Nixon era and who welcomed the conservative movement's promise to let individuals make their own decisions without constraint from government regulation. "Reagan calls for freedom," one Youth for Reagan brochure asserted. "Freedom from harsh government interference in our individual lives, freedom of choice and self-expression, the right of the individual to be master of his own destiny." The government had circumscribed many of these rights, but Reagan would restore them by "transferring power from the government to the private sector." "Individual liberty depends upon keeping government under control," Reagan reminded young voters.[63]

On at least a few issues, Reagan was an ally of the libertarians. In contrast to President Ford and the Republican Party platform, he opposed all restrictions on handgun ownership. In September 1975 he published an article in *Guns & Ammo* magazine criticizing Ford's attorney general for thinking "somehow that banning guns keeps them out of the hands of criminals." "Our country was built and civilized by men and women who used guns in self-defense and in pursuit of peace," Reagan wrote. If people wanted to be safe from crime, they needed more guns, not fewer. "One wonders indeed, if the rising crime rate, isn't due as much as anything to the criminal's instinctive knowledge that the average victim no longer has means of self-protection." Although this position would later become Republican Party orthodoxy, it was not yet mainstream opinion in the GOP, which, as part of its law-and-order image, had officially endorsed efforts to restrict criminal access to "all weapons," especially "readily-obtainable handguns." Reagan wanted to change that. Gun rights advocate Alan Gottlieb sent out a direct-mail fund-raising solicitation under the banner of Sportsmen for Reagan that declared, "If the wrong man is elected president, the Second Amendment could be severely curtailed."[64]

Although Reagan sounded like a libertarian on gun rights, he parted ways with libertarians on several other social issues, beginning with drug policy. He opposed the legalization of marijuana because he considered it a "far more dangerous drug than most people are prepared to admit." He favored a strong military and tougher sentences on criminals. And although his campaign did not mention it in advertising aimed at younger voters, Reagan enjoyed a close alliance with religious conservatives because, by his own admission, he was a moral traditionalist. He had supported school prayer since the early 1960s, and after the Supreme Court's *Engel v. Vitale* decision in 1962 he had joined fellow Hollywood stars John Wayne and Roy Rogers and Dale Evans in support of "Project Prayer." Reagan's denominational affiliation was mainline Protestant, but his strong anticommunism and discussion of his personal faith had earned him the support of a network of California evangelicals that included radio broadcaster George Otis and singer Pat Boone. He also claimed to have much stronger support among Catholics than Ford did.[65] On the abortion issue, at least, Reagan was much closer to the traditional Catholic position than Ford or many other Republicans at the time, and it was this position that most surprised some of his more libertarian-minded associates.

In the mid-1970s most of the nation's leading Republicans on both the right and the left supported *Roe v. Wade*. Nearly all the liberal Republicans in Congress did, but so did the party's conservative elder statesman Barry Goldwater. Reagan himself had signed a liberalized abortion law in California in 1967. But he had become increasingly uncomfortable with the results of such legislation in his own state, and by the early 1970s, he was sympathetic to the right-to-life cause. He still insisted that women experiencing life-threatening pregnancies had the right to abortion as a matter of "self defense," and he would have preferred to allow states to set their own abortion policies, but he was so antipathetic to the Supreme Court's intrusion into state and local matters with its *Roe v. Wade* decision that in 1975 he took the unexpected step of endorsing the pro-life commitment's central goal: a constitutional amendment to ban abortion nationwide.[66]

Even Reagan's closest advisers were taken aback by this move. For most conservative Republicans at the time, there were two possible approaches to the abortion issue: one could endorse *Roe v. Wade* on libertarian grounds (but oppose Medicaid funding for the procedure, since conservatives were opposed to government health care), or one could support efforts to rescind *Roe v. Wade* and return abortion policy to the states on the grounds that *Roe* was yet another example of judicial overreach into matters that should be decided legislatively at the local level. On most issues, Reagan was more of a states' rights conservative than a consistent libertarian, and he was strongly critical of the judiciary, so his advisers expected him to choose the second option. Instead, Reagan went beyond that and took a position held by few conservative Republicans other than Jesse Helms and a handful of Catholics: he endorsed a constitutional amendment not only to repeal *Roe v. Wade* but also to ban abortion in all cases except when a woman's life was in danger. Nofziger was alarmed. "I would hate to see you involved here on something necessitating a Congressional amendment which, in effect, took away one more right from the states," Nofziger told Reagan in a memo dated October 2, 1975. "Perhaps before we formulate a position on the matter of abortion we should have some thorough discussion and legal views."[67]

But Reagan ignored the cautionary advice and pressed ahead with his endorsement of an antiabortion constitutional amendment. Most likely he had been swayed by his meetings with right-to-life activists and the volume of mail he received in the summer of 1975 from conservative Republican pro-lifers who wanted to support his candidacy but insisted that they would vote only for candidates who pledged to support the Human Life Amendment. This had become the pro-life movement's political litmus test. Such a move by Reagan demonstrated a sensitivity to social conservatives (especially socially conservative Catholics)—a group that other political conservatives ignored at their peril. As early as the fall of 1974, research assistant Jeff Bell had noted in a memo to Reagan that one pro-choice conservative Republican congressman—three-term incumbent Roger Zion, who represented a solidly conservative Republican district in Indiana—was in danger of losing his seat to a pro-life liberal Democrat because of the abortion issue. When Zion did lose the race, as Bell had predicted, it seemed to confirm that for some conservative Republicans in the heartland, social issues were more important than fiscal ones. Reagan chose to be conservative on both. When he officially announced his candidacy on November 20, 1975, he was ready with a strong antiabortion position: "Interrupting a pregnancy is the taking of a human life," he said, and can be justified only in cases of "self defense."[68]

The pro-life movement in the 1970s was overwhelmingly Catholic and heavily Democratic, since the majority of Catholics were Democrats at the time. But Reagan's endorsement of their cause convinced some to cross party lines and support him. In December 1975 he received favorable front-page coverage in the *National Right to Life News,* the official publication of the nation's largest right-to-life organization. And throughout his campaign he continued to receive letters from self-identified Democrats who said they were supporting him because of his stance on the abortion issue.[69]

Some of Reagan's staffers failed to understand their boss's position. They were economic conservatives who, in many cases, were to the right of Reagan on business matters but culturally libertarian on social issues. They sought to keep Reagan's position on abortion quiet, perhaps fearing that his deviation from libertarianism and his outreach to socially conservative Democrats on abortion would hurt his candidacy among mainstream Republicans and pro-choice women. "The position paper on abortion is not for distribution," Nofziger instructed another Reagan campaign staffer. "Please provide it only upon request."[70] But to Nofziger's surprise—or perhaps dismay—Reagan's position on abortion brought so many pro-lifers into the campaign that by the summer of 1976, the Reagan delegates had the numerical strength to add antiabortion language to the Republican Party platform for the first time.

Reagan also reached out to antifeminist social conservatives by opposing the ERA. As governor of California, he had endorsed the ERA in 1972, as had many Republicans at the time. But after Phyllis Schlafly mobilized conservative women across the country in opposition to the amendment, Reagan, following Schlafly's argument, decided that the amendment would take away necessary protections that women enjoyed. In particular, he did not want to see women drafted to fight in combat. "I'm old fashioned," he admitted at a town hall in New Hampshire in November 1975. When "we got to go to war, I think we'd like to know that we're fighting for the little girl we left behind." Similar to his position on abortion, Reagan apparently adopted his socially conservative view on the ERA without help from his staff, who did not include the issue in the otherwise comprehensive briefing papers they prepared before his first press conference as a declared candidate.[71]

Reagan's opposition to court-ordered busing also enhanced his appeal to some social conservatives, although it opened him to charges of racism, which he vociferously denied. His opposition to federally ordered busing was consistent with his desire to see an end to all federal involvement in education, and he insisted that it was not racially motivated. It was "insulting to tell a Negro child the only way he could learn anything was to sit him between two white kids," he declared. (By 1975, "black" had replaced "Negro" as the term of choice not only in African American publications but also in the mainstream press, but Reagan still used the earlier nomenclature in some of his speeches.) Reagan evoked the ideal of a color-blind society, and he lauded the heroism of those who had made racial integration possible. In his telling of the story, though, the end of racial segregation in the military had come not through presidential policy but through the loyal service of a black gunner at Pearl Harbor. This historical revisionism fit Reagan's central claim: federal policy was the problem, not the solution, and if the government would just return policymaking to the local level, people would be free to create a meritocratic society. Whether that meritocratic society was fully racially integrated did not concern him as much as getting the federal government out of the business of civil rights enforcement. "The answer to inferior education in the black communities lies *not* in ordering white children into black schools—but in getting the Federal Government out of education so that our local communities—black, white, and inbetween [*sic*]—can regain control of their school districts," he declared in a letter to Republican delegates from Connecticut in 1976.[72]

Many African Americans believed that Reagan was practicing classic dog-whistle politics on race, not only in his opposition to busing but also in his frequent attacks on welfare, one of the centerpieces of his campaign. This was the view of many black Republicans as well; Floyd McKissick, a Ford supporter, called Reagan's campaign "one of the smoothest, racist con games in the history of this nation." Black journalists concurred. "Former California Gov. Ronald Reagan obviously has decided to go all out for the conservative white vote," Simeon Booker wrote in *Jet* magazine in September 1975. "Not a Black serves on his campaign staff."[73]

Nofziger pushed back against this assertion. It was true, he conceded, that Reagan currently had no blacks working on his campaign staff, but there was no reason to think that would be a "permanent situation." As he noted, several African American business leaders in California supported Reagan.[74]

Indeed, Reagan enjoyed support from a few black Republicans, although his support among other black political leaders was minuscule. In a poll of more than three thousand black elected officials conducted by *Ebony* magazine in early 1976, Reagan placed fifteenth in a field of presidential contenders—ahead of George Wallace, but well behind not only eighth-place finisher Gerald Ford (who received 2.9 percent of the vote) but also Pennsylvania's Democratic governor Milton Shapp, whose short-lived campaign had already folded. Even among the small number of African Americans in the Republican Party, Ford received the lion's share of support. Reagan's approval ratings were a little higher among African American voters at large; an Ohio poll in January 1976 predicted that he would get 9 percent of the black vote in Ohio in a hypothetical head-to-head general election matchup against Ted Kennedy and, perhaps surprisingly, as much as 21 percent in a race against Hubert Humphrey.[75] Still, while such polls demonstrated that Reagan could appeal to a small contingent of blacks, his African American critics who accused his campaign of ignoring minority voters and concentrating all its efforts on the white vote were not far off the mark.

The small number of African Americans who did support Reagan usually cited their belief in free enterprise as their principal reason for doing so. Like other black Republican leaders, the African Americans who endorsed Reagan's campaign in its early stages were mostly owners of small businesses who strongly believed in black capitalism as a path to racial uplift. This was not an unusual stance among black Republicans, but what was unusual was their willingness to abandon civil rights advocacy for the sake of free enterprise. Most black businessmen who were active in the Republican Party wanted to couple conservative economic policies with civil rights policies that helped minority-owned businesses as well as other African Americans. They were thus more likely to support Ford than Reagan, and they were even more likely to wish that African American Republican senator Edward Brooke were running for president. But Reagan's African American supporters were different. They were more willing to forgo specific civil rights initiatives and to emphasize that they shared the same concerns as white conservatives—a message that was consistent with Reagan's stated color-blind policies on race. "Minorities are just as interested in unemployment, inflation, high taxes, education, crime as any other citizens," Mel Bradley, the most prominent African American on Reagan's gubernatorial staff, told the press in the fall of 1974. He added, "The Governor has tried not to categorize people into groups, and I think we are realizing more and more that our problems and our needs are the same as those of the majority of the people."[76] From its inception, then, Reagan's campaign pushed a color-blind ideology that, unlike most of the Democratic campaigns and even President Ford's, shunned specific appeals to blacks in favor of general discussions of economic uplift through deregulation, spending cuts, and tax reduction. A few black conservative Republican business owners applauded, but most worried. Reagan had not defended racial segregation in the same defiant terms that George Wallace had, but in the view of many African Americans, his repeated invocations of welfare abusers, his hostility to busing, and his lack of interest in civil rights initiatives made him almost equally dangerous.

On foreign policy, Reagan also tapped into concerns that resonated with Wallace voters and many social conservatives. He had long been active in the grassroots anticommunist movement in California, so it was not surprising that he still viewed the confrontation with the Soviet Union in apocalyptic terms of good and evil, even though President Ford, Secretary of State Kissinger, and most of the Democratic presidential candidates (except for Jackson and Wallace) rejected this view. It was imperative, he believed, for the United States to gain the upper hand in its negotiations with the USSR. He warned that the United States was endangering itself with recent reductions in weapons development expenditures, a consequence of détente and the Strategic Arms Limitation Treaty (SALT I) that President Nixon had negotiated with the Soviet Union. Ford and Kissinger's ongoing negotiations with the USSR threatened to make the situation even worse. "To be second best militarily is to be last," Reagan declared.[77]

Reagan's candidacy thus represented a combination of Jackson's hawkish views on foreign policy (in opposition to both the Ford administration and most other Democrats), Wallace's social conservatism, and Goldwater's opposition to growth of the federal bureaucracy. When packaged with free-market ideology and a promise to restore the nation to military and economic supremacy, this combination appealed to people who were disillusioned with Ford, angry with the federal government's failures, and fearful of Democratic social welfare spending.

REAGAN'S ANNOUNCEMENT

For months leading up to November 1975, Reagan kept his supporters waiting as he quietly allowed his advisers to assemble a campaign operation without directly stating whether he would enter the race. He responded to policy inquiries, traveled the speaking circuit, raised money for a presidential run, and strongly hinted that he would enter the race, even while maintaining the official position that he was not yet a candidate. This charade finally ended on November 20, 1975, with a short speech declaring his candidacy. Given the centrality of anti-Washington rhetoric to his campaign, it was perhaps surprising that he chose Washington, DC, as the venue for his announcement, but he did so, he said, because Washington was "such an intimate part of all our troubles." Calling for the nation to embark on a "new, constructive course," he quickly outlined the major problems the nation faced: inflation, unemployment, dependence on foreign oil, and declining military strength. The real problem, though, was the government itself. "Government at all levels now absorbs more than 44 percent of our national income," he said, using one of his trademark statistics that had become staples of his dinner speeches. "It has become more intrusive, more coercive, more meddlesome and less effective."[78]

The journalists in attendance focused on one central question: what's wrong with President Ford? Invoking what he called the Eleventh Commandment—"Thou shalt not speak ill of a fellow Republican"—Reagan insisted that he would say nothing against the president or his policies, despite implicitly doing so for months. This strategy enabled Reagan to portray himself as a uniter, not a divider, and as a loyal Republican who was simply presenting himself as a candidate who could appeal to independent voters and broaden the party's reach. The Ford campaign immediately tried to negate this message by arguing the opposite. "The simple political fact is that he cannot defeat any candidate the Democrats put up," a Ford campaign press release noted within hours of Reagan's announcement. "Reagan's constituency is much too narrow, even within the Republican Party."[79]

But news reports of the opening day of Reagan's campaign—which involved a whirlwind trip to Miami and New Hampshire following the press conference in Washington—seemed more persuaded by Reagan's carefully crafted centrist image than by the Ford campaign's statements. The press highlighted Reagan's effort to broaden his appeal, noting that he had largely downplayed or avoided mentioning most of his right-wing positions. "The new Ronald Reagan is a centrist," the *San Francisco Chronicle* stated on November 21. "There was not a phrase in his announcement statement or in his newly prepared stump speech that could not be uttered by a liberal Democrat." This was an exaggeration, but it highlighted an important principle: by November 1975, commentary about the ineffectiveness of government bureaucracy had become so commonplace, even among left-of-center

Democrats, that Reagan could sound like a generic moderate as long as he confined his critique to remarks about government's "intrusive" nature and did not echo Wallace's complaints about "welfare bums." This Reagan did. It was clear to many that he was working hard to avoid the "extremist" label that had plagued Goldwater's campaign a decade earlier. Douglas Kiker's newscast on NBC noted Reagan's pledge to run a "gentlemanly" campaign and his insistence that he was not a "right-winger." And Terry Drinkwater's morning commentary on CBS observed that, in the past, Reagan had "talked more conservative than he really was"—implying that he was not as far outside the mainstream as caricatures of his candidacy suggested.[80]

Reagan's sunny approach to his campaign seemed to work. For the next few weeks, he mostly avoided direct attacks on Ford, as he had promised, and his poll numbers continued to rise. Back in June 1975, when he was publicly flirting with the idea of running but had not officially declared, 61 percent of Republican voters still supported President Ford in a two-way contest with Reagan, and only 33 percent favored Reagan. By October, Ford's lead over Reagan had shrunk to 51–40. By mid-December, a few weeks after the official beginning of Reagan's campaign, the two candidates were neck and neck, each receiving the support of 45 percent of Republican voters. This was exactly what the Reagan campaign had expected. Staffers had predicted in the fall of 1975 that they could easily close the gap with Ford by giving their candidate more exposure, and now they were seeing this happen.[81]

THE BEGINNING OF FORD'S CAMPAIGN

When Bo Callaway, a former Georgia congressman, began managing Ford's campaign in the summer of 1975, he made winning back the party's conservatives his top priority. Callaway was a pro-military conservative who was antipathetic to social welfare spending and suspicious of the Rockefeller wing of the Republican Party; he believed that despite Ford's selection of Rockefeller as vice president, at heart, the president was a small-government, midwestern conservative whose views would be acceptable to most white conservative southerners. The Ford campaign's message for conservatives attracted to Reagan's candidacy was that there was no substantive ideological difference between the two candidates, but there was a difference in experience. Ford had the national leadership experience that Reagan lacked, and he was much better positioned to unite the party and win the general election. For those who wanted a conservative in the White House in 1977, their best bet was to stick with Ford.[82]

At the time, even though Reagan's shadow campaign was already well under way, it was not yet apparent that Ford's only substantial primary challenge would come from his right. Several liberal Republicans in Congress were still openly weighing the possibility of running against the president. Charles Percy had suspended his campaign when Ford took office, but he was considering restarting it, and senators Howard Baker and Bill Brock—both party centrists from Tennessee—were likely contenders as well. In June 1975, when White House staffer Max Friedersdorf asked every Republican senator for a pledge to support the president's reelection campaign, only about half were willing to give it. The dissenters included not only conservatives such as Jesse Helms (who would play a central role in Reagan's campaign) but also some of the most liberal members of the party, such as Lowell Weicker, who told Friedersdorf that he "wanted to wait awhile" before committing.[83]

But Callaway correctly determined that if Ford moved to the right to shore up his support among conservatives, the liberals and moderates in the party might grumble, but they would eventually come over to his side because they lacked the voter support to capture the nomination for one of their own. Liberals were overrepresented among Republican senators because of their long-standing foothold in the Northeast, but they could not win the nomination in a national primary system, where more than half the convention delegates came from the South, the Great Plains, the Mountain West, and California. Even the liberals who were thinking about challenging Ford seemed to recognize this. Charles "Mac" Mathias, a liberal Republican senator from Maryland, was slated to appear on the Republican primary ballot in Massachusetts, but he had trouble getting his campaign off the ground, largely because his fellow liberal Republicans were worried that challenging the president would only succeed in throwing the election to Reagan.[84] Callaway mostly ignored Mathias, at least during the fall of 1975.

Instead, Callaway set about courting the conservatives by meeting with each Republican member of Congress individually and asking what his concerns were. He also tried to make inroads into the conservative organizations that were known for their strong support of Reagan. Some, he decided, were so loyal to Reagan that going after them was a lost cause. Young Americans for Freedom, for instance, was so antipathetic to Ford that the campaign decided not to send a representative to its 1975 national convention. Young Republicans National Federation offered greater promise. Although much of the national leadership and local membership was pro-Reagan, the Ford campaign decided that it could work with one member of the board, Paul Manafort, to bring other members over to the Ford camp.[85]

The Ford campaign's biggest prize among conservative activists was the senior statesman of the conservative movement: Barry Goldwater. One might have expected Goldwater to support Reagan, who had gotten his political start with a nationally televised speech in support of the Arizona senator's presidential campaign. The two had long been portrayed in the press as ideological twins, and Goldwater had considered the California governor his "strongest and best supporter." Goldwater had also spoken critically of Ford in the spring of 1975, even going so far as to say that he had not made up his mind whether to support the president for reelection. But, contrary to expectations, Goldwater did not welcome the prospect of a Reagan campaign; he believed it would subject both the party and the nation to unnecessary upheaval. Ideologically, he said, Ford and Reagan were "about equal in every facet that you can look at." Even if Reagan sounded more conservative on the campaign trail, he would have to move toward the center as president, just as Ford had done. With a Democratic Congress, Reagan would be no more successful in trimming the budget deficit than Ford had been. And even if Reagan were elected, his arrival in Washington would mean months of government turnover and a steep learning curve for the new president. The ideological gains would be minimal, and the costs would be great. It was better, Goldwater told the media, for Republicans to stick with Ford but to keep prodding him to move to the right and be true to his conservative principles.[86]

This was exactly what Callaway wanted to hear, and he welcomed Goldwater's suggestions for bringing Reagan-leaning conservatives back to Ford. Like many other conservative members of Congress, Goldwater believed that Ford had to get rid of Rockefeller and select a new running mate. Goldwater favored John Connally of Texas, who was popular among some conservatives in the Sun Belt, but, ultimately, the individual chosen did not matter as long as it was not Rockefeller or another liberal.[87]

Callaway fully agreed with this suggestion, which had been corroborated by his conversations with other conservatives in the party.

Erroneously believing that conservatives' only real concern was Ford's vice president, he embarked on a not-so-quiet campaign to get Rockefeller off the ticket. "This one action of its own would totally take the steam out of the Reagan campaign," he argued in a memo to White House chief of staff Donald Rumsfeld in July 1975. If Callaway had confined his opinion to a memo, presumably it never would have been made public, but what he did next sent shock waves through the Republican Party: he publicly declared that Rockefeller was the "problem among Reagan supporters" and that the president might select a "younger man" as a running mate in 1976. Both Ford and Rockefeller repudiated the comments, leaving journalists to speculate whether Callaway was simply inexperienced and speaking out of turn or whether he was acting on the advice of someone in the White House who might have a vested interest in getting Rockefeller off the ticket (most fingers pointed to Rumsfeld). Rumsfeld denied any collusion, but he had never liked Rockefeller and for months had worked to marginalize the vice president's role in the White House. Despite the antipathy between Rumsfeld and Rockefeller, it seems unlikely that Callaway was taking orders from Rumsfeld or anyone else; he was channeling the advice from Goldwater and other conservatives who believed that Rockefeller's removal held the key to undermining the Reagan campaign. If Rockefeller remained on the ticket, Callaway believed, the president would face a difficult primary fight against Reagan, and conservatives would remain alienated from Ford. If Rockefeller were replaced, conservatives would be appeased and would return to the Ford camp, and Reagan's campaign would be dead in the water.[88]

Ford kept Rockefeller on the ticket for another three and a half months, but during that time, Reagan continued to gain in the polls, and party discontent with Rockefeller continued to mount. A meeting of the Republican National Committee in September 1975 noted that Rockefeller was most popular in New Jersey but was considered a political liability in the West and South. As *American Political Report* noted in October 1975, the regional resentment against Rockefeller reflected more than simply an ideological divide. "One of the big issues of 1976—and we think a party-shattering one—will be popular revolt against the Northeastern Liberal establishment and its symbols." Rockefeller, with his spectacular wealth and privilege, his Manhattan address, and his long-standing support for social welfare spending, seemed to stand for everything that conservatives in the Sun Belt, the Mountain West, and the Midwest heartland distrusted about liberalism, and he neatly encapsulated both the regional and the ideological divide in the GOP. Although Ford personally liked Rockefeller, the anti-Rockefeller forces in the party were too strong, and in early November he delivered the bad news to the vice president: he could not be his running mate in 1976. In announcing the decision to the public, Ford abandoned his usual candor and, to his lasting regret, dishonestly claimed that the decision had been Rockefeller's. But regardless of Ford's handling of the situation, both Goldwater and Callaway were delighted with the outcome. They believed that Rockefeller was the principal reason for conservatives' distrust of Ford, and they thought his removal from the ticket would be sufficient to win them back to the president's side. "I just think Reagan is probably reassessing (his candidacy) because of this," Goldwater told the press immediately after the announcement, erroneously believing that with the removal of Rockefeller, the main impetus for Reagan's campaign had been eliminated. Paul Laxalt quickly corrected him. "The presence or the absence of Rockefeller is of little moment," Laxalt said. "We're not going to reassess."[89] Indeed, in the weeks after the announcement, polls registered no improvement in Ford's prospects; Reagan continued to gain the public's support.

It was clear that Ford could not expect to win back the Reagan supporters. To clinch the nomination, then, he had to appeal to a different type of conservative Republican. Instead of concentrating his efforts on iconoclastic big-*C* conservatives—that is, people who considered themselves part of a self-identified conservative movement whose goal was the purification of the Republican Party along ideological lines and the dismantling of the Great Society—he needed to appeal to small-*c* conservatives—lifelong members of the Republican Party who believed in balanced budgets and fiscal stability. Reagan may have captured the fervor of the party's young ideologues and the support of cultural conservatives who were recent converts to the party, but the Ford campaign knew that it could count on the support of traditionally conservative Republicans who did not want to see a divisive primary season that would fragment their party and prevent them from defeating the Democratic candidate in the general election. Many invoked the memory of Goldwater's landslide defeat in 1964 as a warning of what might happen if they handed the nomination to another conservative extremist.[90]

Business executives—who were, for the most part, fiscally conservative Republicans—were especially concerned, and a solid plurality of these small-*c* conservative industrialists remained in the Ford camp. A survey of 300 company presidents in September 1975 showed that 49 percent supported Ford, while only 28 percent favored Reagan. Steve Forbes, the editor of *Forbes* magazine (and a future Republican presidential candidate himself), gave the president a strong endorsement on the grounds that Reagan would be "anathema to most Democrats." "If the Convention dumps Ford for Reagan, then the GOP will get—and deserve—a thrashing at the polls," Forbes wrote. As tire company CEO and loyal California Republican Leonard Firestone explained in a private letter in May 1975, he was "less than enthusiastic" about the prospect of a Reagan campaign because it would "only be divisive to the Party." "It would be pretty difficult for our Party to get over another Goldwater convention or election," he wrote to a fellow industrialist he hoped to dissuade from supporting Reagan. "I just can't think that there is a majority right wing or conservative vote in the United States."[91] This became the principal argument of the Ford campaign when addressing Republican voters: Ford was a responsible, conservative president who was keeping the Democratic Party in check, and he could be elected to another term in office if Republicans would only unite in support of him. Reagan, in contrast, would only divide the party, and he could not win a general election. Ford was therefore the responsible conservative choice.

This argument was especially popular among monied Republicans, who became the mainstay of Ford's campaign. When discussing possible candidates for finance chair (the person who coordinated the campaign's fund-raising), the Ford campaign selected some of the wealthiest businessmen in the nation; five of the seven candidates mentioned in an April 1975 internal campaign document would appear on the *Forbes* list of the 400 richest people in America. In the end, the Ford campaign chose billionaire David Packard, cofounder of the Silicon Valley electronics giant Hewlett-Packard; by 1982, he would be tied for the rank of third richest person in the United States. Packard had little interest in direct-mail fund-raising, preferring to solicit the largest checks possible from people who already had established histories as loyal Republican donors. He was a "$25,000-a-phone-call kind of guy," the *New York Times* reported—although he had to settle for $1,000 checks in the new era of campaign finance reform. Packard's approach suited the Ford White House perfectly. As Rumsfeld told Packard, he wanted him to raise the maximum amount of money "fast" with "minimum funds," which meant forgoing direct-mail solicitations and pursuing reliable, deep-pocketed donors. The Ford campaign began its fund-raising by contacting Republican Party donors who had contributed $1,000 or more to Nixon's reelection campaign in 1972; then it relied on state finance chairmen—who were almost invariably CEOs of local businesses—to expand that list by organizing fund-raising dinners. By the end of September 1975, Ford led all other candidates except for Wallace in the amount of money accrued; between July and September, the campaign amassed a total of $685,969, versus Reagan's $395,793. But the Ford campaign's money came from only 1,395 individuals, whereas Reagan had collected his from 5,506 donors. The average Reagan campaign contribution was $72, whereas Ford's was nearly $500.[92] The socioeconomic class differences between the two groups of donors were obvious. Ford's strategy, which gave credence to charges that his campaign represented only the wealthy, made for bad publicity, but it helped mobilize a base of party traditionalists whose money and connections could act as a firewall against the Reagan insurgency.

The new system of nomination through primaries presented both a challenge and an opportunity for the Ford campaign. If presidential candidates were selected by party officials, as they had been for decades before the 1970s, Ford probably would have been assured of his party's nomination. In most states outside of the South and a few areas of the West, party officials, congressional delegations, and big-money donors supported Ford over Reagan by overwhelming margins. The primary system changed the equation because those most likely to vote in the primaries were conservative ideologues who were deeply skeptical of the federal government and wanted a radical budget-cutter in the White House who would lead a conservative revolution in favor of free enterprise and a strong defense. They turned out to dump Ford (the symbol of moderate Republicanism and all that was wrong with Washington) and vote for Reagan. But Ford could take comfort in the fact that among all registered Republican voters, he still held the lead because many traditional Republicans were skeptical of the sort of change Reagan promised. If only the most dedicated Republicans voted in a primary, he might lose, but if turnout was high and less energized voters who supported the status quo showed up, he would do substantially better.[93] Open primaries, in which Democrats and independents could cast ballots in Republican contests, were bad for Ford because

Reagan could count on support from culturally conservative blue-collar Democrats who distrusted Ford and were just as anti-Washington as conservative ideologues in the Republican Party. Ford could win only if large numbers of fiscally conservative, traditionally minded Republicans who were not big-*C* conservatives participated in the primaries and neutralized the votes of the iconoclasts who supported Reagan. His strategy was therefore to maximize turnout among traditional centrist Republicans by convincing voters that Reagan's candidacy was dangerous—dangerous for the party because it would throw the election to the Democrats, and dangerous for America because Reagan was a radical right-winger who, in a worst-case scenario, could take the country to the brink of a nuclear confrontation with the Soviet Union. A vote for Ford was a vote for stability, experience, and the status quo. The Republicans who were most risk-averse were likely to back Ford, while those who wanted sweeping change favored Reagan.

By Christmas 1975, with only a few weeks left before the New Hampshire primary, polls showed that the race between the two candidates was a dead heat. It had become a fight between two very different groups of Republicans, with each group struggling to impose its own vision on the party. Would the GOP remain a fiscally conservative, moderately cautious party that focused on balancing the budget and maintaining good relations with the Soviet Union through détente? Or would Republicans become a hard-line anticommunist party supporting rapid military buildup, a radical overhaul of the welfare system, and the imposition of cultural conservatism through constitutional amendments? This is what the Republican voters in New Hampshire would have to decide, and by the end of 1975, the polls were too close for anyone to be certain of the outcome.

5 THE DEMOCRATIC PRIMARIES

On the eve of the Iowa precinct caucuses, where the first votes of the 1976 presidential nomination contests would be cast, the Democratic Party lacked not only a clear front-runner but also, in the view of some observers, any individual with the presidential stature necessary to unify the party. The Republican race had narrowed to a contest between two giants—an incumbent president and a former California governor, both of whom represented large ideological constituencies and had very different visions for the party. But in the Democratic presidential contest, the giants were strangely absent. Despite the gains they were making in the polls by the end of the year, Jimmy Carter and Mo Udall continued to be tagged in the press as "dark-horse" or "long-shot" candidates whose chances of a first-ballot victory at the convention were remote. The two candidates with the longest political résumés—Henry Jackson and George Wallace—alienated large segments of their party with issue positions that liberals considered unacceptable. Several of the governors who had once seemed to be competitive contenders for the White House in 1976—such as Pennsylvania's Milton Shapp and North Carolina's Terry Sanford—decided in early 1976 that they lacked the support to be viable candidates. For much of 1975, many continued to predict that Ted Kennedy would enter the race, despite his disavowals. By the end of the year, when many Democrats were reluctantly coming to terms with the fact that Kennedy would not be their party's nominee, some turned to Hubert Humphrey, who led all declared candidates in the polls, coming in second only to the noncandidate Kennedy.[1]

HUBERT HUMPHREY

Unlike Kennedy, Humphrey wanted to run for president in 1976. The problem was that he wanted to do so without entering the primaries. Humphrey, who turned sixty-five in 1976, had been participating in party conventions for nearly thirty years; he was a veteran of the old system of convention nominations but was uncomfortable with primary campaigns. His track record with primaries was not particularly good. In 1960, during his first presidential campaign, he won only one primary—South Dakota's—and saw his presidential prospects destroyed by a crushing loss to John F. Kennedy in West Virginia. In 1968, after the assassination of Robert Kennedy, he gained his party's presidential nomination at the convention without winning a single primary—but he did so amidst vociferous protests from the floor. And in 1972 he won a few primaries in eastern industrial states but failed to overtake George McGovern in primaries farther west. Humphrey was a three-time presidential loser, and he did not want to be defeated again. "The one thing I don't need at this stage in my life is to be ridiculous," he said. He was also in much poorer health than the public realized at the time. After a lifetime of maintaining a frenetic pace with seemingly boundless energy, he was still projecting an image of health and optimism, but he had undergone a painful operation for bladder cancer in 1973. The cancer returned in 1976, and in October his bladder would be removed. By the end of January 1978, he would be dead.[2]

But after longing for the presidency for decades, Humphrey found it difficult to give up the dream. He expected that none of the presidential aspirants would be able to win enough delegates in the primaries to secure the party's nomination on the first ballot, and the convention would then turn to him as a compromise choice. Although he had made some enemies among the party's progressives because of his identification with President Lyndon Johnson's Vietnam War and his opposition to McGovern in the 1972 primaries, those old scores had been largely forgotten—especially now that Humphrey seemed to be the party's best chance to nominate a 1960s-style liberal who was not Jackson. Because of his lifelong championship of civil rights, Humphrey was popular among African Americans; a poll of black elected officials in 1976 placed Humphrey first among all potential presidential contenders.[3] With his impeccable decades-long record of defending labor unions, Humphrey was also the first choice of organized labor. No

Figure 5.1. Hubert Humphrey with Jimmy Carter at the 1976 Democratic National Convention. (Library of Congress, Prints & Photographs Division, U.S. News & World Report Magazine Collection, LC-DIG-ppmsca-09737)

other candidate was so closely identified with traditional Great Society liberalism; as a senator in the 1960s and as vice president under Johnson, Humphrey had been partly responsible for the War on Poverty. And in the mid-1970s he was still championing the cause of economic uplift through public spending. The Humphrey-Hawkins full employment bill, which was the cornerstone of the Democratic Party's strategy to create jobs, was his legislative project.

Especially in the heavily unionized states of Pennsylvania and New Jersey, party officials begged Humphrey to run and offered to hold uncommitted slates of delegates that would be available to him as soon as he entered the race. Humphrey found it impossible to say no. During the final months of 1975 and the early months of 1976, he delayed a final announcement about his intentions and cast a heavy shadow over the primaries, as Democrats who would have preferred the Minnesota senator wondered whether they should choose among the declared candidates or hold out for a last-minute Humphrey draft.[4] In the meantime, two other candidates entered the race with the intention of appealing to some of the same liberal voters who might have been attracted to Humphrey.

SARGENT SHRIVER

Sargent Shriver had been the Democratic Party's vice-presidential candidate in 1972. He was the founding director of the Peace Corps, and, as director of the Office of Economic Opportunity during the Johnson administration, he was the chief implementer of much of the War on Poverty. But his campaign seemed to be predicated more on his connection to the Kennedys than on his accomplishments. As the husband of Eunice Kennedy Shriver, he was so close to Ted Kennedy that many observers assumed he was simply a "stalking horse" for the Massachusetts senator and that he would drop out of the race as soon as Kennedy decided to run. Shriver, in fact, openly admitted that Kennedy would be the better candidate. On the day he officially announced his campaign in September 1975, he declared that his brother-in-law was "the most able, talented, attractive candidate the party has" and acknowledged that he was running only because Kennedy was not. Perhaps never before had a presidential candidate conceded in his opening campaign announcement that he was not the best person for the job. The tagline of "second-class Kennedy" dogged him throughout the campaign. Shriver filled his campaign staff with Kennedy family members and veterans of President Kennedy's administration, and he used his Kennedy connections to raise money more quickly than most of his rivals, but voters never treated him as a Kennedy.[5]

Because Shriver had never won elected office at any level, he was particularly ill prepared for a presidential run. Although he had spent much of his adult life in government service, all his jobs, culminating with the ambassadorship to France, had been appointed positions. Perhaps as a result, he had never mastered the politician's art of rubbing elbows with the masses. On the campaign trail, he projected the image of a wealthy aristocrat with a cerebral bent. As the only Catholic among the major contenders, Shriver thought he could do well among the heavily Catholic constituencies of New England, but his inability to connect with white working-class voters hampered his efforts. Three years earlier, while campaigning as McGovern's running mate, he had been widely derided for squandering an opportunity to connect with steelworkers at a bar in Youngstown, Ohio. Instead of ordering a Pabst or a Budweiser like all the other men, he had asked for an expensive French cognac. His habits had not changed this time around. When soliciting votes among African Americans in rural Mississippi in early 1976, he showed up wearing handmade Italian shoes, a silk tie, and gold cufflinks.[6]

Despite his weaknesses, Shriver hoped his liberal record and close identification with the Kennedy legacy of the 1960s would allow him to win black votes in the South and do well among Kennedy admirers in New England. He had the potential to offer a liberal Catholic social vision that was reminiscent of Eugene McCarthy's 1968 presidential campaign. Shriver attracted the support of several left-leaning Democratic pro-life activists who were impressed by his long history of antipoverty work, his wife Eunice's speeches against abortion and advocacy for people with disabilities, and his own Catholic piety, as evidenced by his daily attendance at Mass and constant use of his rosary. Shriver also possessed a wide-ranging, detailed knowledge of several centuries of Catholic philosophical and theological writings and could discuss these subjects for hours. One of his speechwriters recalled that Shriver once spent a full twenty minutes explaining the differences between the early, middle, and late writings of the sixteenth-century St. Theresa of Avila. He was also thoroughly conversant with the writings of twentieth-century Catholic intellectuals such as Teilhard de Chardin, Hans Kung, and Thomas Merton. His political candidacy was guided by a lifelong concern for the poor that was rooted in Catholic theologies of social justice. No other candidate had as much potential to recover the liberal ideals of the early 1960s that had sparked the Peace Corps and the War on Poverty and package them with a faith-based, optimistic vision of universal human brotherhood and social obligation. To meet the challenges of the late 1970s, Shriver promised a bevy of new 1960s-style liberal programs, including federally subsidized day care, national health insurance, Social Security benefits for full-time homemakers, and an expanded Health Service Corps to "bring care to the families in under-served America just as the Peace Corps did to the under-served world."[7]

Shriver's proposals for new government programs outstripped those of all the other candidates. He wanted to be seen as left of center, but like Jackson, his views on cultural issues were much more traditional, rooted in the breadwinner liberalism of the New Deal era rather than the new politics of individual rights.[8] The focus of all his proposed programs was strengthening the family, by which he usually meant a traditional two-parent household. "The divorce rate is soaring," he lamented. "Young people are not willing to make commitments—marital or otherwise—to each other or to anything. . . . Something has gone out of the people of this nation." He proposed reforming the welfare system to discourage "family desertion" and called for a part-time and "flexible-hour" jobs program for parents who were juggling child-care responsibilities with employment. He promised to change the military's practice of "moving families from station to station with little regard for family impact." Above all, his "comprehensive governmental strategy for family strength" promised jobs and economic uplift, a goal that accorded well with the New Deal and Great Society liberalism he believed in, as well as the concerns of many working-class Catholics.[9]

Shriver's message might have seemed tailor-made for the culturally conservative but economically liberal Catholic voters of the Northeast, but he found it far more difficult to gain traction among this group than anyone had expected. His liberal stance on busing probably hurt him among the working-class white Catholic voters in Boston who should have been his base of support. His image as a wealthy patrician who lacked the Kennedy charm on the campaign trail probably hurt him everywhere else. Unable to escape Ted Kennedy's shadow and establish a sizable following of his own, he was constantly dogged by unfavorable comparisons with his more famous family members. As late as December 1975, pundits still expected Shriver to win the Massachusetts primary, where his supporters had placed all their hopes, but his campaign quickly tanked, even in Kennedy territory.[10]

BIRCH BAYH

Another late-entry liberal was Senator Birch Bayh of Indiana, who announced his candidacy at the end of October, a month after Shriver. His liberal credentials, especially on women's rights issues, appeared impeccable. He not only supported the Equal Rights Amendment but, as chair of the Senate Constitutional Amendments Subcommittee, had actually helped draft it. He had also coauthored Title IX and played a critical role in blocking proposals for an antiabortion constitutional amendment in committee. He had a reputation as a defender of labor interests and civil rights. Because he was in his third term in the Senate—even though he was only forty-seven years old—he was viewed as an experienced politician and therefore a top-tier candidate, in contrast to most of the rest of the presidential field. He had youth and good looks on his side. The *New York Times* described him as "handsome" and "athletic" and his wife as an "attractive blonde." When he announced his entry into the race, political pundits thought he was the front-runner they had been waiting for, because Bayh's résumé made him look like presidential material. He was "one of only two or three candidates in the crowded Democratic field who achieved instant status among political professionals as 'serious' contenders for the nomination," *Washington Star* reporter Jack Germond observed.[11]

Bayh thought he could win by marketing himself as a pragmatic liberal with a proven track record. Quoting a *Chicago News* columnist who had said that Bayh would not "suffer from the image of his colleagues as so many New Deal retreads" and could "espouse liberal positions" without the "clichés of Hubert H. Humphrey," Bayh claimed that he alone had "broad-based support throughout the Democratic Party" and could unite its various factions. Perhaps he was not a "New Deal retread," but like the other Democratic liberals, his campaign included the New Deal themes of stronger antitrust action (which he thought would curb inflation), an expanded money supply (which Republicans opposed because of their fear of inflation), and a public-sector jobs program. Combined with advocacy of environmental conservation, promise of a tax cut for working-class Americans, and more money for state governments, Bayh's program offered boilerplate Democratic economic liberalism.[12] His ideas were not necessarily innovative, but he hoped his senatorial position and political experience would earn him respect and vault him to the top of the heap of Democratic contenders.

But once Bayh started speaking, many observers decided that he lacked substance. After an all-American, midwestern, small-town boyhood, complete with 4-H tomato-growing contests, Methodist churchgoing, and plenty of baseball, he had spent his entire adult career in elected office and had risen through the political ranks by making the right alliances with power brokers and avoiding offense. "Bayh is all politician," a 1970 *New York Times* profile declared. Five years later, that opinion was unchanged. Bayh was an inveterate glad-hander, greeting young male constituents with "Hiyah, Tiger" as he squeezed their biceps, but his campaign stump speeches were the "worst among the major candidates," in the estimate of the *Times*. Devoid of any real ideas, his speeches had a "juvenile, corny quality," giving the impression that the senator was incapable of speaking with passion or conviction on any issue. The *Washington Post* agreed, calling Bayh a "cautious, calculating political pro" who was much more of a follower than a leader. Even in his personal habits, he always seemed to be looking over his shoulder to gauge audience reaction. After being a teetotaler for much of his early political career, for instance, he began to sip Bloody Marys at political receptions, hoping to ward off snickers about his "Boy Scout image." Regardless of what he did, he could not achieve the gravitas for which he longed. The press mocked him as the forty-seven-year-old who still needed his nightly half pint of chocolate ice cream before bed. "Bayh acts his age . . . only with considerable self-discipline," *Washington Post* reporter Jules Witcover wrote. One Democratic activist declared, "I can't make up my mind whether he is a serious Presidential possibility or only the world's oldest Purdue sophomore." Bayh hardly assuaged doubts about his leadership qualities when, in the midst of his presidential campaign, he began to watch videotapes of his stump speeches to figure out why he was not being taken seriously. "Maybe I joked when I should not have joked," he concluded.[13]

Bayh's reputation for political phoniness was not helped when he announced his candidacy against the backdrop of Indiana farmland. "Those of you who know me longest here know I've never had a burning desire to be President of the United States," intoned the lifelong politician who had entered the Senate at age thirty-four and had already run for president once before. "I feel closer to my God and I felt more fulfilled out in these fields than anything I've done."[14] Bayh tried this folksy, homespun image for a few weeks and then decided, after his campaign failed to catch fire, to proudly proclaim himself a Washington pol after all. "I'm Birch Bayh and I'm a politician," he stated in his most memorable New Hampshire television ad. "It takes a good politician to make a good president." The *New York Times* characterized the unexpected admission as Bayh's attempt to "alchemize the negative sentiments that all politicians are presumed to face this year into grudging respect and support." But in this case, the experiment with political alchemy failed, and the "grudging respect and support" never materialized. Bayh's poll numbers plummeted. He went from being a presumed potential front-runner in October 1975 to an expected distant third-place finisher in New Hampshire by February 1976—and his standing in the polls continued to drop rapidly.[15] Bayh might have had the ideal résumé for a presidential candidate in a previous election, but 1976 was shaping up to be the year of the outsider, and Bayh's lifetime career in Washington was not what voters were looking for.

Nor did Bayh's traditional economic liberalism excite the party's young progressives. Bayh thought he could unite all factions of the party around his candidacy, but it turned out that the party was far too divided. His best chance of winning the nomination probably would have been to seek inroads among the northeastern and midwestern labor vote, where bread-and-butter liberalism and a strong record on unions might have made him a popular candidate. But these working-class constituencies trusted Henry Jackson and Hubert Humphrey far more than they trusted Birch Bayh, who was viewed with suspicion in some northern Catholic circles because of his liberal record on abortion.

ABORTION AND THE DEMOCRATS

The fervor in the Democratic Party over the abortion issue caught several presidential candidates by surprise, but none more than Bayh. Bayh's prominent role in blocking an antiabortion constitutional amendment in the Senate should have endeared him to the party's ascendant pro-choice wing. Pro-choice women's rights advocates had been gaining ground in the Democratic Party ever since the late 1960s, but their influence at the national level was especially evident in 1972, when they helped George McGovern, an abortion rights supporter, win the party's nomination. Some of McGovern's delegates came to the Democratic National Convention prepared to add an endorsement of abortion rights to the party platform, but to their chagrin, the McGovern campaign asked them to drop this proposal for fear of alienating some of the party's culturally conservative voters. After the Supreme Court issued its landmark abortion rights ruling in *Roe v. Wade* in January 1973, the party's pro-choice members assumed that support for legalized abortion would be less controversial, since now it was simply an endorsement of the status quo.[16]

At first, it appeared that this assumption was correct. Before *Roe*, support for the pro-life cause was common among Catholic Democrats, but after that decision, some of these erstwhile pro-life supporters reversed course and came out against an antiabortion constitutional amendment. The most prominent Democrat to switch sides on the issue was Ted Kennedy, a Catholic representing one of the most heavily Catholic—and, at the time, strongly antiabortion—states in the nation. In 1971, when the Massachusetts legislature was overwhelmingly opposed to the legalization of abortion, he had endorsed the pro-life movement with a declaration that the nation had a duty to "fulfill its responsibility to its children from the very moment of conception." But in 1975 he switched positions and fought back attempts to eliminate Medicaid funding for abortion. By that time, the Democratic-controlled

Senate was solidly pro-choice, and the feminist wing of the party even more so. The Democratic Party was home to some of the nation's strongest pro-choice advocates, including National Abortion Rights Action League (NARAL) cofounder and leading feminist Betty Friedan, congresswoman and former presidential candidate Shirley Chisholm, and New York congresswoman Bella Abzug, who earned the nickname "Battling Bella" for her political fights on behalf of women's rights. Pro-lifers had several allies among prominent Democratic senators, including Rhode Island's John Pastore and Missouri's Thomas Eagleton, and many more supporters among Democrats in the House and in state legislatures, so they still had some influence in the party. But the Democrats who aspired to national leadership had already seen the handwriting on the wall, and they were moving into the pro-choice camp. Only George Wallace was willing to endorse the Human Life Amendment, although both Jackson and Shriver expressed strong personal opposition to abortion.[17]

But if the leadership of the Democratic Party was headed in a pro-choice direction, a substantial segment of its membership remained strongly pro-life. In the mid-1970s opponents of abortion were still more likely to be Democrats than Republicans. Opposition to abortion was strongest among white Catholics and African Americans, and both groups were largely Democratic. There were also millions of culturally conservative white Protestants who had serious reservations about abortion, and many of these voters, especially in the South and the Midwest, were also Democrats. With *Roe v. Wade* less than three years old at the beginning of the 1976 campaign season, right-to-life groups were determined to turn the presidential election into a referendum on the Human Life Amendment, which would do more than reverse *Roe*; it would declare conception to be the beginning of human life and ban most abortions nationwide. This was the stated goal of the one million members of the National Right to Life Committee, as well as the nation's Catholic bishops, who made ratification of an antiabortion constitutional amendment the centerpiece of their 1975 Pastoral Plan for Pro-Life Activities. Although public opinion polls showed that approximately half of American Catholic voters dissented from the bishops' view of abortion, the Catholics who supported the constitutional ban accounted for millions of votes, and they were joined by many allies outside of the Catholic Church who also favored the amendment. Support for an antiabortion amendment was often associated with social conservatism, but the idea also gained favor with a few members of the party's left wing, such as Cesar Chavez and Jesse Jackson, who were not normally viewed as conservative on any issue but who considered the defense of fetal life a human rights cause. In total, 48 percent of Democratic voters in 1976 supported the Human Life Amendment.[18]

Unfortunately for Bayh, New Hampshire and Massachusetts, the two critical early-primary states where he focused his initial campaign, were heavily Catholic regions where pro-life sentiment was strong. In Massachusetts, the Democratic-controlled state legislature passed a resolution endorsing the Human Life Amendment immediately after *Roe v. Wade* and remained strongly opposed to abortion for the next several years. The American Civil Liberties Union estimated in 1974 that it would be difficult to find more than thirty pro-choice votes in the 280-seat legislature. Pro-lifers in the state were very well organized, and they were ready to use their muscle to influence presidential candidates. Massachusetts Citizens for Life had fifty thousand members and spent $100,000 on pro-life advertising in 1975—which was almost as much as each of the presidential candidates spent in the state.[19] This did not bode well for a candidate who had played a leading role in defeating pro-life activists' top political priority.

Bayh faced pro-life protesters at nearly every campaign stop. At a rally in New Hampshire, a protester tried to drown out his speech by playing "Taps" on a bugle. At another rally, abortion opponents appeared wearing red-stained surgical gowns. Some called him a "murderer." By January, he was telling the press that abortion was "probably" the most "troublesome" issue of his campaign. Complicating the matter was Bayh's unwillingness to actually endorse abortion rights, as Udall had. Instead, he expressed his personal opposition to abortion and said that while studying proposals for an antiabortion amendment in his Senate subcommittee, he had "wanted to oppose abortion because really we are talking about life," but in the end he felt that he could not impose his own convictions on others.[20] This stance reflected Bayh's habit of trying to win friends on both sides of every issue, but in this case, the effort failed. Pro-lifers gave Bayh no credit for his professed personal opposition to abortion; instead, they treated him as their number-one enemy.

At about the same time Bayh entered the race, pro-life activists decided to run one of their own leaders for president: Ellen McCormack, a forty-nine-year-old housewife and mother of four from Long Island.

McCormack had never run for office before, but she had been an early leader in the New York pro-life movement and was well known among right-to-life activists. The press, however, treated her campaign as an irrelevant sideshow. Even though she lived in Merrick, New York, less than fifty miles from Manhattan, her name appeared in only twelve articles published in the *New York Times* between November 1975 and February 1976. During the same period, Bayh's name appeared in nearly two hundred. In several states, including Massachusetts and Oregon, Democratic Party officials tried (albeit unsuccessfully) to keep her name off the ballot on the grounds that she was not a legitimate national candidate. Even some Catholic bishops were skeptical about her candidacy. The archbishop of Cincinnati sent a letter to his parishes discouraging single-issue voting. That effort to deter voters from supporting McCormack might have been partially offset by a statement from the bishop of neighboring Covington, Kentucky, who said that Catholics should vote for candidates who "clearly and firmly declare themselves defenders of the right to life."[21]

As the internal debate among Catholics about McCormack's candidacy continued to build, the candidate herself began fund-raising at a furious pace. By the middle of February 1976, she had raised enough money to qualify for federal matching funds, and she became the first female candidate ever to qualify for Secret Service protection. It had taken several of the major candidates in the race, including Carter and Udall, more than half a year to secure the requisite $100,000 in small donations from twenty states to qualify for federal matching funds, but McCormack was able to reach that goal within three months of officially kicking off her campaign.[22] She did this by tapping into the fund-raising network of the national pro-life movement, where she had long been an established figure. With one million members, a national newsletter, and a well-orchestrated network of hundreds of state and local chapters, the National Right to Life Committee, along with its allied organizations, offered an ideal recruiting ground for donations and votes from people who wanted to see *Roe v. Wade* overturned with a constitutional amendment.

McCormack's candidacy had originally been devised as a strategy to secure television advertising for the pro-life cause and shift public opinion on the abortion issue, but as the campaign progressed and she began to win far more votes than anyone had expected, it became a quest to preserve a pro-life voice in the Democratic Party. "I don't see anyone on any ticket I could vote for," McCormack said. "If the right to life issue is at the bottom of their priorities, I cannot support them." Critics argued that the law needed to be changed to prevent single-issue candidates from special-interest groups from qualifying for federal matching funds, but McCormack and her supporters responded that the "rights of the unborn" were more important than all other issues and deserved to be the focus of a single-issue campaign.[23]

The Northeast was the strongest bastion of Catholic Democratic pro-life sentiment, but Jimmy Carter's campaign staff believed that antiabortion activism would likely affect the race in Iowa as well. Catholics accounted for less than 20 percent of the population in Iowa, but they constituted a strong interest group within the state's Democratic Party, and many of them cared about abortion. Catholic influence was a principal reason why, before *Roe v. Wade,* the Iowa Democratic Party had taken a more conservative position on abortion than its GOP counterpart and why the state had not liberalized its antiabortion law before it was forced to do so by the Supreme Court in 1973. Although many Democrats in Iowa supported abortion rights, the state's caucus system offered an ideal opportunity for a small but highly motivated contingent of pro-life activists to exercise an outsized influence on the presidential selection process. When Shriver ran a close second to Carter in the Iowa straw poll in October 1975, Rick Hutcheson attributed the former vice-presidential candidate's strength in the state to the "Catholic vote," which he assumed had been mobilized over abortion. "Apparently, anti-abortionists have seized upon packing the Democratic caucuses as a means of working against abortion," he reported to Hamilton Jordan. "This will be an asset to Shriver in the 1976 caucuses as well, it looks like."[24]

But Shriver was not as well positioned among pro-lifers as the Carter campaign assumed. It was true that he had much closer connections to the pro-life movement than any other candidate. His wife had given the keynote addresses at several pro-life rallies and conventions, and he had joined her in some of her pro-life efforts. When Shriver first announced his candidacy, some of his friends from the pro-life movement were ecstatic. Marjory Mecklenburg, founder of American Citizens Concerned for Life, joined his campaign advisory committee immediately, and several other nationally prominent right-to-life advocates also volunteered for the campaign. But Shriver disagreed with the pro-life movement over the best strategy to fight abortion. He believed the Human Life Amendment was not politically possible and would not be effective. Far more useful, he thought, was legislation that offered material assistance and positive alternatives to abortion for women facing crisis pregnancies. The pro-life movement, however, had made support for the Human Life Amendment a political litmus test, and when Shriver refused to endorse it, the *National Right to Life News* warned its readers not to vote for him.[25] Perhaps Carter would not have to worry about Shriver's appeal among Iowa Catholics after all.

THE IOWA CAUCUSES

Because the Iowa caucuses typically attract no more than about 10 percent of eligible voters, they are notoriously difficult to poll for and present a high risk to the presumed front-runner. It is easy for special-interest groups to pack the caucuses and exercise an outsized influence, swinging the vote to a dark-horse candidate. For three months leading up to the January caucuses, Iowa polls had shown Carter ahead of most or all other candidates, but this posed a danger to his candidacy if he underperformed. Before the fall of 1975, his image had been that of an underdog, which suited his campaign well. But now, at least in Iowa, he was the target for the other candidates. Anything less than first place would be viewed as "significant slippage" for Carter, Iowa's Democratic chairman warned, and he "can't finish lower than second or he's finished."[26]

Two weeks before the caucuses, anxiety set in among some of Carter's top campaign staff. The Carter campaign had no organized get-out-the-vote effort in Iowa, Hutcheson told Jordan. Even though polls showed Carter ahead, much of his support came from people who had never participated in a caucus before. How would they know where to find their precinct? What if an insufficient number of Carter supporters showed up? If one of the other Democrats were better organized in Iowa, Hutcheson worried that Carter could be beaten. In actuality, Carter was much better prepared in Iowa than Hutcheson believed. Campaign staffer Tim Kraft, whom the Iowa Democratic chairman called "as good an organizer as ever worked this state," had been monitoring the situation on the ground for nearly a year.[27] But Hutcheson's alarming memo demonstrated the precariousness of the situation.

Two rivals in particular—Fred Harris and Birch Bayh—sensed an opportunity. Harris had been focusing much of his attention on New Hampshire, believing that only a solid performance in the nation's first primary could dispel doubts about his long-shot presidential bid. Then, shortly before the Iowa caucuses, he realized the potential of a voting system that, by default, was dominated by highly energized activists who did not necessarily represent the party's mainstream. He moved his national campaign manager from Washington to Des Moines for the last two weeks of the Iowa campaign and started traveling the roads of the state in his rented camper, covering hundreds of miles in frigid January weather to bring his left-leaning populist economic message to Iowa progressives. Despite his campaign's financial troubles, he bought more radio and television advertising in Iowa than any of his rivals, and he stationed thirty-one national staff members in the state—a much more formidable force than those marshaled by most of the other candidates—to drum up votes and monitor the situation on the ground.[28]

Bayh did not purchase as much media advertising as Harris, but he believed he might be able to pull off an upset by capitalizing on the one group of Democratic voters among whom Carter was weakest: organized labor. Carter was from a right-to-work state where unions had a weak presence, and he gave labor issues little attention on the campaign trail. He only reluctantly endorsed labor unions' highest priority: repealing section 14B of the Taft-Hartley Act. Since its passage in 1947, that provision had paved the way for state right-to-work legislation by depriving unions of the right to require companies to fire workers who refused to join the union. Carter promised to sign legislation repealing section 14B, but only if Congress took the initiative; he would not invest political capital to lobby for it. Bayh sensed an opportunity. Many union leaders favored Jackson or Humphrey, neither of whom was campaigning in Iowa. Bayh was the only candidate with an impeccable reputation among organized labor. Even Udall, considered the most progressive viable candidate in the race, was suspect because he represented a right-to-work state in Congress and had voted for right-to-work legislation in 1965. Thus, while Carter barnstormed the state, Bayh compiled endorsements from labor union leaders.[29]

But Bayh found that midwestern union members were not nearly as liberal as he would have liked. In his home state, more members of the United Auto Workers (UAW) had voted for Nixon than for McGovern in 1972. And in Iowa in 1976, many union members preferred the centrist Carter over the liberal Bayh. Even a few of the more progressive union leaders decided to back Carter because they thought he had more widespread appeal than Bayh, and they wanted a candidate who could decisively defeat Wallace in the primaries and then win the White House. To Bayh's consternation, Carter picked up a coveted endorsement from the Iowa UAW, despite his lackluster record on labor issues.[30]

Bayh also found that his stance on abortion prevented him from reaching out to working-class voters. Carter, by contrast, seemed to enjoy a much greater rapport with these voters, even though his official stance on abortion was hardly different from Bayh's. The press attributed this rapport to Carter's evangelicalism. Iowa had a larger-than-average population of evangelicals compared with other northern states, and Carter's faith played well with many Iowans. Some pro-life Catholics in the state viewed evangelicals as their natural allies, partly because Iowa's best-known evangelical Democratic politician, former governor and senator Harold Hughes, had a pro-life voting record. With pro-life activists viewing Shriver as a turncoat on abortion and Bayh, Udall, and Harris as unacceptable, Carter seemed to be the only suitable alternative among the Democrats. (It helped Carter's cause that the other antiabortion Democrats in the race, McCormack and Wallace, were not running in Iowa.) The Carter campaign's volunteers and enthusiastic supporters in Iowa included a number of Catholic pro-life activists and devout evangelicals and at least one Catholic priest, who campaigned for Carter not only in his hometown of Des Moines but also throughout the state. "Anti-abortion women are volunteers for Carter throughout Iowa," *Washington Post* columnists Rowland Evans and Robert Novak reported. The evangelical Dutch Reformed denominations, which were opposed to abortion and had a strong presence in the state—including three colleges—were "honeycombed with Carter volunteers."[31]

With only a few days to go before the caucuses, Carter solidified his already strong position among pro-life activists by suggesting that he might endorse antiabortion legislation after all. For months, his official position had been that although he was personally opposed to abortion, he did not support the Human Life Amendment. Carter stuck to this line for a while. But right before the caucuses, during a Q&A session at a Catholic church in Creston, Iowa, Carter responded to a question from a pro-life activist a little differently. As Evans and Novak reported it, when asked whether he supported the Human Life Amendment, Carter replied that he did not (as he always had). The activist then asked a follow-up question: would he support a more limited constitutional amendment that imposed the same restrictions on abortion that Georgia had had before 1973—that is, a nationwide ban on elective abortions that were not medically necessary, while allowing limited exceptions for abortions in case of rape, incest, and health concerns? This was not the type of constitutional amendment the pro-life movement had ever supported, but the activist may have been searching for common ground with Carter. To the astonishment of Carter's pro-choice supporters, he seemed to accept the pro-lifer's proposal. "Under certain circumstances, I would [accept it]," he responded. That concession may have seemed limited, but Carter later made a statement to the *Des Moines Catholic Mirror* that he supported a "national statute" to limit abortion, even though he did not support the pro-life movement's Human Life Amendment. Pro-lifers were excited. Carter might not be fully in their camp, but, with the exception of Wallace and McCormack, he was the only Democratic candidate who was now on record supporting restrictive abortion legislation. The executive director of the Iowa Catholic Conference predicted that a strong turnout among Catholics would probably help Carter.[32]

Shriver's campaign, which was better attuned to Catholic politics than most, realized what was happening and tried to stop it. A Shriver campaign manager convinced a Sioux City priest to call Carter campaign headquarters in Atlanta and inquire about the candidate's position on abortion. When the Atlanta headquarters gave him a different line than he had heard Carter use on the campaign trail in Iowa, he issued a statement to the media that pro-lifers were "misinformed" about Carter's position. But the statement did not air on Iowa television until the Monday night of the caucuses, and by then, it was probably too late to dissuade pro-life activists who were supporting Carter. They showed up in full force to caucus for the former Georgia governor. Not until the next morning did some of them find out that their candidate might be less supportive of their cause than they had assumed. "I think I've been sandbagged," said one priest the morning after.[33]

Carter finished ahead of all the other declared candidates, winning nearly 28 percent of the vote. Bayh had to settle for a distant second, with only 13 percent; Harris came in third, at just under 10 percent; Udall finished fourth, with nearly 6 percent; and Shriver received just 3 percent of the vote. Jackson had chosen to bypass Iowa, so when he received only 1 percent of the vote, no one reported it as a loss. But both

Shriver and Udall were dealt serious blows. Shriver had initially polled well in Iowa until the abortion issue thwarted his campaign, and Udall had invested in television advertising to appeal to Iowa liberals only to find himself finishing near the back of the pack. The *New York Times* gave both their campaigns a grade of D, while awarding Carter an A. Carter had won decisively, carrying 38 percent of the black vote, 35 percent of the rural vote, and 37 percent of the blue-collar vote. He did a little more poorly among white-collar workers (winning 32 percent of their vote) and among residents of the state's largest cities (receiving only 18 percent of the urban vote), but even in the cities, he came out ahead of Bayh. The only discordant note for Carter was that 37 percent of the caucus participants had voted "uncommitted," which left a sizable percentage of the state's delegates still in play and suggested that more than one-third of Iowa voters were either waiting for another candidate (perhaps Humphrey or even Kennedy) to enter the race or, for whatever reason, not quite ready to join Carter's campaign. But for the most part, the press downplayed this aspect of the Iowa results and declared Carter the unquestioned winner. "Carter Defeats Bayh by 2–1 in Iowa Vote," "Carter Is Regarded as Getting Big Gain from Iowa Results," and "Iowa Victory Gives Carter Momentum" the national headlines proclaimed.[34]

If, as many analysts believed, the real winner in Iowa was not necessarily the candidate with the most delegates but the one the media proclaimed the victor, then Carter had clearly come out ahead. The one-term Georgia governor wisely tried to temper public expectations, not wanting his candidacy to crest too soon. But his campaign staff, who had been working for months for a candidate the media had written off as a "dark horse" and a "long shot," were eager to make the most of their first taste of success. "Don't fail to mention Jimmy's victory in Iowa when asking for contributions," one internal fund-raising memo instructed—as if Carter's fund-raisers were in any danger of forgetting.[35]

Yet the precinct ballots had hardly been counted before Carter's rivals and the press began to raise questions about his honesty in Iowa. Had Carter distorted his position on abortion in order to win? Before the Iowa campaign, Carter had always insisted that he opposed all antiabortion constitutional amendments, and even during the Iowa campaign, the Atlanta office had continued to reiterate this position. Why, then, did Carter say at the eleventh hour that he supported a "national statute" on abortion or suggest that he might be able to get behind some version of an antiabortion constitutional amendment? If Carter's goal had been to confuse voters, he apparently succeeded. A nationwide *New York Times*–CBS News poll taken during the first week of February showed that 21 percent of voters thought Carter favored a ban on abortion, 36 percent thought he did not, and 43 percent were not sure.[36]

Because Carter had made his credibility the centerpiece of the campaign ever since his official entry into the race in December 1974, his opponents—especially Bayh and Udall—sensed that his perceived dissembling had the potential to derail his candidacy. "If I'd been inconsistent, if I'd been on both sides of the abortion issue, if I got the labor vote [and] the anti-labor vote, someone ought to blow the whistle on me," Udall declared. Bayh, who was affected more directly than Udall by Carter's statements, was even more critical. Asserting that a presidential candidate should "not hold out false hopes and not try to be all things to all people," he said that Carter had been guilty of doing that in Iowa when he misleadingly implied that a "national statute" on abortion was a possibility. "To suggest that we can do by statute something the Supreme Court has said we can't do is holding out false hopes," Bayh said.[37]

Carter brushed off these concerns. He had not lied, he said. By "national statute," he had meant "a general law that would take preventive steps to minimize dependence on abortion" by offering "education programs, family planning programs, contraceptive advice and availability and adoption procedures"—in other words, something very similar to Shriver's approach to the issue, but with more emphasis on contraception than most conservative Catholics were willing to allow.[38]

Regardless of Carter's protestations, some of the journalists who investigated the matter were convinced that Carter had dissembled and that his dishonest outreach to pro-lifers had "made the difference between first and second place for Carter in Iowa," as Evans and Novak asserted. With his once-strong support among Catholics, Shriver had been expected to get at least 10 percent of the vote in Iowa, they wrote, and the only reason he did not was because he clearly indicated that he did not favor an antiabortion constitutional amendment, while Carter falsely suggested that he might. And Bayh, with his relatively strong support among labor, had been polling well in Sioux City until Carter's last-minute statements on abortion deprived him of much of his expected vote.[39]

Without precise issue-based polling at the caucuses, it was difficult to say how much of Carter's vote total was the result of his ambiguity on abortion. After all, he had been in first place in Iowa polls for months, and much of his support came from people who were energized by his image as a Washington outsider or a sensible centrist who would reduce government spending. In a survey of Carter's Iowa delegates, the desire for "honest and competent government" was the primary issue that galvanized them politically, although economic concerns and a desire to reduce government bureaucracy were a close second and third. Carter probably would have won the support of these voters regardless of his position on abortion. But this much was clear: the turnout had been higher than expected, much of that additional turnout had come from pro-lifers, and the pro-lifers who showed up vigorously supported Carter based on misinformation. Carter's support was also exceptionally strong in the most Catholic areas of the state, such as Dubuque. Of the seventeen delegates that Carter won in Iowa, four were white Catholics who listed the "right to life" cause as one of their top three areas of concern on a Democratic National Committee delegate survey.[40] They would come to the Democratic National Convention in June with the intention of keeping their party in the pro-life camp. Carter would be opposed to that effort.

But the convention was still months away. In the short term, Carter's most immediate priority was to convince the public that he was consistent on abortion—an issue that was raised at nearly every campaign stop—and deflect the increasingly hostile questions about his alleged lack of "candor." Evans and Novak were now writing negative columns about him almost every week in the *Washington Post,* and the March issue of *Harper's* featured a scathing article titled "Jimmy Carter's Pathetic Lies." It claimed that Carter's duplicity went far beyond his comments on abortion. He had lied about his record in Georgia, his past relationship to George Wallace, and his position on civil rights—all of which made him the most "sincerely insincere" of any of the candidates, the article charged. Among northern progressives, he positioned himself as a liberal, but, according to the *Harper's* piece, he had long been presenting himself as a conservative to white Georgians who were antipathetic to desegregation. The most damaging aspect of the *Harper*'s story was that its substance was repeated for weeks in the rest of the media, from television shows such as *Face the Nation* and *Tomorrow* to regional magazines such as *Texas Monthly.* Even the

New York Times, which was generally very supportive, conceded that Carter's policy positions did "sometimes seem deliberately ambiguous or evasive."[41]

Members of Carter's campaign staff were not perturbed. The *Harper's* article may have rattled the candidate himself, who denounced it as a "collection of lies, distortions and half-truths," but his campaign aides adopted a cooler, more hopeful view. The "critical" coverage by the media was actually a sign of Carter's success, Rick Hutcheson declared in a strategy memo to Hamilton Jordan and Jody Powell. For most of 1975, when Carter was still largely a political unknown, his press coverage was "by in large [*sic*] highly positive, gushing with surprise at the discovery of a Southerner who was attractive, intelligent, competent, not bigoted and doing far better politically than was his place, as a Southerner," Hutcheson wrote. But now that Carter was the perceived front-runner, journalists were fishing for a new angle on his candidacy, and "the only way to write something new or different from previous glowing accounts is the instant revisionist article—from honest straight-shooter to opportunistic hedger; from southern pro–civil rights wonder to racist-tinged rhetoric—in short, from 'new face' to 'politician.'" And, as Hutcheson conceded, because "JC is, indeed, a successful politician, those who perceived him as a 'non-politician' were bound to be somewhat disappointed." The campaign would thus do well to brush aside these attacks—as Carter was in fact doing—and move forward with the campaign strategy. But Hutcheson warned that Carter needed to shore up some of his issue positions and avoid getting pulled too far from the center on abortion. "We must take great pains not to be too identified with the 'pro-life' extremist right wing of women or else we will lose the moderate, pragmatic center of the 'women's lib' movement," he wrote. "This requires an unequivocal reiteration of JC's position of support for the S.C. decision [*Roe v. Wade*] & opposition to a constitutional amendment. Being personally opposed to abortion & strongly favoring a positive federal program of common sense sex ed & other alternatives to abortion is a highly acceptable middle ground."[42]

Carter followed this course. Even when campaigning in New Hampshire and Massachusetts, where pro-life organizational strength was strong and activists deluged him with questions, he stuck to his standard line of being personally opposed to abortion but also opposed to a constitutional amendment to reverse *Roe v. Wade.*[43] As Hutcheson had expected, this enabled him to deflect Bayh's attacks. For weeks, he continued to face critical questions on abortion from the media, but after a while, the questions about Carter's credibility on the issue started to subside.

The Carter campaign focused more attention than ever on shoring up Carter's brand of truthfulness and morality, hoping that a forceful reiteration of the message would deflect the charges of disingenuousness that his opponents were lobbing against him. "There are a lot of things that I would not do to be elected," Carter declared in a new television ad timed for the early spring primaries. "I'll never make a misleading statement, I'll never betray the confidence that any of you has in me, and I'll never avoid a controversial issue. . . . If you ever see me do any of these things, don't support me, because I would not be worthy to be the President of this country." In the closing seconds of the ad, the camera cut to a scene of Carter kneeling in a field as he invoked his "faith" and "confidence," which came from "people like you."[44]

The reference to "people like you" was a master stroke that redirected the focus from Carter's own credibility to the positive character of the voters themselves. From the moment of Carter's initial campaign announcement, which invoked the "innate quality of our people," to his frequent statements on the campaign trail that Americans deserved a "government as good as its people," the Carter campaign had been about "the restoration of the people's faith in themselves," as *New York Times* columnist Tom Wicker phrased it.[45] In running a populist campaign, Carter had always intended to accentuate the positive and wrap himself in the goodness of the American people. When faced with the charge of disingenuousness, he responded not only by invoking his own character but also by suggesting that any referendum on his own honesty was an indirect judgment on the character of the American people.

This was not enough to persuade all Democrats of his trustworthiness. By a margin of 48 percent to 35 percent, Democratic voters in New York and Wisconsin said that Carter was "too unspecific and fuzzy" about his stances on the issues. But for many Democrats, specificity and consistency on the issues were not the most important determinants of their vote. Voter surveys in six early-primary states showed that those who listed "consistency and honesty" as key concerns were more likely to vote for Udall, but those who wanted an electable candidate who was "not part of the Washington establishment" were more likely to support Carter.[46] In the end, Carter's anti-Washington posture, which remained consistent even if his precise position on the issues did not, may have helped him weather the storm caused by his waffling on abortion.

NEW HAMPSHIRE AND BEYOND

The Carter campaign always considered New Hampshire a top priority, second only to Florida. In January and February the campaign poured approximately six times as much money into New Hampshire as it spent in Iowa, devoting more financial resources to the Granite State than to any other state, with the exception of Florida. Carter had been traveling regularly to New Hampshire for more than a year, and he did so even more often in the last few weeks before the primary. In the estimate of the *New York Times,* the former Georgia governor may have personally talked to more voters in New Hampshire than had any other candidate.[47]

His campaign also brought busloads of volunteers from Georgia to knock on the doors of Democratic voters in New Hampshire and share testimonies about their own personal friendship with Carter and their reasons for believing that he would fulfill his promise to transform the federal government. These personal testimonials, especially when they were delivered in single-digit temperatures by people who had traveled more than a thousand miles, were likely more effective than any television ad, and they also produced valuable information about individual voters that the Carter campaign could use to ensure a high turnout of supporters on primary day. After each conversation, the volunteers estimated the prospective voter's level of support for Carter's candidacy by assigning a numerical score on a five-point scale; they then mailed that information back to Georgia headquarters for additional follow-up.[48] The effort paid off. No other candidate had such a large following of loyalists who could be dispatched to cover the state so thoroughly, and no other campaign invested so much to win the support of individual voters through personal encounters.

The Carter campaigners reported a surprisingly friendly welcome among New Hampshirites, many of whom no doubt considered them a curiosity as they tried to deal with January temperatures. One Atlanta lawyer who volunteered for the trip reported to the Georgia staff that he dressed for his northern door-knocking adventure by wearing long underwear, a wool shirt, a wool sweater, a vest, a scarf, a wool hat, a 60/40 parka (with the hood pulled over the hat), three pairs of socks, two pairs of gloves, and flannel-lined pants tucked into his L. L. Bean boots. "I rarely got cold," he reported.[49]

While Carter's volunteers were trudging across the frozen North, Carter momentarily turned his attention southward to compete in two state caucuses—one in Mississippi and the other in Oklahoma—that were held between the Iowa and New Hampshire voting. It was in Mississippi that his campaign experienced its first major setback. For months leading up to the caucus, Carter's minority affairs desk had been reaching out to African American leaders in Mississippi's Democratic Party, hoping especially to get an endorsement from state NAACP leader Aaron Henry.[50] The favorite candidate among white Mississippians was, to no one's surprise, George Wallace, but the Carter campaign attempted to build a coalition of white moderates who were turned off by Wallace and African Americans who were eager to see a southern governor defeat an Alabama racist.

The attempt was largely a failure. Henry and many other African Americans supported not Carter but Shriver, who had won the affection of poor rural blacks in the state through his antipoverty work during the Johnson administration. Carter managed to win the support of some of the most prominent white liberals in the state, who, along with some of the white moderates, gave him the votes he needed to finish in second place, with nearly 14 percent of the vote. But he trailed Wallace's 44.6 percent and only barely exceeded Shriver's 12 percent. Shriver's vote total in Mississippi, which came almost entirely from African Americans, put him back in the race after his rocky start in Iowa.[51]

The headlines after the caucuses presented the results as a defeat for the Georgian and a clear victory for the Alabaman. "Wallace Defeats Carter by 3 to 1 in Mississippi Test," a *New York Times* headline proclaimed. Carter's "showing was a disappointment to his backers," the *Washington Post* declared. The Mississippi results also demonstrated, in the assessment of *New York Times* reporter R. W. Apple Jr., that Wallace "might do better than previously expected" in the other southern caucuses, such as South Carolina. The conventional wisdom before Mississippi had been that Wallace could win southern primaries when there was a large white turnout, but because caucuses attracted only a small fraction of the electorate and tended to draw from a more liberal, energized Democratic base, he was more vulnerable in that forum. Now it appeared to some observers that Wallace might be a strong candidate in the South regardless of the voting format. He had tried to mobilize his base in Mississippi with the slogan "Stop the Liberal Grab," and it had worked. Who would have predicted, the *Washington Post*'s David Broder asked, that "Jimmy Carter's Georgia charm will wow the voters in chilly Iowa, but leave the good old boys in Mississippi cold"?[52]

But there was a silver lining for Carter: the defeat of Senator Lloyd Bentsen, who had once been considered a serious competitor for moderately conservative white southern voters. Bentsen had publicly stated that he hoped to earn one-third of the delegates in Mississippi, but when he finished with less than 2 percent of the vote, it meant that his campaign was just about over.[53]

Two weeks later, Carter rebounded by eking out a razor-thin first-place victory in Oklahoma, edging out Fred Harris by less than a percentage point. Harris, who had been Oklahoma's senator, still had some support in the state, but he had become a polarizing figure since veering sharply toward the populist left and advocating a near-total nationwide ban on pistols. Harris's campaign depended on a small coterie of highly motivated activist supporters who might be induced to show up in disproportionately high numbers at caucuses, which typically attracted only 4 percent of the state's Democrats, so he thought he had a chance to overtake Carter, but the effort failed.[54] As the final contest before the New Hampshire vote, Oklahoma allowed Carter to regain his momentum just in time for the first major primary of the year.

New Hampshire gave Carter the decisive victory he had been looking for. He carried 31 percent of the vote, taking first place over Udall, who came in second with 23 percent. Bayh took third place, with 18 percent of the vote; Harris came in fourth, with 11 percent; and Shriver finished last, with 9 percent. In some years—including 1972—the candidate who received the most votes in New Hampshire could still be labeled a loser if his vote total was less than expected, but this was not the case for Carter. The press had predicted a close race between Carter and Udall, with possible strong showings by other candidates, and many had suggested that no candidate would receive much more than 25 percent of the vote.[55] Carter exceeded those expectations. After winning three of the first four contests, he was now the race's undisputed front-runner. The identity of his closest challenger, though, was still unknown. The New Hampshire primary put Udall back in the race after his dismal showing in Iowa, but Bayh was still hanging on and hoping to overtake Udall in the Massachusetts primary, which was scheduled to take place the following week. And neither Wallace nor Jackson had run in New Hampshire, so Carter could not yet claim a decisive victory over either of them.

In Mississippi, Carter had tried to win by capturing a share of the moderate and liberal vote, but in New Hampshire, he appealed to the more conservative members of the party, who, according to polls, constituted nearly one-third of the voters in New Hampshire's Democratic presidential primary. These conservatives were mostly working-class Catholic ethnics, and they tended to be Nixon voters who were conservative on cultural issues but also friendly toward labor unions. In Iowa, Carter had won these voters with his southern evangelical charm and his waffling on abortion. After the media backlash that resulted from that strategy, he could not risk reaching out to social conservatives on abortion again, but he could appeal to them by denouncing Washington and promising to balance the budget and reform the welfare system. He was for "minimum taxes and minimum government," he told voters in New Hampshire, a state that was famous for its fiscal austerity. Several of his television and radio ads focused on his promise to reduce government spending while giving jobs to all Americans. Social conservatives were not necessarily conservative on fiscal issues, but in New Hampshire, Carter found that by running to the right on economics, he could win their votes as well, especially when he brought up welfare reform. "It costs about $80 a week now to support a family that's not employed," Carter said in one of his New Hampshire television ads. "All of that comes out of the pockets of people who are working. And it would only cost about $100 a week to give a young person in that family a full-time, 40-hour a week job at the minimum wage." To New Hampshirites who were struggling with an 8 percent unemployment rate, Carter promised the best of all possible worlds: a New Deal–style guarantee of jobs and a promise of national health insurance, combined with lower taxes for working families, higher taxes on the wealthy, reduced government spending, and a reduction in the welfare rolls.[56] It was an appealing combination for moderately conservative working-class Democrats who did not want to dismantle the social safety net or the progressive tax structure created by President Franklin Roosevelt's administration but who wanted to see a reduction in the size of government and an overhaul of the welfare system.

Repeatedly, Carter emphasized his lack of connection to Washington as evidence that he alone, unlike the congressmen and senators running against him, had the fresh perspective and credentials to cut the fat in government and fix the system. "I think it's time to have a non-lawyer in the White House for a change," Carter proclaimed in one of his New Hampshire television ads, reiterating a message that had worked well for him in Iowa. "Someone that's had to work with his hands; someone who has had to run a complicated business; somebody who has actually had to manage the affairs of a large government as I have in my own state. . . . Right now we need a tough, confident, business-like executive who can actually run the government and get the horrible bureaucracy straightened out for change." Another television ad declared, "Jimmy Carter isn't a professional politician," in a not-so-subtle jab at Bayh's image. "I don't think a lot of our Washington officials understand what it means to work for a living," he observed in another New Hampshire TV spot. Carter was the "working man who wants to be our next President," yet another ad intoned.[57]

In presenting his message of deficit reduction and commonsense, anti-Washington solutions, Carter was greatly helped by the absence of the other center-right candidates in the race. Jackson and Wallace had decided not to compete in New Hampshire, and Bentsen's candidacy had folded. All of Carter's opponents—Udall, Shriver, Bayh, and Harris—were splitting the liberal vote, thus giving Carter a clear field to claim the party centrists and conservatives for himself. And he did. A CBS–*New York Times* poll showed that only 18 percent of the New Hampshire Democrats who had voted for George McGovern in the 1972 general election supported Carter, compared with 32 percent who supported Udall. But the New Hampshire Democrats who had voted for Nixon in 1972 were disproportionately likely to support Carter.[58]

Carter's New Hampshire voters had some of the same concerns and issue positions as the New Hampshire voters who supported Reagan, the CBS–*New York Times* poll found. One-third of the Democrats who said the federal budget should be balanced by cutting social welfare spending supported Carter, while only 10 percent of them voted for Udall. Carter also beat Udall by two to one among voters who opposed détente—an issue position they shared with Reagan voters. Most of Carter's voters perceived him to be a center-right candidate: 37 percent considered him a "conservative," 46 percent believed he was a "moderate," and only 17 percent characterized him as a "liberal."[59] The results were clear: Carter's Democratic voters in New Hampshire were more similar to Reagan voters than they were to the McGovern Democrats who supported Udall or one of the other liberal candidates. If McGovern Democrats had been the only ones voting in the New Hampshire primary, Carter would have lost. And if Carter had had to split the conservative vote with Wallace and Jackson, he might have found it more difficult to forge a winning coalition. But as it was, the New Hampshire Democrats who were angry about welfare spending in Washington and who wanted to see a balanced budget gave Carter their vote, propelling him to victory.

For months, Carter had been raising much of his money from the party's progressives, and he continued to call himself a "progressive southerner," but now that the first votes were coming in, his victories seemed to be generated by the party's moderate conservatives—social conservatives in Iowa and economic and foreign policy conservatives in New Hampshire. Perhaps, as Carter's critics charged, this was because he was vague on the issues (or, in the words of the *New York Times*, "candidly ambiguous"), but perhaps it was because Carter's "outsider" image could unite both liberals and conservatives, who, regardless of their many differences, shared a dislike for President Ford and the status quo.[60] Reorganizing (and even shrinking) the government in Washington was not exclusively a conservative or a liberal position in 1976. Nor was opposition to Henry Kissinger's foreign policy. Because Carter capitalized on a broad swath of popular discontent and promised a fresh approach that was as distinct from Great Society liberalism as it was from the Ford administration's austerity policy, observers could not decide whether his anti-Washington campaign was liberal or conservative.

Carter's rivals in the Democratic race accused him of being a conservative. Before New Hampshire, they had been more likely to charge Carter with vagueness than with conservatism, but now that a moderately conservative coalition had propelled Carter to victory in New Hampshire, they thought that tarring Carter with the conservative label would be the easiest way to discredit him among the party's liberals and progressives, whom they believed constituted the majority of Democrats. Bayh's attacks were the most aggressive. A day after the New Hampshire results were announced, he told a press conference that Carter "stands for the wrong things" and charged that he was "running around the country peddling Republican principles." Carter's refusal to take a firm stand against right-to-work laws and his support for a tight money policy at the Federal Reserve, along with his opposition to breaking up the large oil companies, put him at odds with the mainstream wing of the Democratic Party, Bayh asserted. "I believe in the principles of the Democratic Party and unfortunately Governor Carter has been found wanting [on them]," the Indiana senator declared. Udall criticized Carter's stance on busing. Even Jackson, whose position on some issues—including busing—was more conservative than Carter's but who was a thoroughgoing liberal on economic issues, joined the liberals' criticism of the Georgia governor and charged that Carter's tax and economic policies could lead to the "destruction of the working- and middle-class American family."[61]

Udall proposed that the liberal candidates in the race could stop Carter by agreeing to support whichever of them finished first in the Massachusetts primary. The other three liberal candidates—Bayh, Harris, and Shriver—correctly suspected that this move would benefit Udall, and they refused to go along, since none of them was ready to drop out of the race.[62] But in reality, most of them knew that the Massachusetts primary would be a watershed. For Udall, Massachusetts promised an opportunity to build on the success of his second-place finish in New Hampshire and establish himself as the undisputed liberal challenger to Carter. For Shriver, it was a do-or-die moment; if he could not succeed in Massachusetts, the heart of Kennedy country, he could not do well anywhere. For Bayh, it was a last-ditch effort to right his campaign after a disappointing start in Iowa and New Hampshire. With Bayh's message of center-left economic liberalism and strong support for unions, Massachusetts should have been an ideal state for him. And for Harris, Massachusetts—like all other states—was a bit of a long shot, but if he could not earn a sizable percentage of the progressive vote there, he was unlikely to fare any better elsewhere.

MASSACHUSETTS

Massachusetts had a national reputation as a liberal state. It was the only state that had given its electoral votes to McGovern in 1972, and it was the home of the Kennedys, the nation's most prominent liberal family. But as the cultural conservatives in the Democratic presidential race knew, its progressive reputation was greatly exaggerated. The state was strongly Democratic, but its Democrats included not only McGovern-voting progressives but also many blue-collar, working-class Catholic ethnics who were conservative on abortion and race. Because of rising energy costs, a declining manufacturing base, and severe cutbacks to the defense industries as a result of the downsizing of the military following the Vietnam War, Massachusetts was in the throes of a terrible multiyear recession and had an unemployment rate of 11 percent—3 points higher than the national average. The income tax rate in the state dubbed "Taxachusetts" was so high that it would spark a popular revolt at the ballot box only two years later. And the state was being torn apart by a culture war over court-ordered busing. For two years, working-class Catholics in South Boston, led by Boston school board member Louise Day Hicks, had waged a nationally publicized antibusing campaign, facing off against both African Americans and white suburban liberals. Tensions over the issue were so high that in April 1976—only a month after the state's presidential primary—an antibusing protester in downtown Boston would shock the nation by stabbing an African American lawyer with a flagpole bearing a large American flag. Some were predicting that the former hotbed of abolitionism, a state that had prided itself on its progressive reputation on racial issues for nearly two centuries, might give at least 20 percent of its Democratic primary vote to George Wallace.[63] Wallace himself was salivating over this opportunity. What better way to poke a finger in the eye of his media detractors than to win a primary in Ted Kennedy's home state?

This prospect worried the Carter campaign, which had lost to Wallace once already and did not want to do so again. For months, the leaders of Carter's campaign staff had debated how much effort to invest in Massachusetts. Because Massachusetts was significantly larger, with more delegates to be won, than any other state holding a primary or caucus up to that point, all the candidates considered it a significant prize. It would also be the first state primary to feature all the Democratic candidates seeking the presidential nomination. It thus offered an unusual test of strength that the press considered even more important than New Hampshire. Adding to the pressure, word on the street was that Carter did not have the skills to win the state. It was too large to use the strategy of door-knocking and handshaking that had worked so well in New Hampshire.[64] Instead, Carter would be forced to rely on television advertising and compete against seasoned political veterans such as Henry Jackson and Birch Bayh in the Boston media market.

Carter had repeatedly visited Massachusetts, often scheduling brief forays into the state during his trips to New Hampshire. But as early as September, it was clear that his position in Massachusetts was "slipping." He would probably finish behind Shriver, Udall, Bayh, and Wallace, a campaign field report warned. An all-out effort in Massachusetts would be "an extremely high-risk move," Hutcheson declared, because, with such a crowded field, there was no way that Carter could be assured of victory.[65] Yet a loss in Massachusetts only a week before voters went to the polls in Florida could hurt Carter's chances in the Sunshine State—and Florida had always been his highest, "must-win" priority. It was not that Carter needed to win Massachusetts to clinch the nomination, although he certainly would have liked to claim a substantial share of the state's 104 delegates—a massive number when compared with New Hampshire's paltry 17. Rather, the Carter campaign wondered whether its candidate could weather the negative publicity surrounding a loss in the first state primary featuring all the major candidates.

In the end, the Carter campaign decided to make a "token" effort in the state. Carter would compete in the primary, but campaign staff would tell the press that they were not investing much in the state and expected to lose. This would allow them to shrug off defeat with minimal damage. But while downplaying the state's importance, Carter invested a substantial amount on advertising. During the first three months of 1976, his campaign spent more than four times as much money in Massachusetts as it had in Iowa; most of this money was spent in Boston, where television ads could reach voters in both eastern Massachusetts and southern New Hampshire. Then, only hours after his New Hampshire victory was announced, on a day when his meteoric rise was the subject of front-page headlines across the nation, Carter uncharacteristically threw caution to the wind and publicly predicted that he would "finish first, second, or third" in Massachusetts.[66] But he did not have the support in the state to deliver on such a bold prediction.

As the Carter campaign had feared for months, the Massachusetts primary delivered the worst defeat of the season. Carter finished in fourth place. First-place finisher Henry Jackson came from behind by vastly outspending the other candidates on television advertising and focusing much of his campaign on his opposition to busing. This enabled Jackson to finish on top with 23 percent of the vote. Wallace came in second, with 18 percent. Udall captured much of the liberal vote, which gave him a third-place finish, at 17 percent. Carter came in fourth, with 14 percent, followed by Shriver and Harris, each of whom received 8 percent; Bayh at 5 percent; and McCormack at 3 percent. Bayh's performance was so dismal that he ended his campaign. Perhaps most humiliating of all, in the city of Boston he received only eight votes more than McCormack did.[67]

It was not a good day for liberals in Massachusetts. Forty-one percent of the vote went to the two candidates who had made opposition to busing their signature campaign issue. The top vote-getter in the city of Boston was George Wallace. McCormack, whom no one in the press considered a serious candidate, almost outperformed Bayh, forcing him out of the race; she even managed to come in ahead of Pennsylvania governor Milton Shapp, the first Jewish presidential candidate. Shapp's brief foray into presidential politics was now effectively over. Although Shriver did better in Massachusetts than he had elsewhere, his campaign was over, too. He could not continue after finishing only fifth in the state where he had once expected to achieve his strongest victory.[68]

Just as Carter had been vilified by his rivals as unacceptably conservative immediately after his New Hampshire victory, he now leveled similar charges against Jackson. His own record on busing was hardly pure, but he was quick to attack Jackson for exploiting the issue to win votes. "I'm not in favor of mandatory busing, but to run my campaign in Massachusetts on an antibusing issue is just contrary to my basic nature," he told a press conference in Orlando a day after the Massachusetts primary. "If I have to win by appealing to a basically negative, emotional issue, I don't care to win that way." "I don't think Senator Jackson is a racist," he added. "But he exploited an issue with racist connotations."[69]

Carter had won in Iowa and New Hampshire by appealing to conservative Democrats. Now, in preparation for the Florida primary, he attempted to position himself to Jackson's left and discredit him as a Wallace-like racial populist. Jackson hoped his staunch anticommunism and strong support for Israel would enable him to capture the Jewish and Cuban American vote in Miami, and Carter hoped to prevent that. For months, Carter's campaign had expected Florida to be a critical showdown with Wallace, but now it appeared that Jackson might be a formidable force as well—especially if he ended up dividing the anti-Wallace vote and depriving Carter of a much-needed victory.

FLORIDA

Carter spent more than twice as much money in Florida as he did in any other state primary. Throughout the early weeks of 1976, as some groups of Atlanta campaign volunteers headed north to the frozen streets of New Hampshire, other busloads of volunteers headed south to campaign for Carter in Florida. Defeating Wallace in Florida and thus dealing a mortal blow to his candidacy was the centerpiece of Carter's outreach to liberals. Jordan believed it was the main reason why McGovern's young progressive pollster Patrick Caddell had joined Carter's campaign the previous summer. By early 1976, the prospect of defeating Wallace had become so central to the campaign's goals that fund-raising letters designed for northern Democrats treated it as the raison d'être for the Georgia governor's candidacy; they sometimes said little about Carter's own beliefs or qualifications but devoted extensive coverage to the claim that he alone could destroy Wallace. "I am convinced that with your help he can defeat Wallace in Florida," one Carter fund-raising letter designed for New Yorkers declared. "It is an opportunity to make an invaluable contribution to American Democracy."[70]

Florida presented the perfect venue for the Carter campaign to defeat Wallace because it was still widely considered "Wallace country." The Alabama governor had carried the state in the 1972 Democratic presidential primary, winning 42 percent of the total vote and about 60 percent of the white vote. Much of the state—especially the Panhandle and the Jacksonville area—still identified with the cultural values of the South, and the westernmost tip of Florida even bordered Wallace's home state of Alabama. If Carter could defeat Wallace in Florida, he could credibly claim that he had beaten the governor in his own backyard. But, as Carter's campaign also knew, it would be significantly easier to defeat Wallace in Florida than in Mississippi, where he had already tried and failed. Although much of the state still had a culturally southern orientation, its overall flavor was much more New South than Deep South. It was second only to Arizona as the fastest growing state in the Sun Belt; it had experienced a population growth of nearly 25 percent since 1970, with an increase of one and a half million people in only six years. Like Atlanta, Florida had many white progressives who wanted to transcend their state's history of segregation. Governor Reubin Askew had a progressive record on civil rights and was perhaps the most widely admired of the new generation of racially inclusive, progressive, southern Democratic governors. Carter hoped to capitalize on Askew's popularity by asking Floridians to repudiate Wallace to save their state's reputation and endorse their governor's brand of politics. "It's a matter of who best represents the South," Carter told Florida voters. "Is it George Wallace or is it people like myself and Askew?"[71]

When voters went to the polls on March 9, white Floridians in northern Florida voted for Wallace, transplanted Yankees in southern Florida supported Jackson, but central Florida went decisively for Carter. This was enough to give him a first-place finish, with 35 percent of the vote. Wallace came in second, with 31 percent, and Jackson finished third, with 23 percent. Carter carried an impressive 74 percent of the African American vote, but most of his supporters were white and, on average, a little more conservative on racial issues than Jackson's supporters were—though considerably less racially conservative than Wallace voters. Jackson did especially well among Jewish New Yorkers who had retired and relocated to South Florida; they liked Jackson's unequivocal support for Israel, criticism of détente, and long record of supporting New Deal economic liberalism in the Senate. The Washington senator won the support of 47 percent of voters who had moved to Florida from outside the South and 44 percent of voters over age sixty-five but carried only 18 percent of the native Floridian vote. Carter's core support, by contrast, came from young southerners. He won 42 percent of the votes of people under age thirty and more than 50 percent among voters who had moved to Florida from other parts of the South, many of whom were upwardly economically mobile and politically moderate.[72] For the first time, Carter won a primary race by focusing on the theme that was closest to his true political priorities: redeeming the South from its racist past through a centrist, moderate brand of politics. But Carter knew that to win the nomination, he would have to build a coalition that went far beyond his own region. To become the Democratic nominee, he would have to prove that he could win a large northern industrial state, which was a tall order for a southerner who had never been particularly friendly to organized labor. Three big industrial state primaries were scheduled for April—New York, Wisconsin, and Pennsylvania—but Carter was not a favorite to win any of them.

NEW YORK, WISCONSIN, AND PENNSYLVANIA

Now that Birch Bayh was out of the race and Hubert Humphrey was still not in it, the candidate best situated to win the endorsement of labor unions was Henry Jackson. His decades-long record of support for unions, along with his blend of traditional Democratic liberalism on economic questions and moderate conservatism on cultural issues, made him an appealing choice for many blue-collar workers in the Northeast and Midwest. His foreign policy positions made him popular with many Jewish voters, and he had proved in Massachusetts that he could do very well among working-class Catholics. For that reason, he expected to easily carry New York and Pennsylvania and walk away with a large share of the delegates from those two populous states.[73]

In the fall of 1975 the Carter campaign was optimistic about its chances in New York, which happened to be the state that produced the highest number of direct-mail contributions for Carter in November. With liberal New Yorker Midge Costanza as the state campaign coordinator, the Carter forces focused most of their efforts on upstate, thinking they could cede New York City to the opposition but pick up a lot of support among rural voters, just as they had in Iowa. But with Jackson gaining ground in the state, Carter's chances of pulling off a victory in New York started to slip. By March, his campaign decided to settle for the modest goal of "avoid[ing] embarrassment" by limiting the magnitude of the loss.[74]

Jackson, by contrast, became increasingly confident of a landslide victory in New York as the primary date grew closer. He greatly outspent all the other candidates on television advertising in New York City's expensive media market and made repeated trips upstate in an attempt to expand his reach beyond the city, where he was sure he already had overwhelming support. He would win a majority of the state's delegates, he repeatedly predicted.[75] Udall, meanwhile, was working hard for a second-place finish to pick up some needed delegates and solidify his standing as the liberal alternative to both Carter and Jackson.

Udall beat Carter for second place, and Jackson came in first, as expected. But the Washington senator did not win the majority he had predicted; instead, he carried only 39 percent. With 107 of the 274 delegates, Jackson won a substantial prize. But because he had predicted he would do a lot better, the press treated his decisive victory as a defeat. "Jackson Falls Short of 51% Goal that He Had Predicted," the front-page headline of the *New York Times* read the next day. In contrast, Udall's distant second-place showing, with 25 percent of the vote, was what he "needed" to stay in the race, the *Times* declared. And

Carter's third-place finish, at 12 percent—which was actually lower than the number of uncommitted delegates elected—was not treated as a humiliating loss because Carter had given the impression that he had invested little in the state and was not expecting much.[76] In reality, Carter's team had doggedly campaigned in New York for months, but once it became apparent from polling data that their candidate could not win, they pulled back and left the impression that they had largely bypassed the state.

Carter continued to pick up delegates in contests throughout the South and rural Midwest, but he faced another problem: he could not win a majority of a state's Democratic vote, even when he was the only candidate. In Kansas and Virginia, where he faced only token opposition, he still ran behind the uncommitted delegates, just as he had in Iowa and New York. In some states, including New York, a sizable share of the "uncommitted" delegates were really Humphrey backers who were waiting for him to enter the race. In Virginia, the uncommitted delegation was headed by Lloyd Bentsen supporters, who could not figure out which candidate to support once the Texas senator left the race, but they were sure they did not want Carter.[77]

But if Carter had not yet proved his ability to unite the party, Jackson was even less equipped to do so. Jackson tried to run as a centrist liberal with broad appeal among the working class, but his New York victory was due almost entirely to the state's Jewish voters, who liked his forceful, unequivocal support for Israel. Both Udall and Carter professed strong support for Israel, but unlike Jackson, they also favored the idea of a Jordanian-run Palestinian state. Only two and a half years earlier, Israel had been attacked by a coalition of Arab states in the Yom Kippur War, and although Israel beat back this coalition to win a decisive victory, for many American Jews, the attack served as a reminder of Israel's need for American support. Jackson capitalized on this issue, and he built a winning coalition that was based heavily on Jewish voters, who accounted for more than one-third of New York's Democrats. Sixty-one percent of Jackson voters were Jews, and he carried about two-thirds of the state's Jewish vote and 84 percent of those who listed Israel as an issue of concern. Nearly all the remaining Jewish vote went to Udall, who attracted many younger Jewish supporters based on his liberal ideology. Udall's New York voters—whether Catholic, Protestant, or Jewish—tended to be younger and better educated, just as they were in other states. Jackson's tended to be older and more conservative. But contrary to Jackson's expectations, he was unable to broaden his coalition much beyond the Jewish voters in New York City. In Massachusetts, he had won the votes of working-class Catholics based on his strong opposition to busing. In New York, he tried to project a more liberal image on race, and perhaps as a result, he failed to gain much traction among working-class ethnics, who were slightly more likely to support Carter. Jackson's soft-pedaling of the busing issue may have resulted in fewer political gains than he had expected. It may have helped him among Jewish voters who supported civil rights, but it failed to reassure blacks, who had long been suspicious of him. Although blacks constituted 15 percent of New York's Democratic voters, they accounted for only 7 percent of Jackson's support in the state.[78] Jackson ultimately failed to unify a fractious Democratic coalition in New York. After running as a conservative in Massachusetts, he thought he could win as a moderate who was acceptable to all groups, but in the end, he—like many other Democratic candidates—found that he could not transcend the party's divisions and unite factions whose positions on issues such as busing were diametrically opposed.

Jackson's best hope of winning primaries after New York probably would have been to run on his promise of job creation (in keeping with his stated goal of reducing the unemployment rate to only 1 percent in four years) and his appeal to blue-collar workers, his strongest base of support in both Massachusetts and Wisconsin. Exit polls in multiple states showed that the number-one issue for most Democratic voters was jobs. This should have benefited Jackson, who was now the most traditional New Deal–style economic liberal in the race. But Jackson's awkwardness during campaign stops in working-class neighborhoods limited his appeal among a constituency that should have been his natural base of support. Some of the people who turned out for his speeches walked away remarking about his lack of personability and his "condescending" manner; some even compared him to Richard Nixon. Many found his habit of punctuating his speeches with asynchronous, ill-timed finger jabs in the air a little odd. Others were simply bored. "The day Jackson becomes president, Sominex [a sleep aid] goes out of business," one Cincinnati Democrat declared. And when Jackson campaigned in northern urban ethnic neighborhoods, it was sometimes obvious that he had little familiarity with the voters he was trying to reach. At a campaign stop in an Italian neighborhood in Pittsburgh, for instance, he said "*muchas gracias*" instead of "*grazie mille*."

Even some of Jackson's supporters hoped that Humphrey would get in the race. Jackson may have had the right combination of socially conservative views and New Deal–style economic liberalism, but he never inspired the heartfelt loyalty some of the other candidates enjoyed. And after New York, he was running out of money. Jackson had raised more than any of his rivals, but he had also spent more, running an expensive campaign based on a massive amount of television advertising. He had hoped to economize by restricting his campaign to just a few big-state primaries, but even with that strategy, he had burned through his cash too quickly in an all-out media blitz in Massachusetts and New York. His financial troubles forced him to reduce his efforts in Wisconsin, where he might have done well among union members, but where he was also slipping in the polls, partly because of the unpopularity of his pro-military stance.[79]

Jackson's decision to pull back from Wisconsin—and Humphrey's decision not to enter the primary, even though he was very popular among Wisconsin Democrats—turned that race into a head-to-head contest between Carter and Udall. This suited Carter because he would now have little competition from his right as he tried to pick up the votes of rural residents, urban African Americans, and white industrial workers. His campaign staff was confident that he could use the Wisconsin race to finish off Udall before moving on to a head-to-head race against Jackson in Pennsylvania.[80]

Wisconsin was supposed to be Udall's grand prize—his best chance of proving that he could win a primary. He had had a series of second-place finishes, but to have a chance at winning the nomination, he needed to find a state that would give him a first-place victory. Because his campaign was based on his status as the most viable progressive candidate in the race, his best chance of a first-place finish would likely come in a state with a large contingent of liberal voters. Wisconsin, with its large union base and a left-leaning university town as its capital, seemed to offer a better opportunity than most. Despite dwindling financial resources, Udall outspent Carter in the state because he was desperate for victory. Polls showed that Udall could probably win the race if the turnout was low—that is, limited to the most dedicated Democratic voters, who were most likely to be the McGovernite, college-educated, white progressives to whom Udall most strongly appealed. With a high turnout, the race was projected to go to Carter, who had much stronger support among rural whites, African

Americans, and blue-collar workers. Udall gambled and predicted a first-place finish, which he had never done before. His brother and campaign manager Stewart Udall had been telling Mo since January that Wisconsin was one of a handful of states where he should make an all-out effort for "clear-cut victories." Stewart predicted that if Mo failed to win in Wisconsin, he would "probably" have to end his presidential campaign. Udall knew that everything was on the line in Wisconsin, and he became increasingly critical of Carter's "fudging" on the issues. He told voters that his own campaign was predicated on giving people a "choice" that was not the Georgia governor. "Maybe I owe it to the country to keep this process open until Carter can be examined, until his record can be looked at," he said.[81]

Udall almost made it. The race was so close that, with 62 percent of the precincts counted and Udall ahead by 12,000 votes, ABC and NBC called the race for Udall. Based on early returns, the *Milwaukee Sentinel* ran a headline that declared him the winner. That only made things worse for Udall the next day when the results showed that Carter had won by only 7,000 votes out of 553,000 cast. The front page of the *New York Times* featured a grinning Carter holding up the *Milwaukee Sentinel* and doing his best Harry Truman imitation.[82] Carter had managed to become a "comeback kid" because of the newspaper's mistake. And Udall's best performance of the campaign had given him no better than second place.

Udall's central problem, though, was not bad luck. It was that the Democratic electorate was much less progressive than he imagined. Even in what he assumed would be the nation's most liberal states—Massachusetts, New York, and Vermont—there were large numbers of rural voters who were a little too conservative on social issues to be comfortable with Udall, and there were large numbers of urban union members who saw no reason to support him. He was able to pick up a few endorsements from the most liberal union leaders, but he found it very difficult to win the votes of the union members themselves. And, to his bewilderment, Udall had very little support among blacks. Instead, his votes came from young, college-educated, white suburbanites and residents of college towns. Because of McGovern's disastrous defeat in the previous presidential election, even some of Wisconsin's progressives were reluctant to support Udall, believing that Carter had a better chance of winning the general election.[83] Udall, like McGovern, was widely admired among white progressives for his straight-talking honesty, his early opposition to the Vietnam War, and his consistent record of support for the social causes favored by the left wing of the Democratic Party, but he found it impossible to convince many Democrats that he would fare any better than McGovern in a general election against a Republican president. Democrats did not want a reprise of 1972.

Udall was especially annoyed that Carter—who was more conservative on busing and occasionally veered right on racial issues—consistently won a plurality of the black vote in primary after primary, while he never got more than a minuscule percentage. By March, Udall's campaign had made outreach to minorities—both blacks and Hispanics—a priority. He said he was considering a black running mate, and he expressed strong support for the Humphrey-Hawkins bill, the jobs-creation legislation that he saw as the key to economic progress for black communities and that Carter still refused to support.[84] But Carter, with his evangelical faith and southern roots, seemed to have a natural rapport with blacks that Udall lacked.

The Carter campaign realized early on that Udall was unable to speak the language of anyone except white-collar, college-educated liberals, and it strategized accordingly. When Carter's staff acquired one of Udall's fund-raising letters, they were almost exuberant about its narrow focus on environmentalism, a cause that appealed primarily to young white progressives from college towns and the suburbs. Udall's framing of the issue did little to broaden its range of support. Instead of talking about how the location of pollution-spewing plants disproportionately affected poor and minority neighborhoods, he decried "conspicuous consumption" and the "rape" of "the land and our environment to satisfy unlimited greed and desire for luxury." "No longer can we as a nation afford the energy waste of gas-guzzling automobiles and meaningless mobility," he wrote. This might have played well among graduate students in Madison, but not among factory workers in Milwaukee, whether white or black. "This is an excellent mailer *if* it goes *only* to upper-income, white libs," one Carter campaign adviser gleefully noted to Jordan. "Otherwise, it's a waste."[85]

Udall, like Jackson, struck audiences as awkward and stiff. In private settings he was a witty, jocular person at ease in casual attire, but on the campaign trail, his effort to project a sense of presidential gravitas came across as "aloof, reserved, somewhat distant, and formal," one campaign adviser told him. By late March, he had little time to make a course correction, but the adviser made some suggestions. "Avoid wearing three-piece suits except for formal speaking appearances," he counseled. "In street campaigning, take off your jacket (and on warm days loosen your tie). During speeches and plant gate stand-ups, keep your hands out of your pockets." Udall should wade into crowds to shake people's hands, he advised, instead of quickly leaving speaking events without giving people a chance to meet the candidate in person. "Engage people in animated discussion" at campaign dinners, "and even have a beer or take a chicken-wing in hand." "Please try to convey more emotion to black audiences in particular," he concluded. But when Udall tried to loosen up in public, the result was a little bizarre. His campaign released a sixty-second radio commercial of Udall telling a long, rambling joke about a three hundred–pound woman stuck in a church with the devil. "Mo can claim authorship of most of the Wisconsin media [material] himself," Udall's media consultant told the campaign. "With that authorship, however, he must claim responsibility for alienating the 300-pound Fat Lady League." Udall's other radio spots were equally informal but tightly focused on his theme of economic progressivism as the key to job growth. With plenty of attacks on "giant conglomerates," he positioned himself as a trustbuster in the progressive tradition. For a narrow strand of the college-educated electorate, this droll, self-deprecating approach, along with a strong dose of economic populism, seemed to work. But like Eugene McCarthy eight years earlier, Udall was discovering the limits of being an introverted, cerebral liberal on the campaign trail. Carter, Udall's adviser noted, seemed to have no trouble working the crowds, and he was getting better press coverage (and more votes) as a result.[86]

Carter's ability to talk to African Americans and blue-collar workers would receive its greatest test in Pennsylvania, where he would face off against Jackson. With the exception of his narrow victory in Wisconsin—where Jackson had not been a factor—Carter had not yet won a major northern industrial state, and he had finished far behind Jackson in both Massachusetts and New York. Jackson argued that because Carter could not win in the industrial, unionized North he was not qualified to be the nominee. Pennsylvania would be the greatest test of Carter's ability to win the votes of union workers and northern Catholics. If he could defeat Jackson in the heart of northern steel country, he would undermine the central rationale for Jackson's campaign and drive him out of the race, thus almost assuring Carter's nomination.

Polls in March showed Carter running behind Jackson in Pennsylvania. To close the gap, Carter needed a substantial share of the 15 percent of the vote that would come from African Americans. The black vote would be his "greatest edge" in Pennsylvania, Patrick Caddell told Carter in late March.[87]

Only two weeks after Carter received the memo from Caddell, he inadvertently put his expected share of the black vote in grave jeopardy at a press conference in Indiana. The controversy originated with an interview by the *New York Daily News* and a question about where subsidized housing units should be constructed. Carter said they should not be constructed in white neighborhoods that did not want them. "I see nothing wrong with ethnic purity being maintained," Carter told the reporter. "I would not force racial integration of a neighborhood by government action." After the interview was published, reporters at the Indiana press conference seized on the opportunity to press Carter to explain his views, but Carter's clumsy attempt at explanation only made matters worse. "I have nothing against a community that's made up of people who are Polish or Czechoslovakian or French-Canadian, or blacks who are trying to maintain the ethnic purity of their neighborhoods," he said. "This is a natural inclination on the part of people. . . . I see nothing wrong with that as long as it's done freely." He added, "I don't think government ought to deliberately break down an ethnically oriented community, deliberately, by injecting into it a member of another race. That's contrary to the interest of the community. It creates disharmony, it creates hatred, it creates an attitude of unwarranted federal intrusion." "I'm not going to use the Federal Government's authority to circumvent the natural inclination of people to live in ethnically homogenous neighborhoods," he promised.[88]

Carter insisted that he had long supported open housing laws because he believed that people had the right to live wherever they wanted, regardless of race. The government should give people the legal support they needed to move into the neighborhoods of their choice, but it should not deliberately try to change the racial or ethnic composition of a neighborhood by interfering with people's free choice.[89]

In voicing these concerns, Carter appeared to be taking a more conservative position than that reflected by existing housing law. The 1968 Fair Housing Act and the 1974 Housing and Community Development Act prohibited the government from constructing public housing in areas of "minority concentration," except under certain conditions. In other words, federal legislation required public housing to be located in majority-white neighborhoods to encourage integration, although the law also allowed communities to circumvent this requirement if they could demonstrate "overriding housing needs which cannot otherwise be feasibly met"—a loophole that, in practice, had proved large enough to accommodate the desires of communities that preferred not to risk the resentment of the white middle class by constructing public housing units next door.[90] Carter seemed ready to end even this token attempt at affirmative action in housing by abandoning the goal of forced racial integration altogether and suggesting that there was nothing wrong with locating public housing units in low-income, majority-black neighborhoods.

Carter immediately faced a barrage of criticism from his two opponents in the race, as well as from African American leaders and the mainstream press. "He can't have it both ways, preaching 'ethnic purity' and voluntary busing on the white side of town and soul brother on the black side of town," Udall said. But most of Udall's criticism was not directed against the substance of Carter's remarks because, despite his progressive reputation, even Udall was unwilling to defend an affirmative action program in public housing that was extremely unpopular with most voters, including some African Americans. While insisting that he strongly favored open housing—as Carter did—he added, "I do not believe that act [the 1974 Housing and Community Development Act] intends that the Federal Government should go out and bust up a neighborhood to build public housing."[91]

Instead, Carter's opponents denounced his language, especially his use of the term "ethnic purity." "It's not Jimmy Carter's technical position that I question," Udall said. "That is sound and good. But what he has been saying says something about inner attitudes that I find alarming." Carter had not realized how offensive the term "ethnic purity" might be. Even one of his own campaign advisers, Andrew Young, considered it so objectionable that he threatened to withhold his support. "I just think it's an awful phrase," Young said. "I don't think he understood how loaded it is with Hitlerian connotations." Carter's use of the phrase would alienate both blacks and white liberals, Young predicted. "A lot of people who said 'You just can't trust a Southerner' are going to say, 'See, I told you so.'"[92]

Other African American leaders also rebuked Carter. Civil rights veteran Hosea Williams called him a "sophisticated racist." *Philadelphia*

Daily News columnist Chuck Stone labeled Carter a "phony" and said that after winning the black vote in several primaries, he had "quickly moved to reassure white American he was still their 'good ol' boy' and called for a new kind of segregation by homogeneity." Atlanta mayor Maynard Jackson, who had reportedly planned to endorse Carter, backed off and said that he wanted to monitor Carter's response.[93]

Carter was at first defensive. He admitted to an "unfortunate choice of words" but also accused the press of creating a "straw man" by aggressively questioning him on the subject and implying that he might have been fishing for racist votes. But as the damage to his candidacy mounted, he realized that he needed to do something more drastic to put the issue behind him. He sent a written apology to Vernon Jordan, president of the National Urban League, and promised to "support a requirement for affirmative action plans within newly constructed federal funded housing." He met with the Congressional Black Caucus and pledged his support for the Humphrey-Hawkins bill, which he had criticized in a press release only a week earlier. His campaign administrators made it a goal to hire more blacks. Carter also made amends with black civil rights leaders in Atlanta who had been his longtime supporters, and most of them accepted the olive branch. At a rally of black leaders in Atlanta, one of his most loyal supporters, Martin Luther King Sr., clasped Carter's hand and declared, "I have a forgiving heart, so I'm with you all the way."[94]

Some of the African Americans who made peace with Carter did so not because they considered Carter's comments excusable but because they were convinced that the white northern liberals who had charged Carter with double-talk were no better. D. F. Glover, a professor at Atlanta's Morris Brown College, wrote, "Let those who support or aspire to support Morris Udall remind him that he, too, has reflected a white supremacist trend of thought. . . . In my opinion one who is wrong must first admit that he is wrong before he can be expected to do that which is right. Indeed, this may be the difference between a southern moderate and a northern liberal."[95]

African Americans appeared to be in a much worse position in 1976 than they had been in 1972, when the nation's first black major-party presidential candidate, Shirley Chisholm, won 152 delegates and more blacks than ever participated in the Democratic primaries. In 1976 there were no black presidential candidates and, in the midst of the nation's economic recession, there was a noticeable white backlash against the civil rights gains of the previous decade, even within the Democratic Party. Forty percent of Democratic voters in six early-primary states (five of which were in the North) believed that the government "pays too much attention to the needs of minorities." The backlash against federal assistance for African Americans and the widespread white opposition to government measures to guarantee school integration and educational equality for blacks could not have come at a worse time because the burden of the economic downturn of the mid-1970s fell disproportionately on blacks and put an end to the short-lived socioeconomic mobility some of them had experienced in the late 1960s. Black family income had been declining for five years, and it now stood at only 56 percent of white family income. "Black America is in a state of crisis," the National Urban League declared.[96]

National Urban League president Vernon Jordan encouraged blacks to go to the polls to protect their rights. The 1976 presidential contest "could be the most crucial election in recent history for black people," he declared. "The implications of the mass impoverishment of blacks and the massive assault on our newly-won rights demands that every black vote be mobilized in defense of black interests and aspirations." But many blacks were disillusioned with presidential politics and believed the Democratic Party took their votes for granted. The Democrats' official response to President Ford's State of the Union address in January 1976 did not mention blacks once—even though blacks were 25 percent of Democratic voters. And the Republican Party was even worse, most blacks believed, because Ford's cost-cutting measures and his decision to prioritize fighting inflation over reducing unemployment had made their economic situation even more precarious. In a survey of black elected officials taken in the spring of 1976, fewer than 3 percent said they wanted to elect Ford to another term in office. Most were not particularly happy with Carter either. Only 8 percent listed him as their first choice for president—compared with 40 percent who listed Hubert Humphrey.[97]

Throughout Carter's campaign in Pennsylvania, he faced an uphill battle against the noncandidate Humphrey, whether from blacks or working-class whites. At a labor convention in Pittsburgh, his first campaign stop in the state after his arrival from Wisconsin, he was met by shouts of "We want Humphrey." Even worse, numerous articles about a "draft Humphrey" effort began to appear in the press. Two midwestern congressmen—Paul Simon of Illinois and Bob Bergland of

Minnesota—began a campaign to draft Humphrey by recruiting support for him among the uncommitted delegates at the convention. The movement quickly gained ground, especially among Democratic leaders in Congress who respected Humphrey but considered Carter an unreliable unknown. House majority leader Thomas P. "Tip" O'Neill said he would prefer Humphrey to any of the declared candidates. Humphrey, for his part, seemed open to the idea. He declared publicly that he did not believe that Carter would receive the 1,505 delegates needed to clinch the nomination before the convention (he had only 241 on April 8, the day after the Wisconsin primary), and if the former Georgia governor's delegate total fell short, Humphrey would be happy to accept the nomination by acclamation.[98]

In the end, Carter defeated Jackson in Pennsylvania, but only because Humphrey was not on the ballot. Carter ended up with 37 percent of the vote, compared with Jackson's 25 percent. Udall, whose campaign was so strapped for cash that he had to remove the phones in some of his offices in Pennsylvania, still managed to finish with 19 percent of the vote, nearly all of which came from white liberals in the Philadelphia suburbs. Wallace, who had not yet left the race despite a string of defeats, took 11 percent. Carter received 44 percent of the black vote, which accounted for 7 percent of the total in the state. He proved that he could make a comeback among black voters and that he could defeat Jackson in one of the most heavily unionized industrial states in the North. All his declared rivals were now either out of the race or severely weakened. He was the unquestioned front-runner for the nomination. But there was one worrying note: a *Washington Post* poll showed that if Humphrey had been on the ballot in Pennsylvania, he would have beaten Carter by two to one, and Carter's share of the vote would have been reduced to 22 percent. Other polls revealed that Humphrey could have carried Wisconsin and New York if he had been on the ballots there.[99]

With Humphrey's status rising among Democrats, the question was not merely whether Carter could drive Jackson and Udall out of the race; it was whether he could win enough delegates to stave off an open convention, where Humphrey was highly likely to be nominated. "My feeling is that unless we can put together a first ballot victory or damn close to it, this party will deny us the nomination," Caddell told Carter. "Popular with the elites, we are not."[100]

Winning the 1,505 delegates required for the nomination would be a formidable task because all the Democratic presidential primaries allocated delegates proportionately—which meant that Udall and Jackson could continue to chip away and pick up additional delegates, even if they failed to place first in a single additional state. Despite a string of first-place finishes, Carter had rarely won a majority in any state primary, and as a result, his delegate count in mid-April amounted to only 26 percent of the total number of delegates awarded up to that time. The other candidates, along with the perennially popular "uncommitted," had combined to take nearly three-quarters of the delegates under the proportional allocation system.[101] And just when it looked like Carter might have cleared a path to win all the remaining primaries and collect the requisite 1,505 delegates by the narrowest of margins, two new candidates declared their intention to enter the presidential race: Senator Frank Church of Idaho and Governor Edmund G. "Jerry" Brown Jr. of California. Both were liberals who wanted to make sure that a centrist like Carter did not get the nomination. Carter would now have to write off most of California's delegates and those in several other western states as well. His front-runner status was not as secure as it seemed.

6

FORD VERSUS REAGAN

President Gerald Ford's State of the Union address in January 1976 focused on the one theme he had selected as the guiding principle for his reelection campaign: responsible fiscal conservatism as the only way to stop inflation and create jobs. "The Government must stop spending so much and stop borrowing so much of our money," he declared. "To hold down the cost of living, we must hold down the cost of government." For many, Ford was the symbol of the Washington establishment, but he adopted an anti-Washington posture by positioning himself as the enemy of excessive government spending, arguing that he was using his proposed budgets and his veto pen to bring down the cost of government. While all the Democratic candidates were proposing federal jobs-creation programs, Ford believed that the only way to achieve economic recovery was to first get inflation under control by reducing the growth of the federal deficit and then create jobs in a stable economy not through public programs but through tax cuts that would stimulate private industry. His goal was to promote free enterprise and reduce the burden of government in Americans' lives. "We must introduce a new balance in the relationship between the individual and the government," he said, "a balance that favors greater individual freedom and self-reliance."[1]

If this message sounded a lot like Reagan's, that was no coincidence. The Ford campaign believed that the president was just as fiscally conservative as Reagan (if not more so) and that there was no substantive ideological difference between the two candidates. If

Figure 6.1. President Gerald Ford at his desk in the Oval Office. (Courtesy of Gerald R. Ford Presidential Library)

Republicans wanted fiscal conservatism, they should cast their primary election ballots for the president, who had cut the inflation rate in half during his brief time in the White House and was using his political leverage to limit the rate of growth in federal spending. "Quietly and firmly, he is leading us out of the worst recession in years," one Ford television commercial designed for the New Hampshire primary proclaimed. "Rather than loose promises or frantic spending, he has had the courage to say no. He has made the hard decisions." The Ford campaign's plan to win a tough reelection fight was simple: Convince Republican voters that Ford was a proven, responsible champion for fiscal conservatism, while Reagan was not. Then, after defeating Reagan in the early primaries and driving him out of the race, the campaign would persuade voters that the president's Democratic opponent—who was still expected to be Humphrey rather than Carter—was a big-spending liberal whose programs would drive up the deficit and increase inflation, whereas the Republican plan offered a responsible path to economic growth.[2]

The polls in January were not promising: they showed that the contest between Ford and Reagan was a toss-up. Ford's public approval rating had been below 50 percent for months. The unemployment rate was 8 percent nationally and even higher in New England, where the nation's presidential primary contests would begin. With the worst economy in nearly forty years and with his own party divided, Ford faced severe handicaps that were not helped by his poor speaking skills. He "appears to be on weaker footing than any incumbent Presidential candidate since William Howard Taft in 1912," the *New York Times* concluded. Reagan, by contrast, was a master rhetorician and wildly popular on the campaign trail. He was running on his record of a successful, conservative, welfare-cutting gubernatorial administration in California, and he promised a rapid economic turnaround for the nation with his proposal for a massive tax cut and a balanced budget. Reagan enjoyed very strong support in the South and West, and he had a large following in New Hampshire as well.[3]

Both the Reagan and Ford campaigns pinned their hopes on two key early contests: New Hampshire and Florida. Just as Carter believed these two states were must-wins in the Democratic primaries, the two Republican candidates treated these contests as make-or-break efforts for their campaigns. Both Reagan and Ford believed they had a good chance of winning both states. New Hampshire, which was the most libertarian-minded, fiscally conservative state in the East, seemed to be filled with the type of Republicans who would welcome the California governor's anti-Washington message. He also had the support of much of the state's Republican leadership. Governor Mel Thomson, who was very conservative, endorsed Reagan's candidacy, and former governor Hugh Gregg was chairing Reagan's campaign in the state. Reagan also had the support of the state's largest newspaper, the arch-conservative *Manchester Union Leader*. Reagan thought he had good reason to be optimistic about Florida as well, where he was counting on strong support from anticommunist Cuban Americans who thought the Ford administration's policy toward the Soviet Union was too soft.[4] But Ford had better prospects in both states than Reagan's advisers realized because Ford's team was shrewd enough to capitalize on a critical mistake Reagan made in his campaign speeches.

NEW HAMPSHIRE

Reagan's troubles in New Hampshire stemmed from his promise to radically trim the size of the federal budget and give greater decision-making powers to the states—a stance he assumed would appeal to Republicans in the state. If, like Carter, he had simply promised to trim the deficit without saying too much about the size or nature of his proposed cuts, he might have avoided trouble. Instead, he made the mistake of saying that he would trim $90 billion from the federal budget by slashing social programs and returning the responsibility for those programs to the states, a move that he called "creative federalism for America's third century." At the time, this represented a 25 percent reduction in the total federal budget, which would have been more than enough to reduce the budget deficit to zero. But the question was: what would it cost the states to pick up the tab for these social welfare programs, and would state taxpayers be willing to fund them at the local level? This was the question Reagan faced in New Hampshire, which had no state income tax or sales tax.[5]

The plan to balance the budget and reduce federal tax rates by transferring $90 billion of federal social welfare spending to the states was the brainchild of Jeff Bell, a thirty-one-year-old researcher in the Reagan campaign and a conservative ideologue. In the summer of 1975 Bell proposed the plan to some of Reagan's other advisers and to the candidate himself, and they accepted it as a brilliant proposal. Conservative journalist M. Stanton Evans—an editor of *Human Events* (Reagan's favorite magazine), chairman of the American Conservative Union, and an adviser to Reagan's campaign—then incorporated the idea in a speech he wrote for Reagan to give in late September at a meeting of Chicago business executives.[6]

At first, the proposal attracted little scrutiny from the media, but as soon as Reagan made his first trip to New Hampshire as an officially declared presidential candidate in late November, he faced questions about the plan from the local media. His responses were vague. "The states and local governments would undoubtedly have to raise some of their taxes," he said, but taxpayers would probably still save money because there would be a reduction in federal taxes and the states would likely discontinue some of the social welfare programs or administer them far more efficiently and inexpensively than the federal government could. This response reflected Reagan's deep skepticism of the federal bureaucracy and his optimistic view of local control, but it did not satisfy the many New Hampshirites who worried about having to pay income tax or sales tax for the first time. ABC correspondent Bob Clark pressed Reagan on this question a week later on his Sunday morning program *Issues and Answers* and asked him directly whether his proposal would force New Hampshire to levy an income or sales tax. "But isn't this a proper decision for the state to make?" Reagan responded, implying that it was a local matter and therefore not his concern.[7]

Several leading Republican officeholders in New Hampshire expressed concern about Reagan's refusal to take responsibility for his proposal's potential impact on state taxpayers. "I was completely taken by surprise by your presentation on ABC's *Issues and Answers,*" Republican state senate president Alf Jacobson wrote to Reagan. "Bearing in mind that your principal supporters in this state . . . are pledged to a no new tax stand for the State, I find great difficulty in understanding how such a scheme would work satisfactorily in New Hampshire."[8]

Human Events continued to champion the $90 billion plan as "sound in principle" and "politically salable," but mainstream news outlets panned it. The *Washington Post* repeatedly published articles critiquing the plan. Ninety billion dollars, the *Post* pointed out, represented half of all the government's discretionary non-defense-related spending, and if these drastic cuts were made—including cuts to revenue sharing and Medicaid—state governments would be severely burdened. There simply was not enough money in the system to do what Reagan proposed without drastically raising taxes at the local level or forcing massive cuts in social services. And because the effects of Reagan's proposal would be felt most acutely in tax-free New Hampshire, this issue threatened to derail Reagan's campaign in that state, much to the delight of President Ford, who was happy to join the fray with his own criticisms. Ford had proposed $28 billion in federal spending cuts, but cutting the budget by $90 billion and transferring those programs to the states was "totally impractical," he said. "I can't imagine 50 states having all of these programs dumped on them and then having to increase taxes if they want the programs continued."[9]

The Reagan campaign moved quickly to contain the political damage. Pete Hannaford encouraged Reagan to clarify exactly which government programs would be cut from the federal budget and turned over to the states. Reagan should explain to reporters that he was not planning to eliminate Social Security and transfer it to state governments, Hannaford said, but he should propose specific transfers in the areas of education, transportation, welfare, food stamps, law enforcement, and revenue sharing. This list hardly assured Reagan's critics; in fact, it only confirmed their suspicion that Reagan was proposing to create a massive new mandate and tax burden for the states while cutting any federal assistance for carrying out these programs. Hanaford encouraged Reagan to respond to his critics by emphasizing the vast potential for economic growth and cost savings when the federal budget was balanced, federal taxes were cut, and social programs were either eliminated or administered more effectively at the local level, and Reagan did so.[10]

But as criticism of the plan continued to escalate, Reagan also began to back away from it. By mid-December, he was telling the press that implementation would be very gradual, thus giving state governments plenty of time to negotiate the details of the transfer with the federal government and find alternative revenue sources. In late January he renounced the precise financial details of the plan he had previously publicized. "I simply announced a broad program last September," he told the *Los Angeles Times*. "I made no pretense of fleshing it out." The list of specific programs that would be cut, he said, were merely "some stuff the economists gave me. I didn't even agree with all the stuff on that list." To nationally syndicated columnist Garry Wills, this episode only confirmed that "it is unfair to expect accuracy or depth from him." He was dismayed at the number of times Reagan got his facts wrong. "Reagan seems destined to keep playing second lead, even to a bungler like Ford," Wills wrote. It appeared that many voters shared that view. The Reagan campaign's own polling in December showed Reagan ahead of Ford among New Hampshire Republican voters by 8 percentage points—46 percent to 38 percent. But as Reagan continued to experience political fallout over his $90 billion transfer plan, his poll numbers in New Hampshire started to drop. By February 18—six days before the primary—the Reagan campaign's internal polling showed that Reagan's advantage over Ford had shrunk to "a whisper of a lead" that was within the poll's margin of error. It would "be folly to project a winner," the polling report stated.[11]

In the weeks leading up to the New Hampshire vote, the Ford campaign expressed cautious optimism in private but publicly downplayed expectations, realizing that Reagan could still carry the state, despite his gaffes. Ford's team left nothing to chance. Ford had entered the race as the underdog, and his campaign worked hard to close the polling gap in New Hampshire not only by hammering away at the implications of Reagan's $90 billion transfer plan but also by raising questions about Reagan's purported economic miracle in California. Both taxes and the size of government had increased in California during Reagan's two terms as governor, the Ford campaign charged. The Reagan campaign strenuously denied the assumptions used to make these calculations and aggressively pushed back against these assertions.[12]

In reality, Reagan's gubernatorial record was so complex that it was difficult for voters to sort through the competing fact claims. California's economy had done well, and its population had increased. Reagan had indeed balanced California's budget, as he claimed, but only by pushing through the largest income and sales tax increase in the state's history, although much of this tax increase was later offset by a reduction in property taxes. Reagan had doubled education spending—which meant that he was not as much of a conservative budget hawk as some believed—but he had also reduced welfare spending (a fact his campaign regularly highlighted), with a net decrease of nearly 400,000 people from the welfare rolls. In calling for welfare reform, Reagan could thus cite what no other presidential candidate could: proof that he had radically overhauled the welfare system. The Ford campaign was correct to point out that the size of government, along with government spending, continued to increase in California during Reagan's tenure, but Reagan could plausibly claim that, given the state's rapid population growth, the national recession, and high inflation, the increase in taxes and spending on his watch had been less than one might have expected. Reagan was a "pragmatist," not a conservative revolutionary, in his governance of California, so the use of his record as proof that conservative principles worked was perhaps a little misleading. Nevertheless, Bo Callaway almost certainly went too far in asserting that Reagan had a "poor" record as governor. By most measures, the state did reasonably well during Reagan's time in office, with continuous population growth and an unemployment rate that mirrored that of the nation. But the Ford campaign was correct to hammer away at the inconsistency between Reagan's inflated rhetoric about tax cutting and budget balancing and his actual policies. In this, the Ford team was privy to some inside information because Stu Spencer, one of the principal strategists behind Reagan's successful gubernatorial bid in 1966, had turned against his former boss and was now Ford's national campaign director. Spencer had nothing but derisive comments about the man he had helped elect ten years earlier. "He was a nine-to-five governor," Spencer said.[13]

Polls showed that Reagan's greatest weakness among New Hampshire Republicans was the perception that he was just an actor, while

Ford's greatest liability was the perception that he was a weak leader. The Ford campaign therefore did everything possible to capitalize on voters' impression that Reagan might be merely an empty suit, while working hard to showcase Ford as a decisive president. One campaign brochure designed for New Hampshire featured the president saying, "I can't use rhetoric as a solution. I have to deal with reality. . . . Someone who's running for office can use words to express how he's going to meet a problem, whether it's domestic or foreign, and that sometimes is totally unreal, when you have to deal with the actual problems that come into this desk." The image of the president at his desk was especially powerful, Callaway realized, and the campaign took full advantage of it. To improve the president's standing, Callaway advised that televised interviews with Ford should take place in the Oval Office, where he could be shown in full work mode, engaged with the problems of the nation. There were already enough pictures of Ford in golf shirts and in informal settings with his family. At the beginning of his presidency, he had been willing to be photographed in his pajamas and bathrobe, but now it was time to project an image of presidential gravitas, which meant dark suits, serious expressions, and a strategically placed pen or pipe in photos of the president. Voters already found Ford personable, and they liked him as an individual, but to win, Ford would have to convince voters that he was "a strong and decisive leader" and that he was succeeding in his agenda. Accordingly, in New Hampshire nearly all of Ford's television and radio advertising focused on his record of accomplishment. Ford had taken a weak economy and made it stronger, the ads asserted: "Because he stood fast, inflation has been cut in half." But despite all this advertising, some voters remained skeptical. Eighteen percent of the people in a focus group that watched the president's "Accomplishment" ad found it impossible to believe that the economy had improved as much as the Ford campaign claimed. The campaign's internal polling showed the president's approval rating slipping in early February because voters did not believe his claim that he had restored jobs.[14]

For those who were skeptical about Ford's insistence that the economy was improving and that he was working to slow the growth of government, Reagan's optimistic promise to "return government to the people" by balancing the budget, ending inflation, reducing the welfare rolls, and creating an energy-independent, prosperous America had a lot of appeal. The Ford campaign's claim that the president was doing an excellent job demonstrated establishment Republicans' willingness to settle for too little. Reagan encouraged the people of New Hampshire to take a daring step and "make those decisions which will restore confidence in our way of life and release that energy that is the American spirit." "The history of our civilization is a gallant chronicle of the optimists, the determined people, men and women who dreamed great dreams and dared to try to make them come true," he said. It was classic Reagan oratory—the promise of a better nation than any of the centrist Republicans imagined. It was strikingly similar to Carter's promises, but delivered in a more stirring rendition. Throughout the New Hampshire campaign, Reagan insisted that he and Ford agreed on the basic principle of reducing the size of government and cutting deficit spending, but Ford was part of the "Washington establishment" and incapable of making the "hard decisions" required to accomplish that. Ford had proposed a budget deficit of $60 billion—which was less than congressional Democrats' proposed budget but still far too high, in Reagan's opinion. Reagan promised much more immediate results: more drastic budget-cutting measures, more decision-making power returned to the states, larger tax cuts to stimulate the economy and create jobs, a much stronger military, and a tougher line toward the Soviet Union.[15] All these proposals targeted Ford's greatest weakness: the widespread perception that he lacked the qualities of a firm, decisive leader.

In the end, the race came down to whether voters wanted to make the safe choice and stick with Ford or take a risk and bet on Reagan. Not surprisingly, perhaps, Ford's strongest support came from retirees, a largely risk-averse group. The campaign's internal analysis identified Republican voters over the age of sixty as Ford's strongest base of support, so the campaign targeted these voters with ads that highlighted Ford as the safe, responsible choice. It was a "time for facts, not vague promises," one of these ads declared. "President Ford sees the world as it really is." Ford was "promising them no more than we can deliver, and delivering all that we promise." The technique worked: New Hampshire Republican primary voters who were sixty-five or older preferred Ford over Reagan by 61 to 39 percent. Ford also did exceptionally well among college-educated and more affluent Republicans. While those with only a high school diploma chose Reagan over Ford by 58 to 42 percent, college graduates supported Ford over Reagan by a two-to-one margin. Ford also carried the youth vote but lost voters aged forty-five to fifty-four by 39 to 61 percent—a mirror image of the preferences of those over age sixty-five. The Republicans who were most economically secure or most fearful of radical change voted for Ford, while those who were more economically marginalized were willing to take a risk and vote for Reagan. Ford won the votes of those earning more than $15,000 a year (roughly $70,000 in 2018 dollars) but lost among voters with lower salaries. In a pattern that would be repeated in numerous other states, Reagan won the votes of Democrats and independents who had crossed over to vote in the Republican primary, while Ford won a solid 54 percent majority of registered Republicans. Eighty-three percent of Ford voters chose him because he had "done a good job," with 74 percent also citing his experience as an "important" factor. The most important factor for Reagan voters was his record as governor of California (cited by 84 percent of voters)—not necessarily his conservative ideology (cited by only 62 percent).[16] In short, Reagan won among blue-collar, middle-aged New Hampshirites who were struggling economically and believed the California governor's promises. Ford carried the votes of traditional, middle-class, older Republicans who were risk averse. Ford's unexpectedly strong showing among this group allowed him to eke out a narrow victory.

Reagan's lead had been falling continuously since December, but right up until primary day, polls had showed him still slightly ahead of Ford. The voters who made their final decision that morning went for Ford by a two-to-one margin, leading to his slim victory. Reagan was so confident that he had left New Hampshire two days before the vote to campaign in Illinois. Now he had to deal with the shock of a narrow loss. Because some members of his campaign had been predicting victory, his defeat—even though it was a near win—was portrayed in the media as a severe reversal of fortunes.[17] Ford was now back in the game, and Reagan was on the defensive.

FLORIDA

Reagan thought he could win in Florida by highlighting his strong opposition to communism and his allegations that the Ford administration's policy of détente had made too many concessions to the Soviet Union, which he thought would enable him to sweep the Cuban American vote. Although foreign policy issues had always been part of his campaign, Reagan's speeches in other states focused on fiscal issues. In Florida, he doubled down on his foreign policy message and gave increased attention to another issue he had briefly mentioned but rarely discussed at length: his charge that the Ford administration was preparing to give away the Panama Canal. US control of the Panama Canal was vital for the "defense of the Western hemisphere," Reagan said, but Henry Kissinger had acquiesced to Panamanian demands and entered into preliminary negotiations to return the canal to Panamanian oversight, seemingly (in Reagan's view) with no regard for Cold War strategic concerns. "What in the world are we doing—negotiating a giveaway of the Canal to a Marxist, military dictator who seized power eight years ago by means of a coup?" Reagan asked in a speech in Miami.[18]

In reality, the Panama Canal had never been American territory, and Ford and Kissinger were not the first American officials to engage in diplomatic negotiations with Panama over the return of operational rights to it. Many Americans, including Reagan, overlooked these facts. Reagan was simply wrong when he said that the Canal Zone was "sovereign U.S. Territory every bit the same as Alaska and all the states that were carved from the Louisiana Purchase." But for decades, the United States had treated the Canal Zone as if it were American territory. A 1903 treaty gave the United States the right to build the canal and control the Canal Zone "in perpetuity," so the US government generally ignored Panamanian protests against American control. But after the Panamanian government demanded greater sovereignty over the canal, President Lyndon Johnson began the process of negotiating a new treaty that would set a timeline for the end of US control, and Kissinger continued that project as President Richard Nixon's secretary of state. Under the Ford administration, the negotiation process accelerated. Although Ford publicly insisted that "the United States will keep control over the Panama Canal as long as it is essential," the administration continued its dialogue with the Panamanian government, and Ford privately signaled that he would agree to give up American control of the canal as long as it was not scheduled to occur for at least twenty-five years. Even this moderate concession aroused the ire of some conservative activists. M. Stanton Evans filled the pages of *Human Events* with articles such as the one titled "Giving up in Panama" in 1975, and Senator Jesse Helms of North Carolina lambasted Ford on the issue as well.[19]

Reagan, a regular reader of *Human Events* and an ally of Helms, echoed the critique of the Ford administration's Panama Canal policy from the moment he announced his candidacy in November, but because his campaign's message was focused on fiscal issues and welfare reform, the Panama Canal did not become a regular part of his stump speech until the Florida campaign. When Reagan started campaigning in Florida, he pivoted to a foreign policy theme and used the Panama Canal as a symbol of everything wrong with Ford and Kissinger's foreign policy. He called for Kissinger's removal as secretary of state and demanded an end to negotiations with Panama over the canal. "We paid for it, we built it and it is ours," he said. "We intend to keep it."[20]

For Reagan, the Panama Canal was never a stand-alone issue; it pointed to a much larger failure of the Ford administration to defend American interests abroad and stand up to communists. He expressed doubt that Ford and Kissinger were really committed to keeping the military strong and putting the nation's interests first in the Cold War, and he welcomed the prospect of an arms race if it would protect the United States and the world against communism. "There cannot be a peaceful world or a guarantee of our continued existence as a free people unless we start now to build whatever is necessary to ensure that we will never be second to anyone in the ability to defend ourselves," he told Republicans in Melbourne, Florida. The Strategic Arms Limitation Treaty (SALT I) that President Nixon had negotiated and the Ford administration had upheld would have to be revised. And the Ford administration would have to take a tougher line toward Fidel Castro's government in Cuba.[21]

In November, Reagan had promised to observe the "Eleventh Commandment" and refrain from attacking a fellow Republican, but as the date for the Florida primary drew closer, he broke that promise. At the urging of the campaign's coordinator for the South, David Keene, Reagan began to issue scathing denunciations of Ford and Kissinger's record on defense, suggesting that they had left the country vulnerable to a Soviet attack. "I am deeply concerned about our defense posture," he said in Orlando. "Under Messrs. Kissinger and Ford, this nation has become Number Two in military power in a world where it is dangerous—if not fatal—to be second best. . . . The Ford-Kissinger leadership must be held accountable to history for allowing this to happen." He added, "I fear for my country when I see White House indifference to the decline of our military position." Then he ended the speech with a dire warning: if Ford and Kissinger were wrong in allowing the Soviet

Union to gain military superiority over the United States, "there will be no future opportunity to rectify their error."[22]

Such apocalyptic warnings closely echoed lines Reagan had been using against moderate Republicans and liberals for the past twelve years, but they also allowed the Ford campaign to portray Reagan as a dangerous warmonger, just as Lyndon Johnson had done to Barry Goldwater in 1964. In fact, even Goldwater thought Reagan's rhetoric on the Panama Canal went too far, and he warned that Reagan "clearly presented himself in an irresponsible manner on an issue which could affect the nation's security." The Ford campaign thought that Reagan's rhetoric was so over the top that it might actually help the president, giving him a chance to portray himself as a "calm, thoughtful world leader who resists pressures from the left to disarm or weaken America and from the right to substitute confrontation for negotiation." But in reality, Ford was already moving to the right on defense issues. Two weeks before the Florida primary, he gave a tough speech against Castro, which, according to his campaign's internal polling, was so popular with the public that it caused his national approval rating to increase by 10 points.[23]

But the Ford campaign's main weapon against Reagan in Florida was the issue of Social Security. When the president's campaign staff discovered that Reagan had floated the idea of making Social Security "voluntary" in the 1960s and had endorsed that concept as recently as 1974, they decided to make Social Security their main focus in Florida advertising. Every campaign spokesperson in Florida should be "well equipped with talking points on Social Security," Dick Cheney directed. Reagan repeatedly insisted throughout the campaign that he was not going to cut or eliminate Social Security but was going to save the program by increasing the payroll taxes that supported it, but the Ford campaign ignored Reagan's protestations and portrayed him as a threat to the retirement pensions of Florida Republicans. "The President is a firm, unwavering supporter of the Social Security system. Mr. Reagan is not. It's as simple as that," the campaign asserted. The president's advertising specifically targeted Florida retirees and stressed Ford's support for cost-of-living increases in Social Security and his firm commitment to keep the program solvent through increased payroll taxes. "He *does not* favor tampering with the system and opposes any plan that in any way jeopardize the safety of its funds," a Florida newspaper ad declared, accompanied by a picture of a smiling Ford speaking to some older women.[24]

The demographics of Florida's Republican Party favored Ford's strategy over Reagan's. Reagan had planned to win by sweeping the Cuban American vote in Miami, and he did capture a substantial percentage of that vote, carrying the South Florida counties of Dade and Broward, where Cuban Americans were most heavily concentrated. Public opinion polls showed that Reagan's foreign policy message was key to winning the South Florida vote, which shifted markedly toward Reagan in the final ten days of the campaign. Reagan also won in northern Florida, as expected. There, Reagan voters told pollsters that cutting government spending was their top concern, and they cited Reagan's record in California, along with his conservative message, as the most important factor in choosing Reagan over Ford. But voters in central Florida and the state's west coast, which was filled with middle-class retirees who had moved to the Sunshine State from the North, supported the incumbent president. Unfortunately for Reagan, there were more northern retirees in Florida than Cuban Americans or Panhandle Republicans. Thirty-seven percent of Florida's Republicans were over the age of sixty-five, and 70 percent were older than fifty. In St. Petersburg, an area dominated by midwestern Republican retirees, one survey showed that senior citizen Republican primary voters favored Ford over Reagan by a three-to-one margin.[25]

Ford won the Florida primary by 6 points. Before the voting, his campaign had downplayed expectations, as they had in New Hampshire, and predicted a narrow victory, saying that the president would be happy to win "50% plus 1 vote." When he did far better than that, the national media once again portrayed Ford's victory as a major loss for Reagan. "It drastically reduces Mr. Reagan's prospects," the *New York Times* concluded. "If the Californian, even with fierce attacks on the President's policies and leadership, can still go down to defeat in a state once so favorably disposed toward him, it is difficult to think of major states where he can win." The loss in Florida "crippled" Reagan, the *Washington Star* declared. "His position is bad and appears likely to get worse." Goldwater said that Ford's decisive victory in Florida made it clear that the incumbent president would be the party's nominee.[26]

By that time, Reagan had also lost primary contests in Massachusetts and Vermont, and a week later he lost in Illinois. After his loss in New Hampshire, Reagan made no attempt to win elsewhere in New England—a region filled with pro-Ford, moderately liberal Republicans—but for a brief moment, he thought he might do well in Illinois, where he had been born and spent his entire childhood. Instead, Ford trounced him there. Reagan was still popular in much of the West, but primaries in those states were not scheduled until late in the spring. With the Northeast and much of the Midwest arrayed against him, it appeared that Reagan's only hope of staying in the competition until the western primaries was to win some southern states. Because the first southern Republican primary on the schedule was North Carolina's, the Reagan campaign pinned all its hopes on the Tar Heel State.

NORTH CAROLINA

Even the normally ebullient Reagan was a little pessimistic about his prospects in North Carolina. But he had an ally who was determined to help him turn his campaign around: freshman Republican senator Jesse Helms, one of the most conservative members of Congress. Unlike most white southerners, who were generally conservative on social issues but moderate on some economic matters, Helms was a right-wing ideologue on all issues, and he had a crusader's zeal. Although many southern members of Congress in the 1970s were opposed to abortion, Helms was the only southern senator who sponsored a constitutional amendment to ban all abortions from the moment of conception. And although most were strongly anticommunist, Helms was the only one to try to cut funding for the United Nations on the grounds that it aided international communism. His economic conservatism went far beyond that of any other senators from his region; he voted against higher Social Security payments, federal money for highway construction, farm loans, and antitrust legislation. Most white southern politicians opposed civil rights initiatives in the 1960s, but Helms carried his racial conservatism into the 1970s and beyond, sharply decrying busing and affirmative action and appealing to white anxieties about black political and economic power in his campaign advertising. For two decades before entering politics, Helms had run a television station in Raleigh, where he provided conservative news commentary and engaged in a long-standing fight against the national media, which he considered increasingly culturally liberal. When he entered the US Senate in 1973, he was determined to use the power of his office to effect a conservative cultural revolution, and he intended to work with the Republican Party only insofar as it was a useful vehicle for his ideological crusade. Like most southern whites of his generation, he had been a Democrat until the beginning of the 1970s, and he was not entirely comfortable with northeastern Republican moderates. After Nixon's resignation and Ford's selection of Nelson Rockefeller as his vice president, Helms began to openly mull the possibility of forming a third party for discontented conservatives. But when Reagan announced his candidacy for president, Helms decided to stay in the GOP, and he became one of the former California governor's strongest supporters. Reagan, he believed, was the only nationally viable politician who could launch the conservative revolution of his dreams.[27]

Helms's political organization worked closely with the Reagan campaign from the moment the first Reagan volunteers entered the state. As early as the summer of 1975, before Reagan had even officially announced his candidacy, North Carolina's chapter of Citizens for Reagan was buying IBM typewriters for its office through Helms's North Carolina Congressional Club, a fund-raising organization for the senator's campaigns and the broader conservative movement.[28] As the date for the primary drew near, Tom Ellis, the chief campaign strategist in the North Carolina Congressional Club and treasurer of the Citizens for Reagan chapter, took over Reagan's campaign in the state. Ellis and his organization wanted to make Reagan's campaign sharply ideological, and they intended to go for the jugular against Ford. By that point, Reagan's campaign team (with the exception of John Sears) was ready for a sharper fight. But when Ellis decided to play the race card, Reagan's California team was outraged. Ellis produced a flyer that featured Ford's statement that Edward Brooke, the only African American Republican senator at the time, "should be considered" for vice president, and it paired this with a statement from Brooke in favor of busing. Ellis distributed the flyers at several Reagan rallies in the state. David Keene, the Reagan campaign's coordinator for the South, told Ellis to destroy the flyers, but Ellis considered them effective and ignored Keene's instructions. When the *Raleigh News and Observer* ran a story on the flyers, the issue became a national concern for the campaign, and Reagan personally ordered Ellis to "stop this"—at which point he reluctantly did.[29]

The Reagan campaign claimed to take the high ground on the issue of race, but Reagan himself came dangerously close to race-baiting in his attacks on welfare. He told predominantly white audiences that while they were waiting in line at the grocery store to spend their hard-earned money on necessary food items, there was "a strapping young fellow up ahead of you buying T-bone steaks with food stamps." The

New York Times reported that at a campaign rally in Fort Lauderdale shortly before the North Carolina campaign, the "strapping young fellow" became a "strapping young buck" in Reagan's recitation of the story. Carl Rowan, a longtime veteran of civil rights reporting, called it "shameful demagoguery." "It is racism disguised just enough to be palatable to millions of whites," he wrote in the *Atlanta Constitution*. "Everyone knows that 'strapping buck' is a code phrase that conjures up images of Mandingo, of some 'burly' black male, chomping down T-bones courtesy of the food stamp program." Reagan quickly abandoned the line, but his experimental use of the racially charged phrase confirmed for some observers that he was, like George Wallace and Richard Nixon, one of the dog-whistling "exploiters of racism."[30]

Polls showed that southern whites in 1976 were considerably more conservative on race than the rest of the nation. Only 59 percent of voters in the South (and only 49 percent in the Deep South) said they would have "no objection" to a black vice-presidential candidate—compared with 72 percent nationwide who expressed "no objection" to the idea. But it was still unclear whether race-baiting would help or hurt a candidate win a Republican presidential primary in the South, since Republican voters (just like Democratic voters) south of the Mason-Dixon Line were far from monolithic on race. The North Carolina Republican Party contained a growing number of racially conservative white converts to the party of Goldwater and Nixon, but its members also included many northern transplants, upper-middle-class industrialists, native North Carolinian moderate progressives, and even a few African Americans, including Floyd McKissick, a Ford supporter and civil rights advocate who denounced Reagan for running a "racist" campaign.[31] Polls continued to show Ford in the lead in North Carolina, both during and after Reagan's imbroglio over race.

While Reagan was working with Helms and Ellis, Ford's campaign was relying on the services of Governor Jim Holshouser, a lifelong moderate Republican from the state's western mountains. Ford faced his toughest challenge among recent converts to the GOP in North Carolina, and he enjoyed his strongest support among the state's northern transplants and the relatively small number of native North Carolinians who were lifelong Republicans. Most of the latter, like Holshouser, were concentrated in the western mountains from Asheville to the Tennessee border and were fiscally conservative, culturally moderate party loyalists. Reagan's campaign, by contrast, was led by recent converts to the party. Both Ellis and Helms had been registered Republicans for only six years. While Holshouser's political alliances were concentrated in western North Carolina, Helms had a lock on the votes of "Jessecrats" in the Charlotte and Raleigh suburbs and the eastern parts of the state, where the Republican Party was a recent import in response to tensions over busing, school prayer, and welfare that had left many cultural conservatives feeling alienated from the national Democratic Party. Holshouser's Republicans favored a fiscally conservative modification of the status quo, but the Jessecrats wanted a revolution.[32]

If North Carolina's primary had been an open primary that allowed registered Democrats to vote, Reagan might have benefited from the support of the large number of culturally conservative Democrats who had elected Helms to the Senate. But the primary was restricted to the small percentage of voters in the state who were registered Republicans, and a substantial number of them were just as skeptical of Reagan as their Republican governor was. Right up until the week of the primary, polls showed Ford in the lead, even though he had done little advertising in the state. And on his two personal visits to North Carolina, the press had noted that his speeches were bland, even for Ford. But the Ford campaign assumed that its superior organization, which was closely tied to the governor's political network, would be sufficient to turn out the vote for Ford. Some of Ford's supporters not only predicted victory but also suggested that the contest would be so decisive that it would force Reagan to end his campaign.[33] They had not counted on the impact of Reagan's televised speech on foreign policy.

The speech was Ellis's idea. Ellis believed that Reagan's oratorical skills were his greatest asset and his best hope of victory, so he begged the Reagan campaign to release a half-hour speech by the candidate on foreign policy to be used in North Carolina advertising. Reagan's California-based campaign managers were slow to recognize the value of this approach, and they invested little effort in complying with Ellis's request. They thought few voters would tune in to hear a candidate talk for thirty minutes, so a few days before the primary, they sent Ellis a tape of a speech Reagan had given in Florida. This gave Ellis barely enough time to edit out the Florida references and scrub the palm trees from the background and replace them with a backdrop more appropriate to North Carolina. But once he did so, Reagan's defense of US rights to the Panama Canal and his denunciations of

Ford's détente policy worked even better in North Carolina than they had in Florida. Fifteen of the state's seventeen television stations aired the speech in prime time during the final four days of the campaign, and polls showed an immediate benefit for Reagan. The 20 percent of Republican voters who made their decision in the final week before the primary voted for Reagan over Ford by nearly three to one.[34]

The *New York Times* called Reagan's stunning 52 to 46 percent defeat of Ford both a "surprise" and an "upset." He carried every county in the state except for those in the western mountains. His campaign would now have "new life," the *Times* predicted. Even Reagan, who had suggested in a televised interview the previous day that he was prepared for a loss, appeared to be taken aback. When the networks announced his unexpected win, he was on a plane headed to California after a day of campaigning in Wisconsin and was thus unable to deliver a victory speech.[35]

Polls showed that Reagan's surprise victory was due almost entirely to voters who reached a decision during the last week of the campaign. Twenty-seven percent of his support came from people who made up their minds for Reagan in the final seven days. Their number-one concern was fear of détente and Kissinger's foreign policy. Ellis's political instincts saved Reagan's campaign: the revamped speech from Florida changed voters' minds and propelled the former California governor to his first primary victory.[36]

Why did one foreign policy critique accomplish what months of denouncing welfare programs and deficit spending had failed to do? As the *American Political Report* argued, Reagan's fiscal conservatism did not appeal to many Wallace-voting conservative Democrats and recent southern white converts to the GOP, so as long as his campaign message focused on budget slashing, it was easy for Ford to pick off votes from the Reagan coalition by suggesting that Reagan's election would endanger Social Security or result in higher state taxes. But when Reagan denounced détente and discussed the Panama Canal, he tapped into a widely shared bipartisan fear of national decline that resonated with many cultural conservatives in both parties, especially in the South. Wallace's campaign capitalized on this fear, but Reagan's oratorical skills allowed him to do it more effectively. With his soaring rhetoric about national purpose and military strength, he raised cultural conservatives' hopes that he could stand up to the communists and restore the nation's glory days of the 1950s and early 1960s, before the Vietnam War and the cultural conflicts of the late 1960s caused the nation to veer off course. Reagan's rhetoric did not necessarily appeal to a majority. Left-of-center Democrats whose foreign policy views had been shaped by their opposition to the Vietnam War considered Reagan's views anachronistic and dangerous, but they had little influence on a Republican primary. More concerning for Reagan, perhaps, was the fact that a majority of Republicans—62 percent, according to a January 1976 Gallup poll—approved of Kissinger's diplomacy.[37] Especially in the Northeast and parts of the industrial Midwest, Ford's foreign policy approach was more popular among Republicans than Reagan's was. But Reagan's foreign policy views had just enough appeal among conservative Democrats and right-wing Republicans to propel him to victory in some culturally conservative states, starting with North Carolina.

While most pundits still expected Reagan to lose the nomination, it now seemed probable that he had the momentum to stay in the race until California's June primary. And regardless of the ultimate outcome, it was clear that his campaign was already pushing Ford to the right. After the Florida primary, Ford refused to use the word *détente* and began to speak more sharply about international communism, calling Castro's Cuban government an "outlaw" only a few months after mentioning the possibility of normalizing relations with the island nation. In February he adopted a more conservative position on abortion than his advisers (and even his wife) approved of, saying that he would support a constitutional amendment to rescind *Roe v. Wade*. He started to speak out more forcefully against busing. In a nod to the strong right-to-work sentiments in the conservative wing of the Republican Party, he vetoed a common-situs picketing bill that he had once considered signing. He also emphasized more strongly than ever his opposition to deficit spending. Ford's strategy for victory was to woo the party's conservatives away from Reagan. Liberal Republicans were disappointed with the president's new shift to the right, but they felt powerless to stop it because they feared that if they mounted their own primary challenge against Ford from the center-left of the GOP, it would only divide the party's moderates and throw the nomination to Reagan. Senator Mac Mathias had planned to challenge Ford in Massachusetts, a liberal Republican stronghold where he might have had strong support, but with Reagan still a threat, the Ford campaign convinced him to remove his name from the ballot shortly before the primary. Reagan's campaign thus had the unanticipated effect of silencing liberal Republicans' criticism of Ford while simultaneously making Ford more conservative. Some conservatives, such as former Nixon speechwriter William Safire, considered this a victory for their cause, regardless of whether Reagan received the nomination.[38]

BEYOND NORTH CAROLINA

Now that the gloves were off, Reagan continued to blast away at Ford's foreign policy, charging that he had put American freedom and perhaps the nation's very survival at risk. On March 31, in an effort to repeat the magic of North Carolina, the campaign paid $100,000 for NBC to televise a half-hour nationwide broadcast of a Reagan address that functioned as a relentless attack on Ford's record. "Our nation is in danger, and the danger grows with each passing day," he asserted. "We are Number Two in a world where it is dangerous, if not fatal, to be second best." President Ford, he charged, had put "our stamp of approval on Russia's enslavement of the captive nations" in the Helsinki Accords, which recognized the Soviet Union's influence in eastern Europe, and now Kissinger's arms limitation negotiations were possibly "giving away our *own* freedom." Then, warming up to his finale, Reagan painted a vivid picture of America's "rendezvous with destiny" and depicted the choice at the polls in the starkest terms imaginable. "I don't believe the people I've met in almost every State of the Union are ready to consign *this,* the last island of freedom, to the dustbin of history," he declared. "Call it mysticism, if you will, but I believe God had a divine purpose in placing this land between the two great oceans to be found by those who had a special love of freedom and the courage to leave the countries of their birth." He concluded:

> I would like to be President because I would like to see this country become once again a country where a little six-year-old girl can grow up knowing the same freedom that I knew when I was six years old, growing up in America. If this is the America that you want for yourself and your children; if you want to restore government not only of and for but by the people; to see the American spirit unleashed once again; to make this land the shining, golden hope God intended it to be, I'd like to hear from you.[39]

Ford made no attempt to match Reagan's powerful invocation of God, freedom, and national purpose, but he did authorize the State

Department to issue a ten-page, point-by-point rebuttal of Reagan's factual claims. Reagan had badly mischaracterized the realities of foreign policy, the State Department said; he had engaged in a "gross distortion of fact" and was guilty of "total and irresponsible fabrication." Reagan was not deterred. He called the State Department memo an "exercise in creative writing" and asked, "Can we believe any longer what we are told by the State Department?" He then issued a rash of new quotations and statistics to support his original assertions. If a third world war broke out, the Soviet Union would probably win, he warned. The Soviets "are willing to risk their own survival to insure that we do not survive," he said. Ford's "platitudes give little indication that he has thought much about the nature of his potential enemy," he charged.[40]

Reagan had spent the past two decades reading right-wing anticommunist literature, so he took it for granted that the Soviet Union wanted to wipe out the United States in a nuclear war. Ford administration officials, by contrast, viewed the Soviet Union as a rational actor, and they were aghast at such dangerous rhetoric coming from Reagan. At the same time, the administration took pains to emphasize that Ford was not a weak negotiator and had not sold out American interests to the Soviet Union. Contrary to Reagan's claims, the US military under Ford was still "second to none." Ford had proposed a $7 billion increase in the national defense budget that year, and as one of his ads proclaimed in March, "he knows we must maintain our military superiority." Following the advice of White House communications director David Gergen, the campaign portrayed the president as taking a "fairly hard line" against the Soviet Union while still retaining his "commitment to negotiations." Or, as Ford phrased it, he was pursuing "peace through strength"—a line that Reagan would later adopt as his own in the 1980s.[41]

After the North Carolina primary, each successive state contest became a referendum on these competing foreign policy claims. Did voters believe Reagan when he said that Ford and Kissinger had undermined American security by allowing the country to become second best to the Soviet Union, thus exposing the nation to the possibility of nuclear annihilation or manipulation by the communists? Or did they believe Ford's claim that Reagan's rhetoric was "dangerous" and "irresponsible," whereas the president was protecting American security through responsible defense spending, reasonable diplomatic negotiation, and the preservation of peace?

As the Republican race became more acrimonious due to the magnitude of the charges on both sides, the division between the two ideological camps in the Republican Party hardened. Both sides accused the other of lying. *Human Events,* which was solidly in Reagan's camp, refused to believe that Ford took a hard line against communism. The president "purposely tried to mislead the American people," the magazine declared. That same month, John Anderson, a moderate Republican congressman from Illinois and a Ford supporter, punched back and accused Reagan of engaging in "superficial slap-dash analysis that tends to mislead rather than to inform." "Tragic though the implications may be," Anderson charged, "Ronald Reagan has declared war on America's defense posture—and for reasons that are seemingly narrow and political."[42]

Some Ford supporters worried that even if he won the Republican nomination, the bitterness of the primary contest would alienate Reagan voters, split the party, and throw the November election to the Democrats. "We are very sorry that the President didn't win in North Carolina—but if you take the advice of an ignorant State Chairman, please tell those people running the campaign not to attack Reagan," the chair of the New Jersey Republican Party wrote to Rogers Morton, who had replaced Bo Callaway as Ford's campaign manager. "We need Reagan's votes come November."[43] But the Ford campaign ignored these entreaties to pull back, even when they came from Republican congressmen and close allies of the president. This was no longer a gentlemen's campaign; this was a fight for survival, and the president could not afford to cede any ground to Reagan.

For a few weeks, Ford remained ahead. In Wisconsin, Reagan's attack on the president's foreign policy was the central theme of his campaign, and polls showed that it swung voters to his side, with a noticeable shift in sentiment immediately after his national televised address. Nevertheless, it was not enough to prevent Ford from carrying the state by 56 to 43 percent. Ford proclaimed his victory in Wisconsin a vindication of Kissinger. Reagan did not even try to compete with Ford in New York, which held its primary on April 6, the same day as Wisconsin. Nor was he on the ballot in Pennsylvania, which held its primary on April 27.[44]

By the end of April, Ford had won primaries in New Hampshire, Massachusetts, Vermont, Florida, Illinois, Wisconsin, New York, and Pennsylvania. Reagan had won only one state primary: North Carolina.

Ford had 251 delegates, with an additional 184 officially uncommitted delegates from pro-Ford states in the Northeast that were assumed to be in his camp. He was well on his way to the 1,130 delegates needed to win the nomination. Reagan had only 84 delegates. And his campaign was running so low on money that it had to exchange its charter plane for a sixteen-year-old bus that, according to a *New York Times* reporter, "resembled a migrant labor van."[45]

The Reagan campaign was angry about its opponent's financial advantage. Reagan's staff were masters of direct-mail fund-raising, and his campaign had once been near the front of the pack in the amount of money raised. However, the campaign had quickly exhausted its resources, partly because it wasted large sums in states such as Massachusetts, which Reagan had no realistic hope of winning. Reagan had a network of conservative supporters who gladly would have contributed more to his campaign, but campaign finance laws limited the amount he could raise. The Reagan team charged that the Ford campaign was unfairly using the power of incumbency to bypass campaign finance rules. For instance, every time Reagan visited a primary state to make a speech, his travel expenses had to be paid out of his legally limited campaign resources, whereas Ford could use his government-funded plane. In addition, Ford constantly received free news coverage that Reagan had to buy. The Ford campaign typically spent very little on each state primary, relying instead on the local Republican Party apparatus to manage the details in Ford's absence. Its television advertising was likewise limited. While the Reagan campaign spent more than $100,000 to put Reagan's half-hour speech on NBC, the Ford campaign had no need to buy airtime for the president's speeches. As one of the Ford campaign's allies in North Carolina noted before the state primary, "We don't plan to spend a lot on advertising" because "Gerald Ford's got a good free media campaign, courtesy of the television networks, at 6 and 11 every night." The Reagan campaign capitalized on this theme in its fund-raising. Reagan characterized his contest with Ford as "the people" versus the "Washington establishment," and his fund-raisers did the same. Citizens for Reagan did not "control the national media or the machinery of government," and "[we] can only get our message to the people through private contributions to buy TV and radio time and newspaper ads," one Reagan fund-raising letter declared. But a public relations victory could not compensate for a lack of cash, and by the end of April, the campaign was $1 million in debt, with no ability to pay its hotel bills from North Carolina and New Hampshire.[46]

Repeatedly, the Ford campaign called for Reagan to get out of the race. But the North Carolina primary victory gave him just enough hope that his campaign could continue operations until the primary calendar shifted to the West, where Reagan believed he was considerably more popular than he was on the East Coast or in the industrial Midwest. The campaign's new target became Texas, which was scheduled to hold its primary on May 1. Texas was a must-win state for Reagan; if he didn't receive a majority of the votes and get at least half the delegates, John Sears said, they would have to "sit down and talk things over," a euphemism for potentially suspending the campaign.[47]

In March, Senator John Tower, the Ford campaign's main liaison in Texas, had been confident that the president would win the Lone Star State's primary. Although the Ford campaign believed it could lose in Texas and still easily get enough delegates elsewhere, Ford's strategists made a concerted effort to win the state by trying to preempt Reagan's major lines of attack. Tower, a member of the Senate Armed Services Committee, taped commercials arguing that Ford was strong on defense. The Ford campaign once again rolled out its argument that Reagan's $90 billion transfer plan—which he had largely backed away from by that point—would result in "higher taxes for Texas." But the president's campaign leveled its strongest attacks on Reagan's foreign policy, charging that he had engaged in "careless saber-rattling." Voters "must not forget that confrontation between nuclear giants can mean the extermination of mankind," Ford's television advertising declared.[48] Never had the Ford campaign come so close to repeating the message of President Lyndon Johnson's infamous "Daisy" commercial of 1964.

But Ford did not understand the Texas voters as well as Reagan did. When Ford visited the state, he demonstrated his unfamiliarity with its customs by biting into a hot tamale before taking off the corn-husk wrap—prompting the *Washington Star* to run a photo of the incident with the headline, "Oh Shucks, Mr. President." Reagan, by contrast, could easily position himself as the quintessential western conservative. In his campaign advertising, he emphasized the cultural distance between Texas values and the Ford administration, which he labeled part of the "Washington establishment." "One of the biggest failures the Washington establishment has forced on us is forced busing,"

Figure 6.2. First Lady Betty Ford campaigning for her husband in Texas, April 1976. (Courtesy of Gerald R. Ford Presidential Library)

one of his radio ads in Corpus Christi declared. "Control of education should be returned to local school districts." Energy policy was another area where the Ford administration had unwisely attempted to impede local initiative, according to Reagan. "The energy bill Mr. Ford supported and signed into law discourages exploration and cripples our nation's drive for energy self-sufficiency," Reagan's ad declared in this oil-drilling state. "Texas, and the nation, need energy independence and the leadership to get it." Reagan also reached out to ranchers who were angry about federal land-use regulations and promised to get the government off their backs. "Nitpicking EPA and other regulations are a greater threat to the American farmer than any drought or disease," one of his Texas television ads stated. "My administration will get the bureaucrats off the back of American agriculture—and let our farmers and ranchers get back to full-time production as only they know how." And Reagan did not forget the large number of Texas Baptists and other conservative Christians who were upset about the nation's moral drift. Contrasting the culturally permissive Betty Ford with the conservative Nancy Reagan, his print advertising featured headlines such as "Betty . . . or Nancy? A Definitely Different Point of View" and "Nancy Reagan Disagrees with Betty Ford on Sex"—suggesting that Nancy, unlike Betty, would object if her daughter had an "affair."[49]

Reagan won by a landslide in Texas. The Ford campaign's internal polling had predicted the possibility of a narrow victory for the president, but Reagan won approximately two-thirds of the vote and took all ninety-six delegates. At least half the votes came from conservative Democrats and independents, who apparently voted overwhelmingly for Reagan. The Ford campaign had known for a long time that Reagan had an advantage in primaries that allowed crossover voting because he was far more popular than the president among conservative Democrats. In Texas, Reagan's advantage may have been even stronger because the Republican primary was far more competitive than the Democratic contest and may have generated greater interest among voters.[50] Reagan won Texas with an anti-Washington, populist, culturally conservative message that emphasized local control instead of federal oversight. Ford had thought he could win by positioning himself as a traditional conservative who was strong on defense and opposed to high taxes and deficit spending, but he was wrong. The Texans who supported Reagan did not merely want a fiscal conservative in the White House; they wanted a more radical change in the government's direction.

The Texas victory gave Reagan the momentum to win a whole series of primaries. The next week, he won a surprise victory in Indiana. Ford had expected to win that state easily, since the president had solid support among midwestern Republicans. But about one-third of the GOP primary voters in Indiana were Democrats, and although Ford won a majority among Republicans, Reagan carried 75 percent of the Democratic vote—most of which came from cultural conservatives who had supported Wallace in 1972 and now turned to Reagan, since Wallace was out of the race. Reagan also won primaries in Georgia and Alabama, which, like Indiana, allowed crossover voting by Democrats. It was "the most damaging series of electoral reversals suffered by an incumbent President since William Howard Taft lost 12 primaries to Theodore Roosevelt in 1912," the *New York Times* noted. And it sent the Ford campaign into a tailspin. The problem they faced, strategists believed, was Democratic crossover voting, but they had no idea how to prevent it in states where it was allowed. And on occasion, such as in Nebraska, Ford lost primaries where voting was restricted to Republicans. Ford had hoped to win Nebraska, where he had been born and where he was still popular with many centrist Republicans in the eastern cities, but Reagan capitalized on farmers' anger over the Ford administration's embargo on wheat sales to the Soviet Union, and their votes propelled him to victory.[51] Reagan then went on to win caucuses in Oklahoma, Louisiana, and Virginia.

As Reagan racked up these victories, some Republicans began to speculate that Ford might be the first Republican president since Chester A. Arthur to be denied the nomination at the convention, and even the Ford campaign abandoned predictions that the president would arrive at the convention with enough delegates to win on the first ballot. By the middle of May, Reagan had won 476 delegates, compared with Ford's 333. Reagan was now so optimistic that he predicted a first-ballot victory for himself, "barring the unforeseen." And perhaps fittingly, he made the prediction to reporters aboard his newly rented campaign plane, a sign that donations were pouring in and his campaign was once again financially solvent.[52]

But Reagan also made a few missteps. He threw away his lead in Tennessee and Kentucky because of his suggestion that he would privatize the Tennessee Valley Authority.[53] Just as he had lost New Hampshire over the $90 billion transfer plan and Florida over Social Security, he alienated potential allies in the Appalachian states because of the local financial implications of his cost-cutting proposals. Cultural conservatives liked his anti-Washington rhetoric and his attacks on the president's foreign policy, but his suggestions that he might eliminate popular government programs repeatedly got him into trouble.

Because of the possibility that crossover voting might upend predictions, both Ford and Reagan invested a lot in the Michigan primary, which had once seemed safe territory for the president. After Reagan's victories in Texas and Indiana, the Ford campaign worried that there might be enough crossover voting from Wallace Democrats in Michigan to propel Reagan to victory in Ford's home state—which would be a public relations disaster. Ford changed his schedule to include several days of campaigning in Michigan, since, as Rogers Morton said, "He has got to win in Michigan to prove he's viable. He's got to turn this thing around." That campaigning paid off. With an extraordinarily high Republican turnout in support of the president, and with Democratic crossover voting accounting for only 15 percent of the total vote, Ford defeated Reagan 67 percent to 32 percent. Reagan won a majority of the Democratic votes, but with 75 percent of Republican voters supporting Ford, Reagan suffered a far worse defeat than expected.[54]

That same day, Reagan also lost a primary race in Maryland, a strongly pro-Ford, liberal Republican state. But he then went on to win substantial majorities in Arkansas and Nevada, and he took 74 percent of the vote in a landslide victory in Idaho, which for months had been one of his strongest bases of support. Ford had been counting on a solid victory in Oregon to counter Reagan's lead, but he won by a much slimmer margin than expected. Because Oregon's Republican Party was solidly liberal, most pundits had assumed that Ford would easily carry the state, but Reagan's popularity among farmers in eastern Oregon allowed him to take 48 percent of the vote, enough to give him nearly half of Oregon's delegates and counter Ford's strength in the western cities and among higher-earning, better-educated Republicans in the state. Most of the remaining primary results were predictable. Ford won Rhode Island, with 66 percent of the vote, while Reagan carried Montana and South Dakota.[55]

A pattern had clearly emerged: Ford had the support of an overwhelming majority of northeastern Republicans and traditional GOP voters in the industrial Midwest. He also consistently won at least a narrow majority of the Republican vote in most of the remainder of the country, including much of the South. The only regions where a majority of lifelong registered Republicans were firmly arrayed against the president were the Great Plains and the Mountain West, where the unpopularity of his administration's agricultural policies and the appeal of Reagan's challenge to the Washington establishment presented a difficult challenge for Ford.[56] But if this had been his only problem, he could have won the nomination without taking the fight to the convention.

Reagan, in contrast, managed to put together a politically powerful coalition while writing off the entire Northeast and industrial Midwest, regions that had once been the center of the Republican Party. With the exception of Indiana (which he won only with support from Wallace Democrats), he lost every state that had been home to one of the Republican Party's presidential or vice-presidential nominees between 1860 and 1944. Of the seventeen states he won outside of California, nine were former Confederate states, five were in the Mountain West or Southwest, and three were farm states from the Midwest or Great Plains—nearly all of which had not begun voting Republican until after World War II. More than half of the 4.85 million votes he received in all the Republican primaries came from the South and the Sun Belt, whereas approximately 40 percent of Ford's total primary vote came from six states in the traditionally Republican industrial heartland that stretched from Wisconsin to Pennsylvania, with much of the remainder coming from the East Coast.[57] Ford's support came from places that had been voting Republican for more than a century; Reagan's support came from states that were not traditional strongholds of the Republican Party. And even in the states that Reagan carried, many Republican officeholders and the most loyal party members were not supportive of his candidacy. He won primarily by appealing to a new group of Republicans—younger voters, blue-collar workers, rural voters, lower-income earners, those without a college education, former Democrats, and even a large number of voters who were still members of the Democratic Party. Reagan was not simply running for president; he was creating a long-term transformation of the parties.

A year before the primaries, some conservatives who supported Reagan had urged him to run as a representative of a new third party that would meld culturally conservative Democrats with ideologically conservative Republicans—perhaps, they proposed, a Reagan-Wallace ticket. Reagan refused the suggestion, but in essence, his primary campaign accomplished what these conservative ideologues wanted: it brought culturally conservative Democrats into the GOP and propelled Reagan to victory over an incumbent Republican president who had the solid support of most of the voters in his own party. The contest between Reagan and Ford was thus a referendum on whether the GOP would remain a fiscally conservative, culturally moderate, northern-dominated party or whether it would become the southern and Sun Belt anti-Washington party of Ronald Reagan.

The primary contest ended with three states that held their elections on June 8: New Jersey, Ohio, and California. As expected, Ford easily carried New Jersey and Ohio. But Reagan went all out for a California landslide, spending more than $500,000 on advertising, compared with Ford's $200,000. In addition, Reagan received assistance from independent political action committees such as the Reagan California Fund, which were organized by conservative activists and were not restricted by federal campaign spending limits.[58] Although Reagan had been a popular governor, Ford enjoyed support from some of the more liberal Republicans in California, and he was ahead in the polls in April. That lead had vanished by the end of May, and some analysts began to predict the possibility of a Reagan sweep in the state.[59]

As it had done elsewhere, the Reagan campaign warned that a vote for Ford was a vote to surrender America's military superiority and to continue deficit spending unabated. The Ford campaign responded by running radio and television ads that warned about the potentially apocalyptic consequences of Reagan's hawkish approach to foreign policy. "When you vote Tuesday, remember, Governor Ronald Reagan couldn't start a war. President Ronald Reagan could," one ad declared. Reagan was so angry about this "totally dishonest attack" that, at a press conference on the day before the California primary, he repeatedly refused to say whether he would support President Ford in the general election if Ford won the nomination.[60]

The acrimony between the candidates filtered down to their supporters as well. Polls of Republican participants in the New Jersey, Ohio, and California primaries revealed that less than 50 percent of both Reagan and Ford voters said they would vote for the other Republican candidate if he won the nomination. About one-third of the voters in each camp said they would defect to Carter if their nonpreferred Republican candidate was the party's standard-bearer in November, and many others suggested they would find a third-party candidate or not vote at all.[61]

Reagan did better than expected in the last primary of the season: he won 65 percent of the vote in California, which gave him all 167 delegates. But this was not enough to give him the nomination. He finished the primaries with 860 delegates, nowhere near the 1,130 needed to win. Ford had between 895 and 911 delegates, depending on the count. The president also had a lot of support from the officially uncommitted delegations from the Northeast (especially from Pennsylvania and New York, where many pro-Ford delegates were listed as uncommitted). In the estimation of the *Wall Street Journal,* Ford was probably only twenty votes short of receiving the nomination on the first ballot—but only if all his "soft" support from the uncommitted delegates came through, which the Reagan campaign desperately wanted to prevent.[62] The battle would be settled at the Republican National Convention in Kansas City in August. Each campaign now had two months to figure out a strategy to woo uncommitted delegates to their side and win the grand prize. Regardless of the outcome in Kansas City, it appeared that the rift in the party created by Reagan's primary challenge might be irreparable. The GOP would never be the same again.

7

NOMINATING CARTER

For much of Jimmy Carter's campaign, his opponents charged him with vagueness, saying it was impossible to determine his position on issues. While giving a nod to the left on issues such as the environment, he frequently positioned himself somewhat to the right of center on economics and occasionally on social issues and foreign policy as well. In March, for instance, he gave a foreign policy speech that criticized President Ford's policy of détente for conceding too much to the Soviet Union—a line of attack that suggested his own foreign policy might be more hawkish and more staunchly anticommunist. He positioned himself as an aggressive budget-cutter, promising to reduce the federal government's nineteen hundred bureaucratic agencies to only two hundred. He opposed forced busing and government-funded abortions, saying, "abortion is wrong" and "I don't think government should do anything to encourage abortion."[1]

But for a moment in mid-April, Carter seemed to transform himself into a more consistent liberal. It was a sudden turnabout. Until then, he had emphasized balancing the budget and reducing government waste. Although he supported the goals of the Humphrey-Hawkins bill in the abstract, he repeatedly expressed opposition to the bill itself. As late as the beginning of April, he reiterated his reservations about the cost and "bureaucracy" that might be created by some of its specific proposals to reduce unemployment through federal spending. Carter's views on inflation and deficit spending had always sounded more like Gerald Ford than Hubert Humphrey, which is why Birch Bayh accused him in February of running a "Republican" campaign. But the reaction among African Americans and white liberals to his endorsement of the "ethnic purity" of neighborhoods prompted him to immediately tack to the left on economic issues to try to win back their support. At the urging of the Congressional Black Caucus, he somewhat reluctantly pledged support for the Humphrey-Hawkins bill in mid-April, only a few days after the fallout over his controversial comments on "ethnic purity."[2] He learned that he could not retain black support simply by appealing to his alliances with Martin Luther King Sr., Andrew Young, and Atlanta's civil rights leaders; he had to embrace the liberal economic programs that many African Americans wanted.

Carter fulfilled his promise to the Congressional Black Caucus by issuing an economic position paper that made unemployment, not the deficit or inflation, his primary target, and he proposed a massive increase in public works spending. Under the Carter promise of a "progressively managed economy," the government would bolster federal vocational education programs and pay for private companies to provide job training. It would offer tax incentives or other federal aid for businesses to hire more workers, create new public jobs in construction and other fields, and provide temporary summer employment for 800,000 young people. Carter still promised to balance the budget by 1979; by that date, he insisted, the economy would be experiencing such rapid growth that full employment would return and both deficit spending and high inflation would end. This was an astonishingly ambitious goal, but it enabled Carter to harmonize his newly adopted economic liberalism with his long-standing promise to balance the budget.[3]

Carter also endorsed national health insurance that was "universal," "mandatory," and "comprehensive." Citing Reinhold Niebuhr's statement that "the sad duty of politics is to establish justice in a sinful world," he outlined a program of social justice that included "sounder health, a cleaner environment, racial equality and economic fairness."[4] This was not entirely new territory for Carter, who had always positioned himself as a progressive on civil rights and the environment, but it was a new emphasis. For the past few months, he had railed against bureaucratic waste and called for the deficit to be trimmed. Now, without abandoning that earlier message, he pivoted toward more traditional Democratic priorities of "economic fairness" and government-funded jobs.

Some liberals were not convinced that the conversion was genuine. Jeff Greenfield, a young liberal who joined the campaign as a speechwriter in April, decided after only nine days that Carter was not the progressive he had hoped he would be. He suspected that Carter was "more a Republican than a Democrat on social welfare," he wrote in his letter of resignation, but the real problem was that he found Carter disingenuous and accused him of hiding his more conservative positions from the public. "The only thing I am sure he believes in is himself," Greenfield concluded.[5]

While Greenfield's abrupt and angry departure was disconcerting for the Carter campaign, the candidate's more immediate problem was winning the trust of liberal Democrats in Congress. House majority leader Tip O'Neill was officially backing Mo Udall but had suggested that he would support Humphrey if the Minnesota senator entered the race. Few members of Congress were Carter supporters. One campaign consultant noted that Carter could probably improve his standing among Democrats in Congress if he made an effort to communicate with them by sending them his position papers and notifying individual members when he was planning speaking trips to their districts—an expected professional courtesy that he had failed to follow. But Carter's vague and confusing policy proposals were also a barrier to securing the support of congressional Democrats, the consultant noted. "When he starts reaching for definitions on paper it's like dealing with cotton candy," one high-ranking liberal Democrat from the Northeast told the consultant.[6]

Voters who identified with the left wing of the Democratic Party—the wing that had given McGovern the nomination in 1972 and coalesced around Udall in the 1976 race—were especially skeptical of Carter. At the beginning of his campaign, in 1974 and early 1975, some of them were impressed with his civil rights record and his proposal for a human rights–based foreign policy, but as he repeatedly tried to appeal to cultural conservatives in the primaries and only reluctantly supported Democratic economic initiatives, they turned against him. By the late spring of 1976, their disappointment had turned to deep anger; they were outraged that a moderate conservative whom they regarded as a "phony" was about to receive their party's nomination. "Jimmy Carter is a nifty, shifty politician," the *Progressive* declared in May. He is "the most elusive of candidates. His position papers are masterworks of generalized statements allowing room for him to maneuver in almost any direction. He tries hard to be all things to all voters."[7]

Several members of Carter's campaign staff encouraged him to clarify his issue positions and hew to a consistent ideological course—usually farther to the left than he wanted—but Carter was an independent thinker and was reluctant to do this. By this point, his campaign's economic advisers ran the ideological gamut from free-market advocate Martin Feldstein, a Harvard professor who would later serve in the Reagan and George W. Bush administrations, to Massachusetts Institute of Technology professor Lester Thurow, who prioritized narrowing the income gap between rich and poor and lauded European-style government management of the economy. Carter loved to listen for hours to a variety of competing views, but in the end, he made his own policy decisions, often ignoring the suggestions of his advisers. He was involved in every detail of political speechwriting and the drafting of position papers, so to an unusually high degree, the campaign bore the candidate's idiosyncratic ideological imprint and defied the usual categories.[8] Indeed, while Carter was moving to the left on economic questions and embracing more traditional liberal Democratic positions, he was also reaching out to evangelicals by reminding voters that he was a born-again Christian.

THE EVANGELICAL VOTE

Carter's discussion of his faith on the campaign trail was not merely a political act. Anyone who had closely observed his political career knew that his Christian faith had been a central part of his identity long before the presidential campaign, and he had never tried to hide it. Only at the insistence of his inner circle of his advisers had he scaled back his description of his Christian faith in his announcement speech, and even then, he had persisted in identifying himself as a Christian, despite their apprehension about the wisdom of doing so. Throughout the campaign, he tried to attend church each Sunday, regardless of where he was.[9]

Carter's religious commitment was undoubtedly genuine—none of his associates ever doubted this—but the presentation of his faith nevertheless involved political calculations. Throughout 1975 and even into the first few weeks of 1976, during the Iowa and New Hampshire contests, the media barely commented on his religiosity. Not until March and April, when he began to speak more directly about his faith on the campaign trail in North Carolina and Wisconsin and claim that he had been "born again," did reporters take notice and comment on

Figure 7.1. Jimmy Carter shaking hands after leaving church in Jacksonville, Florida. (Library of Congress, Prints & Photographs Division, U.S. News & World Report Magazine Collection, LC-DIG-ppmsca-09751)

that curious phrase, which, according to George Gallup, applied to 34 percent of Americans. According to Carter, these new discussions of his faith were merely responses to questions about the subject and reflected a new determination "not to conceal it but reveal it." But some analysts wondered whether he might reap some political advantages from his evangelical identity. They wondered whether Carter was trying to remake the political landscape by tapping into what Catholic writer Michael Novak called "Carter's natural constituency"—the "huge number of evangelical Protestants" who, by Novak's estimate, accounted for two-thirds of all white Protestants in the United States. Carter's own denomination, the Southern Baptist Convention, was the largest Protestant church body in the United States. At a time when many mainline Protestant churches were shrinking, the Southern Baptist Convention had grown to nearly thirteen million members—mostly in the South, but more than 500,000 in the West—and was adding thousands of new ones every week. Evangelicals were now so numerous in every region of the country and among every social class that *Newsweek* called 1976 the "year of the evangelical."[10] Could Carter, the first viable presidential candidate to publicly wear the "born again" label, pick up votes from this constituency by highlighting his Christian faith?

Complicating the issue was the fact that evangelicals were not a single political constituency; they were almost as divided as the rest of the country along regional, cultural, and political lines. In the North, many were Republicans. In the South, they tended to be registered Democrats, even if most of them had voted for Richard Nixon in 1972. The nation's best-known evangelical, Billy Graham, was a registered Democrat, although most of the presidential candidates he favored were Republicans. In 1976 he was believed to prefer Gerald Ford, despite his statements of political neutrality.[11]

Carter was not as theologically or politically conservative as Graham. A few years later, in the 1980s, when the Southern Baptist Convention experienced a fissure, Carter would side not with the conservatives but with the significantly smaller number of moderates who favored strict church-state separation, a less literal interpretation of some biblical passages, and an egalitarian view of gender roles. Unlike some of the conservatives in the denomination, Carter was not interested in creating a "Christian nation" through laws that mirrored biblical standards; instead, he saw his Christian faith primarily as a mandate for social justice, human rights, and personal morality.[12]

In another political context (1980, for example), Carter's differences with the majority of Southern Baptists and other white evangelicals might have cost him votes, but in 1976 most evangelicals cared more about a presidential candidate's personal faith and ethical behavior than his policy positions. Carter's habits of weekly church attendance, daily Bible reading, and frequent prayer, along with his conversion experience and personal testimony of his faith in Jesus, endeared him to evangelicals across the theological spectrum and assuaged whatever doubts they might have had about his positions on particular political issues. Most evangelical leaders in the North opposed abortion, and although Southern Baptists also expressed grave reservations about it, they did not yet support an absolute ban on abortion in all circumstances. Very few evangelicals wanted to make abortion policy a political litmus test, and they rarely asked Carter about his stance on this or any other policy issue. Instead, they just were excited to find a candidate who identified with their faith. "Christians in particular ought to be concerned about the ethical and religious convictions of those who aspire to the presidency," *Christianity Today* declared in April 1976. "The basis upon which a leader makes his decisions is more important than what side he takes in current transient controversies."[13]

This widespread evangelical attitude of ambivalence toward policy positions—but a strong commitment to vote only for candidates who demonstrated the highest personal values and Christian faith—worked to Carter's advantage because he had always wanted to base his campaign on personal trustworthiness and leadership ability rather than particular policy views. Carter's references in campaign speeches to "trust," "honesty," and "decency" solidified his credentials among evangelicals, even when he was not speaking directly about his faith. His language of moral conviction and faith in the American people was naturally evangelical. Even without direct outreach to white evangelicals, Carter picked up their support, especially in the South. By the summer, about 75 percent of Southern Baptist voters supported his candidacy, according to Gallup. But the Carter campaign also experimented with direct appeals to evangelicals that highlighted the candidate's personal Christian testimony. His campaign autobiography *Why Not the Best?* was published by the Southern Baptist Convention's Broadman Press, and it included extensive discussions of his personal faith. In June 1976 the evangelical Logos Publishers released an even more directly religious biography, *The Miracle of Jimmy Carter.* This celebratory book, which Logos called a "chronicle of faith," was cowritten by Pulitzer Prize–winning *Baltimore Sun* reporter Howard Norton and evangelical Christian journalist Bob Slosser, a board member of Pat Robertson's Christian Broadcasting Network, and it combined traditional biographical analysis with a detailed discussion of the spiritual power of Carter's trust in God. Ads for the book appeared in leading evangelical magazines throughout the summer and fall, and *The Miracle of Jimmy Carter* sold 1.5 million copies by October. Carter also solidified his appeal to fellow born-again Christians by granting interviews to the evangelical magazines *Christian Life* and *Eternity,* in which he discussed his conversion in detail and noted his daily reliance on "Christ and the Holy Spirit."[14]

Carter's faith was especially useful in winning the trust of blacks, a highly religious demographic group that knew how important Baptist churches and the Christian faith had been in the civil rights struggle. "Black folks feel that Carter is deep in their corner," T. Garrott Benjamin, pastor of the predominantly black Second Christian Church in Indianapolis, explained to the *Washington Post.* "What I mean is that he speaks from roots. He's a born-again Christian and he's out of the South. . . . It's a spiritual thing—the fact that he claims the church. When he talks about the Lord Jesus Christ, he talks about Him as somebody he knows, and the people believe him."[15]

Perhaps, as the Ford campaign believed, it was Carter's faith that enabled him to unite white conservative Democrats with politically liberal blacks. Baptist marketing consultant Gaylord Briley told the Ford campaign, "The [white] evangelicals assume that because he uses the right words, he must be a conservative, while the blacks assume that if he really is a Christian he must really be concerned about and willing to help the poor and downtrodden."[16]

Carter was aware that overt discussions of his Christian beliefs might also have negative political costs, since many on his campaign staff and in the media assumed that he would lose votes among Jews and secular Americans if he discussed his evangelical faith on the campaign trail. Stu Eizenstat frequently cautioned Carter against evangelical politicking. While Carter's religious views "undoubtedly have helped in many states," he noted in a May 3 memo, "they have hurt among liberals and particularly Jews. We have gathered all of the support we will get from it and can expect more negative reaction." From this point on, Eizenstat advised, Carter needed to answer all questions about his religious faith by saying, "My religious views, like yours, are personal and are something I keep to myself. Because of this it would be inappropriate for me to discuss in a Presidential campaign my religious beliefs, except to say they are quite normal Baptist views." He needed to issue a JFK-like statement on the subject and affirm his commitment to the "separation of Church and State" while also declaring that his "beliefs on religion" did not "influence [his] decision-making."[17]

Carter did not do this. Instead, he found a way to reaffirm his religious beliefs while reassuring Jews and secular voters that a strong commitment to church-state separation was a central tenet of his Baptist faith. To voters who might be skeptical about an overtly evangelical Christian president, he pointed out that Baptist churches were the ultimate democratic institutions in their affirmation of the right of conscience and their repudiation of all church hierarchy. His evangelical faith would make him a more honest president but not a more intolerant one, he said; he strongly affirmed religious liberty for all and was committed to a pluralistic society.[18] With this explanation of his religious faith, Carter managed to mollify most of his critics while also winning support from both black and white born-again Protestants for whom Udall's secular campaign had little attraction. Carter recognized what Udall (and McGovern) had not: most Democratic voters were religious, and the vast majority of Democrats outside of college towns and affluent suburbs were not drawn to secular candidates. As Udall's attempt to unite Democrats under a progressive banner continued to founder, Carter expanded his hold on the center of the Democratic Party.

FRANK CHURCH AND JERRY BROWN

So far, for liberal Democrats, 1976 had not been a good year. Although Carter had moved slightly to the left by the end of April, many McGovern liberals still did not trust him. They had hoped Udall could stop him, but the Arizona congressman had not won a single primary outside of his own state. The liberals in the party therefore welcomed the announcement that two new liberal candidates from the West—Senator Frank Church of Idaho and Governor Jerry Brown of California—would make a last-gasp effort to stop Carter in the remaining primaries in May and June. Both Church and Brown were unconventional liberals who did not fit neatly into ideological categories, but many progressives viewed them as potential allies.

The press consistently described Church as a "liberal," but his liberalism was infused with a strong dose of western-style libertarian thinking and, in some respects, seemed far removed from the East Coast economic liberalism of the New Deal. In some ways, Church was the polar opposite of Henry Jackson, a consistent advocate of government programs. Church wanted to trim the bureaucracy, but not merely for the sake of balancing the budget. What motivated him above all else was a belief in individual freedom and conscience, and he viewed bloated government bureaucracies as a corrupting force and an impediment to individual liberty.

Church was a third-generation Idahoan whose values reflected the independent spirit of the Mountain West. His grandfather had come to Idaho City in the 1860s to look for gold, and the family had been in the state ever since. When Church was born in 1924, the family was living in Boise and was strongly Republican. Politics became an obsession for Church from an early age. As a teenager in the late 1930s, he considered Idaho senator William Borah, who was known for his isolationist views on foreign policy, his political hero, and he memorized several of Borah's speeches. Church's childhood friends remembered that he wanted to serve on the Senate Foreign Relations Committee, as Borah did, but he also frequently talked about becoming president. By the age of fifteen, he had already picked much of his future cabinet. After excelling in high school debate, Church earned a bachelor's degree at Stanford University, won a Bronze Star for his military service in World War II, and then headed to Harvard Law School. It was there that he experienced a debilitating cancer that nearly took his life. The six-foot-tall Church shriveled to ninety pounds during radiation treatments and surgery, but he ultimately regained full health and finished his law degree at Stanford, after which he immediately headed back to Idaho and entered politics. At age thirty-two, he was elected to the Senate.

As an adult, Church became a Democrat, despite growing up in a Republican home and serving a predominantly Republican constituency. But in some respects, his views still bore a certain resemblance to those of his boyhood hero Borah. Church was one of the Senate's earliest opponents of the Vietnam War, and he was critical of foreign aid programs. In 1976, when he decided to run for president, he was using his position as chair of the Senate Intelligence Committee to recommend tight controls on the CIA's covert activities, as well as on the FBI's domestic spying. Civil liberties were a passion for him. He consistently supported civil rights legislation and was one of the co-sponsors of the Equal Rights Amendment. Contrary to most of his party, he opposed all federal restrictions on guns, insisting that gun control measures should be passed only at the state and local levels. On abortion, he insisted on the primacy of the right of conscience. Although he supported abortion rights, he opposed all measures to require federally funded hospitals to provide abortions, and he authored legislation to allow doctors and nurses to refuse to assist in abortions for reasons of conscience.

In several areas in which Church's libertarian leanings clashed with Democratic Party orthodoxy, he chose the path of personal freedom. He opposed national health insurance, at least in the immediate future, and he disliked the idea of "forced busing" to achieve integration, except as a last resort and when absolutely necessary to protect civil rights. But he was also suspicious of the corporate power that some Republicans favored. He wanted to "give free enterprise some breathing room" through an aggressive antitrust policy that reined in the power of large multinational corporations and broke up some of the large oil companies. "Big government," "big business," and "big labor" were all equally problematic, he believed, and he wanted to limit their size and influence. He was running for president, he said, because he wanted to see greater transparency in Washington and hoped to create "better, not bigger, government" by "turning the decision-making homeward again."[19]

The press's consistency in describing Church's anti-Washington campaign agenda as "liberal," with its emphasis on individual freedom in opposition to several programs long favored by the Democrats, was a sign that antiwar sentiment and support for feminism and civil rights now served as a litmus test for progressive orthodoxy in the minds of many journalists and young suburban white liberals. These liberals had not objected to Udall's vote for right-to-work legislation, nor did they raise eyebrows when Church complained about "big labor." Church's views on national health insurance, labor unions, and gun control were well to the right of Jackson's, but Jackson was culturally conservative and, in the view of many progressives, wrong on foreign policy. Church's record of going after the CIA and the FBI appealed to progressives who were still outraged about the Vietnam War, the military-industrial complex, and the abuse of power in the Nixon White House.

Many McGovern liberals also appreciated Church's candor and precision. He invariably gave long, detailed answers to policy-related questions, leaving voters with no doubts about where he stood—even though his positions might be unpopular. "I have never believed in the politics of style over substance," he said. As he told the press in a not-so-subtle dig at Carter, he refused to sugarcoat his answers to suit a particular audience or to gloss over hard truths. When speaking to pro-choice feminists, he pledged to support doctors' right to exempt themselves from performing abortions, and when visiting a synagogue, he expressed skepticism about American support for Israel. "The people of Idaho have given me much latitude to be my own man," he said.[20] He intended to extend this political independence to his presidential campaign.

Church knew that it was too late for him to win the nomination outright, but he hoped that if he could win Nebraska and Oregon and get at least 20 percent of the vote in California and a few other states, he could deprive Carter of a first-ballot nomination at the convention and perhaps win the nomination for himself on a subsequent ballot. Many observers thought the convention was more likely to give the nomination to Hubert Humphrey than to Church, but for some liberals, that did not matter. A vote for Church was a vote against Carter, and that was all that counted. Church himself acknowledged the long-shot nature of his bid. Calling his approach the "late, late strategy," he wore tortoise ties on the campaign trail in an overt reference to Aesop's fable of the tortoise and the hare. It would be a "miracle" if he won Nebraska, he said, but he was holding out hope for the improbable.[21]

Church did win the Nebraska primary. He spent three times as much money in the state as Carter did and devoted a full two weeks to his Nebraska campaign, while Carter spent only two days there.[22] Still, his victory came as a surprise to those who thought Carter had a clear path to the nomination, and it gave hope to those who were desperate to stop Carter before the convention. Church then turned his attention to the other remaining western primaries. By then, there was another westerner in the race: California governor Jerry Brown.

Edmund G. "Jerry" Brown Jr. was perhaps the most unconventional presidential candidate yet to emerge, and many journalists had trouble figuring out whether they should treat him as a serious contender. His political credentials suggested that he would be a candidate of the highest caliber. He was a highly popular first-term governor of the nation's largest state. After just fifteen months on the job, his cost-conscious management had resulted in impressive budget surpluses, prosperity, and improved efficiency—all of which had eluded his predecessor in Sacramento, the self-proclaimed budget-cutter Ronald Reagan. Brown had also endeared himself to many liberal Democrats by bringing a record number of African Americans, Hispanics, and other minorities into state regulatory agencies and the California judiciary. He fought for the rights of migrant workers and became an ally of Cesar Chavez. He also had a respected political pedigree: his father, Edmund G. "Pat" Brown Sr., had served as governor of California in the early 1960s. Educated at Berkeley and Yale Law School, Jerry Brown was an avid reader and was widely described as intelligent and articulate. He also had good looks and what some viewed as Kennedyesque charisma on the campaign trail. At his rallies of thousands, young women swooned. Having just turned thirty-eight, he was the youngest of the presidential contenders—and would have been the youngest president ever elected had he won the White House that year. Some reporters viewed him as politically immature, but what really confused them was Brown's utter refusal to speak or act like a politician. He was given to ironic detachment, not political glad-handing, and on the campaign trail, he insisted on playing the part of a melancholy poet or doom-and-gloom prophet, not the gregarious office-seeker or policy expert.[23]

Earlier in life, Brown had fled politics, and he never became entirely comfortable with it. As a young man, he defied his father's wishes by enrolling in a Catholic seminary, intending to become a Jesuit. After three and a half years he dropped out, complaining that seminary life was "too rigid" and "too dogmatic." He then went to law school and eventually entered the political world he had once eschewed. But, as *New York Times* reporter James Reston phrased it, he "didn't leave the Church after his Jesuit studies; he merely switched pulpits." Although Brown rarely went to Mass as governor, he spent weekends in Zen and Trappist monasteries. His preferred form of spirituality became more Buddhist than Thomistic, and meditation rather than conventional prayer became his favorite spiritual exercise, but he was constantly asking the deep questions about meaning, existence, and human flourishing that had animated his seminary studies. Existentialist philosophy especially interested him. He memorized verbatim a section of Albert Camus's novel *The Stranger* and quoted Dylan Thomas's poetry with such ease that the *New York Times* observed such recitations were as "natural" to him "as breathing." But he did not enjoy newspapers very much and was loath to watch television. He had a deep antipathy to simple solutions but little interest in policy details; it was the philosophy behind the policies that fascinated him. He pursued environmental causes with an almost religious zeal because he was convinced that the planet was being destroyed. One of his early legislative achievements was a law requiring that all toilets sold in California be water-saving, low-flush models.[24]

A recognition of "limits" was the theme of Brown's governorship, and it became the central focus of his presidential campaign as well. He was convinced that the era of economic growth had ended and that Americans would have to get used to living with less. But more importantly, nothing less than the "survival of the planet" was at stake. As Brown tried to live out the ecological values he preached, his personal austerity became legendary. When he was elected governor, he refused to use the governor's mansion or limousine and insisted on living in a small bachelor apartment and driving a Plymouth. Rather than investing in a bed, he slept on a mattress on the floor. Reporters noticed that he was even too frugal to buy new razor blades; the telltale splotches on his face revealed that he was scratching his cheeks with dull shaving equipment. Brown applied his personal philosophy of frugality to the state government, engaging in rigorous cost-cutting. Brown had a hatred for government bureaucracy, but his hatred had more in common with the New Left critiques of the 1960s than with Reagan's conservative philosophy of the 1970s. Brown did not want to reduce the size of government merely to create more space for free enterprise, as Reagan did; he wanted to "reduce the role of the Federal Government" (as well as the role of the state government) to save resources in a shrinking planet and to give people the space to pursue things that were personally meaningful. To explain his approach, he gave away copies of E. F. Schumacher's *Small Is Beautiful: Economics as If People Mattered,* which included chapters titled "Peace and Permanence," "Buddhist Economics," "The Proper Use of Land," and "New Patterns of Ownership." The large government programs that had characterized the liberalism of the 1960s—and that still characterized Hubert Humphrey's policy views—made no sense in the new ecology. "The future to a large extent is not within your control," Brown said. "That's one of the problems with planning. There's an organic, natural flow to things."[25]

Perhaps it was characteristic of Brown's melancholy, conflicted approach to politics that he insisted in February that he had no interest in joining the presidential race but then decided in mid-March, after missing the filing deadlines for most of the state primaries, that he wanted to be a candidate after all. No other presidential candidate had succeeded in "capturing the imagination of the Democratic Party or the American people," he said, so he intended to enter the race to ask the questions no one else was asking. The other candidates gave their audiences false hope; Brown would speak hard truths to them about "limits." "The [political] competition is based on an escalation of promises which are now so far removed from people's ordinary experience of what government gives them that there's very little credibility," he said. "People in their own heart of hearts know that we are in a limited world. We all sense it in our own personal vibes. I think that if there's any response to what I'm doing, it's that . . . the refashioning of those limits is the work of politics now."[26]

Brown's father advised him to restrict his candidacy to a "favorite-son" campaign in his own state of California, whose primary was scheduled for June 8. California controlled 280 Democratic delegates, and if Brown could win a majority of them, he might be able to prevent Carter from winning the nomination on the first ballot at the convention or, at the very least, extract some concessions. Favorite-son candidacies had been popular for decades. But Brown decided to take his message to the East as well. Some of Sargent Shriver's former supporters in Ohio encouraged him to enter that state's primary because they saw in him the same liberal, values-centered, cerebral, Catholic approach that had originally attracted them to Shriver. And when Maryland governor Marvin Mandel, a Humphrey supporter, encouraged his state's political machine to support Brown as a way to block Carter from getting the nomination, the California governor was suddenly catapulted to a position of national influence in the presidential race. He arrived in Maryland and received a red-carpet welcome from the governor and thousands of cheering supporters. In one of the oddest political matches of the entire primary season, grizzled machine politicians from Baltimore united with baby-boomer idealists to turn Brown into a serious contender in their state.[27] Brown's political platform was, in most respects, the polar opposite of Humphrey's traditional liberal agenda of expanded government programs, increased spending to create jobs, and strong support for labor unions, but that no longer mattered in the eleventh-hour rush to stop Carter.

Brown looked on all this with the detached bemusement that characterized his approach to life. He seemed disdainful of the work of campaigning, taking little joy in the crowds that thronged about him. When a wealthy Democratic donor in New York sent a chauffeured Mercedes to take him to a fund-raiser, he turned down the ride and insisted on driving a borrowed Ford instead. "I cannot relate to that material possessory consciousness," he said. Journalists alternately described him as "humorless" in private or as seeming to take nothing seriously. In reality, his ironic and cynical humor was the sort that had rarely been seen on the political trail because it represented the new, postmodern approach of a young generation that had barely begun to enter the political scene. Brown constantly spoke about the value of authenticity, but most journalists who interviewed him found him elusive and "enigmatic," and they noted that he seemed to take delight in throwing them off the trail when they questioned him. Sometimes he would repeat their questions back to them and pontificate without providing any real answers; at other times he would toss out ridiculous deadpan responses just to see if they would take the bait. When a reporter at a press conference asked Brown to name his favorite political philosopher, for instance, he answered, "Thomas Hooker." After the journalists dutifully scribbled the answer in their notebooks, Brown explained that he was just being "facetious"; Thomas Hooker was the seventeenth-century Puritan founder of Connecticut, and he had simply picked the name at random. "You have to have a certain sense of the absurd to be in politics," he said. "Absurd is seeing the process, standing back from it, commenting on it like in plays where someone comes out and explains. It's a way of trying to say something that is true. The grooves are so worn in public discourse that you must find ways of breaking through that give a sense of what you are."[28]

It was this ironic, emotional distance from his audience that always seemed to throw reporters off. They followed him on the campaign trail as he ate his airport lunches of orange juice and granola bars (a newly invented snack that had appeared on the market less than a year earlier) or sipped white wine at fund-raising events that he derisively mocked. They noted that whether he was greeting supporters or speaking at large rallies, his "quizzical" expression never seemed to leave his face. "He is not unlikeable, but there is something about him that gives one the impression that he doesn't care personally about people," *Washington Post* reporter Sally Quinn wrote. "He cares intellectually but doesn't exude that concern, that feeling of human compassion that one would expect from someone with his humanitarian beliefs."[29]

Reporters quickly learned that Brown would shut down the conversation if they asked him about his past or his personal life. Questions about his own habits particularly galled him. When reporters inquired about his love life or wondered how he would respond to rumors that he was a "homosexual," he denied the rumors and disclosed that he was not currently dating but refused to say whether he had ever been in love. When they asked why he slept on a mattress on the floor, he became visibly irritated. "The human species faces extinction, and we're worrying why my mattress is on the floor," he snapped at one reporter. "Look, I lived a certain way before, and I still live that way. It's not uncommon among people of my generation."[30]

Seasoned reporters may have had trouble understanding Brown, but he proved wildly popular with Democratic voters under the age of thirty, especially on the West Coast. For a generation that had been shaped by the environmental message of Rachel Carson's *Silent Spring* and the warnings about declining resources presented in Paul Ehrlich's *The Population Bomb,* Brown's campaign made sense. And for a voting group that was yearning for an anti-Washington message delivered in a style that was contemptuous of conventional politics, Brown was the perfect antipolitician. Many voters had once looked to Carter to be the anti-Washington candidate, but with Carter's vacillations receiving extensive scrutiny in the press, some were looking for a fresh face, and they found it in Brown. As the press noted, Brown was even less specific than Carter on most policy issues, but he did not take both sides of an issue, and his supporters seemed not to mind his vagueness. Those who wanted specific policy detail could get it from Frank Church, but for people who cared less about issue positions than about vision and authenticity, Brown's campaign was an attractive option.

Brown won the Maryland primary with 49 percent of the vote, leaving only 37 percent for Carter. Bolstered by this success, he then launched a write-in campaign in Oregon, since he had missed the filing deadline to put his name on the ballot there. Under normal circumstances, no candidate who was not on the ballot had any chance of winning, but Brown had been such a sensation on the campaign trail that he thought he could pull it off. He spoke to exuberant crowds in Oregon and earned an enthusiastic following among younger Democrats, which enabled him to carry nearly 25 percent of the vote. It was "one of the best-organized and best-financed write-in campaigns in Presidential primary history," the *New York Times* proclaimed. Despite his "sardonic humor" and low-key demeanor on the campaign trail, Brown proved to have more political acumen and a wider political following than anyone had suspected. He ultimately finished with the second-highest primary vote total of any Democrat in the 1976 presidential race.[31]

Squeezed by both Brown and Church, Carter was now unexpectedly on the defensive. He was still winning primaries in the South, but the magic had ended for him in the West. Church won Oregon, relegating Carter to second place; Church also carried his own state of Idaho, as expected. Brown took first place in the Nevada primary. The next week, Church continued his winning streak by defeating Carter by an almost three-to-one margin in Montana, but the real surprise of the night came in Rhode Island, where Brown, who was not on the ballot, endorsed an uncommitted slate of delegates and claimed an unexpected victory when that slate finished ahead of Carter's delegates. Because of the proportional allocation system, Carter continued to increase his delegate count even while losing primaries, but the momentum had left his campaign. He barely beat Udall in Michigan, defeating the Arizona congressman by only 43 to 42 percent, even while outspending him. He also defeated Udall in South Dakota, but only by investing far more campaign resources in the state than he had initially planned. The Carter campaign had expected to knock Udall out of the race in early April, but, buoyed by Carter's new vulnerability, the Arizonan's cash-strapped campaign experienced a sudden resurgence in late May and early June.[32]

The last Democratic Party contests of the season came on June 8, when voters went to the polls in Ohio, New Jersey, and California. Carter decisively defeated Udall in Ohio, winning 52 percent of the vote in his one victory of the night. Brown won by a landslide in California, carrying 59 percent of the vote, compared with Carter's 21 percent. And in New Jersey, a slate of uncommitted anti-Carter delegates who were supporters of either Brown or Humphrey took first place with 42 percent of the vote, compared with Carter's 28 percent.[33] Carter had expected to win New Jersey, so the outcome came as a disappointment. By his own count, he finished the primaries with about 1,250 delegates, although the *New York Times* could verify only that he had "over 1,125."[34] Regardless of the exact count, he had not locked up the nomination because he needed 1,505 delegates to win. It was time to start making phone calls.

THE CARTER CAMPAIGN'S DELEGATE STRATEGY

Jimmy Carter was not the first choice of most Democratic voters. Although he won many primary victories, most of his first-place finishes came only by earning a plurality (not a majority) of the vote in a divided field. He received only 39 percent of the sixteen million votes cast in all the Democratic primaries from February's New Hampshire contest to the California primary in June, and much of his support was regionally concentrated. Ohio, Indiana, and Kentucky were the only nonsouthern states where he received a majority of the vote, and each of these states had southern-leaning regions.[35] If the 61 percent of Democratic primary voters who cast their ballots for another candidate had united around one of Carter's opponents, his campaign would have been in trouble. But Democratic voters were divided among Wallace's cultural conservatives, Jackson's pro-Israel and antibusing advocates, Church's freedom-loving westerners, Udall's college-educated suburban liberals, and Brown's young environmentalists, and there was no other candidate who could unite them.

Many Democrats had thought that Hubert Humphrey would be the most viable alternative to Carter. Although Humphrey almost certainly would have won primaries in northern industrial states if he had been a candidate, he did not have the support of a majority of Democrats. He was not popular among whites in the South, and he held little appeal for the younger voters who liked Brown. And as Jackson had found, a strong defense of large government programs was out of step with the anti-Washington mood of many voters. Even as some Democrats were entreating Humphrey to enter the race, polls showed him barely running even with President Ford in a hypothetical matchup, with Carter running ahead.[36]

Perhaps Humphrey realized these liabilities. After keeping his party waiting for months while he hinted at the possibility of a convention challenge, he announced on June 9, a day after the last primaries, that he would not attempt to stop Carter's nomination at the convention. Carter, he said, was "virtually certain to be our party's nominee." Brown insisted that he would stay in the race and take his challenge to the convention, but with only a fraction of the number of delegates that Carter controlled, this seemed to be a quixotic quest.[37]

With no other candidate waiting in the wings to claim the nomination, Carter's task of convincing delegates for rival candidates to join his side was a lot easier. If he was not their preference, he was, for the majority of Democratic delegates, an acceptable second choice. The stop-Carter campaign had the support of only a minority of Democrats. With the exception of the Brown and Udall progressives who worried that Carter might betray their ideals, most Democratic Party activists' greatest desire was not to create an ideologically pure ticket but to unify the party around a candidate who could win the general election and avoid the debacle of 1972. Carter seized on this desire and appealed to delegates to unite around him as quickly as possible to avoid an intraparty fracture. He argued that, as a centrist, he was the candidate who represented the concerns of every faction in the Democratic Party. Weeks earlier, his campaign team had already started calling uncommitted delegates, along with delegates pledged to candidates who had dropped out of the race. They divided up the rival delegates ideologically, assigning each delegate to a prominent pro-Carter political figure who most closely matched the delegate's political views and would therefore be able to make an individually scripted, personal appeal to that delegate's issues of concern. Senator Bennett Johnston of Louisiana, for instance, called some of the conservative delegates, while Andrew Young was assigned to phone blacks and liberals. Birch Bayh, who was now on Carter's side, was assigned to round up support from pro-labor delegates, and Representative Pat Schroeder of Colorado was assigned some liberal female delegates to call. Senator Joe Biden of Delaware, a strong supporter of Carter, volunteered to call any Pennsylvania delegates he thought he could influence. Wallace delegates received calls from Carter's cousin, Georgia state senator Hugh Carter, whose rural South Georgia heritage and worm-farming business were expected to endear him to some of Wallace's supporters.[38]

Carter's campaign staff worried that, with Udall delegates still united against him, their most likely converts might be Wallace delegates, which would not help Carter's image at the convention. They made a special appeal to the Udall delegates, sending out a letter that encouraged them to unite behind Carter to defeat the Republicans in November. Even if they did not personally like Carter, it was important for Democrats to regain the White House and control judicial and federal administrative appointments, the letter declared. But even with these appeals—and even with their preferred candidate out of the race—a number of delegates were reluctant to switch to Carter. In Massachusetts, Carter's volunteers noted, "We have worked the Shriver delegates pretty hard, and no more movement there." And Udall continued to hold out for days, refusing to officially end his candidacy or give his delegates to Carter, even though he knew he could not prevent Carter from winning the nomination. Udall's campaign staff urged him not to cede his delegates because they believed those delegates could be a bulwark of support for the progressive wing of the party and prevent Carter from moving the platform too far toward the political center. Udall was the only one, they thought, who would "act as the 'conscience' of the Democratic Party, to remind delegates of our commitment to progressive ideals." They even held out the vain hope that, with a substantial number of delegates under his control, Udall would be a more attractive candidate for vice president, giving him an opportunity to continue his efforts to push Carter to the left.[39]

As some of Carter's campaign staff had feared, George Wallace proved easier to persuade than the liberals. At 2:15 a.m. on Wednesday, June 9—almost immediately after the California primary results were announced—Wallace telephoned Carter and offered him his delegates; the next day he gave the Georgia governor an enthusiastic public endorsement. Faced with a somewhat embarrassing situation—that is, the impression that Wallace had delivered the nomination to him—Carter decided not to tell reporters about the call until the next day. Fortunately for him, Chicago mayor Richard Daley, who controlled a small group of uncommitted delegates from Illinois, offered on Wednesday morning to give those delegates to Carter, and Henry Jackson, though not yet formally endorsing Carter or explicitly offering him his delegates, suggested that he would probably do so within a few days. Carter could thus claim the nomination without acknowledging his dependence on Wallace's support.[40]

This left some unanswered questions: Why had Wallace been so quick to endorse Carter after his bitter race against him? Why did he not run against Carter as an independent candidate, as many observers, including Wallace's own campaign manager, had expected? Part of the reason, no doubt, was that Wallace's showing in the primaries had been disappointing. The Alabama governor had won 12.5 percent of the primary vote nationwide, but both the press and Democratic Party officials had predicted the previous year that he would likely earn 20 or even 30 percent of the vote. Wallace's lower-than-expected performance took the wind out of his sails. He would never run for president again. Wallace blamed his poor showing on his paralysis, saying that his followers did not want to vote for a man confined to a wheelchair. There was probably some truth to Wallace's speculation. At home in Alabama, he had raised record amounts of money in a direct-mail operation that appealed to his followers' anger and discontent through the written word. But when Wallace's supporters came to his campaign rallies, they were disappointed. Expecting to see the old rabble-rousing master of colorful invective who had goaded them to action in 1968 and 1972 by shouting down protesters and waving his fist at the audience, they saw instead a "quiet immobile man protected by a sea of Secret Service men," as the *Washington Post* phrased it. It appeared that the fire had gone out of him. And he was no longer quite sure how to handle the issue of race in the new postsegregationist, post–civil rights era. The issue of busing had worked for him in 1972, but outside of Massachusetts and a few other locations, it no longer aroused much passion in voters. And besides that, other candidates—Jackson and, to a lesser degree, Carter—also opposed busing. Indeed, both Carter and Reagan, it seemed, had appropriated most of Wallace's anti-Washington message, with both candidates complaining at length about government bureaucracy and deficit spending, and with Reagan mounting a campaign against détente that was just as strong as Wallace's. "All of them done stole my water," Wallace told a reporter. "They're drinking out of my dipper." As Wallace's direct-mail guru Richard Viguerie noted, Reagan's campaign "siphoned" much of Wallace's support.[41]

But Wallace, unlike a few of his supporters, was not attracted to Reagan's candidacy. He had cut his political teeth as a southern New Deal Democrat, and he intended to remain in the Democratic Party. What he wanted above all was to earn respect for the white South and respect for himself as a political visionary. Carter, he thought, might deliver those goods. The candidate from Georgia represented a new generation of southern political leadership that differed in many ways from Wallace's brand, but like Wallace, he connected with white southerners and understood their values. In 1972 Wallace had hated the McGovern campaign's alleged scorn for poor whites of the Deep South. Carter, he thought, would never do that, so he felt comfortable endorsing him. Best of all, he could claim credit for giving Carter the nomination by introducing the anti-Washington populist themes the Georgian had ridden to victory. "I paved the way for a Jimmy Carter," he boasted.[42]

Most Wallace voters seemingly felt the same way. Although Reagan benefited from the votes of Wallace Democrats in several state primaries, Wallace supporters were far more likely to switch to Carter than to support either of the Republican presidential candidates. A *New York Times*–CBS poll in June 1976 found that the one-third of Democrats who identified themselves as supportive of Wallace's ideas preferred Carter over either Ford or Reagan by a five-to-one ratio. But among the much narrower group of Wallace's core supporters—that is, the longtime donors to his campaigns and the people who had read his newsletters and attended his campaign rallies for years—there was a great deal of anger about his decision to endorse the Georgia governor. Hundreds wrote to express their dismay, saying that they would never again donate money to his campaigns because he had betrayed their cause. Carter, they argued, was a liberal in disguise. "This November when Carter is elected and in January when he continues forced bussing, rams the E.R.A. down our throats, registers our guns, sells out the independence of America to internationalism—you will be to blame," one of the many angry Wallace voters wrote to their erstwhile champion. Many begged him to reconsider. Most thought he should run on an independent ticket, although some believed he could find common cause with the one remaining populist conservative presidential candidate: Reagan. "At least, will you help what is left of America by supporting the Ronald Reagan campaign?" one Texas couple pleaded.[43] But Wallace viewed the issue differently. Although his campaign had attracted the support of some conservative movement activists—as well as those outside the boundaries of respectable conservatism, who were prone to conspiracy theories or the speculations of the John Birch Society—Wallace had never been one of those people himself; his loyalties were always to the white South rather than to the conservative movement. Carter's rural upbringing in Georgia was something that Wallace could relate to, and when it was clear that Carter would get the nomination, Wallace wanted to get the credit for delivering the delegates that made it possible.

Carter tried to distance himself from Wallace's racist image, but he continued to channel his populist politics. When Carter convened a press conference to announce that he now had the nomination in hand, he showed up to this important event wearing jeans, boots, and a tieless casual shirt—a highly unusual wardrobe choice for the occasion. Even Jerry Brown donned a conservative suit and tie on the campaign trail. But Carter wanted to make it clear that he was running a people's campaign against the establishment and that he was his own man. Amassing enough delegates to clinch the nomination before the convention meant that "we won't have to wheel and deal or trade away any responsibilities except to the people themselves," he told the press.[44]

CREATING A PLATFORM

Carter's delegates were not ideologically uniform, but for the most part, they were more conservative than the McGovern delegates four years earlier. Ranging in age from seventeen to eighty-four, they included a few students, some elected officials, and a large number of people from outside of government. Thirty-nine percent had graduate degrees, while 38 percent had never graduated from college. Eighty-four percent of the Carter delegates were white, and 13 percent were black. (In early May only 11 percent of Carter's delegate slate—and only 7 percent of all Democratic convention delegates—were black, but after complaints from black political leaders and an effort by Carter's team to increase black representation on his delegate slate, they managed to raise the total to 13 percent.) "Attorney" was the most common occupation listed on the campaign's delegate survey; 18 percent of the delegates had law degrees. The second most commonly listed occupation was "housewife." Churches were the most common organizational affiliation listed; the only labor union that made the list was the National Education Association. The delegates' top issues of concern, according to a survey, were "employment," "economy," "honest and efficient government," and "government reorganization."[45]

In keeping with these themes—and with the message of his entire campaign—Carter proposed a platform that offered a vision for government reorganization and job creation that he called "a new beginning." A government characterized by "openness, compassion, and efficiency" was his primary goal, he said. Ethics reforms were a top priority, followed by a promise of full employment, low inflation, and a balanced budget. Like his recent speeches on the economy, Carter's proposed platform promised expansionary spending during his first year in office—including endorsement of the Humphrey-Hawkins bill's proposals for job creation—and assumed that after one or two years of this plan, the nation's economic growth would be sufficient to make a balanced budget feasible. Carter's letter to the Platform Committee also endorsed national universal health insurance, an increase in federal aid to cities and education, and more federal investment in transportation. He called for increased environmental protection, energy conservation, and antitrust prosecution of large oil companies (which had been a popular cause among Udall supporters and other liberals in the Democratic Party). Social Security payments should be increased, he said. The income tax system should be made more progressive. And the welfare system should be overhauled. "No one able to work, except mothers with preschool children, should be continued on the welfare rolls unless they accept a job," he wrote. He did not want to perpetuate a system that was "wasteful to the taxpayers of America" and "demeaning to the recipients," or one that "encourage[d] the breakup of families." But this was a rare proposal of a budget cut. Although Carter devoted two and a half pages of his thirty-seven-page document to a discussion of budget efficiency, and although he reiterated his promise of a balanced budget, the only other explicit spending cuts he called for were in the defense budget. He said defense spending should be reduced by up to $7 billion per year but claimed that these cuts would not endanger American military preparedness; they would merely cut unnecessary projects and personnel from a Pentagon that had become "wasteful and bloated."[46]

For the most part, then, Carter's proposed platform leaned to the left and endorsed the sort of large-scale spending projects liberal Democrats had long called for. He preserved his vow to balance the budget by arguing that high economic growth and the reduction of waste would allow him to eliminate deficit spending even while pursuing a rapid expansion in domestic social programs. His promise of an overhaul of the welfare system might have appealed to Wallace conservatives (indeed, Wallace himself submitted a very similar proposal to the Platform Committee), but on most other issues, Carter's platform was more in line with the priorities of Mo Udall and Hubert Humphrey than with budget-conscious critics of federal bureaucracy.[47]

On foreign policy, he attempted to split the difference between the hawkish views of Henry Jackson and the dovish leanings of Jerry Brown and Frank Church. He criticized Ford and Kissinger's policy of détente for conceding too much to the Soviets, especially in eastern Europe. "To the Soviets, détente is an opportunity to continue the process of world revolution without running the threat of nuclear war," he declared in a line that some of Jackson's and Wallace's supporters would have applauded. But he also promised to continue the project of arms reduction and to make détente "broader and more reciprocal," even while working toward eastern European states' independence from Soviet control.

Foreign policy must be multilateral, he said, and the CIA should not "effect violent change" in a foreign government. Future US military action should be limited to situations in which "our own security is endangered." But foreign aid needed to be reformed and potentially expanded so that "it meets the human needs of the greatest number of people."[48] In short, Carter's platform strongly suggested a more humanitarian foreign policy, with appeals both to liberals who wanted to avoid another Vietnam War and to Jackson-style hawks who were afraid that the United States had conceded too much to the Soviet Union.

There were a few glaring omissions from Carter's proposed platform statement. It did not mention the concerns of labor unions or call for the repeal of section 14B of the Taft-Hartley Act, which was a top priority for labor interests. Although it endorsed the Equal Rights Amendment, federally subsidized child care, and "family planning," it said nothing about abortion. It did not mention marijuana decriminalization—an issue of interest to some of Carter's younger supporters and a subject of frequent media inquiry. It said nothing about amnesty or pardon for Vietnam War draft evaders. It said nothing about busing. There was relatively little in the document about civil rights for African Americans. The only new legislation that Carter proposed to address racial discrimination was a law to make redlining by the Federal Housing Authority and federally subsidized savings and loans institutions illegal. His proposed platform said nothing about affirmative action or the location of public housing—the issue that had caused him so much trouble in Pennsylvania and Indiana two months earlier. In short, Carter's proposed platform avoided nearly all the polarizing social issues that had damaged George McGovern's campaign four years earlier, and instead it focused more narrowly on economic uplift and government management. This was a program, Carter hoped, that could unite almost all sections of the party, from Wallace conservatives to Brown progressives. Wallace, in fact, began his own statement to the Platform Committee by noting, "The greatest continuing problem we have in this country today is the unemployment of more than 7 million of our fellow Americans."[49] On that, all Democrats could agree.

The Platform Committee accepted most of Carter's recommendations. As Carter proposed, the platform adopted by the convention called for a "complete overhaul of the present tax system" to create greater equity. It endorsed a system of welfare reform, with work requirements for benefits, as Carter advocated. To no one's surprise, the platform also called for national universal health insurance, which had been a top priority of congressional Democrats throughout the decade.[50]

The leading theme of the platform was a promise to rejuvenate the economy and create jobs, which had been the focus of several primary candidates' campaigns. Beginning with a pledge to create a "fairer distribution of wealth, income and power," the platform presented a detailed plan to reduce the unemployment rate to only 3 percent in four years. This was an astonishing promise: the US unemployment rate had not been that low since World War II, and there were no signs that it could get there again in the foreseeable future. But a 3 percent unemployment rate was the target set by Hubert Humphrey and Augustus Hawkins, and as the *New York Times* observed, "the economic plank [of the proposed Democratic Party platform] reads like a description of the Humphrey-Hawkins bill pending in Congress."[51] Even without getting the nomination, Humphrey managed to put his stamp on the Democrats' presidential campaign. Carter entered the general election connected to a platform that strongly endorsed a measure he had expressed skepticism about as recently as early April but that he now officially supported.

The platform went beyond Carter's stated goals in a few cases. The party retained its historical repudiation of right-to-work legislation and its endorsement of repeal of section 14B of the Taft-Hartley Act. The platform also included a paragraph on equal opportunity in housing that had not been part of Carter's draft, and it went beyond Carter's proposed language on gun control by endorsing a ban on "Saturday night specials"—though this was something he supported. Carter would have preferred to keep some of the platform language a little less liberal, but he did not object to any of the policy stances the Platform Committee adopted.

On foreign policy, the platform largely endorsed Carter's views, even though his approach was more hawkish and more sharply critical of the Soviet Union than some progressives would have liked. The party was "morally opposed" to "the continued U.S.S.R. military dominance of many Eastern European countries," the platform stated. While endorsing détente and nuclear disarmament (as Carter had), the platform criticized the Republican administration for making too many concessions to the Soviet Union. "Pursuit of détente will require maintenance of a strong military deterrent" and "hard bargaining for our own interest," the platform declared. In keeping with Carter's proposal, the platform called for reduced military expenditures and a more streamlined military to meet the nation's defense needs. But even on this point, both the platform and Carter insisted that modest reductions in military expenditures would not diminish the nation's defense capabilities. Some Wallace and Jackson delegates would have preferred an even stronger anticommunist, more hawkish stance, but in suggesting that the United States needed to take a harder line with the Soviet Union, the platform was already staking out a position to the right of the Ford administration, just as Carter had.[52]

The Platform Committee's greatest deviations from Carter's preferred platform language were related to the polarizing cultural issues he had avoided discussing in his statement to the committee. While the members of the committee acquiesced to Carter's wishes to say nothing about gay rights—which was a key concern for some convention delegates, such as Bella Abzug—they refused to ignore busing, which the Democrats had endorsed in the 1972 platform. They likewise insisted on mentioning abortion. Both issues were controversial among Democrats, and there were plenty of delegates on both sides. On busing, the Platform Committee decided to endorse the practice, but only as a "judicial tool of the last resort." The 1972 Democratic Party platform had enthusiastically endorsed busing as "another tool to accomplish desegregation" and stated that "it must continue to be available." By 1976, the delegates were not ready to repudiate that stand altogether, but they were clearly retreating on the issue, just as Carter had during his primary campaign. The abortion issue was still sufficiently controversial in the Democratic Party to prompt the Platform Committee to avoid a ringing endorsement of abortion rights, as some of the California delegates wanted. In fact, by a vote of ten to three, a drafting subcommittee decided not to include any language on abortion, on the grounds that it would be "divisive." But when feminist organizations and pro-choice groups complained, the Carter campaign team, which at first tried to duck the issue, worked with the subcommittee to find language that would be broadly acceptable to most Democrats. "We fully recognize the religious and ethical nature of the concerns which many Americans have on the subject of abortion," the platform stated. "We feel, however, that it is undesirable to attempt to amend the U.S. Constitution [to] overturn the Supreme Court decision in this area." The subcommittee adopted this language by a vote of eight to four, and the full Platform Committee approved the statement by a vote of seventy-five to twenty-eight. But even though this two-line compromise statement had the support of approximately three-quarters of the delegates, it generated more objections from Democrats than anything else in the party platform that year. Ten thousand antiabortion demonstrators, led by Ellen McCormack, protested against the platform statement outside the convention hall.[53]

The conflict over abortion was the exception rather than the rule that year. Determined to avoid the intraparty divisions that had damaged McGovern's campaign four years earlier, the Platform Committee avoided involvement in most of the cultural flash points that had arisen during the campaign. When Wallace asked the Platform Committee to endorse a constitutional amendment allowing school prayer, the committee ignored his request. Nor did the committee mention anything about the decriminalization of marijuana, which many cultural liberals supported but the committee "overwhelmingly" rejected. The committee likewise ignored the seven hundred gay rights demonstrators who lobbied for platform language supporting their cause. Committee members held a long debate about amnesty for Vietnam War draft evaders but ultimately stopped short of endorsing the idea, saying instead that "deserters" should "be considered on a case-by-case basis." Even on abortion and busing, the Platform Committee made a concerted effort to adopt language that respected differing views within the party, while taking a middle-of-the-road position that it hoped would be broadly acceptable. The long minority rights section of the 1972 platform—which included multiple paragraphs on the "rights of children," "rights of women," "rights of youth," "rights of American Indians," "rights of the physically disabled," "rights of the mentally retarded," "rights of the elderly," and even "the right to be different"—was now largely eliminated and replaced with a short section on "civil and political rights" that deliberately adopted a moderate tone. The platform writers needed to avoid "purple language that's going to give the Republicans pot shots," Stu Eizenstat told the committee. Led by Carter's delegates, and working closely with Carter's campaign team, the Platform Committee brought the party's stances on cultural issues back to the political center, while retaining a traditionally liberal stance on economic issues. Progressive delegates who would have liked the party to take a more liberal stance on cultural issues surrendered their own preferences for the sake of party unity and the prospect of winning in the fall with a platform that, at least on economic issues, was much closer to Humphrey's views than Carter initially preferred.[54]

When Carter first entered the presidential race in 1974, he described himself as a fiscal conservative, but after a year and a half on the campaign trail, he moved closer to where the heavyweights of his party stood on budgetary matters and endorsed a platform that promised a lot more government programs and greater federal spending than he originally envisioned. Perhaps most significantly, he was now pledged to run on a platform that focused heavily on the central economic principle of the postwar Democratic Party: the Keynesian belief that the government had a social responsibility to engage in deficit spending to stimulate job creation during economic downturns. While Carter had never directly repudiated this notion, he had been such a strong deficit hawk that some Keynesian economists questioned his support for Democratic Party economic orthodoxy. The platform now committed him to a stance that was the opposite of both Ford's and Reagan's. Republicans believed that the government had a responsibility to cut spending and reduce taxes to end high inflation and give private industry the tools it needed to rejuvenate the economy. Thus, the 1976 election would be, in part, a contest between two different visions for economic recovery. Carter, the erstwhile anti-Washington deficit hawk, was now the champion of a platform that, thanks to Humphrey and other traditional liberals, envisioned a revived New Deal and an extension of the federal spending programs of the 1960s. As the Ford campaign recognized, Carter now appeared to be "conservative on social issues and liberal on economic issues"—the opposite of his image at the beginning of his presidential campaign.[55]

CHOOSING A LIBERAL RUNNING MATE

All of Carter's advisers recognized that he needed to pick a northerner or a westerner to balance the ticket. Most also thought that he should select a senator (not a fellow governor) who was significantly more liberal than Carter or could at least earn the respect of northern liberals who, despite the liberal Democratic platform, were still somewhat suspicious of him. Internal polling in June found that Carter was receiving unusually strong support from Republicans, independents, and southern whites, but he was facing opposition from the left wing of his own party. He was especially unpopular among liberal Jews and voters under the age of twenty-five. Many of these cultural liberals, who had supported Udall or Brown in the primaries, were threatening to vote for Eugene McCarthy, who had sought the Democratic presidential nomination in 1968 and was now running a third-party campaign to advance progressive principles that, in his opinion, Carter did not support. The Carter campaign's internal polling showed that McCarthy had the backing of 17 percent of all Democratic voters at the end of June—including 30 percent of Democrats who were Jewish, 30 percent of those who were eighteen to twenty-five years old, and 22 percent of those who lived on the Pacific coast. McCarthy was the first-choice candidate for 71 percent of voters who described themselves as "very liberal" and for 14 percent of those who called themselves "liberal." Some of Carter's progressive champions tried to stave off this hemorrhaging of liberal support by reassuring their fellow social liberals that Carter's views were compatible with theirs. Massachusetts governor Michael Dukakis defended Carter on this front, saying that his "social justice stands which are commendable . . . have linked him to the liberal wing of the party." Carter, after all, described himself as a "strong" advocate of the Equal Rights Amendment, and he had long touted his civil rights credentials and support among African Americans. But for some progressives, this was not nearly enough. Pollster Patrick Caddell advised Carter to pick a liberal running mate who could cut into McCarthy's margin and regain some of the votes from progressive demographic groups that were reluctant to support him.[56]

The two potential running mates who would produce the greatest political gains, Caddell said, were Senators Ted Kennedy and Ed Muskie. Muskie, the 1968 Democratic vice-presidential nominee, was known for his pro-environmentalist stances. Both men were popular with McGovern liberals but also had widespread support among all Democrats, and both were Catholic. Because Carter's internal polling suggested a potential problem with northern Catholics, selecting a Catholic running mate with liberal credentials would be a good move, Caddell thought. But Hamilton Jordan gave the scandal-ridden Kennedy a low rating for "integrity," which was one of the most important criteria Carter should consider in selecting a running mate, he said. Carter shared Jordan's views about a running mate's personal character. He wanted a vice-presidential candidate whose values were similar to his own and who could be a full partner in his administration—not merely a vote-getter on the campaign trail. He never gave Kennedy any serious consideration. Nor is it likely that Kennedy, who had turned down the vice presidency in 1972 and refused to run in 1976, would have accepted. Carter initially viewed Muskie, whose integrity Jordan believed was impeccable, as a much more viable running mate. The Maine senator had already served as Humphrey's running mate in 1968, and it was highly unusual for a presidential candidate to consider him for the same role again, but Carter treated him as a front-runner among seven finalists until a private interview convinced him that Muskie's volatile temper might make him a difficult partner.[57]

Carter also gave strong consideration to Senator John Glenn of Ohio, a former astronaut who was popular among centrists and conservatives in the party. But negative public reaction to Glenn's lackluster keynote speech at the beginning of the convention led to speculation that he would be a weak campaigner. In any case, Glenn did not have the pull among northern liberals and Humphrey backers that Carter needed at this stage of his campaign.[58]

In the end, Carter selected forty-eight-year-old Senator Walter "Fritz" Mondale, a Protestant from Minnesota and a Humphrey protégé. He was popular with organized labor and had solid liberal credentials, especially on traditional bread-and-butter economic issues and federal social welfare programs. Mondale did not poll particularly well among the young cultural progressives that Caddell had identified as a target group, but the pollster was most concerned about the Minnesota senator's unpopularity among white southerners. Carter, though, was still running very strong in the South, and he was prepared to risk losing a few votes among moderately conservative white southerners if he could gain a much stronger footing in the large industrial states, which Jordan had identified as the key to winning the election. If Carter could retain the South from Virginia through Texas, run well in the Northeast, and sweep the industrial heartland of the Midwest, he could easily win the election without carrying any state in the West other than California. That was Jordan's strategy, and Mondale might help realize this goal. If Carter wanted to find a traditional Great Society liberal in the Humphrey mold (which he did) and thus win over the pro-labor Humphrey backers who had opposed his nomination until the very end, he could not have made a better choice.[59]

But Carter's main reason for choosing Mondale was personal rather than political. He could envision Mondale as a genuine partner in his administration. The son of a Methodist minister and a schoolteacher,

Mondale shared Carter's concern for moral rectitude and social justice, even though he was far more enamored of Great Society–style economic liberalism than Carter was. Mondale identified poverty as his main concern. He had spent his eleven years in the Senate fighting for open-housing laws, federally funded child care, and other liberal measures. Jordan, like Caddell, had some concerns about how Mondale would poll among voters and suggested that Senator Alan Cranston of California or Frank Church might be a more politically savvy choice, but he gave the Minnesota liberal high marks for integrity and ability. Mondale had the congressional experience and detailed knowledge of federal policymaking that Carter lacked. *New York Times* reporter David Rosenbaum called him "perhaps, the best-informed member of the Senate on the entire gamut of legislative issues." Though witty and personable, Mondale was not a gregarious backslapper or a fiery campaigner, but he was well regarded as a compassionate, decent person. For a campaign that had made personal probity and ability its main criteria in evaluating potential vice-presidential selections, Mondale fit the bill. He was "one of the least wealthy members of the Senate," the *New York Times* reported, and had the "lowest net worth of any major party candidate for the Presidency or the Vice Presidency," partly because of his scrupulous efforts to avoid any financial investments that would represent a potential conflict of interest. His long, happy marriage to a minister's daughter had given him the picture-perfect family with three children. With the possible exception of his habit of smoking six cigars a day, he seemed to have no obvious vices. The press reaction to Carter's choice was mostly positive. Mondale had the potential to help Carter expand his base of support on the campaign trail and become even more useful as an experienced Washington insider once Carter reached the White House.[60]

Both the Ford and Reagan campaigns seized on the selection of Mondale, who had one of the Senate's most liberal voting records (with a 94 percent rating from the Americans for Democratic Action), as proof that Carter was actually a "big-government" liberal. Citing Mondale's left-of-center votes on child care, welfare, defense, and busing—all of which were likely to be unpopular with both culturally conservative and fiscally conservative voters—the Ford campaign accused the Minnesota senator of being "a 100 percent, bona fide liberal." "It gives us a tangible target," Ford campaign spokesperson Peter Kaye told the press as he explained why Carter would be easier to defeat now that the "liberal" Mondale was on the ticket. "We're not just running against this peanut farmer who walks on water." Carter was "no longer running against the Washington establishment; he's embracing it," Reagan campaign aide Lyn Nofziger said. Republicans thought that Mondale's selection, combined with the Democrats' economically liberal platform, gave the GOP an opportunity to win back some of the anti-Washington Republican and conservative Democratic voters who had turned to Carter but now might be nervous that he was just another "big-government" liberal Democrat. But the Carter campaign was not concerned. Because Democrats outnumbered Republicans nationwide by more than two to one, the Carter team never gave loyal members of the GOP much consideration.[61] Their strategy for victory rested on winning back the Democrats who had defected to Nixon in 1972, and they thought they could do that as long as Mondale retained the votes of Humphrey-supporting blue-collar workers in the industrial North and Carter maintained a lock on the South.

The Democratic strategy assumed that most voters were far more supportive of government social programs than Republicans believed. Although complaints about wasteful government spending were ubiquitous, few Americans wanted a rollback of the government social programs on which they depended, and few objected to Mondale's liberalism. Within days of Mondale's selection, the Carter campaign reported that it was receiving grateful letters from party liberals whose skepticism about Carter had turned to enthusiasm now that Mondale was on the ticket. Polls also showed that Carter's lead was nearly as large as Lyndon Johnson's before his landslide victory in 1964. Immediately before Carter's selection of Mondale, he led Ford by 53 percent to 36 percent in a Gallup survey. But a week after the convention and Mondale's addition to the ticket, a Harris survey showed that the gap had widened to 66 percent to 27 percent. If Reagan received the GOP nomination, Carter's margin of victory might be even greater, polls suggested; he led Reagan in the Harris poll by 68 percent to 26 percent. The Carter campaign's own polling showed that its candidate would likely pick up even solidly Republican states such as South Dakota, where he led Ford by 14 points in August. Not only was Carter expected to win, but it now seemed that he might sweep the country in a Democratic landslide as large as LBJ's in 1964.[62]

THE CONVENTION

Carter used the Democratic National Convention at Madison Square Garden in New York City primarily to solidify his unification of the party and touch the heartstrings of traditional Democrats by grafting his anti-Washington populist campaign onto the Democratic Party's track record of providing jobs for all. Despite a few discordant notes from liberals, which included a floor vote on Jerry Brown's and Mo Udall's nominations and some tension between Carter and the party's feminists over gender quotas to ensure equal representation for female delegates (which Carter opposed), the convention largely served as a Carter rally. The 1968 and 1972 Democratic conventions had been characterized by angry divisions among delegates in the convention halls and, in the case of the 1968 convention, violent confrontations in the streets. The 1976 convention, by contrast, was marked by unity and excitement among Democrats that they might finally recapture the White House after eight years of Nixon and Ford. It was the "smoothest-running [Democratic] convention in a dozen years," the *Washington Post* reported.[63] The ticket that Carter created went a long way toward bridging divisions in the party. Carter could continue to reiterate the populist themes that resonated not only with his core supporters but also with Wallace voters and many white southerners, while Mondale could appease the Humphrey backers and the northern labor interests.

The prime-time speeches at the convention offered a blend of Carter's promise to restore government to "the people" and the platform's pledge to produce full employment. John Glenn's keynote address provided the former; George McGovern, Hubert Humphrey, and Ed Muskie offered the latter, especially in their criticism of President Ford's veto of spending bills passed by the Democratic Congress. Ford and the other Republicans, the speakers alleged, had behaved like President Herbert Hoover, plunging the nation deeper into economic stagnation because of a commitment to penny-pinching. But Carter and the Democrats would return the nation to the low-inflation, high-growth era of the Kennedy administration, and they would do so with a public jobs creation program analogous to the New Deal. "Let's elect a President who will not veto public works programs, anti-recession grants to cities, youth employment and the other valuable and necessary programs contained in our platform," Muskie declared. Carter won the nomination, but it seemed that the Humphrey-style economic

Figure 7.2. Jimmy Carter and Walter Mondale at the 1976 Democratic National Convention. (Library of Congress, Prints & Photographs Division, U.S. News & World Report Magazine Collection, LC-DIG-ppmsca-09739)

liberals triumphed after all. With 59 percent of Americans citing "the economy" as the most important election-year issue, according to a recent Associated Press poll, this theme seemed likely to carry the Carter-Mondale ticket to victory.[64]

In addition to cementing his newly formed alliance with the Humphrey-style liberals who had been nervous about his candidacy only weeks before, the convention offered Carter an opportunity to showcase his endorsement of civil rights for African Americans and solidify his support among blacks, which had briefly been called into question earlier that spring with the public uproar over his use of the phrase "ethnic purity." The convention began with a keynote address by African American congresswoman Barbara Jordan of Texas, who brought the house down with a reminder that the Democratic Party was an "inclusive not an exclusive party" for "all the people." In fact, the reaction to Jordan (the first female African American keynoter at any major-party convention) was so enthusiastic that several black delegates insisted on nominating her for vice president, even though she said she was not interested in the position. Later in the convention,

Coretta Scott King offered an address that quoted liberally from her late husband's "I Have a Dream" speech and called on Democrats to live out their "commitment to human rights." Andrew Young also spoke from the podium, declaring, "For almost 200 years now and more our country has stumbled along the path to greatness under the burden of race and economic deprivation. I don't know about you, but I'm ready to lay those burdens down. . . . If you would vote to lay down the burdens of race, you will vote with me for Jimmy Carter as president." And the minister who closed the convention in prayer was none other than Martin Luther King Sr. "Surely the Lord sent Jimmy Carter to come on out and bring America back where she belongs," Daddy King declared. After the final benediction from King, the band played "We Shall Overcome," and some of the delegates joined arms and sang the old civil rights theme song in unison, closing the convention with a show of racial unity that made it hard to believe that George Wallace had just endorsed the ticket.[65] But perhaps the old segregationist's conversion to the cause only accentuated the evangelical appeal to forgiveness Daddy King had offered. There was room at the altar for everyone.

President Ford's television consultant, Bob Mead, watched such overtly religious themes with a mixture of envy and disgust, knowing that Ford and the Republicans could never match the Democrats' evangelical style when they met in Kansas City for their own convention later that summer. "I realized during the nomination speeches that an air of the Gospel was flowing from my television set," he told White House director of communications David Gergen. "Speeches were more like testimonials or confessionals."[66] Carter had masterfully used the language of evangelical Christian faith, which appealed to both black and white southerners, to bridge the racial and ideological divides in the party and unite all Democrats around his candidacy.

The evangelical language of values and moral causes also infused Carter's acceptance speech, which focused on the central theme of his campaign: the moral imperative of returning the government to "the people" so that it would represent their values once again. "It is time for the people to run the government, and not the other way around," he declared. He promised that he would be a "President who's not isolated from the people, but who feels your pain and shares your dreams and takes his strength and his wisdom and his courage from you." He spoke once again of the "simple decency of our people" and said that "the tragedy of Vietnam and Cambodia, the disgrace of Watergate, and the embarrassment of the CIA revelations could have been avoided if our government had simply reflected the sound judgment and good common sense and the high moral character of the American people."[67] This was the campaign Carter had always wanted to wage—a campaign based on values rather than specific policy proposals. While the platform was a policy-specific reiteration of Great Society–style economic liberalism, the convention speech was Carter's opportunity to reclaim the vision that had animated his campaign and to wrap it in the package of traditional Democratic priorities, from the New Deal to the 1960s. The Republicans tried to characterize the Carter-Mondale ticket as a return to failed programs of the mid-twentieth century, but Carter argued that those thirty years of Democratic programs had produced America's glory days and that the country had lost its way only when the government lost touch with the common virtues of the American people. Now Carter would return the government to the people, and the "high moral character of the American people" would once again be allowed to shine.

Walter Mondale's acceptance speech, which preceded Carter's, presented a similar message, though with a more sharply partisan tone. The Republicans, he said, "have tried to paralyze the momentum for human justice in America" by promoting policies that "further comfort the comfortable," but a Carter administration, working with a Democratic Congress, would "restore honesty and decency and hope in American life" by listening to the people and promoting the policies of compassion. Like Carter, he had great faith in the virtues of the American people. "We are a compassionate people, a peaceful people, and we believe in the dignity of work," he said. Carter had frequently promised to make the government as good as the American people, and Mondale reiterated that pledge. "Obeying the law," he said, would be "the fundamental principle of the Carter Administration." He concluded with a promise to enact the Democratic legislative priorities that he had spent his entire senatorial career working toward: the "right of everyone to have a job," a "reformed tax system," and "decent health care and good education and good housing and a secure and decent retirement for all." "The other party is trying to prove that government cannot work," he said. "We are pledged to make it work and it will work."[68]

Republican strategists who viewed Mondale as a big-government liberal heard much in the speech to confirm their views. If Mondale had been the presidential nominee in 1976, he might have lost the South and much of the rest of the nation, as Humphrey had in 1968 and as Mondale himself would in 1984. But with Carter occupying the leading spot on the ticket, many southerners—both blacks and whites—thought they could trust the Democrats to share their values. Carter skillfully tapped into moderately conservative voters' concerns about government, and he expressed those concerns in language that resonated with voters—the language of ethical concerns, faith, and moral fervor. The real reason many moderately conservative voters objected to "liberal" government programs, Carter recognized, was that they thought those programs did not share their values. By speaking in the language of moral values, Carter won the support of many cultural conservatives. And even for fiscal conservatives, who might have been most worried about some of Mondale's promises, Carter offered reassurance by reminding them that he was a fiscally conservative businessman himself, and he was going to balance the federal budget and protect the right of small businesses to operate free from government interference. "As an engineer, a planner, a businessman, I see clearly the value to our nation of a strong system of free enterprise based on increased productivity and adequate wages," he said. "We Democrats believe that competition is better than regulation, and we intend to combine strong safeguards for consumers with minimal intrusion of government in our free economic system."[69]

The magic worked. Not since 1944 had the entire South voted for the Democratic ticket, but it seemed likely to do so in 1976 because Carter had managed to reassure white southerners while winning the support of blacks, labor union members, and northern liberals. Carter "has united the Democratic Party more completely than at any time since Franklin Roosevelt's great victories," the *Christian Science Monitor* declared.[70]

In the view of many Republicans, including the editors of *Forbes* magazine, Carter did this by offering a "mirage." It was impossible to simultaneously create a national health insurance program, reduce taxes for the working class, promote the free-enterprise system, lower the unemployment rate to 3 percent, end inflation, and balance the budget within three years, they believed. If Carter was running on such a platform, he was offering false promises to the American people. "Barring a miraculous change in him, he can be counted on within three years to challenge Richard Nixon as one of the most unpopular

Presidents in American history," Republican consultant Powell Moore predicted.[71]

But most American voters did not agree with the Republicans' assessment. President Ford had been ineffective, they thought. Faced with worse-than-average inflation and unemployment, they welcomed the promise of a successful southern governor who gave voice to their moral concerns while identifying with their skepticism of the Washington establishment. A vote for Carter was a vote for both economic hope and moral values. He promised a return to the optimism of JFK, the compassion of FDR, and the honesty of Harry Truman. Though many voters had seen news reports about Carter's vacillating policy positions, most were still willing to trust him. He was a fresh face—the first Washington outsider to win a major-party nomination for the presidency in a generation, and the first Deep South major-party candidate in more than a century. Most Americans, it appeared in July, were willing to give him a try. After all the setbacks of the spring, he now had a united party behind him, and he was polling better than any Democratic presidential candidate had in decades. With the Republicans badly divided between an unpopular, unelected incumbent and a right-wing challenger who was also deeply unpopular with large sections of the electorate, it looked like Carter's path to the White House was assured. This illusion would not last for long.

8 THE REPUBLICAN CONVENTION

As President Ford prepared for the Republican National Convention in Kansas City, his campaign advisers were in a grim mood. As recently as April, they had been hopeful that the convention could be a celebration of Ford's achievements and a rallying point for Republicans to unify around the banner of the president's centrist conservatism. After all, the convention would be under the control of Republican National Committee (RNC) chair Mary Louise Smith, a liberal Republican and Ford loyalist. Key committee chairs, such as Platform Committee chair Bob Ray, the moderate Republican governor of Iowa, were also Ford supporters who worked in close consultation with the White House. But by the middle of May, after a string of primary losses, Ford's campaign strategists realized that they would not be able to win enough delegates to ensure the president's nomination before the convention. This meant that the convention itself, no matter who controlled it, would likely turn into a bitter nomination fight between the Ford and Reagan delegates. And even if the president won the nomination, they knew that he would face nearly insuperable odds in the general election against Jimmy Carter, who was, by some measures, more popular than any Democratic presidential nominee since Franklin Roosevelt. "You face a unique challenge," Mike Duval, Ford's lead campaign strategist, told him in July. "No President has overcome the unique obstacles to election which you will face following our Convention this August." Ford liked to compare himself to Harry Truman, another straight-talking midwesterner who had ascended to the White House through the vice presidency and had been widely expected to lose his 1948 campaign but pulled off an upset victory. But as Duval pointed out, Ford's situation was significantly worse. Truman had been running 11 points behind his Republican opponent, Thomas Dewey, in August 1948, whereas Duval expected Ford to be 20 points behind Carter after the GOP convention. And that was an optimistic prediction; a recent Harris poll placed Ford nearly 40 points behind.[1]

The convention would thus be a fight for survival, not a coronation. But it would also be a battle for the future direction of the party. The Reagan and Ford campaigns represented two regionally and ideologically distinct wings of the Republican Party, and their supporters had different visions of the principles the party should stand for. Should the party support détente and Kissinger's arms reduction negotiations with the Soviet Union, or should it support the hawkish policies that Reagan promoted? Should the party support or oppose gun control? And what stance should the party take on abortion and the Equal Rights Amendment? The delegates in the two camps envisioned very different platforms for the GOP. The convention would determine not only the GOP presidential nominee but also the principles that would guide the party well beyond 1976.

THE QUEST FOR DELEGATES

Both the Ford and Reagan campaigns spent the months of June and July calling uncommitted delegates—and even delegates ostensibly committed to the other candidate—to try to persuade them to join their camp. In this endeavor, the Ford campaign had the advantage, not only because Ford finished the primaries with more delegates than Reagan but also because, as the incumbent president, he had a lot more influence over the state Republican Party chairs who controlled the delegations. For instance, the Ford campaign convinced the Mississippi party chair to give more than half the state's GOP delegates to Ford, even though Reagan was far more popular than the president among Mississippi Republicans. In other cases, the president and his campaign team contacted wavering delegates directly to identify their concerns and make whatever promises or assurances were needed to get them to support the president on the first ballot. The Ford campaign invited delegates to the White House for formal receptions and photos with the president, hoping to win them over with the "red-carpet" treatment.

Figure 8.1. Ford delegates and supporters from Massachusetts at the Republican National Convention in Kansas City. (Library of Congress, Prints & Photographs Division, U.S. News & World Report Magazine Collection, LC-DIG-ppmsca-08486)

The Reagan campaign complained that it could not compete with White House prestige or presidential patronage. Reagan's strategists were frustrated because they believed (incorrectly) that their candidate had won more votes than Ford in the primaries, but because of party rules and presidential influence over state delegations, they ended up with fewer delegates. And now, because of the White House's ability to dispense favors, they were losing the fight for uncommitted delegates. Several of New York's uncommitted delegates told the president that their support depended on the receipt of federal money for a sewer construction project in Long Island's Suffolk County, and Ford assured them that the project proposal would receive a "fair appraisal." Reagan argued that this crossed an ethical line, and although the White House denied that there was any quid pro quo, seven previously uncommitted delegates from Suffolk County committed to Ford immediately after the meeting.[2]

Above all else, most Republican delegates wanted to pick a nominee who could win in November, so both the Reagan and Ford campaigns spent a lot of time trying to convince delegates that their candidate was more electable than the other. The Ford campaign claimed that Reagan was an extremist who would lose by a landslide, just as Goldwater had. Reagan's primary successes, Ford's team argued, had mainly been due to an energized conservative minority. Citing a June 1976 Harris poll that showed Republicans and independents supporting Ford over Reagan for the GOP nomination by 60 to 30 percent, they argued that Ford's centrist conservatism offered the only hope of retaining the White House. Polls also consistently predicted that Ford would receive a larger share of the vote than Reagan in a head-to-head match with Carter.[3]

The Reagan campaign responded that its candidate was the only one who could compete with Carter for votes in the South and that he was the GOP's only hope of countering Carter's anti-Washington image. If Carter was running on the claim of being a successful Sun Belt governor and a deficit hawk, the GOP's best hope of defeating him was to nominate another successful Sun Belt governor who promised to balance the budget. In an anti-Washington year, the Republicans would not be competitive if they nominated a Washington politician who had little appeal outside his own party—especially since that party accounted for only 22 percent of the electorate. Nor could they win the election without making inroads into the South and carrying California. Ford seemed unlikely to do this, but Reagan could.[4]

The Ford campaign countered that Reagan's supposed transpartisan appeal was limited, as national polls indicated. He had captured the support of a few Wallace voters, but his appeal did not extend much beyond the Sun Belt. The GOP would lose not only the Northeast but also most of the industrial North if the party gave Reagan the nomination. And even if Reagan could counter Carter's greatest strength—his image as a Washington outsider and a successful governor—he was in no position to attack Carter's greatest weakness: his inexperience. President Ford had the national governing record that Carter lacked, and he was also well situated to attack Carter's "fuzziness" on issues, the Ford campaign asserted.[5]

The debate in the GOP about the two candidates' electability reflected a larger debate about what voters wanted. The Republicans who supported Ford generally valued experience and stability in a chief executive and thought other voters would do the same. They tended to be older, wealthier, better educated, more moderate in their views, more committed to the Republican Party, and much more resistant to political change. They probably underestimated the strength of the anti-Washington mood in much of the country outside of the white, upper-middle-class suburbs of the North. Reagan supporters understood this because they shared the Wallace and Carter campaigns' antipathy to the "Washington establishment" and the political status quo. In the end, the debate revolved around this question: did the delegates want to endorse the current Republican Party and its leader, President Gerald Ford, or did they want to radically reshape the party and take it in a new geographic and ideological direction, as Reagan would likely do? If they chose the latter course and nominated Reagan, the northern moderate Republicans would likely bolt. "A Reagan nomination—representing, as it would, a repudiation of Republican leadership—would split the party so badly it is very questionable whether the GOP could be put back together again," White House communications director David Gergen warned.[6]

Whether through persuasive argument or political pressure, the Ford campaign was quickly gaining the upper hand in the race for delegates. It brought some of the uncommitted delegates from the Northeast officially into the Ford camp and even picked off a few Reagan delegates in other parts of the country. One of the greatest coups came in Mississippi, where Reagan had expected to receive at least twenty-five of the state's thirty delegates. But after long conversations with Ford campaign liaison Harry Dent, Mississippi Republican Party chair Clarke Reed said he would probably give Ford a majority of the state's delegates. In late July the Ford campaign announced that it had 1,119 delegates, and the Reagan campaign feared that Ford might be just hours away from getting the required 1,130 delegates to secure the nomination. Reagan campaign manager John Sears claimed that Reagan had 1,140 delegates, but the Ford campaign thought he was bluffing—which he undoubtedly was. *Newsweek* estimated that Reagan had only 1,079 delegates, and most other news agencies produced similar estimates.[7]

At that point, Sears decided on a desperate gambit: he suggested that Reagan name one of Ford's Pennsylvania delegates, Senator Richard Schweiker, as his running mate in advance of the convention. Schweiker, who was a close friend of Pennsylvania delegate chair Drew Lewis, could use his influence to bring the state's Ford-leaning delegation into the Reagan camp and secure the nomination, Sears believed. Schweiker was considered one of the most liberal Republicans in the Senate (he had earned an 89 percent rating from Americans for Democratic Action), but Sears considered the ideological difference an asset. If Reagan were going to have any chance of winning in the general election, he had to unify the Republican Party by appeasing the Ford-supporting moderates, and he had to do well in the Northeast and win some industrial states. Selecting a northeastern liberal senator might do the trick.[8]

Candidates normally did not announce their running mates before the convention, and campaign managers did not take the initiative in selecting them, so Sears's action was certainly unexpected—even though it had the support of Reagan campaign chair Paul Laxalt. Both the Ford and Carter campaigns had spent weeks drawing up preliminary lists of possible vice-presidential picks and debating their merits. Sears's circumvention of the traditional process took only a few days. He met with Schweiker to gauge the senator's willingness to accept a place on the ticket if asked, and then he suggested the plan to Reagan. Reagan had one question for Sears: "Will he do it?" Sears was convinced that Schweiker would agree, so Reagan gave him the go-ahead. Schweiker flew to California to meet with Reagan the next day, and Reagan offered him the number-two spot, which Schweiker accepted. Two days later, on Monday, July 26, the campaign held a press conference to announce Schweiker's addition to the ticket.[9]

The press reaction ranged from incredulous to severely critical. Reagan had repeatedly pledged to pick a running mate who was ideologically compatible—a pledge that made sense, given that much of the conservative opposition to Ford had initially centered on his own selection of liberal Nelson Rockefeller as vice president. (In fact, Sears claimed that he briefly toyed with the idea of asking Rockefeller to join the ticket, but he never mentioned the idea to Reagan and quickly settled on Schweiker instead.) The Schweiker selection, engineered by the nonideological, calculating Sears, seemed like a cynical, patently transparent ploy to co-opt Pennsylvania delegates. It called into question the ideological premise of Reagan's campaign—which, for most of his supporters, was the reason for his candidacy. It also made Schweiker look unprincipled because, until being selected by Reagan, he had been a liberal Ford delegate pledged to support the president. Only four weeks earlier, he had written to the White House, "I look forward to participating in the Republican Convention on the winning side as a Ford delegate."[10] But now, he had not only agreed to be Reagan's running mate; he was also shifting some of his issue positions to match Reagan's conservatism.

Angry letters began to pour into campaign headquarters from disappointed Reagan supporters who had decided to abandon the California governor and switch to Ford.[11] Some conservative Reagan delegates from South Carolina, Louisiana, and a few other southern states where northeastern liberal Republicans were especially unpopular expressed disgust with the whole charade and announced that they would probably support Ford at the convention. Even New Hampshire governor Mel Thompson, who had chaired Reagan's primary campaign in the state and had been one of his earliest supporters, announced that because of Schweiker, he was abandoning Reagan. And the Pennsylvania delegates that Sears had expected to win never materialized, partly because Drew Lewis refused to abandon his commitment to Ford and partly because both conservative and liberal Republican delegates in the state viewed the Schweiker selection as a cynical move. The Ford campaign could hardly believe its good fortune: Reagan had foolishly forfeited some of his delegates with a vice-presidential choice that undermined his credibility, making Ford's path to the nomination easier than ever. The Ford team immediately renewed their efforts to pry southern delegates away from Reagan while simultaneously using their influence over Lewis and other northeastern state party leaders to prevent any defections from their own camp in Pennsylvania and neighboring states.[12]

But Sears insisted he made the right decision, a conviction from which he never wavered. Reagan's main selling point, for Sears, had never been his conservative ideology. Reagan's electability, he thought, depended not on his issue positions—which were actually a political liability—but on his leadership qualities and his fresh vision. His conservative ideology had been useful only insofar as it had helped him solidify a base of support in the primaries. But he could not win the Republican nomination—let alone the general election—by relying only on Sun Belt conservatives. To secure the nomination, he would need the support of northern moderate Republicans, and to win the general election, he would need the support of centrist suburban Catholic Democrats and others in the industrial Northeast. Schweiker could get those votes for Reagan, Sears thought. According to the press, by selecting Schweiker, Reagan proved himself a cynical politician rather than a statesmanlike president-in-the-making, but in Sears's view, the Schweiker selection proved just the opposite. It demonstrated that Reagan was not a right-wing extremist but a sensible, pragmatic consensus builder who could unite the Republican Party and the nation. A Reagan-Schweiker ticket was a winning ticket: it would carry the West and the Great Plains, pick up Texas and several states in the southern periphery, and carry Pennsylvania and parts of the industrial Midwest and Northeast. "It was time to shake hands across an invisible border (to the Northeast states) and bring a section of the U.S. and two sections of the Republican Party together," Reagan explained.[13]

As Reagan's campaign pointed out, there was actually more similarity between Reagan's and Schweiker's ideological positions than the senator's ADA rating suggested. Schweiker's liberalism was largely confined to his support for labor unions and government social programs, and on these issues, his voting record was certainly a far cry from the Reagan wing of the Republican Party. He had received an AFL-CIO endorsement in his 1974 Senate race, prompting his conservative critics in Pennsylvania to call him "the Senator from Big Labor." But, as Reagan pointed out in a letter to Republican delegates, Schweiker was also a hawk on defense and a cultural conservative who supported a school prayer amendment and opposed abortion and gun control.[14] He was not a Catholic, but as a dedicated member of the tiny, regional Schwenkfelder Church (a historically German Protestant denomination with a couple thousand adherents in central Pennsylvania), he shared many of the religious and family-centered values of the culturally conservative Catholics who made up much of his Pennsylvania constituency. Perhaps in a general election he could simultaneously position himself as an economic liberal and social conservative who would appeal to northern Catholic Democrats; as a religiously devout, socially concerned Protestant who could win over politically moderate evangelicals; and as a northeastern liberal Republican who would appeal to other moderate Republicans in the North. He could reinforce Reagan's positions on foreign policy and cultural issues—which had been the key to many of his primary victories—while also broadening the Reagan coalition to reach several key voter groups the Californian could not have won on his own.

Schweiker failed to live up to these expectations. He could not win over the Pennsylvania delegation, and he struck many as a poor campaigner who was unsure of his own issue positions. Even some members of the Reagan campaign were somewhat taken aback when he quickly reversed himself on labor issues to bring his position into alignment with Reagan's. Such a sudden and complete switch on a matter of principle made him appear untrustworthy, they thought, and it undermined his appeal among the northern voters they needed to attract. "We can't have RS [Richard Schweiker] looking like a complete pimp," Larry Uzzell explained in a memo to other Reagan campaign staffers. "He's got to show some rightward movement while also demonstrating that on some matters of principles he's unbudgeable." The "key to repackaging Schweiker," he said, was to market him as "an economic liberal but a social conservative"—a political blend that would appeal to the culturally conservative northern Catholic Democrats that Reagan would need in a general election.[15] With an "economic liberal" on the ticket, Reagan might still alienate some of the strong free-market advocates who had been the backbone of his campaign in the early days, such as Mel Thompson. But those people could probably be won back with assurances that Reagan, not Schweiker, would be setting policy.

Ford picked up several delegates immediately after Schweiker joined the Reagan ticket, but then Reagan gained a few delegates of his own, as the campaign had hoped. Even though the large gains expected from Pennsylvania never materialized, Reagan eventually managed to get a few additional delegates from the state. By the time the Republican convention began, the delegate counts for the two campaigns were almost exactly where they had been before Schweiker's addition to the ticket. In the estimate of the *Washington Post,* Ford had 1,126 delegates on the opening day of the convention (only 4 short of the total needed to win the nomination), and Reagan had 1,084. There were still 99 uncommitted delegates who refused to ally with either camp. The chance that nearly all the uncommitted delegates would end up voting for Reagan was remote, but the Reagan campaign and its supporters still had a few tricks they could try to finagle an upset victory. When Reagan arrived in Kansas City, he was greeted by a cheering crowd of two thousand supporters who hoped he could still pull off a miracle and wrest the nomination from Ford. As the convention began with a speech by eighty-eight-year-old former Kansas governor Alf Landon, who had run against Franklin Roosevelt forty years earlier, the Reagan and Ford delegates readied themselves for a showdown that would involve every parliamentary trick they could muster.[16]

The major tactic the Reagan campaign tried was to pass a resolution, known as Rule 16-C, requiring each presidential candidate to name his running mate in advance of the nomination vote. Reagan, of course, had already done this, so the hope was that regardless of who Ford selected, a few of his delegates would be prompted to switch sides. For instance, if Ford chose liberal Republican Elliott Richardson, who had been mentioned in the press as a vice-presidential possibility, he would almost certainly lose the support of some conservative delegates. And if he chose former Texas governor John Connally, the favorite of many of his conservative backers (including Goldwater), some of the moderate northerners might decide that the Reagan-Schweiker ticket was a better option. The Maine delegation had already stated that it would not vote for Ford if Connally were on the ticket. In any case, the resolution would force Ford's hand and put him in the same uncomfortable position Reagan had found himself in after selecting Schweiker. But Ford did not take the bait. His delegates voted against the resolution, and it was defeated in a largely partisan vote, with nearly all the Reagan delegates supporting it and the Ford delegates opposing it. The defeat of this resolution was seen as an important show of force for Ford, and it seemed to indicate that Reagan's chances of winning the nomination were remote.[17] But Reagan's supporters were not ready to give up yet.

A few Reagan supporters, including Senator Jesse Helms and Illinois congressman Phil Crane, thought that if they could get conservative senator James Buckley of New York to enter the contest, he could peel a few votes away from Ford and deprive him of a first-ballot majority. That would free delegates to vote their preference on a second ballot, where it was widely believed that Reagan could pick up approximately thirty-five votes. But Buckley, who had been warned by the New York delegation chair not to run, decided not to go along with the Reagan supporters' plan.[18]

Some in the Reagan camp thought they might have a chance of winning if they could win all thirty Mississippi delegates. Traditionally, Mississippi delegates voted as a bloc according to the "unit rule," and the delegation had been leaning heavily toward Reagan at the beginning of the summer. But this time the Mississippi delegates voted to suspend the unit rule, which allowed sixteen delegates to vote for Ford and fourteen for Reagan. Once again, the Reagan campaign was stymied.[19]

The Ford campaign feared that the Reagan forces, having exhausted all other options, would encourage delegates to vote for the candidate of their choice on the first ballot, regardless of the primary results. Nine hundred delegates came from states whose laws required them to vote in accordance with the results of the state primary, regardless of their personal preferences. Of those nine hundred, a significant number were pledged to Ford but privately supported Reagan. Because the Ford campaign was not sure whether the state laws binding delegates' choices would hold up in court—and because it suspected that the Reagan campaign would be willing to test those laws if it were the only option remaining—it asked the convention to adopt a rule requiring delegates to follow their state laws and vote in accordance with primary results on the first ballot. Reagan insisted that he would not encourage any delegate to violate the law, but he opposed the proposed rule on the grounds that it was superfluous. Nevertheless, it passed overwhelmingly on a voice vote—another victory for Ford.[20]

When the moment came for the roll-call vote for the nomination, the Reagan forces knew they were going to lose. Some Reagan delegates, angry about the expected outcome, protested by blowing horns to disrupt the process, making it impossible for the parliamentarian to hear and record the votes as the delegates called them out. But the voting could not be delayed forever. When the final votes were tallied, Ford was the winner: 1,179 to 1,068.[21] Even so, Reagan and his delegates exerted an enormous influence over the platform, which was arguably just as important as the nomination in shaping the future direction of the party.

Figure 8.2. Gerald and Betty Ford celebrating his victory over Ronald Reagan after receiving the Republican presidential nomination at the convention in Kansas City, August 1976. (Library of Congress, Prints & Photographs Division, U.S. News & World Report Magazine Collection, LC-DIG-ppmsca-08487)

THE BATTLE OVER THE PLATFORM

The platform was originally supposed to be under the control of the Ford campaign. Four months before the convention, when White House chief of staff Dick Cheney met with Platform Committee chair Bob Ray to coordinate strategy, they agreed that the platform should highlight the president's record and suggest some broad goals that would appeal to Democrats and independents as well as Republicans. The platform should not be a "legislative laundry list," they decided, but should focus on general principles. Above all, it should emphasize Ford's main campaign themes, which Cheney believed were broadly acceptable to all Republicans, as well as to many Democrats: "fiscal responsibility, reduced Federal government intervention, and a strong defense and foreign policy."[22]

But only a month later, the Ford campaign realized that its optimism about the platform had been premature. Reagan had surged ahead of Ford in the number of committed delegates, and the momentum was on his side. Although the Ford campaign still believed the president would receive the nomination, staffers knew that the fight for the nomination would consume so much of their attention that they might have to cede control of the platform to conservative ideologues who would try to undermine Ford and advance their own agenda. "I don't see any way we can win with the Platform issues, and it may be so bad that the President will be in the position of having to repudiate the Platform prior to being nominated," a Ford campaign strategy paper glumly predicted in late May.[23]

The problem, as one of Vice President Rockefeller's assistants explained, was that the Reagan delegates would likely want to introduce platform statements on abortion, busing, the Equal Rights Amendment, gun control, capital punishment, the Panama Canal, and détente that were well to the right of Ford's positions. If Ford opposed those planks, he might lose a few of the conservative delegates that were still in his camp, which he could not afford to do.[24] Because the nomination was the most urgent priority, Ford was willing to make concessions on the platform if that was the only way to keep Reagan from winning. He intended to do what he could to secure a moderate, centrist platform, but he was also prepared to give a lot of ground to the conservatives if necessary. This gave the Reagan forces an opening.

The pro-Ford Republican National Committee produced a draft platform that affirmed the party's commitment to the principles Cheney and Ray had agreed on earlier that year: "less government, less taxes, less inflation." The platform was certainly conservative—arguably more conservative than the 1972 platform, which had endorsed a number of federal spending programs that the 1976 draft omitted—but it avoided most of the controversial issues that divided the Reagan and Ford campaigns.[25]

Reagan wanted a platform that was more in line with his own views. A few days before the convention began, he sent a telegram to the members of the Platform Committee encouraging them to create a platform that would oppose abortion and gun control, support school prayer and welfare reform, and, above all, "insure that our national defense is number one in the world." Reagan's call for a strong defense was not controversial, since Ford was already committed to increasing the defense budget. Even the liberal Rockefeller encouraged the Platform Committee to endorse increased defense spending. Reagan's stance on welfare was also widely shared in the party, but some of his other proposals represented at least a modest shift in party policy. The

Republican Party had never before taken an official position on abortion, and a sizable group of pro-choice feminists wanted to make sure the party did not go on record as opposing abortion rights. In fact, in February a group of GOP feminists had hoped to add an endorsement of abortion rights in the platform. By August, after the party's shift to the right during the primaries, they realized there was no chance of that happening, but they thought they could at least keep antiabortion language out of the platform. Finally, Reagan's opposition to gun control represented a direct reversal of party policy; in 1972 the GOP platform had endorsed measures that would reduce criminal access to "cheap, readily-obtainable handguns"—which was still Ford's position.[26]

Jesse Helms wanted to go a lot further than Reagan in revising the platform draft. At the beginning of the convention, he released a list of more than twenty planks he wanted the Platform Committee to approve. He then relied on Reagan delegates on the Platform Committee—especially his protégé John East, a staunchly conservative North Carolina political science professor who would later become a US senator—to persuade other committee members to support his proposals.[27] Covering a wide range of conservative movement priorities, the resolutions opposed détente, busing, affirmative action, and national health insurance, while endorsing the priorities Reagan had outlined in his telegram.

The committee was narrowly divided on Helms's proposals. His resolution opposing US "policies which undercut the stability and sovereignty of certain select nations in Africa through unrealistic and impractical demands which are not expected of other African nations"—a thinly veiled reference to policies designed to promote change in apartheid in South Africa and Rhodesia—failed on a tie vote.[28] But several of his other proposals made it into the platform, even though the committee toned down his language in some cases. The result was a platform that was markedly to the right of the draft the Ford forces had originally proposed.

The final version of the Republican platform affirmed US control over the Panama Canal and supported school prayer and antibusing constitutional amendments. It included stronger language on welfare reform than that contained in the original draft, stipulating that "work requirements" needed to be strengthened. It also expressed opposition to "compulsory national health insurance" and included the first Republican platform statement against gun control. The Republican

National Committee's original platform draft retained a statement from the 1972 platform supporting measures to limit access to "cheap, readily obtainable handguns," but the Platform Committee voted to replace that statement with a resolution that opposed gun control of any sort: "We support the right of citizens to keep and bear arms. We oppose federal registration of firearms. Mandatory sentences for crimes committed with a lethal weapon are the only effective solution to this problem."[29]

On two issues—abortion and the Equal Rights Amendment—the platform subcommittees proved to be more socially conservative than most party leaders expected. RNC chair Mary Dent Crisp was strongly pro-choice, as were Vice President Nelson Rockefeller, First Lady Betty Ford, and a large number of Republicans in Congress. But both Reagan and Helms called for platform statements against abortion, and even the Ford campaign decided that an antiabortion platform statement might be desirable, since it would placate some of the culturally conservative Reagan delegates and attract Catholic votes from the must-win states in the industrial North in November. There was some nervousness among Ford campaign strategists about this concession to social conservatives. "It is a mistake to think that Republicans have nothing to lose by taking a strong stand against abortion," Jim Reichley told Dick Cheney in June. "Many middle-class Republicans and independents, particularly among women, are strong pro-abortionists, and some will vote on this issue alone."[30] But after the Democrats alienated some pro-life members with their platform statement on abortion, some in the Ford campaign decided that the prospect of winning the votes of a few pro-life, traditionally Democratic Catholics outweighed the risk of offending pro-choice Republican women.

Senator Bob Dole, a Ford ally who was serving as temporary chair of the Republican National Convention, took the lead in implementing the president's new conservative strategy on abortion. He announced at the beginning of the convention that the platform should include language supporting an antiabortion constitutional amendment and "protesting the Supreme Court's intrusion into the family structure." Because he wanted to make sure that the platform would be useful in winning over some traditionally Democratic pro-life Catholics in the general election, Dole took the unusual step of discussing the proposed plank with representatives of Democratic presidential candidate Ellen McCormack before showing it to his fellow Republicans. He then secured the support of some moderately pro-choice Republicans by marketing the plank as a resolution against judicial activism and a promise to return the matter to the states. "If the Democrats are going to carry the label of the 'abortion party' into this election, then I would hope that the Republicans might be known as the 'submit it to the people party,'" Dole said. "The majority of those who identify with our Party's philosophy . . . want the abortion controversy settled by other than nine men in long black robes." With both the Ford and Reagan campaigns on board, the call for an antiabortion plank passed in subcommittee by a vote of thirteen to one. Twenty-nine pro-choice delegates led by Ann Peckham and Millicent Fenwick, Ford delegates from Wisconsin and New Jersey, respectively, mounted a floor challenge to delete the platform plank on abortion, but their effort failed.[31] The Republican Party was now officially opposed to *Roe v. Wade*.

Republican feminists at the convention were not happy about the abortion vote, but it hardly came as a surprise. The subcommittee vote against the Equal Rights Amendment was a greater shock. Although anti-ERA activist Phyllis Schlafly gave impassioned testimony urging the Platform Committee to oppose President Ford's "intimate involvement with the radical women's lib movement," the news media predicted that the GOP would narrowly reaffirm its support for the ERA, which the party had endorsed since 1940. Instead, endorsement for the ERA failed by one vote in the human rights subcommittee, with Ford delegates voting in support and Reagan delegates voting as a bloc against it. Betty Ford, a strong ERA supporter, was aghast and called the vote "incredible." The next day, though, the full Platform Committee voted fifty-one to forty-seven to reaffirm the party's long-standing support for the ERA. The anti-ERA activists in the party were not quite ready to give up, however. Led by Alabama Reagan delegate Frances Wideman, they attempted to take the fight to the floor for a vote by all 2,259 delegates, but without Reagan's support, the effort failed. Schlafly complained that the "Reagan forces" were "more interested in his candidacy than in principle," and she predicted that the Reagan campaign's failure to support the anti-ERA effort at the convention would hurt the party among social conservatives. Reagan, however, ignored the criticism and maintained that there should be a floor fight on only one platform plank: "Morality in Foreign Policy."[32]

Reagan's criticism of President Ford's foreign policy had become the defining issue of his campaign, so it was not surprising that he chose this topic for his only requested floor vote. The proposed platform plank, which was an attack on Ford and Kissinger's policy of détente, was the creation not of Reagan or his campaign staff but of John East and Jesse Helms. Even so, Reagan decided to endorse the measure as an accurate statement of his views. Ford chose not to fight the measure; at the time of the floor vote, he was still trying to secure enough votes to win the nomination, and he thought that appeasing conservatives on the foreign policy issue might prevent right-leaning delegates in his camp from shifting to Reagan. The measure passed—which meant that the party platform now contained a commendation of Alexander Solzhenitsyn (with whom Ford had refused to meet the previous year) and a warning that "agreements that are negotiated, such as the one signed in Helsinki, must not take from those who do not have freedom the hope of one day gaining it."[33]

Both Ford and Reagan found the platform acceptable, and both campaigns claimed victory in the fight to have their positions adopted.[34] In a sense, both were right—though Reagan's forces gained more than Ford's did. The Ford delegates prevented the Reagan delegates from making as many changes to the platform as they wanted, but the Reagan supporters succeeded in shifting the platform markedly to the right. Many of the conservative policies that would guide the party for the rest of the twentieth century and beyond—such as opposition to abortion and gun control, along with criticisms of détente—were now part of the party platform for the first time. As a final touch, the platform even included a few references to God, who had not been mentioned at all in 1972. Liberal Republicans were deeply disappointed. The Ripon Society called it an "unenlightened and in some areas regressive platform" that was "filled with the emotional pet proposals of the far right." Senator Lowell Weicker was even more scathing. "When the conservatives get through in Kansas City, there may be nothing left of the Republican Party," he lamented.[35] If by "Republican Party" Weicker meant the liberal wing of the GOP, he was right. The liberal Republicans had permanently lost control of their party, and they would soon disappear altogether. Eventually, Weicker would change his party affiliation.

Black Republicans, who accounted for just under 3 percent of the convention delegates, were especially worried about the direction of the party. In 1972 the Republican Party platform had included several paragraphs touting federal aid to minority-owned businesses and black colleges, as well as affirmative action programs to promote minority hiring. The National Black Republican Council urged the Platform Committee at the 1976 convention to expand on these ideas and to endorse affirmative action to reduce the black unemployment rate, college scholarships for low-income students, welfare reform so that "people can work their way to independence," and a "comprehensive national health care plan." The council supported "majority rule in southern Africa" and "increased assistance to Africa." Above all, black Republicans at the convention wanted more black representation among party leadership and more federal assistance for black capitalism. They believed that hard work and free enterprise, not government handouts, were the tickets to success, but unlike many of the Reaganites, they believed that government should continue to play a role in helping people to help themselves—which meant the expansion of affirmative action programs. These demands were out of step with the direction of the party. The 1976 platform contained no references at all to "black Americans" or to "blacks," and it reduced the 1972 platform's multiparagraph pledge to promote specific affirmative action programs to a single sentence that affirmed a few of the general goals favored by black Republicans: "Wiping out past discrimination requires continued emphasis on providing educational opportunities for minority citizens, increasing direct and guaranteed loans to minority business enterprises, and affording qualified minority persons equal opportunities for government positions at all levels."[36]

Some black Republicans noted the contrast with the Democratic convention, which featured keynote speaker Barbara Jordan and gave center stage to several heroes of the civil rights movement. "I am seriously disturbed by the extreme lack of sensitivity displayed by our National leadership relative to blacks and Republicanism," wrote Ethel Allen to President Ford. Allen, a Philadelphia doctor and city council member, was also chair of the Philadelphia President Ford Committee and one of the most prominent black Republican activists. Her detailed, two-page letter continued:

> The fact that the hierarchy of the Republican Party permits Barbara Jordan to stake out a Goliath-like claim on party representation without offering up a David or Davida especially when there is the Honorable Edward Brooke, the Honorable Dr. Ethel Allen and the Honorable Joanne Collins [a Republican Kansas City council

member] to offer Blacks and other persons in America living proof that there are viable alternatives to the Democratic Party who are equally skilled practitioners and orators . . . is appalling, to say the very least! It gives one pause to wonder whether the Grand Old Plantation has surfaced once more or whether this year G.O.P. is the acronym for "Going Out Party."[37]

Ford received numerous similar complaints from black Republicans, but he was too busy fending off the Reagan attack from the right to give them much consideration. Instead, Allen's passionate lament received a rather cold response from presidential assistant John Calhoun. "President Ford has asked me to thank you for your letter," Calhoun wrote to Allen. "He understands the concerns you expressed, however, there were never plans other than those you were aware of and participated in during the Republican National Convention. . . . The President appreciated your strong leadership on his behalf, and he is counting on your support during the next eight weeks and the next four years."[38]

Earlier in the year, Ford had received strong support from the small number of black Republicans who voted in the primaries, and he was far more popular than Reagan among black members of the GOP. In Florida, 65 percent of black Republicans voted for him over Reagan, as did 78 percent in Chicago. Ford was also the overwhelming favorite among the small number of black delegates at the party convention. Edward Brooke estimated that of the seventy-six Republican delegates who were black, perhaps as many as seventy supported Ford, which meant that black delegates who supported Ford outnumbered those who supported Reagan by approximately nine to one. Before the convention, some black Republicans were optimistic about Ford's prospects among African Americans. In the summer of 1975 Maurice Dawkins, a black Republican minister who would later run for the US Senate from Virginia, predicted that if Ford appointed more blacks to key positions in his administration, he might receive 20 to 25 percent of the black vote in the 1976 presidential election. But the convention and the platform left many black Republicans feeling angry and ignored. By the end of the summer, it looked like Ford would fail to win even 20 percent of the black vote. The Ford campaign's Black Desk decided in September that 16 percent would be a more realistic target.[39]

CHOOSING A RUNNING MATE

Having barely survived the nomination fight—and having ceded some important ground on the platform just to avoid being rejected by the party—Ford knew he would have to tread carefully when selecting his running mate. He did not finalize that choice until the early hours of the last day of the convention. He had started the process months earlier. Proceeding methodically—and with the goal of getting as close as possible to achieving a party consensus—he asked all Republican convention delegates and party leaders to submit their suggestions for a vice-presidential pick. Numerous Republicans urged Ford to select Reagan as his running mate, but Ford's personal antipathy toward Reagan made him reluctant to do so, and Reagan had repeatedly said he would never accept the position. Not surprisingly, some of the liberals in the party urged him to choose a liberal such as Charles Percy or even Nelson Rockefeller, and the conservatives wanted him to choose a conservative, which for many, meant John Connally. After Reagan selected Schweiker, Ford's team insisted that the president could not do worse, no matter who he selected. "The person he picks is *bound* to be left of Reagan [and] right of Schweiker, so we'll all be content," the campaign staff declared.[40] But this was merely campaign rhetoric; privately, the staff knew they might face a party revolt if the president selected a polarizing running mate.

Shortly before the convention, Ford requested personal financial and health data from nearly twenty finalists who ranged in ideology from Lowell Weicker and Edward Brooke on the liberal end of the spectrum to John Connally on the conservative end. Brooke and Weicker were not interested. Connally was a highly controversial figure, not only because of his ideological position but also because of his polarizing personality, his association with the Nixon White House, and persistent rumors of personal financial scandals, despite his acquittal on bribery charges the previous year.[41]

The press assumed that Ford's solicitation of liberal candidates was merely "window dressing" to satisfy the liberal Republicans scorned by his rejection of Rockefeller, some of whom had seriously considered challenging the president in the primaries. Ford did not want to alienate the liberals in his party, but few expected him to go so far as to appoint another liberal stalwart in the Rockefeller mold. Instead, they thought he would choose a party centrist acceptable to both liberals and conservatives.[42]

The name mentioned most often as a possibility was Howard Baker, a self-described "moderate to moderate-conservative" senator from Tennessee who had a reputation for being honest and hardworking; his main claim to fame was his aggressive investigation of the Watergate scandal as a member of the Senate Intelligence Committee. If lingering concerns about the Nixon pardon were still an issue, Baker could help Ford distance himself from Watergate. And perhaps he could help Ford make inroads in the South, which the president was preparing to cede to Carter. Best of all, Baker was a safe choice. He was well liked by some of the most liberal members of the party, but even conservatives had no substantial objections to him. Known for his fiscal conservatism, support for increased defense spending, and advocacy for environmental regulations, Baker was closely in line with most of Ford's policy positions, which meant that he was somewhat to the left of the newly adopted right-leaning Republican Party platform, including on the issue of abortion (Baker, like most moderate and liberal Republicans, was pro-choice). But if Baker did not alienate any group within the Republican Party, he did not excite them either. The fear was that Baker would reinforce Ford's image of blandness. He was not popular enough in the South to counteract Carter's appeal. At best, he would help Ford carry his home state of Tennessee, and even that was not a sure thing. And for Reagan supporters in the South, Baker was not an acceptable consolation prize.[43]

Even though the press assumed that Baker was the favorite, the president was strongly leaning toward William Ruckelshaus, the first Environmental Protection Agency (EPA) administrator and a former deputy attorney general in the Nixon White House. In 1973 he had resigned from the Justice Department rather than carry out President Nixon's order to fire the special prosecutor who was investigating the Watergate scandal. This principled move temporarily ended his government career, but it earned him plaudits as a man of courage and led some people to call him "Mr. Clean." "If Hollywood ever shoots a sequel to 'All the President's Men,' two of the good guys will be named Ruckelshaus," *People* magazine declared. Theoretically, Ruckelshaus could help Ford put the Nixon pardon behind him, and some speculated that he could also help the president pick up Catholic votes in the Midwest. But whether he could have delivered the culturally conservative Catholic vote is questionable. By his own admission, his religious practice had lapsed since marrying an Episcopalian pro-choice feminist. "The example my father set as a deeply religious man is not one that I am setting for my children," he told an interviewer earlier that year.[44]

Ruckelshaus had several troubling strikes against him. He had never won elected office; in fact, he had lost a Senate race in the Republican-leaning state of Indiana. He was considered a poor campaigner, which was a serious liability for a campaign that was desperate to excite the voters. He was also a moderately liberal Republican whom many conservatives in the party would never accept. His wife, Jill, was a strong supporter of feminism; she had served as a special assistant on women's rights in the Nixon White House and was a member of the policy council of the bipartisan National Women's Political Caucus. At the 1972 Republican National Convention, she had been a leader of the women delegates' campaign to secure GOP platform endorsements of the Equal Rights Amendment, a female appointment to the Supreme Court, and abortion rights.[45] Ruckelshaus himself was the architect of environmental regulations that did not necessarily meet the approval of free-market Reaganites.

Ford knew that if he picked Ruckelshaus, he might face a revolt from conservatives at the convention; they had been outraged about his selection of Rockefeller and had been warning him for more than a year not to pick a liberal running mate. And in the general election, internal polling suggested that the results of adding Ruckelshaus to the ticket could be catastrophic. A Ford-Ruckelshaus ticket was guaranteed only 25 percent of the vote in a matchup against Carter-Mondale, compared with 31 percent for a Ford-Reagan ticket and 33 percent for Ford-Baker. Nevertheless, Ford was leaning toward Ruckelshaus as late as one day before the end of the convention, when he was scheduled to announce his choice. One of his campaign advisers, Doug Bailey, suggested that if he picked Ruckelshaus or another liberal and provoked an open revolt from conservatives on the floor, he could win the fight and come out looking stronger. Ford could prove that he was his own man who refused to be pushed around by Reagan. Anything that enhanced Ford's image as a decisive leader, his advisers thought, would help him in the general election.[46]

If Ford wanted a bold choice, though, some of his advisers thought he should nominate the one woman on his list of finalists: Anne Armstrong, who was currently serving as ambassador to the United Kingdom. Like Ruckelshaus, Armstrong had never held elected office, but as conservative columnist George Will told Ford campaign strategists in a private meeting, she was "a great campaigner, bright and from Texas"—a state Ford would love to peel away from Carter. Four years earlier, she became the first woman to give a keynote address at a national party convention when she addressed the GOP delegates in Miami. She was also the first woman to ever serve as counselor to the president—a position she held in both the Nixon and Ford administrations. She was, the *Washington Post* later said, "one of the most prominent women in the Republican Party." She was well liked by nearly all her associates and had succeeded in every political task she had undertaken. For the most part, her political work focused on women's causes, but she was capable of wearing other hats as well. After a long career in the Texas Republican Party, she was fluent in Spanish and had served as a Nixon campaign liaison to Hispanics. For those who wanted to see a woman on the ticket, Armstrong was the logical choice. But the Ford campaign worried that a female running mate—whether it was Armstrong or anyone else—would cost the president even more votes than he had already lost. In a Ford campaign poll taken immediately before the convention, 33 percent of all voters—including 32 percent of women and 43 percent of Republicans—said that Ford's running mate "should not be a woman." According to the *Washington Post,* Armstrong was one of the top five finalists for the position, but most news analysts expected her to be bypassed for a safer choice.[47]

The only right-of-center candidate on Ford's list of finalists was Treasury Secretary William Simon, a wealthy investment banker who was a staunch defender of the free market. Simon was a northeastern Catholic, a plus if the Ford campaign was seriously considering a Catholic strategy in the general election. Some conservatives, such as William Casey (who would serve as CIA director in the Reagan administration), thought that because economic concerns were likely to be paramount, Ford needed a successful free-market advocate like Simon to aggressively make the case for a Republican jobs creation program centered on tax cuts, fiscal prudence, and deregulation. But Simon, like Armstrong and Ruckelshaus, had never won elected office. His campaign skills were unknown. It was unclear whether a millionaire investment banker would be able to secure a substantial number of traditionally Democratic Catholic votes in the Northeast and Midwest, as the campaign expected. Despite conservative support for Simon, pundits thought he might be a distant fourth or fifth choice at best. Even those who supported Simon thought Ford was unlikely to choose him.[48]

On the night before Ford was scheduled to announce his choice, Ford invited Reagan to his hotel suite to discuss vice-presidential options. Dick Cheney had told the press the day before that Ford would offer the vice presidency to Reagan as a matter of courtesy, but he expected Reagan to refuse it, given his repeated declarations that he was not interested in the number-two position. John Sears went further: he told Ford's people that Reagan would meet with the president only on the condition that he was *not* offered the vice presidency. Ford agreed. When Reagan arrived at 1:30 a.m.—after an exhausting day at the convention, where he had been denied the nomination in a close vote—Ford was ready to discuss the real issue of concern: which of Ford's vice-presidential candidates would Reagan accept? He did not want a floor fight with the Reagan delegates.[49]

Reagan quickly settled on Bob Dole, who was one of the sixteen to twenty people contacted as a potential vice-presidential candidate but not one of the finalists. The Ford campaign had not even polled for a Ford-Dole ticket because it was considered an unlikely scenario. But Ford was intrigued by the suggestion. Dole was more conservative than most of the other finalists (his Senate voting record in the previous year had earned him a 67 percent approval rating from the conservative Americans for Constitutional Action and only 17 percent from the ADA), but he was a strong Ford supporter, and the president liked him. As temporary convention chair, he had done yeoman's work to advance the president's agenda while building bridges with the Reagan delegates. And he was eager to help Ford win back the support he had lost in the farm states because of his embargo on grain sales to the Soviet Union. Under normal conditions, Dole's strongly Republican home state of Kansas would never be considered a swing state, but this was not a normal year. South Dakota, a state that had voted Republican in eight of the last nine presidential elections, was projected to support Carter over Ford by 52 to 38 percent, according to an internal Carter campaign poll taken that month.[50] Whether Dole would be able to steer the Ford campaign to victory was questionable, but at the very least, he could potentially avert a catastrophic loss by keeping the Great Plains in the Republican column.

Dole's most valuable potential contribution to the campaign, Ford thought, was his reputation as an aggressive attacker on the campaign

Figure 8.3. President Gerald Ford with Bob and Elizabeth Dole. (Courtesy of Gerald R. Ford Presidential Library)

trail. As Ford's campaign staff realized, the president needed someone who could effectively cut Carter down to size in a way that Ford could not. "The first criteria for a VP nominee is that he must be an excellent campaigner, and a super attackman," Mike Duval's strategy memo had advised only a few weeks earlier. There might be no one better equipped to perform that task than Dole, who pulled no punches when going after his opponents with one-line zingers. He had already blasted Carter as "a Southern-fried McGovern or a Southern-fried Humphrey," and he had told midwestern farmers that a Carter-Mondale administration would lead to a "farm program controlled from Washington with prices fixed by bureaucrats."[51] Dole's zeal for the Ford ticket and his willingness to come out swinging against his opponents might be just what the campaign needed.

The meeting with Reagan was enough to vault Dole to the top of Ford's list of finalists, but the president remained undecided. After Reagan left the hotel, Ford summoned his closest campaign advisers—a group that included the liberal Rockefeller, conservatives Cheney and John Tower, and six others who fell somewhere in the middle of the ideological spectrum. It was 3:15 a.m. when the group met, and the opening speeches of the last day of the convention were only a few hours away, yet Ford still had not reached a decision. He had narrowed the list to four candidates: Dole, Armstrong, Ruckelshaus, and Baker. Tower, the lone Texan at the meeting, argued for Connally, but Ford had already crossed him off the list. Most of the participants were not excited about Baker, and they questioned his usefulness on the campaign trail. Ford's campaign manager, Stuart Spencer, argued for Armstrong. Prior to the meeting, Ruckelshaus had been Ford's first choice, but Spencer almost persuaded him to name the first female vice-presidential candidate. In the end, he could not bring himself to make such a potentially unpopular move. "She came close. Very close," he wrote in his autobiography three years later. "Naming her was something I really wanted to do, but I found myself drawing back every time I thought about it. (In retrospect, if given the opportunity to make that decision again, I might well have said, 'Damn the torpedoes,' and gambled on Anne.)"[52]

Much of the meeting was spent discussing one question: should Ford acquiesce to the conservative delegates at the convention or defy their expectations and make a bold choice? Bryce Harlow, a White House aide from Oklahoma, was sensitive to the damage a liberal running mate would do to Ford's chances in the South and the conservative Midwest, and he urged the president to select a conservative. Bob Teeter, the campaign's pollster, urged Ford to take the bold, unconventional path and pick Ruckelshaus. Rockefeller likewise encouraged Ford to ignore the conservative naysayers and select Ruckelshaus if the former EPA administrator was really his first choice. According to several people who were there, including Harlow, Ford left the meeting at 5:00 a.m. leaning toward Ruckelshaus—the choice that would defy the conservatives.[53]

But then Ford had second thoughts. After sleeping for three hours, he recalled his aides and told them, "Assume it's Bob Dole. I am not clear what happens next." Most of those in the room had nothing but positive words to say about Dole, even though he had not been their top choice. Within an hour, Ford was ready to make the next move. He called Dole at 10:00 a.m. to offer him the job, which he accepted.[54]

At the time, no one in the media knew why Ford switched from Ruckelshaus to Dole in less than four hours. He expressed concern that Ruckelshaus had never won elected office; he said he felt comfortable with Dole and thought he would appeal to farmers who were angry about the embargo on grain sales to the Soviet Union. But later, journalists found out that behind-the-scenes lobbying from southern conservatives may have influenced Ford's choice. Apparently, discontented conservative delegates were planning to draft Reagan as the vice-presidential nominee, but shortly before Ford's second meeting with his campaign staff, Clarke Reed told Cheney that the southern delegates would abandon the effort to draft Reagan if the president selected Dole. Other southern delegates called the president's aides with similar messages, and according to press secretary Ron Nessen's personal notes, their influence determined the president's decision.[55] A year earlier, conservatives in the party had forced Ford to remove Rockefeller from the ticket. Now they succeeded in preventing the selection of another moderately liberal vice-presidential candidate.

Dole had already addressed the convention earlier in the week, but as Ford's newly chosen running mate, he gave another speech that night. Reporters thought it fell flat, perhaps because he had little time to prepare it. Three hundred seventy-eight delegates—most of whom were still holding out for Reagan, despite his repeated refusal to accept the vice presidency—cast protest votes for Jesse Helms and other conservatives, but their dissent was not enough to make a difference. Despite Reed's assurances to the contrary, Dole had no real following at the convention, especially among the diehard southern conservatives who were supposed to be appeased by his selection. "What's a Dole?" groused Helms campaign manager Tom Ellis. "A pineapple?" Even some of Ford's delegates were disappointed, especially those from Sun Belt states, where a Kansas senator would have little appeal. The Dole selection was "not exactly what we had in mind, not as strong as a Ford-Reagan ticket would have been," the chair of Ford's Florida delegation told the press.[56]

Dole was actually a much more accomplished politician than these criticisms would suggest. He had served in Congress for fifteen years and was well versed in the processes of both policymaking and campaigning. A decorated World War II combat veteran, Dole had sustained severe injuries that nearly killed him and left his right arm permanently incapacitated. Dole was extremely determined, a hard worker and a scrappy fighter known for what the *New York Times* called his "aggressive partisanship and a savage wit." He had served in the Kansas state legislature, the US House of Representatives, and the US Senate and had chaired the Republican National Committee. Few people were better versed than Dole in parliamentary and party procedure.

He was a champion of fiscal conservatism, opposing much of the Great Society (including Medicare) in the 1960s, but on agricultural issues that appealed to his Kansas farming constituency, he could make alliances with liberals. He joined George McGovern in advocating an expansion of the food stamp program in the early 1970s, for instance. He got along well with his colleagues and was personable in private, but he was best known for his long workdays, his wholehearted dedication to politics, and, above all, his willingness to go after his political opponents on the campaign trail. "He's the first man we've had around here in a long time who will grab the other side by the hair and drag them down the hill," Goldwater said. Other colleagues called him "a real gut fighter," a "hungry Doberman Pinscher," and a "hatchet man." Connally had no doubt that Dole would "carry the fight to Carter and Mondale." But when Dole addressed the delegates on the last night of the convention, he spoke somewhat blandly about the need to "free the free-enterprise system." He avoided his usual direct attacks on the Carter-Mondale ticket, perhaps because he had been cautioned against appearing too irascible.[57] There would be plenty of opportunity for his characteristic feistiness later, on the campaign trail.

Following Dole's speech, President Ford addressed the convention and gave what most people consider the best speech of his life. It was hard for a president who had served in Congress for decades to present himself as a Washington outsider, but Ford attempted to do so, waging an uncharacteristically fiery attack on the Democratic Congress that was reminiscent of President Truman's assault on the "do-nothing" Republican Congress during his 1948 campaign. But rather than criticizing Congress for refusing to spend money to help people, as Truman had done, Ford castigated the Democratic majority for wasting people's money, and he cast himself as a lone figure wielding his veto pen to put the brakes on runaway spending in Washington. "For two years I have stood for all the people against a vote-hungry, free-spending congressional majority on Capitol Hill," he said. "Fifty-five times I vetoed extravagant and unwise legislation; 45 times I made those vetoes stick. Those vetoes have saved American taxpayers billions and billions of dollars. I am against the big tax spender and for the little taxpayer." It was a stirring defense of fiscal conservatism—Ford's favorite issue—and Ford wanted to make sure that the Americans who were watching him on television realized that it was not only a wise policy but also a compassionate one. Jimmy Carter might claim to represent the people, but in the end, the candidate who refused to waste the people's money was the true populist, he argued. "You at home, listening tonight, you are the people who pay the taxes and make the system work," Ford said. "You are the people who make America what it is. It is from your ranks I come and on your side I stand."[58]

Then, remarkably, as a gesture of unity, Ford invited Reagan to join him at the podium and address the delegates. He seemed to genuinely want a reconciliation with the man who had nearly deprived him of the nomination, almost splitting the party in the process. "Let me say this from the bottom of my heart," Ford told the delegates. "After the scrimmages of the past few months, it really feels good to have Ron Reagan on the same side of the line."[59] The invitation appeared to catch Reagan off guard, but he gave what many thought was his most memorable performance of the campaign. Speaking without notes for less than six minutes, he captured the hearts of the conservatives in the audience and made some of them regret nominating Ford. Some reporters noted that it could have been his acceptance speech, and perhaps he did use some of the words he might have been planning to speak in the event he received the nomination. Although he briefly endorsed Ford, Reagan said little about the president himself, focusing instead on the conservative principles reflected in the Republican Party platform. Near the end of his speech, he launched into the tear-inducing apocalyptic imagery he had been using since his 1964 speech for Barry Goldwater. Whether people one hundred years from now will be free depends on "what we do here," he said. "Will they look back with appreciation and say, thank God for those people in 1976 who headed off that loss of freedom; who kept us now a hundred years later free; who kept our world from nuclear destruction?" he asked. He concluded:

> This is our challenge. And this is why we are here in this hall tonight. Better than we've ever done before, we've got to quit talking to each other and about each other and go out and communicate to the world that we may be fewer in numbers than we've ever been. But we cry the message they've been waiting for. We must go forth from here united, determined, that what a great general said a few years ago is true: There is no substitute for victory.[60]

And so, Reagan had the last word. The band broke into the Michigan fight song, the president stood waving to the crowd, and the delegates cheered for fourteen minutes. But it was unclear whether the

Figure 8.4. Ronald Reagan addressing the 1976 Republican National Convention as Bob Dole, Nancy Reagan, Nelson Rockefeller, and Gerald and Betty Ford look on. (Courtesy of Gerald R. Ford Presidential Library)

delegates were cheering for Ford or for Reagan. Ford had hoped for reconciliation and an endorsement from Reagan that would unify the party after a bruising primary fight. What he received instead was a conservative call to arms that would perpetuate the party's divisions. Some delegates—including a few who had cast their ballots for Ford—immediately exclaimed that the convention had nominated the wrong candidate. "The first real emotion of the night wasn't for the ticket, but for the man who wasn't on it," Sam Donaldson reported for ABC.[61]

"We're not going to lose next time," one Reagan delegate from South Carolina told journalist Elizabeth Drew at the close of the convention. "Next time, we'll control the Party. . . . The sentiment of this party is with Ronald Reagan. The professionals of this party were for Ford, but we're going to pull the conservative citizens into this movement. We're going to win next time. There is a conservative tide in this nation. . . . Four years from now, the conservative position can prevail again, with a true conservative."[62]

Reagan and his supporters did not reconcile with Ford. Reagan went back to his nationally syndicated radio program and resumed criticizing Ford's policies. He endorsed the president and made a number of campaign appearances on his behalf, but in his speeches he focused not on the president but on the conservative Republican Party platform—just as he had in his closing speech at the convention. And although the Ford campaign periodically consulted with some of Reagan's campaign staff, it did not have much contact with the former California governor himself. Ford was deeply upset not only about the damage Reagan's primary campaign had done to the Republican Party but also about Reagan's refusal to provide anything more than tepid support in the general election. To the end of his life, he blamed the election results on Reagan.[63]

Part of the problem, no doubt, was that Reagan and his supporters viewed the 1976 contest as a beachhead for a larger conservative assault on the moderate wing of the Republican Party that was just beginning. In contrast, Ford and his supporters considered the Reagan conservatives defeated rivals who had a duty to put party loyalty ahead of ideology or personal preferences. Unlike the Ford campaign team, which consisted almost entirely of party loyalists whose highest concern was the good of the GOP, many of the Reagan supporters valued ideology above party. In their view, they were leading a revolution, and they were not sure that Ford's election would do much to advance their cause.

This revolutionary mind-set scared the moderate Republicans in the Ford camp, and it increased their determination to elect the president to another term in office. They believed this was their last chance to save the centrist and liberal wings of the Republican Party from a takeover by the Reaganites. The primary fight, the convention, the platform, and the vice-presidential selection had already pushed Ford to the right, but this was nothing compared to what would happen if Ford lost the election to the Democrats and the Reagan forces took over at the next convention. "If President Ford loses, not only will the country be worse off, but the party will clearly be left to those right wing radicals who would rather lose elections than have an open party," declared Frank Kent, executive director of the Minority Contractors Resource Center and a prominent black Republican. "If he loses, for all intents and purposes we will have one party rule. That is the reason, for me at least, why I consider the election of President Ford a 'must win' situation."[64] The election, in other words, would be the last chance for the socially moderate, fiscally conservative, big-tent, midwestern Republicanism that Ford favored.

9 CARTER STUMBLES OVER CULTURAL ISSUES

With the convention behind them and Election Day less than three months away, members of the Ford campaign team finally had what they wanted: a unified party and a chance to go head-to-head with the Democratic nominee. But after the exhausting nomination fight, Ford now faced the most challenging presidential race of any incumbent since Herbert Hoover. As his campaign advisers pointed out, no candidate had ever accomplished what Ford would need to do: erase a nearly 40-point lead by his opponent.[1] This would call for a strategy like no other. Closing such a massive gap might be impossible, but to have any chance of succeeding, Ford would have to adopt the same type of values-based politics that Carter had pioneered and convince socially conservative voters that he shared their concerns and was more trustworthy than Carter.

FORD'S SOCIALLY CONSERVATIVE STRATEGY

Ford's only hope of victory, his advisers thought in the summer of 1976, was to hold on to the Midwest, a moderately socially conservative heartland that included a mix of Democratic-leaning industrial cities and Republican-leaning farm country. His campaign managers assumed that he would lose most of the South to Carter because it was inconceivable to them that southerners would vote against a fellow southerner, especially a politically centrist Southern Baptist who was poised to become the first president from the Deep South in

Figure 9.1. A meeting of the Ford campaign team at Camp David in early August 1976. White House chief of staff Dick Cheney is speaking to President Ford. (Courtesy of Gerald R. Ford Presidential Library)

more than a century. But if Ford captured nearly all of the eastern and midwestern industrial states "from New Jersey to Minnesota," and if he carried the Great Plains, the Mountain West, and the Pacific coast as well—with the swing state of California a must-win—he could amass a narrow majority of electoral votes. Ford could even afford to lose one large industrial state, such as Pennsylvania, if he could pick up Virginia or Florida. New England was a secondary priority, but if Ford could pick up a few historically Republican states from that region, as his campaign strategists thought he could, the president would be even better situated. But the "key" to winning the election, Jim Reichley and other strategists repeatedly asserted, was the industrial heartland, which was traditionally a battleground.[2] To win these states, Ford's advisers thought, he needed to reprise President Nixon's outreach to Catholics and appeal to upwardly mobile suburban Catholic voters who had become more politically conservative (and more Republican) than their parents.

Ford's advisers thought the president's best hope of capturing the culturally conservative Catholic vote in the nation's industrial heartland was to position himself as a "social conservative and economic moderate," just as Nixon had in 1972. Carter seemed far less vulnerable to the charge of being a cultural liberal than McGovern had been in 1972, but Carter's earlier waffling on abortion—followed by a declaration that he would not support a constitutional amendment to overturn *Roe v. Wade*—offered a narrow opening that the Ford campaign thought it might be able to exploit. More important, Carter's cultural background was unfamiliar to northern Catholics. At the beginning of the summer, the Ford campaign's polls showed Carter 10 percentage points ahead of the president, but compared with Carter's support among other demographic groups, this was a lower margin than expected among traditionally Democratic Catholic voters. To win them over, the president's campaign team believed, Ford simply needed to maintain his quiet honesty, his commitment to family, and his moderately conservative stances on social issues such as abortion, busing, marijuana decriminalization, and amnesty for Vietnam War draft evaders. If Ford promoted what Reichley called "family values," which he defined as fostering a "moral atmosphere in which families can flourish," he could do well among Catholics and other religious voters. Accordingly, the Ethnic Desk—a campaign office for outreach mainly to northern white Catholics—would play a central role in Ford's campaign strategy. And to pick up socially conservative votes on the abortion issue, the director of the Minnesota-based American Citizens Concerned for Life was brought in to send targeted campaign advertising to leaders of the nation's pro-life organizations that highlighted the Republican Party's new antiabortion platform.[3]

The Ford team expected Carter to win the southern Protestant vote, but they considered it imperative to keep the northern Protestants in their camp. In early August, Ford was running stronger among Protestants than Catholics, but a Harris poll showed him still losing the Protestant vote to Carter by 21 points. To close this gap, Ford's strategists believed they had to shore up support among Protestants who were probably Republican already—that is, those in the North. This meant appealing both to mainline Protestants—Episcopalians, Congregationalists, Lutherans, and other venerable, moderately liberal, socially influential denominations—and to evangelicals—Southern Baptist transplants to the North, along with numerous other theologically conservative Wesleyan, Reformed, and Pentecostal Christians. The best strategy to reach both groups was for the president to "stress the moral objectives of his policies" and to convince his fellow Protestants that "his attitudes are shaped by the same basic beliefs that they hold."

Ford should "seek to establish cultural identification with middle-class Protestants whenever possible," Reichley suggested.[4]

As a moderately conservative Episcopalian, Ford was not one to wear his faith on his sleeve, but he had long represented the Dutch Calvinists of Grand Rapids in Congress, and he was comfortable with the quiet piety of culturally conservative Christians in the North. One of his sons was a student at Gordon-Conwell Theological Seminary, a leading evangelical institution in Massachusetts. Like many other Republicans whose political careers began during the early years of the Cold War, Ford was familiar with the civil religion of the Eisenhower years, and he believed that American democracy was based on a strong moral and religious foundation that must be preserved. Carter might get much of the southern "born-again" vote with his personal testimony, but Ford needed to do whatever he could to limit the impact of Carter's religious image among voters who might otherwise lean Republican. As Baptist marketing consultant Gaylord Briley told the Ford campaign team in June, "religious people" were "'conservatives' in the classical sense," and they were often suspicious of the Washington establishment because of their growing "feeling that the government is out to push religion completely out of public life." As both conservative Catholics and evangelical Protestants lamented the sexual revolution and other culturally liberal trends in the nation, it was more important than ever for Ford to imitate President Eisenhower and revive an image of civil religion in the nation. There could be no more controversial expressions of cultural liberalism from the First Lady. Instead, the president had to project an image of quiet but heartfelt faith, coupled with plenty of public references to God and country.[5]

Ford found plenty of opportunities that summer to speak at religious forums in defense of conservative moral values. In June he became the first American president to address the annual meeting of the Southern Baptist Convention. The invitation was opposed by some Carter supporters in the convention who wondered why the Democratic candidate had not been asked to speak, but Ford used the opportunity to promote civil religious themes. Southern Baptist leaders had requested a "nonpartisan Bicentennial speech" when they invited Ford, and he complied by avoiding any partisan references, but he probably exceeded their expectations in his sermonizing on behalf of a "strong moral foundation" for America. Excoriating the "situation ethics" of moral relativism and "a new code of conduct which rivals the basic truths and mocks the basic beliefs that this nation and much of religion were founded" on, he called for public officials to practice the kind of "personal integrity" that had been lacking in Washington in recent years.[6]

The bicentennial offered Ford an ideal opportunity to solidify his support among religious conservatives by employing civil religious rhetoric that was not explicitly partisan or sectarian. This appealed to Ford's ecumenical inclinations. In preparation for the bicentennial, he called for four days of "celebration, thanksgiving and prayer . . . so that people of all faiths, in their own way, may give thanks for the Divine Providence through 200 years, and pray for the future safety and happiness of our nation." And when he addressed a crowd at Philadelphia's Independence Hall on July 4, 1976, he reminded the one million spectators that "perhaps the greatest basis for our strength was our continuing belief in the principle set forth by the writers of the Declaration of Independence and the Constitution that the source of all our blessings is a belief in a living God." Unbeknownst to most Americans at the time, Ford had also sent a videotaped bicentennial message to televangelist Jerry Falwell's Thomas Road Baptist Church, which was even more direct in its invocation of civil religious themes. He had spoken at the annual gathering of the National Association of Evangelicals earlier that year, and he addressed the National Religious Broadcasters convention later that fall.[7]

Even as the Ford campaign strategized about how to reach particular religious, ethnic, and demographic groups, it recognized that the president—in keeping with the tradition of the Republican Party—had never been comfortable presenting himself as the candidate of special interests or particular groups. That was why civil religious rhetoric appealed to him more than outreach to sectarian minorities. If he changed course now, his campaign would suffer, some of his advisers believed. "President Ford's greatest single advantage is his appeal to the American people *as a whole,*" Reichley noted in a memo to Dick Cheney. "If he should be perceived as deviating from this course to favor a particular group or groups, his chances for reelection would be greatly reduced." Although Carter strongly denied it, Reichley believed the Democrats were the party of "special interests," while the Republicans were the party of the "national interest."[8]

With its ambivalence about appealing to "special interests," the Ford campaign ran on two parallel tracks: while the national campaign, under the management of James Baker, focused on a national or regional strategy and publicly eschewed appeals to "special interests," a parallel volunteer effort called People for Ford, headed by liberal Michigan Republican Elly Peterson, coordinated particular "desks" that made targeted appeals to women, blacks, Catholic ethnics, Jews, youths, farmers, veterans, and other demographic groups that the national campaign avoided discussing in detail. The Black Desk, for instance, emphasized Ford's consistent record of support for civil rights both as a congressman and as president. The Older Americans Desk emphasized Ford's concern for senior citizens and his desire to maintain the strength of the Social Security program. Peterson, however, faced ideological challenges within the campaign that stymied her efforts. Although the Ford campaign purchased advertising on black radio stations and in black newspapers in eighteen states, the volunteers at the Black Desk complained that their efforts were a low priority. And the director of the Labor Desk complained that Dole's spirited defense of right-to-work laws on the campaign trail made it very difficult to gain support from labor unions. Some People for Ford volunteers saw themselves as defenders of a moderate Republican vision that was swiftly being eroded as the party moved to the right. But if a number of the African Americans, women, and labor supporters in the campaign worried that the Ford-Dole ticket and the platform were too conservative, the Youth for Ford organizers encountered the opposite ideological problem: campus Republican organizations were filled with Reaganites who were not excited about working for the more moderate, more traditional Ford.[9]

The primary architects of Ford's campaign ignored these internal dissensions and focused on the campaign's national message, which was "America Together"—an appropriate theme, they thought, for the nation's bicentennial. The Ford campaign needed to "create a mind-set among our swing voters that America has come together, and the divisiveness and fears of the past are abating," a strategy memo declared. The campaign attributed this "healing" to President Ford's leadership and suggested that his pardon of Nixon—though politically costly at the time—had been the right decision because it helped heal the nation.[10]

In essence, the campaign against Carter followed the pattern of many incumbents seeking reelection. The president argued that the nation was recovering both economically and emotionally and that conditions had improved under his leadership. This was a difficult position for Ford to take, given that the unemployment rate was still above 7 percent. For months, the Democrats had portrayed Ford and the Republicans as the cause of the nation's poor economy, and Ford had let them get away with it by focusing most of his public rhetoric on balancing the budget and fighting inflation rather than creating jobs. On inflation, he could legitimately claim some measure of success: during his time in office, the inflation rate had dropped from 11 percent to less than 6 percent, which Ford attributed to his efforts to rein in deficit spending. But Carter was still criticizing the president on inflation while simultaneously launching major attacks on his administration's failure to provide jobs. Even though the unemployment rate was slowly decreasing (it had hit 9 percent the previous year), Ford found it difficult to convince Americans that jobs were a priority for him, especially since he opposed the Humphrey-Hawkins bill, the Democrats' major jobs creation proposal.[11]

Some conservative Republicans, such as Representative Jack Kemp, urged Ford to give more publicity to Republican proposals to stimulate the economy through tax cuts. Ford, who had the same aversion to unbalanced budgets as Presidents Hoover and Eisenhower, had been cautious about cutting taxes too quickly. In fact, the previous year he had supported a tax increase (which the Democratic Congress rejected) because he wanted to balance the budget, which he believed was the key to controlling inflation. But during the campaign he began to talk more about lowering taxes as a way to stimulate economic growth—although he promised that any tax cuts would be offset by equivalent reductions in spending.[12]

Opposition to deficit spending had always been one of Ford's major issues, and he intended to make it a focus of his campaign, regardless of Kemp's desire to emphasize tax cuts. His campaign staff believed that the image of Ford as a budget-cutter would have widespread appeal because, according to a Gallup poll, 78 percent of Americans (and 84 percent of Republicans) in 1976 supported a constitutional amendment requiring a balanced budget. Because the Democrats' platform and convention had promised large, expensive federal programs to create jobs and provide health care for all, the Ford campaign had an easier time arguing that Carter—who had long claimed to be a deficit hawk—was really a big-spending liberal. "The combined costs of Humphrey-Hawkins, Kennedy-Corman health insurance, and federalization of welfare would be astronomical," Reichley noted in a strategy memo to Cheney. "These costs can be paid only through inflation or higher taxes or both." The problem for the Ford campaign, Reichley thought, was that most voters were not aware of the costs of these programs, and they still believed that Carter was a budget-cutter because that was how he portrayed himself. Reichley was not sure whether Carter really believed in some of the expensive federal programs his party's platform advocated, but he advised, "We should hang the liberal program on him to the extent that we can. We should nail him with Humphrey-Hawkins, which he privately opposes but publicly endorsed after 'ethnic purity.'" Mike Duval concurred. In the campaign's official strategy handbook, he wrote that the Ford team needed to brand Carter as a "liberal, well to the left of center and part of the old-line Democratic majority."[13]

By "liberal," Duval meant one thing: someone who would overspend, driving up both the deficit and the inflation rate and ultimately increasing taxes and slowing the economy. Carter had long insisted that he would never do this, but the Democratic platform, the choice of Mondale as a running mate, and Carter's own public shift to the left on economic questions allowed the Ford campaign to argue that he would. Carter's "regional and religious background have developed a conservative base of support while his running mate and platform are basically liberal," Duval wrote. "We must mount an attack on him on conservative issues, both economic and social. . . . We must make it a race between a liberal (Carter/Mondale) and a moderate (the President)."[14]

The tactic succeeded in rebranding Carter and diminishing his support. In the spring, before the Democratic National Convention, a Gallup poll had shown that Americans were evenly divided on the question of whether Carter was a liberal or a conservative: 46 percent labeled him a conservative, and 48 percent thought he was a liberal. But in the fall, after the Ford campaign had spent several months branding Carter as a liberal because of the Democratic Party platform and the selection of Mondale, Americans' perceptions shifted: 60 percent now viewed Carter as a liberal, while only 32 percent considered him a conservative. "Liberal" was a problematic label for many Americans outside of major urban areas; for some, it conjured up images of both excessive cultural permissiveness and fiscal irresponsibility. Because the political labels "liberal" and "conservative" were not yet firmly defined in many people's minds, polls in the fall of 1976 showed wide variation in the percentage of Americans who used these labels to describe their own ideology, but one thing was clear: more Americans called themselves "conservative" than "liberal." As the Democratic Party's own polling showed, even Americans who were worried about their own economic future and who wanted an expanded social safety net were worried about the long-term costs of continued deficit spending. By labeling Carter a liberal, the Ford campaign capitalized on those fears and diminished Carter's standing in the areas where he had been strongest. By September, the farming states of the Great Plains were no longer in Carter's camp; the Midwest was now considered a toss-up; and even the South, though still solidly behind Carter, was beginning to show signs of wavering. As one conservative Democratic state legislator in Louisiana told the Carter campaign in mid-September, "Governor Carter's position has deteriorated badly in this state over the past two months. His image is more and more that of a liberal, and that's not good in Louisiana. . . . To improve our position here we must appear more conservative than Ford on at least some issues."[15]

Despite its successful branding of the Carter-Mondale ticket as too "liberal" for most Americans, the Ford campaign believed that issues alone would be of limited value. According to a majority of the nation's newspaper editors, voters would ultimately base their decision on their perception of the candidates' leadership abilities. Ford, they thought, had not yet convinced Americans that he was an effective leader. "There is a clear public perception that no one is in control of this Administration," Ford strategist Duval wrote. "This is a major negative." Ford's White House team believed that the public perception of the president as dimwitted, clumsy, and inept was terribly unfair, but they knew from extensive polling data that these views were widespread. No matter what the Ford campaign did to highlight the president's achievements, the message never seemed to sink in. "People don't seem to be interested in specific issues or in the President's record," one campaign staff member lamented in July. "They seem to yearn for a change and to be attracted to personality, the promise of leadership, spirituality, a vision for the future." This was the main reason why Carter had surged ahead in the polls, the Ford team believed. Duval was blunt: "Until the voters perceive that President Ford has the personal characteristics of a strong, decisive leader, no strategy can be expected to close the Ford-Carter gap."[16]

In an effort to showcase Ford as a leader, his campaign settled on an unusual strategy: the president would not campaign at all. The "no-campaign strategy" was a result of the staff's calculation that Ford was a "poor communicator" on the campaign stump and that he would win more votes by staying in the White House and projecting an image of presidential gravitas. When Ford had actively campaigned against Reagan, his poll numbers had dropped because voters reportedly viewed him as a Republican partisan.[17] In addition, whenever Ford traveled, he risked the embarrassing gaffes that undermined his claim to leadership. The campaign did not need any more photos of the president biting into the corn husk on a hot tamale.

In the television era, this strategy of avoiding the campaign trail made a lot of sense. As president, Ford would receive constant media coverage anyway, and he had a better chance of controlling the message. A few well-rehearsed television speeches could more effectively depict the president as "in control, decisive, open and candid" than weeks of campaigning.[18]

In executing this strategy, the president's campaign staff realized that they had to disguise the real reason for taking the president off the campaign trail. "It is essential that the announcement be characterized as the President's personal decision, against the advice of his campaign managers," one strategy memo noted. The speech written for Ford's announcement of his no-campaign strategy emphasized the imperative of presidential duty. "I would prefer to be judged on the basis of my actions and proven leadership rather than on the empty rhetoric of promise," he declared. "The business of this Nation cannot be neglected."[19]

Ford would thus remain above the fray for most of the campaign. This did not mean that there were no negative attacks on Carter—just that they were not made through general media advertising or through the president's own words. The Ford team had known since the summer that if they wanted to win, they had to undercut Carter's image as a miracle-worker. They needed to portray him as "an amateur at the business of governing, a hungry type, perhaps, ambitious for power," and a duplicitous "closet liberal" who "talks out of both sides of his mouth," one campaign aide suggested in August. That was why Duval and some of his associates had encouraged Ford to pick a running mate who was an "attackman." Attacking Carter and Mondale now became Dole's primary responsibility, and he was eager to oblige. Ripping into Carter's support for pardoning Vietnam War draft dodgers, Dole told a Seattle American Legion chapter a week after the convention that

Carter was "declaring that those who served this nation in her armed forces deserve no greater consideration than those who turned their backs and scurried away." The next week he was in North Carolina railing against the Democratic Party platform as one of "special interests—big labor, big government and big spending." And he was quick to point out Carter's inconsistencies on controversial issues. "I don't fault him for having a position," Dole said. "I fault him for having two or three positions."[20]

Whether because of Dole's campaigning, the president's convention speech, or Carter's weaknesses, Ford gained steadily in the polls. The campaign was also under new management. Immediately after the convention, Ford, who had changed campaign managers several times already, made his final appointment: he entrusted leadership of the campaign to Texas lawyer James Baker, who consulted closely with Cheney in crafting strategy. The previous campaign manager, Rogers Morton, had stated publicly that the president had written off the "Cotton South," but Baker reversed that position and decided that the Ford campaign would invest resources even in the Deep South. Within days, Dole was headed to Georgia, North Carolina, and other southern stops, where he warned that Carter and Mondale were running on a platform "so far to the left that many of us would slide right off." "As soon as Governor Carter is revealed as the liberal he is, we think there will be a big shift in the South," he predicted.[21]

When Dole traveled to Salisbury, North Carolina, he brought along the person he called his "southern strategy"—his new bride, Elizabeth (better known as "Liddy" at the time), who had been born and raised in Salisbury. It had been nearly two decades since Elizabeth lived in North Carolina. After graduating Phi Beta Kappa from Duke University and earning a degree from Harvard Law School, she had spent most of her time in Washington, DC, working for the Johnson and Nixon administrations, followed by a stint on the Federal Trade Commission. But North Carolinians still treated her as one of their own, and she milked the local connection for all it was worth. She was determined to win the South for the Ford-Dole ticket. "Jimmy Carter may be their geographical neighbor," she said about southerners, "but Ford and Dole are the philosophical neighbors. I think Southerners can perceive that difference—they're too sophisticated to be fooled."[22]

This was a new role for Elizabeth, who had been married to Bob for less than a year (his first marriage had ended in divorce in 1972).

She was also a recent convert to the Republican message, having been a Democrat for most of her political career. In fact, even at the beginning of the 1976 campaign, her partisan conversion was still a work in progress. Bob had convinced her to renounce her long association with the Democratic Party and become an independent, but according to an Associated Press article in early September, "she claims she's still not ready to go that extra step and become a Republican." Despite being new to GOP politics, she proved to be both an eager defender of the president's record and an indefatigable campaigner—perhaps one of the few who could surpass her husband's capacity to endure grueling speaking schedules. She shared her husband's ambition and his ability to deliver biting political attacks. She had a high-profile career of her own; in fact, no other candidate's wife—either in the general election or the primaries—had been appointed to as many high-level federal government positions as Elizabeth Dole. She was a women's rights advocate and strongly supportive of the Equal Rights Amendment, but she did not position herself as a feminist on the campaign trail. Instead, when she traveled to some of the most socially conservative regions of the country, she turned on her southern charm. She was quite capable of playing to more traditional gender stereotypes and using the twinkle in her hazel eyes to connect with voters on the campaign trail and take the edge off her husband's more acerbic style. The *Washington Star* called her a "Southern strategy that can cuddle."[23]

Dole viewed himself as the president's "bridge" not only to the conservative Reaganite wing of the Republican Party but also to rural America and farmers in the Midwest and the South. At Dole's request, the president made him a senior policy adviser on agricultural matters during the campaign—a position Dole used to woo the wheat-farming states back into the Republican column. "If I bring anything to the ticket, it's, I think, a close identification with agriculture, small towns, rural America, and that would appeal, I think, in those areas to Democrats and independents," he said.[24]

A Harris poll taken at the beginning of October indicated that despite Dole's efforts, he was personally disliked everywhere outside of the Great Plains states and Wisconsin. In the industrial midwestern states such as Ohio and Illinois, which the Ford campaign considered a must-win, Dole was considerably less popular than Ford and less popular than Mondale as well. It seemed that voters were turned off by his political attacks, even though they were usually delivered with a wisecrack that had audiences laughing along with him. To Dole's consternation, Mondale engaged in regular attacks against Ford and Dole with few negative repercussions, perhaps because he did not have Dole's reputation as a "hatchet man."[25] Dole's attacks on the Democratic ticket made him personally unpopular, but they may have played a role in driving down Carter's poll numbers.

By early September, polls showed that Ford had regained the support of most voters who identified themselves as "conservative" (a self-description that applied to 34 percent of all voters, according to a *New York Times*–CBS poll). Earlier that summer, polls had shown that as many as 44 percent of self-identified conservatives were planning to support Carter, perhaps because of Ford's divisive primary campaign against Reagan, combined with the freshness of Carter's anti-Washington message. By early September, Ford also had the support of 85 percent of all Republicans. Perhaps the Ford campaign's efforts to label Carter a "liberal" and to link him with Mondale's Senate voting record were starting to pay off. Ford's support from conservatives and Republicans was not enough to propel him to victory (registered Republicans accounted for only 22 percent of the electorate), but it meant that he would not have to waste valuable campaign time trying to consolidate his base, as he had feared might be necessary back in July and August.[26]

Carter was still ahead in the polls, but his lead was slipping. He had been more than 30 points ahead in a Gallup poll taken at the end of the Democratic National Convention in July, and immediately before the Republican convention, he had still been 23 points ahead. By the end of the GOP convention, Carter's lead had shrunk to 10 points. This in itself did not provoke much anxiety in the Carter camp. As the *New York Times* explained, "The polls tend to follow the television cameras . . . so the President is likely to fall back again as the Democrats get organized and registered in the key industrial states of the East and Middle West. The major political trends are still with the Democrats." Indeed, only a week after the Republican convention, Carter started to experience a rebound, and his lead over Ford increased to 15 points. But in September, the substantial Democratic gains expected by both the *New York Times* and the Carter campaign never materialized. By the third week of September, Ford was ahead of Carter in Illinois, and the race was too close to call in New Jersey, California, and New York. Nationally, the *New York Times* observed, the race had become a "virtual toss-up." Even when Carter had been solidly in the lead, his strong margins in the polls had depended on his overwhelming popularity in the South, where he led Ford 64 to 28 percent at the end of August. But outside the South, the two candidates were statistically tied in late August: Carter with 44 percent, and Ford with 43 percent.[27] This lopsided regional support for Carter meant that Ford's chances of eking out a bare majority of the electoral vote—even if he ran slightly behind in the national popular vote—might be much better than the Carter campaign had assumed.

CARTER'S STRUGGLE TO BALANCE COMPETING INTERESTS

Despite slippage in the polls, Carter and his campaign staff were confident that they could easily win the election. They believed that the number of "safe" states in their camp far exceeded the number of solidly Republican states that Ford could count on. Carter's campaign strategists thought that the South was solidly behind the Democratic ticket and could be largely ignored, as long as Carter made occasional trips there to "show the flag." Liberal, traditionally Democratic states outside the South, such as Massachusetts and Minnesota, could also be counted on to support the Carter-Mondale ticket. This freed the Carter campaign to concentrate on the same battleground states the Ford campaign wanted to win—the industrial Midwest and California—with some occasional forays into solidly Republican territory to throw the Ford team off guard. Carter wanted to wage a national campaign that would secure a landslide victory with support from every region (thus giving him a national mandate for his agenda), but Hamilton Jordan thought that, given the legal limits on campaign spending, it was important not to overextend the campaign's scarce resources. Even in July, when Carter was more than 30 points ahead of Ford in the polls, he advised caution. The campaign's "clear and single goal must be to simply win 270 electoral votes," he said.[28]

Votes for Carter would come from all points on the ideological spectrum, which meant that to build a winning coalition, Carter would have to use campaign "surrogates" who appealed to particular demographic or ideological groups that might ordinarily be at odds with one another. Carter and Mondale family members would campaign on behalf of the ticket—with the Mondales being particularly useful in northern and pro-union states—but the campaign would also rely heavily on the targeted use of some recently defeated Democratic rivals. Mo Udall would be sent to "liberal areas and college communities" in Michigan, Wisconsin, Connecticut, and Colorado. Hubert Humphrey would campaign in Pennsylvania, Illinois, New York, and New Jersey—where he likely would have won the primaries if he had been on the ballot. Jerry Brown would be an important campaigner in California, and Frank Church would also be useful in the West. Ted Kennedy could be sent to Chicago to reach "suburban liberals" and "Catholic ethnics"—two groups that were currently giving Carter only "weak" support. Henry Jackson could handle the Carter campaign's outreach to Jews in New York, Miami, and Los Angeles. Barbara Jordan, whose keynote address at the Democratic convention had inspired such fervent support among blacks, could be sent to Chicago to "work the media and black communities." Most of the campaign's efforts focused on solidifying liberal support for Carter—especially since a third-party candidacy by Eugene McCarthy was still a threat—but even as he worked to convince northern Democrats that he shared their concerns, Carter did not completely ignore the southern conservative vote. Hamilton Jordan wanted to send George Wallace to the Florida Panhandle and Jackson, Mississippi, to bring out the white southern conservative vote for Carter. "It is important that you have Wallace campaign for you and have him public early in the campaign," Jordan wrote. "Most of the other surrogates are liberals and it will help to have him active for you."[29]

Recognizing that each targeted group of voters had somewhat different concerns, the campaign decided to assign each constituency to a separate campaign committee that would tailor a message appropriate for that particular group. The Hispanic Affairs Desk produced Spanish-language advertising for Carter, while the Asian Pacific Desk reached out to Chinese, Japanese, Filipino, and Korean immigrants. In the first week of October the Carter campaign distributed 800,000 copies of Spanish-language campaign brochures and posters—mostly in California, Texas, and New York, but also in ten other states. Carter was in favor of giving work permits to the nation's eight million undocumented immigrants (most of whom were Hispanics living in the Southwest), and his Spanish-language advertising highlighted this promise, but it also focused on his pledge to reduce unemployment. For most of the demographic-specific campaign desks—especially the Black Affairs Desk—maximizing turnout was the major concern. Carter strategists assumed that Hispanics, Asian Americans, and especially blacks would vote Democratic if they participated in the election, but they feared that a substantial number of these prospective voters would not show up at the polls. Black voter turnout had been declining in the 1970s, and the Carter campaign feared that if an insufficient number of blacks voted in northern cities, Carter might fail to carry some of the industrial states he needed to win.[30] The campaign was confident that if all the Democratic-leaning voters turned out, Carter would easily defeat Ford, but the danger was that some of them might not.

The campaign's biggest signs of trouble came from women and Catholics. Carter was polling better among men than among women, and some of the women in his coalition questioned his commitment to their most important issues. At the convention, where women accounted for only 33 percent of the delegates, a group of female delegates had urged Carter to support a requirement that half the delegate seats at the 1980 convention be reserved for women, but he refused to support a firm quota, even after meeting with the women for an hour. Carter strongly supported the Equal Rights Amendment, but in the view of some members of the 51.3% Committee, the group handling his campaign's outreach to women, his position on abortion was too moderate. Although polls showed that both men and women were closely divided on the abortion question, the 51.3% Committee had a pro-choice, feminist tilt, and the committee members spent so much time analyzing Carter's position on abortion that some of the women who attended the meetings reported feeling "bored by extended and aimless abortion discussions." Carter attempted to downplay abortion and unite his female campaign volunteers around the issue of discrimination against women, especially in employment, health insurance, financial credit, and education. He called for "improved child care services for working parents" and pledged to appoint "substantial numbers" of "qualified women" to "jobs of importance" in his administration. Many women were impressed with this commitment, and his advisory board included many women's rights activists ranging in ideology from iconic feminist Gloria Steinem to liberal pro-life Catholic Sidney Callahan.[31]

But still, the Carter campaign found it difficult to counter the appeal of the outspoken, pro-ERA First Lady and the Ford campaign's outreach to women across the ideological spectrum, from Republican feminists to anti-ERA social conservatives. Within the Carter campaign, some women grumbled that Carter was not practicing the nondiscrimination he preached. A slight majority of the campaign staff were men, and they held the top positions. The average woman employed by Carter's campaign in October 1976 earned only 79 percent of the salary earned by the average male campaign staff member, Sarah Hertel pointed out to Hamilton Jordan. This was better than the national gender wage gap, and it was an improvement over the campaign's salary figures for August, when the average woman had earned only 73 percent of the average male's salary, but it was still far from parity.[32]

Although the Carter campaign was concerned about the women's vote, it also feared that too many concessions to feminists might alienate socially conservative Catholics, especially on the abortion issue. Catholics, the Carter campaign believed, were the key to winning the industrial Midwest and California, and those states were the key to winning the election. For months, both internal polling and media reports had indicated that Carter's support among Catholics was unusually low for a Democratic presidential candidate, and that situation had not improved by September. Carter had ignored his pollster's advice to select a Catholic running mate, and as New York lawyer Adam Walinsky told him, "The campaign, thus far, has not yet dealt directly with a single Catholic issue in a remotely positive way. . . . So far as Catholics are concerned, the Convention was a negative." Earlier that year, during the primaries, Carter had tried to reach Catholic voters with his moderation on abortion, his middle-of-the-road stance on busing, and his indication that he might oppose affirmative action in public housing, but after facing criticism from progressives—especially after the widespread backlash against his "ethnic purity" comment in early April—he had moved to the left on all these issues, making socially conservative northern Catholics more suspicious of him than ever. The platform's modest endorsement of abortion rights—despite its careful phrasing and acknowledgment of a range of views on the issue—alienated some strongly pro-life Catholics. Although some Catholics appreciated Carter's open discussion of his Christian faith, many in the media thought his evangelical language might alienate some cultural Catholics who were less devout or who remembered the anti-Catholic statements emanating from southern evangelicals in the 1960 presidential election, when John F. Kennedy was running.[33]

To address these concerns and reach out to Catholic voters, the Carter campaign created an Urban Ethnic Affairs Desk in late August and put it under the coleadership of a nun and an administrative assistant from the National Conference of Catholic Bishops (NCCB). But campaign staff complained that the office was disorganized and unproductive. Five weeks after the Urban Ethnic Affairs Desk was created, Carter campaign offices in Rhode Island and Connecticut—two of the most Catholic states in the nation—had not yet heard from it.[34]

Members of the Carter campaign staff were divided about how to reach Catholics. The nation's Catholic bishops cited abortion, along with other social justice issues, as a leading concern in their official statement on Catholic political priorities issued in February. Most of Carter's campaign advisers, however, counseled him not to worry about abortion or complaints from the bishops about that issue; instead, they recommended that Carter bypass the church leadership and appeal directly to Catholic voters on issues of jobs and urban uplift. Most of all, they said, he needed to ally himself with experienced Catholic Democratic congressmen such as Tip O'Neill of Massachusetts or Peter Rodino of New Jersey and let them take him to Catholic neighborhoods. According to pollster Patrick Caddell, less than 10 percent of Catholic voters would base their presidential choice on the abortion issue. "The hierarchy speaks principally for itself, and it is far more likely to follow than to lead its parishioners," Walinsky told Carter. "The only real way to gain support from Catholic voters is to go to them yourself, in the toughest places you can find: in the Holy Name societies and American Legion halls of Brooklyn and Buffalo, South Milwaukee and South Boston." Bob Burns, editor of *U.S. Catholic,* agreed. "Nearly all Catholics will vote along 'bread and butter' lines," he wrote. "A tiny minority might be swayed by the abortion issue. As for the bishops, I would wager that 95% of the Catholics in the United States have never heard of the six bishops who met with Mr. Carter."[35]

But the nation's highest-ranking bishops, who had been criticizing Carter on abortion ever since the Democratic platform was adopted, wanted to talk with the candidate, and eventually, Carter agreed to do so, despite misgivings among his staff. Carter tried to use the meeting to discuss his common ground with the bishops on a wide range of economic and social policies, but the bishops wanted to talk about abortion. This did not surprise Carter's advisers; in fact, it was what they had feared. "The abortion issue to the Catholic clergy is like 14-B is to labor leadership," Landon Butler told Hamilton Jordan and Rick Hutcheson a few days before the meeting.[36]

Aides were dismayed to discover that Carter appeared to give ground to the bishops by pledging not to block an antiabortion constitutional amendment if it were proposed in Congress. Even though that statement was technically consistent with Carter's repeated assertions that he was opposed to an antiabortion constitutional amendment, the pledge of neutrality looked like more waffling, and it did not help Carter's cause. It also failed to mollify the bishops. They emerged from the meeting saying that they were "disappointed" with Carter's position.[37]

This gave the Ford campaign an opening to reach out to Catholics on the abortion issue. Earlier in the year, Ford had been reluctant to say much about abortion, but he reiterated his party's support for the antiabortion amendment when he met with the same representatives of the NCCB who had spoken to Carter. The bishops expressed their approval, saying they were "encouraged" by the meeting. That fall, the Ford campaign purchased full-page ads in Catholic diocesan newspapers, reminding Catholics of the president's support for an antiabortion constitutional amendment. Ford's move to the right on the abortion issue provoked a negative reaction among some pro-choice members of the party, as advisers had feared. John D. Rockefeller III, a leading population-control advocate and the older brother of the vice president, published an editorial in *Newsweek* protesting the Republican Party's move to the right on the issue and wrote a personal letter to the president to express his concerns. "I am distressed to find that our party appears to be rapidly becoming the party opposed to a woman's right to choose abortion," he told Ford. But Ford was not particularly worried about Rockefeller's vote; he was far more interested in winning the votes of culturally conservative Catholics in the Midwest. As Ford's analysts pointed out, internal polling showed that even though both Democrats and Republicans were evenly split on an antiabortion constitutional amendment, voters who said they were "very interested" in the abortion issue—and who would therefore be more likely to base their votes on that issue alone—were more likely to support the amendment than oppose it. Thus, Ford's stance in favor of an antiabortion constitutional amendment would probably attract more voters than it would repel. Indeed, this seems to be exactly what happened. Despite some murmurs of discontent, very few pro-choice Republicans abandoned the Ford-Dole ticket in the fall (perhaps partly because Betty Ford was such a strong advocate of abortion rights), while at least a few pro-life proponents, especially among Catholics, voted Republican specifically because of the party's platform on abortion. An October poll taken by the Catholic periodical *Our Sunday Visitor* showed that 61 percent of readers favored Ford, while only 33 percent supported

Figure 9.2. Jimmy Carter campaigning in Pittsburgh in September 1976, while a protester waves an antiabortion sign. (Library of Congress, Prints & Photographs Division, U.S. News & World Report Magazine Collection, LC-DIG-ppmsca-09742)

Carter, and abortion was cited as the number-one factor affecting their choice.[38]

Among all Catholics, Carter still enjoyed a lead over Ford, but his flat-footed efforts to reach out to Catholics were failing, and his poll numbers among this voter demographic were falling. He campaigned in heavily Catholic areas, as his advisers suggested, and he emphasized his opposition to Medicaid funding for abortion when speaking to Catholic audiences. At a time when Congress was preparing to vote on the Hyde Amendment, which would prohibit federal funding for most abortions, Carter signaled to pro-lifers that he was on their side. "Last year, I understand we had 300,000 abortions paid for by the federal government, and I don't think that's right," he told a crowd in Pittsburgh. "I think abortion is wrong and that government ought not ever do anything to encourage abortion," he declared in another forum. He even tried to distance himself from the party's platform on abortion, which his own aides had helped create. He said he objected to the platform's opposition to an antiabortion constitutional amendment and would have preferred neutrality on the issue. "My own position on abortion is much more conservative than the opinion expressed in the platform," he told reporter Jim Castelli of the *National Catholic News*.[39]

This tactic failed to raise his poll numbers among Catholics. Prolife conservatives in the Catholic Church viewed Carter's new conservative statements on abortion as a replay of what had happened in Iowa a few months earlier, and they did not intend to fall for the same trick twice. The Albany, New York, diocesan paper accused him of having a "forked tongue." Carter's statements also alarmed some of the pro-choice people in his coalition, such as Birch Bayh and numerous other Democratic members of Congress, and they urged Carter not to make his position on abortion any more conservative. "The greatest damage," according to one adviser, "may be with respect to voters who could care less about abortion but are concerned about whether he is a political opportunist because he seems to be trying to come down on all sides of the issue." Carter did not think he had engaged in doublespeak. He honestly believed that abortion was "wrong," and he did not think taxpayer dollars should be used to fund it. He had always intended to take a somewhat neutral stance on an antiabortion constitutional amendment, not supporting it personally but taking no direct action to block it. This had been his position for months, so there was no inconsistency. But few in his coalition believed that Carter would score any political points by highlighting these nuances. They encouraged him to move on from the abortion issue as quickly as possible.[40]

If anything would win Catholic voters back to the Democratic Party that year, it would probably be economic issues, according to some of Carter's campaign advisers. Following the lead of the Democratic Party platform, Carter had made the economy a central focus of his campaign. But by mid-October, polls indicated that Carter's support from Catholics was still lower than the 60 percent threshold ordinarily needed to win. It was likely that large numbers of disaffected urban working-class Catholics would not vote at all, while the suburban Catholic vote would be split between Carter and Ford. The pollsters could not determine the exact reason for Catholics' hesitancy to embrace Carter, other than to suggest that perhaps they felt he could not be trusted.[41]

Regardless of the reason, Carter could not count on Catholic support, and those lost votes would have to be offset by a stronger-than-average performance among southern Protestants. But in late September, the publication of an interview Carter did with *Playboy* magazine suddenly put this once-solid base of southern evangelical support in question and nearly erased his lead over Ford.

THE *PLAYBOY* INTERVIEW

When Jody Powell agreed to *Playboy* magazine's request to interview Carter in the summer of 1976, it had seemed like a good way to boost his credentials among cultural liberals who were still suspicious of a Southern Baptist presidential candidate. *Playboy* routinely interviewed political figures, and some of them had benefited as a result. Jerry Brown, for instance, had conducted an interview with *Playboy* immediately before his presidential campaign, and in the opinion of several journalists, the publicity had enhanced his reputation as a culturally progressive, innovative governor who was ready for the national political scene. In the summer of 1976, when Carter was enjoying a 30- or 40-point lead over Ford but was still trying to overcome a lingering suspicion of his candidacy among college-aged voters and northern progressives, an interview with *Playboy* seemed to offer an opportunity to expand his base of support and reach out to a culturally liberal wing of the Democratic Party that was still not completely reconciled to his candidacy. As Hamilton Jordan told *Playboy* editor Barry Golsom, "We wouldn't do it [the interview] if it weren't in our interest. It's your readers who are probably predisposed toward Jimmy—but they may not vote at all if they feel uneasy about him."[42]

Interviewer Robert Scheer was particularly interested in questioning Carter about the relationship among his religion, his moral views, and his policy positions. As an outspoken opponent of the Vietnam War and editor of the New Left magazine *Ramparts* in the 1960s, Scheer was especially interested in pressing Carter on his foreign policy views and asking him why he did not call for an American withdrawal from Vietnam until 1971—long after others in his party had publicly spoken out against the war.[43]

But more than anything, Scheer wanted Carter to talk about how he would square his religiously conservative Baptist beliefs on sexual morality with his stated commitment to pluralism as a Democratic candidate for president. In a series of interviews conducted in July, he repeatedly circled back to that theme. He started by asking Carter about homosexuality. A few weeks earlier, while campaigning in San Francisco ahead of the California primary, Carter had said he supported adding "sexual persuasion" (today, the term would be "sexual orientation") to the categories enumerated in the Civil Rights Act of 1964, thus protecting gays from discrimination. But when asked whether he believed that homosexuality was a sin, Carter said, "I believe in the Bible. The Bible teaches against homosexuality." The response did not create any national controversy at the time. If there was anything surprising in his statements, it was his willingness to offer gays the same federal protections accorded minorities and women, since that idea did not yet have widespread support. Other candidates in the Democratic primaries, such as Henry Jackson, opposed gay rights much more forcefully. Carter's views on gay rights—he supported expanded legal protections, even though he had personal reservations about the sexual behavior in question—closely paralleled his approach to abortion, and the media were much more interested in covering the politically charged issue of abortion than gay rights, which was considered a narrowly focused, regionally specific issue.[44] Neither the *New York Times* nor the *Washington Post* covered Carter's comments in San Francisco. The story received more coverage on the West Coast but was soon forgotten by most people outside of the gay community—though not by Scheer.

Scheer asked Carter, "Wouldn't we expect a puritanical tone to be set in the White House if you were elected?" Carter responded that he looked at homosexuality no "differently from the way I look on other sexual acts outside marriage," and he spoke of the Christian imperative "not to judge other people." There was nothing to fear from a Southern Baptist in the White House, he said. "Harry Truman was a Baptist," he noted. "Some people get very abusive about the Baptist faith. If people want to know about it, they can read the New Testament. The main thing is that we don't think we're better than anyone else."[45]

During five hours of questions and answers, Scheer continued to press Carter on this theme. How could he square his friendship with the drug-using, profane Hunter Thompson with his self-professed Christian morality? Did he feel a sense of cultural "estrangement" at rock concerts? What would he say to a "woman who said her vote would depend on how you stood on abortion"? To each question, Carter gave a similar response: he was comfortable with people of all types, he did not consider himself better than others, and his faith motivated him to love other people and to be humble, not to adopt a self-righteous attitude. Though he occasionally expressed irritation with Scheer's repeated probing on questions he thought he had already answered, he mostly adopted an attitude of quiet confidence in his own beliefs and persona.

Carter had a deep personal faith and a close relationship with his wife. He admitted in the interview to praying regularly throughout the day—perhaps twenty-five times a day, he said. He also had clear ideas about right and wrong that informed his political positions. For instance, he stated, "I think abortion is wrong and I will do everything I can to minimize the need for abortions." But he added that he would abide by the Supreme Court ruling in *Roe v. Wade,* just as he would protect the civil rights of homosexuals. He insisted that he shared liberals' progressive views on many issues. "On human rights, civil rights, environmental quality, I consider myself to be very liberal," he said. "On the management of government, on openness of government, on strengthening individual liberties and local levels of government I consider myself a conservative. And I don't see that the two attitudes are incompatible." A quotation that *Playboy* featured on the first page as a summation of Carter's views suggested the general message Scheer took away from interview: "We Baptists are taught not to judge other people. . . . Anybody can come and look at my record as governor. I didn't run around breaking down people's doors to see if they were fornicating."[46]

As Scheer and his assistants packed up to leave after the last interview session, he stood in the doorway and asked Carter one final question: "Do you feel you've reassured people with this interview, people who are uneasy about your religious beliefs, who wonder if you're going to make a rigid, unbending President?" Carter gave a lengthy, somewhat impassioned response, which the interview team captured on tape. He talked about his love of going to church, his Baptist beliefs, and his conviction that "what Christ taught about most was pride, that one person should never think he was any better than anybody else." After discussing the importance of humility at some length, he then talked about the "almost impossible standards" set by Jesus and acknowledged that he, too, had sinned because "I'm human and I'm tempted." He gave a specific example: Jesus said that "anyone who looks on a woman with lust has in his heart already committed adultery." Carter admitted:

> I've looked on a lot of women with lust. I've committed adultery in my heart many times. This is something that God recognizes I will do—and I have done it—and God forgives me for it. But that doesn't mean that I condemn someone who not only looks on a woman with lust but who leaves his wife and shacks up with somebody out

> of wedlock. Christ says, Don't consider yourself better than someone else because one guy screws a whole bunch of women while the other guy is loyal to his wife. The guy who's loyal to his wife ought not to be condescending or proud because of the relative degree of sinfulness.

Carter then added, "But I don't think I would *ever* take on the same frame of mind that Nixon or Johnson did—lying, cheating and distorting the truth. Not taking into consideration my hope for my strength of character, I think that my religious beliefs alone would prevent that from happening to me. I have that confidence. I hope it's justified."[47]

Playboy's November issue, featuring the interview, did not reach newsstands until October 14, but during the third week of September, the magazine released excerpts to the media, creating an immediate sensation. Nearly all the commentary focused on Carter's response to *Playboy*'s final question. Outside of evangelical Christian circles, some were surprised by Carter's confession that he had "committed adultery in my heart many times," and this was the lead in articles from the Associated Press, the *New York Times*, the *Washington Post*, and other national news outlets. "Guilty of Adultery in My Heart Many Times, Carter Says," was the *Atlanta Constitution*'s front-page headline. Reporters immediately asked Rosalynn Carter for comment. "Jimmy didn't tell me about that," she replied. "I only heard about it this morning." But she said she was not concerned.[48] Neither were most evangelicals, who were thoroughly familiar with Jesus's statement in the Sermon on the Mount and were not surprised to hear that a fellow Christian who was deeply in love with his wife admitted to struggling with "lust" for other women. But to those outside of evangelical circles who were perhaps less familiar with biblical language, the phrase "adultery in my heart" sounded strange. If Carter's goal had been to reassure secular cultural liberals that they had nothing to fear from his religious beliefs, he had probably failed. Reporters thought Carter had confessed to a secret sin, only to discover that they had missed the real story: the presidential front-runner had just jeopardized support among his core constituency by speaking to a magazine that many conservative Protestants viewed as pornographic.

Indeed, the real damage to Carter's candidacy occurred among more religious Americans, especially among the conservative evangelicals whose views Carter had attempted to translate into a secular vernacular for *Playboy* readers. They did not appreciate his somewhat vulgar paraphrase of Jesus's teaching—"Christ says, Don't consider yourself better than someone else because one guy screws a whole bunch of women while the other guy is loyal to his wife"—and they wondered why Carter, a born-again Southern Baptist Sunday school teacher, was talking to *Playboy* magazine in the first place. "Here's a man, who like us, professes to be a Christian," Harold Lindsell, editor of *Christianity Today,* the nation's largest evangelical magazine, told a Baptist congregation in Arlington, Virginia. "And then he gets himself all tied up in speaking words which at best are most questionable. How can the words he speaks be consistent with the Christianity he professes?"[49]

At first, the Carter campaign assumed that conservative evangelicals were upset mainly because their candidate had used the word "screw," which was considered a vulgarity in some circles. Some news outlets, including the *Atlanta Constitution,* declined to print the word. Even Carter's own pastor, who tried to be supportive, expressed reservations about the language, saying, "I would have used other words to describe the same thing." Jody Powell tried to shrug off the controversy over Carter's vocabulary and focus instead on the candidate's message of humility. "We have had a president who expressed himself in much more earthy terms," he told the press. Indeed, both Lyndon Johnson and Richard Nixon had been much more liberal in their private use of vulgarity. To many voters, a presidential candidate's profanity did not matter. "If there are people who think Jimmy Carter shouldn't be president because he uttered a commonplace vulgarity for the public prints, they shouldn't be allowed to vote," the *Omaha World-Herald* editorialized.[50]

But Carter had marketed himself as a Southern Baptist church deacon—a man who would never lie—and voters held him to a different standard. The issue was not whether vulgar speech disqualified a candidate for the presidency (hardly anyone thought it did) but whether Carter's use of vulgarity cast doubt on his self-described character and, ultimately, on his integrity. Throughout the campaign, he had made his own character and ethical commitments the primary justification for his candidacy. Many of his supporters had not imagined that within days of his speech on morality and honesty at the Democratic National Convention, he would be talking to *Playboy* magazine about sex and using a term that some publications considered unprintable. Even some of Carter's campaign staff, who had never seen that side of Carter, were taken aback. He was immediately criticized by several southern Democratic members of Congress. And among Democratic voters in Carter's home state, the reaction was "uniformly negative," the chair of the Georgia Democratic Party declared.[51]

In private, Powell fumed that Scheer had not honored their agreement to allow the campaign staff to review the interview transcript before it was printed. Powell certainly would have crossed out the word "screw" and perhaps one or two other phrases before allowing the interview to go to press. Scheer later said he had tried repeatedly to contact Powell but had been unable to reach him; this remained a point of disagreement.[52] In any case, the excuse that Carter's team had not reviewed the transcript before it was printed was unlikely to assuage anyone's concerns.

Perhaps more important, the Carter campaign misjudged the damage a *Playboy* interview would do to Carter's standing among religious conservatives, regardless of what he said. During the interview, Scheer asked Carter if he had "any problems with appearing in *Playboy*." "Do you think you'll be criticized?" Scheer asked. "I don't object to that at all," Carter responded. "I don't believe I'll be criticized." Carter badly underestimated the extent to which conservative evangelicals had mobilized against pornography and the "*Playboy* philosophy." They regularly heard sermons denouncing the sexual licentiousness of the culture. The same week Carter's interview with *Playboy* made front-page headlines, Southern Baptists in Arkansas, for instance, read an editorial in their denomination's state periodical lamenting the "pornography" and "less than desirable language" that had "invaded the parlor by way of the TV and adjacent newsstands." For these social conservatives, Carter's *Playboy* interview placed him on the wrong side of the sexual revolution. Shortly after the story broke, W. A. Criswell, a former president of the Southern Baptist Convention and pastor of Dallas's First Baptist Church, the denomination's largest congregation, preached a sermon denouncing the *Playboy* interview and then, on the steps of his church, personally endorsed President Ford.[53]

Ford considered Criswell's support so important that he traveled to Dallas to attend the Sunday morning service and then used Criswell's endorsement in a television commercial. Ford reiterated the charge that a *Playboy* interview was beneath the dignity of a presidential candidate, saying that he had refused to give an interview to *Playboy* because "I don't think the President of the United States ought to have an interview in a magazine featuring photographs of unclad women." Dole was quick to bring up the *Playboy* interview on the campaign trail, calling it a "weird performance" that raised doubts about Carter's "judgment." The Ford campaign even designed an anti-Carter print ad with an image of the *Playboy* cover—a tactic that Carter called a "highly misleading sort of advertising campaign" that reflected poorly on the Ford campaign.[54] But, for the most part, the Ford campaign did not have to fan the flames of controversy; the national news media had already taken care of that.

The *Playboy* controversy forced Carter to try to shore up support among conservative white southern evangelicals. Indeed, the week before news of the interview broke, the campaign staff had already sensed that Carter's support among evangelical Protestants was slipping. In response, they created a Protestant Desk because they believed that evangelicals and Southern Baptists had begun to doubt Carter's evangelical commitment, owing to his moderate stance on abortion, his willingness to drink alcohol (in spite of the Southern Baptist Convention's opposition to the practice), and his liberal political views. If evangelical support for Carter continued to soften, they thought, their candidate could lose both Texas and California, which would be catastrophic. They envisioned the Protestant Desk, led by the Texas Baptist Convention's Christian Life Commission director Phil Strickland, as an outreach arm that could solidify evangelical support for the Democratic ticket by talking about Carter's support for Israel, his born-again testimony, and issues of concern to evangelicals. But within days of the Protestant Desk's formation, its work was consumed by damage control over the *Playboy* interview. As numerous nationally prominent evangelical leaders—ranging from Pat Robertson and Jerry Falwell to future Southern Baptist Convention president Bailey Smith—weighed in with criticism of Carter, the campaign scrambled to stop the hemorrhaging of evangelical support. The Protestant Desk compiled a list of nationally known mainline Protestant and evangelical leaders who had not yet endorsed Ford and called them, hoping they might be persuaded to support Carter. Carter still had the support of many "moderates" among the Southern Baptist Convention's leadership because they appreciated his concern for human rights and economic justice; they believed that although the *Playboy* interview may have demonstrated poor judgment, it was essentially a presentation of Jesus's teachings translated into secular language. Carter's own pastor wrote a public letter that attested to Carter's Christian commitment and explained that the *Playboy* interview, which had included several references to the Bible and the teachings of Jesus, had actually been an attempt to "share [his] faith in Christ." "Jimmy, of course, is not perfect," Carter's pastor wrote. "However, I am convinced that he is a sincere Christian and I do not believe he is using religion to win votes."[55]

The Ford campaign acted quickly to pick up some of the evangelical support that Carter was losing. Richard Brannon, an ordained Southern Baptist minister who was a special assistant to Secretary of Defense Donald Rumsfeld, arranged for several Southern Baptist clergy to join the president on a Mississippi River campaign cruise. Ford also used an interview with the National Religious Broadcasters, carried on Christian radio stations across the nation, to talk about his own personal faith and denounce the "secularism" that, in the opinion of many evangelicals, Carter had failed to adequately oppose. "I have a deep concern about the rising tide of secularism," Ford said. "There is an apparent increase of irreverence for life. I do not believe in abortion on demand."[56]

Ford's campaign organizers in the South were also quick to adopt the new strategy of reaching out to white evangelicals with religiously based attacks on Carter's character. The state chair of Ford's campaign in Kentucky mailed a letter to all Baptist ministers in the state citing Baptist televangelist Jerry Falwell's warnings about Carter. In Tennessee, the Ford campaign distributed copies of a conservative evangelical book titled *What about Jimmy Carter?* that used Carter's statements on abortion, homosexuality, and other issues to argue that he was not the theologically conservative Christian that southern evangelicals assumed him to be. Though not particularly attuned to the nuances of theological differences among evangelicals, the Ford team was discovering, whether they realized it or not, that the more "fundamentalist" white conservative evangelicals in the South, such as Falwell and Bob Jones Jr., were especially worried about pornography and sexual licentiousness and were quick to criticize Carter, whereas many of the more economically liberal, socially moderate Southern Baptist Convention leaders, who thought that poverty relief and racial justice were more important than vulgar language, were still in the Carter camp.[57] Ford's southern campaign staff hoped that if they enlisted the support of enough of these fundamentalist ministers, they would be able to swing a sizable part of the southern evangelical population into the

Ford camp and crack the "solid South." The fallout over the *Playboy* interview, combined with continued attacks on Carter's alleged cultural and economic liberalism, could be the key to winning over a large percentage of the religious group that the Ford team had once considered impervious to their message.

Before the *Playboy* interview, Carter's lead in the South seemed insurmountable. An NBC poll taken on September 16–19, immediately before news of the *Playboy* interview was released, showed Carter with a 22-point lead in the southern states. After the existence of the interview became public, all that changed. A Yankelovich poll taken a week and a half later, on September 25–29, showed that Carter's lead in the South was only 8 points. Although other polls showed Carter with somewhat higher levels of support, they all suggested that he was rapidly losing ground south of the Mason-Dixon Line. An Atlanta-based Darden poll of voters in seven southern states showed Carter slipping 11 percentage points between early September and early October. For the first time, Carter's support in the South dropped below 50 percent.[58]

Carter initially tried to defend his statements to *Playboy*, saying three days after the story was released that his intention had been to show that "I would not foist my own religious beliefs on others using the authority of the White House."[59] But after weeks of fallout, he was ready to admit by late October that he had demonstrated poor judgment. "If I should ever decide in the future to discuss my deep Christian beliefs and condemnation and sinfulness, I'll use another forum besides *Playboy*," he said.[60] By then, however, the political damage had been done. The interview with *Playboy* had given the Ford campaign an opening to appeal to religious conservatives and pick up votes from southern evangelicals who had once been Carter's most enthusiastic supporters. It appeared that the only viable path to victory for either candidate was to win the votes of social conservatives among both Protestants and Catholics. Now, for the first time, it seemed that Ford might be better positioned than Carter to do this.

10 FORD VERSUS CARTER

THE FINAL WEEKS

In late September, six weeks before Election Day, Ford's campaign managers were jubilant about their good fortune. In July the president had been between 30 and 40 points behind Carter in the polls, and even in late August he had been more than 20 points behind, but now that Carter's missteps had alienated some of the culturally conservative voters who were supposed to be his core supporters, Ford was lagging by only a few points. He was running ahead in some critical midwestern states such as Illinois, and even in New York, which had voted Democratic in three of the last four presidential elections, he was nearly neck and neck with Carter. "I think we have the momentum now," Ford pollster Robert Teeter told the press. Some in the Carter camp glumly agreed. The Democratic nominee "has to regain the momentum or it won't even be close," one Carter campaign aide who wished to remain nameless told the *New York Times*.[1]

The Ford campaign's sudden turnaround was largely due to Carter's failures, although the president's cautious efforts to reach out to the cultural conservatives Carter had offended while avoiding any major gaffes of his own had clearly helped. But only two days after the news about Carter's *Playboy* interview broke, Ford faced a test that no other incumbent president had ever experienced: debating his opponent on live television in front of tens of millions of voters. The presidential debates were supposed to be an opportunity to refocus the national attention on the economy and foreign policy, rather than the values-driven issues that had dominated much of the September media coverage of the campaigns. But as both candidates discovered, economics and foreign policy were never far removed from cultural issues for many voters.

THE FIRST PRESIDENTIAL DEBATE

Televised presidential debates had been held only once before—in 1960, when John F. Kennedy famously impressed television audiences with his relaxed, confident demeanor and gained an advantage over Richard Nixon. After that defining moment, to which some attributed Nixon's razor-thin defeat, no incumbent president had wanted to risk a televised debate. Lyndon Johnson was far ahead in the polls in 1964 and saw no need to subject himself to the uncertainties of a debate, and Nixon had no wish to relive his performance of 1960 when he ran again in 1968 and 1972. But Ford was so far behind in the polls in the summer of 1976 that he thought the potential gain from a debate was worth the risk. So he challenged Carter to a debate during his convention acceptance speech in August. Carter's team, believing that their candidate would easily trounce Ford in a verbal sparring match, eagerly accepted the challenge.[2]

The Ford campaign acknowledged that debating was a "risky" idea because Ford was not a naturally gifted speaker. He did not think quickly on his feet, nor was he very eloquent; his frequent verbal gaffes had been the butt of numerous jokes. Carter, by contrast, was widely lauded for his detailed command of policy issues and his razor-sharp mind. He had performed well in small-scale debates against some of his opponents in the Democratic primaries, whereas Ford had turned down the opportunity to debate Reagan and therefore had no experience with presidential debates. In addition, because of the president's "no-campaign" strategy, the media were likely to focus even more attention on the debates, which would be voters' only opportunity to hear the president answer tough questions and directly engage his opponent on the issues. Ford's aides knew that the president had some substantial handicaps, but they also believed that Carter's vulnerability in a debate would be far greater than many observers assumed. They believed that Carter's meteoric rise in the polls during the summer had been based on a rhetorical sleight of hand that attempted to convince voters they could have a jobs creation program, a national health care system, and numerous other expensive big-government programs while balancing the budget, eliminating unemployment and inflation, and shrinking the size of government. A debate would give Ford the opportunity to confront Carter with these contradictions. It would also allow him to correct the public impression that he lacked the requisite intelligence for the job. "The debates, while risky, are the quickest way to close the perception gap," Mike Duval said. "But needless to say, if the President loses the debates, he loses the election."[3]

Ford spent two weeks practicing for the first debate. His advisers made detailed notes about every question they thought the moderators might ask, and he memorized the answers. He watched tapes of the 1960 Kennedy-Nixon debates and Carter's debate performances in the Democratic primaries. He practiced delivering the answers in front of campaign aides and responded to video clips of Carter addressing some of the same points. He even agreed to let his aides videotape his responses and then review the tapes with him, hoping to improve his on-camera appearance. Although Ford did not engage in the detailed preparation that would become standard by the end of the twentieth century—with mock rehearsals in which the candidate faced off against someone playing his or her opponent—his twenty hours of preparation vastly exceeded Carter's. As communications director Dave Gergen reminded Ford's advisers, they could not afford to leave anything to chance. Carter "is one of the shrewdest politicians in America today, and he has a very precise understanding of the English language," Gergen noted. "I am convinced that Carter has the capacity to put the President's record in the worst possible light—while being totally respectful—and also presenting a very positive, very concrete (and very phoney) program of his own. We cannot give him a free ride."[4]

The Ford campaign did not underestimate Carter, but Carter probably underestimated Ford. Confident that he would win, the Democratic nominee decided to forgo practice sessions entirely and simply studied a campaign briefing book to brush up on his responses to questions. He spent the final three hours before the debate relaxing over dinner with his wife, seeing no need to engage in last-minute cramming. Ford, by contrast, had dinner with Dick Cheney and two other aides who used the time to coach him in final preparation for his meeting with Carter.[5]

Some of Carter's aides were less confident than their candidate. They urged Carter to prepare for the debate with mock practice sessions, but to no avail. Rick Hutcheson warned that Carter could not win

Figure 10.1. Gerald Ford and staff assistant Dorrance Smith preparing for the president's first televised debate with Jimmy Carter, September 1976. (Courtesy of National Archives and Records Administration)

the debate merely by "rolling off dry statistics," as he likely intended to do. They also worried about the format of the debate. Their greatest fear was that Ford would use the office of the presidency to gain an unfair advantage by awing voters. They asked the moderators to avoid using the title "Mr. President" and to refer to the two candidates as "Mr. Ford" and "Mr. Carter," but the Ford campaign overruled them, and the concession was not granted. The network did agree, however, not to show the two candidates standing side by side, which meant there would be no shot of the six-foot-tall Ford appearing to tower over the five-foot-nine-and-a-half-inch Carter. Carter's team also prevailed with regard to the sequence of the debates. The Ford team had wanted to hold the foreign policy debate first; because Carter lacked experience in international affairs, they thought that debate would be Ford's strongest.[6] But they reluctantly agreed to the sequence the Carter campaign requested: the first debate would focus on domestic issues, the second on foreign policy, and the third would be open to questions on any topic. All three debates would be moderated by a panel of journalists from several news agencies. There would be no questions from the audience.

Ninety-four million American adults—more than 70 percent of the voting-age population—tuned in to watch the first ninety-minute debate, which was held on a Thursday night at the Walnut Street Theater in Philadelphia. Both the candidates and the journalists questioning them treated the event with the utmost seriousness. Ford wore a dark blue three-piece suit, and Carter chose a similarly colored two-piece suit for the occasion. When the moderator, NBC news anchor Edwin Newman, opened the broadcast, he noted its historic importance: it was the first presidential debate in sixteen years and the first ever between an incumbent president and his challenger—which was why it was fitting, he noted, that the debate was taking place in historic Philadelphia, "just three blocks from Independence Hall."[7]

For weeks leading up to the event, the media had been commenting on the historic nature of the exchange, and viewers had been expressing the hope that the forum would answer their questions about the candidates' positions. The questions, as expected, focused strictly on policy, with no exploration of tangential matters that were currently receiving front-page headlines, such as Carter's *Playboy* interview or Ford's decision not to leave the White House to campaign. The questioners did not bring up abortion, even though it had recently received a lot of press following the candidates' meetings with Catholic bishops. Instead, the three journalists on the panel—ABC News anchor Frank Reynolds, *Wall Street Journal* reporter James Gannon, and Elizabeth Drew of the *New Yorker*—asked a series of questions that invited the two candidates to explain their contrasting economic platforms. The resulting exchange was largely a point-by-point comparison of the Republican and Democratic visions for economic growth. By the end of the evening, voters learned (if they did not know already) that both candidates planned to cut taxes, but in different ways. Carter would cut taxes for the working class and raise taxes on the wealthy, while Ford proposed an income tax cut accompanied by a corporate tax cut. Both candidates also promised to balance the budget (Ford by 1978, and Carter by the end of his first term), but they disagreed on how to accomplish that goal. Carter planned to rely heavily on economic growth, along with cuts to the bloated government bureaucracy, to provide the necessary revenue to balance the budget, while Ford would focus more directly on cutting social welfare spending, although he was rather vague about how he would do this. Carter emphasized the Democratic Party's promise to create jobs through government programs, whereas Ford, in keeping with Republican Party philosophy, planned to reduce unemployment by refunding money to the private

Figure 10.2. Jimmy Carter and Gerald Ford in their first televised presidential debate at the Walnut Street Theater in Philadelphia, September 1976. (Courtesy of Gerald R. Ford Presidential Library)

sector through tax cuts. Both candidates performed to script in articulating the economic views of their respective political parties. Ford said that Carter's proposals for new government spending would add $100 billion to $200 billion to the deficit, while Carter claimed that Ford had already added record amounts to the deficit while failing to address unemployment and inflation. Most of this only reiterated points made in the convention speeches a few weeks earlier, but perhaps voters had not understood the contrast between the two parties at the time. Before the debate, they told pollsters they were confused about the issues in the campaign. The first debate seemed to clarify the differences between the two candidates, and it helped some voters finalize their choice. Immediately after the debate, polls showed a sharp reduction in the number of undecided voters.[8]

Both the media and the campaigns themselves had expected the debate to force the candidates to answer tough questions related to their policy claims. However, neither Ford nor Carter went much beyond their standard campaign scripts or the promises of their party platforms. Because the journalists on the panel restricted themselves to only one follow-up question for each candidate's reply—and because there was limited opportunity for the candidates to respond to each other—the debate turned out to be little more than a policy-oriented, side-by-side television interview. The journalists rarely used their designated follow-up questions to press a candidate for a more in-depth explanation, and both Ford and Carter were surprisingly deferential toward each other, seldom challenging the other directly. Beginning with Frank Reynolds's question to Carter about the specific steps he would take to reduce unemployment, and continuing with James Gannon's query to Ford about how he would fulfill his promise to balance the budget while cutting taxes, the journalists' questions rarely went beyond standard points of clarification about the party platforms; nor did the candidates' answers.

Both candidates—but especially Carter—were probably overly optimistic about the economic growth their policies would produce and the ease of balancing the federal budget. Carter assumed that his rather vague plans—which included targeted research and development funding, a partnership between the public and private sectors in housing construction, and tax reform—could reduce the unemployment rate to between 3 and 4.5 percent during his first term in office, and he believed the resulting economic growth would enable him to balance the budget while creating large new government programs. He had been saying this for months, and the debate did not force him to answer any new questions about this prediction. He reiterated his promise to return the nation to the vibrant economic conditions that had existed during Kennedy's presidency, with no acknowledgment that changing global economic conditions over the past fifteen years might make that pledge difficult to fulfill. Ford was less optimistic about future economic growth than Carter, but he, too, displayed unfounded optimism when he pledged to balance the budget by 1978 while passing a $28 billion tax cut. The total federal budget at the time was $372 billion, with an annual deficit of $73 billion, so Ford's plan would have required an across-the-board 25 percent reduction in government spending, assuming that economic conditions remained constant.[9] The questioners did not ask Ford to stipulate which federal programs he was planning to cut.

While Carter was answering the final question before closing arguments, the sound system malfunctioned, so the candidates had to stand on the stage, frozen at their lecterns, for twenty-seven minutes until the audio was restored. Then the candidates gave their closing statements. Some of Carter's staff thought the delay caused Carter to lose his momentum, but in reality, the debate was almost over by that point, and the delay was not a serious detriment to either candidate.[10]

Carter's closing statement was a call for a "government as good as our people," a line that had been the theme of his campaign for nearly two years. "It's time for government to understand and to cooperate with our people," he said. "For a long time our American citizens have been excluded, sometimes misled, sometimes have been lied to." This was "not compatible with the purpose of our nation," he said. "The government needs to be well-managed, efficient, economical. We need to have a government that's sensitive to our people's needs—to those who are poor, who don't have adequate health care, who have been cheated too long with our tax programs, who've been out of jobs, whose families have been torn apart. We need to restore the faith and trust of the American people in their own government."

At first, Ford's closing statement was slow and lumbering, but he seemed to gain confidence as he looked directly into the camera and sketched his vision of traditional Republican conservatism. "One of the major issues in this campaign is trust," he said. "A president should never promise more than he can deliver and a president should always deliver everything that he's promised." This was Ford's major attack on the Democratic Party platform: it promised the impossible. He then talked about individual freedom and the need to contain the size of government. "We should never forget that a government big enough to give us everything we want is a government big enough to take from us everything we have."

Although both candidates probably made promises they could never fulfill, neither made an obvious gaffe. But neither gave the other a "knock-out" blow, in the opinion of most editorialists. Democrats and blacks thought Carter had won. Republicans, by an overwhelming margin, picked Ford as the winner. Pundits commented on Ford's apparent confidence and Carter's seemingly unsure footing, and they concluded that Ford had outperformed expectations. Carter demonstrated a quick recall of a wide variety of specific statistics and policy details, but he also made statements that were clearly erroneous (and this was in the days before instant fact-checking or the ability to look up information on the internet). For instance, he said, "We've never had a president since the War between the States that vetoed more bills" than President Ford, but in reality, Franklin Roosevelt, Harry Truman,

Dwight Eisenhower, and several others had vetoed a larger number. Probably more damaging to his performance was Carter's verbal tic, consisting of frequent "ums" and "uhs," and his habit of rarely looking into the television camera while shifting back and forth on his feet, as though he were intensely uncomfortable. Ford's delivery was slow and by no means eloquent, but it sounded more confident than Carter's.

A Gallup poll taken immediately after the debate showed that 32 percent of viewers thought Ford had won, 25 percent gave the prize to Carter, and 33 percent declared it a draw. An Associated Press poll also showed that viewers considered Ford the winner (but by an even smaller margin than the Gallup poll); it revealed that those who gave the win to Ford usually based that decision on his confidence, likability, and delivery, while those who awarded the debate to Carter cited his discussion of the issues. Polls also showed that independent and undecided voters were likely to think that Ford had won the debate. This boded well for his prospects of winning the votes of independents, a group that had not been supportive of him in August.[11]

Ford experienced a net gain of 2 percentage points in the polls immediately following the debate, which meant that, according to an Associated Press poll, he was now only 2 points behind Carter, with 47 percent of voters favoring the Democratic ticket and 45 percent favoring the Republican. A Gallup poll also showed that Carter's lead had shrunk to only 2 points. At that point, the Associated Press declared that the numbers were within the margin of error and the election was therefore "too close to call." Other polls showed that Carter maintained a slightly larger lead, so Ford was still the underdog, but there was no doubt about the momentum of the race. Ford was rapidly gaining, and Carter's 30- to 40-point summer lead had almost entirely disappeared. "In the 40 years we've been in the business, we've never reported this kind of comeback," George Gallup Jr. said. "This is history-making." Ford was "within striking distance of an upset victory on Nov. 2," the *Christian Science Monitor* reported.[12]

THE SECOND DEBATE

Carter resolved to come to the second debate much better prepared. This time, he did not merely study briefing books but practiced his answers in front of his aides. Ford, in contrast, neglected the preparation that had been so critical to his success in the first debate, partly because other urgent matters demanded his attention, and partly because he was confident that he was well versed in his own administration's foreign policy.[13] He studied the briefing book his aides created, and he met with Kissinger to discuss foreign policy issues, but he did not engage in the lengthy practice sessions that had characterized his earlier preparation. When Ford and Carter arrived for the second debate, which took place in San Francisco on October 6, their positions were almost exactly reversed: Ford was overconfident but underprepared, whereas Carter had spent two weeks cramming for the test.

Both candidates arrived at the debate looking polished and comfortable, and this time, the panel of journalists seemed more willing to grill the candidates and press them for clarification in their follow-up questions. Both men looked directly at the camera and addressed each other more often. Carter largely eliminated his excessive "umms" and "uhhs," and he was quick to challenge Ford when he thought the president was distorting his position. This occurred early in the debate when Ford said that Carter would "look with sympathy" on a communist government in Italy. In fact, Carter had said once that if a government comprised partially of communists formed in Italy, the United States should befriend it to avoid having it "driven into the Soviet orbit irrevocably." Ford distorted the intent of Carter's remarks, and Carter was quick to call the president on this, demonstrating a degree of forcefulness he had not shown in the first debate. "Mr. Ford, unfortunately, has just made a statement that's not true," he said.[14]

Ford also misstated his administration's position on companies that participated in the Arab boycott of American businesses that engaged in trade with Israel. When Carter criticized him for blocking legislation that would have revealed the names of companies participating in the boycott—thus subjecting them to public pressure that, in his view, would have stopped the boycott from continuing—Ford responded with a pledge to "announce tomorrow that the Department of Commerce will disclose those companies that have participated in the boycott." After the debate, the Commerce Department announced that it would not release this information because it was "confidential," which left Ford struggling to explain his clearly erroneous statement. Some Democratic members of Congress claimed that Ford had lied. The Carter campaign saw this as an opportunity not only to undermine the president's credibility but also to win support from Jewish voters who were upset that the Ford administration was not taking action to stop the anti-Israel boycott.[15]

But Ford's biggest gaffe in the debate came when he was questioned about eastern Europe. Eastern Europe was a particularly thorny topic for Ford, and his advisers had warned him that Carter would likely "try to out-conservative the President" on communism by arguing that he had made too many concessions to the Soviet Union, leaving America in a weaker position. Indeed, that is exactly what Carter did. Early in the campaign, Carter's calls for a reduction in the defense budget and for a human rights–based foreign policy had given some analysts the impression that he was a left-leaning progressive on foreign affairs, but now he was nearly as critical of the president's concessions to the Soviet Union as some of the conservative Reaganites were. Carter had made the strongly anticommunist Zbigniew Brzezinski, a Polish American Columbia University professor, his leading foreign policy adviser, and it was largely Brzezinski's views that he echoed in the debate.[16] Ford's challenge was to defend his record of détente while positioning himself as stronger than Carter in defending against communism. This challenge was similar to the one that had nearly tripped him in his primary campaign against Reagan. Now Carter was using Reagan's lines to score political points against Ford. "Even the Republican platform has criticized the lack of leadership in Mr. Ford and they've criticized the foreign policy of this administration," he pointed out in his opening statement. "This is one instance where I agree with the Republican platform." Carter went after Ford aggressively in every subsequent statement, charging that the president had made "a political football out of the defense budget," demonstrated "an absence of leadership," and conducted foreign policy in secret while abdicating important responsibility to his secretary of state.

By the time Ford was questioned directly about his policy of détente, he was ready to punch back with what he thought was a strong defense of his diplomatic negotiations with the Soviet Union, but he did so ham-fistedly. When Max Frankel of the *New York Times* said, "We've virtually signed, in Helsinki, an agreement that the Russians have dominance in Eastern Europe," Ford responded, "There is no Soviet domination of Eastern Europe and there never will be under a Ford administration," looking directly into the camera. The moderator, Pauline Frederick of National Public Radio, turned to Carter, intending to give him a chance to speak, but Frankel broke in and insisted on a clarification. "I'm sorry, I—could I just follow—did I understand you to say, sir, that the Russians are not using Eastern Europe as their own sphere of influence in occupying most of the countries there and in—and making sure with their troops that it's a—that it's a Communist zone, whereas on our side of the line the Italians and the French are still flirting with the possibility of Communism?" Frankel asked incredulously.

Ford doubled down on his inept response. "I don't believe, Mr. Frankel, that the Yugoslavians consider themselves dominated by the Soviet Union," he said. "I don't believe that the Rumanians consider themselves dominated by the Soviet Union. I don't believe that the Poles consider themselves dominated by the Soviet Union. Each of those countries is independent, autonomous; it has its own territorial integrity and the United States does not concede that those countries are under the domination of the Soviet Union." He then added, "As a matter of fact, I visited Poland, Yugoslavia and Rumania to make certain that the people of those countries understood that the president of the United States and the people of the United States are dedicated to their independence, their autonomy and their freedom."

Ford's response was a bungled recitation of the answer his staff had prepared for him. The answer he was supposed to give, according to his briefing book, was: "To say that my policies accept Soviet domination over Eastern Europe is patent nonsense. The United States recognizes no spheres of influence nor the hegemony of any people over another and it never will. For me this is more than a rhetorical exercise however. I have carried this message in personal visits to the people of Eastern Europe—to Poland, Yugoslovia [*sic*] and Romania."[17] But instead of saying that his policies did not "accept" or "recognize" the domination of the Soviet Union, he suggested that Soviet domination of eastern Europe did not actually exist, and this is what Frankel seized on. Carter seemed to recognize the mistake as well. When the moderator asked for his response, he replied, "I would like to see Mr. Ford convince the Polish-Americans and the Czech-Americans and the Hungarian-Americans in this country that those countries don't live under the domination and supervision of the Soviet Union behind the Iron Curtain."

Despite the exchange, most viewers did not immediately recognize Ford's verbal stumble as a serious mistake. A Market Opinion Research poll taken immediately after the debate ended at 11:00 p.m. Eastern time showed that 44 percent of viewers considered Ford the winner of the debate, while only 33 percent thought Carter had won.

An Associated Press poll that night showed a slight edge for Carter—38 percent versus 35 percent. A Roper poll showed a somewhat stronger preference for Carter, with differences of opinion falling mainly along partisan lines. According to the Wednesday night Roper poll, Democrats gave the debate to Carter by a margin of 65 percent to 10 percent, while Republicans gave the debate to Ford, 56 percent to 16 percent. Undecided voters gave a slight edge to Carter over Ford, 33 percent versus 25 percent, and 42 percent called the debate a tie. Although the polls varied slightly, there was clearly no indication on the night of the debate that Ford's statement on eastern Europe had been catastrophic. A Teeter poll showed that viewers did not consider the eastern Europe statement the worst thing Ford said that evening; they were far more concerned about Ford's defense of arms sales to Iran. (The Ford campaign's internal polling showed that many Americans were against selling arms to other countries because they feared it would lead to another war like the one in Vietnam.) But many journalists considered Ford's statement on eastern Europe a fatal error, and as soon as the debate was over, this line of criticism dominated the news coverage. Ford just "kissed off the Polish vote," Bob Schieffer of CBS remarked.[18]

Dick Cheney and national security adviser Brent Scowcroft, who were watching the debate in San Francisco, knew they would have to do immediate damage control. After the debate ended, they convened a press conference. Most people on the East Coast had gone to bed by then, but it was only 9:15 p.m. in California, and journalists there were eager to grill Cheney and Scowcroft about the president's misstatement on eastern Europe. As soon as the press conference began, they demanded an explanation for the president's remark. "Are there Soviet troops in Poland?" someone asked. "Yes," Cheney responded. "Do you think that would imply some Soviet dominance of Poland?" came the follow-up question. "I think what the President was trying to say," Scowcroft replied, "is that we do not recognize Soviet dominance of Europe and that he took his trip to Eastern Europe—to Poland, to Romania, to Yugoslavia—to demonstrate, to symbolize their independence, and their freedom of maneuver." That was, in fact, more or less what Ford had intended to say. His debate briefing book used the words "accept" and "recognize," and if he had stuck to the prepared text, he would have said almost exactly what Scowcroft told the press. But the journalists were not satisfied; they wanted to force Cheney and Scowcroft to either admit that the president had made a mistake or do the impossible and reconcile his answer with their own. "Do you think he succeeded in saying what you just said he said?" one journalist asked. "Did he misspeak himself? Is that what you are saying?" another queried. Cheney dodged the question, but the journalists held his feet to the fire. "But he did misspeak himself. That is fair enough to say, isn't it?" Cheney would not admit that the president had misspoken. "I understood exactly what he was saying, and I think the American people will understand exactly what he was saying, too," he insisted.[19]

The press was sure the American people would *not* understand, and to some extent, they were right. Newspapers across the country highlighted the president's blunder and called the debate a win for Carter. After seeing this commentary, most Americans no longer believed that Ford had won the debate or even that it had been a close match. A Market Opinion Research poll taken between 9:00 a.m. and 12:00 p.m. on October 7—approximately twelve hours after the debate ended—showed that Americans now awarded the debate to Carter by a margin of 44 to 33 percent. By that evening, the results were even more lopsided: 62 percent of respondents surveyed after 5:00 p.m. on October 7 thought Carter had won the debate, versus only 17 percent who thought the winner was Ford.[20]

The gaffe itself probably did not hurt Ford all that much; his refusal to admit the mistake compounded the damage and was much more costly. Misstatements, at least on a small scale, were not uncommon in the Ford-Carter debates. In the first debate, for instance, Carter had referred to the "Great Depression of the 1940s," but this was an obvious slip of the tongue and no one seemed to care. Ford obviously bungled the line about eastern Europe he had memorized for the debate, but instead of admitting his mistake, he compounded it in his answer to Frankel's follow-up question. Cheney and Scowcroft then defended the president's answer and refused to admit that he had misspoken, even as they vainly attempted to limit the damage caused by the remark. After the press conference, Cheney could see that this strategy was not working, and he told Ford that he needed to admit his error. Ford refused. "I told him [Cheney] I didn't see any need for that," Ford recalled in his autobiography. "If the critics didn't understand what I had meant to say, then that was their problem, not mine. And in my own mind I was sure what I had meant to say. Although the Soviet Union dominated Polish territory by stationing troops there, it didn't dominate the heart, soul and spirit of the Polish people. No, I reiterated, I wasn't going to retract what I had said. . . . I can be very stubborn when I think I'm right, and I just didn't want to apologize for something that was a minor mistake."[21]

Although Ford attributed his refusal to correct the error to mere stubbornness, it is possible that his decision to dig in his heels and refuse to admit a simple slip of the tongue was a sign of his frustration with the political attacks on his policy of détente, which had started with Reagan's primary challenge and were continuing with Carter. Ford had withstood these attacks all the way to the Republican National Convention, where he had been forced to accept a humiliating amendment to the party platform rebuking his administration's foreign policy, especially as it concerned the people in the Soviet bloc. In his debate with Carter, he had given a spirited defense of his administration's diplomatic negotiations with the Soviet Union and had tried to rebut the charge that he had betrayed the interests of the eastern European people. Now he was being asked to apologize for the language he had used and to admit that the Soviet Union dominated eastern Europe. He found this difficult to do.

The Carter campaign immediately seized on this issue. The day after the debate, Carter declared that he was "shocked by the insensitivity and lack of knowledge which Mr. Ford displayed in his remarks about Eastern Europe." "To declare as he did that 'there is no Soviet domination of Eastern Europe' is beyond belief," Carter said. "It is an affront to the people of Poland, Czechoslovakia, Hungary and East Germany, who have strived so long for some small measure of freedom." The next day, Carter went even further and suggested that Ford might have been "brainwashed" by communist propaganda during his trip to Poland the previous year—a deliberate evocation of the word that had derailed George Romney's presidential campaign ten years earlier. Hamilton Jordan instructed all campaign staff to "react strongly" to Ford's gaffe in their discussions with the media and prospective voters. "Please give this reaction a top priority," a campaign communiqué instructed.[22]

The deluge of criticism, coupled with the repeated urgings of his own staff, finally convinced Ford that he needed to do something to stop the damage to his campaign. He began the process of walking back his comments the day after the debate, but he waited until October 12—six days after his misstatement—to issue a full-throated mea culpa. At that point, he invited leaders of numerous Polish American,

Lithuanian American, Ukrainian American, and other ethnic groups to the White House and, wearing a lapel pin that spelled "Ford" in Ukrainian, declared that he supported the cause of freedom in eastern Europe. "I did not express myself clearly; I admit it," he said. "The original mistake was mine." "The countries of Eastern Europe are, of course, dominated by the Soviet Union," he said. But "the United States never has, does not now and never will recognize, accept, or acquiesce in this Soviet domination of Eastern Europe."[23] This is what he had intended to say in the debate, and now that he had finally said it—six days after the fact—he hoped he could put the matter behind him.

For most voters, the matter had been put to rest. Indeed, it appears that most Americans cared much less about Ford's gaffe than news commentators did. Polls showed only a very modest drop in support for Ford during the week following the debate. Gallup showed Carter's lead widening from 2 points to 6 points. An NBC poll showed only a 3-point lead for Carter, and a Harris poll showed a 4-point lead.[24] Carter's lead, in short, was still only barely above the margin of error, and Ford's statements in the debate had been only a minor setback, at least as far as the national polls were concerned.

Why did Ford's misstatement on eastern Europe, though widely covered, change so few voters' minds? It appears from polling data that, despite his gaffe, Ford's statements were a reminder that his administration had kept the nation at peace. And for a country that had only recently emerged from the Vietnam War and had not seen a presidency without war since the Hoover administration, that counted for a lot. A *San Francisco Examiner* poll taken on the day after the debate showed that Bay Area voters rated Ford more highly than Carter on nearly all the issues discussed—even détente and eastern Europe. Only on the Panama Canal and arms sales to Iran did they think Carter's position was better than Ford's. Prior to the debate, American voters had believed, by a five-to-three ratio, that Ford was stronger than Carter on foreign policy, and although the debate damaged his public image on international issues, it did not completely erase his lead. Nothing that either candidate said in the debate changed the fact that the nation was at peace and the military draft was over. Ford's advisers had encouraged him to stress this theme in the debate, and in spite of his stumbles, that message came through. A Gallup poll taken during the five days after the debate showed that Americans still believed, by a margin of 46 to 34 percent, that Ford would do a better job than Carter of "keeping the U.S. out of war." Americans also believed, by a margin of 42 to 38 percent, that Ford would do a better job than Carter of "dealing with the Soviet Union."[25]

The only real concern for the Ford campaign was whether white "ethnics"—the second- and third-generation eastern European immigrants who lived in the cities and suburbs of the northern industrial states—would turn against the president because of his remarks. Ford needed these ethnic voters to win the election, and after his apology, the campaign hoped he could still count on them. Among Republicans, at least, Ford's position seemed secure. Reagan, who had made a career of issuing hard-line denunciations of communism and was still antipathetic toward Ford, could have easily capitalized on this opportunity to criticize the president, as he was already doing on Ford's tax policy. Instead, Reagan defended the president's remarks on eastern Europe, saying that Ford had intended "to express the independent spirit of the Polish people."[26] There would be no division among Republicans on foreign policy during the final weeks of the campaign.

TROUBLE FOR FORD IN THE FINAL MONTH

The Ford campaign had hoped to use the month of October to capitalize on its momentum and overtake Carter in the polls, but a series of setbacks threatened to damage the campaign. At the beginning of the month, *Rolling Stone,* followed by *New Times* magazine and then every major national media outlet, released a story about crude remarks made by one of Ford's cabinet officials. *Rolling Stone* reported that, on a flight back from the Republican National Convention in August, a member of Ford's cabinet—soon identified as Secretary of Agriculture Earl Butz—had told a sexually crude, racist joke that was so vulgar that the nation's wire services considered it "not fit to print." This story caused an uproar among Republican officials. Senator Edward Brooke demanded Butz's resignation, as did several other liberal Republican senators. Ford reprimanded Butz but was reluctant to fire the secretary, who was popular among midwestern farmers and whom he considered a "close personal friend." The campaign's Black Desk, which was receiving numerous calls from black Republicans demanding that Ford fire Butz, found itself in a difficult situation. To avoid contradicting the president, it issued a terse "no comment" on Butz's remarks. For two days, the controversy dominated the front-page headlines and gave Carter and Mondale an opportunity to criticize the

Ford administration's record on race. "When people in high public office cast despicable racist slurs, it's like poison, cancer in the society," Mondale said. "Respect for people of different races and backgrounds" was an essential aspect of "decency and humanity"—and certainly a requirement for any cabinet official. After two days, Butz resigned. But when Ford called him a "decent and good" man in spite of his racist remarks, it raised questions about the president's commitment to the rights of African Americans.[27]

Ford's reputation for honesty was temporarily called into question by two allegations of scandal, although he was quickly cleared of the charges against him. At the end of September, the FBI acted on an accusation by the Marine Engineers Beneficial Association (MEBA) that Ford had failed to disclose campaign contributions from that union during his congressional campaigns years earlier. The FBI reported the matter to the attorney general, who appointed Watergate special prosecutor Charles Ruff to investigate the allegation. Ford insisted that he had accurately disclosed all campaign contributions from MEBA and claimed that MEBA had leveled this charge only because he had vetoed a bill the union supported. Ford's innocence was verified when Ruff cleared him of all charges only three weeks after the investigation began.[28]

But as soon as this threat of scandal abated, Ford faced another accusation: John Dean, the former White House counsel who had turned against Nixon to provide damaging information to Congress about the president's role in the Watergate scandal, said that Ford, as House minority leader, had blocked early hearings related to Watergate at the request of a White House congressional liaison. During Ford's confirmation hearings for vice president, he had denied under oath that he had conferred with the White House about the Watergate hearings. If Dean's accusation were true, it would mean that Ford had not only possibly obstructed justice but also perjured himself. Ford denied Dean's charges, as did the White House congressional liaison that Dean named as the intermediary. Dean claimed he had telephone logs to prove his charges, and some Democrats in Congress found the accusation sufficiently credible to merit further investigation. But neither Ruff nor the attorney general thought an investigation was justified, so nothing was done. Three days before the election, the *Washington Post* suggested that there was no scandal and the matter should be dropped. Ford had been an ardent defender of Nixon, the *Post* said, but there was no reason to believe he had committed perjury or acted unethically in the manner described by Dean.[29] But the two weeks of national media attention surrounding Dean's accusations, coming immediately after several weeks of reporting on Ford's campaign contributions from MEBA, did not help the president's campaign.

If voters needed any additional reminders of Watergate, they received one at their local theaters: two weeks before the election, Warner Brothers re-released *All the President's Men* in six hundred theaters across the country. The movie, starring Robert Redford and Dustin Hoffman as intrepid *Washington Post* reporters Bob Woodward and Carl Bernstein investigating the crimes of the Nixon White House, had originally been released earlier in the year. Some Ford supporters suspected that this preelection re-release was a partisan move to remind voters of Ford's connection to Nixon.[30]

Carter was not entirely sure how to capitalize on voters' anger over Watergate. The basis of his candidacy had always been his promise to introduce honest, efficient government and to never lie to the American people. As he reminded voters of this promise at each campaign stop, he implicitly drew a contrast between his own character and Nixon's. He had even said it directly in his *Playboy* interview when he clenched his fist and declared emphatically, "I don't think I would *ever* take on the same frame of mind that Nixon or Johnson did—lying, cheating, and distorting the truth. . . . I think that my religious beliefs alone would prevent that from happening to me." But making this point required caution, because he did not want to seem mean-spirited in attacking Ford. He avoided suggesting that Ford was linked to Watergate, and he directly ruled out attacks on the Nixon pardon, saying that it was not a valid topic for the campaign. He often spoke of the "Nixon-Ford administration," but in the summer of 1976 Hamilton Jordan advised him not to do this, arguing that it might undermine Carter's image among an electorate that largely respected Ford's personal honesty. Carter did not completely follow Jordan's advice—he still linked Ford to Nixon's economic policies in his campaign speeches—but he did not accuse Ford of being associated with Nixon's scandals. Even in the final presidential debate in late October, when Ford was asked directly about his involvement in Watergate, Carter refused to discuss the issue. When Ford faced ethical questions related to his personal finances and his disclosure of congressional campaign contributions, Carter called on Ford to "tell the truth, the whole truth, and nothing but the truth" to the American people, but he largely left attacks to his running mate.[31]

Mondale was not bound by the same reservations that kept Carter out of the fray, and he lambasted Ford for standing with Nixon as his vice president and then pardoning Nixon after he became president himself. "To the bitter end, Mr. Ford strongly defended Mr. Nixon, long after it was obvious to many members of his own party, as well as most of the American people, that the Administration was obstructing justice," he charged in a speech at a Missouri law school in October. By pardoning Nixon, Ford "made a mockery of the notion that in America, there is no sovereign who stands above the law," Mondale declared. A pardon might have been justified after a trial, but by pardoning Nixon before the evidence of his guilt could be assessed, Ford had "snuffed out that process" for which the judicial system was designed. Mondale highlighted Carter's promise of a transparent administration and a clean government, and he contrasted the Democratic candidate's commitment to governmental reforms with Ford's failure to uphold the rule of law in his association with Nixon. A Gallup poll from earlier that summer showed that 55 percent of Americans still objected to Ford's pardon of Nixon, so pundits expected that Mondale's attacks would resonate with voters and that the issue would hurt Ford in the election.[32]

THE VICE-PRESIDENTIAL DEBATE

With both Mondale and Dole playing the role of hatchet man on their respective campaign teams, the debate between the two vice-presidential candidates, which was held in Houston on October 15, was a feisty affair. Dole claimed afterward that he had a "bad cold," but he nevertheless came out swinging against Mondale, never letting up on his attacks throughout the seventy-five-minute exchange. In his opening statement, Dole briefly acknowledged his friendship with Mondale but then leveled his usual charge, calling Mondale "probably the most liberal senator in the United States Senate." "And that's really what this debate's all about," he said. "If by some tragic circumstance one of us should become president of the United States, where do we stand on the issues? . . . My opponent has a record of voting for every inflationary spending program except on defense, where he votes for every cut." Observers later noted that, against the advice of the campaign team, Dole had spent little time practicing for the debate.[33]

Mondale, for his part, opened by attacking the Ford administration's economic record, evoking the Great Depression of the 1930s for comparison. He called Ford's debate stumble on eastern Europe "probably one of the most outrageous statements made by a president in recent political history." "I'm glad the president finally apologized for that remark, but it's surprising that it took six days and several attempts before we finally received that apology," he said. Mondale also castigated Ford and Dole for refusing to stand up against Nixon when he fired the special prosecutor. "In the night of the Saturday Night Massacre, perhaps the most treacherous moment in the history of American liberty, when the high officers—Richardson and Ruckelshaus—were fired for enforcing the law, fired by the president of the United States, both Mr. Ford and Mr. Dole stood up and defended Mr. Nixon."

Dole brought up every accusation against Carter and Mondale he could think of. He criticized Mondale's record of absences in the Senate. He mocked Carter's *Playboy* interview. "I couldn't quite understand what Governor Carter meant in *Playboy* magazine," he said. "I couldn't understand frankly why he was in *Playboy* magazine. But he was, and we'll give him the bunny vote." He also tried to defend himself against Mondale's charge that he and Ford had failed to stand up against Nixon in the Watergate scandal, but the accusation seemed to rattle him, and his somewhat bizarre retort became the most memorable line of the debate. Watergate, he said, was "not a very good issue any more than the war in Vietnam would be or World War II or World War I, or the war in Korea, all Democrat wars, all in this century. I figured up the other day, if we added up the killed and wounded in Democrat wars in this century, it'd be about 1.6 million Americans—enough to fill the city of Detroit." Mondale sensed that Dole had overreached and made a serious blunder. Perhaps if he had confined his criticism to President Johnson's policies in the Vietnam War, the charge would not have seemed so outrageous, but to imply that World War II was the fault of the Democrats was beyond the pale, and Mondale knew it. "I think Senator Dole has richly earned his reputation as a hatchet man tonight, by implying, and stating, that World War II and the Korean Wars were Democratic wars. Does he really mean to suggest to the American people that there was a partisan difference over our involvement in the war to fight Nazi Germany? I don't think any reasonable American would accept that." Mondale then reiterated his charge against Ford and Dole: "We're not charging, and he knows it, his involvement in

Watergate. What we're saying is that they defended Mr. Nixon up to the last."

Some commentators initially characterized the debate as good "entertainment" and unusually "caustic" but observed that it had probably changed no one's vote. That was not quite true; for some previously undecided voters, Dole's sharp-tongued retorts and harsh invectives were enough to drive them into the Democratic camp. "At last I have found a reason for voting in this presidential election: Robert Dole," one Southern California resident declared in a letter to the editor of the *Los Angeles Times*. "The vice presidential debate revealed a clear and present and ominous danger, namely the possibility that Dole might accidentally become President of this country." A Santa Barbara Republican agreed. "To me, Dole's cynical behavior is reminiscent of Joe McCarthy and Richard Nixon in the early 1950s," he wrote. "Nevertheless, I planned to vote for the Ford-Dole ticket until I viewed the vice presidential debate. His worse-than-usual behavior made me seriously question Ford's ability to make decisions. I am voting for Carter." It is difficult to say how widespread these sentiments were because—in contrast to the first two presidential debates—no polling agency conducted a voter survey afterward. With only seventy million viewers, the vice-presidential debate was seen by fewer people than had watched either of the first two presidential debates. Some blamed this on the fact that few voters cared about the views of prospective vice presidents, but others pointed out that the debate was held on a Friday, when television viewing audiences were usually smaller than on other nights of the week.[34]

Within days, though, a consensus developed in the media: even though both candidates had lobbed sharp attacks, Dole's charges had been more reckless, and the Carter campaign quickly picked up on this theme. The debate showed that Dole was a "dirty campaigner," Rosalynn Carter said. After the debate, the Carter campaign's internal polling found that a plurality of respondents agreed with the statement "Bob Dole is not qualified to be president." And when polls asked voters whether they preferred the Ford-Dole ticket or the Carter-Mondale ticket, the latter scored 3 percentage points higher than when voters were simply asked whether they preferred Ford or Carter. The Carter campaign began to highlight Mondale's name in its advertising, and Carter started to mention Mondale in nearly every speech—not only because of Dole's unpopularity but also because many liberal Democrats in the North trusted the reliably liberal, Humphrey-like Mondale more than they trusted Carter. "Among Democrats especially, Mondale is probably the most popular of the four men on the national ticket," one Carter campaign aide told the *New York Times*.[35]

THE FINAL APPEALS

The vice-presidential debate clarified much more than the contrasting temperaments of the two vice-presidential candidates; it also highlighted the contrasting economic positions of the two parties and suggested that the election might come down to which message particular groups of voters found more persuasive. In keeping with the theme of the Republican Party platform, Dole attempted to paint the Democrats as the party of runaway inflationary spending, while Mondale, reflecting his deeply rooted belief in the economic liberalism of the New Deal and the Great Society, argued that unemployment was a more urgent problem than inflation and that government spending programs were the best way to get the economy moving again. "The economy today is in very, very bad shape," he declared in his opening statement at the debate. The United States was facing "the highest unemployment since the Great Depression, 50 percent higher than when Mr. Ford took office."[36]

The contrasting claims highlighted a class divide in the Republican and Democratic appeals. Mondale's bleak description of national joblessness was much more likely to ring true for lower-income voters than for midlevel managers and other white-collar workers. In reality, the unemployment rate, which was 7.7 percent in October 1976, had been somewhat worse the previous year, so Mondale's statement was not entirely accurate. After hitting a high of 9 percent in May 1975, the unemployment rate slowly dropped to a low of 7.4 percent in May 1976 and then ticked up slightly in the fall. But the economic gains of the modest recovery under Ford were not evenly distributed. The white-collar unemployment rate was below 5 percent, but the blue-collar unemployment rate was twice as high. Most of the jobs that had been added during the summer of 1976 went to women rather than men. For male blue-collar workers in the nation's Industrial Belt—which was rapidly becoming known as the Rust Belt because of the number of factories being shuttered and workers laid off—Mondale's attacks on the Ford administration's economic record were likely more persuasive than Dole's warnings about the negative effects of liberal Democratic spending. This was especially true in northern manufacturing cities. Buffalo, New York, one of the cities most severely affected by the recession of the mid-1970s, experienced a 16 percent decline in manufacturing employment between 1973 and 1975.[37] Many Americans feared that worker productivity was declining, that jobs were uncertain, and that the good life their parents had enjoyed in the 1950s and 1960s might be unavailable to the younger generation. Carter's promise to restore the prosperity of the Kennedy years and Mondale's evocations of FDR's solutions to the Great Depression resonated with voters who felt vulnerable in a stagnant economy where jobs were much more difficult to find than during the previous decade.

Dole's warning about runaway inflation if government spending were not kept in check was likely to appeal to middle-class voters who had jobs and who felt that, despite the uncertain economy, the monetary stability they had experienced during the last year was preferable to the economic risks if a Democrat were elected. The inflation rate in October 1976 was only 5.5 percent—exactly half what it had been when Ford took office. The United States had experienced double-digit inflation rates during the first few months of Ford's presidency, but he had made it his highest priority to fight inflation through deficit reduction, and he could proudly claim by 1976 that he had won the battle. Wages, for the most part, were keeping up with inflation. Union contracts achieved average salary gains of 7 to 9 percent in 1976, and although wage increases for nonunionized workers were smaller, the increase in the Social Security wage index—perhaps the best measure for measuring salary growth among nearly all the nation's workers—was just under 7 percent. Partly because of the power of labor unions, benefits for both white-collar and blue-collar workers remained generous. Approximately two-thirds of workers in the mid-1970s were covered by retirement plans. Even among "production workers" (blue-collar factory employees), 90 percent had employer-provided basic medical insurance, according to a 1975 study.[38] The economy was certainly in much worse shape than it had been in the early 1960s, and both Ford and Carter promised to improve the economy substantially by the end of the next presidential term. But for many voters in the middle-income bracket, the stability of the Ford economy—as lackluster as it had been—was preferable to the uncertainties of a Democratic administration.

As Ford and Dole emphasized during their final weeks on the campaign trail, a vote for the Republican ticket was a vote for low inflation, a balanced budget, and across-the-board tax relief. A vote for the Democrats, they argued, was a vote for high spending that would wreck the economy by producing runaway inflation. Carter and Mondale countered that a vote for the Republican ticket was a vote for economic stagnation, continued joblessness, and policies that would benefit only the rich. By contrast, they said, a vote for the Democrats was a vote for jobs, universal health insurance, tax relief for the working class, and a return to the prosperity of the early 1960s.[39]

The other theme reiterated by Ford and Dole during the final weeks of the campaign was peace. "The most telling point you made," Ford told Dole in a telephone conversation immediately after the vice-presidential debate, was that "we are at peace and our foreign policy has achieved it and will maintain it. And the comment that you made tonight that not a single American is fighting or dying on foreign soil tonight ought to give great reassurance to the American people that our policy of peace through strength is the highest policy of morality in foreign policy." This was the theme Ford had tried to highlight in his second debate with Carter, albeit rather unsuccessfully, and it may have been the idea behind Dole's clumsy attempt to blame the Democrats for the wars of the twentieth century. But in the final two weeks before the election, the Ford-Dole campaign conveyed the message of peace and economic stability much more effectively. A final blitz of television ads portrayed the president as a steady leader who had kept the nation at peace and set the country on the road to recovery in difficult times. With upbeat songs such as "I'm Feeling Good about America" and images of smiling, racially diverse faces juxtaposed with picture-postcard American landscapes, Ford's campaign ads encouraged Americans to be optimistic about their country and to associate its progress with his leadership. "Under President Ford, America is on a steady course," one television ad proclaimed. "Keep him."[40]

"There has been a restoration of faith and confidence and trust in the presidency because I've been open, candid and forthright," Ford told the audience in his final televised debate with Carter on October 22. "I have never promised more than I could produce and I have produced everything that I promised. We are at peace. Not a single young American is fighting or dying on any foreign soil tonight. We have peace with freedom."[41]

The theme of peace and stability counted for a lot, but polls showed that voters still found the Democratic economic message more credible than Ford's. So the president began to focus on one issue where the polls showed him ahead: his own trustworthiness. Despite Carter's two-year-long focus on personal character and honesty as the hallmarks of his campaign, polls in late October revealed that voters trusted the affable and experienced Ford more than the vague and untested Carter. The allegations of scandal at the beginning of October may have briefly threatened the president's public image, but Ford weathered the storm, and by the end of the month, it seemed possible that he could achieve a narrow victory based on the public's growing uncertainty about Carter's ability to deliver on his promises. Without resorting to direct attacks, the Ford campaign doubled down on the theme of trust by airing a series of half-hour television interviews between Ford and baseball veteran and sportscaster Joe Garagiola, which highlighted the president's compassion, experience, and fundamental decency. Even though the conversations were carefully orchestrated, they seemed informal and unscripted, and they gave the president an opportunity to play to his strengths. When Garagiola asked Ford to describe the difference between his own approach and that of his predecessor, Ford noted that his White House, unlike Nixon's, contained "no pomp," "no ceremony," and "no dictatorial authority." "We've tried to run the White House as the people's White House," he declared. "I think the average guy in the street knows that on Aug. 9 there was a distinct break between the previous administration and between my administration."[42] For months, pundits had predicted that the Watergate issue would damage Ford, and at the beginning of October, allegations of scandal almost made this a reality. But Ford rebounded and effectively put Watergate to rest by reminding voters of his openness and credibility. Polls at the end of the month showed Ford running nearly even with Carter in what the *New York Times* called "the most stirring political comeback in decades."[43]

For the final weeks leading up to Election Day, Ford broke with his "no-campaign" strategy and took his message of peace, stability, and trustworthiness directly to the voters. He campaigned across the Midwest and South aboard a presidential train named "Honest Abe." Ford's campaign team thought he had a good chance of winning Virginia, Mississippi, Louisiana, Florida, and the Carolinas, so they concentrated much of their effort in those states, along with Southern California and the midwestern industrial heartland. Ford was polling only 4 points behind Carter in Florida and only 2 points behind in

Figure 10.3. President Ford campaigning in Gulfport, Mississippi, October 1976. (Library of Congress, Prints & Photographs Division, U.S. News & World Report Magazine Collection, LC-DIG-ppmsca-08515)

North Carolina, they noted; with a concentrated campaign effort in the South, they hoped to close that gap. Their best strategy for picking up southern votes, they decided, was to suggest that Carter would raise taxes and leave the nation unprotected militarily. Carter was too much of a risk, they argued; Ford, by contrast, had demonstrated steady, reliable leadership. Accordingly, when Ford was asked at a news conference in San Diego what he planned to "emphasize in this final week of blitz," he replied, "trust, peace and prosperity." Jimmy Carter "wavers," "waffles," and "wiggles," Ford pointed out in his campaign speeches, and he and the Democrats had made promises they could not keep. The proposed programs in the Democratic Party's platform would add between $100 billion and $200 billion in new spending each year, the president claimed. A Carter administration would "borrow more money, spend more money, have higher taxes, and lead us down the road to more and more inflation," Ford declared in Oklahoma. But "as long as Jerry Ford is President . . . we will have a strong Government at home with less taxes, less inflation, less Federal spending, and we will have a Government that is strong enough to preserve the peace and to maintain our deterrent forces and to look at each other and say we are proud of America."[44]

Ford made few specific policy promises and mainly reiterated his basic philosophy of fiscal conservatism and summarized his record of success. "You know where I stand," he told an audience in Raleigh, North Carolina. "I stand on your side for fiscal responsibility, for rising prosperity, for lower taxes, for military strength and for peace in the world." Ford occasionally referenced some of his culturally conservative issue positions as well, especially since he spent most of the final days of his campaign in the religiously conservative South, Midwest, and Southern California. He noted his support for a constitutional amendment to restore prayer in public schools, and he regularly mentioned his address to the Southern Baptist Convention and his commitment to maintaining the example of "private morality" as a public servant. But his primary focus remained the issues he had always stressed: his fiscal conservatism, personal honesty, and commitment to "peace through strength." His advisers were mindful that any statements on abortion had the potential to alienate some part of the Republican coalition, so they urged him not to mention the GOP's antiabortion position, even on a campaign stop in Louisiana, a strongly pro-life state that Republicans thought they had a strong chance of carrying.[45]

Some of his advisers believed that Ford's promised tax cut needed to be a more central theme in the last stage of the campaign.[46] But Ford was at heart a deficit hawk, and regardless of the advice he received, the theme of preventing unnecessary spending and balancing the budget was a favorite of his. Perhaps he could have won over more southerners with a Reagan-like message that stressed cultural conservatism, tax cuts, and opposition to an out-of-control government bureaucracy, but these ideas did not interest Ford. After months of tilting to the right to stave off the threat of Reagan's primary challenge and then, in the general election, to attract the votes of culturally conservative Catholics and evangelical Protestants, Ford finally reverted to type and campaigned as the candidate he really was: a centrist Republican who wanted to balance the budget and preserve international stability.

Carter faced a greater challenge in his attempt to campaign on the themes he cared most about. His coalition was more ideologically diverse than Ford's, and he found it difficult to assure those competing factions that he was not moving off course. For instance, the businessmen in his coalition became nervous when the Carter campaign embraced the Democratic platform's commitment to economic liberalism, including the Humphrey-Hawkins full employment bill, and their anxiety increased as the election grew closer. Bert Lance, the Georgia banker who served as the Carter campaign's liaison to business interests and fiscal conservatives in the South, traveled to Dallas and Houston in mid-October to reassure wealthy Texans at the Petroleum Club that they could trust Carter to keep a tight rein on the federal budget. Business interests outside the South were mostly allied with Ford, and Carter devoted a substantial effort to attracting some of them to his camp. The campaign launched a Business Desk to remind voters that Carter was a small businessman who believed in balanced budgets and who wanted to free entrepreneurs from unnecessary government regulation. The head of the effort, Frank Saunders, had impeccable conservative business credentials: he was a New York–based public relations executive for Philip Morris and had served for five years as an editor of *Fortune* magazine.[47]

But this outreach to business interests worried some of the liberals in the Carter coalition, who feared their candidate was going to renege on his commitment to the economic liberalism of the Democratic platform and that the campaign would suffer as a result. "We're getting killed with our move to the right or center or wherever it is we thought we were going," Patt Derian told Rick Hutcheson. "It isn't clicking." Derian, a liberal Mississippi civil rights activist, played a leading role in mobilizing southern liberal populists for Carter. For his part, Hutcheson thought Carter should focus solely on the Democratic Party's promise of jobs. "The most important thing for JC to do in these last two weeks is to stick to the economic message," he told Jody Powell and Hamilton Jordan in a memo on October 20.[48]

To a large extent, Carter did this. In September the unemployment rate fell by 0.1 percentage point to reach 7.8 percent, but this was still the highest unemployment rate in any election year since the Great Depression. In addition, a slight decrease in the growth rate of the gross national product (GNP) raised questions about the economic recovery Ford insisted was occurring. Carter continued to hammer away at Ford's economic record, especially on campaign stops in northern industrial cities. "The economic news is bad," he told a crowd of thirty thousand in Philadelphia four days before the election. "We simply cannot depend on those who created this economic mess to clean it up." But Carter also continued to emphasize his promise of clean government and fiscal responsibility. He saw no contradiction between his support for the expensive jobs creation programs that appealed to liberals in his coalition and his promise to balance the budget, which mollified the fiscal conservatives associated with Lance. "From the start of this campaign, I have been saying that it *is* possible to afford to begin the types of programs Americans need *without* increased taxes, budget deficits, or massive unemployment," Carter declared in late October. "I know this is so because it happened in Georgia while I was governor."[49]

Carter's economic promises were never far removed from his appeal to cultural values, especially in the South. In the final days of the campaign, Carter attempted to shore up flagging support from white southerners with television advertising that highlighted regional pride. Conservative white southerners might disapprove of Carter's *Playboy* interview and might be worried about his endorsement of economic liberalism, but in the end, they would not pass up an opportunity to elect the first president from the Deep South since Zachary Taylor. This was, after all, the main reason why George Wallace was campaigning for Carter. And if Wallace could endorse the Democratic ticket (despite Mondale's presence) because of his pride in the South, other white southerners could be won over with the same appeal. "On November 2, the South is being readmitted to the Union," one of Carter's ads declared. It continued:

> If that sounds strange, maybe a southerner can understand. Only a southerner can understand years of coarse, anti-southern jokes and unfair comparison. Only a southerner can understand what it means to be a political whipping-boy. But, then only a southerner can understand what Jimmy Carter as President can mean. . . . November 2 is the most important day in our region's history. Are you going to let it pass without having your say? Are you going to let the Washington politicians keep one of our own out of the White House?[50]

In the final week before the election, as Carter was bringing white southerners back into the Democratic fold, his standing among black voters was suddenly called into question with another distracting news story about race: Carter's home church in Plains, Georgia, voted not to accept a black pastor as a member of the church, thus preserving its all-white membership policy. Carter, who was campaigning in Texas at the time, opposed the church's decision and insisted that the church should be open to members of all races. When the news story broke, most of Carter's black allies, including Martin Luther King Sr., Ralph

David Abernathy, and Andrew Young, reaffirmed their support for Carter and warned black voters not to use this event as an excuse to stay home on Election Day. As questions continued to swirl over the issue, Carter was traveling in California with Coretta Scott King at his side on Monday, November 1, the day before voters went to the polls. Martin Luther King Jr.'s widow disagreed with Carter's decision not to resign from the church to protest its segregationist policies, but she reaffirmed her strong support for the Democratic presidential nominee. "If I'm ever needed, I'm sure needed now," she said.[51]

With the black unemployment rate at 12.7 percent (down from 14 percent in January, but still nearly 5 percentage points higher than the national unemployment rate), many blacks were more concerned about the economy than the controversy over Carter's church. For months, black politicians had been telling Carter that if he wanted the black vote, he needed to support the Humphrey-Hawkins bill. Indeed, in the spring, Hubert Humphrey had been far more popular than Carter among many African American political leaders, and in the final stages of the campaign, some were still wistfully longing for Humphrey and wondering whether Carter was really on their side. The *San Francisco Sun Reporter,* a black-owned newspaper, refused to endorse Carter in the final week before the election because, the editors believed, he was not committed to the social safety net that protected America's poor and he considered the Humphrey-Hawkins bill a "secondary agenda item" that might have to give way to "fiscal responsibility." "Carter has not earned the votes of Black America," the *Sun Reporter* declared. The view that neither Ford nor Carter paid sufficient attention to the concerns of blacks was widespread. Jesse Jackson and Vernon Jordan accused both candidates of ignoring the black vote—a view that 32 percent of black respondents endorsed, according to an October poll. If many low-income African Americans were disillusioned with both candidates, a few members of the black middle class were supporting Ford. One hundred black clergy, led by Los Angeles minister E. V. Hill, endorsed Ford, as did the black-owned *Atlanta Daily World,* on the grounds that the "overriding issue is who can best keep the peace."[52] But support for the president was confined mainly to a small segment of the black population that appreciated the Republican Party's support for black capitalism. The vast majority of blacks were not convinced that another term for Ford was a better option than the election of a Democrat who had pledged (however reluctantly) to support the Humphrey-Hawkins bill and had allied himself with most of the South's leading civil rights advocates.

By the last week of the campaign, pundits knew that the black vote could decide the outcome of the race, because all the major polls suggested that the election would be extremely close. A Harris poll taken two days before the election showed Ford only 1 percentage point behind Carter, at 45 to 46 percent. A Gallup poll put Ford 1 percentage point ahead, at 47 to 46 percent. An NBC News poll showed that the two candidates were tied at 41 percent. Only a PBS Burns Roper poll suggested that Carter was solidly ahead of Ford, at 47 percent versus 43 percent. Most polls indicated that 6 percent of voters were still undecided, which meant that the election could be determined by individuals who made up their minds at the last minute. What made the election particularly difficult to predict was that an unusually high number of electoral vote–rich states were toss-ups. In California, Ohio, Pennsylvania, New Jersey, Texas, and Illinois, Ford and Carter were tied in the polls or separated by only the slimmest of margins.[53]

There was also the question of how Eugene McCarthy's independent campaign would influence the race. In mid-October he was still projected to receive 6 percent of the vote nationally and possibly as much as 10 percent in California. Despite Democrats' legal battles to keep McCarthy off state ballots—an effort that had already succeeded in New York—his name was slated to appear on the ballot in approximately forty states, and he was expected to be a potential spoiler in at least five: California, New Jersey, Illinois, Michigan, and Ohio. The Carter campaign dispatched Mo Udall and other surrogates to persuade liberals that a vote for McCarthy was a vote for Ford, and perhaps it worked. By the end of October, McCarthy's poll numbers were dropping rapidly. At the last possible moment, and after several court battles, Democrats succeeded in limiting McCarthy's ballot reach to only twenty-nine states. Their biggest success was keeping McCarthy off the ballot in California, although that did not prevent more than fifty-eight thousand California voters from writing in his name, giving him 0.7 percent of the vote in that state.[54]

With questions looming about black turnout, liberal defections to McCarthy, and southern white votes, the Carter team was also worried about two other groups: women and Catholics. Polls indicated that despite efforts to win them over, Carter would likely lose a majority of women voters to Ford. According to internal polling in October,

Carter's biggest problem was among married Catholic women. Perhaps this was related to Carter's long-standing challenges in appealing to northern Catholics, but Patrick Caddell suggested there might be another problem: even though married Catholic women were more economically liberal than their male counterparts, they were going to base their votes primarily on the issue of security. Ford's campaign message of peace and a steady economic course had won them over. They did not want to take a risk by voting for Carter. The problem was so bad that Carter's internal polls were projecting that he could lose the women's vote even in Rhode Island, one of the most solidly Democratic states. If that also proved to be the case in the industrial Midwest, Carter's failure to appeal to married Catholic women could be fatal to his chances.[55]

Journalists noticed that Carter seemed unusually "subdued," "pensive," and "troubled" on his last day of campaigning, which they attributed to the allegations of racial discrimination in his home church and to polls that showed, for the first time, a real possibility that he could lose the election. But he pressed on with his bid for votes from the swing states, starting with campaign rallies in California and ending with a final stop in Flint, Michigan. The choice to finish his campaign in Flint, where unemployment was above the national average, suggested both an appeal to the industrial labor vote in the president's backyard and a reminder that Carter's campaign was about the economy.[56] Carter had not initially positioned himself as an economic liberal, nor had his early campaign been primarily about creating jobs, but now it seemed that his best chance of winning a tight race might be to remind voters of his party's New Deal legacy.

Ford ended his campaign only a few miles away in Grand Rapids, where he was greeted by fifty thousand people in a large homecoming celebration. He was treated to a hero's welcome, knowing that he had done the unprecedented: he had erased his opponent's lead of nearly 40 points and was, he hoped, within sight of an election win. In contrast to Carter, he and his campaign managers were in a buoyant mood, even though his voice had given out on the campaign trail, and even though the outcome of the race was still far from certain.[57] Ford, like Carter, went to bed on the night before Election Day believing that he was likely to pull off an upset victory.

11 WHY CARTER WON

The election that was too close to predict turned out to be the tightest presidential race, at least in terms of electoral votes, since 1916. At 3:00 on the Wednesday morning after Election Day, the television networks had not yet called the election. An exhausted President Ford, his voice now completely hoarse after two weeks of nonstop campaigning, walked away from his TV set and went to bed. Poll workers at that late hour were still counting votes in Ohio, where the candidates were separated by only two-tenths of a percentage point. And in Maine, a mere thirty-one votes separated Carter and Ford in the early hours of the morning when the Wednesday edition of the *New York Times* went to press. The vote in California was too close to call as well, and neither candidate had enough electoral votes to win. The pundits were waiting on late returns from Hawaii to see whether its four electoral votes would give Carter a winning margin. A few minutes later, when Hawaii announced that Carter had carried the state by fewer than eight thousand votes, the networks called the election for the Democratic candidate.

Carter then walked onto the stage at the Georgia World Congress Center in Atlanta and claimed the presidency in front of five thousand cheering supporters. It was after 4:00 a.m. when he gave his victory speech. The contest had been a nail-biter up until the end, and only a few hours earlier, his closest aides had been afraid he might lose to Ford. But now Carter was headed to the White House after all. He had defied the odds to capture the nomination in primary contests

Figure 11.1. President Jimmy Carter and First Lady Rosalynn Carter walk down Pennsylvania Avenue in the inaugural parade, January 1977. (Courtesy of National Archives and Records Administration)

against better-known members of his party and to become the first candidate in more than forty years to defeat an incumbent president. Now he was the first president-elect from the Deep South in more than a century.[1]

WHY DID CARTER WIN—AND FORD LOSE?

Carter finished the race with 50.1 percent of the popular vote to Ford's 48 percent, and he won 297 electoral votes, with Ford carrying 240. A closer look at the state popular vote totals reveals an even closer margin: in an election in which eighty million Americans participated, the results could have been reversed if only ten thousand Democratic voters in Ohio and Hawaii had switched their ballots to Ford. The Democrat's razor-thin margin of victory made the Republican incumbent's election team feel even more despondent as they contemplated what might have been. The title of one of the Ford campaign memoirs expressed it well: *We Almost Made It.*[2]

In popular memory, there are two reasons for Ford's loss: his pardon of Richard Nixon and his debate gaffe on eastern Europe. These historical myths have an element of truth, in the sense that both the pardon and the gaffe probably had a marginal effect on some voters. But neither factor was the major issue in the election. The Carter campaign's postelection survey showed that no more than 2 percent of voters cited either the Nixon pardon or Watergate as their primary or secondary reason for voting against Ford. In an election as close as the Ford-Carter race, any single factor—no matter how small the impact—could have determined the outcome of the election. So in that sense, one could say that had Ford not pardoned Nixon, the 2 percent of voters who expressed concern about this issue in an exit survey might have voted Republican, and Ford could have won the race. But even this is doubtful. According to CBS News exit polls, Ford won the votes of 89 percent of Republicans and 52 percent of independents, indicating that there was very little Republican defection to Carter over Watergate. Ford even won the votes of 20 percent of Democrats—more than enough to counter the loss of the 11 percent of Republicans who voted for Carter. The idea that Ford sealed his fate when he pardoned Nixon in September 1974 is not supported by the polling data. His action did result in an immediate 22-point drop in his public approval rating at the time, and it may have contributed to a Democratic sweep in the midterm elections of 1974.[3] But by 1976, the economy had become a much more important concern for most voters.

The argument that the president's debate gaffe on eastern Europe gave the election to Carter gained currency among the Ford campaign staff almost immediately after Election Day. According to internal polls, the president had been receiving a majority of Catholic support shortly before the second debate, but right after his gaffe on eastern Europe, his support among Catholics dropped from 53 to 48 percent, and he never recovered. The Ford campaign's postelection analysis indicated that he had carried only 41 percent of the Catholic vote. Although other surveys showed that as many as 45 percent of Catholic voters had supported Ford, it was clear that Carter had won a majority of the Catholic vote. According to some of Ford's supporters, the president's losses among Catholics were enough to make the difference in the electorally rich, heavily Catholic states of New York (where Carter won 51.9 percent of the vote), Pennsylvania (50.4 percent for Carter), Wisconsin (49.4 percent for Carter), and Ohio (48.9 percent for Carter, versus 48.7 percent for Ford). If Ford had won New York alone—or any two of the other three states—he would have won the election. He could have carried those states if he had not alienated Catholic ethnics with his garbled statement about eastern Europe, Ford's pollsters argued. "When you have a margin of one or two points in an election,

Figure 11.2. Gerald and Betty Ford comfort each other as they watch election returns on the night of November 2, 1976. (Courtesy of Gerald R. Ford Presidential Library)

anything that was worth a point or two was the crucial thing," Bob Teeter declared.[4]

But the debate gaffe was certainly not a primary consideration for most voters outside of ethnic enclaves in a few northern cities, and even in those places, there is no firm evidence that the last-minute Catholic defections to Carter—especially in the final week of the race, more than two weeks after the debate—were due to Ford's misstatement on the stage in San Francisco. After all, Ford won several heavily Catholic eastern states, including New Jersey and Connecticut, in addition to Maine (home of the Catholic, Polish American senator Edmund Muskie) and Illinois (home to the largest urban concentration of Polish Americans outside of New York City). Ford lost Ohio, Pennsylvania, and Wisconsin by narrow margins, yet even in those states, it does not appear that Catholic ethnic voters were the chief reason for his defeat.

Ford actually ran much stronger among Catholics in the industrial North than most previous Republican presidential candidates had. He carried the city of Cincinnati, where Catholics outnumbered Protestants. He received nearly 47 percent of the vote in Pittsburgh and its surrounding county, which Nixon had lost with only 39 percent of the vote in 1968. Catholics in the suburbs were even more supportive of Ford. Indeed, there is some evidence of a slight shift in Catholic votes toward Ford in Ohio during the final days of the campaign; only a few days before the election, polls had projected that Carter would win the state by a much higher margin than he actually did. A *Columbus Dispatch* poll published two days before the election showed Carter with a 7-point lead, and the Ford campaign's own polling in Ohio showed that Carter was ahead by 4 points. Carter's actual margin of victory in Ohio was far narrower—only 0.2 percent. To the extent that Ford experienced unexpected losses in the state, they came not from last-minute Catholic defections but from a surprisingly high black voter turnout in Cleveland (where 95 percent of African Americans voted Democratic) and from strong Democratic voting among white Protestants in several Appalachian counties on the state's southern border that had long leaned Republican but voted for Carter in 1976. Likewise, in Pennsylvania, Ford's real problem came not from Catholic ethnics in the steel towns but from Philadelphia's blacks and others who were mobilized by Mayor Frank Rizzo's Democratic machine. Ford came out ahead of Carter in the heavily Catholic industrial counties where the cities of

Bethlehem, Allentown, and Altoona were located, but in Philadelphia he received less than a third of the vote. If not for Philadelphia, Ford would have won Pennsylvania.[5]

And nationally, as exit polls demonstrated, the best predictor of whether Catholics would support Ford was not their ethnic heritage or religion but rather the size of their salary and whether they were union members. Ford lost 61 percent of the union vote to Carter. Union members were considerably more likely than working-class nonunion members to vote Democratic, but even aside from union membership, Ford had trouble appealing to lower-income voters. A majority of voters who earned less than $12,000 a year cast their ballots for Carter, but 61 percent of those whose annual salaries were greater than $20,000 voted for Ford.[6]

CLASS, RACE, AND REGION IN THE 1976 ELECTION

Among both Catholics and non-Catholics, the election was a contest between security and employment. Those who favored security supported Ford, and those who prioritized job creation voted for Carter. This class-based division in the vote largely reflected the candidates' own messages during the final month of the campaign. After experimenting with cultural appeals to social conservatives, during the last month of campaigning Ford largely eschewed such discussions and ran as a centrist Republican with a message of fiscal prudence and international stability. In contrast, Carter, in spite of his original desire to run as a fiscal conservative, spent the final weeks of the campaign focusing on the Democratic Party's traditional New Deal–style message of jobs and economic relief. There was a general feeling among voters, regardless of party, that Ford's foreign policies had produced peace and security, but the Democrats were more likely than the Republicans to create jobs. By a margin of 51 to 25 percent, voters of both parties thought Ford was better qualified than Carter to manage foreign policy, and by a margin of 42 to 28 percent, they trusted the incumbent president, rather than Carter, to "keep the United States at peace." By a margin of 47 to 22 percent, they thought Ford was more capable of handling the Soviet Union. But by a margin of 57 to 23 percent, they believed Carter was more likely to reduce unemployment. Ford won the votes of those who were most concerned about international and monetary stability, while Carter was elected primarily with the support of those who were most concerned about jobs. Fifty-seven percent of white working-class voters supported Carter, compared with only 39 percent of white middle-class voters. Ford won a majority of college-educated voters and a strong majority of white mainline Protestants, who tended to be upper-income voters in the North. Manual laborers supported Carter, as did those who had not attended college.[7]

Because Ford was equated in the public's mind with stability and security, he won the votes of older Americans—especially those over the age of sixty-five—as well as the "housewife" vote. A majority of women who were employed full time voted for Carter, but an overwhelming number of women who did not work outside the home voted for Ford—reflecting a generational, economic, and cultural divide. The youngest cohort of American voters—those under the age of thirty—split their vote sharply along economic lines, with young working-class whites strongly supporting Carter and young college-educated professionals voting for Ford.[8]

This class-based division in the vote extended even to the South, Carter's strongest source of support. Despite Carter's popularity in the South, Ford won 55 percent of the southern white vote and about 60 percent of the middle-class white vote, and he carried the state of Virginia by a narrow margin. Yet Carter's overwhelming support from African Americans as well as a majority of white working-class southerners (especially in rural areas) allowed him to win every other southern state. In the days leading up to the election, the Ford team optimistically expected to carry Louisiana and thought he had a chance of winning Mississippi and perhaps Florida. But a strong turnout from blacks and lower-income rural whites enabled Carter to carry all these states by slim (but higher than expected) margins—Louisiana by 51.7 percent, Mississippi by 49.6 percent, and Florida by 51.9 percent. In North Carolina, the Ford campaign invested substantial resources in the hope that Elizabeth Dole's hometown connection and the support of the Republican governor would lead to a slim majority, but Carter carried North Carolina with 55.2 percent of the vote.[9]

Carter's victory in the South was due partly to strong support from African Americans, partly to his economic proposals, and partly to the effectiveness of his deliberate appeal to white southern regional pride. Many whites who might have been unenthusiastic about his political ideology decided they could not pass up the opportunity to elect the first southern president in more than a century. While many northern Republican voters were nervous about Carter, southerners, as a whole, were attracted to his born-again Baptist faith and his promise to redeem the South. In his own state of Georgia, he carried every county. In the rest of the South, his support varied along racial and socioeconomic class lines, but he retained enough support even from better-educated or more affluent white southerners to counteract Republican defections among the white middle class. McGovern had experienced catastrophic losses among southern whites, but 45 percent of them supported Carter, including 56 percent of working-class white southerners and 40 percent of those who were middle class. Carter likely won approximately 90 percent of the black vote nationwide, with some studies indicating that the percentage was even higher. Both black and white southerners were excited about Carter's candidacy, and as a result, voter turnout in much of the Deep South was substantially higher than it had been in 1972, with an increase of 24 percent in Louisiana and 28 percent in Mississippi.[10]

The high turnout worked to Carter's advantage, and it was largely due to the effectiveness of his campaign's get-out-the-vote effort and the Democratic National Committee's voter registration drive. In the months leading up to the election, some pundits had predicted a national turnout of less than 50 percent, but after a massive effort by the Carter campaign and the excitement of an unusually close race, voter turnout was nearly 55 percent. This was still lower than the 56 percent turnout in 1972, and many pundits noted that voter "apathy" was more prevalent than was healthy for a representative democracy. Yet even as voting rates declined in some northern states, such as New York, they increased in the South. This higher-than-expected turnout in Carter's own region undoubtedly helped him and may have been a deciding factor in the election. Analysts noted that the increased turnout was likely more than enough to account for Carter's margin of victory in Texas, for instance.[11]

A larger number of blacks voted in 1976 than in any previous presidential election, and their votes were more than enough to put Pennsylvania, Ohio, Maryland, Missouri, Mississippi, Louisiana, and Texas in the Carter column. Carter lost the white vote nationwide, but his support from blacks and Hispanics carried him to victory.[12] The Ford campaign made a concerted effort to target black voters through advertisements on black radio stations, and unlike several other Republican campaigns of the late twentieth century (including Reagan's North Carolina primary campaign earlier that year), Ford and his team eschewed any race-based appeals to whites, even when trying to win southern white votes. But by their own admission, they attempted to win the support of only middle-class blacks, and even in their most optimistic moments, they never expected to win more than 25 percent of the black vote. The Carter campaign appealed to the vast majority of blacks who were not part of the black elite, and these voters deprived Ford of victory. Ford's support for fiscal austerity, his willingness to embrace a right-leaning Republican platform that alienated even black Republicans, and his failure to counteract Carter's cultural appeal for evangelical Protestants prevented him from doing as well among black voters as his campaign had hoped. Carter stumbled at times in his outreach to blacks—especially during the primaries, when he used the phrase "ethnic purity"—but in the end, his own religious faith, his enlistment of numerous civil rights veterans as campaign surrogates, and his willingness to champion the Democratic Party's economic message (despite his doubts about it) won over a record number of black voters, thus giving him the presidency.

This same blend of cultural and economic appeals ensured Carter's success among white working-class voters, whose support he needed to counteract the Republican votes from more affluent southerners. In Alabama, the impoverished rural counties along the Tennessee border gave Carter some of his strongest support and allowed him to carry the state with 56 percent of the vote, even though Ford won the urban and suburban vote in Mobile, Birmingham, Auburn, and Montgomery. In Mississippi, Carter lost Jackson, Vicksburg, and much of the Gulf Coast to Ford, but he swept the poorer northern part of the state. In Florida, Ford won Pensacola, Orlando, and most of the southwestern coast, with especially high vote totals in Naples and Sarasota, but Carter received strong support from most of northern Florida as well as Miami. Carter carried most of the counties in the Carolinas and Tennessee outside of the historically Republican mountain regions, which gave him strong margins of victory in these states even though he lost several university towns and more affluent areas such as Raleigh-Durham and Davidson, North Carolina, and Greenville and Aiken County, South Carolina. In Texas, Carter lost Houston and the Dallas–Fort Worth area, as well as the oil-producing cities of Odessa and Midland, but he carried much of the rest of the state.[13]

With the vote falling largely along predictable partisan and socioeconomic class lines, Ford's claim that he could have won several southern states if Reagan had endorsed him more enthusiastically and campaigned for him in the South is doubtful. Reagan was popular in Mississippi, a state that Ford narrowly lost, so if Reagan had brought out the white conservative vote in Mississippi, Louisiana, and southern Ohio, one could speculate that Ford might have carried these states and thus won the election. But the supposition that Reagan could have swayed more conservative southern voters to Ford's side fails to take into account the southern regional pride that kept many southern whites loyal to Carter, despite their doubts about his political ideology. Dole's concerted campaigning and his wife's local connections failed to win North Carolina for Ford, and Ford managed to peel away only a bare majority of the southern white vote even after months of portraying Carter as a liberal. Whether Reagan could have accomplished more with a southern campaign is questionable. The Reagan campaign team claimed that their efforts on Ford's behalf gave the president California—a state he carried with only 49.3 percent of the vote—and they resented Ford's attempt to blame his loss in the South on Reagan.[14]

The racial and socioeconomic class divisions that characterized southern voting were also reflected in the voting patterns of the Northeast and the Midwest. In Michigan, Ford lost Detroit, Flint, and parts of northern Michigan and the Upper Peninsula, but because of exceptionally high support in Grand Rapids and other parts of western Michigan, he won his home state with 51.8 percent of the vote. In New England, Ford lost the declining paper-mill towns of western Maine; the city of Hartford, Connecticut; all of Rhode Island; and most of Massachusetts, a solidly Democratic state. But he carried Cape Cod and Connecticut's affluent southern shoreline. In fact, despite losing Hartford, Ford received enough votes from the rest of Connecticut to carry the state, which had rarely voted Republican in recent elections. In Illinois, Ford lost much of the rural southern part of the state as well as Chicago, but he managed to eke out a slim victory of 50.1 percent by carrying most of the historically Republican counties of north-central Illinois, where the descendants of nineteenth-century Yankee settlers had been voting Republican for decades. In California, Ford carried many of the state's more affluent counties, such as San Diego, Ventura, Santa Barbara, and San Jose, as well as the strongly Republican Orange County, but he fared poorly among Hispanics and blacks—which contributed to his failure to carry the state's largest cities. He also lost the rural white vote in California's poorer northeastern counties.

As Ford had feared, he lost a substantial number of votes in the farm states, where voters were still angry with him because of the wheat embargo, but in the end, he managed to hold on to nearly all these states, perhaps thanks to Dole's help. He carried North Dakota by 51.6 percent of the vote, South Dakota by 50.4 percent, Kansas by 52.5 percent, and Iowa by 49.5 percent. With the exception of Ohio, Ford carried nearly every traditionally Republican state in the nation. He held on to traditionally Republican northern New England and swept the West, carrying seventeen states west of the Mississippi, compared with Carter's five. For his part, Carter reclaimed the once-solid South for the Democrats and also held on to Appalachia, New York, and much of the industrial Midwest. Carter received almost twice as many white Protestant votes as McGovern had in 1972, and he performed 10 points better among white Catholics. He also carried 64 percent of the Jewish vote, which was not as high as he had hoped but equaled McGovern's percentage in 1972, and it was enough to prevent losses in New York, Pennsylvania, and Florida.[15]

Ford, in essence, received the votes of the historically Republican constituency of college-educated, middle-class whites, along with western farmers and ranchers, while Carter forged a coalition of rural whites, northern and western immigrants, the working class, those without a college education, and blacks throughout the nation. Carter's coalition looked very much like the one that had elected Franklin Roosevelt to his third and fourth terms in the early 1940s.Because Americans had become more suburban and more affluent in the intervening thirty years, a biracial coalition of working-class voters was not as large as it had been in the 1940s. But as Carter demonstrated, it was still large enough to win.

Because the election results were based on social class and racial and regional identity, explanations that focus on serendipitous events or particular contingencies probably miss the import of the larger economic and political trends that determined the election. Although the Ford campaign wondered what would have happened if the debates had gone differently or if Reagan had been more helpful, the Republican ticket actually did much better than expected in the circumstances. Faced with the worst economy the United States had experienced since the Great Depression and running as the candidate of an unpopular party in the aftermath of the Watergate scandal, Ford won 48 percent of the popular vote.

Although Ford agonized over the razor-thin margin of defeat in a handful of states that could have put him over the top, the electoral vote outcome could have been worse, given that he had only a tenuous hold on most of the states he did carry. One hundred twenty-eight of his 240 electoral votes came from states he carried by less than 51 percent. If only one or two out of every fifty Republican voters across the nation had switched their ballots to Carter, the former Georgia governor's electoral vote landslide would have been substantially greater than that of any Democratic president after that point, including Barack Obama's triumph of 2008. And if Eugene McCarthy had not been on the ballot in Illinois, Iowa, Maine, Oklahoma, and Oregon, Carter likely would have carried all those states, since Ford's margin of victory in each of them was lower than McCarthy's vote totals. Conversely, if only one out of every three hundred Democratic voters in Ohio, along with one out of every fifty-seven Democratic voters in Wisconsin, had switched their ballots to the Republican incumbent, Ford would have won the election. Because the electorate was nearly evenly divided, the slightest shift in either direction would have changed the election results. The Carter campaign could take credit for bringing the South back into the Democratic fold and putting together a winning New Deal–style coalition, but Ford deserved plaudits for successfully projecting an image of stability and competence that, though not quite enough to win, made Carter's margin of victory one of the narrowest possible. In the contest between security and the economy, security concerns came tantalizingly close to winning, but the working-class interracial coalition that was motivated by the promise of jobs and economic change triumphed in the end.

THE CULTURAL VALUES BEHIND CARTER'S ECONOMIC APPEAL

Why did Carter succeed in forging a working-class coalition of blacks and whites when several previous candidates—most notably, George McGovern—had failed? In 1972 only 43 percent of people who earned less than $8,000 a year voted for McGovern, but Carter won 62 percent of their vote in 1976.[16] He reclaimed the votes of the historically Democratic working-class constituency for the Democratic Party. The poor economy—which was in much worse shape in 1976 than it had been in 1972—played a role in Carter's ability to win back the working class, but so did his insistence that the party platform had to

Figure 11.3. Gerald Ford with Jimmy and Rosalynn Carter after the first debate. (Courtesy of Gerald R. Ford Presidential Library)

avoid the rights-conscious, culturally liberal rhetoric that had alienated many southern evangelicals and socially conservative Catholics four years earlier. Carter convinced working-class voters that he shared their values. Like many of them, he was a Christian. Like many of them, he had worked with his hands. And like some of them, he came from a poor rural county in the South. One survey showed that 5 percent of Carter's voters cited his Christianity and moral commitments as the principal reason for supporting him.[17] For many others, these attributes may not have been the deciding factor, but they gave Carter credibility and reassured voters that they could trust him with their economic future.

Through both the party platform and his own conservative image, Carter made the Democratic Party palatable to wavering cultural conservatives who had found McGovern objectionable. Thirty percent of self-described conservatives voted for Carter in 1976. Forty-one percent of white Protestant voters supported Carter, compared with only 22 percent who had supported McGovern in 1972. Among the subset of white Protestant voters who identified as evangelicals, Carter nearly won a majority, with 49 percent of their vote; McGovern, by contrast, had received less than 20 percent. Without Carter's concerted effort to appear more moderate than McGovern, some of the cultural conservatives who supported his candidacy—most of whom were Democrats, many of them from the South—may not have felt comfortable casting their ballots for the Democratic ticket. Carter's *Playboy* interview offended a few of the culturally conservative Protestants he needed to attract, and his clumsy attempts to reach out to Catholics may have backfired, but in the end, he won over enough social conservatives to sweep the South and make substantial inroads in the Midwest. At the same time, he won 73 percent of the liberal vote and prevented large-scale defections to McCarthy.[18] Even though he lost California by the slimmest of margins, he kept New York and Massachusetts in the Democratic column.

Carter, in essence, did what most observers only two years earlier had wondered whether any Democratic candidate (with the possible exception of Ted Kennedy) could do: he found a way to make conservatives and liberals, southerners and northerners, and blacks and whites feel comfortable in the same party, and he did so by taking most of the contentious cultural issues off the table and refocusing on the economic promises that had created the New Deal coalition of the mid-twentieth century. He did that by projecting an image of personal trustworthiness rooted in his southern Christian values. Low-income voters trusted him with the economy only because they trusted him as a person.

But this dream of a united, winning Democratic coalition based on Carter's personal character would be short-lived because Carter could not deliver on his economic promises and because the Democratic Party was moving in a very different direction from the one his culturally conservative voters wanted. Within four years, Carter's coalition would collapse. Never again would a Democratic candidate win nearly the entire South—or even a majority of the region. And not until 2008 would another Democrat win a majority of the popular vote. By the time the Democrats took control of the White House again, the idea that a Democrat could replicate Carter's coalition of southern whites and African Americans, of cultural conservatives and northern liberals, would be unimaginable.

EPILOGUE
WHAT HAPPENED TO CARTER'S COALITION?

Forty years after Jimmy Carter defeated President Gerald Ford with his anti-Washington message, another antiestablishment presidential candidate won an unexpected victory with a similar promise to bring clean and efficient government to Washington. This time, the candidate was a Republican. But despite the differences in party label and in issue positions, the regions of the country that gave Carter their vote in 1976 were, for the most part, the same ones that put Donald Trump in the White House.

Indeed, the 2016 presidential election map was almost a mirror image of the 1976 map: the regions that were once the strongest Democratic bastions of support were now firmly in the Republican camp, and those that were once Republican were now solidly Democratic. All six of the East Coast states that Ford carried in 1976—Maine, New Hampshire, Vermont, Connecticut, New Jersey, and Virginia—went to the Democrats in 2016. And all ten of the states of the old Confederacy that Carter carried in 1976 voted Republican forty years later. Similarly, the Pacific coast states, which voted Republican as a bloc in 1976, voted Democratic in 2016. Only in some of the central states of the Mountain West, Great Plains, and Midwest was there partisan continuity in the two elections, but even there, several large states switched parties. Illinois, which voted Republican in 1976, cast its electoral votes for Democrat Hillary Clinton in 2016, as did Colorado, which in 1976 had been a bastion of support for Ford.

Even more strikingly, a county-by-county analysis of the two elections reveals a similar partisan reversal.[1] Some of the counties that were Carter's strongest sources of support in 1976 went for Trump in 2016, and some of the counties where Ford received the most votes were firmly behind Clinton forty years later. In Alabama, for instance, Carter lost several of the state's largest cities to Ford, even though he carried the state; Birmingham, Mobile, and Montgomery voted Republican. Carter's strongest support in Alabama came from the poor rural areas, just as it did in the rest of the South. Jackson County, a majority-white rural county on the Tennessee border, gave Carter 72 percent of its vote in 1976—which was one of his strongest showings in the state. But in 2016 nearly 80 percent of Jackson County's votes went to Trump. By contrast, Clinton won the two largest metropolitan areas in Alabama that went for Ford in 1976; she carried both Birmingham and Montgomery. This shift in partisan loyalties did not result from a shift in the economic fortunes or racial demographics of these regions. Jackson County was still 93 percent white and just as impoverished as it had been in 1976. Its 2016 per capita income was nearly $5,000 below the state average. And the Birmingham metropolitan region was still one of the wealthiest areas in the state.[2]

Other states showed similar results. In California, for instance, all the West Coast cities that Ford carried in 1976—San Diego, Ventura, Santa Barbara, and San Jose—went for Clinton in 2016, usually by overwhelming margins. Even Orange County, which gave Ford 62 percent of its vote in 1976, voted for Clinton in 2016. But just as in Alabama, the poorest white rural areas of the state that voted for Carter in 1976 supported Trump in 2016. Trump's highest percentage—an astonishing 72 percent of the vote—came from Lassen County, a majority-white desert region on the Nevada border and one of California's poorest counties, with a per capita income of $21,000.[3] In 1976 Lassen County gave Carter a comfortable 55 percent of its vote. Carter lost California but carried the poor rural areas of the state. He won Alabama, but lost the affluent, educated white vote in the cities and suburbs. Trump did the same.

Such a striking partisan reversal—in state after state, the regions that voted Democratic switched to Republican, and vice versa—suggests that a substantial shift in the parties' ideological orientations occurred between 1976 and 2016. The seeds of this change might have been evident in the party platforms of 1976, although no one realized it at the time because the results of the election looked like a throwback to the election maps of the previous generation, which had been forged in the politics of the New Deal. The 1976 election map would have seemed familiar, for instance, to anyone who remembered the election of 1960, when Democrat John F. Kennedy carried most of the South, southern New England, New York, Pennsylvania, Illinois, Minnesota, and Texas, while losing most of the West, northern New England, and the Great Plains states. With only a few exceptions, the election map of 1976 looked identical; most of the states that voted for Kennedy in 1960 voted for Carter in 1976, and most of the states that Nixon carried in 1960 voted Republican again and supported Ford. Indeed, with only a few variations, the 1976 partisan leanings of most regions reflected long-standing preferences that dated back to the late 1930s. Ford carried every state that Wendell Willkie won in 1940, and he carried all but three of the fifteen states that Thomas Dewey won in his race against Truman in 1948.

These party preferences were based primarily on income and education, with religion, ethnicity, race, and region also playing a role. As a general rule, wealthier and more educated people voted Republican, while those in poorer, more rural regions voted Democratic. Carter's strongest showings in 1976 outside of his home state of Georgia and the District of Columbia were in Arkansas and West Virginia, two of the poorest, most rural, and least educated states in the nation. By contrast, much of the Republican vote—and an even greater share of its financial support—came from affluent northern suburbs and from upwardly mobile professionals, although Republicans could also count on some votes from rural westerners; fiscally conservative and libertarian-minded ranchers and farmers had supported the GOP for decades.

But the class-based partisan divide was already changing in the 1970s, even though the election map of 1976 masked that change. African Americans, who, for the most part, had been barred from voting at the beginning of the New Deal era, were now strong supporters of the Democratic Party. That was why Carter's best showing in any region came from the majority-black District of Columbia. And a younger generation of educated professionals who had come of age in the rights-conscious 1960s were skeptical of the Republican Party, especially after Nixon's presidency. Although they were too young to share their parents' admiration for FDR, their own positive memories of JFK, Bobby Kennedy, and the antiwar movement endeared them to the Democrats. But they had no use for older, big-government Democrats like Henry Jackson; they wanted the Democratic Party to stand for efficient government, environmentalism, and women's rights. Sexually tolerant and moderately fiscally conservative, these individuals looked very different from the culturally conservative white rural southerners and northern urban Catholics who had formed the New Deal Democratic coalition of the mid-twentieth century. In 1972 it appeared that these younger cultural liberals had gained control of the Democratic Party and then caused it to crash and burn. In 1976 the party experienced a course correction with Jimmy Carter, who, because of his regional and religious background, was able to reach out to the white rural southerners and northern Catholics who had supported the party before McGovern and bring them back into the fold for one last election. He managed to do so without alienating the blacks or the young progressives who had supported McGovern. It was a difficult balancing act, but on the morning after Election Day, it appeared that Carter had restored the New Deal coalition and forged a winning path for Democrats once again.

In fact, Carter had not done so. He had barely eked out a majority, and he had managed to do that only by being vague enough about his own political ideology to forge a coalition of very different demographic groups. The one thing uniting the white rural southerners, African Americans, and northern urban Catholic labor union members who supported Carter was a desire for economic relief, but Carter's commitment to fiscal conservatism meant that whatever economic programs he pursued would be markedly different from those of the Great Society and the New Deal. In addition, Carter's campaign had received support from culturally liberal McGovern Democrats—some of whom, in fact, had occupied key spots on Carter's campaign staff—and their priorities were often very different from those of the West Virginia coal miners and southern textile mill workers who had trusted Carter with their vote. While the 1976 party platform focused primarily on promises of economic uplift through government guarantees of full employment and national health insurance, it also included a modest endorsement of abortion rights and a stronger affirmation of the Equal Rights Amendment.

Carter supported promises of full employment only reluctantly, and his fiscal conservatism made him cautious about national health care. He wanted to put people back to work, but he thought he could do so on the cheap, and he greatly overestimated the degree to which productivity could rise and bring in new revenue. As a fiscal conservative who had been elected on a liberal Humphreyite party platform, he entered the White House with neither the courage to spend money like a Great Society liberal nor the party mandate to tighten the budget. Nor was Carter any better equipped than Ford to address the international forces that were preventing the American economy from growing, which turned out to be far more complex than he had assumed. As a result, the already lackluster economy worsened. During his four years in office, the unemployment rate remained unchanged at 7.5 percent, while the inflation rate more than doubled and the federal budget deficit experienced a modest increase.[4] The 1976 Democratic Party platform, which had promised an unemployment rate of 3 percent by 1981, government action to end high inflation, welfare reform, and federally financed comprehensive national health insurance, had seemingly been forgotten.

What was not forgotten was the Democratic Party's commitment to individual rights. In 1980 the party gave an even stronger endorsement of the Equal Rights Amendment than it had in 1976, denying funding to any candidate who did not support it. The party added an endorsement of gay rights as well, and over the course of the 1980s, it strengthened its platform language on reproductive rights. Gradually, the party of bread-and-butter liberalism became the party of rights-based liberalism.[5] In the mid-twentieth century, many people had voted for Democrats because of the party's economic promises, but by the second decade of the twenty-first century, the most reliable predictors of Democratic Party affiliation were cultural rather than economic. LGBT voters, single women, racial minorities, immigrants, non-Christians, and people with PhDs were much more likely to vote Democratic, while white evangelical Christians, less educated voters, and those in rural areas were more likely to vote Republican.[6]

Signs of this cultural divide were already beginning in 1976, as Ronald Reagan's primary campaign demonstrated. Reagan's campaign was explicitly antiestablishment, and it promised to remake the Republican Party. Although Reagan's campaign staff consisted of economic libertarians who viewed his campaign as a defense of free enterprise, his greatest appeal for many voters was values based, and his delegates came to the convention determined to move the party over to their side on cultural issues. They partly succeeded. The 1976 platform was more conservative on both gender issues and foreign policy than the 1972 platform had been, and the 1980 platform would be more conservative still. Perhaps if Reagan had gained the nomination—and especially if he had been running against a culturally progressive candidate such as Jerry Brown instead of Carter—the 1976 election map would have looked very different, and the cultural divide that remade both parties would have been evident. In the end, because both Ford and Carter presented themselves as moderate conservatives on matters of cultural controversy, those issues played a limited role in the final vote. Voters who favored the Democratic Party's economic stance but had voted Republican in 1972 because they felt alienated by McGovern's values decided they could trust Carter. And some culturally liberal northern voters who disliked the GOP's new direction on social issues nevertheless voted for Ford.

The vote was divided primarily along lines of traditional economic and partisan loyalties, with the battle over cultural issues seemingly tabled for at least one election cycle. But because Carter never delivered on the party's economic promises—and because the contingent in the Democratic Party that demanded an endorsement of rights-based causes continued to grow—the party continued to move to the left on cultural issues, even as it became less committed to Great Society–style economic liberalism. As this happened, northern liberal Republicans, who had combined moderate economic conservatism with social liberalism, became more comfortable with the Democratic Party and less comfortable with the GOP, which, by the early twenty-first century, had become the party of tax cuts, deficit spending, and cultural conservatism—none of which the liberal Republicans favored. By the beginning of the twenty-first century, liberal Republicanism had disappeared, and what had been Ford's centrist wing of the party was rapidly vanishing. George H. W. Bush, who had been a centrist Republican in the 1970s, voted for the Democratic presidential nominee in 2016.[7] No longer was the Republican Party the party of the economic and cultural establishment.

Reagan's insurgent campaign of 1976 united the self-styled "conservatives" of the West and the South against what they called the "liberal establishment" of the Northeast. To Reagan's original campaign staff, this meant a defense of free enterprise against government regulation. But on the campaign trail, Reagan found that his attacks on Ford and Kissinger's foreign policy, along with his defense of "traditional values," generated more votes. It was only when he started to attack welfare in more racially charged language and promised to keep America from "giving away" the Panama Canal that he began to win southern primaries. And many of the Reagan delegates elected to the Republican convention seemed to care more about abortion than tax cuts. Reagan's voters, in short, cared about economic uplift, but their vote for Reagan was about more than just keeping a bigger part of their paychecks; it was a vote to change the cultural direction of the country by attacking the "establishment." That was what Reagan's campaign advertising promised, and it was what voters thought they would get with the California governor in the White House.

By the time Reagan ran for president in 1980, the culturally conservative wing of the GOP had expanded, and new Christian Right organizations such as the Moral Majority had the influence to secure party platform statements in support of school prayer and against the ERA. With the Republican Party now opposed to the "liberal establishment," all but the most economically impoverished of the culturally conservative regions of the country that had voted for Carter in 1976 supported Reagan in 1980 and again in 1984. Although it would take another decade, the white rural South eventually became solidly Republican as it came to accept not only Reagan's patriotic and cultural message but also the gospel of tax cuts and deregulation. But the antiestablishment fervor that had propelled Reagan's candidacy in 1976—and resulted in such strong support for Carter in the country's economically impoverished rural areas—never disappeared. From the 1990s through the second decade of the twenty-first century, the messages of Rush Limbaugh, Glenn Beck, Bill O'Reilly, and Sean Hannity channeled their listeners' anger against a "liberal establishment" that was supposedly threatening their well-being—as though the Republican victories of the 1980s and beyond had never happened. And indeed, for many voters, those victories had failed to bring the changes they expected. Their income levels had not changed, and the cultural liberalism they feared had continued unabated.[8]

In 2016 Donald Trump capitalized on this antiestablishment message. His economic platform was a little different from Reagan's, since he promised economic protection rather than merely free enterprise. But like both Reagan and Carter, he ran an explicitly anti-Washington campaign, and he combined an economic promise with a conservative cultural appeal. The message worked. Trump won most of the states Carter had carried—and those Reagan had won in the 1976 Republican primaries. Trump even won over one key veteran of Carter's campaign staff: Patrick Caddell, the progressive pollster who had helped shape Carter's antiestablishment message and advised him how to reach out to both liberals and culturally conservative Catholics. Caddell, who served as an adviser to Trump campaign aide Stephen Bannon, rejected the Democratic Party when, according to him, it became a party of the "elites" rather than "a party of the people" and when it refused to allow pro-life members to speak against abortion at its national conventions.[9] Like Caddell, the culturally conservative whites who left the Democratic Party often accused it of failing to represent not only their cultural values but also their economic interests, and for many voters, the two were intrinsically related.

In contrast to Carter's careful attempt to stake out a centrist position on polarizing cultural issues to create as broad a coalition as possible, Trump championed the politics of cultural division, and perhaps as a result, both his popular vote total and his public approval rating were somewhat lower than Carter's. But regardless of what happens to his administration, both the Republicans and the Democrats will continue to face the two questions that both Ford and Carter wrestled with in 1976. They will have to figure out how to manage an economy so that it experiences a predictably high rate of growth, with jobs for all. And they will have to find a way navigate the cultural divides that threaten to destroy the coalitions that are based on economic concerns. Carter was unusually creative (and successful) in forging an electoral coalition that straddled the cultural divide with a clear economic promise. But by failing to deliver on that promise, he ended up destroying his coalition, setting in motion a process by which the cultural divisions he had tried to keep in check would fragment his party. And Ford, by failing to convince Americans that his administration could provide jobs, failed to save culturally inclusive, moderate Republicanism from oblivion.

The 1976 election was the last stand of Ford's brand of midwestern moderate Republicanism, and it was the last opportunity to restore the Democratic New Deal coalition. It was thus a pivotal turning point in the nation's political history—a moment when neither candidate was sure whether to embrace the traditional political formulas of the past or to exploit the forces of cultural polarization that seemed to be a harbinger of the nation's political future. Ford, after toying with the idea of campaigning on a platform of cultural conservativism, decided to embrace a traditional moderate Republican platform focused on economics—a platform that ultimately failed him. And Carter, despite his initial reluctance, decided to at least halfheartedly embrace a New Deal–style platform of government intervention to create jobs—a promise that won him the election, even though he was unable to fulfill it once he took office. In the end, then, perhaps the real winner of the 1976 election was neither Ford nor Carter but the forces that polarized the two parties along cultural lines. The Ford and Carter administrations are now distant memories, but the changes in the parties produced by the 1976 election are with us still.

NOTES

ABBREVIATIONS

AC	*Atlanta Constitution*
ADAH	Alabama Department of Archives and History
CCEJC	Records of the 1976 Campaign Committee to Elect Jimmy Carter (also listed in the Jimmy Carter Library's finding aid under the title Carter/Mondale Campaign Committee—1976)
CFR	Citizens for Reagan Records
CSM	*Christian Science Monitor*
GCWCR	Snider/Dauphin Inc., George C. Wallace Campaign Records, 1962–1984
GRFL	Gerald R. Ford Library
Hoover	Hoover Institution, Stanford University
JCL	Jimmy Carter Library
LAT	*Los Angeles Times*
MKU	Morris K. Udall Papers, University of Arizona
MRD	Michael Raoul-Duval Papers
NYT	*New York Times*
PFC	President Ford Committee Records
PHF	President's Handwriting File, 1974–1977
RRPC	Ronald Reagan 1980 Presidential Campaign Papers, 1964–1980
RRPL	Ronald Reagan Presidential Library
WHCF	White House Central Files
WP	*Washington Post*
WSJ	*Wall Street Journal*

PREFACE

1. Franklin D. Roosevelt served as governor of New York before his election as president in 1932, but he also served as assistant secretary of the navy before his governorship. Before Carter's election, the last governor to win the White House without prior experience in Washington was Woodrow Wilson.
2. The best (and most thorough) journalistic study of the 1976 presidential election is Jules Witcover's *Marathon* (New York: Viking Press, 1977). Others include Elizabeth Drew, *American Journal: The Events of 1976* (New York: Random House, 1977); Martin Schram, *Running for President: A Journal on the Carter Campaign* (New York: Stein & Day, 1977); Kandy Stroud, *How Jimmy Won: The Victory Campaign from Plains to the White House* (New York: Morrow, 1977). Shortly after the election,

memoirs by campaign managers also began to appear, and new ones continue to be published. For the Ford campaign, see Malcolm MacDougall, *We Almost Made It* (New York: Crown, 1977). Donald Rumsfeld's *When the Center Held: Gerald Ford and the Rescue of the American Presidency* (New York: Free Press, 2018) does not focus on the 1976 election, but the material on Ford's campaign presents a valuable firsthand perspective by one of the architects of the president's political strategy. For a similar resource on Carter, written by one of his top campaign advisers, see Stuart E. Eizenstadt, *President Carter: The White House Years* (New York: Thomas Dunne Books, 2018). Most of these books attribute Carter's victory to a combination of luck, persistence, and the unpopularity of the incumbent president. By contrast, historians who have analyzed the election have been much more interested in larger explanations for Carter's seemingly improbable rise. Judith Stein's *Pivotal Decade: How the United States Traded Factories for Finance in the Seventies* (New Haven, CT: Yale University Press, 2010) treats the 1976 election only in passing but posits an economic explanation for Carter's victory. In *Invisible Bridge: The Fall of Nixon and the Rise of Reagan* (New York: Simon & Schuster, 2014), Rick Perlstein presents a narrative of the 1976 election that focuses on how it facilitated Reagan's national political career and led to a rightward shift in American politics.

3. Jim Merriner, "Carter Assured Nomination as Ex-Foes Join Bandwagon," *AC*, 10 June 1976.
4. Kenneth L. Woodward, "Born Again!" *Newsweek*, 25 October 1976.
5. Bruce J. Schulman, *The Seventies: The Great Shift in American Culture, Society, and Politics* (New York: Free Press, 2001); Thomas Borstelmann, *The 1970s: A New Global History from Civil Rights to Economic Inequality* (Princeton, NJ: Princeton University Press, 2012); Rick Perlstein, *Nixonland: The Rise of a President and the Fracturing of America* (New York: Scribner, 2008); Perlstein, *Invisible Bridge*; Laura Kalman, *Right Star Rising: A New Politics, 1974–1980* (New York: W. W. Norton, 2010); Bruce J. Schulman and Julian E. Zelizer, eds., *Rightward Bound: Making America Conservative in the 1970s* (Cambridge, MA: Harvard University Press, 2008). For the role that crises of the 1970s played in producing a conservative shift in the nation, see Meg Jacobs, *Panic at the Pump: The Energy Crisis and the Transformation of American Politics in the 1960s* (New York: Hill & Wang, 2016); Philip Jenkins, *Decade of Nightmares: The End of the Sixties and the Making of Eighties America* (New York: Oxford University Press, 2006).
6. Daniel T. Rodgers, *Age of Fracture* (Cambridge, MA: Harvard University Press, 2011); Marjorie J. Spruill, *Divided We Stand: The Battle over Women's Rights and Family Values that Polarized American Politics* (New York: Bloomsbury, 2017); Natasha Zaretsky, *No Direction Home: The American Family and the Fear of National Decline, 1968–1980* (Chapel Hill: University of North Carolina Press, 2007); Andrew Hartman, *A War for the Soul*

of America: A History of the Culture Wars (Chicago: University of Chicago Press, 2015); Stein, *Pivotal Decade*; Jefferson Cowie, *Stayin' Alive: The 1970s and the Last Days of the Working Class* (New York: New Press, 2010). Other studies of the cultural fragmentation of the 1970s include Robert O. Self, *All in the Family: The Realignment of American Democracy since the 1960s* (New York: Hill & Wang, 2012); Edward D. Berkowitz, *Something Happened: A Political and Cultural Overview of the Seventies* (New York: Columbia University Press, 2006); and the essays in Beth Bailey and David Farber, eds., *America in the Seventies* (Lawrence: University Press of Kansas, 2004).

7. See, for instance, Kevin M. Kruse and Julian E. Zelizer, *Fault Lines: A History of the United States since 1974* (New York: W. W. Norton, 2019), 34–38.
8. For journalists' analyses of Carter's appeal, see David E. Rosenbaum, "Carter's Position on Issues Designed for Wide Appeal," *NYT*, 11 June 1976; Louis Harris, "'New Face' and 'Integrity' Carter's Foremost Draws," *AC*, 17 June 1976.
9. For Wallace's fund-raising, see "Wallace Raises $1.3-Million, Widening Fund Lead," *NYT*, 15 July 1975.
10. Some might object that the presidential elections of the 1990s, which featured the centrist Democrat Bill Clinton against the relatively moderate George H. W. Bush and Bob Dole, were also contests between moderates. It is true that Clinton was less liberal than Michael Dukakis or John Kerry, and Bush did not lean nearly as far right as Ronald Reagan. However, there was a difference between the elections of 1992 and 1996 and the election of 1976. In 1976 Carter had a reputation as a social conservative, unlike Clinton, whose policy positions on abortion and gay rights angered many religious conservatives. In 1976 Bush might have been ideologically indistinguishable from Ford, but he followed other Republicans in moving to the right in the 1980s and early 1990s to placate his base—especially the growing number of Religious Right voters in the Republican Party. Because of this, Pat Robertson and Ralph Reed's Christian Coalition, along with a sizable right-wing talk-radio constituency (led by Rush Limbaugh), supported the Republican ticket in 1992 and strongly opposed Clinton. This was very different from the situation Ford and Carter faced in 1976, when Carter handily won the socially conservative vote in Alabama, Arkansas, and West Virginia, while Ford carried Cape Cod, Massachusetts; Long Island, New York; every county in Vermont; and the coastal California counties of San Diego, Santa Barbara, and Santa Clara. This did not happen in the 1990s: no Republican presidential candidate in the 1990s, no matter how moderate, won the state of California (which Ford carried in 1976), and no Democratic ticket—not even one with two Southern Baptists—could win the state of Alabama (which Carter won in 1976). By the 1990s, the two parties were too ideologically polarized along cultural lines to permit a repetition of

the 1976 electoral map. My argument in this book is that the groundwork was laid in 1976 for a polarizing change in party positions on cultural issues that prevented any future presidential election from featuring candidates who were as centrist as Carter and Ford. Carter and Ford were thus the "last moderates."

1. TWO-PARTY CHAOS

1. For the cultural divisions of the 1970s, see Bruce J. Schulman, *The Seventies: The Great Shift in American Culture, Society, and Politics* (New York: Free Press, 2001). For the debate over women's rights, see Marjorie J. Spruill, *Divided We Stand: The Battle over Women's Rights and Family Values that Polarized American Politics* (New York: Bloomsbury, 2017). For analyses of the economic problems of the 1970s, see Judith Stein, *Pivotal Decade: How the United States Traded Factories for Finance in the Seventies* (New Haven, CT: Yale University Press, 2010); Jefferson Cowie, *Stayin' Alive: The 1970s and the Last Days of the Working Class* (New York: New Press, 2010). For the energy crisis, see Meg Jacobs, *Panic at the Pump: The Energy Crisis and the Transformation of American Politics in the 1970s* (New York: Hill & Wang, 2016).
2. Richard Bergholz, "Reagan Future: Which Office to Aim For?" *LAT,* 13 August 1974.
3. For histories of conservatism in the 1960s and 1970s, see Jonathan Schoenwald, *A Time for Choosing: The Rise of Modern American Conservatism* (New York: Oxford University Press, 2001); Donald T. Critchlow, *The Conservative Ascendancy: How the Republican Right Rose to Power in Modern America* (Lawrence: University Press of Kansas, 2011), 1–103; Rick Perlstein, *Before the Storm: Barry Goldwater and the Unmaking of the American Consensus* (New York: Hill & Wang, 2001).
4. For social conservatism and anticommunism among grassroots conservatives, see Lisa McGirr, *Suburban Warriors: The Origins of the New American Right* (Princeton, NJ: Princeton University Press, 2001); Michelle M. Nickerson, *Mothers of Conservatism: Women and the Postwar Right* (Princeton, NJ: Princeton University Press, 2012). For conservatism and libertarianism on college campuses in the 1960s, see Rebecca E. Klatch, *A Generation Divided: The New Left, the New Right, and the 1960s* (Berkeley: University of California Press, 1999); John A. Andrew III, *The Other Side of the Sixties: Young Americans for Freedom and the Rise of Conservative Politics* (New Brunswick, NJ: Rutgers University Press, 1997).
5. Jim Squires, "'U.S. Needs New Course'; Reagan to Oppose Ford," *Chicago Tribune,* 21 November 1975; Howard "Bo" Callaway to Rogers Morton, Information for President's Meeting with Members of Congress, 29 February 1976, folder "Congressional Support (2)," box A1, PFC, GRFL; Tom Wicker, "The More They Run," *NYT,* 4 February 1975.
6. George Gallup, "Ford's Approval Rating Declines to 50–28 Pct.," *WP,* 13 October 1974.

7. James M. Naughton, "Congress Begins with Unity Vows," *NYT*, 15 January 1975; Andrew J. Glass, "Ford Bailing out of 'Cotton South,'" *AC*, 22 August 1976; John Micklethwait and Adrian Wooldridge, *The Right Nation: Conservative Power in America* (New York: Penguin Press, 2004), 71.
8. R. W. Apple Jr., "Democrats' Outlook Is Hurt by Wounds of '68 and '72," *NYT*, 2 September 1974.
9. There are numerous analyses of these trends, but for an introduction, see Steve Fraser and Gary Gerstle, eds., *The Rise and Fall of the New Deal Order, 1930–1980* (Princeton, NJ: Princeton University Press, 1989); E. J. Dionne Jr., *Why Americans Hate Politics*, 2nd ed. (New York: Simon & Schuster, 2004); Robert O. Self, *All in the Family: The Realignment of American Democracy since the 1960s* (New York: Hill & Wang, 2012).
10. "Wallace Raises $1.3-Million, Widening Fund Lead," *NYT*, 15 July 1975; Joseph Kraft, "The Cast: With Teddy out and New Rules in, You Can't Tell the Democratic Players without a Playbill," *NYT*, 17 November 1974; George H. Gallup, *The Gallup Poll: Public Opinion, 1972–1977*, 2 vols. (Wilmington, DE: Scholarly Resources, 1978), 1:43.
11. Rick Perlstein, *Nixonland: The Rise of a President and the Fracturing of America* (New York: Scribner, 2008), 745.
12. Richard M. Scammon and Ben J. Wattenberg, *The Real Majority* (New York: Coward-McCann, 1970), 279–305; "National Exit Polls Table," *NYT*, 5 November 2008, www.nytimes.com/elections/2008/results/president/nationalj-exit-polls.html.
13. National Urban League, "The State of Black America," 28 January 1976, folder "Black Affairs, 3/76–10/76," box 2, CCEJC, JCL; Vernon Jordan, statement at "The State of Black America" press conference, 28 January 1976, ibid.; "Distress Signal," editorial, *NYT*, 2 February 1976. For the black unemployment rate, see "Unemployment Rate: Black or African American," Federal Reserve Bank of St. Louis, https://fred.stlouisfed.org/series/LNS14000006, which reproduces historical statistics from the US Bureau of Labor.
14. "Special Ebony Poll: Black Elected Officials' Choices for U.S. President," *Ebony*, May 1976, 88.
15. Alan Flippen, "Black Turnout in 1964, and Beyond," *NYT*, 17 October 2014.
16. For the alienation of blacks from the Republican Party in the mid-1970s, see Jeremy D. Mayer, *Running on Race: Racial Politics in Presidential Campaigns, 1960–2000* (New York: Random House, 2002), 96–149.
17. James M. Naughton, "Senate and House Margins Are Substantially Enlarged," *NYT*, 6 November 1974; Roy Reed, "The South: G.O.P. Is Set Back in Region as the Democrats Stress Economic Issues," *NYT*, 7 November 1974.
18. Brookings Institution, Vital Statistics on Congress (2014), https://www.brookings.edu/wp-content/uploads/2016/06/Vital-Statistics-Chapter-8

-Political-Polarization-in-Congress-and-Changing-Voting-Alignments .pdf; Apple, "Democrats' Outlook Is Hurt by Wounds of '68 and '72."

19. Gallup, *Gallup Poll,* 2:648; Harold D. Clarke and Motoshi Suzuki, "Partisan Dealignment and the Dynamics of Independence in the American Electorate, 1953–88," *British Journal of Political Science* 24 (1994): 60; "National General Election VEP Turnout Rates, 1789–Present," United States Elections Project, http://www.electproject.org/national-1789-present; Yanek Mieczkowksi, Gerald Ford and the Challenges of the 1970s (Lexington: University Press of Kentucky, 2005), 21.
20. Gallup, *Gallup Poll,* 2:621–622, 645–647.
21. Wicker, "The More They Run."
22. Jules Witcover, "Campaign Finance without the Fat Cats," *WP,* 10 November 1975; Stephen M. Travis, memo to Carter campaign, 28 July 1976, folder "Memoranda, General Election [1]," box 411, CCEJC, JCL.
23. Kraft, "The Cast"; J. F. terHorst, "Who Made New Hampshire Divine?" *AC,* 2 November 1975.
24. Douglas E. Kneeland, "Democratic Contest in New Hampshire Viewed as 3-Man Race," *NYT,* 12 February 1976.

2. THE DEMOCRATIC FIELD IN 1974

1. For the chilling effect McGovern's landslide defeat had on some of the young liberals who supported him, see Bruce Miroff, *The Liberals' Moment: The McGovern Insurgency and the Identity Crisis of the Democratic Party* (Lawrence: University Press of Kansas, 2007).
2. Joseph Kraft, "The Cast: With Teddy out and New Rules in, You Can't Tell the Democratic Players without a Playbill," *NYT,* 17 November 1974.
3. Kraft, "The Cast"; B. Drummond Ayers Jr., "Doubts Rise on Wallace's '76 Strength," *NYT,* 2 January 1976.
4. President Ford Committee, Report of Current Level of Fundraising for Each Presidential Candidate, July 1–September 30, 1975, folder "Advisory Committee, 11/17/75," box A3, Callaway Subject Files, PFC, GRFL.
5. "Wallace Campaign Plans for 1975–76 Period," [1975], folder 13, box 260, GCWCR, ADAH; George Wallace, direct mail, 29 May 1975, folder 1, box 12, ibid.; George Wallace, direct mail, 1 May 1976, folder 12, box 2, ibid.; Jonathan Moore and Janet Fraser, eds., *Campaign for President: The Managers Look at '76* (Cambridge, MA: Ballinger, 1977), 89; Jeff Frederick, *Stand up for Alabama: Governor George Wallace* (Tuscaloosa: University of Alabama Press, 2007), 358.
6. Dan T. Carter, *The Politics of Rage: George Wallace, the Origins of the New Conservatism, and the Transformation of American Politics* (New York: Simon & Schuster, 1995), 456–457; Chris Kenrick, "George Wallace—Voters Know 'Where He Stands,'" *CSM,* 8 March 1976; George C. Wallace, *Stand up for America* (Garden City, NY: Doubleday, 1976), 166; Frederick, *Stand up for Alabama,* 358; George C. Wallace campaign

advertisement, "A New Day for America," January 1976, folder "Public Relations—Public Opinion Polls," box 42, PHF, GRFL.

7. For a scholarly biography of Wallace that links him to the rise of the culturally conservative right, see Carter, *Politics of Rage.*
8. Gus Tyler, "Third-Party Capers," *New Leader,* 12 April 1976, 7; Carey McWilliams, "Scenario for '76," *Nation,* 1 February 1975, 98–100; Wallace, *Stand up for America,* 178; Frederick, *Stand up for Alabama,* 341; Wallace campaign advertisement, "New Day for America."
9. Jody Carlson, *George C. Wallace and the Politics of Powerlessness: The Wallace Campaigns for the Presidency, 1964–1976* (New Brunswick, NJ: Transaction Books, 1981), 230–231.
10. Cambridge Reports Inc., "Jimmy Carter: A Political Analysis," May 1975, folder "Political Analysis of Jimmy Carter," box 33, Jody Powell Papers, JCL.
11. Douglas E. Kneeland, "Jackson Is Out," *NYT,* 2 May 1976; Douglas E. Kneeland, "Jackson Is Endorsed by Rustin in New Push for Black Voters," *NYT,* 2 April 1976; Kraft, "The Cast"; "Sen. Jackson at Apex of His Career," *WP,* 6 July 1974. For Jackson's political career, see Robert G. Kaufman, *Henry M. Jackson: A Life in Politics* (Seattle: University of Washington Press, 2000). In writing this book, I debated whether to call Senator Jackson "Scoop," as journalistic accounts of the 1976 election generally do, including Jules Witcover's *Marathon,* or to identify him more formally as "Henry M. Jackson," as newspapers and print sources of the 1970s almost invariably did. Because it seems that Jackson always used his formal name in print, I decided to follow Kaufman's lead and identify him as "Henry Jackson" throughout this book.
12. Kneeland, "Jackson Is Out."
13. Kraft, "The Cast"; Kneeland, "Jackson Is Out"; Christopher Lydon, "Jackson Pays a Visit to New Hampshire and Considers Trying a Primary Race There in 1976," *NYT,* 7 October 1974; "Jackson to Decide Soon on Candidacy for 1976," *NYT,* 7 November 1974; R. W. Apple Jr., "Jackson Now Sets Early Primary Bid," *NYT,* 20 November 1975.
14. "Wallace Campaign Plans for 1975–76 Period."
15. Thomas M. Fletcher, DNC, Analysis of Recent Polls, 19 January 1976, 11, folder "Poll Analysis," box 412, CCEJC, JCL. For debates over busing in the 1970s and their effect on national politics, see Matthew F. Delmont, *Why Busing Failed: Race, Media, and the National Resistance to School Desegregation* (Berkeley: University of California Press, 2016); Ronald P. Formisano, *Boston against Busing: Race, Class, and Ethnicity in the 1960s and 1970s* (Chapel Hill: University of North Carolina Press, 1991); Matthew D. Lassiter, *The Silent Majority: Suburban Politics in the Sunbelt South* (Princeton, NJ: Princeton University Press, 2006).
16. Paul Delaney, "Blacks' Issues Are Slighted in Campaign, Leaders Say," *NYT,* 8 February 1976; "Black Elected Officials' Choices for U.S. President," *Ebony,* July 1974, 132.

17. Robert Sherrill, "Senator Jackson Enters Right," *Nation,* 1 February 1975, 110.
18. Michael Stern, "Low-Cost Eximbank Loans to Soviet Hit by Jackson," *NYT,* 4 June 1974; "Jackson Links Aid for Soviet to Arms," *NYT,* 15 July 1974; Kraft, "The Cast"; Sherrill, "Senator Jackson Enters Right," 111.
19. Kraft, "The Cast."
20. George H. Gallup, *The Gallup Poll: Public Opinion, 1972–1977,* 2 vols. (Wilmington, DE: Scholarly Resources, 1978), 2:668; "Lead Us to Our Leader," *New Republic,* 28 December 1974. McGovern won the support of 67 percent of Democratic voters in the 1972 election; Nixon carried 33 percent of the Democratic vote. See http://www.gallup.com/poll/9457/election-polls-vote-groups-19681972.aspx.
21. Kneeland, "Jackson Is Endorsed by Rustin."
22. R. W. Apple Jr., "Democrats' Outlook Is Hurt by Wounds of '68 and '72," *NYT,* 2 September 1974; "Kennedy's 44 Pct. Leads Democrats," *NYT,* 8 April 1974.
23. Clayton Fritchey, "Looking to the '76 Finals: Mondale vs. Jackson?" *WP,* 23 March 1974.
24. Stuart Auerbach, "The Health Insurance Struggle," *WP,* 11 April 1974; Fletcher, Analysis of Recent Polls, 19 January 1976.
25. Gallup, *Gallup Poll,* 2:641–643.
26. "Transcript of Kennedy Statement on 1976 Plans: Responsibilities at Home," *NYT,* 24 September 1974.
27. "Transcript of Kennedy Statement on 1976 Plans"; Edward M. Kennedy, *True Compass: A Memoir* (New York: Twelve, 2009), 345–346; "Kennedy Is Ahead of Ford in Poll Despite Disavowal of Candidacy," *NYT,* 10 August 1975; George Gallup, "Kennedy Moves into Lead While Denying Race," *Montgomery (AL) Advertiser,* 10 August 1975; "Poll Finds Jackson Strongest Ford Challenger," *NYT,* 6 April 1975. Kennedy also did well in polls that matched him against Reagan. An Ohio poll taken in January 1976 showed Kennedy defeating Reagan in that state if Reagan were the Republican nominee; it also indicated that Hubert Humphrey would lose to Reagan in a head-to-head contest there. The Ohio poll, press release, 30 January 1976, folder "Ohio," box 5, Rogers Morton Files, GRFL.
28. Susan Donaldson James, "Ted Kennedy's Wife Joan Kennedy: Casualty of Camelot," ABC News, 28 August 2009, http://abcnews.go.com/Politics/TedKennedy/story?id=8428638; Kennedy, *True Compass,* 344.
29. Paul Lutzker and Thomas M. Fletcher, DNC, Analysis of Recent Polls, 13 June 1975, folder "Poll Analysis," box 412, CCEJC, JCL; Kennedy, *True Compass,* 294, 343–346; Rowland Evans and Robert Novak, "Sen. Kennedy: The Burden of Chappaquiddick," *WP,* 13 February 1974; Mary Russell, "Concern on Morality Hurts Kennedy," *WP,* 23 September 1974.
30. Kennedy, *True Compass,* 344.

31. William Chapman, "Busing Foes Boo Kennedy in Boston," *WP*, 10 September 1974.
32. Fritchey, "Looking to the '76 Finals"; Jules Witcover, "Sen. Mondale Won't Seek Presidential Nomination," *WP*, 22 November 1974; Kraft, "The Cast."
33. Molly Ivins, "Liberal from Goldwater Country," *NYT*, 1 February 1976; William V. Shannon, "A Good Man Is Not Enough," *NYT*, 30 August 1974; Richard Pearson, "Environmental Leader Rep. Mo Udall Dies," *WP*, 14 December 1998; William Connell to Terry Bracy, 2 December 1975, folder 8, box 40, MKU; "Morris K. Udall—A Biography," [1975], folder 8, box 40, MKU; Charles Mohr, "Abortion Dispute Troubling Bayh," *NYT*, 12 February 1976.
34. Terry Bracy to Mo Udall, 4 February 1974, folder 4, box 40, MKU; Mo Udall to staff, 9 October 1973, folder 3, box 40, MKU.
35. Mo Udall, draft of fund-raising letter, 21 May 1975, folder 6, box 40, MKU.
36. R. W. Apple Jr., "Morris Udall, Backed by 27 in House, to Explore Presidential Bid," *NYT*, 17 May 1974.
37. Mo Udall, "Mo Udall Statement on the Mormon Church," [1975], folder 6, box 40, MKU; Lois Romano, "Ella Udall, Congressman's Wife, Found Dead at McLean Home," *WP*, 14 August 1988; Judy Klemesrud, "Wives in '76 Campaign Find the Going Difficult," *NYT*, 12 April 1976; Morris K. Udall to Mrs. Kenneth H. Johns, 2 April 1975, folder 6, box 40, MKU.
38. Apple, "Morris Udall, Backed by 27 in House, to Explore Presidential Bid"; Richard Severo, "Morris K. Udall, Fiercely Liberal Congressman, Dies at 76," *NYT*, 14 December 1998.
39. Udall's brand of liberalism was especially appealing to young, college-educated whites in the suburbs of Boston, Philadelphia, and other cities. For an insightful regional study of northeastern suburban liberalism during the 1970s, see Lily Geismer, *Don't Blame Us: Suburban Liberals and the Transformation of the Democratic Party* (Princeton, NJ: Princeton University Press, 2015).
40. UPI, "Harris Will Announce," *NYT*, 13 December 1974.
41. Jules Witcover, *Marathon: The Pursuit of the Presidency, 1972–1976* (New York: Viking Press, 1977), 212.
42. For analyses of how events of the 1970s produced an increasingly individualistic, pro-capitalist ideology among American voters, see Thomas Borstelmann, *The 1970s: A New Global History from Civil Rights to Economic Inequality* (Princeton, NJ: Princeton University Press, 2012), 122–174; Daniel T. Rodgers, *Age of Fracture* (Cambridge, MA: Harvard University Press, 2011), 41–76.
43. Frank Lynn, "Bayh, Harris, Shapp and Udall Are Fighting Hard for Democratic Liberal Bloc's Endorsement for '76," *NYT*, 21 November 1975; Warren Weaver Jr., "Shapp Basing Campaign on Revamping Economy,"

NYT, 30 December 1975; Kraft, "The Cast"; Wayne King, "Sanford Pins Victory Hope on His Nonpolitical Stance," *NYT,* 29 December 1975; Wayne King, "Sanford Is Leaving Presidential Race; 'Realities' Are Cited," *NYT,* 22 January 1976.

44. Kraft, "The Cast."
45. Kraft, "The Cast."

3. JIMMY CARTER ENTERS THE RACE

1. Hamilton Jordan to Jimmy Carter, 4 November 1972, folder "Memorandum—Hamilton Jordan to Jimmy Carter, 11/4/72," box 199, CCEJC, JCL.
2. Saul Pett (AP), "President of What?—of the United States," *High Point (NC) Enterprise,* 15 July 1976.
3. Comparisons between Kennedy and Carter were common in the press during the early days of Carter's campaign. For an example, the *New York Times* described him as a candidate with a "crinkled pearly grin, blue eyes, Kennedy-style blond hair, and soft Dixie voice." B. Drummond Ayres Jr., "1976 Surprise: Carter Is Running Well," *NYT,* 26 December 1975.
4. Unless otherwise noted, the following biographical details about Carter's life come from Peter G. Bourne, *Jimmy Carter: A Comprehensive Biography from Plains to Postpresidency* (New York: Scribner, 1997); Kenneth E. Morris, *Jimmy Carter: American Moralist* (Athens: University of Georgia Press, 1996); Betty Glad, *Jimmy Carter: In Search of the Great White House* (New York: W. W. Norton, 1980).
5. Howard Norton and Bob Slosser, *The Miracle of Jimmy Carter* (Plainfield, NJ: Logos International, 1976), 4; transcript of Bill Moyers's interview with Jimmy Carter, 16 May 1976, in *Conversations with Carter,* ed. Don Richardson (Boulder, CO: Lynne Rienner, 1998), 9.
6. "Jimmy Carter on Small Business," [October 1976], folder "Business, 10/76," box 2, CCEJC, JCL; Jimmy Carter, ad for Missouri caucus, April 1976, folder "State file—Missouri," box 239, ibid.
7. Bourne, *Jimmy Carter,* 99, 115–116.
8. Morris, *Jimmy Carter,* 161; Glad, *Jimmy Carter,* 119.
9. Bourne, *Jimmy Carter,* 192–193.
10. Kenneth Reich, "Gov. Carter Urges End to Discrimination," *WP,* 13 January 1971; Howell Raines, "'One of Us': King Portrait Is a First at Capitol," *AC,* 18 February 1974.
11. Patrick Anderson, "Peanut Farmer for President," *NYT,* 14 December 1975.
12. James T. Wooten, "Carter's Drive from Obscurity to Front," *NYT,* 15 March 1976.
13. Bourne, *Jimmy Carter,* 232.
14. Jimmy Carter, *Why Not the Best?* (Nashville, TN: Broadman Press, 1975).
15. Peter Bourne to Jimmy Carter, 1 August 1974, folder "Correspondence,

Jimmy Carter, 7/73–11/74," box 7, CCEJC, JCL; Jordan to Carter, 4 November 1972.

16. Rick Hutcheson to Hamilton Jordan, 3 April 1975, folder "Memoranda, March–June 1975," box 411, CCEJC, JCL; Anderson, "Peanut Farmer for President."
17. Richard D. Lamm, "Whither the Democratic Party?" *NYT,* 1 February 1976; Graeme Starr, "Carter and the Federal Power," *Sydney Morning Herald,* 12 August 1976; Roy Reed, "Sunbelt Still Stronghold of Conservatism in U.S.," *NYT,* 10 February 1976. For more on the economics and politics of the postwar Sun Belt, see Bruce J. Schulman, *From Cotton Belt to Sunbelt: Federal Policy, Economic Development, and the Transformation of the South, 1938–1980* (New York: Oxford University Press, 1991); Ann Markusen and Peter Hall, *The Rise of the Gunbelt: The Military Remapping of Industrial America* (New York: Oxford University Press, 1991); Numan V. Bartley, *The New South, 1945–1980: The Story of the South's Modernization* (Baton Rouge: Louisiana State University Press, 1995); James C. Cobb, *The Selling of the South: The Southern Crusade for Industrial Development, 1936–1990* (Urbana: University of Illinois Press, 1993); Michelle Nickerson and Darren Dochuk, eds., *Sunbelt Rising: The Politics of Space, Place, and Region* (Philadelphia: University of Pennsylvania Press, 2011).
18. Rick Lyman, "Hamilton Jordan, Carter's Right Hand, Dies at 63," *NYT,* 21 May 2008; Hamilton Jordan, *A Boy from Georgia: Coming of Age in the Segregated South,* ed. Kathleen Jordan (Athens: University of Georgia Press, 2015), 220–221; Hamilton Jordan, *No Such Thing as a Bad Day* (Atlanta: Longstreet Press, 2000).
19. David Stout, "Jody Powell, Trusted Aide to Jimmy Carter, Dies at 65," *NYT,* 15 September 2009.
20. John Dillin, "Who Are the Men behind Jimmy Carter?" *CSM,* 5 May 1976; Ken Auletta, "Jimmy Carter's 'Mafia': What the Men around the Man Say about the Candidate," *Village Voice,* 28 June 1976.
21. Kandy Stroud, *How Jimmy Won: The Victory Campaign from Plains to the White House* (New York: William Morrow, 1977), 214; Art Harris, "The Fall of a Maverick," *WP,* 24 July 1978; Peter G. Bourne, biography, http://petergbourne.co.uk/bio.html; Bourne, *Jimmy Carter,* 231.
22. Mary E. King to Jimmy Carter, 9 March 1976, folder "Black Affairs, 3/76–10/76," box 2, CCEJC, JCL.
23. Matt Schudel, "Bert Lance, Banker and Carter Budget Director," *WP,* 16 August 2013; Robert D. Hershey Jr., "Bert Lance, Carter Advisor, Dies at 82," *NYT,* 15 August 2013; "Carter Concerned about His Image," *AC,* 18 October 1976; Stroud, *How Jimmy Won,* 199; Albert R. Hunt, "Jimmy Carter's Advisers," *WSJ,* 25 May 1976; "Charles Kirbo Dies at Age 79," *WP,* 4 September 1996; Dillin, "Who Are the Men behind Jimmy Carter?"; Lawrence Van Gelder, "Charles H. Kirbo, 79, Is Dead; Was Carter's Closest Advisor," *NYT,* 4 September 1996.

24. Hamilton Jordan to Jimmy Carter, March 1975, folder "Memoranda, March–June 1975," box 11, CCEJC, JCL; Auletta, "Jimmy Carter's 'Mafia.'"
25. Bourne, *Jimmy Carter,* 240–243; Gloria Duffy, "Shaping Carter's World View," *WP,* 15 August 1976.
26. Jimmy Carter, speech, National Press Club, 12 December 1974, folder "Issues Statements," box 410, CCEJC, JCL.
27. Carter speech, 12 December 1974.
28. Jimmy Carter, first draft of Carter's announcement speech, 20 November 1974, folder "Announcement speech, 9/74–12/74," box 1, CCEJC, JCL; Stuart Eizenstat to Jimmy Carter, Hamilton Jordan, Jody Powell, and Jerry Rafshoon, 26 November 1974, ibid.
29. Jimmy Carter, third draft of Carter's announcement speech, 1 December 1974, folder "Announcement speech, 9/74–12/74," box 1, CCEJC, JCL.
30. Jody Powell, notes to Jimmy Carter on third draft of Carter's announcement speech, [December 1974], folder "Announcement speech, 9/74–12/74," box 1, CCEJC, JCL.
31. Stroud, *How Jimmy Won,* 183.
32. Carter speech, 12 December 1974.
33. Wayne King, "Georgia's Gov. Carter Enters Race for President," *NYT,* 13 December 1974; Eric McCrossen, "Jimmy Carter Hits Bureaucracy," *Albuquerque Journal,* 26 January 1975; John McCormally, "Jimmy Carter for President," *Burlington (IA) Hawk Eye,* 20 December 1974.
34. Roscoe Drummond, "Meet Governor Carter," *Cincinnati Enquirer,* 21 December 1974; "'A Man Who' Named Carter," *Red Wing (MN) Republican Eagle,* 17 December 1974.
35. AP, "Carter Accuses Senators of Violating Law's Spirit," *NYT,* 16 December 1974.
36. Rick Hutcheson to Hamilton Jordan et al., 23 July 1975, folder "Memoranda, July–August 1975," box 411, CCEJC, JCL; Carter campaign, weekly report of contributions by state, 25 August 1975, ibid.
37. Andrew Young, telegram to *Village Voice,* 9 January 1976, folder "Jimmy Carter's Position Papers," box 291, CCEJC, JCL.
38. Knox to Jimmy Carter and Hamilton Jordan, 7 May 1975, folder "Memoranda, March–June 1975," box 411, CCEJC, JCL.
39. Bourne, *Jimmy Carter,* 275–276.
40. Stu Eizenstat and Issues Group to Carter, re: The economy, 2 October 1974, folder "Economics, 6/74–11/74," box 11, CCEJC, JCL.
41. Jimmy Carter, press release, statement on full employment, 1 April 1976, folder "Issues Statements," box 410, CCEJC, JCL; "Jimmy Carter on the U.S. Economy and Business: A *Fortune* Interview," *Fortune,* May 1976, 84–86.
42. Jimmy Carter, press release, issue statement on taxes, 3 October 1975, folder "Issues Statements," box 410, CCEJC, JCL; Jimmy Carter, issue position statements, 15 March 1976, ibid.

43. Jimmy Carter, press release on foreign policy, 28 May 1975, folder "Issues Statements," box 410, CCEJC, JCL; Carter, issue position statements, 15 March 1976. For support for Israel among liberals, see Judith M. Hughes and H. Stuart Hughes, "A Clear and Present Commitment," *Nation,* 26 April 1975, 486.
44. Carter, press release on foreign policy, 28 May 1975. For similar themes in an earlier speech by Senator Ted Kennedy, see Edward M. Kennedy, address at University of California, Berkeley, 11 April 1975, folder "Foreign Policy, 9/74–4/75," box 16, CCEJC, JCL.
45. Leslie H. Gelb, "Carter's Foreign Policies in Liberal Democratic Vein," *NYT,* 7 July 1976. For liberal views of foreign policy in the mid-1970s, see Judith M. Hughes and H. Stuart Hughes, "Notes for a Foreign Policy," *Nation,* 7 June 1975, 691.
46. Rick Hutcheson, notes from meeting with field staff, 17–18 June 1975, folder "Memoranda, March–June 1975," box 411, CCEJC, JCL; Godfrey Sperling Jr., "'Stop-Carter' Move under Way," *CSM,* 2 February 1976; Carter, press release, issue statement on taxes, 3 October 1975; Jimmy Carter, press release, issue statement on employment, 9 September 1975, folder "Issues Statements," box 410, CCEJC, JCL.
47. Anderson, "Peanut Farmer for President"; Carter, issue position statements, 15 March 1976; "Julian Bond Recalls: Carter Pushed for Integration Busing Ban," *Milwaukee Star-Times,* 8 April 1976.
48. John Dennis, "Jimmy Carter's Fierce Campaign," *Nation,* 17 May 1975, 595; Robert Healy, "Carter Ready to Run Country," *Boston Globe,* 14 March 1975; Anderson, "Peanut Farmer for President."
49. Paul Lutzker and Rick Hutcheson, DNC, Analysis of Recent Polls, 8 January 1975, folder "Poll Analysis," box 412, CCEJC, JPL.
50. Cambridge Reports Inc., prepared for Rafshoon Advertising, "Jimmy Carter: A Political Analysis," May 1975, folder "Political Analysis of Jimmy Carter," box 33, Jody Powell Papers, JCL; NBC News poll of NH voters, 16 September 1975, folder "Poll Analysis," box 412, CCEJC, JCL; "2 Democrats Low on Funds for '76," *NYT,* 15 October 1975.
51. Hamilton Jordan to Jimmy Carter, 5 July 1975, folder "Memoranda, July–August 1975," box 411, CCEJC, JCL; Chris Brown, political strategy memo to Carter campaign, [7 September 1975], folder "Field Reports, Primaries, 1975," box 409, ibid.
52. Hutcheson to Jordan et al., 23 July 1975.
53. Tim Kraft to Hamilton Jordan, re: Iowa campaign, 28 August 1975, folder "Field Reports, Primaries, 1975," box 409, CCEJC, JCL; David Frye to Marc Cutright et al., field report for midwestern states, 14 October 1975, ibid.; R. W. Apple Jr., "Carter Appears to Hold a Solid Lead in Iowa as the Campaign's First Test Approaches," *NYT,* 27 October 1975.
54. Mark Pinsky, "Sanford: Everyone's Second Choice," *Nation,* 22 February 1975, 213; Christopher Lydon, "Carter's Support in South Is Broad," *NYT,* 2 November 1975.

55. Ezra Mintz to Jerry Rafshoon, re: Campaign strategy, 19 December 1974, folder "Campaign Planning and Strategy, 12/74–5/76," box 2, CCEJC, JCL; Knox to Carter and Jordan, 7 May 1975; Hutcheson to Jordan et al., 23 July 1975.
56. Knox to Carter and Jordan, 7 May 1975.
57. John Dillin, "A New Political Style Erodes Old South Ways," *CSM,* 16 April 1976.
58. Theodore C. Sorensen, draft basic campaign speech for Jimmy Carter in primaries, 31 January 1976, folder "Campaign Planning and Strategy, 12/74–5/76," box 2, CCEJC, JCL.

4. THE REPUBLICANS

1. There are many studies of Goldwater's coalition and the Arizona senator's relationship to a broader conservative movement; they include Rick Perlstein, *Before the Storm: Barry Goldwater and the Unmaking of the American Consensus* (New York: Hill & Wang, 2001); Jonathan M. Schoenwald, *A Time for Choosing: The Rise of Modern American Conservatism* (New York: Oxford University Press, 2001); Donald T. Critchlow, *The Conservative Ascendancy: How the GOP Right Made Political History* (Cambridge, MA: Harvard University Press, 2007), 1–76. Although liberal Republicans of the late 1960s and 1970s viewed Goldwater's campaign as a disaster, recent historians have generally seen it as a harbinger of the party's conservative future. See, for example, Mary C. Brennan, *Turning Right in the Sixties: The Conservative Capture of the GOP* (Chapel Hill: University of North Carolina Press, 1995). For liberal Republicans, see Nicol C. Rae, *The Decline and Fall of the Liberal Republicans: From 1952 to the Present* (New York: Oxford University Press, 1989).
2. For a study of Nixon's pragmatic, centrist Republicanism, see Robert Mason, *Richard Nixon and the Quest for a New Majority* (Chapel Hill: University of North Carolina Press, 2004).
3. For conservative discontent and factionalism in the Republican Party in the early 1970s, see Critchlow, *Conservative Ascendancy,* 77–152.
4. Lou Cannon, "Old, New Agnew Seen Keyed to Top Job," *WP,* 5 November 1972; George Gallup, "Agnew, Reagan Top GOP List," *WP,* 29 April 1973.
5. Rae, *Decline and Fall of the Liberal Republicans,* 93; "Agnew Acts to Stop Incendiary Talks in Maryland," *NYT,* 31 July 1967. For Agnew's early career as a liberal Rockefeller Republican, see Justin P. Coffey, "Spiro T. Agnew: The Decline of Moderates and Rise of the Republican Right," in *The Right Side of the Sixties: Reexamining Conservatism's Decade of Transformation,* ed. Laura Jane Gifford and Daniel K. Williams (New York: Palgrave Macmillan, 2012), 243–259.
6. Lou Cannon, "Agnew, Still Nixon's Man, Looks toward '76 Succession," *WP,* 20 January 1973; Don Fulsom, *Nixon's Darkest Secrets: The Inside Story of America's Most Troubled President* (New York: St. Martin's Press,

2012), 170–171; George H. Gallup, *The Gallup Poll: Public Opinion, 1972–1977*, 2 vols. (Wilmington, DE: Scholarly Resources, 1978), 1:115.

7. "A Chronology of Events in Agnew Case," *NYT*, 11 October 1973; James M. Naughton, "Judge Orders Fine, 3 Years' Probation," *NYT*, 11 October 1973.
8. Mason, *Richard Nixon and the Quest for a New Majority*, 130; John Herbers, "Nixon Reported to Favor Connally in '76," *NYT*, 31 January 1973; James Reston, "Nixon and Connally," *NYT*, 21 September 1973; Rowland Evans and Robert Novak, "John Connally: Slipping on the Road to the White House," *WP*, 3 October 1973.
9. Robert D. McFadden, "Rockefeller Is Dead at 70," *NYT*, 27 January 1979; Jeffrey Frank, "Big Spender: Nelson Rockefeller's Grand Ambitions," *New Yorker*, 13 October 2014.
10. Richard Norton Smith, *On His Own Terms: A Life of Nelson Rockefeller* (New York: Random House, 2014), 363–365, 403–409, 517–518, 575–607, 629–634; Lou Cannon, "Rocky Is Welcomed by Southern GOP," *WP*, 8 December 1973.
11. *Human Events* editorial quoted in David S. Broder, "The New 'Centrist' Rockefeller," *WP*, 27 January 1974; Gallup, *Gallup Poll*, 1:115, 173, 230, 242.
12. Joel D. Weisman, "Percy, in '76 Move, Scores Others," *WP*, 9 February 1974; AP, "$135,000 Is Raised by Percy," *WP*, 22 March 1974.
13. For Mathias's civil rights record, see Adam Clymer, "Charles Mathias, Former U.S. Senator, Dies at 87," *NYT*, 25 January 2010.
14. Rae, *Decline and Fall of the Liberal Republicans*, 109–110.
15. Douglas Martin, "Edward W. Brooke III, 95, Senate Pioneer, Is Dead," *NYT*, 3 January 2015; "Random Notes from All Over: Of Bomfog, Moat and Goveclop," *NYT*, 25 May 1964; Rae, *Decline and Fall of the Liberal Republicans*, 196–204.
16. These statistics are based on a biographical analysis of the senators listed in the Americans for Democratic Action's 1972 voting record, http://www.adaction.org/media/votingrecords/1972.pdf. The ADA rated members of Congress based on their legislative voting records; this was the most widely used method of determining how liberal or conservative a politician was in the 1970s. Those with higher ratings on the 100-point scale were considered more liberal.
17. Jacob K. Javits, "GOP Survival Linked to Progressive Broad-Based Party," 26 April 1975, folder "Political Affairs—Ford (1)," box 36, PHF, GRFL.
18. ADA's 1972 voting record.
19. Javits, "GOP Survival Linked to Progressive Broad-Based Party."
20. For Reagan's early political career and activities during the 1970s, see Steven F. Hayward, *The Age of Reagan: The Fall of the Old Liberal Order, 1964–1980* (Roseville, CA: Forum, 2001); Rick Perlstein, *The Invisible Bridge: The Fall of Nixon and the Rise of Reagan* (New York: Simon & Schuster, 2014); Lou Cannon, *Governor Reagan: His Rise to Power* (New

York: Public Affairs, 2003). For a study of the conservative coalition that elected Reagan in the 1960s, see Lisa McGirr, *Suburban Warriors: The Origins of the New American Right* (Princeton, NJ: Princeton University Press, 2001).

21. Lou Cannon, "GOP Hopefuls Stir," *WP*, 4 November 1974.
22. Ronald Reagan, speech to Young Americans for Freedom (YAF), San Francisco, 20 July 1974, folder "Tony Dolan Files [RR Speeches], July 20, 1974, YAF, San Francisco," box 874, RRPC, RRPL.
23. John P. Sears to Majetta Bozeth, 9 September 1975, folder "Individual Responses to Issues Letters (Misc. Subjects)," box 9, CFR, Hoover.
24. Peter D. Hannaford, memo re: Dick Wirthlin luncheon, 3 July 1974, folder "Correspondence, 1974–2000," box 1, Peter Hannaford Papers, Hoover; Reagan speech to YAF, 20 July 1974.
25. Cannon, "GOP Hopefuls Stir"; Reagan staff, "Ronald Reagan: A Program for the Future," 4 November 1974, folder "Office of Ronald Reagan—Reagan for President—Miscellaneous, 1974–1976 (1/4)," box 573, RRPC, RRPL.
26. Lou Cannon, "Support for Reagan Grows in South," *WP*, 18 November 1973; G. Spruce McCain to Ronald Reagan, 24 July 1975, folder "Correspondence—Incoming—No Responses (Miscellaneous)," box 7, CFR, Hoover; Ronald M. Joyce to Ronald Reagan, 28 July 1975, ibid.
27. McCain to Reagan, 24 July 1975; Bill Vaughn to Ronald Reagan, [July or August 1975], folder "Correspondence—Incoming—No Responses (Miscellaneous)," box 7, CFR, Hoover.
28. DMI, "A Fourth Survey of Republican Voters in New Hampshire for the Citizens for Reagan," 18 February 1976, box 179c, RRPC, RRPL.
29. Alfred M. Skolnik and Sophie R. Dales, "Social Welfare Expenditures, 1950–1975," *Social Security Bulletin*, January 1976, 3.
30. Erven J. Geeck to Ronald Reagan, 10 June 1975, folder "Correspondence—Incoming—No Responses (Miscellaneous)," box 7, CFR, Hoover.
31. For examples of correspondence from Reagan supporters who also supported Wallace, see Joseph Bazzeghin to Reagan, 29 December 1974, folder "Misc. Correspondence—Jan.–June 1975," box 7, CFR, Hoover; Vaughn to Reagan, [July or August 1975]; Lloyd O. Chase to Reagan, 28 March 1975, folder "Michigan, 1975–76," box 7, CFR, Hoover.
32. Karel A. Smith Jr. to Ronald Reagan, 21 August 1975, folder "Correspondence—Incoming—No Responses (Miscellaneous)," box 7, CFR, Hoover; William A. Rusher to Ronald Reagan, 7 October 1975, folder "Rusher Letter Re: Third Party Comm.," box 13, ibid.; Ronald Reagan to H. R. Garvey, 24 June 1975, folder "Misc. Correspondence—Jan.–June 1975," box 7, ibid.
33. Jules Witcover, *Marathon: The Pursuit of the Presidency, 1972–1976* (New York: Viking Press, 1977), 66; Jeff Bell, memo to Ronald Reagan, 3 August 1974, folder "Bell Memos to RR, 1974 (GRF's VP Selection)," box 4,

CFR, Hoover; R. W. Apple Jr., "'76 Hopes Revive for Gov. Reagan," *NYT,* 13 October 1974.

34. Lou Cannon, "'76 Bid Hinted by President," *WP,* 13 August 1974; US Senate, "Vetoes: Summary of Bills Vetoed, 1789–Present," https://www.senate.gov/reference/Legislation/Vetoes/vetoCounts.htm. Ford's vetoes included forty-eight regular vetoes and eighteen pocket vetoes.
35. Lou Cannon, "Amnesty and Health Plan Stir Disenchantment," *WP,* 26 August 1974.
36. Smith, *On His Own Terms,* 643–645; Laura Kalman, *Right Star Rising: A New Politics, 1974–1980* (New York: W. W. Norton, 2010), 8–9.
37. Ted Kennedy to Gerald Ford, 20 August 1974, folder "PL/Rockefeller, Nelson," box 16, WHCF, GRFL; Richard A. Viguerie, *The New Right: We're Ready to Lead* (Falls Church, VA: Viguerie, 1981), 50; Linda Charlton, "A Conservative to Oppose Rockefeller in Senate Vote," *NYT,* 18 October 1974; Ken Cole, memo to Gerald Ford, re: Abortion, 6 September 1974, folder "Welfare—Abortions," box 51, PHF, GRFL; Christopher Lydon, "Ford Gets Recommendations for a Vice President," *NYT,* 14 August 1974.
38. Linda Charlton, "Rockefeller Woos Southern G.O.P.," *NYT,* 29 August 1974; Linda Charlton, "Goldwater Now Undecided on Rockefeller Nomination," *NYT,* 25 October 1974.
39. Smith, *On His Own Terms,* 647–658.
40. Kalman, *Right Star Rising,* 6–8; Gallup, *Gallup Poll,* 1:351; Jeffrey M. Jones, "Gerald Ford Retrospective," Gallup News Service, 29 December 2006, http://www.gallup.com/poll/23995/gerald-ford-retrospective.aspx; Yanek Mieczkowski, *Gerald Ford and the Challenges of the 1970s* (Lexington: University Press of Kentucky, 2005), 47.
41. Gallup, *Gallup Poll,* 1:354–357; John Robert Greene, *The Presidency of Gerald R. Ford* (Lawrence: University Press of Kansas, 1995), 59–64; Mieczkowski, *Gerald Ford and the Challenges of the 1970s,* 31–37, 47–55. See also Scott Kaufman, *Ambition, Pragmatism, and Party: A Political Biography of Gerald R. Ford* (Lawrence: University Press of Kansas, 2017), 177–195, 264–266.
42. Kimberly Amadeo, "U.S. GDP by Year Compared to Recessions and Events," *The Balance,* 1 August 2017, https://www.thebalance.com/us-gdp-by-year-3305543; Edwin L. Dale Jr., "Inflation: Now It Really Is the No. 1 Problem," *NYT,* 18 August 1974.
43. Gallup, *Gallup Poll,* 1:360, 365–366; Donald Rumsfeld, *When the Center Held: Gerald Ford and the Rescue of the American Presidency* (New York: Free Press, 2018), 63–70; Dale, "Inflation."
44. "US Inflation Rate by Year," http://www.multpl.com/inflation/table; Gallup, *Gallup Poll,* 1:415, 2:805, 887.
45. DNC, "Issue Analysis: Federal Government Budget Policy," 1976, folder "Democratic National Committee (DNC), Issues Analysis—Target '76 Publications," box 11, CCEJC, JCL; "Big Business Has a Friend in the

White House," Carter-Mondale Campaign Daily Bulletin, 22 September 1976, folder "Internal Memos [1]," box 279, ibid.

46. Cannon, "GOP Hopefuls Stir"; "The US Federal Budget," Inside Gov, http://federal-budget.insidegov.com/.
47. "US Federal Budget," Inside Gov.
48. President Ford Committee campaign plan, 29 August 1975, folder "Campaign Strategy—August 1975 (1)," box A1, PFC, GRFL.
49. Leo Thorsness to Bo Callaway, re: Congressman Bob Shuster (PA), 17 December 1975, folder "Pennsylvania," box 5, Rogers Morton Files, GRFL.
50. Stan Parris to Bo Callaway, re: Congressman Steve Symms (ID), 8 December 1975, folder "Idaho," box 4, Rogers Morton Files, GRFL.
51. Gallup, *Gallup Poll,* 1:461, 2:756.
52. Gallup, *Gallup Poll,* 2:806; President Ford Committee, Guide to Primary Campaign Strategy in Colorado, [April 1976], folder "Colorado," box 4, Rogers Morton Files, GRFL; Foster Chanock to Mike Duval, re: Polling information on foreign policy/national defense, 1 October 1976, folder "Polling Information," box 16, MRD, GRFL.
53. Catherine E. Rymph, *Republican Women: Feminism and Conservatism from Suffrage through the Rise of the New Right* (Chapel Hill: University of North Carolina Press, 2006), 188–238. For more on Schlafly's campaign, see Donald T. Critchlow, *Phyllis Schlafly and Grassroots Conservatism: A Woman's Crusade* (Princeton, NJ: Princeton University Press, 2005); Marjorie J. Spruill, *Divided We Stand: The Battle over Women's Rights and Family Values that Polarized American Politics* (New York: Bloomsbury, 2017).
54. UPI, "Betty Ford Would Accept 'an Affair' by Daughter," *NYT,* 11 August 1975; "Monthly Picketing Set at White House," *National Right to Life News,* December 1975, 1.
55. UPI, "Betty Ford Would Accept 'an Affair' by Daughter"; Bo Callaway to Sheila Rabb Weidenfeld, 18 September 1975, folder "Ford, Betty," box A2, PFC, GRFL; Leo Thorsness to Bo Callaway, 8 March 1976, folder "California," box 4, Rogers Morton Files, GRFL; Daniel K. Williams, *God's Own Party: The Making of the Christian Right* (New York: Oxford University Press, 2010), 123–124.
56. Bo Callaway and Stu Spencer to Rogers Morton and Dick Cheney, 11 February 1976, folder "New Hampshire," box 5, Rogers Morton Files, GRFL.
57. Lyn Nofziger to Joseph J. Tribble, 20 August 1975, folder "Lyn Nofziger," box 10, CFR, Hoover; Citizens for Reagan, fund-raising totals, folder "Election Law," box 102, ibid.; Lyn Nofziger to David LeRoy (Republican Congressional Committee), description of Citizens for Reagan, [24 October 1975], folder "Formation of CFR, Announcement of," box 9, ibid.
58. "Reagan's Team: A California Touch," *U.S. News and World Report,* May 31, 1976, 25; Witcover, *Marathon,* 374; Craig Shirley, *Reagan's Revolution:*

The Untold Story of the Campaign that Started It All (Nashville, TN: Nelson Current, 2005), 23–24.

59. David Keene to Ronald Reagan, re: Florida briefing, 29 October 1975, folder "Florida," box 4, CFR, Hoover; David Keene to John Sears, Report on Southern Campaign Strategy, [October 1975], ibid.; "An Easy Rider on the Campaign Trail," *New York Sunday News*, 9 May 1976; Delegate Picture, n.d. [1975], folder "Office of Ronald Reagan—Reagan for President—Miscellaneous, 1974–1976 (2/4)," box 573, RRPC, RRPL; George F. Will, "The Danger of Underestimating Reagan," *WP*, 22 August 1975.
60. Ronald Reagan, "Tax Cuts Spur Inflation," 24 January 1975, folder "Ronald Reagan File—Writings and Speeches—Writings—Newspapers Columns—Copley News Service, 1975 Jan.–Feb.," box 8, Peter Hannaford Papers, Hoover; John P. Sears to W. F. Hudson, 30 September 1975, folder "Individual Responses to Issues Letters (Misc. Subjects)," box 9, CFR, Hoover.
61. Paul Laxalt, direct mail on behalf of Citizens for Reagan, n.d. [ca. 1975–1976], folder "Julian Gingold," box 9, CFR, Hoover.
62. Clarence E. Warner, direct mail on behalf of Oklahoma Citizens for Reagan, 31 July 1975, folder "Reagan, Ronald," box A4, Callaway Subject Files, PFC, GRFL.
63. Roger Stone, direct mail from Citizens for Reagan, n.d. [ca. 1975–1976], folder "Reagan—Current Clippings," box 53, CFR, Hoover; Youth for Reagan brochure, "Reagan Cares about What Young America Thinks," n.d. [ca. 1976], folder "Leaflets and Pamphlets," box 9, ibid.
64. Ronald Reagan, "Ronald Reagan Champions Gun Ownership," *Guns & Ammo*, September 1975, 34; Republican Party Platform of 1972, http://www.presidency.ucsb.edu/ws/index.php?pid=25842; Alan Gottlieb, direct mail from Sportsmen for Reagan, n.d. [ca. late 1975 or early 1976], folder "Solicitations," box 13, CFR, Hoover.
65. Transcript of Ronald Reagan's interview with George Otis, n.d. [ca. 1976], folder "Hannaford/CA HQ—Religion [Interview Excerpts]," box 49, RRPC, RRPL; Donald H. Gill, "Will the Bible Get Back into School?" *Eternity*, May 1964, 9; David Keene to Ronald Reagan, 2 July 1976, folder "Hannaford/CA HQ—General—[Convention]—Delegate Memos, 1976 (1/2)," box 39, RRPC, RRPL.
66. For Reagan's views on abortion in the late 1960s and early 1970s, see Daniel K. Williams, *Defenders of the Unborn: The Pro-Life Movement before* Roe v. Wade (New York: Oxford University Press, 2016), 80–84, 230–233.
67. Lyn Nofziger, memo to Ronald Reagan on abortion, 2 October 1975, folder "Abortion," box 1, CFR, Hoover.
68. Jeff Bell, state briefing memo for Ronald Reagan, [fall 1974], folder "State Briefing Memos," box 53, CFR, Hoover; transcript of town meeting with Ronald Reagan, Manchester, NH, 20 November 1975, folder "Speeches—Campaign," box 103, ibid.

69. Alice Hartle, "Reagan Likes HLA, Gives Views on Abortion, Euthanasia," *National Right to Life News,* December 1975, 1. Examples of pro-life correspondence with Reagan include Barbara Latine to Citizens for Reagan, [July 1976], folder "Correspondence—Misc.," box 7, CFR, Hoover; Fran Watson to John Sears, 30 July 1976, folder "Endorsement of RR by Ellen McCormick, 30 July 1976," box 10, ibid.
70. Lyn Nofziger to Jan McCoy, 17 February 1976, folder "1976 Correspondence—Jan.–Feb.," box 101, CFR, Hoover.
71. Transcript of town meeting with Reagan, Manchester, NH, 20 November 1975; Reagan campaign aides, briefing on questions likely to be asked by the press at announcement of campaign, 20 November 1975, folder "Announcement of Candidacy, 11/75," box 1, CFR, Hoover.
72. Transcript of town meeting with Reagan, Manchester, NH, 20 November 1975; transcript of press conference with Ronald Reagan, Charlotte, NC, 21 November 1975, folder "Speech Files (Garrick)—1975 (Copies of press conferences and statements) (2/2)," box 431, RRPC, RRPL; Ronald Reagan, letter to Republican delegates from Connecticut, [July 1976], folder "Hannaford/CA HQ—1976 Campaign—Delegates—Other States (6/6)," box 36, ibid.
73. F. B. McKissick to Rogers Morton, 18 June 1976, folder "North Carolina," box F17, PFC, GRFL; Simeon Booker, "Ticker Tape U.S.A.," *Jet,* 11 September 1975, 10.
74. Lyn Nofziger to Simeon Booker, 24 September 1975, folder "Individual Responses to Issues Letters (Misc. Subjects)," box 9, CFR, Hoover.
75. "Special *Ebony* Poll: Black Elected Officials' Choices for U.S. President," *Ebony,* May 1976; Ohio poll, 30 January 1976, folder "Ohio," box 5, Rogers Morton Files, GRFL.
76. "Governor Reagan Years Assessed," *Los Angeles Metropolitan Gazette,* 5 December 1974.
77. Transcript of town meeting with Reagan, Manchester, NH, 20 November 1975.
78. Ronald Reagan, campaign speech, 20–21 November 1975, folder "Announcement," box 102, CFR, Hoover; Ronald Reagan, speech announcing presidential candidacy, Washington, DC, 20 November 1975, folder "Campaign Materials," box 4, ibid.
79. Transcript of press conference with Ronald Reagan, Washington, DC, 20 November 1975, folder "Speech Files (Garrick)—1975 (Copies of press conferences and statements) (1/2)," box 431, RRPC, RRPL; President Ford Committee, response to Reagan's announcement, 20 November 1975, folder "Reagan, Ronald," box A4, Callaway Subject Files, PFC, GRFL.
80. Joseph Albright, "Reagan's Swing to the Center," *San Francisco Chronicle,* 21 November 1975; Douglas Kiker, NBC, transcript of remarks on Reagan's announcement of candidacy, 20 November 1975, and Terry Drinkwater, CBS television commentary on Reagan's declaration of candidacy,

20 November 1975, folder "PL/Reagan, Ronald 8/9/75–11/30/75," box 16, WHCF, GRFL.

81. Fred Slight to Bo Callaway, re: Gallup poll on GOP nomination preference, 31 March 1976, folder "Pres. Ford Committee: General," box 3, Rogers Morton Files, GRFL; Dave Keene to John Sears, [October 1975], folder "Florida," box 4, CFR, Hoover.
82. President Ford Committee, campaign plan, 29 August 1975, folder "Campaign Strategy—August 1975 (1)," box A1, Callaway Subject Files, PFC, GRFL.
83. Max Friedersdorf, memo to Gerald Ford, 11 June 1975, folder "Political Affairs—Ford (1)," box 36, PHF, GRFL.
84. Philip Shabecoff, "Maryland Senator Might Seek G.O.P. Presidential Candidacy," *NYT,* 31 October 1975; R. W. Apple Jr., "Little Time Remains for a Challenge on the Left: Ford May Be the G.O.P.'s Only 'Liberal' Alternative," *NYT,* 18 January 1976.
85. Bo Callaway to Don Rumsfeld, 14 August 1975, folder "Rumsfeld, Don," box A4, Callaway Subject Files, PFC, GRFL; Carolyn Booth to Gwen Anderson and Mimi Austin, 8 January 1976, folder "Spencer, Stu," ibid.
86. Transcript of PBS TV interview with Barry Goldwater, 30 September 1975, folder "Misc.," box 10, CFR, Hoover; Barry Goldwater to Laurence Schaeffer, 7 April 1975, folder "Goldwater," box 9, ibid.
87. Bo Callaway to Don Rumsfeld, re: Meeting with Barry Goldwater, 23 July 1975, folder "Rumsfeld, Don," box A4, Callaway Subject Files, PFC, GRFL.
88. Callaway to Rumsfeld, 23 July 1975; Allan Cromley, "Bo's Candor Incredible," *Oklahoman,* 27 July 1975; Fred Barnes, "Is Divorce the Next Step for Ford and Rockefeller?" *Washington Star,* 25 July 1975; Rowland Evans and Robert Novak, "Deepening the Rocky Dilemma," *WP,* 28 July 1975.
89. *American Political Report,* 31 October 1975; UPI, "Goldwater Says Rockefeller Decision Will Hurt Reagan," *Orlando (FL) Sentinel,* 5 November 1975.
90. See, for instance, David Gergen, "President Ford: 10 Reasons Why He Should Carry the GOP Banner in November," 11 June 1976, folder "Political Affairs—Ford (6)," box 37, PHF, GRFL.
91. "Company Presidents Assess Key Issues in 1976 Presidential Campaign," *Gallagher Presidents' Report,* 3 September 1975; M. S. Forbes Jr., "Can Gerald Ford Avoid Political Extinction?" *Forbes,* 15 July 1976, 17; Justin Dart to Leonard K. Firestone, 19 May 1975, folder "Office of Ronald Reagan—Reagan for President—Miscellaneous, 1974–1976 (2/4)," box 573, RRPC, RRPL.
92. President Ford Committee, outline of campaign strategy, April 1975, folder "Campaign Strategy—April 1975," box A1, Callaway Subject Files, PFC, GRFL; Christopher Lydon, "Jimmy Carter's Dark-Horse Campaign Adds Gains in New England to Those in the South and Iowa," *NYT,* 3 November 1975; Bo Callaway, memo regarding discussion with Donald

Rumsfeld, 31 July 1975, folder "Rumsfeld, Don," box A4, Callaway Subject Files, PFC, GRFL; President Ford Committee, finance committee meeting minutes, 8 July 1975, folder "Finance (1)," box A2, ibid.; David Packard, General Strategy for Fund-raising for the President Ford Committee, 15 August 1975, folder "Finance (2)," ibid.; President Ford Committee, financial report showing current level of fund-raising for all candidates through 30 September 1975, folder "Advisory Committee, 11/17/75," box A3, ibid. Other presidential campaigns, by contrast, entrusted their fund-raising to much less well-heeled individuals. The Carter campaign's finance chair was Alabama attorney Morris Dees, founder of the Southern Poverty Law Center. In the Reagan campaign, Senator Paul Laxalt handled much of the fund-raising.

93. George Van Cleve to Dave Gergen, re: Voter turnout in the remaining GOP presidential primaries, 15 April 1976, folder "Pres. Ford Committee: General," box 3, Rogers Morton Files, GRFL.

5. THE DEMOCRATIC PRIMARIES

1. Christopher Lydon, "Jimmy Carter's Dark-Horse Campaign Adds Gains in New England to Those in the South and Iowa," *NYT,* 3 November 1975; Andrew J. Glass, "10 Democrats Off, Running," *AC,* 16 November 1975; R. W. Apple Jr., "Democratic Chiefs Beginning to Rate Presidential Rivals," *NYT,* 12 January 1976; James T. Wooten, "Shapp Drops out as '76 Contender," *NYT,* 13 March 1976; Wayne King, "Sanford Is Leaving Presidential Race; 'Realities' Are Cited," *NYT,* 22 January 1976; Christopher Lydon, "Humphrey, at 30% in Poll, Widens Democratic Lead," *NYT,* 14 December 1975.
2. Iric Nathanson, "The Final Chapter: Hubert Humphrey Returns to Public Life," MinnPost, 26 May 2011, https://www.minnpost.com/politics-policy/2011/05/final-chapter-hubert-humphrey-returns-public-life; Arnold A. Offner, *Hubert Humphrey: The Conscience of the Country* (New Haven, CT: Yale University Press, 2018), 375–380.
3. "Special *Ebony* Poll: Black Elected Officials' Choices for U.S. President," *Ebony,* May 1976, 88–90.
4. Jules Witcover, *Marathon: The Pursuit of the Presidency, 1972–1976* (New York: Viking Press, 1977), 297–298, 310–316; Myra MacPherson, "Humphrey Gamble: Senator Takes to Sidelines in Long-Shot Try for President," *WP,* 14 March 1976.
5. Warren Weaver Jr., "Shriver Enters the '76 Presidential Race," *NYT,* 21 September 1975; Lucinda Franks, "Shriver Stressing 'Kennedy Connection,'" *NYT,* 31 December 1975. See also Scott Stossel, *Sarge: The Life and Times of Sargent Shriver* (Washington, DC: Smithsonian Books, 2004).
6. Stossel, *Sarge,* 596; Lucinda Franks, "Shriver Evokes Warm Memory for Poor Blacks in Mississippi," *NYT,* 24 January 1976.
7. Colman McCarthy, "Sargent Shriver, a Loved and Loving Man," *National Catholic Reporter,* 19 January 2011, https://www.ncronline.org/news

/sargent-shriver-loved-and-loving-man; Shriver for President, press release, "Shriver Announces Comprehensive Program to Restore the Authority of American Families," 15 January 1976, folder "Shriver, Sargent, 11/75–9/76," box 27, CCEJC, JCL; Sargent Shriver, "Restoring the Authorities of American Families: A New Focus for National Policy," 15 January 1976, ibid.

8. For a discussion of the contrast between the rights-based liberalism of the 1970s and the breadwinner liberalism of earlier decades, see Robert O. Self, *All in the Family: The Realignment of American Democracy since the 1960s* (New York: Hill & Wang, 2012), 17–46.
9. Franks, "Shriver Stressing 'Kennedy Connection'"; Shriver for President press release, "Shriver Announces Comprehensive Program to Restore the Authority of American Families."
10. Franks, "Shriver Stressing 'Kennedy Connection.'"
11. R. W. Apple Jr., "Bayh Runs for President," *NYT,* 22 October 1975; Robert Sherrill, "Birch Bayh Isn't a Household Word—Yet," *NYT,* 5 February 1970; Jack W. Germond, "Indiana's Birch Bayh as a Presidential Contender—Four Years Later," *Boston Globe,* 6 August 1975.
12. Bayh for President, campaign brochure, [fall 1975?], folder "Bayh, Birch," box G15, PFC, GRFL.
13. Sherrill, "Birch Bayh Isn't a Household Word—Yet"; Charles Mohr, "Bayh's Main Premise: That He's Electable," *NYT,* 24 December 1975; Charles Mohr, "How the Bayh Race Deteriorated," *NYT,* 4 March 1976; Jules Witcover, "Bayh Stressing His Experience," *WP,* 29 January 1976.
14. Bill Peterson, "Bayh: Toward an Indiana Camelot," *WP,* 8 February 1976.
15. Joseph Lelyveld, "TV Spot Ads Selling Presidential Hopefuls in Primaries," *NYT,* 5 February 1976; David Schultz, "Demo Placing Third Will Breathe Easier," *AC,* 22 February 1976.
16. Daniel K. Williams, *Defenders of the Unborn: The Pro-Life Movement before* Roe v. Wade (New York: Oxford University Press, 2016), 186–187, 219–229.
17. Edward M. Kennedy to Mrs. Edward J. Barshak, 3 August 1971, folder 31, "MORAL (Mass. Organization to Repeal Abortion Laws), 1970–1974," box 2, Patricia Gold Papers, Schlesinger Library, Harvard University; Stuart Auerbach, "Kennedy Backs Abortion Aid," *WP,* 11 April 1975; Williams, *Defenders of the Unborn,* 220–225; Stephen Wermiel, "Kennedy Leads Defeat of Anti-Abortion Provision," *Boston Globe,* 11 April 1975; AP, "Jackson Abortion Stand Is Disputed by His Wife," *NYT,* 11 March 1976; David Morrison, "Abortion Issue Faces Carter," *AC,* 1 April 1976.
18. Williams, *Defenders of the Unborn,* 171, 212–219; Gallup poll on constitutional amendment to prohibit abortions, 18 March 1976, in Gallup Organization, *America's Opinion on Abortion, 1962–1992* (Washington, DC: Gallup, 1992). For opposition to abortion among African Americans in the 1970s, see Michael W. Combs and Susan Welch, "Blacks, Whites,

and Attitudes toward Abortion," *Public Opinion Quarterly* 46 (1982): 510–520.

19. Rachelle Patterson, "Citizens for Life Replace Catholic Church as Leader in Mass. Abortion Battle," *Boston Globe,* 15 May 1974; Craig Waters, "Pro Life: Movement or Madness?" *Boston Magazine,* May 1975, 52.
20. Charles Mohr, "Abortion Dispute Troubling Bayh," *NYT,* 12 February 1976; Warren Weaver Jr., "Bayh Accuses Carter of Raising 'False Hopes' of Abortion Foes," *NYT,* 30 January 1976.
21. Jane Gilroy, "Changing the Culture through Politics and Media: Ellen McCormack's 1976 Presidential Campaign," *Life and Learning* 15 (2005): 367. For McCormack's presidential campaign, see Stacie Taranto, *Kitchen Table Politics: Conservative Women and Family Values in New York* (Philadelphia: University of Pennsylvania Press, 2017), 129–161; Stacie Taranto, "Ellen McCormack for President: Politics and an Improbable Path to Passing Anti-Abortion Policy," *Journal of Policy History* 24 (2012): 263–287.
22. Phyllis Bernstein, "Anti-Abortion Candidate for President," *NYT,* 30 November 1975; Douglas Martin, "Ellen McCormack, Anti-Abortion Presidential Candidate, Dies at 84," *NYT,* 29 March 2011; Gilroy, "Changing the Culture through Politics and Media," 357–363; "Delegate Votes in Both Parties," *NYT,* 25 May 1976; Hamilton Jordan to Jimmy Carter, March 1975, folder "Memoranda, March–June 1975," box 411, CCEJC, JCL; Carter campaign, weekly report of contributions by state, 27 June 1975, ibid. In 1976, any candidate who raised $100,000 from twenty different states qualified for both federal matching funds and Secret Service protection; as a result, nineteen individuals (including both the candidates and their spouses) were assigned Secret Service details during the 1976 presidential race. To save funds, the qualifying criteria for Secret Service protection were tightened considerably in the late 1970s, which meant that in the future, no candidate with poll numbers as low as McCormack's would be eligible. Karen De Witt, "Guarding Notables Makes Secret Service Very Public," *NYT,* 14 October 1979.
23. Bernstein, "Anti-Abortion Candidate for President"; George Vecsey, "Antiabortion Candidate Sparks Funding Debate," *NYT,* 9 February 1976.
24. James C. Mohr, "Iowa's Abortion Battles of the Late 1960s and Early 1970s: Long-Term Perspectives and Short-Term Analyses," *Annals of Iowa* 50 (1989): 71–81; Rick Hutcheson to Hamilton Jordan, 17 October 1975, folder "Memoranda, September–December 1975," box 411, CCEJC, JCL.
25. Williams, *Defenders of the Unborn,* 155, 221–223; Dexter Duggan, "Still Waiting for Shriver," *National Right to Life News,* December 1975, 8.
26. "Carter Is First in Iowa Poll," *Atlanta Daily World,* 2 November 1975; Lyn Martin, "Carter Trails 2 in Iowa Poll," *AC,* 24 November 1975; Jules Witcover, "Rivalry Fierce for Iowa Caucus Vote," *WP,* 11 January 1976.
27. Rick Hutcheson to Hamilton Jordan, 6 January 1976, folder "Mem-

oranda, January–March 1976," box 411, CCEJC, JCL; R. W. Apple Jr., "Carter Is Regarded as Getting Big Gain from Iowa Results," *NYT,* 21 January 1976; Tim Kraft to Hamilton Jordan, Jody Powell, and Knox, 24 March 1975, folder "Memorandums [2]," box 30, Jody Powell Papers, JCL.

28. Charles Mohr, "Harris Encouraged by Iowa Support of Campaign," *NYT,* 8 January 1976; Joseph Lelyveld, "Cheap TV Time in Iowa Aids Drives by 3 Democrats," *NYT,* 17 January 1976.
29. Witcover, *Marathon,* 228; R. W. Apple Jr., "Labor Playing Key Role in Iowa as Democrats Vie for Delegates," *NYT,* 16 January 1976.
30. Martin Halpern, "Jimmy Carter and the UAW: Failure of an Alliance," *Presidential Studies Quarterly* 26 (1996): 755–756.
31. Rowland Evans and Robert Novak, "Carter 'Whispers' on Abortion," *WP,* 17 January 1976.
32. Evans and Novak, "Carter 'Whispers' on Abortion"; R. W. Apple Jr., "Carter and Bayh Favored in Iowa," *NYT,* 19 January 1976.
33. Rowland Evans and Robert Novak, "Carter and Abortion," *WP,* 22 January 1976.
34. R. W. Apple Jr., "Carter Defeats Bayh by 2–1 in Iowa Vote," *NYT,* 20 January 1976; Apple, "Carter Is Regarded as Getting Big Gain from Iowa Results"; Jules Witcover, "Iowa Victory Gives Carter Momentum," *WP,* 21 January 1976.
35. Apple, "Carter Is Regarded as Getting Big Gain from Iowa Results"; National Finance Organization of Carter Campaign to State Campaign Coordinators and State Finance Coordinators, 30 January 1976, folder "Memoranda, January–March 1976," box 411, CCEJC, JCL.
36. Robert Reinhold, "Poll Finds Voters Judging '76 Rivals on Personality," *NYT,* 13 February 1976.
37. Helen Dewar, "Carter Dubs Himself Washington 'Outsider,'" *WP,* 20 February 1976; Charles Mohr, "Bayh Finds Carter Posing an Obstacle to His Plans for Victory by a Liberal," *NYT,* 8 February 1976; Weaver, "Bayh Accuses Carter of Raising 'False Hopes' of Abortion Foes."
38. Jules Witcover, "Carter Finds His Words Are Watched," *WP,* 27 January 1976.
39. Evans and Novak, "Carter and Abortion."
40. Computer printout of survey of all delegates to DNC, [June 1976], folder "Delegate Information Computer File [1]," box 206, CCEJC, JCL.
41. Steven Brill, "Jimmy Carter's Pathetic Lies," *Harper's,* March 1976, 77–88; James Fallows, "Turning the Other Chic," *Texas Monthly,* May 1976, 29–30; B. Drummond Ayres Jr., "Carter's Candor Is Becoming an Issue in the Campaign," *NYT,* 26 January 1976.
42. James T. Wooten, "As Carter Moves into the Limelight, He Becomes Highly Visible and Vulnerable," *NYT,* 4 February 1976; Rick Hutcheson to Hamilton Jordan and Jody Powell, re: Image and issues, 2 February 1976, folder "Memoranda, January–March 1976," box 411, CCEJC, JCL.

43. David E. Rosenbaum, "Democrats Mostly Agree, Emphasis Differs," *NYT*, 18 February 1976.
44. Script for Carter television ad, [February–April 1976], folder "Campaign Planning and Strategy, 12/74–5/76," box 2, CCEJC, JCL.
45. Jimmy Carter, speech to National Press Club, 12 December 1974, folder "Issues Statements," box 410, CCEJC, JCL; Tom Wicker, "Jimmy Carter's Appeal," *NYT*, 25 April 1976.
46. Robert Reinhold, "G.O.P. Crossover a Help to Carter," *NYT*, 8 April 1976; Robert Reinhold, "Democrats Found More Conservative than 4 Years Ago," *NYT*, 21 April 1976.
47. Carter campaign, expenditures by state, January–March 1976, folder "Memoranda, April–July 1976," box 411, CCEJC, JCL; Tom Wicker, "Mr. Carter's Formula," *NYT*, 23 January 1976.
48. Author's interview with Dorothy Padgett, 13 August 2018.
49. Richard A. Denny Jr., excerpt from report on Georgians' trip to NH, 4–9 January 1976, 10 January 1976, folder "Georgians for Carter—Ohio and New Hampshire Trip Reports," box 37, Carter Family Papers, JCL.
50. Bill Samuels to Allen Miller, 9 December 1975, folder "Field Reports, Primaries, 1975," box 409, CCEJC, JCL; Rick Hutcheson to Hamilton Jordan et al., 23 July 1975, folder "Memoranda, July–August 1975," box 411, ibid.
51. R. W. Apple Jr., "Wallace Defeats Carter by 3 to 1 in Mississippi Test," *NYT*, 26 January 1976.
52. Apple, "Wallace Defeats Carter by 3 to 1 in Mississippi Test"; David S. Broder, "Gov. Wallace Victorious in Miss. Voting," *WP*, 25 January 1976; David S. Broder, "A Campaign Trail of Confusion," *WP*, 28 January 1976.
53. Apple, "Wallace Defeats Carter by 3 to 1 in Mississippi Test."
54. R. W. Apple Jr., "Carter Apparent Winner in Oklahoma's Caucuses," *NYT*, 8 February 1976.
55. Douglas E. Kneeland, "Ford-Reagan Race Appears Close in New Hampshire Primary Vote; Democrats for Carter; Udall 2d," *NYT*, 25 February 1976; Douglas E. Kneeland, "Democratic Contest in New Hampshire Viewed as 3-Man Race," *NYT*, 12 February 1976.
56. Tom Wicker, "A Race for the 'Top 3,'" *NYT*, 27 January 1976; Tom Wicker, "Mr. Carter's Formula," *NYT*, 23 January 1976; scripts for Carter's television advertisements in New Hampshire, [February 1976], folder "Campaign Planning and Strategy, 12/74–5/76," box 2, CCEJC, JCL.
57. Scripts for Carter's television advertisements in New Hampshire.
58. Robert Reinhold, "Reagan Voters Viewed as Similar to Carter's," *NYT*, 26 February 1976.
59. Reinhold, "Reagan Voters Viewed as Similar to Carter's."
60. Kneeland, "Ford-Reagan Race Appears Close"; Wicker, "Mr. Carter's Formula."
61. R. W. Apple Jr., "Carter Target of Liberals after New Hampshire Gain," *NYT*, 27 February 1976.

62. Apple, "Carter Target of Liberals after New Hampshire Gain."

63. R. W. Apple Jr., "New Political Universe," *NYT*, 3 March 1976; John Kifner, "Massachusetts Held Key Test for Wallace and Liberals," *NYT*, 23 February 1976. For tensions over busing and race in Massachusetts, see Ronald P. Formisano, *Boston against Busing: Race, Class, and Ethnicity in the 1960s and 1970s* (Chapel Hill: University of North Carolina Press, 1991). For liberalism in Massachusetts, see Lily Geismer, *Don't Blame Us: Suburban Liberals and the Transformation of the Democratic Party* (Princeton, NJ: Princeton University Press, 2015).

64. George B. Merry, "Massachusetts Next: Splitting Vote More Ways," *CSM*, 27 February 1976.

65. Chris Brown, weekly field report from New England, September 1975, folder "Field Reports, Primaries, 1975," box 409, CCEJC, JCL; Rick Hutcheson to Hamilton Jordan, 10 July 1975, folder "Memoranda, January–March 1976," box 411, ibid.

66. Hamilton Jordan to Jimmy Carter, 5 July 1975, folder "Memoranda, July–August 1975," box 411, CCEJC, JCL; Carter campaign, expenditures by state, January–March 1976; William Chapman and David S. Broder, "Predicts Top-3 Finish," *WP*, 26 February 1976.

67. John Kifner, "Jackson Beats Wallace and Udall, Carter Is 4th in Massachusetts Vote," *NYT*, 3 March 1976; "Massachusetts Tally Finalized," *AC*, 14 March 1976; R. W. Apple Jr., "Bayh and Shriver Expected to Quit Democratic Race," *NYT*, 4 March 1976.

68. Kifner, "Jackson Beats Wallace and Udall."

69. Roy Reed, "Jackson's Victory Spurs Lagging Florida Campaign," *NYT*, 4 March 1976.

70. Hamilton Jordan to Jimmy Carter, August 1975, folder "Memoranda, July–August 1975," box 411, CCEJC, JCL; Carter campaign, fund-raising letter for New York, 29 January 1976, folder "Memoranda, January–March 1976," ibid.

71. Robert Reinhold, "Voting Reflects Shift in Florida," *NYT*, 11 March 1976; James T. Wooten, "Carter Now Aims to Win in Florida," *NYT*, 1 March 1976. For a study of Reubin Askew's politics, see Gordon E. Harvey, *The Politics of Trust: Reubin Askew and Florida in the 1970s* (Tuscaloosa: University of Alabama Press, 2015). Askew shared Carter's disdain for Wallace, but this did not make him a Carter supporter. He maintained a stance of neutrality in the Florida primary and later volunteered to be a delegate for Henry Jackson. "Gov. Askew Endorses Jackson," *WP*, 18 April 1976.

72. Roy Reed, "Ford Defeats Reagan in Florida; Carter Is Winner over Wallace in Democratic Vote, Jackson 3d," *NYT*, 10 March 1976; Reinhold, "Voting Reflects Shift in Florida."

73. Maurice Carroll, "Jackson Optimistic as He Seeks to Build State Coalition," *NYT*, 16 March 1976; R. W. Apple Jr., "Jackson, Carter and Udall Turn to Pennsylvania," *NYT*, 8 April 1976.

74. Brock Greene, field report from New York and New Jersey, 21 October 1975, folder "Field Reports, Primaries, 1975," box 409, CCEJC, JCL; Brock Greene, field report from New York and New Jersey, 12 November 1975, ibid.; Pat Caddell to Jimmy Carter et al., 24 March 1976, folder "Memoranda, January–March 1976," box 411, ibid.
75. Douglas E. Kneeland, "Jackson Seen Aiming at Big State Victory," *NYT,* 3 April 1976; Frank Lynn, "Jackson's Hopes Face Major Test in New York Race," *NYT,* 4 April 1976; Maurice Carroll, "Jackson and Udall Push New York Drive," *NYT,* 5 April 1976.
76. Frank Lynn, "Georgian Is Third: Jackson Falls Short of 51% Goal that He Had Predicted," *NYT,* 7 April 1976.
77. Carroll, "Jackson and Udall Push New York Drive"; "Carter Takes the Lead in Delegate Selections in Kansas Counties," *NYT,* 5 April 1976; "Carter Is Victor in Two State Races," *NYT,* 4 April 1976.
78. Maurice Carroll, "Jackson Won in New York by Narrowly Based Voting," *NYT,* 8 April 1976; Reinhold, "G.O.P. Crossover a Help to Carter."
79. Andrew Mollison, "Wisconsin Blitzed by the Campaigners," *AC,* 5 April 1976; Reinhold, "Democrats Found More Conservative than 4 Years Ago"; Lucinda Franks, "How Rally Audiences Size up the Candidates," *NYT,* 3 April 1976; Joseph Kraft, "The Cast," *NYT,* 17 November 1974; James T. Wooten, "Carter Is Victor in Pennsylvania," *NYT,* 28 April 1976; Andrew Mollison, "Carter's Biggest Test: Udall on Brink in Wisconsin—Jackson Leads in New York," *AC,* 4 April 1976.
80. Hamilton Jordan to Jimmy Carter, [late March 1976], folder "Memoranda, January–March 1976," box 411, CCEJC, JCL.
81. Stewart Udall to Mo Udall, 6 January 1976, folder 9, "Memos: Strategy, 1973–1976," box 40, MKU; Caddell to Carter et al., 24 March 1976; Stewart L. Udall to Mo Udall, 5 January 1976, folder 9, "Memos: Strategy, 1973–1976," box 40, MKU; Jules Witcover, "Udall Predicts Victory in Wisconsin Primary," *WP,* 3 April 1976.
82. Andrew Mollison and David Schultz, "Carter Trailing Udall in Wis.," *AC,* 7 April 1976; Apple, "Jackson, Carter and Udall Turn to Pennsylvania"; George Moneyhun, "The Computer Misses Calling Wisconsin Election," *CSM,* 8 April 1976.
83. "Carter Gains among Wisconsin Liberals and Unions," *NYT,* 2 April 1976.
84. Gabriel Guerra-Mondrajon to Thomas Kiley, memo on New York primary, [March 1976], folder 9, "Memos: Strategy, 1973–1976," box 40, MKU; "Udall Tells Black Press Jobs for All a Must," *Milwaukee Star-Times,* 1 April 1976.
85. Morris K. Udall, fund-raising letter, [1975], folder "Udall, Morris K.," box 59, Jody Powell Papers, JCL.
86. Ira Jackson to Mo Udall, 27 March 1976, folder 9, "Memos: Strategy, 1973–1976," box 40, MKU; script for Morris Udall's sixty-second

Wisconsin radio ad, [March 1976], ibid.; Dan Payne to Morris Udall et al., 31 March 1976, ibid.

87. Caddell to Carter et al., 24 March 1976.
88. UPI, "Carter Retracts 'Ethnic Purity' Remark," *New York Daily News,* 9 April 1976; Peter Milius, "Housing Integration a Tough '76 Issue," *WP,* 10 April 1976; Christopher Lydon, "Carter Defends All-White Areas," *NYT,* 7 April 1976; Joel D. Weisman, "Carter Supports 'Ethnic Purity' of Neighborhoods," *WP,* 7 April 1976.
89. Joel D. Weisman, "Ethnic Purity Statement Tails Carter," *WP,* 10 April 1976.
90. Milius, "Housing Integration a Tough '76 Issue."
91. David S. Broder and Myra MacPherson, "Carter Accused of 'Racial Division,'" *WP,* 8 April 1976; Seth S. King, "Udall Backs Carter's View on Housing," *NYT,* 16 April 1976.
92. King, "Udall Backs Carter's View on Housing"; Christopher Lydon, "Carter Issues an Apology on 'Ethnic Purity' Phrase," *NYT,* 9 April 1976.
93. "Carter's 'Ethnic Purity' Comments Spark Unusually Strong Reactions," *Atlanta Daily World,* 11 April 1976; Robert Reinhold, "Carter Mounts Campaign to Win Blacks' Backing," *NYT,* 14 April 1976.
94. Lydon, "Carter Issues an Apology on 'Ethnic Purity' Phrase"; Jimmy Carter to Marie Brookter, 9 April 1976, folder "Correspondence, Jimmy Carter, 2/76–4/76," box 8, CCEJC, JCL; Jimmy Carter, press release on full employment, 1 April 1976, folder "Issues Statements," box 410, ibid.; Paul Hemmann to Rick Hutcheson, 8 April 1976, and Rick Hutcheson to Paul Hemmann, 8 April 1976, folder "Memoranda, April–July 1976," box 411, ibid.; Reinhold, "Carter Mounts Campaign to Win Blacks' Backing."
95. D. F. Glover, "Candidates Criticized for Racial Comments," *Atlanta Daily World,* 16 April 1976.
96. Reinhold, "Democrats Found More Conservative than 4 Years Ago"; "N.A.A.C.P. Report on Labor Is Grim," *NYT,* 18 January 1976; National Urban League, "The State of Black America," 28 January 1976, folder "Black Affairs, 3/76–10/76," box 2, CCEJC, JCL.
97. Vernon Jordan, statement at "The State of Black America" press conference, 28 January 1976, folder "Black Affairs, 3/76–10/76," box 2, CCEJC, JCL; "Special *Ebony* Poll," 88–90.
98. Apple, "Jackson, Carter and Udall Turn to Pennsylvania"; Warren Weaver Jr., "Humphrey Draft May Be Renewed," *NYT,* 10 April 1976; Christopher Lydon, "After Worrisome Week for the Carter Campaign, a Key Test in Pennsylvania," *NYT,* 12 April 1976; Jules Witcover and Robert G. Kaiser, "Carter Says He'd Beat Humphrey," *WP,* 29 April 1976.
99. Wooten, "Carter Is Victor in Pennsylvania"; R. W. Apple Jr., "Humphrey May Attempt to Stop Carter, but Few in Party Think He Can Succeed," *NYT,* 29 April 1976; Barry Sussman and William Chapman, "Post's Pa. Survey," *WP,* 29 April 1976; Robert Reinhold, "Contrast in Appeal Shown by Carter and Humphrey, *NYT,* 29 April 1976.

100. Caddell to Carter et al., 24 March 1976.
101. Carter campaign, summary of delegate count, 11 April 1976, folder "Memoranda, April–July 1976," box 411, CCEJC, JCL; "Delegate Votes for President," *NYT,* 27 April 1976.

6. FORD VERSUS REAGAN

1. "Transcript of President's State of the Union Message to Joint Session of Congress," *NYT,* 20 January 1976.
2. Script for Ford campaign's New Hampshire television commercial, "Accomplishment," 6 February 1976, folder "Pres. Ford Committee: Campaign '76 Media Comm., Inc. (1)," box 2, Rogers Morton Files, GRFL; Gerald R. Ford, *A Time to Heal: The Autobiography of Gerald R. Ford* (New York: Berkley Books, 1979), 365; President Ford Committee, campaign plan, 29 August 1975, folder "Campaign Strategy—August 1975 (1)," box A1, Callaway Subject Files, GRFL.
3. "Presidential Approval Ratings—Gallup Historical Statistics and Trends," https://news.gallup.com/poll/116677/presidential-approval-ratings-gallup-historical-statistics-trends.aspx; R. W. Apple Jr., "G.O.P. Seems Evenly Split over Ford-Reagan Contest," *NYT,* 11 January 1976; James L. Rowe Jr., "Jobless Rate Falls to 7.8% in January," *WP,* 7 February 1976; "Mass. Unemployment up .1%," *Boston Globe,* 28 February 1976; Christopher Lydon, "Ford's First National Campaign: Incumbent in Role of Underdog," *NYT,* 22 December 1975; Citizens for Reagan, "Reasons for Reagan" brochure, [1976], folder "Hannaford/CA HQ—1976 Campaign—Positions (3/3)," box 37, RRPC, RRPL; James M. Perry, "Ford's No Shoo-in to Be GOP Nominee," *National Observer,* 15 November 1975; DMI, "Fourth Survey of Republican Voters in New Hampshire for the Citizens for Reagan," 18 February 1976, box 179c, RRPC, RRPL.
4. AP, "Reagan and Thomson Pat Each Other's Backs," *Portsmouth (NH) Herald,* 12 February 1976; Reagan campaign, list of state chairmen of Citizens for Reagan, [1976?], folder "Staff," box 103, CFR, Hoover; UPI, "Publisher Raps Kennedy, HHH," *Nashua (NH) Telegraph,* 2 February 1976; David Keene to Reagan, re: Florida briefing, 29 October 1975, folder "Florida," box 4, CFR, Hoover.
5. Philip Sharecoff, "Reagan Disavows $90 Billion Figure," *NYT,* 14 January 1976; AP, "Reagan May Bring N.H. Sales Tax," *Portsmouth (NH) Herald,* 2 January 1976.
6. Rowland Evans and Robert Novak, "Ronald Reagan's '$90-Billion Scheme,'" *WP,* 9 December 1975.
7. Richard T. Stout, "Reagan's $90 Billion Misunderstanding," *WP,* 21 December 1975; transcript of press conference with Reagan, Manchester, NH, 21 November 1975, folder "Speech Files (Garrick)—1975 (Copies of press conferences and statements) (2/2)," box 431, RRPC, RRPL; "Reagan: The Tax Man," editorial, *Nashua (NH) Telegraph,* 8 January 1976; Evans and Novak, "Ronald Reagan's '$90-Billion Scheme.'"

8. Alf E. Jacobson to Ronald Reagan, 1 December 1975, folder "New Hampshire," box 10, CFR, Hoover.
9. "Reagan off to Good Start in New Hampshire," *Human Events,* 17 January 1976; Peter Milius, "Balancing $90 Billion Cut," *WP,* 1 February 1976; Hobart Rowen, "Reagan's Plan Is Shot Full of Holes," *Philadelphia Inquirer,* 25 January 1976.
10. Pete Hannaford to Martin Anderson and Jeff Bell, 2 December 1975, folder "Transfer Proposal ($90 Billion)," box 103, CFR, Hoover; AP, "Reagan Explains, Explains, Explains," *Portsmouth (NH) Herald,* 8 January 1976.
11. Kenneth Reich, "$90 Million [*sic*] U.S. Cutback Would Take Time—Reagan," *LAT,* 15 December 1975; Richard Bergholz, "Reagan Disparages Own Funds Shift Lift as 'Some Stuff the Economists Gave Me,'" *LAT,* 28 January 1976; Garry Wills, "Reagan's Facts Just Aren't There," *Washington Star,* 26 January 1976; DMI, telephone survey of Republicans in New Hampshire for Citizens for Reagan, December 1975, box 179a, RRPC, RRPL; DMI, "Fourth Survey of Republican Voters in New Hampshire for Citizens for Reagan," 18 February 1976.
12. Bo Callaway to Rog Morton and Dick Cheney, New Hampshire election night, 2 February 1976, folder "Pres. Ford Committee: Callaway, Bo," box 2, Rogers Morton Files, GRFL; Lou Cannon, "Callaway Hits Record of Reagan," *WP,* 14 December 1975.
13. "Reagan's Real Record in California," *U.S. News & World Report,* 9 February 1976; Ronald Reagan, draft of stump speech, 22 January 1976, folder "Speech Files (Garrick)—Jan.–Feb. 1976 (Copies of statements) (1/2)," box 431, RRPC, RRPL; Reagan campaign brochure, "Reasons for Reagan," [1976], folder "Pres. Ford Committee: Campaign '76 Media Comm., Inc. (1)," box 2, Rogers Morton Files, GRFL; Cannon, "Callaway Hits Record of Reagan"; Dennis Farney, "Changing Sides: Two Men Who Helped Reagan in His '66 Race Try to Break Him in '76," *WSJ,* 1 March 1976.
14. Draft copy of Ford campaign brochure, "President Ford vs. Candidate Reagan," 11 February 1976, folder "Pres. Ford Committee: Campaign '76 Media Comm., Inc. (1)," box 2, Rogers Morton Files, GRFL; Bo Callaway to Dick Cheney, 19 January 1976, folder "Pres. Ford Committee: Callaway, Bo," ibid.; script for New Hampshire radio commercial, 9 February 1976, folder "Pres. Ford Committee: Campaign '76 Media Comm., Inc. (1)," ibid.; Bruce Wagner to Bo Callaway, 17 February 1976, folder "Pres. Ford Committee: Campaign '76 Media Comm., Inc. (2)," ibid.; Dave Gergen to Dick Cheney, approval ratings for president, 2 March 1976, folder "Pres. Ford Committee: Strategy," box 3, ibid.
15. Reagan campaign brochure, "Reasons for Reagan," [January or February 1976], folder "Pres. Ford Committee: Campaign '76 Media Comm., Inc. (1)," box 2, Rogers Morton Files, GRFL; "Interview with Ronald Reagan: Reducing Washington's Role," *Business Week,* 9 February 1976, 73.

16. President Ford Committee, draft report on campaign strategy, [February 1976?], folder "Pres. Ford Committee: Strategy," box 3, Rogers Morton Files, GRFL; script for Ford campaign radio commercial, "Older Americans," 6 February 1976, folder "Pres. Ford Committee: Campaign '76 Media Comm., Inc. (1)," box 2, ibid.; Market Opinion Research, New Hampshire postelection study, prepared for President Ford Committee, February 1976, folder "2/76 New Hampshire Post-Election Study (1)," box 4, PFC, GRFL.
17. Market Opinion Research, New Hampshire postelection study, February 1976; Craig Shirley, *Reagan's Revolution: The Untold Story of the Campaign that Started It All* (Nashville, TN: Nelson Current, 2005), 126–127; Rowland Evans and Robert Novak, "And Reagan Prepares for His Last Stand," *WP,* 26 February 1976.
18. Ronald Reagan, statement on the Panama Canal, 10 February 1976, folder "Hannaford/CA HQ—1976 Campaign—Positions (3/3)," box 37, RRPC, RRPL; Ronald Reagan, excerpts from speech in Miami Springs, FL, 10 January 1976, folder "Speech Files (Garrick)—Jan.–Feb. 1976 (Copies of statements) (1/2)," box 431, ibid.
19. Ronald Reagan, draft of speech in Asheville, NC, 24 March 1976, folder "Speech Files (Garrick)—March 1976 (Copies of statements) (2/2)," box 431, RRPC, RRPL; Adam Clymer, *Drawing the Line at the Big Ditch: The Panama Canal Treaties and the Rise of the Right* (Lawrence: University Press of Kansas, 2008), 3–35; "Where Ford and Reagan Stand on the Issues—in Their Own Words," *U.S. News & World Report,* 1 March 1976, 16.
20. Transcript of press conference with Ronald Reagan, Miami, FL, 20 November 1975, folder "Speech Files (Garrick)—1975 (Copies of press conferences and statements) (1/2)," box 431, RRPC, RRPL; Ronald Reagan, speech to Southern Republican Conference banquet, Houston, TX, 13 December 1975, folder "Speech Files (Garrick)—1975 (Copies of press conferences and statements) (2/2)," ibid.; Ronald Reagan, excerpts from remarks in Illinois, 12 March 1976, folder "Speech Files (Garrick)—March 1976 (Copies of statements) (1/2)," ibid.
21. Ronald Reagan, excerpts from speech in Miami Springs, FL, 10 January 1976, and excerpts from speech in Melbourne, FL, 30 January 1976, folder "Speech Files (Garrick)—Jan.–Feb. 1976 (Copies of statements) (1/2)," box 431, RRPC, RRPL.
22. Clymer, *Drawing the Line at the Big Ditch,* 27; Ronald Reagan, transcript of speech in Orlando, FL, 4 March 1976, folder "Speech Files (Garrick)—March 1976 (Copies of statements) (1/2)," box 431, RRPC, RRPL.
23. Transcript of Barry Goldwater's press conference on the Panama Canal, 4 May 1976, folder "Panama Canal," box 16, MRD, GRFL; Peter Kaye to Bo Callaway, 2 February 1976, folder "Pres. Ford Committee: Strategy," box 3, Rogers Morton Files, GRFL; Gergen to Cheney, approval ratings for president, 2 March 1976.

24. Dave Gergen to Warren Hendricks, talking points on Social Security, 4 March 1976, folder "Florida (1)," box 4, Rogers Morton Files, GRFL; Ford campaign, senior citizen ad for Florida, [February 1976], folder: "Reagan—New Hampshire/Florida—Newsclippings," box G19, PFC, GRFL.
25. Market Opinion Research, Florida postelection study prepared for President Ford Committee, March 1976, folder "3/76—Florida Post-Election Study (1)," box H4, PFC, GRFL; David E. Rosenbaum, "Florida's Elderly Raise Hopes of Ford and Jackson," *NYT*, 6 March 1976.
26. Bo Callaway to Rogers Morton, 6 March 1976, folder "Florida (1)," box 4, Rogers Morton Files, GRFL; R. W. Apple Jr., "Impact of Florida Vote," *NYT*, 10 March 1976; James R. Dickenson, "Reagan Drive Stalled," *Oakland (CA) Tribune*, 10 March 1976 (reprinted from *Washington Star*); Bo Callaway, memorandum for the record, 11 March 1976, folder "Pres. Ford Committee: Callaway, Bo," box 2, Rogers Morton Files, GRFL.
27. William A. Link, *Righteous Warrior: Jesse Helms and the Rise of Modern Conservatism* (New York: St. Martin's Press, 2008), 138–139, 147. For Helms's television career, see Bryan Hardin Thrift, *Conservative Bias: How Jesse Helms Pioneered the Rise of Right-Wing Media and Realigned the Republican Party* (Gainesville: University Press of Florida, 2014).
28. Sara Williamson to Arlene Triplett, 16 August 1975, folder "North Carolina," box 10, CFR, Hoover. For a study of Jesse Helms and the North Carolina Congressional Club, whose name was later changed to the National Congressional Club, see Thomas Edmund Packer, "Jesse Helms and North Carolina Politics, 1972–1984" (PhD diss., University of Oxford, 2012).
29. Link, *Righteous Warrior*, 152–153; James M. Naughton, "Reagan Halts a Pamphlet Linking Ford to Brooke," *NYT*, 21 March 1976.
30. Jerry Shinn, "Reagan Ridicules Social Programs," *Charlotte (NC) Observer*, 28 January 1976; Jon Nordheimer, "Reagan Is Picking His Florida Spots," *NYT*, 5 February 1976; Carl Rowan, "Sly Racism of Reagan," *AC*, 16 February 1976. See also Richard Scott Primuth, "Election 1976 and 1980: The Reagan Campaign's Use of Race" (master's thesis, University of West Georgia, 2009).
31. Louis Harris, "The Harris Survey," 24 May 1976, folder "Public Relations—Public Opinion Polls," box 42, PHF, GRFL; F. B. McKissick to Rogers Morton, 18 June 1976, folder "North Carolina," box F17, PHC, GRFL.
32. Link, *Righteous Warrior*, 149–157.
33. R. W. Apple Jr., "Reagan, Wallace Facing Key Tests," *NYT*, 21 March 1976; Philip Shabecoff, "Momentum to Win Claimed by Ford," *NYT*, 21 March 1976; Edward Walsh, "White House Writers under Fire for Speech," *WP*, 27 March 1976.
34. Shirley, *Reagan's Revolution*, 169–170; Joseph Lelyveld, "Reagan's Upset Victory in North Carolina Attributed to Impact of Last-Minute TV Speech," *NYT*, 29 March 1976.

35. R. W. Apple Jr., "Reagan Tops Ford in N. Carolina for First Triumph in a Primary," *NYT,* 24 March 1976; Shirley, *Reagan's Revolution,* 174–175.
36. Lelyveld, "Reagan's Upset Victory in North Carolina."
37. "The Ford Administration," *American Political Report,* 28 May 1976; George Gallup, "Kissinger's Popularity Down, but More Approve than Disapprove," 29 January 1976, folder "Foreign Policy," box 1, Rogers Morton Files, GRFL.
38. William Safire, "Life of the Party," *NYT,* 18 March 1976; "Ford Asks States' Rule on Abortion," *Minneapolis Star,* 4 February 1976; transcript of White House press conference, 2 February 1976, folder "President's Position (2)," Sarah C. Massengame Files, GRFL; Callaway to Rogers Morton, information for president's meeting with members of Congress, 29 February 1976, folder "Congressional Support (2)," box A1, Callaway Subject Files, PFC, GRFL; Phil Buchen and Jim Cannon, memo to President Ford on abortion, 15 January 1976, folder "Welfare—Abortions," box 51, PHF, GRFL.
39. Ronald Reagan, nationwide television address, 31 March 1976, folder "Hannaford/CA HQ—1976 Campaign—Miscellaneous Items," box 37, RRPC, RRPL.
40. Ford campaign, "The Reagan Speech and the Facts," [April 1976], folder "RR 3/31/76 Speech & GRF Response to Foreign Policy Charges," box 11, CFR, Hoover; Ronald Reagan, remarks at a press conference in Dallas, TX, 5 April 1976, ibid.; Ronald Reagan, excerpts from speech in Seattle, WA, 10 April 1976, ibid.
41. Gerald R. Ford, telegram to Hampden Township (PA) Republican Association, 5 April 1976, folder "Pennsylvania," box 5, Rogers Morton Files, GRFL; President Ford Committee, script for newspaper ad in Wisconsin, 26 March 1976, folder "Pres. Ford Committee: Campaign '76 Media Comm., Inc. (5)," box 2, ibid.; Dave Gergen to Dick Cheney, 11 March 1976, folder "Gergen, David," box 16, MRD, GRFL; Gerald Ford, remarks at a briefing for representatives of military organizations on defense and foreign policy, 10 February 1976, www.presidency.ucsb.edu/ws/index.php?pid=6321.
42. "Should Republicans Trust Jerry Ford?" *Human Events,* 13 March 1976; John B. Anderson, press release, "Anderson Scores Reagan's Defense Critique," 4 March 1976, folder "Reagan (3)," box 39, PHF, GRFL.
43. Webster Todd to Rogers Morton, 24 March 1976, folder "PL/Reagan, Ronald, 9/9/74–1/20/77," box 20, WHCF, GRFL.
44. Market Opinion Research, postelection analysis of Wisconsin, April 1976, folder "4/76 Wisconsin Post-Election Analysis (1)," box H6, PFC, GRFL; Stephen S. King, "Ford Easy Victor," *NYT,* 7 April 1976; James M. Naughton, "Ford Sees Wisconsin Vote as Kissinger Endorsement," *NYT,* 8 April 1976; Lou Cannon, "Reagan Seeking New Start in Texas," *WP,* 5 April 1976.
45. Jon Nordheimer, "Reagan Still Says He Can Beat Ford," *NYT,* 12 April 1976.

46. R. W. Apple Jr., "Early Losers Will Get Second Chance in North Carolina Primary," *NYT,* 15 February 1976; Loren A. Smith, direct mail on behalf of Citizens for Reagan, [late March or early April 1976], folder "Newsletter," box 10, CFR, Hoover; Jon Nordheimer, "Reagan Nears Fund Crisis over Lack of Federal Aid," *NYT,* 4 May 1976.
47. Nordheimer, "Reagan Still Says He Can Beat Ford."
48. Leo Thorsness to Bo Callaway, 1 March 1976, folder "Texas," box 5, Rogers Morton Files, GRFL; Ford campaign, script for newspaper ad in Texas, 20 April 1976, folder "Pres. Ford Committee: Campaign '76 Media Comm., Inc. (6)," box 3, ibid.; Ford campaign, script for five-minute TV documentary, "Faces," in Texas, 24 April 1976, ibid.
49. "Oh Shucks, Mr. President," *Washington Star,* 10 April 1976; text of Reagan campaign ads in Texas, April 1976, folder "Ronald Reagan File—Campaign File, 1976—Republican Primaries," box 6, Peter Hannaford Papers, Hoover; Citizens for Reagan, "Reasons for Reagan," [April 1976], folder "Texas," box 5, Rogers Morton Files, GRFL.
50. James P. Sterba, "Democratic Vote Propels Reagan to Texas Sweep," *NYT,* 3 May 1976.
51. Robert Reinhold, "Indiana Indicates Growing G.O.P. Rift," *NYT,* 6 May 1976; R. W. Apple Jr., "Ford Is Reviewing Strategy in Light of Reagan's Gains," *NYT,* 6 May 1976; Seth S. King, "Reagan Wins in Nebraska, Church Is Leading Carter; Ford West Virginia Victor," *NYT,* 12 May 1976.
52. Apple, "Ford Is Reviewing Strategy"; AP, "Reagan Gets 46 Delegates in Five States," *NYT,* 17 May 1976; Lou Cannon and David S. Broder, "Aide Predicts Early Victory," *WP,* 13 May 1976.
53. "The Ford Administration," *American Political Report,* 28 May 1976.
54. Edward Walsh, "Ford Takes W. Va.," *WP,* 12 May 1976; William K. Stevens, "Ford Beats Reagan in Michigan and Maryland," *NYT,* 19 May 1976; R. W. Apple Jr., "Ford Stems the Tide," *NYT,* 19 May 1976.
55. Joseph Kraft, "Ford and Carter: Limping Frontrunners," *WP,* 27 May 1976; Wallace Turner, "Church Got Oregon Votes of Elderly and Unionists," *NYT,* 26 May 1976; "Vote Results in Primaries," *NYT,* 2 June 1976.
56. For survey data and an analysis of the regional differences in Ford's and Reagan's support among Republican delegates and party activists, see Perry, "Ford's No Shoo-in to Be GOP Nominee."
57. Total Republican presidential primary votes, state by state, [June 1976], folder "Total Republican Primary Votes," box 44, CFR, Hoover.
58. Robert Lamb, "California, Here They Come," *AC,* 3 June 1976; Reagan California Fund, direct mail, [May 1976], folder "Gun Control," box 16, MRD, GRFL. The Reagan California Fund was directed by Ron Robinson, a young conservative activist who would become president of Young Americans for Freedom the next year.
59. Mervin D. Field, "California Poll: Ford Again Leads Reagan," *San Francisco Chronicle,* 15 April 1976; Lou Cannon, "Reagan Confident: Sure of Calif., He Turns to Ohio," *WP,* 31 May 1976.

60. Script for Reagan California Fund campaign ad narrated by Efrem Zimbalist, [May 1976], folder "Gun Control," box 16, MRD, GRFL; Jon Nordheimer, "Ford, in Ad Shift, Describes Reagan as Peace Threat," *NYT,* 6 June 1976; Lou Cannon and Edward Walsh, "Reagan Assails Ford," *WP,* 8 June 1976.
61. Robert Reinhold, "Defection to Carter in G.O.P. Is Hinted," *NYT,* 10 June 1976.
62. Dennis Farney, "Primaries Leave GOP in a Tight Race and Hurt Party's Chances in November," *WSJ,* 10 June 1976.

7. NOMINATING CARTER

1. Jimmy Carter, speech to the Chicago Council on Foreign Relations, 15 March 1976, folder "Jimmy Carter's Position Papers," box 291, CCEJC, JCL; Jimmy Carter, statement of position on issues, 15 March 1976, folder "Issues Statements," box 410, ibid.
2. Stu Eizenstat to Jimmy Carter, re: Proposed answers to questionnaire to be summarized on the Robert MacNeil Report on his April 12 program, 6 April 1976, folder "Economics, 4/76–7/76," box 12, CCEJC, JCL; Carter campaign, "The Carter Program," [early 1976], folder "Economics, 1/76–3/76," ibid.; Carter campaign press release, "Statement by Jimmy Carter at Full Employment Press Conference," 1 April 1976, folder "Issues Statements," box 410, ibid.; R. W. Apple Jr., "Carter Target of Liberals after New Hampshire Gain," *NYT,* 27 February 1976; "Black Caucus Blasts Carter," *San Francisco Sun Reporter,* 17 April 1976; Hobart Rowen, "Full Employment: Carter's Top Priority," *WP,* 29 April 1976; David S. Broder, "Carter Details Economic Plan," *WP,* 24 April 1976.
3. Jimmy Carter, "The Economy: An Economic Position Paper for Now and Tomorrow," 22 April 1976, folder "General Business," box 293, CCEJC, JCL.
4. Jimmy Carter, speech on national health policy, 16 April 1976, folder "Jimmy Carter's Position Papers," box 291, CCEJC, JCL.
5. [Jeff Greenfield], letter explaining resignation of speechwriter from Carter's campaign on 27 April 1976, folder "Campaign Planning and Strategy, 12/74–5/76," box 2, CCEJC, JCL.
6. Henry Hall Wilson to Landon Butler, 7 and 8 April 1976, folder "Correspondence," box 204, CCEJC, JCL.
7. Thomas W. Ottenad, "Jimmy Carter: A Smile and a Shoeshine," *Progressive,* May 1976, 24.
8. Jimmy Carter, "The Economy: An Economic Position Paper for Now and Tomorrow," 22 April 1976, folder "General Business," box 293, CCEJC, JCL; Richard Corrigan and Joel Havemann, "The Issues Teams: The People Who Prepare Jimmy Carter for the Presidency," *National Journal,* 21 August 1976, 1167.
9. Vicki Rogers to field staff and advance people, 20 October 1975, folder "Memoranda, September–December 1975," box 411, CCEJC, JCL.

10. George Gallup, "Half of Protestants 'Born Again,'" *Montgomery (AL) Advertiser,* 26 September 1976; Kenneth A. Briggs, "Carter's Evangelism Putting Religion into Politics for First Time since '60," *NYT,* 11 April 1976; Michael Novak, "The Hidden Religious Majority," *WP,* 4 April 1976; Kenneth A. Briggs, "Religion: The Baptists Have Done More than Survive," *NYT,* 20 June 1976; Kenneth L. Woodward, "Born Again!" *Newsweek,* 25 October 1976.
11. William Martin, *A Prophet with Honor: The Billy Graham Story* (New York: William Morrow, 1991), 462–463. For a comprehensive study of American evangelicalism in the 1970s, including evangelical political culture, see Steven P. Miller, *The Age of Evangelicalism: America's Born-Again Years* (New York: Oxford University Press, 2014).
12. For detailed analyses of Carter's religious views in relation to larger trends in the Southern Baptist Convention, see Randall Balmer, *Redeemer: The Life of Jimmy Carter* (New York: Basic Books, 2014); J. Brooks Flippen, *Jimmy Carter, the Politics of Family, and the Rise of the Religious Right* (Athens: University of Georgia Press, 2011). For Carter's own discussion of his faith, see Jimmy Carter, *Faith: A Journey for All* (New York: Simon & Schuster, 2018). For the split between "moderates" and "conservatives" in the Southern Baptist Convention, see Barry Hankins, *Uneasy in Babylon: Southern Baptist Conservatives and American Culture* (Tuscaloosa: University of Alabama Press, 2002).
13. "Carter's Credibility," *Christianity Today,* 9 April 1976, 31.
14. Myra MacPherson, "Evangelicals Seen Cooling on Carter," *WP,* 27 September 1976; Jimmy Carter, *Why Not the Best?* (Nashville, TN: Broadman Press, 1975); Howard Norton and Bob Slosser, *The Miracle of Jimmy Carter* (Plainfield, NJ: Logos, 1976); ad for *The Miracle of Jimmy Carter* in *Eternity,* October 1976, 73; "Obituary: Howard Norton Dies; Pulitzer Prize Winner," *WP,* 13 March 1994; "In Memory: Bob Slosser," Christian Broadcasting Network, September 2002, www.cbn.com/spirituallife/churchandministry/bobslosser; "Jimmy Carter Explains His Faith," *Eternity,* September 1976, 80–81; "Turning Point with Jimmy Carter," *Christian Life,* March 1976, 50.
15. Warren Brown, "Carter's Special Appeal among Blacks," *WP,* 20 June 1976.
16. George Van Cleve to Dave Gergen, 18 June 1976, folder "Van Cleve, George," box 24, MRD, GRFL.
17. Stu Eizenstat to Jimmy Carter, 3 May 1976, folder "Religion, 2/75–6/76," box 27, CCEJC, JCL.
18. Charles Mohr, "Carter Gets an Ovation after Assuring Jews in Jersey on His Religious Views," *NYT,* 7 June 1976.
19. Linda Charlton, "Senator Church Joins Presidential Race," *NYT,* 19 March 1976; George Lardner Jr., "Frank Church's Presidential Dreams," *WP,* 18 April 1976; David S. Broder, "Frank Church: The Unbeaten Candidate," *WP,* 30 May 1976; Jack Anderson and Les Whitten, "Frank Church—A Study in Courage," *WP,* 15 March 1976.

20. Les Ledbetter, "Church Opens Bid for Oregon Votes," *NYT,* 21 May 1976; Les Ledbetter, "Church's Race Takes the Tortoise's Cue," *NYT,* 23 May 1976; Charlton, "Senator Church Joins Presidential Race."
21. Charlton, "Senator Church Joins Presidential Race"; Ledbetter, "Church's Race Takes the Tortoise's Cue"; R. W. Apple Jr., "Church Says Miracle He Needs 'May Be in the Making,'" *NYT,* 12 May 1976.
22. R. W. Apple Jr., "Nebraska Victory by Church Buoys Stop-Carter Bloc," *NYT,* 13 May 1976.
23. David S. Broder, "Brown's Run for the Presidency Puzzles Some of His Associates," *WP,* 4 June 1976; Jon Nordheimer, "Brown Bets on California in Thrust for Nomination," *NYT,* 22 March 1976; Kandy Stroud, "On Hustings with an Enigmatic Brown," *NYT,* 14 May 1976.
24. James Reston, "Governor Brown's America," *NYT,* 18 February 1976; Stroud, "On Hustings with an Enigmatic Brown"; Joseph Lelyveld, "Brown, on Stump, Reveals Style Marked by Paradox," *NYT,* 9 May 1976.
25. "Jerry-Come-Lately," editorial, *NYT,* 11 May 1976; Ben A. Franklin, "Brown, Ali Spar Near Baltimore," *NYT,* 1 May 1976; Reston, "Governor Brown's America"; Richard D. Lamm, "Whither the Democratic Party?" *NYT,* 1 February 1976; Stroud, "On Hustings with an Enigmatic Brown"; E. F. Schumacher, *Small Is Beautiful: Economics as If People Mattered* (New York: Harper & Row, 1973).
26. Lelyveld, "Brown, on Stump, Reveals Style Marked by Paradox"; Anthony Lewis, "Ice on a Hot Stove," *NYT,* 12 April 1976.
27. Stroud, "On Hustings with an Enigmatic Brown"; Bill Peterson, "Support of Brown Called Mandel Ploy," *WP,* 14 May 1976; Ben A. Franklin, "Brown Opens Drive in Maryland Race; Is Greeted by 3,000," *NYT,* 29 April 1976.
28. Stroud, "On Hustings with an Enigmatic Brown"; Sally Quinn, "Jerry Brown: He Thinks, He Wants to Be President," *WP,* 9 May 1976.
29. Quinn, "Jerry Brown."
30. Stroud, "On Hustings with an Enigmatic Brown."
31. R. W. Apple Jr., "Ford Takes Kentucky and Oregon, Leads Tennessee; Reagan Gains 3; Carter Wins 3, Loses 2 to Church," *NYT,* 26 May 1976; Wallace Turner, "Church Got Oregon Votes of Elderly and Unionists," *NYT,* 26 May 1976; Joseph Lelyveld, "Brown Cites Differences with Carter in Quest for Oregon Write-in Victory," *NYT,* 23 May 1976; *Congressional Quarterly's Guide to 1976 Elections* (Washington, DC: Congressional Quarterly, 1977), 30.
32. Apple, "Ford Takes Kentucky and Oregon"; Turner, "Church Got Oregon Votes of Elderly and Unionists"; R. W. Apple Jr., "Carter Wins One, Loses 2d, Jolted by Brown in 3d," *NYT,* 2 June 1976; William K. Stevens, "Ford Beats Reagan in Michigan and Maryland," *NYT,* 19 May 1976.
33. "Effects of Tuesday Voting," *NYT,* 10 June 1976; Ronald Sullivan, "Carter Victory Is Forecast in Jersey Vote Tomorrow," *NYT,* 7 June 1976.

34. Jules Witcover, "Carter Plan for Primaries Is Vindicated," *WP,* 9 June 1976; R. W. Apple Jr., "Carter Scores Delegate Gains, Wins Ohio, Is Beaten in New Jersey," *NYT,* 9 June 1976.
35. *Congressional Quarterly's Guide to 1976 Elections,* 30.
36. Robert Reinhold, "Gallup Finds Ford Is Trailing Carter, Tied with Humphrey," *NYT,* 25 April 1976.
37. R. W. Apple Jr., "Shift to Georgian," *NYT,* 10 June 1976; AP, "Carter Picks up More Delegates," *NYT,* 11 June 1976.
38. Carter campaign, list of political endorsers who have been assigned to call delegates, [May or June 1976], folder "Convention File, 1976," box 204, CCEJC, JCL; Carter campaign, "Where We Can Pick up Delegates," [early June 1976], ibid.
39. Carter campaign, "Wooing Liberal Delegates," folder "Convention File, 1976," box 204, CCEJC, JCL; Stephen I. Schlossberg, letter to all Udall delegates, [May 1976?], folder "Correspondence," box 204, CCEJC, JCL; Carter campaign, "Where We Can Pick up Delegates"; James T. Wooten, "Udall Concedes to Carter, Ends Delegate Search," *NYT,* 15 June 1976; Morris Udall's campaign staff to Morris K. Udall, 4 June 1976, folder 10, box 40, MKU.
40. Jim Merriner, "Carter Assured Nomination as Ex-Foes Join Bandwagon," *AC,* 10 June 1976.
41. Myra MacPherson, "A Final Irony for George Wallace," *WP,* 10 June 1976.
42. MacPherson, "Final Irony for George Wallace."
43. Robert Reinhold, "Election Held Turning on Traditional Issues," *NYT,* 25 June 1976; William Zeitz to George Wallace, 8 July 1976, folder 12, box 2, GCWCR, ADAH; Mr. and Mrs. Edmund L. Etlinger to George Wallace, 12 July 1976, folder 13, ibid.
44. Merriner, "Carter Assured of Nomination as Ex-Foes Join the Bandwagon."
45. Rick Hutcheson to Jimmy Carter, 1 May 1976, folder "Memoranda, April–July 1976," box 411, CCEJC, JCL; "Carter Delegate Profile," results of survey of delegates, [June 1976], folder "Delegate Selection Demographics," box 208, ibid.
46. Jimmy Carter, "A New Beginning," presentation to the Democratic Party Platform Committee, [June 1976], folder "Democratic National Committee, 1/75–10/76," box 11, CCEJC, JCL.
47. For Wallace's welfare reform proposal, see George C. Wallace, statement to Democratic Party Platform Committee, 11 June 1976, folder 5, "Issues—1976," box 259, GCWCR, ADAH.
48. Carter, "A New Beginning."
49. Wallace, statement to Democratic Party Platform Committee.
50. 1976 Democratic Party platform, www.presidency.ucsb.edu/documents/1976-democratic-party-platform.
51. David E. Rosenbaum, "Democratic Platform Unit Calls for 3% Jobless Rate," *NYT,* 13 June 1976.

52. 1976 Democratic Party platform; Joseph S. Clark, "The Decision Making Process," 13 August 1976, folder "Defense, 7/27/76–8/76," box 10, CCEJC, JCL.
53. 1972 Democratic Party platform, www.presidency.ucsb.edu/documents/1972-democratic-party-platform; Planned Parenthood Washington memo, 18 June 1976, folder "Abortion," box 294, CCEJC, JCL; 1976 Democratic Party platform; Peter Kihss, "10,000 Antiabortionists Attend a Protest Rally," *NYT,* 12 July 1976.
54. UPI, "Democratic Platform Tailored for Carter," *AC,* 16 June 1976; 1972 Democratic Party platform; 1976 Democratic Party platform; David E. Rosenbaum, "Democrats Adopt a Platform Aimed at Uniting Party," *NYT,* 16 June 1976.
55. Robert Healy, "Carter Ready to Run Country," *Boston Globe,* 14 March 1975; Bill Leonard to Stuart Eizenstat, 30 September 1976, folder "Economics, 8/76–9/76," box 12, CCEJC, JCL; [Mike Duval], Ford campaign strategy handbook, [July 1976], folder "Campaign Plan—Final Copy, 4 of 4," box 13, MRD, GRFL.
56. Pat Caddell to Jimmy Carter, Charles Kirbo, and Hamilton Jordan, re: Vice presidency, 23 June 1976, folder "Survey: General Election," box 36, Jody Powell Papers, JCL; Pat Caddell to Carter et al., 3 July 1976, ibid.; Religious News Service, "Catholic Democrats and Others See No Major Problems for Jimmy Carter," 19 July 1976, folder "Abortion [1]," box 304, CCEJC, JCL.
57. Caddell to Carter, Kirbo, and Jordan, re: Vice presidency, 23 June 1976; Caddell to Carter et al., 3 July 1976; R. W. Apple Jr., "Carter Promises No. 2 Spot Will Go to 1 of 7 Queried," *NYT,* 12 July 1976; Hamilton Jordan, General Election Strategy Manual, [June 1976], folder "Memorandums—Hamilton Jordan to Jimmy Carter, General Election," box 39, Carter Family Papers, JCL; author's interview with Stuart E. Eizenstat, 27 August 2018.
58. Andrew Alexander, "More Data Sought on Glenn," *AC,* 14 July 1976.
59. Jordan, General Election Strategy Manual; Arlen J. Large, "Mondale Will Help Carter with Liberals; GOP Is Also Happy," *WSJ,* 16 July 1976.
60. Stuart E. Eizenstat, *President Carter: The White House Years* (New York: St. Martin's Press, 2018), 90–92; Jimmy Carter, *A Full Life: Reflections at Ninety* (New York: Simon & Schuster, 2015), 114–116; Jack W. Germond and Martha Angle, "VP Pick Concession to Liberals," *AC,* 16 July 1976; Jordan, General Election Strategy Manual; David E. Rosenbaum, "A Hard-Nosed Dreamer," *NYT,* 16 July 1976; Nicholas M. Horrock, "Mondale's Assets Relatively Modest," *NYT,* 25 July 1976.
61. Richard L. Madden, "Mondale's Liberal Vote Rating Exceeds Humphrey's and Kennedy's," *NYT,* 17 July 1976; Spencer Rich, "Democrats' Slate Hit by GOP as 'Liberal,'" *WP,* 16 July 1976; James M. Naughton, "G.O.P. to Portray Carter as Liberal," *NYT,* 16 July 1976; Andrew J. Glass, "Ford Bailing out of 'Cotton South,'" *AC,* 22 August 1976.

62. George Gallup, "Gallup Report," *Cincinnati Enquirer,* 11 April 1976; "Poll Shows Carter Leads; Best Margin in 40 Years," *NYT,* 16 July 1976; Barry Gussman, "Carter Routs Foes in Poll," *WP,* 26 July 1976; Carter campaign, state-by-state survey data for Ford-Carter race from internal campaign polling, August 1976, folder "Survey: General Election," box 36, Jody Powell Papers, JCL; Helen Dewar, "Buoyed by Polls, Carter Plans Tour of GOP Farm Belt," *WP,* 15 August 1976. Lyndon Johnson's 56-point lead over Barry Goldwater in the summer of 1964 was wider than Carter's lead over Ford, but Johnson was an incumbent at the time, while Carter was running as a challenger to an incumbent president (George Gallup, "Goldwater Chances Viewed beside Dewey's Defeat," *AC,* 19 July 1964). The *New York Times* noted that Carter enjoyed "the widest lead a challenger has ever held over an incumbent since the advent of scientific polling more than 40 years ago" ("Poll Shows Carter Leads").
63. Eileen Shanahan, "Women Fail to Agree with Carter on Their '80 Role," *NYT,* 12 July 1976; Austin Scott and Peter Milius, "Carter's Forces Move to Smooth Convention Path," *WP,* 14 July 1976.
64. "Excerpts from Some of the Addresses Delivered at Democratic Convention," *NYT,* 15 July 1976; AP, "Poll Shows Voters Confused on Issues; Real Focus Is on Personalities," *Baltimore Sun,* 3 June 1976.
65. "Excerpts from Some of the Addresses Delivered at Democratic Convention"; David S. Broder, "Carter Sweeps to Nomination," *WP,* 15 July 1976; B. Drummond Ayres Jr., "Democratic Unity Reflects Changes in South," *NYT,* 16 July 1976; Celestine Sibley, "Memorable Convention," *AC,* 19 July 1976.
66. Bob Mead to Dave Gergen, 15 July 1976, folder "Carter, Jimmy," box 14, MRD, GRFL.
67. Jimmy Carter, "Our Nation's Past and Future," speech at Democratic National Convention, 15 July 1976, www.jimmycarterlibrary.gov/assets/documents/speeches/acceptance_speech.pdf.
68. "Transcript of Address by Mondale Accepting the Democratic Nomination for Vice President," *NYT,* 15 July 1976.
69. Carter, "Our Nation's Past and Future."
70. Roscoe Drummond, "Is Carter a Certain Winner?" *CSM,* 14 July 1976.
71. "Fact and Comment: Time to Try Fathoming the Jimmy Carter Phenomenon," *Forbes,* 1 April 1976, 17; Powell Moore, memo on Carter for Ford campaign, [May 1976], folder "Carter, Jimmy," box 14, MRD, GRFL.

8. THE REPUBLICAN CONVENTION

1. Dick Cheney to Gerald R. Ford, 8 April 1976, folder "PL 1–2, Platforms 8/9/74–5/30/76," box PL76, Subject Files, WHCF, GRFL; [Mike Duval], campaign strategy book, [July 1976], folder "Campaign Plan—Final Copy, 4 of 4," box 13, MRD, GRFL; Barry Gussman, "Carter Routs Foes in Poll," *WP,* 26 July 1976.

2. Rudy Abramson, "Ford Phoning Personal Appeals to Key GOP State Delegates," *LAT,* 15 June 1976; Peter C. Stuart, "Ford, Reagan Target: Committed Delegates," *CSM,* 28 July 1976; "RR Best Hope This November," *Reagan-Schweiker, They'll Beat Carter, News* [Reagan campaign newsletter], 15 August 1976, folder "RR/Schweiker, 'Convention News,'" box 53, CFR, Hoover; Frank Lynn, "Some New York Delegates Making Demands on Ford," *NYT,* 26 July 1976; David S. Broder, "Ford's Forces Claim to Add 16 Delegates," *WP,* 21 July 1976. Paul Laxalt claimed in August 1976 that Reagan finished the primaries with 400,000 more votes than Ford received. *Reagan-Schweiker, They'll Beat Carter, News,* 15 August 1976. But this was incorrect. *Congressional Quarterly* calculated that Ford finished the primaries ahead of Reagan by more than 771,000 votes. The vote totals from all Republican primaries, according to *Congressional Quarterly,* were: Ford, 5,529,899; Reagan, 4,758,325. *Congressional Quarterly's Guide to 1976 Elections* (Washington, DC: Congressional Quarterly, 1977), 30.
3. David Gergen, "President Ford: 10 Reasons Why He Should Carry the GOP Banner in November," 11 June 1976, folder "Political Affairs—Ford (6)," box 37, PHF, GRFL; Louis Harris, "Ford's Still Well Ahead of Reagan," *Chicago Tribune,* 7 June 1976.
4. Dick Bryan to Larry Uzzell, 10 June 1976, folder "Ford Electability," box 51, CFR, Hoover; Andrew J. Glass, "Ford Bailing out of 'Cotton South,'" *AC,* 22 August 1976.
5. Gergen, "President Ford."
6. Gergen, "President Ford."
7. "Delegates Reported Shifting to Ford," *Washington Star,* 22 July 1976; David M. Alpern, "The Ford-Reagan Psy-War," *Newsweek,* 2 August 1976, 22–23; "Counting the Delegates," *Washington Star,* 9 July 1976.
8. Author's interview with John Sears, 6 August 2018; Craig Shirley, *Reagan's Revolution: The Untold Story of the Campaign that Started It All* (Nashville, TN: Nelson Current, 2005), 267–273; Richard L. Strout, "What Emerges from Reagan's 'Daring Gamble,'" *CSM,* 30 July 1976.
9. Interview with Sears; Shirley, *Reagan's Revolution,* 274–275.
10. Jack W. Germond, "Politics Today: Speculation on VP Fruitless Exercise," *Washington Star,* 1 July 1976; interview with Sears; William Randolph Hearst Jr., "Monumental Insult," *San Francisco Examiner,* 1 August 1976; David S. Broder, "The Schweiker Miscalculation," *WP,* 1 August 1976; Richard S. Schweiker to Gerald Ford, 28 June 1976, folder "PL 1–1/ST 34–ST 51–4," box PL76, Subject Files, WHCF, GRFL.
11. For examples of these letters, see Janice E. Johnson to Ronald Reagan, 29 July 1976, and Kendall F. Query to Ronald Reagan, 28 July 1976, folder "Schweiker Whites—with Incoming Correspondence," box 47, CFR, Hoover.
12. Jim Field to Gerald Ford, 6 August 1976, folder "PL 1–1/ST 34–ST 51–4," box PL76, Subject Files, WHCF, GRFL; Jim Baker to President,

6 August 1976, folder "PL 1–1/FG1–6–ST 18—Delegates," ibid.; Rudy Abramson and John H. Averill, "Connally Backs Ford, Deals Blow to Reagan," *LAT,* 28 July 1976; Christopher Lydon, "Ford's Position Still Firm with Pennsylvania G.O.P., *NYT,* 8 August 1976; Margot Hornblower, "Reagan, Schweiker Find Pa. Delegates Hard to Persuade," *WP,* 7 August 1976; Jack Marsh, memos to Gerald Ford, 26 July 1976, folder "Reagan (3)," box 39, PHF, GRFL; Jim Field to Jim Baker, 26 July 1976, folder "Schweiker, Richard—Selection by Ronald Reagan," box J2, PFC, GRFL.

13. Interview with Sears; "Ronald Reagan Arrives for Convention," *Reagan-Schweiker, They'll Beat Carter, News,* 16 August 1976, folder "RR/Schweiker, 'Convention News,'" box 53, CFR, Hoover.
14. Dennis Farney, "Reagan Names Liberal Sen. Schweiker as Choice for Running Mate in Bold Move," *WSJ,* 27 July 1976; "Schweiker for VP? It's a Smart, Bold Move by Reagan," editorial, *Bryn Mawr (PA) Suburban and Wayne Times,* 28 July 1976; Ronald Reagan to Republican delegates on Schweiker, [late July 1976], folder "Schweiker, Sen. Richard," box 103, CFR, Hoover.
15. Larry Uzzell to Martin Anderson, Peter Hannaford, and Edwin Meese, re: Repackaging Schweiker, 1 August 1976, folder "Memo 'Repackaging Schweiker,' 8/1/76," box 53, CFR, Hoover.
16. Lou Cannon and William Claiborne, "Ford Gains Votes as Sessions Open," *WP,* 17 August 1976; Jon Nordheimer, "Californian Gears for Battle," *NYT,* 16 August 1976; Richard L. Madden, "Veterans of Past Struggles on Hand to Watch Reagan-Ford Showdown," *NYT,* 19 August 1976.
17. Richard L. Madden, "Platform Panel Votes to Endorse Equal Rights Plan," *NYT,* 13 August 1976; "GOP Doesn't Need V.P. 'Pig-in-the-Poke,'" *Reagan-Schweiker, They'll Beat Carter, News,* 18 August 1976, folder "RR/Schweiker, 'Convention News,'" box 53, CFR, Hoover; roll-call vote on amendment 16-C, 17 August 1976, folder "Rule 16C (GOP Platform)," box 53, CFR, Hoover; Philip Shabecoff, "'Delighted' Ford Says Victory on Rules Points to His Nomination on First Ballot," *NYT,* 18 August 1976.
18. Lou Cannon, "Buckley Hints He Would Run as 'Compromise,'" *WP,* 12 August 1976; Frank Lynn, "Buckley Abandons Presidential Effort after Support Lags," *NYT,* 17 August 1976.
19. Shirley, *Reagan's Revolution,* 283–296; presidential nomination, roll-call vote, 18 August 1976, folder "Convention Roll Calls—16C/Pres. Nom.," box 53, CFR, Hoover.
20. Stuart, "Ford, Reagan Target"; James M. Naughton, "Reagan Leaders Raiding Delegates Pledged to Ford," *NYT,* 17 June 1976; Reagan campaign, press release, 10 August 1976, folder "RR/Schweiker, 'Convention News,'" box 53, CFR, Hoover; "Reagan and Rules," *CSM,* 17 August 1976; R. W. Apple Jr., "Reagan Men Seek Way to Deal Ford a Damaging Blow," *NYT,* 11 August 1976.

21. R. W. Apple Jr., "Ford Takes Nomination on First Ballot," *NYT,* 19 August 1976.
22. Dick Cheney to Gerald Ford, re: Meeting with Governor Robert Ray, 8 April 1976, folder "PL 1–2, Platforms 8/9/74–5/30/76," box PL76, Subject Files, WHCF, GRFL.
23. Ford campaign, draft strategy paper for convention, 21 May 1976, folder "Convention Strategy," box 14, MRD, GRFL.
24. Peter J. Wallison to Nelson Rockefeller, 9 June 1976, folder "Political Affairs—Ford (6)," box 37, PHF, GRFL.
25. RNC, original draft of Republican Party platform of 1976, [August 1976], folder "Platform—Original Draft," box 58, CFR, Hoover.
26. Ronald Reagan, telegram to Platform Committee members, 6 August 1976, folder "PL 1–2, 8/31/76," box PL76, Subject Files, WHCF, GRFL; "Rockefeller: More Dollars for Defense," *Kansas City Times,* 10 August 1976; "Republican Feminists Prepare to Fight for Conversion Delegates, Rights Amendment and Abortion," *NYT,* 19 February 1976; Christopher Lydon, "Abortion Plank Is Fought by Republican Feminists," *NYT,* 18 August 1976; 1972 Republican Party platform, www.presidency.ucsb.edu/documents/republican-party-platform-1972; William J. Baroody Jr. to Gerald Ford, 16 September 1976, folder "Political Affairs—Ford (11)," box 37, PHF, GRFL.
27. Jules Witcover, "Reagan Forces and Helms' 'Rebels' Get Together," *WP,* 12 August 1976.
28. Jesse Helms, proposed platform plank on Africa, [11 August 1976], folder "Platform—Helms Statement," box 58, CFR, Hoover.
29. Reagan campaign, point-by-point comparison between RNC platform draft and final platform, [August 1976], folder "RR/Schweiker, 'Convention News,'" box 53, CFR, Hoover.
30. Jim Reichley to Dick Cheney, 25 June 1976, folder "Constituency Analysis," box 2, A. James Reichley Files, GRFL.
31. George Van Cleve to Mike Duval, re: Conversation with Senator Dole's A.A.," 28 July 1976, folder "Van Cleve, George," box 24, MRD, GRFL; Bob Dole, press release, "Dole Urges Republican Convention to Support Constitutional Convention on Abortion," 10 August 1976, folder "Platform Presentations," box 58, CFR, Hoover; UPI, "Subcommittee Platform Backs Ban on Abortions," *Salina (KS) Journal,* 11 August 1976; Richard L. Madden, "Reagan's Plank Criticizes Ford-Kissinger Policies," *NYT,* 17 August 1976.
32. AP, "Platform Committee Faces Dispute over Issues," *Iowa City Press-Citizen,* 12 August 1976; Richard L. Madden, "Platform Panel Endorses Equal Rights Plan," *NYT,* 13 August 1976; Don Phillips (UPI), "Foreign Policy, Abortion Floor Fights Are Assured," *Shreveport (LA) Times,* 17 August 1976; Robert H. Spiegel, "Uncommitteds Guard Their Status," *Wisconsin State Journal,* 17 August 1976.
33. Reagan campaign, press release, 15 August 1976, folder "Ronald Reagan

File—Campaign File, 1976—Republican Party Platform," box 6, Peter Hannaford Papers, Hoover; Richard L. Madden, "Reagan's Forces Prevail on Foreign Policy Plank," *NYT,* 18 August 1976; 1976 Republican Party Platform, www.presidency.ucsb.edu/documents/republican-party-platform-1976.

34. Reagan campaign, press release, 14 August 1976, folder "RR/Schweiker, 'Convention News,'" box 53, CFR, Hoover; Gerald Ford to Ray Barnhart, 15 September 1976, and Michael Raoul-Duval to Robert D. Ray, 25 October 1976, folder "PL 1–2, 9/1/76–1/20/77," box PL76, Subject Files, WHCF, GRFL.
35. "GOP Platform," *CSM,* 16 August 1976; AP, "Dole and Platform Both Disappointing to Ripon Society," *Emporia (KS) Gazette,* 27 August 1976; AP, "Republican Platform Panel Backs ERA," *Tucson (AZ) Daily Star,* 13 August 1976.
36. Henry Lucas, "National Black Republican Council Issues Statement Presented to Platform Committee at National Republican Convention," 10 August 1976, folder "Platform Testimony," box 58, CFR, Hoover; Samuel C. Jackson, "Testimony of the Council of 100—an Organization of Black Republicans—to the Republican National Convention," 10 August 1976, ibid.; 1972 Republican Party platform; 1976 Republican Party platform.
37. Ethel Allen to Gerald Ford, 8 July 1976, folder "PL 1, 8/17/76–1/20/77," box PL75, Subject Files, WHCF, GRFL.
38. John Calhoun to Ethel Allen, 10 September 1976, folder "PL 1, 8/17/76–1/20/77," box PL75, Subject Files, WHCF, GRFL.
39. *The Black Vote: Election '76* (Washington, DC: Joint Center for Political Studies, 1977), 5; UPI, "Ford Pledges Blacks Will Be in Campaign," *AC,* 18 August 1976; Maurice A. Dawkins to Donald Rumsfeld, 27 July 1975, folder "Black Voters," box A1, PFC, GRFL; People for Ford Black Desk national budget, [September 1976], folder "Black Desk—Budget," box F14, PFC, GRFL.
40. Ford campaign, talking points for campaign, [August 1976], folder "Political Affairs—Ford (9)," box 37, PHF, GRFL.
41. Jules Witcover, "Ford Follows Carter's Lead on No. 2 Spot," *WP,* 11 August 1976; Dick Barnes, "Party Unity," *South Bend (IN) Tribune,* 9 August 1976.
42. Jules Witcover, "Ford's Long No. 2 List Believed Cut to around 5," *WP,* 16 August 1976.
43. David Stout, "Howard H. Baker Jr., a Senate Republican Bridge-Builder, Dies at 88," *NYT,* 27 June 2014; Rowland Evans and Robert Novak, "The Search for a Vice President," *WP,* 18 August 1976; Rowland Evans and Robert Novak, "Why It Probably Won't Be Baker," *WP,* 9 May 1980; Jules Witcover, *Marathon: The Pursuit of the Presidency, 1972–1976* (New York: Viking Press, 1977), 507.
44. Yanek Miezkowski, *Gerald Ford and the Challenges of the 1970s* (Lexington: University Press of Kentucky, 2005), 320; Clare Crawford, "From

Watergate to Womankind, Bill and Jill Ruckelshaus Fight for Their Ideas," *People,* 12 April 1976.

45. Eileen Shanahan, "Women's Unit Broke and Split on Future," *NYT,* 28 August 1972; Catherine E. Rymph, *Republican Women: Feminism and Conservatism from Suffrage through the Rise of the New Right* (Chapel Hill: University of North Carolina Press, 2006), 198–219.
46. Witcover, *Marathon,* 508.
47. Stef Halper to Dave Gergen, re: Luncheon with George Will, 11 June 1976, folder "Vice Presidential Selection," box 24, MRD, GRFL; Joe Holley, "Obituary: Leading Texas Republican Anne Armstrong," *WP,* 31 July 2008; William Grimes, "Anne Armstrong, Presidential Adviser and Pioneering Politician, Dies at 80," *NYT,* 31 July 2008; Robert Teeter to Gerald Ford, 16 August 1976, folder "Political Affairs—Ford (8)," box 37, PHF, GRFL; Witcover, "Ford's Long No. 2 List Believed Cut."
48. William J. Casey to Gerald Ford, 29 July 1976, folder "Political Affairs—Ford (7)," box 37, PHF, GRFL; Evans and Novak, "Search for a Vice President"; David S. Broder and Edward Walsh, "Ford Reportedly Won't Ask Reagan to Serve as No. 2," *WP,* 19 August 1976.
49. Charles Mohr, "Ford Said to Plan Talk to Reagan," *NYT,* 18 August 1976; Gerald R. Ford, *A Time to Heal: The Autobiography of Gerald R. Ford* (New York: Berkley Books, 1979), 386–388; Witcover, *Marathon,* 504–506.
50. Marjorie Hunter, "Ford and Dole Found in Harmony on Issues," *NYT,* 21 August 1976; Carter campaign, state-by-state survey data for Ford-Carter race from internal campaign polling, August 1976, folder "Survey: General Election," box 36, Jody Powell Papers, JCL.
51. [Mike Duval], "Campaign Strategy—GRF vs. JEC—November 2, 1976," folder "Campaign Strategy, 7/2/76 draft," box 13, MRD, GRFL; AP, "Carter Is Described by Dole as 'Southern-Fried McGovern,'" *Baltimore Sun,* 19 July 1976; AP, "Mondale Says He and Carter Would End Embargoes on Grain Shipments," *Arizona Republic,* 1 August 1976.
52. Ford, *Time to Heal,* 388–389.
53. Witcover, *Marathon,* 506–508.
54. John Robert Greene, *The Presidency of Gerald R. Ford* (Lawrence: University Press of Kansas, 1995), 173; Witcover, *Marathon,* 507–509.
55. Ford, *Time to Heal,* 390–391; Greene, *Presidency of Gerald R. Ford,* 173.
56. James M. Naughton, "Delegates Voice Doubts on Ford-Dole Prospects," *NYT,* 20 August 1976.
57. R. W. Apple Jr., "Ford Picks Senator Dole as Running Mate," *NYT,* 20 August 1976; Christopher Lydon, "A Tough Infighter: Robert Joseph Dole," *NYT,* 20 August 1976; Elizabeth Drew, *American Journal: The Events of 1976* (New York: Random House, 1977), 403, 406.
58. Apple, "Ford Picks Senator Dole as Running Mate"; Gerald Ford, speech at Republican National Convention, 19 August 1976, https://millercenter.org/the-presidency/presidential-speeches/august-19-1976-republican-national-convention.

59. Ford, speech at Republican National Convention.
60. Witcover, *Marathon,* 509–510; Shirley, *Reagan's Revolution,* xxi–xxii; "Transcript of Reagan's Remarks to the Convention," *NYT,* 20 August 1976.
61. Shirley, *Reagan's Revolution,* xxii–xxiii.
62. Drew, *American Journal,* 405.
63. Ronald Reagan, "Tax Cuts and Increased Revenue," 8 October 1976, folder "Memoranda, 1974–1983 and undated," box 1, Peter Hannaford Papers, Hoover; Lou Cannon, *Governor Reagan: His Rise to Power* (New York: Public Affairs, 2003), 433; Douglas Brinkley, *Gerald R. Ford* (New York: Times Books, 2007), 145.
64. Frank C. Kent to Richard Cheney, 16 September 1976, folder "Black Desk—Correspondence (1)," box F14, PFC, GRFL.

9. CARTER STUMBLES OVER CULTURAL ISSUES

1. [Mike Duval], Ford campaign strategy handbook, [July 1976], folder "Campaign Plan—Final Copy, 4 of 4," box 13, MRD, GRFL.
2. David W. Belin, "The Election of President Ford: Basic Strategy Paper No. 7," May 1976, folder "Political Affairs—Ford (6)," box 37, PHF, GRFL; Jim Reichley to Dick Cheney, 25 June 1976, folder "Campaign Strategy—Suggestions (2)," box 13, MRD, GRFL.
3. [Duval], Ford campaign strategy handbook; Reichley to Cheney, 25 June 1976; Patrick Riley, "Pro-Life Leader Marjory Mecklenburg Joins Ford-Dole Campaign Committee," *National Catholic Register,* 10 October 1976; Marjory Mecklenburg, DM to pro-life group leaders on behalf of President Ford Committee, [October 1976], folder "Abortion Issue (1)," box C25, PFC, GRFL.
4. John Dillin, "Pollsters Tell Ford: Look North," *CSM,* 20 August 1976; Reichley to Cheney, 25 June 1976; Jim Reichley to Dick Cheney, 5 June 1976, folder "Reichley, Jim," box 23, MRD, GRFL.
5. Wesley G. Pippert, "Where Do They Stand? Issues Significant to Christians," *Christian Life,* November 1976, 14–15; George Van Cleve to Dave Gergen, 18 June 1976, folder "Van Cleve, George," box 24, MRD, GRFL; Reichley to Cheney, 25 June 1976.
6. AP, "Baptist Convention Hears Ford," *Montgomery (AL) Advertiser,* 16 June 1976; Alice Murray, "Ford Attacks Sex Scandal," *AC,* 16 June 1976.
7. "President's Proclamation," *NYT,* 4 July 1976; Ray Morgan, "Ford: Fight for Liberty Must Always Continue," *Kansas City Times,* 5 July 1976; transcript of Gerald Ford's videotaped speech for use at Thomas Road Baptist Church, Lynchburg, VA, 21 June 1976, folder "6-21-76—Thomas Rd. Baptist Church," box 61, Paul Theis and Robert Orben Files, GRFL; "The Word in Washington," *Christianity Today,* 12 March 1976, 39; Kenneth Briggs, "Ford, in Appeal to Evangelists, Stresses His Religious Beliefs," *NYT,* 10 October 1976.
8. Reichley to Cheney, 25 June 1976.

9. People for Ford organizational chart, [September 1976], folder "People for Ford—Staff Roster," box F16, PFC, GRFL; Ford campaign, list of advertising purchased from black radio stations and black newspapers, [October 1976], folder "Black Desk—Budget," box F12, ibid.; Robert J. Keyes to Elly Peterson, 10 November 1976, folder "People for Ford—Post-Election Analysis," box F3, ibid.; Ned Shreve (Labor for Ford) to Elly Peterson, [November 1976], folder "People for Ford—Post-Election Analysis (3)," box F4, ibid.; Oklahoma State Report for Youth for Ford, 27 September 1976, folder "Oklahoma—General," box F20, ibid.; Oregon State Report for Youth for Ford, 19 September 1976, folder "Oregon—General," box F70, ibid.
10. [Mike Duval], additions to strategy book, [July 1976], folder "Campaign Strategy—'Truncated Campaign Strategy'—Notes & Outlines," box 13, MRD, GRFL.
11. Unemployment rates come from the Bureau of Labor Statistics. Inflation rates come from inflationdata.com.
12. Jack Kemp to Rogers C. B. Morton, 17 March 1976, and T. Coleman Andrews III to William F. Gorog, 14 April 1976, folder "Job Creation," box 1, Rogers Morton Files, GRFL; Jim Reichley to Jim Cavanaugh, re: Tax statement, 25 October 1976, folder "Gergen, David," box 16, MRD, GRFL.
13. George Gallup, "Public Favors Budget Law," *AC*, 11 April 1976; Reichley to Cheney, 25 June 1976; [Duval], Ford campaign strategy handbook.
14. [Duval], Ford campaign strategy handbook.
15. "The Carter Tailspin," editorial, *WSJ*, 1 November 1976; R. W. Apple Jr., "Poll Shows Ford Trailing in Bid for 2 Voter Groups G.O.P. Needs," *NYT*, 10 September 1976; Eva Lubalin, DNC, Analysis of Recent Polls, 8 August 1976, folder "Democratic National Committee, 5/75–10/76," box 199, CCEJC, JCL; Louis "Woody" Jenkins to Gary Smith, 13 September 1976, folder "Memorandums—Campaign Staff, 9/76," box 199, ibid.
16. [Duval], Ford campaign strategy handbook; Ford campaign memo, Additional Thoughts on Fall Campaign Travel Schedule, [June–July 1976], folder "Campaign Travel," box 14, MRD, GRFL.
17. George Van Cleve to Mike Duval, 30 July 1976, folder "Campaign Strategy—Suggestions (3)," box 13, MRD, GRFL.
18. [Duval], Ford campaign strategy handbook.
19. Draft of speech for Gerald Ford on "No Campaign" strategy, [July 1976?], folder "Campaign Strategy—'Truncated Campaign Strategy'—Notes & Outlines," box 13, MRD, GRFL.
20. Andrew J. Glass, "Ford Bailing out of 'Cotton South,'" *AC*, 22 August 1976; James M. Naughton, "Ford's Aides Say Dole Will Assume Big Campaign Role," *NYT*, 23 August 1976; "Ford against Draft-Dodger Pardons—Dole," *AC*, 26 August 1976; UPI, "Dole Campaigns in Carter Territory," *Fort Lauderdale (FL) News*, 2 September 1976; Douglas E. Kneeland, "Embargoes at Issue," *NYT*, 27 August 1976.

21. James M. Naughton, "Voting Surprise by Ford Forecast," *NYT,* 29 August 1976; AP, "Dole: Carter Too Liberal," *Jackson (TN) Sun,* 2 September 1976; Douglas E. Kneeland, "Dole Predicts Carter Losses in the South," *NYT,* 1 September 1976.
22. Carol Wilson Utley, "Liddy Dole Best Southern Strategy," *High Point (NC) Enterprise,* 30 October 1976.
23. AP, "Salisbury Honors Liddy," *High Point (NC) Enterprise,* 2 September 1976; AP, "Elizabeth Dole to Take Leave to Help Campaign," *Great Falls (MT) Tribune,* 5 September 1976; Martha Angle, "Dole's Tarheel Wife Helps Party Heal Southern Wound," *Tallahassee (FL) Democrat,* 3 September 1976.
24. Jim Cavanaugh to Gerald Ford, 11 October 1976, folder "Political Affairs—Ford (13)," box 37, PHF, GRFL; Douglas E. Kneeland, "Dole Believes He Was Nominated to Span G.O.P. Gap," *NYT,* 23 August 1976.
25. Louis Harris, "Harris Survey: Mondale More Help than Dole," *Chicago Tribune,* 7 October 1976; Godfrey Sperling Jr., "V-P Impact: Mondale Rated Stronger 'Where It Counts,'" *CSM,* 7 October 1976.
26. Carter campaign, polling data for Ford-Carter race, 1 August 1976, folder "Survey: General Election," box 36, Jody Powell Papers, JCL; Apple, "Poll Shows Ford Trailing."
27. "Carter's Margin in Gallup Poll Now 2–1 over Ford or Reagan," *NYT,* 1 August 1976; "Gallup Poll Reports Ford Has Cut Lead of Carter to 49–39," *NYT,* 26 August 1976; James Reston, "Ford up in the Polls," *NYT,* 27 August 1976; "Carter Gains in the Gallup Poll," *NYT,* 3 September 1976; R. W. Apple Jr., "Debate on Tonight; Ford-Carter Battle Seen as Close," *NYT,* 23 September 1976; "Ford-Carter Race Found about Even outside the South," *NYT,* 29 August 1976.
28. Hamilton Jordan to Jimmy Carter and Walter Mondale, July 1976, folder "Memorandum/Analysis—Hamilton Jordan to Jimmy Carter, 7/76," box 199, CCEJC, JCL.
29. Jordan to Carter and Mondale, July 1976.
30. Kenneth Reich, "Carter Backs 'Legitimate Status' for Nation's Long-Time Illegal Immigrants," *LAT,* 2 July 1976; Carter campaign, Spanish-language print ad: "Vote por Jimmy Carter y Walter Mondale," [September–October 1976], folder "Mailings," box 306, CCEJC, JCL; Rick Hernandez to Curtis Allen, 5 October 1976, folder "Memoranda, General Election [2]," box 411, ibid.
31. Eileen Shanahan, "Compromise Reached on Women's Role," *NYT,* 13 July 1976; Carter campaign, Political Desk's daily report, 17 September 1976, folder "Political Desk Reports, General Election," box 412, CCEJC, JCL; Jimmy Carter, speech to women's rights activists, Los Angeles, 7 October 1976, folder "Carter Statements on the Issues," box 294, ibid.; 51.3% Committee, "51.3% for Jimmy Carter and Fritz Mondale," September 1976, folder "Advisory Group—Handbooks," ibid.; 51.3% Committee Advisory List, [September 1976], folder "Advisory Group—Handbooks," ibid.

32. Sarah Hertel to Hamilton Jordan et al., Comparison of Male, Female, and Minority Salaries for 1/31/76, 8/15/76, and 10/15/76, [October 1976], and Sarah Hertel to Hamilton Jordan et al., Comparison of Men and Women's Salaries per 8/31/76 Payroll, [September 1976?], folder "Memoranda, General Election [2]," box 411, CCEJC, JCL.
33. Adam Walinsky to Jimmy Carter, [July 1976], folder "Catholics, 8/23/76–10/76," box 3, CCEJC, JCL; Religious News Service (RNS), "Carter's Baptist Faith Held a Plus: Editor of Catholic Paper: 'I Like the Idea of a Praying President,'" 20 July 1976, and RNS, "Catholic Democrats and Others See No Major Problems for Jimmy Carter," 19 July 1976, folder "Abortion [1]," box 304, ibid.; Albert R. Hunt, "Carter and the Catholics," *WSJ*, 8 July 1976.
34. Landon Butler, memo to all department heads, 24 August 1976, folder "Memoranda, General Election [1]," box 411, CCEJC, JCL; Scott Burnett to Hamilton Jordan, 5 October 1976, folder "Memoranda, General Election [2]," ibid.
35. Adam Walinsky to Jimmy Carter, [July 1976], folder "Catholics, 8/23/76–10/76," box 3, CCEJC, JCL; David Murray, "Carter Decides to Stonewall Position on Abortion Issue," *Chicago Sun-Times*, 5 September 1976; Bob Burns to Stuart Eizenstat, 7 September 1976, folder "Catholics, 8/23/76–10/76," box 3, CCEJC, JCL.
36. Landon Butler to Hamilton Jordan and Rick Hutcheson, 28 August 1976, folder "Memoranda, General Election [1]," box 411, CCEJC, JCL.
37. Lou Cannon, "Carter: Abortion Amendment," *WP*, 2 September 1976.
38. James M. Naughton, "Bishops 'Encouraged' by Ford on Abortion," *NYT*, 11 September 1976; John D. Rockefeller III, "No Retreat on Abortion," *Newsweek*, 21 June 1976; John D. Rockefeller III to Gerald Ford, 31 August 1976, folder "Welfare—Abortions," box 51, PHF, GRFL; Ford campaign internal document for the president, "Abortion," [September 1976], folder "Religious Matters—Catholic," box 42, ibid.; *Our Sunday Visitor*, press release, 21 October 1976, folder "Catholics, 8/23/76–10/76," box 3, CCEJC, JCL.
39. David S. Broder, "Effort to Court Catholic Gains," *WP*, 9 September 1976; Carter campaign, press release, "Carter-Catholics," 5 September 1976, folder "Abortion, 9/76," box 1, CCEJC, JCL; transcript of Jim Castelli's interview with Jimmy Carter, *National Catholic News*, 9 August 1976, folder "Catholics, 5/76–8/20/76," box 3, ibid.
40. "Forked Tongue," editorial, *Albany (NY) Evangelist*, 22 July 1976; Birch Bayh to Jimmy Carter, 16 September 1976, folder "Abortion, 9/76," box 1, CCEJC, JCL; Frank Moore to Jimmy Carter, 3 September 1976, folder "Catholics, 8/23/76–10/76," box 3, ibid.; Bob Havely and Doug Robinson to Stu Eizenstat, 6 September 1976, folder "Abortion, 9/76," box 1, ibid.
41. Sam Popkin to Patrick Caddell, [September 1976], folder "Survey: General Election," box 36, Jody Powell Papers, JCL; Dennis Farney, "New

Converts? Blue-Collar Catholics Become Less Skeptical of a President Carter," *WSJ*, 17 October 1976.

42. Peter G. Bourne, *Jimmy Carter: A Comprehensive Biography from Plains to Postpresidency* (New York: Scribner, 1997), 345–346; "*Playboy* Interview: Jimmy Carter," *Playboy*, November 1976, 64.
43. "*Playboy* Interview," 70. For Scheer's brief professional biography, see his faculty webpage at the University of Southern California's Annenberg School for Communication and Journalism, https://annenberg.usc.edu/faculty/communication/robert-scheer.
44. AP, "Carter Hits Prosecution of Gays," *Albany (OR) Democrat-Herald*, 22 May 1976. In 1977 (the earliest year for which Gallup survey data are available) Americans were evenly divided (43 percent versus 43 percent) over whether "homosexual relations between consenting adults should or should not be legal." Sixty-five percent of all Americans (and 71 percent of southerners) said that "homosexuals" should not be hired as elementary school teachers. George H. Gallup, *The Gallup Poll: Public Opinion, 1972–1977*, 2 vols. (Wilmington, DE: Scholarly Resources, 1978), 2:1136–1155. Carter's proposal to create federal civil rights protections for gays and lesbians was thus more liberal than the policies most Americans—and certainly most Southern Baptists—favored at the time. For more on gay rights policy debates of the 1970s, see Dudley Clendinen and Adam Nagourney, *Out for Good: The Struggle to Build a Gay Rights Movement in America* (New York: Simon & Schuster, 1999). For a discussion of Carter's moderately liberal views on gay rights in 1976, see R. Brooks Flippen, *Jimmy Carter, the Politics of Family, and the Rise of the Religious Right* (Athens: University of Georgia Press, 2011), 83–85.
45. "*Playboy* Interview," 69.
46. "*Playboy* Interview," 63–86.
47. "*Playboy* Interview," 86.
48. AP, "Guilty of Adultery in My Heart Many Times, Carter Says," *AC*, 21 September 1976.
49. Myra MacPherson, "Evangelicals Seen Cooling on Carter," *WP*, 27 September 1976.
50. "Remarks on Sexuality Draw Mixed Response," *WP*, 21 September 1976; Robert Lamb and Fay S. Joyce, "Carter *Playboy* Talk Starts 'em Buzzing," *AC*, 22 September 1976; "The Ridiculous Factory," editorial, *Omaha World-Herald*, 22 September 1976.
51. Lamb and Joyce, "Carter *Playboy* Talk Starts 'em Buzzing"; Lee Dembart, "Carter's Comments on Sex Cause Concern," *NYT*, 23 September 1976.
52. Jules Witcover, *Marathon: The Pursuit of the Presidency, 1972–1976* (New York: Viking Press, 1977), 561–570.
53. "*Playboy* Interview," 86; Charles H. Ashcraft, "The Pig-Sty in the Parlor," *Arkansas Baptist Newsmagazine*, 23 September 1976, 2; "Dallas Baptist Backs Ford," *AC*, 11 October 1976.
54. "Dallas Baptist Backs Ford"; President Ford Committee, "Criswell"

commercial, livingroomcandidate.org; Deirdre Carmody, "Ford and Carter Forces Dispute G.O.P. Ad Showing *Playboy* Cover," *NYT,* 22 October 1976; UPI, "Carter, Ford Are Facing New Campaign Headaches," *Naples (FL) Daily News,* 3 October 1976; Sandy to Tim Kraft, Carter campaign report from Plains and Rockies, 20 October 1976, folder "Field Reports, October 1976," box 409, CCEJC, JCL.

55. Lynn Darden to Chuck Parrish and John Carlin, 15 September 1976, folder "Protestants [2]," box 280, CCEJC, JCL; Landon Butler to Jimmy Carter et al., re: Telephone calls to Protestant leaders, 16 October 1976, folder "Protestants [1]," ibid.; [Bruce Edwards], open letter supporting Carter, 19 October 1976, ibid.
56. Andrew J. Glass, "Clergy Answering Call from Carter," *AC,* 3 October 1976; MacPherson, "Evangelicals Seen Cooling on Carter."
57. Carter campaign, daily report from the southern region, 26 October 1976, folder "Field Reports, October 1976," box 409, CCEJC, JCL; MacPherson, "Evangelicals Seen Cooling on Carter"; Glass, "Clergy Answering Call from Carter"; Ron Boehme with Rus Walton, *What about Jimmy Carter?* (Washington, DC: Third Century, 1976).
58. "The Phillips-Singdingler Report: Putting Polls in Time Context," *Longview (TX) News-Journal,* 12 October 1976; David Morrison, "Carter's Support Slipping in South," *AC,* 6 October 1976.
59. UPI, "Carter Explains More about *Playboy* Article," *Tampa (FL) Tribune,* 25 September 1976.
60. Transcript of third presidential debate, Williamsburg, VA, 22 October 1976, www.debates.org/voter-education/debate-transcripts/october-22-1976-debate-transcript/.

10. FORD VERSUS CARTER

1. R. W. Apple Jr., "Debate on Tonight; Ford-Carter Battle Now Seen as Close," *NYT,* 23 September 1976.
2. Jules Witcover, *Marathon: The Pursuit of the Presidency, 1972–1976* (New York: Viking Press, 1977), 570–573.
3. Dorrance Smith to Mike Duval, 3 September 1976, folder "Carter Primary Forums," box 25, MRD, GRFL; [Mike Duval], "Campaign Strategy—GRF vs. JEC—November 2, 1976," [2 July 1976], folder "Campaign Strategy, 7/2/76 draft," box 13, ibid.
4. Mike Duval, debate preparation schedule, 3 September 1976, folder "Debate Preparation," box 25, MRD, GRFL; Gerald R. Ford, *A Time to Heal: The Autobiography of Gerald R. Ford* (New York: Berkley Books, 1979), 401; Dave Gergen to Dick Cheney and Mike Duval, 18 September 1976, folder "Strategy," box 31, MRD, GRFL.
5. Witcover, *Marathon,* 573–575.
6. Stuart E. Eizenstat, *President Carter: The White House Years* (New York: Thomas Dunne, 2018), 57; Rick Hutcheson to Hamilton Jordan, 18 September 1976, folder "Memoranda, General Election [2]," box 411,

CCEJC, JCL; Martin Schram, *Running for President 1976: The Carter Campaign* (New York: Stein & Day, 1977), 295–296.

7. David E. Rosenbaum, "Mondale and Dole Campaign Again after Claiming a Victory in Debate," *NYT,* 17 October 1976; "Ford Seen Winning Debate 32%–25% in Gallup Poll," *LAT,* 30 September 1976; Louis Harris, "Debate-Winner Ford Still Lags in Race," *Chicago Tribune,* 27 September 1976. All quotations from the first debate are from transcript of first Ford-Carter presidential debate, 23 September 1976, folder "Debate Working Papers—First Debate, 9/23/76—Transcript," box 27, MRD, GRFL, or video footage of the debate.
8. R. W. Apple Jr., "Voter Poll Finds Debate Aided Ford and Cut Carter Lead," *NYT,* 27 September 1976.
9. Office of Management and Budget, Historical Tables for 1976, www.whitehouse.gov/omb/historical-tables/. In recent decades, presidents who have proposed tax cuts have usually predicted that they would produce economic growth and increased revenue that would at least partially offset any immediate reduction in tax revenue. But because Ford's administration preceded the Republican Party's adoption of supply-side "Reaganomic" views, he did not necessarily expect a tax cut to increase government revenue; he therefore insisted that any tax cuts had to be offset by equivalent reductions in spending to produce a balanced budget. James P. Gannon, "Ford Proposes $28 Billion of Tax Cuts Linked to New $395 Billion Spending Lid," *NYT,* 7 October 1975.
10. Witcover, *Marathon,* 578–579.
11. "Ford Seen Winning Debate 32%–25% in Gallup Poll"; AP, "Poll Indicates Ford Is Inching Closer," *Tampa (FL) Tribune,* 25 September 1976; Apple, "Voter Poll Finds Debate Aided Ford and Cut Carter Lead."
12. AP, "Poll Indicates Ford Is Inching Closer"; Barry Sussman, "Widely Varying Voter Polls May Befog Election Outlook," *WP,* 19 October 1976; John Dillin, "Gallup Says Swift Climb Gives Ford Upset Chance," *CSM,* 20 October 1976.
13. Ford, *Time to Heal,* 407.
14. All quotations from the second Ford-Carter debate are from transcript of the second Ford-Carter debate, 6 October 1976, folder "Debate Working Papers—Second Debate, 10/6/76—Transcript," box 28, MRD, GRFL, and from video footage of the debate.
15. Philip Shabecoff, "Ford Seems to Retreat on Pledge of Disclosures in Arabs' Boycott," *NYT,* 8 October 1976; Carter campaign, Political Desk's daily report, 7 October 1976, folder "Political Desk Reports, General Election," box 412, CCEJC, JCL.
16. Rob Quartel to Mike Duval, 3 October 1976, folder "Debate Working Papers—First Debate, 9/23/76—Comments & Analysis," box 26, MRD, GRFL; Leslie H. Gelb, "Brzezinski Viewed as Key Advisor to Carter," *NYT,* 6 October 1976.
17. Bud McFarlane to Dave Gergen, 1 October 1976, folder "Debate Working

Papers—Second Debate, 10/6/76—Multiple Topics (1)," box 27, MRD, GRFL.

18. Market Opinion Research poll, 6–7 October 1976, folder "Debate Working Papers—Second Debate, 10/6/76, Market Opinion Res.—Post Deb Poll," box 27, MRD, GRFL; "Roper, AP Polls List Carter as Debate Winner," *Boston Globe,* 7 October 1976; Teeter tape printout of instant reaction to the second debate, 6 October 1976, folder "Debate Working Papers—Second Debate, 10/6/76—Teeter Tape (Instant Reaction)," box 28, MRD, GRFL; Foster Chanock to Mike Duval, re: Polling information on foreign policy/national defense, 1 October 1976, folder "Polling Information," box 16, ibid.; Martin Plissner, *The Control Room: How Television Calls the Shots in Presidential Elections* (New York: Free Press, 1999), 138.
19. Transcript of press conference with Richard Cheney, Brent Scowcroft, and Michael Duval after second debate, San Francisco, CA, 6 October 1976, folder "Press Conferences—Campaign Advisers," box 17, MRD, GRFL.
20. Market Opinion Research poll, 6–7 October 1976.
21. Ford, *Time to Heal,* 409–410.
22. Carter campaign, press release, "Carter Blasts Ford Insensitivity on Eastern Europe," 7 October 1976, folder "Newspaper Questionnaire Replies," box 306, CCEJC, JCL; James M. Naughton, "Carter Demands that Ford 'Tell the Truth,'" *NYT,* 9 October 1976; Dick Moe to state and regional coordinators, 7 October 1976, folder "Memoranda, General Election [2]," box 411, CCEJC, JCL.
23. "Ford Tells Ethnics He Erred in Eastern Europe Remark," *Washington Star,* 12 October 1976.
24. Sussman, "Widely Varying Voter Polls May Befog Election Outlook."
25. "Carter's 1st, but Ford's 3rd," *San Francisco Examiner,* 7 October 1976; second debate preparation, questions for President Ford, [October 1976], folder "Debate Working Papers—Second Debate, 10/6/76—Key Questions," box 27, MRD, GRFL; Foster Chanock to Mike Duval, 1 October 1976, folder "Polling Information," box 16, ibid.; George Gallup, "Carter Gains on President on 4 Foreign Policy Issues," *WP,* 17 October 1976.
26. "The Great Flap," *AC,* 12 October 1976.
27. Marty Dinkins to Robert Keyes, 2 October 1976, folder "Butz, Earl," box F15, PFC, GRFL; Warren Brown, "Ford Raps Butz for Race Slur," *WP,* 2 October 1976; Morton Mintz, "Critics Urge Resignation or Firing of Butz for Remarks about Blacks," *WP,* 3 October 1976; James M. Naughton, "Ford Termed Ready to Let Butz Resign If Dispute Widens," *NYT,* 3 October 1976; Jules Witcover, "Butz Resigns," *WP,* 5 October 1976.
28. Ford, *Time to Heal,* 404–405; Godfrey Sperling Jr. and Richard L. Strout, "Prosecutor Clears Ford; Dean Charge Still a Threat," *CSM,* 15 October 1976.

29. "Ford Plays Defense: Cleared in Fund Case, but Now Faces John Dean," *NYT*, 17 October 1976; George Moneyhun, "Dean Defends 'New' Watergate Charge," *CSM*, 28 October 1976; "Mr. Ford's Confirmation Testimony," editorial, *WP*, 30 October 1976.
30. UPI, "Pre-election Showings of 'President's Men,'" *WP*, 7 October 1976.
31. "*Playboy* Interview: Jimmy Carter," *Playboy*, November 1976, 86; Hamilton Jordan to Jimmy Carter and Walter Mondale, July 1976, folder "Memorandum/Analysis—Hamilton Jordan to Jimmy Carter, 7/76," box 199, Presidential Campaign Records, JCL; Naughton, "Carter Demands that Ford 'Tell the Truth.'" For an example of Carter's use of the phrase "Nixon-Ford administration" on the campaign trail, see Jack Zaiman, "Carter Says 'Fumbles' Hurt Campaign," *Hartford (CT) Courant*, 2 October 1976.
32. Linda Charlton, "Mondale Says Ford Has Failed to Heed Watergate Lesson," *NYT*, 6 October 1976; George H. Gallup, *The Gallup Poll: Public Opinion, 1972–1977*, 2 vols. (Wilmington, DE: Scholarly Resources, 1978), 2:799.
33. Transcript of phone conversation between Ford and Dole after vice-presidential debate, 15 October 1976, folder "Presidential Statements & Remarks (2)," box 17, MRD, GRFL; Witcover, *Marathon*, 613. All quotations from the vice-presidential debate come from "Transcript of Debate between the Vice-Presidential Candidates," *NYT*, 16 October 1976.
34. Raymond Marcus (Tarzana, CA) and Tom Weverk (Santa Barbara, CA), letters to the editor, *LAT*, 31 October 1976; AP, "Dole, Mondale Debate No Vote-Getter," *AC*, 17 October 1976; David S. Broder and Jules Witcover, "Mondale, Dole Exchange Broadsides," *WP*, 16 October 1976; Rosenbaum, "Mondale and Dole Campaign Again."
35. Rosenbaum, "Mondale and Dole Campaign Again"; R. W. Apple Jr., "Carter Emphasizing Mondale as an Asset," *NYT*, 29 October 1976.
36. "Transcript of Debate between the Vice-Presidential Candidates."
37. Robert W. Bednarzik and Stephen M. St. Marie, "Employment and Unemployment in 1976," *Monthly Labor Review*, February 1977, 3–5; "US Unemployment Rate by Month," https://www.multpl.com/unemployment/table/by-month; US Department of Labor, *Industry Wage Survey: Machinery Manufacturing, Winter 1974–75*, Bulletin 1929 (1977), 1–2. For the economic crises of the 1970s, see Judith Stein, *Pivotal Decade: How the United States Traded Factories for Finance in the Seventies* (New Haven, CT: Yale University Press, 2010); Jefferson Cowie, *Stayin' Alive: The 1970s and the Last Days of the Working Class* (New York: New Press, 2010).
38. "Improvement on the Wage Front," *Business in Brief*, October 1976; Social Security Administration, "National Average Wage Index," https://www.ssa.gov/oact/cola/AWI.html; US Department of Labor, *Industry Wage Survey: Machinery Manufacturing, Winter 1974–75*, 1.
39. Richard J. Levine, "Ford Finds a Comfortable, Effective Style of Campaigning as Homestretch Begins," *WSJ*, 26 October 1976; Jimmy

Carter, speech in Portland, OR, 27 September 1976, folder "Economics, 8/76–9/76," box 12, CCEJC, JCL.

40. Transcript of phone conversation between Ford and Dole after vice-presidential debate, 15 October 1976; Sophie Gilbert, "The Year Political Advertising Turned Positive," *Atlantic,* 9 June 2015; Gerald Ford TV ad, "Future," 1976, www.youtube.com. See also the Ford campaign ads "Accomplishment," www.youtube.com, and "Peace," http://www.livingroomcandidate.org/commercials/1976, for similar themes.
41. Transcript of third presidential debate, Williamsburg, VA, 22 October 1976,https://www.debates.org/voter-education/debate-transcripts/october-22-1976-debate-transcript/.
42. Lou Cannon, "Ford Talks of Nixon, Draws a Favorable Contrast to Him," *WP,* 28 October 1976.
43. Robert Reinhold, "Independents' Swing Spurs Ford Comeback," *NYT,* 31 October 1976.
44. "Things Looking up in Carolinas," President Ford Committee newsletter, 19 October 1976, folder "President Ford Committee Newsletters (4)," box F13, PFC, GRFL; Joe Jenckes to Max Friedersdorf and Jack Marsh, re: Campaign meeting with selected senators and governors, 18 October 1976, folder "Debate Preparation," box 25, MRD, GRFL; transcript of Q&A with press, San Diego, CA, 24 October 1976, folder "Presidential Statements & Remarks (4)," box 17, ibid.; Gerald Ford, transcript of campaign speech in Joliet, IL, 16 October 1976, folder "Presidential Statements & Remarks (3)," ibid.; transcript of Q&A session with Ford at San Fernando Valley Business and Professional Association, Los Angeles, CA, 8 October 1976, folder "Presidential Statements & Remarks (1)," ibid.; Gerald Ford, remarks at Lawton Municipal Airport, Lawton, OK, 8 October 1976, ibid.
45. Gerald Ford, transcript of campaign speech in Raleigh, NC, 23 October 1976, folder "Presidential Statements & Remarks (3)," box 17, MRD, GRFL; Gerald Ford, campaign speech, Cincinnati, OH, 28 October 1976, folder "Presidential Statements & Remarks (5)," ibid.; Gerald Ford, campaign speech, Fountain Valley, CA, 24 October 1976, folder "Presidential Statements & Remarks (4)," ibid.; Dave Gergen and Jerry Jones to Gerald R. Ford, 24 September 1976, folder "Political Affairs—Ford (11)," box 37, PHF, GRFL.
46. Mike Duval to Ford, re: Last debate, 18 October 1976, folder "Debate Preparation," box 25, MRD, GRFL; Jim Reichley to Jim Cavanaugh, 25 October 1976, folder "Gergen, David," box 16, ibid.
47. Jim Merriner, "Politics and People: Carter Concerned about His Image," *AC,* 18 October 1976; schedule for Bert Lance, 14–15 October 1976, folder "Press Releases," box 293, CCEJC, JCL; Steve Selig to Hamilton Jordan, 27 August 1976, folder "General Business," ibid.; Carter campaign, press release, "Carter Campaign Announces Business Liaison," [August 1976], folder "Press Releases," ibid.
48. Patt Derian to Rick Hutcheson, re: Basic campaign strategy, [October 1976],

folder "Memoranda, General Election [2]," box 411, CCEJC, JCL; Rick Hutcheson to Jody Powell and Hamilton Jordan, 20 October 1976, ibid.

49. "Jobless Rate Fell 0.1 Point to 7.8% for September," *WSJ*, 11 October 1976; Peter Milius, "A Low-Key Voter Issue," *WP*, 9 October 1976; Robert D. Hershey Jr., "G.N.P. Growth Rate Slows to 4% Level; Housing Starts to Rise," *NYT*, 20 October 1976; Helen Dewar, "Carter Says Trend Mocks Ford Forecast," *WP*, 30 October 1976; Carter-Mondale campaign, press release, "Carter Statement Corrects Distortions of His Record in Georgia," 21 October 1976, folder "Carter's Record as Governor, 10/76," box 3, CCEJC, JCL.
50. Schram, *Running for President 1976*, 332.
51. Wayne King, "Carter's Church May Dismiss Pastor for His Role in Dispute over Blacks," *NYT*, 2 November 1976; Charles Mohr, "Democrat's Aides Concerned," *NYT*, 2 November 1976.
52. "Black Jobless Rate Edged Down," *Tri-State Defender* (Memphis, TN), 23 October 1976; Pat Patterson, "Black Unemployment," *Black Enterprise*, November 1976; "The Presidency: Is There a Choice?" editorial, *San Francisco Sun Reporter*, 28 October 1976; "Will Black Voters Sit out the Presidential Election?" *New York Daily Challenge*, 14 October 1976; "100 Black Clergymen Support Pres. Ford," *Atlanta Daily World*, 24 October 1976; "Vote Today," editorial, *Atlanta Daily World*, 2 November 1976.
53. R. W. Apple Jr., "Ford and Carter Give Final Appeals in Race Still Viewed as Close," *NYT*, 2 November 1976.
54. Brock Brower, "Lean, Mean Gene," *NYT*, 24 October 1976; Wallace Turner, "Carter Ahead in California Poll, with Smaller Edge," *NYT*, 7 October 1976; Patt Derian to Hamilton Jordan et al., 18 October 1976, folder "Memorandums—Campaign Staff, 9/76," box 199, CCEJC, JCL; Patt Derian to Hamilton Jordan, Pat [Caddell?], Rick [Hutcheson], Landon Butler, re: McCarthy roundup, 14 September 1976, folder "Memoranda, General Election [2]," box 411, ibid.; "M'Carthy Ruled off Ballot in New York," *NYT*, 23 October 1976; *Congressional Quarterly's Guide to 1976 Elections* (Washington, DC: Congressional Quarterly, 1977), 23.
55. Pat Caddell to Carter campaign, 20 October 1976, folder "Survey: General Election," box 36, Jody Powell Papers, JCL; Lori and Alicia [Smith] to Tim Kraft et al., summary of daily political reports, 29 October 1976, folder "Field Reports, October 1976," box 409, CCEJC, JCL.
56. Mohr, "Democrat's Aides Concerned"; Jim Merriner, "Ford State Last Carter Stop," *AC*, 2 November 1976.
57. Edward Walsh, "An Emotional Homecoming in Grand Rapids," *WP*, 2 November 1976.

11. WHY CARTER WON

1. R. W. Apple Jr., "Georgian Wins South," *NYT*, 3 November 1976; Martin Schram, *Running for President 1976: The Carter Campaign* (New York: Stein & Day, 1977), 352–359.

2. Warren J. Mitofsky and Catherine C. Krein, *Campaign '76: A Reference of Official Vote Returns* (New York: Arno Press, 1977), 78, 288; Malcolm D. MacDougall, *We Almost Made It* (New York: Crown, 1977).
3. Cambridge Survey Research (CSR), "An Analysis of Political Attitudes in the United States of America," vol. 1, prepared for Democratic National Committee, January 1977, folder "Cambridge Survey Research (CSR): Analysis of Political Attitudes in the US volume #1," box 15, Jody Powell Papers, JCL; Robert Reinhold, "Carter Victory Tied to Democrats Back in Fold, Plus Independents," *NYT*, 4 November 1976; "Support for Ford Declines Sharply," *NYT*, 12 September 1974.
4. Market Opinion Research, 1976 presidential election, postelection analysis, [November 1976], folder "National Surveys—Post Election Analyses, November 1976—MOR Summary Report," box 62, Robert Teeter Papers, GRFL; Jonathan Moore and Janet Fraser, eds., *Campaign for President: The Managers Look at '76* (Cambridge, MA: Ballinger, 1977), 150.
5. R. W. Apple Jr., "Presidential Race Called Very Close on Eve of the Vote," *NYT*, 1 November 1976; "1968 Presidential General Election Results—Pennsylvania," in Dave Leip's Atlas of US Presidential Elections, https://uselectionatlas.org; "Black Voters Put Carter in White House," *Oakland (CA) Post*, 7 November 1976; Paul Delaney, "Blacks Expect Gains for Help to Carter," *NYT*, 7 November 1976; Apple, "Georgian Wins South"; Mitofksy and Krein, *Campaign '76*, 294–295, 311.
6. Reinhold, "Carter Victory Tied to Democrats Back in Fold"; James M. Naughton, "Key States '76," *NYT*, 3 November 1976; Roper Center, "How Groups Voted in 1976," https://ropercenter.cornell.edu/how-groups-voted-1976; "A Look at the Carter Coalition," *National Journal*, 6 November 1976, 1589. A salary of $12,000 a year in 1976, adjusted for inflation, would be equivalent to about $54,000 in 2019, and a 1976 salary of $20,000 would be equivalent to about $90,000.
7. CSR, "Analysis of Political Attitudes in the United States of America"; George H. Gallup, *The Gallup Poll: Public Opinion, 1972–1977*, 2 vols. (Wilmington, DE: Scholarly Resources, 1978), 2:887, 909; Paul R. Abramson, "Class Voting in the 1976 Presidential Election," *Journal of Politics* 40 (1978): 1070.
8. CSR, "Analysis of Political Attitudes in the United States of America"; Abramson, "Class Voting in the 1976 Presidential Election," 1070–1071.
9. Barry Sussman, "East, South, and Labor Provided Carter's Thin Margin," *WP*, 4 November 1976; Mitofsky and Krein, *Campaign '76*, 62, 128, 203, 279, 393.
10. CSR, "Analysis of Political Attitudes in the United States of America"; Abramson, "Class Voting in the 1976 Presidential Election," 1070; *The Black Vote: Election '76* (Washington, DC: Joint Center for Political Studies, 1977), 10–11; Sussman, "East, South, and Labor Provided Carter's Thin Margin." Estimates of Carter's share of the black vote range from

83 to 95 percent, depending on the survey. The Roper Center's figures, which are based on CBS News exit polls, indicate that Ford received 17 percent of the black vote and Carter 83 percent, but other studies suggest that black support for Carter was considerably higher. The extensive state-by-state analysis of the black vote published by the Joint Center for Political Studies in 1977 suggests that Carter received 90 percent of the black vote nationwide. Political scientist Paul Abramson's analysis of postelection survey data collected by the University of Michigan's Center for Political Studies led him to conclude that Carter received 96.3 percent of the black major-party vote in the South and 93.8 percent in other regions of the country. Abramson, "Class Voting in the 1976 Presidential Election," 1071.

11. Richard D. Lyons, "Turnout of Voters Largest in History," *NYT,* 4 November 1976.
12. "Blacks Gave Carter Victory in South," *AC,* 8 November 1976; "Black Vote Won for Carter, *Skanner* (Portland, OR), 18 November 1976.
13. The regional voting analysis in this chapter is based on data from "Election of 1976," American Presidency Project, www.presidency.ucsb.edu; Dave Leip's Atlas of US Presidential Elections; and Mitofsky and Krein, *Campaign '76.*
14. Douglas Brinkley, *Gerald R. Ford* (New York: Times Books, 2007), 145; Moore and Fraser, *Campaign for President,* 133.
15. "National Exit Polls Table," *NYT,* 5 November 2008, www.nytimes.com/elections/2008/results/president/nationalj-exit-polls.html.
16. Judith Stein, *Pivotal Decade: How the United States Traded Factories for Finance in the Seventies* (New Haven, CT: Yale University Press, 2010), 151. Eight thousand dollars would be equivalent to approximately $35,000 in 2019.
17. CSR, "Analysis of Political Attitudes in the United States of America."
18. "Look at the Carter Coalition," 1589; "National Exit Polls Table"; Lyman Kellstedt et al., "Faith Transformed: Religion and American Politics from FDR to George W. Bush," in *Religion and American Politics: From the Colonial Period to the Present,* ed. Mark A. Noll and Luke E. Harlow (New York: Oxford University Press, 2007), 273.

EPILOGUE

1. County election data are from Dave Leip's Atlas of US Presidential Elections, uselectionatlas.org.
2. US Census Bureau, QuickFacts: Jackson County, Alabama, https://www.census.gov/quickfacts/jacksoncountyalabama; US Census Bureau, QuickFacts: Alabama, https://www.census.gov/quickfacts/al.
3. US Census Bureau, QuickFacts: Lassen County, California, https://www.census.gov/quickfacts/lassencountycalifornia.
4. For studies of Carter's economy, see W. Carl Biven, *Jimmy Carter's Economy: Policy in an Age of Limits* (Chapel Hill: University of North Carolina

Press, 2002); Burton I. Kaufman, *The Presidency of James Earl Carter, Jr.* (Lawrence: University Press of Kansas, 1993); Judith Stein, *Pivotal Decade: How the United States Traded Factories for Finance in the 1970s* (New Haven, CT: Yale University Press, 2010); Thomas Borstelmann, *The 1970s: A New Global History from Civil Rights to Economic Inequality* (Princeton, NJ: Princeton University Press, 2012).

5. For this transformation, see Robert O. Self, *All in the Family: The Realignment of American Democracy since the 1960s* (New York: Hill & Wang, 2012); Gareth Davies, *From Opportunity to Entitlement: The Transformation and Decline of Great Society Liberalism* (Lawrence: University Press of Kansas, 1996); John D. Skrentny, *The Minority Rights Revolution* (Cambridge, MA: Harvard University Press, 2002); E. J. Dionne Jr., *Why Americans Hate Politics,* 2nd ed. (New York: Simon & Schuster, 2004).
6. "How to Forecast an American's Vote: All Politics Is Identity Politics," *Economist,* 3 November 2018.
7. Greg Price, "Trump Is a 'Blowhard,' 'I Don't Like Him,' and I Voted for Hillary, George Bush Says in New Book," *Newsweek,* 4 November 2017.
8. For an analysis of conservative Republican administrations' inability to deliver what their supporters expect, see E. J. Dionne Jr., *Why the Right Went Wrong: Conservatism—From Goldwater to Trump and Beyond* (New York: Simon & Schuster, 2016).
9. Will Lester, "Patrick Caddell, Carter Pollster Who Later Advised Trump Strategists, Dies at 68," *WP,* 18 February 2019.

BIBLIOGRAPHIC ESSAY

The most comprehensive, detailed book on the 1976 presidential election is Jules Witcover's *Marathon: The Pursuit of the Presidency, 1972–1976* (New York: Viking Press, 1977). As a *Washington Post* correspondent, Witcover wrote numerous articles on the candidates throughout their campaigns, and shortly after Jimmy Carter's election, he published a definitive journalistic account that has not been surpassed. Other useful journalistic analyses published immediately after the election include Elizabeth Drew's *American Journal: The Events of 1976* (New York: Random House, 1977), Martin Schram's *Running for President 1976: The Carter Campaign* (New York: Stein & Day, 1977), and Kandy Stroud's *How Jimmy Won: The Victory Campaign from Plains to the White House* (New York: Morrow, 1977).

CAMPAIGN MEMOIRS AND BIOGRAPHIES

Many of the managers and other staff members involved in the 1976 presidential campaigns published memoirs of their experiences. Malcolm D. McDougall's *We Almost Made It* (New York: Crown, 1977) is a firsthand account of the Ford campaign from one of his advertising directors. Donald Rumsfeld's *When the Center Held: Gerald Ford and the Rescue of the American Presidency* (New York: Free Press, 2018) includes the 1976 campaign as part of a study of Ford's entire presidency, and it offers an insider's perspective. Stuart E. Eizenstat's *President Carter: The White House Years* (New York: Thomas Dunne, 2018) offers a similar study of the Carter campaign and presidency, as told by a member of the campaign team who joined the White House staff. Carter's campaign manager, Hamilton Jordan, published two memoirs that say disappointingly little about the campaign: *No Such Thing as a Bad Day: A Memoir* (Atlanta: Longstreet, 2000) and *A Boy from Georgia: Coming of Age in the Segregated South* (Athens: University of Georgia Press, 2015). Several other Carter campaign staff members published more revealing memoirs. Speechwriter Patrick Anderson offers an insider's perspective in *Electing Jimmy Carter: The Campaign of 1976* (Baton Rouge: Louisiana State University Press, 1994). Dorothy Padgett's *Jimmy Carter: Elected President with Pocket Change and Peanuts* (Macon,

GA: Mercer University Press, 2016) is a personal campaign memoir from a native Georgian and longtime Carter admirer who helped orchestrate the Peanut Brigades that conducted door-to-door canvassing in New Hampshire and other states. One of the best sources for campaign managers' recollections of the 1976 election is *Campaign for President: The Managers Look at '76* (Cambridge, MA: Ballinger, 1977), edited by Jonathan Moore and Janet Fraser. It consists of a transcript of interviews conducted in December 1976 with managers not only from the Ford and Carter campaigns but also from the Reagan campaign and the campaigns of some of the Democratic primary contenders.

Shortly after his presidency, Gerald Ford published a detailed memoir, *A Time to Heal: The Autobiography of Gerald R. Ford* (New York: Harper & Row, 1979), that includes a significant amount of information about his unsuccessful campaign. It is an essential primary source for anyone seeking to understand his decision-making process. Jimmy Carter has published numerous memoirs and books. Unfortunately, none of them provides extensive information about his campaign for the presidency in 1976, but there is at least a limited discussion of his path to the White House in one of his most recent memoirs, *A Full Life: Reflections at Ninety* (New York: Simon & Schuster, 2015). Carter's campaign autobiography, *Why Not the Best?* (Nashville, TN: Broadman, 1975), is a useful primary source for anyone who wants to understand how the Georgia Democrat presented his own life story to prospective voters during the 1976 campaign.

Several good biographies of Jimmy Carter and Gerald Ford, both academic and popular, have been published. Well-researched studies of Ford that feature discussions of his 1976 presidential campaign include Scott Kaufman's *Ambition, Pragmatism, and Party: A Political Biography of Gerald R. Ford* (Lawrence: University Press of Kansas, 2017), John Robert Greene's *The Presidency of Gerald R. Ford* (Lawrence: University Press of Kansas, 1995), and Yanek Miezckowski's *Gerald Ford and the Challenges of the 1970s* (Lexington: University Press of Kentucky, 2005). The most comprehensive and informative Carter biography is Peter G. Bourne's *Jimmy Carter: A Comprehensive Biography from Plains to Post-Presidency* (New York: Scribner, 1997). Bourne was a close associate during Carter's governorship and presidency, so he offers an insider's perspective, but he is also an academic who supplements his own memories with extensive primary source research. Kenneth E. Morris's *Jimmy Carter: American Moralist* (Athens: University of Georgia Press,

1996) also offers an informative, analytic survey of Carter's life, written from an academic perspective. For a succinct, thoughtful analysis of Carter's presidency and life, Julian E. Zelizer's brief biography for the American Presidents series, *Jimmy Carter* (New York: Times Books, 2010), is recommended.

The role of Carter's evangelical Christian faith in the formation of his political convictions and in his presidential campaigns is the subject of Randall Balmer's *Redeemer: The Life of Jimmy Carter* (New York: Basic Books, 2014) and J. Brooks Flippen's *Jimmy Carter, the Politics of Family, and the Rise of the Religious Right* (Athens: University of Georgia Press, 2011). Any serious study of Carter's faith should include his own extensive writings on the subject, including *Faith: A Journey for All* (New York: Simon & Schuster, 2018) and *Living Faith* (New York: Times Books, 1996).

Most studies of Carter's presidency say little about the 1976 campaign, but they are still useful sources for an understanding of Carter's politics and the end result of his successful run for the White House. For a succinct but comprehensive overview of his administration, Burton I. Kaufman's *The Presidency of James Earl Carter, Jr.* (Lawrence: University Press of Kansas, 1993) is unsurpassed.

Biographical studies are available for most of the unsuccessful contenders in the 1976 presidential primaries. The number of studies of Ronald Reagan is vast and impossible to survey here, but for a portrait of Reagan in the 1970s, one of the best biographies is Lou Cannon's *Governor Reagan: His Rise to Power* (New York: PublicAffairs, 2003). Craig Shirley's *Reagan's Revolution: The Untold Story of the Campaign that Started It All* (Nashville, TN: Nelson Current, 2005) focuses solely on Reagan's 1976 campaign, which also receives extensive treatment in Rick Perlstein's *The Invisible Bridge: The Fall of Nixon and the Rise of Reagan* (New York: Simon & Schuster, 2014). Biographies of Carter's rivals in the Democratic primaries include Robert G. Kaufman's *Henry M. Jackson: A Life in Politics* (Seattle: University of Washington Press, 2000), Donald W. Carson's *Mo: The Life and Times of Morris K. Udall* (Tucson: University of Arizona Press, 2001), Chuck McFadden's *Trailblazer: A Biography of Jerry Brown* (Berkeley: University of California Press, 2013), and Scott Stossel's *Sarge: The Life and Times of Sargent Shriver* (Washington, DC: Smithsonian Books, 2004). George Wallace's effort to galvanize a populist movement of conservative Democrats has received extensive scholarly attention, but the best and most comprehensive study is Dan T. Carter's *The Politics of Rage: George Wallace, the Origins of the New Conservatism, and the Transformation of American Politics* (New York: Simon & Schuster, 1995). Hubert Humphrey ultimately decided not to enter the 1976 Democratic primaries, but he exercised enormous influence over the presidential contest and the party platform, so anyone wishing to understand the Democratic Party in 1976 would benefit from reading a good Humphrey biography such as Arnold A. Offner's *Hubert Humphrey: The Conscience of the Country* (New Haven, CT: Yale University Press, 2018).

POLITICAL CULTURE AND THE ISSUES THAT SHAPED THE 1976 ELECTION

Several studies of conservatism during the 1970s chronicle the social and political changes that formed the backdrop for the primary contest between Ronald Reagan and Gerald Ford. Laura Kalman's *Right Star Rising: A New Politics, 1974–1980* (New York: W. W. Norton, 2010) is one of the most detailed studies of conservative politics and presidential history during the Ford and Carter administrations. Donald T. Critchlow's *The Conservative Ascendancy: How the GOP Right Made Political History* (Cambridge, MA: Harvard University Press, 2007) includes an excellent analysis of the battle between conservatives and moderates in the Republican Party in the mid-1970s. Senator Jesse Helms played such a pivotal role in the rise of the New Right and the success of Reagan's primary campaign in North Carolina that a study of conservatism in the 1976 election should probably include William A. Link's definitive biography *Righteous Warrior: Jesse Helms and the Rise of Modern Conservatism* (New York: St. Martin's, 2008). Other useful studies of the internal struggles in the Republican Party during the 1970s include Catherine E. Rymph's *Republican Women: Feminism and Conservatism from Suffrage through the Rise of the New Right* (Chapel Hill: University of North Carolina Press, 2006) and Nicol C. Rae's *The Decline and Fall of the Liberal Republicans: From 1952 to the Present* (New York: Oxford University Press, 1989). *Rightward Bound: Making America Conservative in the 1970s*, a collection of essays edited by Bruce J. Schulman and Julian E. Zelizer (Cambridge, MA: Harvard University Press, 2008), covers a wide range of social and cultural issues that shaped the growth of conservatism during the Nixon, Ford, and Carter administrations.

For liberalism and the Democratic Party in the 1970s, Lily Geismer's *Don't Blame Us: Suburban Liberals and the Transformation of the*

Democratic Party (Princeton, NJ: Princeton University Press, 2015) offers one of the best historical analyses. Eric Alterman and Kevin Mattson's *The Cause: The Fight for American Liberalism from Franklin Roosevelt to Barack Obama* (New York: Viking, 2012) situates the liberalism of the 1970s in the larger context of the entire postwar era. Although Bruce Miroff's *The Liberals' Moment: The McGovern Insurgency and the Identity Crisis of the Democratic Party* (Lawrence: University Press of Kansas, 2007) focuses on the election of 1972, this analysis is helpful for understanding the internal debates in the Democratic Party in the months leading up to the 1976 election. The shift toward rights-based liberalism in the Democratic Party is well chronicled in John D. Skrentny's *The Minority Rights Revolution* (Cambridge, MA: Harvard University Press, 2002). To understand the backdrop of the Democratic presidential primary in Massachusetts and working-class Catholic ethnics' disillusionment with rights-based liberalism, consult Ronald P. Formisano's *Boston against Busing: Race, Class, and Ethnicity in the 1960s and 1970s* (Chapel Hill: University of North Carolina Press, 1991). For an analysis of southern Democrats and the social and cultural changes that facilitated Carter's political rise and transracial appeal in the South, see Earl Black and Merle Black's *Politics and Society in the South* (Cambridge, MA: Harvard University Press, 1987). White Democrats' growing alienation from their party over issues of race, welfare, and taxes has been the subject of extensive scholarly analysis, much of which helps explain the desire of many Democrats to nominate a candidate in 1976 who was less liberal than George McGovern. For an introduction to this topic, see Molly C. Michelmore's *Tax and Spend: The Welfare State, Tax Politics, and the Limits of American Liberalism* (Philadelphia: University of Pennsylvania Press, 2012) and Thomas Byrne Edsall and Mary D. Edsall's *Chain Reaction: The Impact of Race, Rights, and Taxes on American Politics,* 2nd ed. (New York: W. W. Norton, 1992). E. J. Dionne Jr.'s *Why Americans Hate Politics,* 2nd ed. (New York: Simon & Schuster, 2004), which describes Carter's victory as a sign of liberalism's weakness in 1976, presents a detailed analysis of the reasons why liberalism was struggling in the 1970s and conservatism was ascendant.

Recent studies of the particular economic, cultural, and social issues that divided Americans in the mid-1970s have greatly expanded our understanding of the issues at play in the 1976 election. For analyses of the causes and political and social consequences of the economic stagnation of the 1970s, see Judith Stein's *Pivotal Decade: How the United States Traded Factories for Finance in the Seventies* (New Haven, CT: Yale University Press, 2010), Jefferson Cowie's *Stayin' Alive: The 1970s and the Last Days of the Working Class* (New York: New Press, 2010), and Thomas Borstelmann's *The 1970s: A New Global History from Civil Rights to Economic Inequality* (Princeton, NJ: Princeton University Press, 2012). Meg Jacobs's study of the energy crisis, *Panic at the Pump: The Energy Crisis and the Transformation of American Politics in the 1970s* (New York: Hill & Wang, 2016), offers an excellent treatment of one particular aspect of the American economy during the Nixon, Ford, and Carter administrations. For histories of the national anxieties and increasingly conservative political culture of the 1970s, Natasha Zaretsky's *No Direction Home: The American Family and the Fear of National Decline, 1968–1980* (Chapel Hill: University of North Carolina Press, 2007) is recommended. For debates over sexuality and gender roles, see Marjorie J. Spruill's *Divided We Stand: The Battle over Women's Rights and Family Values that Polarized American Politics* (New York: Bloomsbury, 2017) and Robert O. Self's *All in the Family: The Realignment of American Democracy since the 1960s* (New York: Hill & Wang, 2012). Stacie Taranto's *Kitchen Table Politics: Conservative Women and Family Values in New York* (Philadelphia: University of Pennsylvania Press, 2017) is a useful source of information on gender politics of the 1970s, and it includes one of the best treatments of antiabortion activist Ellen McCormack's 1976 presidential campaign. For evangelical political culture during the 1970s—a religious movement that influenced both conservative Republican supporters of Reagan and more liberal Democratic supporters of Carter in 1976—see Steven P. Miller's *The Age of Evangelicalism: America's Born-Again Years* (New York: Oxford University Press, 2014). There is some discussion of the role of abortion, evangelical politics, and other religious issues in the 1976 election in two of my own books: *God's Own Party: The Making of the Christian Right* (New York: Oxford University Press, 2010) and *Defenders of the Unborn: The Pro-Life Movement before* Roe v. Wade (New York: Oxford University Press, 2016). Adam Clymer's *Drawing the Line at the Big Ditch: The Panama Canal Treaties and the Rise of the Right* (Lawrence: University Press of Kansas, 2008) is the best study of the foreign policy issue that became the focal point of Reagan's campaign in the spring of 1976.

For the role of race in the 1976 presidential campaigns, see chapter 6 of Jeremy D. Mayer's *Running on Race: Racial Politics in Presidential*

Campaigns, 1960–2000 (New York: Random House, 2002). Alton Hornsby Jr.'s *Black Power in Dixie: A Political History of African Americans in Atlanta* (Gainesville: University Press of Florida, 2009) may be useful background reading to gain an understanding of the broader historical context of Carter's own experiences with race as a Georgia politician in the fifteen years preceding his presidential campaign. To understand the broader context of the Republican Party's abandonment of the African American vote in the 1976 election—as well as the decisions of the small minority of African Americans who supported Ford—Joshua D. Farrington's *Black Republicans and the Transformation of the GOP* (Philadelphia: University of Pennsylvania Press, 2016) and Leah Wright Rigueur's *The Loneliness of the Black Republican: Pragmatic Politics and the Pursuit of Power* (Princeton, NJ: Princeton University Press, 2015) are helpful.

Because the rise of the Sun Belt played a central role in Reagan's primary challenge and Carter's primary and general election victories, studies of the Sun Belt's political ascendancy during the 1970s are useful sources of background information on the 1976 election. The historical scholarship on this topic is too extensive to survey here, but for a representative anthology of recent work in this area, see Michelle Nickerson and Darren Dochuk's *Sunbelt Rising: The Politics of Place, Space, and Region* (Philadelphia: University of Pennsylvania Press, 2011).

More broadly focused histories of the political and cultural changes of the 1970s include Bruce J. Schulman's *The Seventies: The Great Shift in American Culture, Society* (New York: Free Press, 2001), Edward D. Berkowitz's *Something Happened: A Political and Cultural Overview of the Seventies* (New York: Columbia University Press, 2006), and Daniel T. Rodgers's *Age of Fracture* (Cambridge, MA: Belknap Press, 2011).

ARCHIVAL MATERIALS AND OTHER PRIMARY SOURCES

Archival sources on the 1976 presidential election are readily accessible at the Gerald R. Ford Presidential Library in Ann Arbor, Michigan, and the Jimmy Carter Presidential Library in Atlanta, Georgia. Both libraries house hundreds of boxes of archived documents from their respective campaigns. The Ford Library has digitized a few of these materials, but for research purposes, the vast majority of the collection is available only onsite.

The records from Ronald Reagan's presidential campaign are split between the Ronald Reagan Presidential Library in Simi Valley,

California, and the Hoover Institution at Stanford University, which has acquired the papers of Citizens for Reagan, the organization that orchestrated his campaign. Some of the unsuccessful Democratic presidential contenders have also archived their papers. The Morris K. Udall Papers at the University of Arizona were useful sources for this book, as were George C. Wallace's campaign papers at the Alabama Department of Archives and History. I also found helpful material in Sargent Shriver's presidential campaign papers, which are housed at the John F. Kennedy Presidential Library in Boston.

Although the ability to conduct digital research in presidential libraries' archival collections is still very limited, anyone with access to historical newspaper databases can easily conduct primary source research on media coverage of the 1976 campaigns. I relied heavily on articles from two national newspapers with reputations for excellent political coverage in the 1970s: the *New York Times* and the *Washington Post.* I supplemented these materials with articles from a number of other regional papers. The *Atlanta Constitution* (which is now the *Atlanta Journal-Constitution*) was a particularly good source of information on Carter and his supporters. For Republican perspectives, I looked at editorials from a few conservative syndicated columnists, as well as business and conservative periodicals such as *Forbes* and *Human Events.* For liberal or progressive perspectives, I looked at magazines such as the *Nation,* the *Progressive,* the *New Republic,* and *Harper's. Ebony* was a useful source for African American opinion, as were historical databases of black newspapers. For religious opinion, I looked at the Catholic Jesuit magazine *America,* the liberal Protestant periodical the *Christian Century,* and evangelical magazines such as *Christianity Today.* National newsmagazines such as *Time, Newsweek,* and *U.S. News & World Report* were occasionally useful supplementary sources, although their articles on the campaign rarely went beyond the information found in the *New York Times.*

Polling data and county-level election returns are easily accessible in several sources published shortly after the 1976 election. George H. Gallup's two-volume *The Gallup Poll: Public Opinion, 1972–1977* (Wilmington, DE: Scholarly Resources, 1978) compiles the results of Gallup polls on numerous topics, both political and social. The best one-volume resource on voting returns from the 1976 election is Warren J. Mitofsky and Catherine C. Krein's *Campaign '76: A Reference of Official Vote Returns* (New York: Arno Press, 1977). Some of this information can be found in *Congressional Quarterly's Guide to 1976 Elections* (Washington, DC: Congressional Quarterly, 1977), which also features information on presidential primary vote totals that may be difficult to locate elsewhere. *The Black Vote: Election '76* (Washington, DC: Joint Center for Political Studies, 1977) offers detailed state-level data on black voting patterns. Some of these statistics, public opinion survey results, and voting returns are also available online from the Roper Center, Gallup, the *New York Times,* and Dave Leip's Atlas of US Presidential Elections.

Other useful online primary sources for the 1976 presidential election include the Living Room Candidate (which has archived the major television advertisements from every presidential election from 1952 to the present) and the American Presidency Project, which presents the complete text of numerous presidential speeches, as well as the platforms of both parties. Complete video footage of the presidential debates and party convention speeches can also be found online.

The 1976 presidential campaigns were exceptionally well documented, and anyone who wants to study this topic will find a plethora of print, archival, and online resources.

INDEX